Walk in the Ways of Wisdom

Walk in the Ways of Wisdom

ESSAYS IN HONOR OF ELISABETH SCHÜSSLER FIORENZA

EDITED BY
SHELLY MATTHEWS,
CYNTHIA BRIGGS KITTREDGE,
AND MELANIE JOHNSON-DEBAUFRE

TRINITY PRESS INTERNATIONAL
A Continuum imprint
HARRISBURG • LONDON • NEW YORK

Trinity Press International, P.O. Box 1321, Harrisburg, PA 17105

Trinity Press International is a member of the Continuum International Publishing Group.

Cover design: Corey Kent

Library of Congress Cataloging-in-Publication Data

Walk in the ways of wisdom : essays in honor of Elisabeth Schüssler
  Fiorenza / edited by Shelly Matthews, Cynthia Briggs Kittredge, and
  Melanie Johnson-DeBaufre.
      p. cm.
  Includes bibliographical references.
  ISBN 1-56338-406-X
    1. Feminist theology. 2. Theology. I. Schüssler Fiorenza,
  Elisabeth, 1938– II. Matthews, Shelly. III. Kittredge, Cynthia Briggs.
  IV. Johnson-DeBaufre, Melanie.
  BT83.55 .W35 2003
  230′.082–dc21

                                                                    2003011975

Contents

Acknowledgments

We would like to thank all of the current and former Harvard faculty and doctoral students who have contributed to this volume in honor of Elisabeth Schüssler Fiorenza.

We acknowledge with gratitude the support of Dean William A. Graham whose financial contribution on behalf of Harvard Divinity School was crucial for the success of this project. We would also like to thank the institutions where we teach for the generous support of this volume: Furman University, the Episcopal Theological Seminary of the Southwest, and Luther College.

We thank the many individuals who have contributed to the successful completion of this project. We list their names on the following page. Final thanks for the preparation of the bibliography go to Mary F. Vano, Master of Divinity student at the Episcopal Seminary of the Southwest, Mary E. Fairbairn, reference librarian at Furman University, and especially Deborah Whitehead, doctoral student at Harvard Divinity School.

SHELLY MATTHEWS
CYNTHIA BRIGGS KITTREDGE
MELANIE JOHNSON-DEBAUFRE

The following individuals join with the editors and contributors to this volume in bringing their well wishes and congratulations to Elisabeth Schüssler Fiorenza on the occasion of her 65th birthday.

Leila Ahmed

Katherine Bain

Kimberley Patton & Bruce Beck

Anne Braude

Laura Beth Bugg

Ruth Clements

Valerie C. Cooper

Carly Daniel-Hughes

Sylvia & Arthur Dyck

Diana Eck & Dorothy Austin

Linda Ellison

Eldon Jay Epp & ElDoris B. Epp

Kenneth Fisher

Georgia Frank

Peter Gomes

Claudia Highbaugh

Caroline Johnson Hodge

William & Virginia Hutchison

Cathie Kelsey

S. Zohreh Kermani

Nami Kim

Helmut & Gisela Koester

Michelle Lelwica

Elizabeth Lemons

David Little

AnneMarie Luijendijk

Kevin Madigan

Joseph A. Marchal

Edgar & Shirley McKnight

Margaret R. Miles

Julie B. Miller

Lyn J. Miller

Anne Monius

Irene Monroe

Emily R. Neill

Nancy Nienhuis

Robert Orsi

Tovis Page

Catherine Playoust

Nancy Richardson & Elaine Huber

Ilene Standford

Krister Stendahl

Margot Stevenson

Margaret Studier

Yuko Taniguchi

John Townsend

Sze-kar Wan

Deborah Whitehead

Preston Williams

Lawrence M. Wills

C. Conrad Wright

Introduction

Walk in the Ways of Wisdom

Shelly Matthews, Cynthia Briggs Kittredge,
and Melanie Johnson-DeBaufre

> Wisdom calls
> from the highest places in the town,
> "You that are simple minded, turn in here!"
> To those without sense she says,
> "Come, eat of my bread
> and drink of the wine I have mixed.
> Lay aside immaturity, and live,
> and walk in the way of Wisdom."
> — Proverbs 9:3b–6

Feminist biblical inquiry is best understood as a practice in the horizon of Divine Wisdom, as searching for Her presence and sustenance on the way, as learning Her ways or as engaging in the steps and moves of Her spiraling circle dance of interpretation. To walk in the ways of Wisdom is to walk in the ways of justice.
> — Elisabeth Schüssler Fiorenza, *Wisdom Ways*

It seems appropriate in a volume of essays celebrating the work of Elisabeth Schüssler Fiorenza to begin with Sophia-Wisdom's call to walk in her ways. As the quotation from Schüssler Fiorenza's *Wisdom Ways* explains, the biblical and extrabiblical traditions of divine Wisdom provide a rich imaginative and theoretical space for feminist biblical interpretation and theology. By articulating Sophia-Wisdom's call to "walk in the ways of Wisdom" as a call to "walk in the ways of justice," Schüssler Fiorenza presses us to see that Wisdom's invitation to her open table is also Wisdom's imperative to imagine and create a radical democratic space of well-being for all people. Ostensibly, this collection of essays from current and former Harvard University colleagues and students honors the remarkable achievements and invaluable contributions of Schüssler Fiorenza on the occasion of her sixty-fifth birthday. As each contributor situates her or his essay in relation to Schüssler

Fiorenza's critical insights and emancipatory framework, however, the process of celebrating this influential scholar becomes a way of participating in the ongoing critical debate and struggle for justice that she has sought to foster. The greatest honor we can give to our colleague and teacher, therefore, is to join with her in the public, interreligious, and open-ended debate that seeks to articulate the invitation and realize the imperative to walk in the ways of Wisdom.

Forging the Path

It is well known that Schüssler Fiorenza's scholarship has been a pioneering force in twentieth-century feminist biblical interpretation. It is important to note, however, that the pioneering character of her scholarship is matched by her path-breaking professional career. In the 1960s, she was the first woman admitted to the University of Würzburg's program of theological studies, previously reserved for candidates to the priesthood. In the 1970s, she and Carol Christ were the first co-chairs of the Women's Caucus for Religious Studies in the American Academy of Religion and the Society of Biblical Literature. In 1987, she was the first woman to serve as president of the Society of Biblical Literature. And in 1988, she was appointed as the first Krister Stendahl Professor of Scripture and Interpretation at Harvard Divinity School. She and Margaret Miles were the first women to be tenured at the Divinity School.

Schüssler Fiorenza has never been content, however, with her own professional successes, but has also been instrumental in creating structures and programs that empower feminists and wo/men in the academy and in ministry. She initiated a doctor of ministry program for Feminist Liberation Theology and Ministry during her tenure at Episcopal Divinity School. She put extensive time and energy into developing the Religion, Gender, and Culture concentration at Harvard Divinity School into a strong program for both Th.D. and Ph.D. candidates. Schüssler Fiorenza also co-founded the *Journal of Feminist Studies in Religion* and continues to be the co-editor of that journal. She also co-initiated and co-edited the issues on feminist theology in the international journal *Concilium*.

As Schüssler Fiorenza is keenly aware, however, there is still much to be done, and there is still much structural resistance to the work of feminists in the field. The standard reference books and introductions in biblical studies rarely give thorough treatment to feminist biblical scholarship. Program sections at the American Academy of Religion and the Society of Biblical Literature still reflect the marginalization of feminist scholarship as solely interested in women's issues or as ideological in contrast to "scientific" biblical criticism. The Society of Biblical Literature has had only two women — and as yet no women or men of color — in the office of president in the fifteen years since Schüssler Fiorenza's election. And despite the path-breaking work of Schüssler Fiorenza and others, the tenure percentages for women and marginalized men at major research institutions are still very low.

In this light, it is not surprising that Schüssler Fiorenza adopts a model of struggle to conceptualize both historical and contemporary efforts to resist kyriarchal systems of domination and to transform them with a vision of the radical democratic *ekklēsia* or public assembly. She turns her critical and incisive analysis, therefore, not only to the rhetoric and contexts of biblical texts and their ongoing interpretation but also to the frameworks and presuppositions of biblical studies as an academic discipline with the power to exclude or include. She argues that biblical studies must understand itself as a public discourse that seeks "not just to describe and understand but to change and transform the unjust situation of wo/men's religious and academic silencing, marginalization, and exploitation."[1]

Transforming the Discipline

Schüssler Fiorenza issued a challenge to the dominant paradigm in the discipline of biblical studies in her presidential address to the Society of Biblical Literature in 1987 entitled "The Ethics of Biblical Interpretation: Decentering Biblical Scholarship."[2] There she called for a change in the ethos and practice of biblical scholarship, a shift that called for the discipline to rearticulate itself as a public discourse. Noting that no president of the Society of Biblical Literature had ever used a presidential address to ask scholars to "consider the political context of their scholarship and to reflect on its public accountability,"[3] Schüssler Fiorenza challenged her audience to consider whether "we ask and teach our students to ask in a disciplined way how our scholarship is conditioned by its social location and how it serves political functions."[4] Articulating the theoretical underpinnings and methodological implications of this challenge has been a central feature of Schüssler Fiorenza's scholarly work in the past decade.

It is appropriate, therefore, that Schüssler Fiorenza's work is linked with that of Krister Stendahl through her appointment as the Krister Stendahl Professor of Scripture and Interpretation at Harvard Divinity School. In 1982, Stendahl called for biblical studies to attend to the "public health" aspects of its teaching and interpretation. Responding to a question about his repeated attention to women and Jews in his scholarship, Stendahl said that

---

1. Elisabeth Schüssler Fiorenza, *Rhetoric and Ethic: The Politics of Biblical Studies* (Minneapolis: Fortress), 8.

2. Elisabeth Schüssler Fiorenza, "The Ethics of Biblical Interpretation: Decentering Biblical Scholarship," *Journal of Biblical Literature* 107 (1988): 3–17; repr. in idem, *Rhetoric and Ethic*, 17–30.

3. Schüssler Fiorenza, *Rhetoric and Ethic*, 23.

4. Ibid.

from a New Testament scholar's point of view, these are two rather striking issues on which the Christian tradition, and in the case of women, the whole scriptural tradition has had a clearly detrimental and dangerous effect. There is no question that the way the New Testament material about Judaism contains within itself the seeds of much anti-Judaism; and that the male community has found aid and comfort in its chauvinism in the name of the Bible is relatively easy to document in western culture. . . . I have come to believe that the problem calls for frontal attention to what I have called the public health aspect of interpretation. How does the church live with the Bible without undesirable effects?[5]

Speaking within a feminist theoretical framework, Schüssler Fiorenza echoes and amplifies Stendahl's call for attention to the contemporary consequences of biblical interpretation. While Stendahl made a distinction between exegesis ("what it meant") and application ("what it means"), Schüssler Fiorenza consistently presses for a dynamic and self-reflexive relationship between imagining the past and engaging the present:

A critical feminist hermeneutics does not simply "apply" or translate the solutions of the past to the problems of the present; its historical imagination seeks to reconstruct the sociopolitical worlds of biblical writings and contemporary biblical interpretations in order to open them up for critical inquiry and theological reflection. Studying the biblical past in order to name the destructive aspects of its language and symbolic universe as well as to recover its unfulfilled historical possibilities becomes a primary task for biblical scholarship today.[6]

This combination of the historical-exegetical work of biblical scholarship, reflection on the social location of scholars, and attention to the impact of our discourse on "public health" is the hallmark of Schüssler Fiorenza's work. It is also characteristic of the rich contribution that she has made to students in the New Testament doctoral program at Harvard Divinity School. The fruit of this labor is apparent in many of the contributions from her doctoral students in this volume.

There are two areas in which Schüssler Fiorenza surely makes an enormous impact but which are not reflected or traced in the pages of this book. The first is among the master's students at the Divinity School. Because she is dedicated to feminist pedagogical praxis, classrooms for Gospel Stories of Wo/men and Feminist Biblical Interpretation are always abuzz with group projects, creative textual interpretations, and intense intellectual debates. As

---

5. Krister Stendahl, "Ancient Scripture in the Modern World," in *Scripture in the Jewish and Christian Traditions: Authority, Interpretation, and Relevance* (ed. Frederick E. Greenspahn; Nashville: Abingdon, 1982), 204–5.
6. Schüssler Fiorenza, *Rhetoric and Ethic*, 32.

several contributors to this volume will attest, Schüssler Fiorenza's classroom has no need for "teaching fellows" but rather "teaching facilitators" who are available as resources for the students' ongoing work. Schüssler Fiorenza's classrooms are always made up of diverse faces and diverse voices. These classes are not always peaceful or without conflict. However, the intensity of the students' involvement in Schüssler Fiorenza's classes speaks volumes about how these classes raise critical questions and empower students to engage issues that matter for their intellectual and spiritual lives.

The second arena of influence that must be recognized is the international community of scholars and activists with whom Schüssler Fiorenza joins in conversation and common cause. In her most recent book, *Wisdom Ways,* she thanks the participants in workshops on Feminist Biblical Interpretation in India, the Philippines, Brazil, Chile, Switzerland, Australia, New Zealand, and South Africa. Since being at Harvard, she has had visiting professorships in Germany, Switzerland, and Brazil. She has given lectures in all of these countries plus Canada, Norway, England, Argentina, the Netherlands, Belgium, Spain, Mexico, Austria, Scotland, Hong Kong, Israel, Sweden, Australia, Ireland, Korea, and all over the United States. In addition, *In Memory of Her* has been translated into ten languages and has been a force for change in how women and men in churches, seminaries, and graduate schools think about and imagine the biblical text.

In order to recognize and honor the complex and far-reaching influence of Schüssler Fiorenza's scholarly work, the essays in this volume are arranged around four major themes. Drawing on the titles of her books and the language of her scholarship, these sections highlight four aspects of her methodological contributions to biblical interpretation in particular and to religious studies in general. Taken together these emphases represent Schüssler Fiorenza's distinctive and compelling vision of the scholar of religion as a public intellectual engaged in discourses that foster social and religious transformation for justice.

Toward a Contemporary Discipleship of Equals

Schüssler Fiorenza places the radical democratic concept of the "discipleship of equals" at the center of her work. Another name for the "*ekklēsia* of wo/men," the discipleship of equals expresses a vision of reality in opposition to hierarchical structures of domination both within the church and in society at large.[7] The idea links emancipatory struggles in early Christianity and in biblical religion with those throughout history and in the present. In the essays in the first section, three faculty colleagues and two former students contribute to realizing this vision in their own fields of expertise. With

---

7. Elisabeth Schüssler Fiorenza, *Jesus: Miriam's Child, Sophia's Prophet: Critical Issues in Feminist Christology* (New York: Continuum, 1994), 24–31.

its own particular subject, each of the five essays exemplifies the hallmarks of Schüssler Fiorenza's work: its call for the interpreter to be forthrightly engaged as an advocate for the promotion of the vision of the discipleship of equals, the understanding of interpretation as a constructive or reconstructive enterprise, and the ultimate goal of the creation of a democratic *ekklēsia*.

In the opening essay, Francis Schüssler Fiorenza places Elisabeth Schüssler Fiorenza's feminist biblical hermeneutics within current discussion about the task of systematic theology. He describes how Elisabeth's critical rhetorical analysis challenges conceptions of theology such as that of David Tracy, for whom systematic theology is the interpretation of classics, and that of Hans Frei and George Lindbeck, who understand theology as "thick description." Her advocacy of critical rhetorical analysis challenges the idealistic assumptions of both positions by taking into account the relation between author and addressees, argumentative strategies, and the text's diverse receptions. Francis further points to the influence of Elisabeth's work on his own understanding of systematic theology as constructive and normative.

Harvey Cox traces the development of the main alternative to liberation theology with which both he and Schüssler Fiorenza identify. The New Christendom strategy, represented in his discussion by Josef Ratzinger and Marie-Dominique Chenu, advocates building a new religiously grounded civilization that takes into account changes that happen in the world. This stands in contrast with the Restored Christendom approach—championed by Leo XIII in the nineteenth century—that seeks to restore the age where the values of the church guided the world. Cox evaluates the continuities between the New Christendom strategy and its predecessor, and he points to the common problems in the modern world that both liberation theology and the New Christendom must address.

John R. Lanci's essay develops a model of pedagogy as collaborative work inspired by Schüssler Fiorenza's assertion about the connection between feminist biblical education and pastoral practice, between learning and fostering critical thinking and self-esteem. With a series of imagined conversations, Lanci demonstrates the interaction of teacher and students in the spiraling dance of interpretation. Acting as companion, resource to the community, and advocate, the educator assists the community in the dialogical method of reflection that leads to action.

Putting historical research into conversation with modern debates, Barbara R. Rossing explores the ancient associations around the word *oikoumenē* and their implications for its use in contemporary ecumenical discussions. Rossing argues that in the literature of the Roman era, the word *oikoumenē* carried an imperial meaning. She traces the use of the word in the Septuagint, Greek and Roman historians, Revelation, the Gospels, and Acts and shows that the New Testament authors gave no ecological connotation to the word; it represents, rather, the world under Roman imperial rule. Rossing discusses critiques of the word raised by critics of globalization and reflects on the need to develop images of church unity that reject kyriarchal associations and encompass diversity.

Ronald F. Thiemann explores the role of the public intellectual through the discussion of the poet Anna Akhmatova. A person both deeply identified with and prophetically critical of her own society, Akhmatova exemplifies the public intellectual as connected critic. By exercising her poetic craft, she chronicles the story of her own time through the lives of women. Through his discussion of the Russian poet's work, Thiemann reflects on the kind of communities of faith that would allow a genuine public intellectual to emerge within our "fragmented, shallow, media-saturated culture" (see p. 103 below).

As mentioned above, Schüssler Fiorenza's call for ethically engaged biblical scholarship, forcefully given in her 1987 presidential address to the Society of Biblical Literature, challenges academic biblical scholarship to shift its self-understanding and public profile. Thiemann's reflection on the role of the public intellectual as "connected critic" shares with Schüssler Fiorenza the dissatisfaction with scholars who restrict their attention to obscure academic questions and deny the connection of their work with wider political discourse. Similarly, Lanci presents the role of the educator as a "critical transformative intellectual" in the learning community who must take an advocacy stand for or against the oppressed. Rossing's exegetical questions about the imperial context of *oikoumenē* arise explicitly from her commitment to the ecumenical movement. In their emphasis on the necessity of connection between scholarship and justice, these essays indicate the potential power of scholarship that reflects upon and articulates its ethical and political commitments.

The forthright claim that interpretation is constructive characterizes Elisabeth's work. This insight is clearly articulated in Francis's essay, in which he argues strongly that systematic theology is primarily normative and reconstructive rather than descriptive and hermeneutical. Rossing proposes that it may be necessary to move beyond "(re)claiming" *oikoumenē* to develop other images of unity that encompass diversity in our thinking about the church. This exemplifies the constructive move that follows the feminist hermeneutics of suspicion and critical evaluation. Claiming one's creative role as constructor of tradition as well as interpreter is closely linked to positioning oneself as an advocate for the oppressed. Such a reconception of the task of biblical interpretation is a difficult one for many New Testament scholars who are rehearsed in the methods of "scientific" exegesis. But as these essays show, taking up the task of the public intellectual yields fruitful insights for envisioning the contemporary discipleship of equals.

This discipleship of equals is part of a larger vision of a radical democratic *ekklēsia*. A similar emphasis on the ideal of democracy arises in Thiemann's discussion of the role of public intellectual, in Lanci's vision of the college classroom, in Rossing's image of the ecumenical movement, and in Cox's discussion of the differences between liberation theology and the New Christendom strategy. The essays presented in this section share with Schüssler Fiorenza the vision of church and of society as an assembly of free citizens engaged in public debate and discussion from which truth and justice emerge.

In Memory of Wo/men

Schüssler Fiorenza has made key contributions to feminist historical reconstruction and the process of writing wo/men back into history. She argues that doing so requires adopting a theoretical framework that understands early Christian history as one of struggle between dominant patriarchal discursive practices and competing discourses that articulate egalitarian visions of discipleship. Both François Bovon and Ann Graham Brock focus on texts that give evidence of this struggle, texts that preserve discourses that advocate the right of women to assume authoritative roles in the *ekklēsia*. Steven J. Friesen's essay on wo/men leaders in the imperial cults of Asia Minor illustrates how analysis of the discursive practices of interpreters contributes to the process of reconstructing ancient wo/men's lives.

Bovon's essay traces a struggle between hierarchical and egalitarian ecclesial impulses through a study of various witnesses to the apocryphal *Acts of Philip*. While the best known and relatively late manuscript of *Acts of Philip* demonstrates a tendency to censure "heretical" aspects of the original and to eradicate evidence for women's ministry, Bovon focuses on an earlier manuscript in which women are depicted as engaged in all aspects of ministerial leadership, including sacerdotal ones. He argues that this manuscript is the product of a minority ascetic community in conflict with "the Great Church." Noting that the "orthodox" church claimed the threefold hierarchical system of bishops, priests, and deacons as biblical, Bovon argues that the author of this document, who relies on the biblical witness of Philip's prophesying daughters, "has the same right and the same authority to defend a church order that includes both men and women in priestly ministry" (see p. 121 below).

Brock focuses on a collection of apocryphal texts in which the struggle over authority in the church is also in evidence. Her main concern is to argue that the identity of Mary in *Pistis Sophia* is most often Mary Magdalene and not Mary the mother of Jesus. Arguing on the basis of a variety of internal and external clues, Brock shows that whenever Mary is portrayed in conflict with Peter, the Mary in question is Mary Magdalene. These conflict scenes, in which Peter and Mary Magdalene function as ciphers, are evidence of the struggle between the emerging orthodox church with its exclusively male leadership and Christian communities that pointed to Mary Magdalene as legitimizing women's authority in the *ekklēsia*.

Schüssler Fiorenza repeatedly argues that all historical reconstruction is rhetorical practice and not merely the scientific practice of presenting the data. Friesen applies this insight to his own work in the field of archeology, faulting the discipline for its "cultivated aura of neutrality" that belies its biased scholarship. In a survey of the history of interpretation of inscriptions indicating female leadership roles in the imperial cults of Asia, he shows how kyriarchal reasoning undergirds this scholarship and most often results in the unwarranted conclusion that a woman's cultic status must have depended on her husband's religious rank. By employing Schüssler Fiorenza's neologisms *wo/men* and *kyriarchy,* he is able to call for an emancipatory rhetoric in the field of classical archeology, which would undertake a multidimensional discussion of high priestesses as "oppressed oppressors" and would shift the focus in the field from antiquity's elite minority to the impoverished majority.

Rhetoric and Ethic:
The Practice of Interpretation

Schüssler Fiorenza calls scholars' attention to the importance of reflection on the presuppositions of scholarly discourse, noting that different frameworks will produce different results. She argues that the most adequate historical reconstruction emerges from frameworks that can account for viewpoints routinely submerged in dominant discourses. The essays in both this section and the next call into question dominant scholarly frameworks. These exegetical essays also offer alternative reading strategies to make sense of the rhetoric of the text.

Bernadette J. Brooten, for example, draws attention to the unspoken framework guiding much mainstream thinking on sexual ethics as she focuses on Augustine's *On the Good of Marriage.* She notes that assumptions in such ancient texts are "simultaneously strangely archaic to our own way of thinking and yet deeply embedded in it" (see p. 181 below). She exposes the presupposition of sexual hierarchy that undergirds Augustine's classification of sexual acts and the cultural embeddedness of Augustine's category of "the natural."

Melanie Johnson-DeBaufre demonstrates how framing early Christianity as "a response to the work and vision of one great man" cannot adequately account for the rhetoric of the sayings material in Q. In her essay on the children in the marketplace saying in Q 7:31–35, she notes that mainstream scholarship, constrained by presuppositions of Jesus' centrality and difference, cannot account for the various components of the pericope. Rather than inscribing relationships between Jesus and other characters in the pericope as relationships of othering, Johnson-DeBaufre concludes that "John/Jesus and 'this generation' " are "actors in the same group rather than foes.... [The pericope] argues for solidarity in the group across differences without calling for the obliteration of differences" (see pp. 231–32 below).

In her work on three early Christian texts concerned with prophecy, Laura S. Nasrallah calls into question the predominant narrative of early Christian history that posits an originary spark of charisma that devolves into routinization or institutionalization. Employing both Schüssler Fiorenza's method of rhetorical analysis and her historiographic model of struggle, Nasrallah argues that the anti-Phrygian source in Epiphanius's *Panarion*, Tertullian, and 1 Corinthians should not be read straightforwardly. They are best read, Nasrallah argues, as "fragments of a discursive struggle over history, interconnected to issues of epistemology and authority" (see p. 264 below).

Other contributions in this section also adopt Schüssler Fiorenza's method of rhetorical analysis for early Christian texts. Denise Kimber Buell uses rhetorical analysis in her reading of Clement of Alexandria's *Who Is the Rich Person Who Is Saved?* Buell first identifies both kyriarchal and potentially subversive elements of Clement's own views regarding material possessions, wealth, and status. She then reads against the grain to suggest that the emancipatory materialist readings against which Clement argues may indicate an alternative egalitarian ethos — "one that interprets Mark [10:17–31] to negotiate economic differences among Christians differently, with seemingly greater insistence on material redistribution of wealth" (see p. 200 below).

Building on Schüssler Fiorenza's understanding of the visionary rhetoric of apocalyptic texts, Ellen Bradshaw Aitken sets her essay on the *Apocalypse of Paul* within the context of the literary and visual world of Roman landscapes. Attuned to questions of rhetoric and ethic, Aitken focuses on the persuasive strategy of the text. This enables her to see the text not as one concerned primarily with a theological problem — the fate of the dead — but as an ethical exhortation, a map that seeks to guide the Christian community in the ways of covenantal faithfulness.

As in the next section, several of the contributions in this section answer Schüssler Fiorenza's call to reflect on "the ethical consequences and political functions of biblical texts and their interpretations in their historical as well as in their contemporary sociopolitical contexts."[8] For example, in their essay on the Gospel of John, Rita Nakashima Brock and Rebecca Ann Parker offer historical-critical exegesis of a biblical text that is coupled with sustained ethical and theological reflection. The essay situates the Gospel of John within a pro-Samaritan community and explains the anti-Jewish polemic in John as owing in part to a long history of enmity between Samaritans and Jews. Their argument does not, however, seek to explain away John's anti-Judaism. Rather, they fault the gospel for its "duplicitous

---

8. Schüssler Fiorenza, *Rhetoric and Ethic*, 28.

theology," its positioning of Jesus as calling down violent wrath on Jews and all who do not believe in him, and its masking of Roman imperial violence.

Karen L. King reflects on the ethics of the negation of the body and material world in her essay on the *Gospel of Mary*. While acknowledging the often harmful consequences of such negation and transcendence, King revisits the gospel to scrutinize more carefully its subversive potential. She asks, "What if transcendence and justice are linked?" Because the transcendent perspective in the *Gospel of Mary* is one from which the reigning ideology of violence and domination is critiqued, King concludes that it is not escapist, but rather transformative. She suggests that its readers are enabled to "rise above the current system and discern how leadership should be exercised among those who follow the teachings of the Savior" (see p. 243).

Ethical consequences and political locations are acknowledged by several authors in this section. Buell locates the impetus for her task expressly in modern-day struggles against socioeconomic oppression. Her interpretation of Clement both exposes kyriarchal views and practices and identifies alternative visions and struggles for justice. Johnson-DeBaufre makes the connection between contemporary and social-political context and interpretation of early Christian texts by situating her own reading of Q within contemporary debates over religious pluralism and particularity. Brooten advocates for a sexual ethic based on consent and mutuality and thus calls for the wholesale rejection of Augustine's hierarchically framed sexual ethic. Brock and Parker's work on violence in John stems from their long-standing concern for victims of violence and their feminist theological agenda of exposing links between Christian violence and doctrines of atonement.

Rhetoric and Ethic: The Politics of Meaning

Schüssler Fiorenza's reconceptualization of biblical studies as a public and political discourse entails analyzing the hermeneutical lenses in which texts are read and exploring the rhetoricity of texts within their political contexts. As a critical discourse, biblical studies must then also exercise the same critical awareness with respect to its own arguments and claims. The goal of such public discourse is "to further the well-being of all the inhabitants of the *cosmo-polis* today."[9] The essays in the final section demonstrate in different ways the critical activities that contribute to biblical studies as a rhetorical-ethical discourse. Aware of how biblical studies is embedded in its own social-historical context, the authors ground their arguments in urgent ethical questions. The essays of Allen Dwight Callahan and Demetrius Williams attend to the way New Testament texts have been used as a force for liberation by different faith communities in particular historical periods. The essays of Cynthia Briggs Kittredge and Shelly Matthews aim to

---

9. Ibid., 11.

describe the hermeneutical lenses used by historians who study the letters of Paul and the Gospel of Matthew. Dieter Georgi and Richard Horsley illustrate the important process of scholarly reflection that is attuned to the unexpressed political dimensions of biblical criticism.

Three of the authors speak explicitly to the pressing ethical issues that give rise to the questions raised in their essays. The transformation of the global economy and the violence it engenders constitute the interpretive context for Callahan's analysis of Latin American exegetes' reading of the economic rhetoric in Rev 18. Callahan contrasts Marxist, feminist, and premillennialist readings of chapter 18 of the Apocalypse with those of Latin American exegetes. Callahan argues that unlike the readings that de-emphasize the economic and political features of the Apocalypse, readings by Latin American exegetes Pablo Richard, Néstor Míguez, Günther Wolf, Ricardo Foulkes, and Dagoberto Ramírez Fernández interpret Rev 18 as an indictment of economic structures that perpetuate the oppressive system of an imperial economy.

The present hegemony of global capitalism is the immediate context in which Horsley seeks to recover submerged histories of movements of resistance within the Roman imperial order. Building upon the postcolonial and feminist critique of Western theological readings of the New Testament, Horsley reads the Gospel of Mark as a story of peoples' struggle for renewal of village life against the Roman imperial order in Palestine. In contrast to those who see Hellenistic syncretism in an undifferentiated manner, Horsley argues that syncretism took diverse forms in the Roman Empire. He reconstructs Paul and the other leaders of the Jesus movement as those who reject their previous Hellenistic hybridity and seek to renew Israelite tradition in a movement sharply opposed to the Roman order.

Christian complicity in anti-Jewish violence provokes Matthews's treatment of the construction of Jewish persecutions of Christians in first-century history. Matthews first identifies and describes the dualistic inscription of Jew as persecutor and Christian as persecuted that underlies reconstructions of early Christian violence in the Gospel of Matthew. She then notes the literary, theological, and psychological impulses that also compel early Jesus followers to script themselves as suffering persecution. In order to move away from arguments that posit persecution of Jesus followers as originary/essential, Matthews proposes a reconstruction that sees a continuum of hostile acts directed toward sectarian groups before, during, and after the writing of the Gospel of Matthew. She concludes with a discussion of Josephus's account of the death of James, a text that presents a more complex picture of sympathetic friendship among Christian and non-Christian Jews.

Analyzing how texts function in the ongoing struggle between kyriarchal domination and egalitarian vision is an important task of Schüssler Fiorenza's vision of critical biblical studies. The essays by both Williams and Callahan explore the interrelationship between texts and their reception by faith communities. Williams explores the appropriations of the baptismal formula of Gal 3:28 by African American preachers and leaders. Williams notes that among the interpretations, some thinkers emphasize common humanity, others race, class, and gender. Williams observes that the implications for women of biblical teachings on equality have not been fully actualized in the African American religious tradition.

Clarification of the dominant hermeneutical frameworks and proposal of alternative frames of reference are important elements in biblical criticism as a critical public discourse. Kittredge examines the way that theologians of Paul treat the issue of authorship of earlier traditions within Paul's letters. She contrasts the perspective of Pauline theologians who focus on Paul as the single authoritative author with the work of feminist scholars who conceive of communities of Christians in the *ekklēsia* as the origin of those traditions. Kittredge finds the basis of these different approaches in assumptions about the authority and centrality of Paul. In spite of the high value placed on Paul by the Protestant theological tradition, Kittredge argues for the benefits of an approach that decentralizes Paul. She emphasizes the role of the community as source of Christian language in order to create dialogical communities of interpretation in the present.

Schüssler Fiorenza calls scholars both to restore the submerged voices of early Christianity and to trace the reinscription of early Christianity's dominant voices in contemporary scholarship. Georgi identifies such a reinscription in the marginalization of gnosis scholarship in contemporary European New Testament scholarship. He shows the ways in which scholarly descriptions of Gnosticism mirror the views of the ancient heresiologists and the way that certain theories sympathetic to gnostic texts have been silenced by scholarly editing. In order to give voice to the submerged voices in gnostic texts, Georgi suggests rejecting the sharp evaluative divide between Gnosticism and the New Testament writings. Instead, he argues that scholarship should give primary attention to the rhetoric and themes of the texts themselves, particularly focusing on their antiobjectifying language and their critique of power.

Conclusion

There has always been a kind of urgency in Schüssler Fiorenza's work, an awareness that humanity's well-being is at the heart of the matter. She has repeatedly said that the Bible should come with a warning label: "While commonsense wisdom asserts 'sticks and stones may break my bones but words can never hurt me,' we all know this is not true. Words, especially sacred words full of authority like those of the Bible, have great power to harm or to encourage."[10] She calls biblical scholars to be trained and ready

---

10. Ibid., 14.

to "reflect on what kind of role the Bible plays today in the social construction of reality and in the discursive formations that determine individuals, religious communities, and society on the whole."[11] This is a large task to be sure, but a vital one. In a recent letter, Krister Stendahl spoke of the crucial importance of Elisabeth's contribution to the discipline:

> Every time I hear Elisabeth referred to as the [first] "Krister Stendahl Professor" there is a smile inside me, a smile of recognition, of exegetical kinship. Just imagine that our names would be linked together. What I stammered in my hermeneutical writings 50 years ago, I now hear a hundred times clarified, amplified, and intensified in hers. And her critical acumen I read as powerfully constructive, driven as it is by a moral pathos without which there can be no future for those of us who cannot help but love the Bible.[12]

It is in recognition of Elisabeth Schüssler Fiorenza's significant contribution to biblical scholarship and in celebration of her sixty-fifth birthday that we offer this volume of essays from her colleagues and students at Harvard Divinity School. The editors of this volume and the scholars who have been inspired by Elisabeth's vision of emancipatory interpretation look forward to many more years of walking together in the ways of Wisdom.

---

11. Ibid., 11.
12. Personal correspondence with the editors, 3 January 2003.

Part 1

Toward a Contemporary Discipleship of Equals

I

From Interpretation to Rhetoric

The Feminist Challenge to Systematic Theology

Francis Schüssler Fiorenza

I begin this essay with a personal story. Before traveling to Germany in 1964 for doctoral studies at the University of Münster, I was advised to look for Mary Buckley, a member of the Grail in Brooklyn (an international organization of women dedicated to church ministry). Soon after my arrival, we met and engaged in a discussion of Karl Rahner's theology.[1] Mary Buckley strongly recommended that I talk with Elisabeth Schüssler. Having met Elisabeth during her year of study at the University of Würzburg, she was convinced that Elisabeth was an exceptionally brilliant young scholar: she had a licentiate degree in practical theology; she was pursuing a doctorate in New Testament studies; and, most important, she had some very important criticisms of Rahner's theology. Mary argued that if I wanted to become a good systematic theologian, then I just had to take into account Elisabeth's challenging criticisms.

Several months later we finally met (at Mary's initiative) and debated Rahner's theology. Our first discussion after a lecture lasted so long that we missed lunch: the student mensa at Collegium Marianum, my residence, had closed. We went to a coffee shop, where the discussion continued until it was time for supper at Marianum. That day was the beginning of a long friendship that has been intertwined with continued theological discussions. Elisabeth had just published in 1964 *Der vergessene Partner* (The Forgotten Partner), which dealt with foundations, realities, and possibilities for the ministerial role of women in the church.[2] The first part of that book historically retrieved the role of women in ministry, offered criticisms of Gertrude von Le Ford's "theology of woman," and inspired the structure

---

1. After receiving her doctorate with Professor, now Cardinal, Walter Kasper, Dr. Buckley became a professor first at the University of San Francisco and then at St. John's University in New York.

2. Elisabeth Schüssler Fiorenza, *Der vergessene Partner: Grundlagen, Tatsachen und Möglichkeiten der Beruflichen Mitarbeit der Frau in der Heilssorge der Kirche* (Düsseldorf: Patmos, 1964).

and basis of Mary Daly's *The Church and the Second Sex*.[3] The second part of *The Forgotten Partner* gives a detailed description of the de facto ministerial practice and experience of women in diverse pastoral ministries in the German church. Elisabeth appeals to this practice to challenge not only the traditional theological understanding of church office and ministry, but also Rahner's contemporary reconceptualization of ministry. I left our meeting convinced that she and Rahner had indeed very different theological visions of the church and its ministry. Though she did not convince me that day, in the years to come her insights and arguments have increasingly persuaded me of the significance of her theological vision.

From the very beginning, two elements characterized Elisabeth's vision: one is an egalitarian vision of the church that affirms the equality of all human persons and the full discipleship of women; the other is a critical method of interpretation that is evident in her feminist hermeneutics and rhetorical analysis. The first comes to the fore in her licentiate on the ministry of women in the church, in her dissertation analyzing the biblical affirmation of equal dignity of the members of the Christian community as kings and priests[4] in her feminist interpretation of the role of women within early Christianity,[5] and in her systematic and practical reflections on the struggle of women for equality in the church.[6] The second is a method of feminist hermeneutics and critical rhetorical analysis that she has developed in several books.[7] Such an approach takes into account that historical and religious writings come into existence within a social and political context permeated with power and polemics. Such a rhetorical analysis demonstrates that the belief that knowledge that can achieve objectivity by transcending its social historical embeddedness is at best a chimera or an illusion and at worst an ideology. Because of this hermeneutical awareness, Elisabeth avoids any appeal to women's experience as foundational; she refuses to appeal to an original golden age history; and she eschews a feminist theology based upon a gender dualism. Such a rhetorical analysis is required not only for interpretation, but also for construction and practice. Her work undercuts any idealistic conceptions of the hermeneutical task, and she herself illustrates the connection between historical interpretation and systematic theology. If I may be permitted to modify Rahner's term *anonymous Christian*, I would

---

3. Mary Daly, *The Church and the Second Sex* (New York: Harper & Row, 1968).
4. Elisabeth Schüssler Fiorenza, *Priester für Gott: Studien Zum Herrschafts- und Priestermotiv in der Apokalypse* (Münster: Aschendorff, 1972).
5. Elisabeth Schüssler Fiorenza, *In Memory of Her: A Feminist Theological Reconstruction of Christian Origins* (10th anniv. ed.; New York: Crossroad, 1994).
6. Elisabeth Schüssler Fiorenza, *Discipleship of Equals: A Critical Feminist Ekklēsia-Logy of Liberation* (New York: Crossroad, 1993).
7. Elisabeth Schüssler Fiorenza, *Bread Not Stone: The Challenge of Feminist Biblical Interpretation* (Boston: Beacon, 1985); idem, *But She Said: Feminist Practices of Biblical Interpretation* (Boston: Beacon, 1992); idem, *Sharing Her Word: Feminist Biblical Interpretation in Context* (Boston: Beacon, 1998); and idem, *Wisdom Ways: Introducing Feminist Biblical Interpretation* (Maryknoll, N.Y.: Orbis, 2001).

claim that Elisabeth Schüssler Fiorenza is "an anonymous systematic theologian." As such, her scholarship has constantly influenced my own thinking about theology. In appreciation for her contribution, this essay will show the significance of her methodological analyses for systematic theology by analyzing the inadequacies of contemporary understandings of systematic theology and the significance of her hermeneutical stance.

Many theologians understand the task of systematic theology primarily as interpretative or hermeneutical. Such a definition leads me to ask both what is the implied understanding of hermeneutics and whether the theological task and the hermeneutical task are identical.[8] Even though hermeneutics is central to systematic theology, and even though the hermeneutical task is crucial to all aspects of theology, systematic theology cannot be reduced to hermeneutics. The theological endeavor entails much more than the interpretive task, no matter how broadly this task is construed. This claim that there are other functions besides the hermeneutical also suggests limits on the role of hermeneutics within theology. In this essay, I would like to take up the challenges that Elisabeth Schüssler Fiorenza's proposals for feminist hermeneutics and critical rhetorical analysis raise for the understanding of systematic theology as hermeneutical.

Theology is a complex endeavor, and the term *theology* has a long and varied history.[9] At first the term *theologia* was used to refer more to the opinions of those outside Christianity and more specifically to the philosophical doctrine of God in contrast to the "Christian teaching" that dealt with the economy of salvation. Only since the thirteenth century has the term *theologia* become the customary umbrella term. Moreover, only in modernity has theology fragmented into the standard fourfold division: biblical, historical, systematic, and practical.[10] Within this division, systematic theology takes on the tasks of a specific discipline. It is within this framework that one should examine definitions of the discipline of systematic theology as "hermeneutical" and "interpretive" and explore the critical significance of Elisabeth Schüssler Fiorenza's understanding of rhetorical analysis for such conceptions of systematic theology.

Two significant contemporary conceptions of theology specify the theological task as hermeneutical. David Tracy defines systematic theology via its hermeneutical task and appropriates for theology the hermeneutical theories of Hans-Georg Gadamer and Paul Ricoeur. The other approach of the "Yale School" was developed by Hans Frei, George Lindbeck, and some

---

8. Francis Schüssler Fiorenza, "Theology: Transcendental or Hermeneutical?" *Horizons* 16 (1989): 329–41.

9. Francis Schüssler Fiorenza, "Systematic Theology: Tasks and Methods," in *Systematic Theology: Roman Catholic Perspectives* (ed. Francis Schüssler Fiorenza and John Galvin; Minneapolis: Fortress, 1991), 1.3–87.

10. Edward Farley, *Theologia: The Fragmentation and Unity of Theological Education* (Philadelphia: Fortress, 1983).

of their former students at Yale Divinity School.[11] Even though they criticize the appropriation of a general and universal theory of interpretation
within theology, they too basically understand theology as hermeneutical.
The differences between these two approaches are significant, and yet both
conceive of theology as primarily hermeneutical. Consequently, both can be
challenged by a critical feminist approach to theology.

Elisabeth Schüssler Fiorenza's development of the ethics of interpretation, feminist hermeneutics, and critical rhetorical analysis questions and
challenges such conceptions of systematic theology. Moreover, I argue that
systematic theology should appropriate the method of broad reflective
equilibrium that includes hermeneutical tasks, but understands systematic
theology as combining four distinct tasks: a reconstructive interpretation of
the tradition, a weighing of relevant background theories, an assessment of
warrants drawn from ongoing experience, and a taking into account of diverse communities of discourse. This essay will argue that a critical rhetorical
analysis challenges the understanding of systematic theology as hermeneutical and raises significant questions for an understanding of the method of
broad reflective equilibrium.

Systematic Theology as a Hermeneutics
of Christian Classics

David Tracy distinguishes systematic theology from two other types of theology: fundamental theology and practical theology. They differ in terms of
primary reference group, mode of argument, ethical stance, personal commitment, and what counts as meaning and truth claim. For Tracy, systematic
theology starts from a particular religious tradition that is assumed to be true
or whose truth has been already argued in fundamental theology. Systematic
theology will, therefore, "focus upon reinterpretations and new applications
of that tradition for the present. In that sense, systematic theologies are
principally hermeneutical in character."[12]

Systematic Theology as Hermeneutical

The nature of systematic theology as hermeneutical is illustrated by two
analogies: art and the classic. Religion is analogous to art insofar as both
provide resources so that the disclosure of meaning of truth is also received
as such. Just as interpreting a work of art draws out its disclosure of new
possibilities for human life, so too does the interpretive task of systematic

---

11. See Mark I. Wallace, "The New Yale Theology," *Christian Scholar's Review* 17.2 (1987):
154–70. For the more recent developments, see Gary Dorrien, "Truth Claims," *Christian
Century* 118 (18–25 July 2001): 22–29.

12. David Tracy, *The Analogical Imagination: Christian Theology and the Culture of
Pluralism* (New York: Crossroad, 1981), 58.

theology.[13] Tracy's argument relies centrally on the function of the classic in its diverse forms (broadly interpreted to include events, persons, images, rituals, symbols, and texts) to disclose and manifest "permanent possibilities of meaning and truth."[14] Though Tracy includes more than texts as classics, his explanation of the method of interpretation primarily focuses upon the textual classic. His analysis begins with the literary classic in general, then progresses to the religious literary classic, and finally arrives at the Christian classic, especially, the "norming norm" of the Christian Scriptures.[15]

The systematic theologian's interpretation of classic texts in the Hebrew and Christian traditions performs a function analogous to the philosopher's interpretation of philosophical classics and the literary critic's interpretation of the major literary classics. The systematic theologian interprets the classic in a way that articulates the disclosure of God embedded in these classics for the contemporary situation. The disclosure of truth and meaning is central to the hermeneutical task of systematic theology that interprets the religious tradition in order to disclose the meaning of tradition for the present situation. An appropriate interpretation seeks to retrieve not simply a historical meaning of a classic, but to uncover (using a disclosure model of truth) both its meaning and truth. The results are a "mutually critical correlation" between the interpretations of the tradition and the present situation. This correlation involves application and response.[16]

Although Tracy defines systematic theology as hermeneutical, he avoids totally collapsing theology in general into hermeneutics in two ways. First, he distinguishes but does not separate systematic theology from fundamental and practical theology. Fundamental theology formulates its arguments primarily in harmony with rules of argument that are usually articulated in a specific philosophical approach. Whereas fundamental theology argues for the cognitive claims of a religious tradition, systematic theology assumes the truth of the classic and hermeneutically discloses it. Since systematic theology is hermeneutical, its task is limited to disclosing the meaning and truth of what is demonstrated as true in fundamental theology according to a distinct mode of argument. Therefore, the decisive question remains: how does systematic theology exercise or relate to the fundamental theological task? Whereas Elisabeth Schüssler Fiorenza's rhetorical analysis brings the ethical and practical evaluation into the interpretive task, Tracy's conception limits systematic interpretation to the criteria of appropriateness and leaves other criteria to the other theological disciplines.

---

13. Ibid., 67.

14. Ibid., 68.

15. The progression in chaps. 3–7 in ibid., 99–338.

16. Ibid., 68. See also Tracy's treatment of Scripture in Robert M. Grant and David Tracy, *A Short History of the Interpretation of the Bible* (2d ed.; London: SCM, 1984). See Tracy's response to Frei, Lindbeck, and Tanner in "On Reading the Scriptures Theologically," in *Theology and Dialogue: Essays in Conversation with George Lindbeck* (ed. Bruce Marshall; Notre Dame: University of Notre Dame Press, 1990), 35–68.

Second, Tracy further nuances the hermeneutical task of systematic theology by adopting Ricoeur's criticisms of Gadamer's hermeneutical theory.[17] In contrast to Gadamer's de-emphasis of method, Ricoeur incorporates the methodic and explanatory mode within interpretation.[18] He underscores that interpretation requires both understanding and interpretation. The text objectifies the meaning in the event of discourse. The objectification that takes place through the spoken word becomes further objectified through the production of a written text.[19] In addition, this objectification makes a structural analysis of the text possible. As a structured work, the text, like a musical score, gives its own clues for interpretation. The structure not only displays the sense, but also projects and creates a world of reference. This makes it possible to analyze the meaning of a text within a new context that differs from the original event and situation.

For Tracy, the systematic-theological interpretation of a classic involves interpretation, explanation, and appropriation.[20] He divides these into four steps: (1) theologians as interpreters of the classic begin with some preunderstanding of the subject matter; (2) they recognize and acknowledge the religious classic as a manifestation of meaning and truth; (3) they engage in the logic of questioning in relation to the subject matter of the text; and (4) they attend to the structured form of the text in a way that takes into account the explanatory methods dealing with the structure and sense of the text. In this fourth step, Tracy's approach contrasts with Gadamer's de-emphasis upon method. He seeks to overcome Gadamer's contrast between method and truth by appropriating Ricoeur's account of explanation. The explanatory mode is brought to bear in the fourth step upon the text as structured.

The Truth of Classics

Tracy's definition of systematic theology as the interpretation of the Christian classics rests on some basic assumptions. One assumption is a specific understanding of truth; the other involves the suitability and adequacy of the

---

17. For a discussion of Tracy's work in relation to the hermeneutical theories of Gadamer and Ricoeur, see my chap. 9, "History and Hermeneutics," in James Livingston and Francis Schüssler Fiorenza, *Modern Christian Thought*, vol. 2: *The Twentieth Century* (Upper Saddle River, N.J.: Prentice-Hall, 2000), 341–85.

18. Paul Ricoeur, "Hermeneutics and the Critique of Ideology," in Ricoeur's *From Text to Action: Essays in Hermeneutics* (trans. Kathleen Blamey and John B. Thompson; Evanston, Ill.: Northwestern University Press, 1991), 270–308.

19. The major difference between Elisabeth Schüssler Fiorenza's rhetorical analysis and Ricoeur's analysis is that Ricoeur locates the critical element in the element of objectification that makes possible a scientific structural analysis of the text, whereas she places the critical element in the rhetorical analysis of the embedded character of the text within a sociopolitical context that produces certain strategies of argumentation.

20. Tracy, *Analogical Imagination*, 233–47; idem, "The Uneasy Alliance Reconceived: Catholic Theological Method, Modernity, and Postmodernism," *Theological Studies* 50 (1989): 548–70.

notion of "classic" for understanding the task of systematic theology. The disclosure model of truth that conceives of truth as unconcealment is interrelated with the understanding of the classic as historical and yet extending beyond its historical context. Consequently, one needs to analyze the conception of systematic theology as the interpretation of Christian classics with reference to its specific model of truth and with reference to the centrality given to the classic. The disclosure model of truth underlies the interpretation of the classic within the framework of the definition of systematic theology as hermeneutical.

The understanding of systematic theology as hermeneutical relies on a specific model of truth, namely truth as disclosure, which developed within philosophical hermeneutics. This hermeneutics radicalized the linguistic turn within the tradition that began in Germany with Johann Hamann, Johann Gottfried Herder, and Wilhelm von Humboldt and was further developed by Martin Heidegger and Hans-Georg Gadamer.[21] This philosophical hermeneutics makes two significant assumptions that are relevant to the conception of systematic theology as hermeneutical: the first concerns truth as world disclosure and unconcealment; the second revolves around the relationship between truth and the meaningfulness of classics.

Disclosure Model of Truth: The disclosure model of truth is articulated within Heidegger's phenomenological hermeneutics as an institution, event, and happening of truth that involves a giving, a grounding, and an originating of truth. In *Being and Time* Heidegger contends that truth as unconcealment is much more fundamental than truth as assertion and has a priority over truth as correspondence.[22] In his later works, especially in his lectures "On the Essence of Truth" and "On the Origin of the Work of Art," Heidegger radicalizes his view of truth as disclosure and unconcealment.[23] Previously, he had claimed that truth as disclosure was merely more foundational than truth as assertion.[24] Now, truth as disclosure replaces truth as assertion. From downplaying external conditions, Heidegger moves to eradicating correspondence and a cognitive orientation.[25] His view of

---

21. Cristina Lafont, *Heidegger, Language, and World-Disclosure: Modern European Philosophy* (New York: Cambridge University Press, 2000); idem, *The Linguistic Turn in Hermeneutic Philosophy* (Cambridge: MIT Press, 1999); and Ingrid Scheibler, *Gadamer: Between Heidegger and Habermas* (Lanham, Md.: Rowman & Littlefield, 2000).

22. Martin Heidegger, *Being and Time* (trans. Joan Stambaugh; Albany: State University of New York Press, 1996), 44.

23. Heidegger's lecture on art was given on 13 November 1935, but was published only in 1950. See Martin Heidegger, *Pathmarks* (ed. William McNeill; Cambridge: Cambridge University Press, 1998). For the other essays, see idem, *Basic Writings* (New York: Harper & Row, 1976).

24. See Ernst Tugendhat, *Der Wahrheitsbegriff bei Husserl und Heidegger* (Berlin: de Gruyter, 1967). See Tugendhat's essay "Heidegger's Idea of Truth," in *Hermeneutics and Truth: Northwestern University Studies in Phenomenology and Existential Philosophy* (ed. Brice R. Wachterhauser; Evanston, Ill.: Northwestern University Press, 1994), 83–97.

25. See the disagreement with Tugendhat's interpretation in Lafont, *Heidegger, Language, and World-Disclosure*, 109–75.

language is that meaning determines reference, and he replaces the subject-object distinction with that of a symbolically structured world. The tendency of later writings is to equate truth and meaning so that what is true becomes tantamount to what is meaningful.

Gadamer's hermeneutics fully develops this view for cultural phenomena. The truth entailed in the appropriation of esthetic and religious phenomena goes beyond scientific knowledge and logically reasoned argument. It does not stem from a cognitive orientation toward what is objectively the case, but it transcends such an orientation. Gadamer, thereby, breaks not only with the subject-object dichotomy of historicism, but also with the scientism underlying the Enlightenment's attitude toward truth. This break in turn enables him to rehabilitate tradition and the authority of classics: "That which has been sanctioned by tradition and custom has an authority that is nameless, and ... not just what is obvious on the grounds of reasons ... and is valid without foundations."[26] The authority of tradition that needs to be rehabilitated is not so much a question of obedience, but of knowledge, but a knowledge that is other than a reasoned knowledge.[27] Moreover, in his response to Jürgen Habermas's application of ideology critique, Gadamer claims that hermeneutics has as its basic task "the appropriation of superior meaning."[28]

Truth and the Meaningfulness of the Classic: In this hermeneutical view, a classic is a classic because it discloses truth and meaning in an extraordinary way. This extraordinariness makes a classic that is temporal and historical and, at the same time, atemporal and ahistorical. Although a classic was created within a specific historical period, a classic transcends its own historical time and place as its endurance through time and its acceptance by successive generations demonstrates. It is precisely this endurance through generations that displays the extraordinary and atemporal character of a classic. But ambiguity emerges here. On the one hand, a classic was created within a specific context, and this context is part of the original horizon of the author and audience of the classic. On the other hand, a classic transcends its original horizon insofar as a classic endures through successive generations and through new applications. The original horizon and context of a classic is integral to its interpretation. Nevertheless, a classic transcends its own context and horizon. A classic demands of the succession of interpreters that they expand their own horizons and merge with the horizon of the classic. They come to interpret and to understand a classic when expanding their own horizons; they acknowledge the meaning of the classic in applying its significance to their own situation.

---

26. Hans-Georg Gadamer, *Truth and Method* (2d rev. ed.; New York: Continuum, 1993), 281. See Lafont, *Linguistic Turn*, 113–14.

27. Gadamer, *Truth and Method*, 279.

28. Hans-Georg Gadamer, *Gesammelte Werke* (Tübingen: Mohr, 1993), 2.264.

Critical Questions

A decisive question is this: What are the implications of these two presuppositions for the definition of systematic theology as the interpretation of classics? Does the emphasis upon the disclosure model of truth play down, devalue, or deny the cognitive dimension within systematic theology? Does the practical equation of truth and meaningfulness influence the evaluation of the role that religious classics have within such a conception of systematic theology? Consequently, one has to raise these and other questions about this approach. Although Tracy's view of systematic theology as the interpretation of Christian classics recognizes that classics are not simply texts, its method and the steps for interpreting classics are outlined primarily in relation to the interpretation of texts. This emphasis on the literary classic makes systematic theology appear primarily as a "great books" program — a great books program of religious classics and, in the case of Christian systematic theology, a great books program of Christian classics. Systematic theology seeks to uncover the religious dimension of texts and to apply its meaning and truth to the contemporary situation.

Moreover, one can question the adequacy of such an understanding of systematic theology. Granted that it is important to interpret religious and Christian classics in order to uncover their disclosive religious and Christian meaning, nevertheless the decisive question remains: Does the systematic theological task stop there? Is that sufficient for the cognitive task of systematic theology? How does such an approach deal with the diversity of such religious classics? The Reformation and post-Tridentine Christian classics on the nature of the church differ considerably. Take, for example, the contrasting conceptions of the church in Martin Luther's *Babylonian Captivity of the Church,* Cardinal Bellarmine's writings on the church, and John Calvin's *Institutes of the Christian Religion,* which differ not only in their conceptions of ecclesial structures and practices, but also in regard to the very the nature of the church.

One can argue that all three conceptions are disclosive of religious truth and that one should learn from each — an important theological task for a systematic theology seeking to be ecumenical and irenic. Yet is it not an equally important task for a systematic theologian within a specific church community to ask: Which structure, practice, and self-understanding should my community have? Which conception of the church is more adequate to my tradition? Which conception is more adequate to my experience and to the changing organizational structures of society? Answers to these questions cannot simply celebrate a pluralism of readings. A community may want to make decisions about what kind of a community it wants to be. Women can ask what impact these texts have upon the lives and experiences of women. Such questions demand much more than the interpretation of classics. The problem of conflict among diverse classics cannot be simply reconciled through a pluralist account of either interpretation or application.

In addition, the question emerges: How does systematic theology deal with new theoretical issues, new communities of discourse, and new experiences arising from differences in gender, class, social location, and cultural location? How does systematic theology carry out its task when it not only looks backward but also looks forward and faces new questions? Systematic theology performs an invaluable task in asking: What is the religious significance of the Genesis narrative, Augustine's commentary on Genesis, Aquinas's commentary on the *Book of Causes,* and Calvin's commentary on Genesis? These questions are indeed important, but they do not touch upon other questions: What is the meaning of creation when the background conceptions of the ancient Orient that underlie the Genesis account are no longer valid? How do the narratives about the creation of male and female reflect a specific social and cultural constellation? How does one reconstruct a doctrine of creation within a completely different natural scientific worldview? How does one understand the creation of human beings in the post-Darwinian evolutionary worldview? What meaning should be given to accounts of original sin, or should it be demonstrated without a shadow of a doubt that the human race descends not from one Eve but seven Eves? These questions, proper to systematic theology, go beyond the interpretative task. If systematic theology has to ask what it means to believe in creation under the conditions of scientific knowledge today, then it does not suffice, as someone might object, that this question is sufficiently raised when, in interpreting religious classics, one uses explanatory theories to locate classics through historical criticism, to provide a structural analysis of the text, to determine the linguistic meaning of terms, or to specify the rhetorical context of the text. Even the exploration of the subject matter as understood by both author and reader of the classic or exploration of the trajectory of the classic's reception does not suffice in raising the systematic theological issues at stake. One has to go beyond interpretive retrieval to deal with the subject matter at hand, for ethical and cognitive issues are at stake. The inadequacies of the disclosure model of truth come to the fore in the reduction of systematic theology to the hermeneutical retrieval of religious classics. Systematic theology should, however, deal systematically with the subject matter at hand in relation to cognitive and ethical claims.

Systematic Theology as Thick Description

The term *hermeneutical* might appear as a misnomer for the theological approach labeled "thick description," for Frei criticizes much of nineteenth- and twentieth-century hermeneutical theory and contests the applicability of a general theory of interpretation to biblical texts.[29] Nevertheless, if one takes hermeneutics in the sense of a way of reading and interpreting, then this position, even in its polemic against the strictures of general theories of interpretation, does indeed offer a specific understanding of theology and hermeneutics and a distinctive view of their interrelation.[30] Despite differences among them, Frei, Lindbeck, Kelsey, Thiemann, Wood, and Tanner exhibit common traits in their interpretative approach to the Scriptures and in their understanding of systematic theology as thick description. They take over the category of thick description from philosophy and cultural anthropology, but use it in a very specific and unique way.

Since Schleiermacher, hermeneutical theorists have emphasized that biblical texts share with other texts in the general problems of understanding. They do not require a special hermeneutic, but are subject to the same general rules and practices as other texts. It is to this modern hermeneutical view that Frei and Lindbeck object. Because of their objection, their initial position seems at face value to be "antihermeneutical." But this needs to be qualified. It is a critique of modern hermeneutics, and this critique brings to the fore their specific views of both hermeneutics and theology. Frei and Lindbeck take up Barth's attempt to emphasize God's absolute freedom and sovereignty in God's self-revelation in order to criticize modern hermeneutical theory. Consequently, Frei argues that to the extent that modern hermeneutics subjects the biblical texts to general rules of understanding and interpretation, it runs the risk of subjecting the revelation expressed in those texts to external standards.[31] However, he does not eliminate all rules, but allows those rules that are low level, modestly appropriate, and used in an ad hoc manner.[32] What is excluded are those hermeneutical rules that might "serve globally and foundationally, so that the reading of the biblical material would simply be a regional instance of the universal procedure."[33] In order to avoid this external grounding, Frei develops an intratextual and

---

29. Hans W. Frei, *The Eclipse of Biblical Narrative: A Study in Eighteenth and Nineteenth Century Hermeneutics* (New Haven: Yale University Press, 1974). Although Frei advocates his study as a critique of hermeneutics, the major theorists of hermeneutics in the nineteenth and twentieth centuries are neither mentioned nor discussed. His criticisms of Ricoeur and Tracy are in his essay "The 'Literal Reading' of the Biblical Narrative in the Christian Tradition: Does It Stretch or Will It Break?" in *The Bible and the Narrative Tradition* (ed. Frank McConnell; New York: Oxford University Press, 1986), 36–77. For my analysis of Frei, see Livingston and Schüssler Fiorenza, *Modern Christian Thought*, 2.369–77.

30. One of the best analyses of Frei's work in relation to that of Ricoeur's is James Fodor, *Christian Hermeneutics: Paul Ricoeur and the Refiguring of Theology* (New York: Oxford University Press, 1995).

31. Frei rightly argues against an Enlightenment hermeneutics of the eighteenth or early nineteenth century; unfortunately, he does not confront the extent to which Gadamer's hermeneutical theory seeks to avoid such pitfalls.

32. Frei, "Literal Reading," 71. See also Paul Schwartentruber, "The Modesty of Hermeneutics: The Theological Reserves of Hans Frei," *Modern Theology* 8 (1992): 181–95.

33. Frei, "Literal Reading," 59.

literal view of reading in a way that is both formal and functional: It is formal insofar as the meaning of the text is internal; it is functional insofar as its use and meaning are interrelated.

Intratextual and Literal Reading as Formal and Functional

Frei's understanding of the interpretation of biblical texts developed or shifted in time from a formal description to a functional one. A formal description of the text explicates its meaning and truth, thereby giving the sense of the text. In his view, Christians should think of the Scriptures not so much as sources, but rather as texts that are configured in intrinsically meaningful narrative structures. Christians read the Bible as a realistic narrative that made figural interpretation possible. The meaning of these texts has an internal sufficiency; that is, it is inherent in the texts themselves rather than in a reference to some extrabiblical universal moral truth or to the truth to which the texts refer. This emphasis on formal description and internal sufficiency stems from different resources.

This theory draws on the formal literal theory of New Criticism, on Erich Auerbach's interpretation of realistic narratives,[34] and theologically on the Reformation emphasis on the autonomy, sufficiency, and perspicuity of the text. New Criticism emphasizes that a text should be interpreted from its own internal formal narrative structures rather than from external sources in contrast to psychoanalytic interpretations focusing on the author's psychology or social interpretations examining a text's economic and social context. Auerbach's tracing of the historical lineage of realistic narratives provides not only a specific way of reading a text, but also a historical justification. This combined literary and interpretive theory is further buttressed and theologically justified through the Reformation belief in the sufficiency and perspicuity of the text.[35] This combination constitutes the "general hermeneutical theory" of the Yale School despite all protests against general hermeneutical theories. Likewise, Lindbeck characterizes "intratextuality" as an approach that takes into account literary considerations for their meaning and so provides an "internal" interpretation. The internal meaning is described as immanent to the text insofar as it depends on literary considerations and literary form for its meaning.[36] However, it is this immanent meaning that specifies the "theological controlling sense of scripture."

In advocating that the literal reading of the Bible is internal to the text, Frei is also arguing that the literal sense should not be associated with any

---

34. Erich Auerbach, *Mimesis: The Representation of Reality in Western Literature* (Princeton: Princeton University Press, 1953); idem, *Gesammelte Aufsätze zur romanischen Philologie* (Munich: Francke, 1967); idem, *Literary Language and Its Public in Late Latin Antiquity and in the Middle Age* (Princeton: Princeton University Press, 1993).

35. See Hans W. Frei, *Theology and Narrative: Selected Essays* (ed. George Hunsinger and William C. Placher; New York: Oxford University Press, 1993), 108.

36. George Lindbeck, *The Nature of Doctrine: Religion and Theology in a Postliberal Age* (Philadelphia: Westminster, 1984), 120.

one specific theory of reading so that that theory does not become the criterion or standard by which the literal reading of the Bible is measured and judged. In order to avoid this view, he argues that any account of how Christian communities understand the primary and plain sense of the Scripture has to be based instead on a "thick descriptive analysis of communal ruled use and only secondarily and in a low-keyed way to any literary theory."[37] Frei's appeal to thick description of the "communal ruled use" constitutes his hermeneutical key that seeks to eschew any a priori standard or interpretive theory. The plain sense of Scripture follows from the actual and fruitful use that a religious community makes of a biblical text as its communal sense.[38] In other words, instead of privileging a particular hermeneutical theory as normative, one privileges a de facto use and meaning of the Scripture as normative. The way that Scripture is used and read in the community is the literal and plain sense of Scripture. This communal practice rather than any general hermeneutical theory is the basis of the plain sense.

Frei's equation of a community's de facto use and the plain sense of the Scripture constitutes the major point of an approach that equates a community's functional use of Scripture with its meaning. This approach was picked up and developed by other members of the Yale School, especially David Kelsey, Charles Wood, and Kathryn Tanner. The plain sense of the Scripture is the way the text is used in the community. Tanner defines the scriptural plain sense as what a community "automatically or naturally takes a text to be saying on its face insofar as he or she has been socialized in a community's conventions for reading that text as scripture."[39] As the sense of a text functioning as Scripture, the plain sense, Tanner adds that once the use of a community has become "sedimented," it shapes belief and practice and becomes normative for future interpretation of Scripture.

Several basic problems exist with this position: It overlooks the diversity of Christian communities and the pluralism of their readings of the Scriptures. In many instances, it would be more accurate to speak not of *the* Christian community, but of diverse Christian communities. Yet this position appears to presuppose not only that there is one use and meaning of the Scriptures in "the Christian community," but also that, despite theological differences and differences in the various narratives, the biblical narratives present a "coherent narrative" with a corresponding world. As Ronald F. Thiemann argues, "The stories are coherent and they function to invite the reader into the world of the tale."[40] One has to ask whether

---

37. Frei, "Literal Reading," 51, 64, 72.

38. Ibid., 61–62.

39. Kathryn E. Tanner, "Theology and the Plain Sense," in *Scriptural Authority and Narrative Interpretation* (Festschrift for Hans W. Frei) (ed. Garrett Green; Philadelphia: Fortress, 1987), 59–78, quotation on 63.

40. Ronald F. Thiemann, "Radiance and Obscurity in Biblical Narrative," in *Scriptural Authority and Narrative Interpretation* (Festschrift for Hans W. Frei) (ed. Garrett Green; Philadelphia: Fortress, 1987), 21–41, quotation on 38.

the Scriptures present a diversity of worlds and whether throughout Christian tradition there are a diversity of uses and multiple normative receptions of the Scriptures. At this point a rhetorical analysis becomes important because it underscores the diversity of meaning in relation to diverse audiences and diverse argumentative strategies and also because it brings into consideration a rhetorical and evaluative analysis of contemporary readings. A rhetorical analysis requires an interpretive pluralism, which in turn requires that systematic theology take into account that pluralism without reducing the meaning of Scriptures simply to literal sense and their de facto use and thereby assuming a single normative reading.

Second, and more important, this interpretive view of normativity is a theological version of what modern ethics labels the "naturalistic fallacy." Such a fallacy argues from what is to what should be. The crucial question is whether the de facto use and interpretation of the Scriptures necessarily provides an adequate basis for the normative meaning of the Scriptures within the ongoing life of the Christian communities.[41] For example, in the twentieth century, in the light of the Holocaust, many Christian communities retrospectively and critically reflected on the traditional and sedimented theological, religious, and liturgical use of the Scriptures. The distinction between a reading in the spirit and a reading in the flesh was traditionally understood and used in the life of Christian communities in an explicitly anti-Jewish polemic. Such a use became sedimented in an interpretation that contrasted Christian and Jewish readings of the Scriptures, labeling the latter as a reading according to flesh. It is quite clear that such a de facto use of the Scriptures contributed to the anti-Jewish mentalities within Christian communities. Likewise, many Christian communities have only in the last decades taken out of their Good Friday liturgies those anti-Jewish texts of the Gospel of John's passion narratives in order to correct a previous de facto use and meaning of those Scriptures within the communities. The de facto use in the Christian communities of the household codes tended to justify the subordination of women to males and slaves to their masters throughout many centuries of the Christian past.[42] To make normative the plain sense and the de facto use of the Scriptures is to overlook these significant historical examples of the use of the Scriptures in a way that can no longer be justified as normative. The theological understanding of the community as a wandering people of God and as a sinful community needs to find its expression in a hermeneutics that leaves open the possibility for testing and reevaluating de facto use and appropriation of the Scriptures within diverse Christian communities.

---

41. Francis Schüssler Fiorenza, "The Conflict of Hermeneutical Tradition," *Journal of Chinese Philosophy* 27 (2000): 3–31.

42. On the household codes, see Schüssler Fiorenza, *Bread Not Stone,* 65–92.

Thick Description as the Hermeneutics of Christian Identity

"Thick Description" is the term that characterizes the procedure and "method" that both Frei and Lindbeck use to characterize their distinctive view of theology as hermeneutics. Theology should not be philosophically grounded in a universal worldview, a metaphysics, or an anthropology. Likewise, Christian language should not be translated into another language, as if that language were somehow more foundational, more grounding, and more universal than Christian language itself. As Frei maintains: "Christianity has its own distinctive language, which is not to be interpreted without residue into other ways of thinking and speaking."[43] This critique limits the theological task and sets the parameters for the understanding of theology as hermeneutical. It blocks taking into account the experience of women today as a normative instance in their interpretive and evaluative reception of the traditional Christian ways of thinking and speaking. Consequently, Christian theology is descriptive or redescriptive. Theology does not have the task of arguing the "possibility of Christian truth any more than the instantiation or actuality of that truth."[44] Instead, theology should be confessional rather than apologetic.[45] The content or logical structure of the Christian belief and the logic of coming to belief should be kept distinct. As Frei emphasizes: "I should want to draw a sharp distinction between the logical structure as well as the content of Christian belief, which it is the business of theologians to describe but not to explain or to argue, and the totally different logic of how one comes to believe."[46] Similarly, Lindbeck argues for the interpretive rule that a religious object should not be described from the outside, but only in and through the concrete and symbolic structured life practices of a specific religious community (church). Systematic theology as hermeneutical explicates the immanent logic of the Christian community. From that perspective it provides a corresponding Christian understanding of reality.[47]

The systematic import of this argument leads Lindbeck to characterize his position as "postliberal" and to use the category "thick description" to describe the task of theology. The question, however, is: What is liberal, and which theological positions exemplify liberalism against which these postliberal interpretive proposals are directed? His characterization of these opponents, if taken to be liberalism, would be a misleading and even unconventional understanding of liberalism. Lindbeck takes as an example of liberalism not Ernst Troeltsch's individualism, relativism, and historicism,

---

43. Hans W. Frei, *Types of Christian Theology* (New Haven: Yale University Press, 1992), 38.
44. Frei, *Theology and Narrative,* 30.
45. Frei, *Eclipse of Biblical Narrative,* xi.
46. Frei, *Theology and Narrative,* 30.
47. Christof Gestrich and Till Hüttenberger, "Zur Einführung: Theologie und Hermeneutik ums Jahr 2000," *Berliner theologische Zeitschrift* 16 (1999): 153.

but rather Bernard Lonergan, a Roman Catholic transcendental Thomist. Lindbeck objects to Lonergan's reliance on Catholic phenomenologist Friedrich Heiler, and in a similar vein he takes issue with Rahner, another contemporary Catholic theologian, for his emphasis on the experiential horizon in the interpretation of Christianity.

Evidently, postliberal theology contrasts itself primarily with the emphasis upon an anthropological and experimental horizon (a long-standing Roman Catholic tradition) rather than with the individualism and historicism of Protestant liberalism. Liberalism becomes for Lindbeck the label for an appeal to the normative instance of experience, especially within the contemporary theological turn toward the subject. In its critique, the postliberalism of the Yale School primarily continues the Protestant liberal Ritschlian polemic (which needs to be distinguished from Reformed and Calvinist approaches to theology) against the more metaphysical and more expressive experiential claims of modern theology rather than against the individualism and relativisms of the more historicist forms of Protestant liberalism.[48] Yet it is precisely this turn to the subject that has had such a powerful influence upon contemporary liberation theologies, even in their challenge to modern bourgeois understandings of subjectivity. Feminist liberation theologians took up this approach but argued that the subject should not be conceived in terms of male experience. To the extent that liberation theologians, postcolonial theologians, and feminist theologians appeal to experiences and practices that challenge traditional descriptions and practices, the question can be raised whether systematic theology can be defined primarily as a thick description of the languages, practices, and logic of a particular community.[49]

The understanding of systematic theology as an interpretive thick description can be profiled against the original use of the term *thick description* in philosophical and anthropological literature. Gilbert Ryle first used *thick description* to characterize an interpretation that explicates the meaning of human actions not by merely describing the superficially observable action, but by viewing the action as an expressive act that exhibits an intentionality that is not immediately evident. His example is a youth's mimicking to poke fun at another youth. A thick description does not merely describe the external actions, but interprets them as a mimicking.[50] Clifford Geertz adopts from Ryle the term *thick description* for social and cultural anthropology in order to express an interpretation that exhibits the symbolic and

48. Francis Schüssler Fiorenza, "Theological Liberalism: An Unfinished Challenge," *Harvard Divinity Bulletin* 28 (1998): 9–12.

49. Francis Schüssler Fiorenza, "Being, Subjectivity, and Otherness: The Idols of Gods," in *Questioning God* (ed. John D. Caputo, Mark Dooley, and Michael Scanlon; Indianapolis: Indiana University Press, 2001), 320–50.

50. Gilbert Ryle, *Collected Papers*, vol. 2 (London: Hutchinson, 1971).

meaningful structure of human actions.[51] A thick description is, however, only one half of the theoretical interpretative framework. Geertz makes a relative distinction (even more relative in anthropology than in the observational or experiential sciences) between inscription (thick description) and specification or diagnosis. The former (inscription or thick description) tries to ascertain as clearly as possible the meaning that social actions have for the actors or agents of these actions. The anthropologist seeks to inscribe or describe the meaning of the action based on the clues that the actors give the anthropologist. The specification or diagnosis seeks to construct "a system of analysis in whose terms what is generic to those structures, what belongs to them because they are what they are, will stand out against the other determinants of human behavior."[52] One moves from a description of small and densely textured facts to broad assertions about culture and societal life. Such ethnographic descriptions include interpretative elements of action as well as the interpretative flow of social discourses. They also seek to rescue what people have said in such discourses and to fix it in usable categories.

Geertz advocated his interpretive approach to culture against objectivist and functionalist approaches to the anthropology and the social sciences that dominated in the 1950s in the United States. Moreover, similar to some currents in social history, Geertz's approach does not rest on the thoughts of intellectual elites or the actions of political elites, but rather sought to decipher the meaning in the rituals, practices, and conventions of ordinary people. Against any reductionist approach, Geertz proposes that culture should be interpreted as expressing the multiple webs of meaning in which people live. Further, anthropologists should interpret symbolic systems (language, ritual, arts, practices) that encode these webs of meaning. Since for Geertz the activity of the cultural anthropologist is similar to that of the literary critic, it might seem at first glance that a hermeneutical affinity exists between Geertz's resistance to reductionism and those theological approaches that model their method of theological interpretation on the New Criticism's adherence to the structured code and autonomy of the text.

A couple of significant differences exist in the appeal to thick description. Geertz's understanding of a cultural anthropological approach combines both expressive and structural elements. Lindbeck, however, appeals to the cultural linguistic primarily in critique of an expressive approach (and also a propositional approach to theology).[53] Ryle and Geertz do not so much criticize expressive approaches as they focus on culture as laden with the expressive symbolic actions. Thick description relates in their view to the meaning that agents give their actions. Moreover, though Geertz is

51. Clifford Geertz, "Thick Descriptions: Towards a Theory of Interpretation of Cultures," in Geertz's *The Interpretation of Cultures* (New York: Basic Books, 1973), 3–30.

52. Ibid., 27.

53. Francis Schüssler Fiorenza, "Schleiermacher and the Construction of a Contemporary Roman Catholic Foundational Theology," *Harvard Theological Review* 89 (1996): 175–94.

even criticized for reacting too excessively to Parson's functionalism, his analysis does appropriate structural and anthropological methods that go beyond the Wittgensteinian interpretation of social reality that dominates this theological approach.[54]

In addition, one can ask whether the criticisms that have been brought against Geertz's interpretative theory can also be addressed to the theological appropriation of thick description. The notion of culture as text often leaves unclear who is speaking in the text, to whom it is addressed, and about what it speaks.[55] Such a treatment of culture-as-text separates the text from its social context, isolates it from its historical context, and fails to address its entailment within social processes, social formation, and societal differentiation. Such a criticism is most pointedly formulated in Edward Said's arguments against the construal of anthropology dealing merely with textuality, ethnographic fact, or hermeneutical construct. "The vogue for thick descriptions," as Said asserts, "acts to shut out and block out the clamour of voices on the outside asking for their claims about empire and domination to be considered."[56] A rhetorical analysis, which requires that one take into account the relation between the author and addressee (both real and implied), the respective argumentative strategies, and the diverse receptions both in the past and present, offers a corrective to the idealism of the theological use of thick description.

Critical Questions

Not only are the questions about the adequacy of Geertz's own conception of thick description applicable, but a specific problem exists with the way that some limit systematic theology's task to thick description or redescription. They presuppose that Christian theology and interpretation relate to one another in a one-directional way. Both Frei and Lindbeck reject a general hermeneutics because, in their view, such a hermeneutics assumes that Christian theological ideas are translated into a common public discourse in order to interpret and to justify them. They argue in contrast that Christian theological language is a particular discourse, whereas philosophical hermeneutics entails a translation of this language into a general discourse. One cannot translate the particular into the general without a loss of specificity

---

54. See criticisms of Geertz in Talal Asad, "Anthropological Conceptions of Religion: Reflections on Geertz," *Man* 18.2 (1983): 237–59. See also Clifford Geertz, "Anti-Anti-Relativism," *American Anthropologist* 86 (1984): 263–78; repr. in idem, *Available Light* (Princeton: Princeton University Press, 2000), 42–67; Jeffrey C. Alexander, *Twenty Lectures* (New York: Columbia University Press, 1987).

55. See William Roseberry, "Balinese Cockfights and the Seduction of Anthropology," *Social Research* 49 (1982): 1013–28; and Roger M. Keesing, "Introduction," in *Rituals of Manhood* (ed. G. H. Herdt; Berkeley: University of California Press, 1982), 1–43.

56. E. W. Said, "Representing the Colonised: Anthropology's Interlocutors," *Critical Inquiry* 15 (1989): 219–20.

and particularity. In addition, as some suggest, they imply that various discourses are incommensurable with each other and should not be interpreted in terms of some common generic discourse or some common foundation.

However justified the critique of any appeal to a generic discourse or common foundation may be, it is questionable whether the philosophical hermeneutics (as represented, for example, by Gadamer) does indeed require such a translation or rather, as Gadamer's own criticisms of Schleiermacher and Dilthey indicate, explicitly develop hermeneutical theory in a way to avoid any such translation into the generic. What is presented as the procedure of hermeneutics is in fact a caricature of contemporary hermeneutics. In addition, such a critique in itself does not provide a sufficient justification that the understanding of systematic theology as a thick description is an adequate theological method. The alternative between "thick description" and "some common foundation" is a false alternative and a misguided description of the issues at stake.[57]

Since both Frei and Lindbeck write from a Protestant theological perspective, one can, therefore, ask them whether Martin Luther's execution of the theological task can be adequately described as thick description or as redescription. His *Babylonian Captivity of the Church* does not perform the theological task by providing a thick description of the Roman Catholic community's current beliefs, communal practices, and sedimented interpretation of the plain sense of Scripture. Instead, he gives a reconstructed and new interpretation of the law/gospel distinction, and he interprets God's prevenient grace in a way that challenges sedimented meaning and a consistent interpretation of that grace. Furthermore, he offers a new interpretation of the flesh/spirit distinction that decisively differs from the early Christian interpretation; Luther draws out the implications of this theological view in order to challenge certain current beliefs, practices, and interpretations. He, therefore, offers a Reformation understanding of the Christian community, the self, and the world. Luther's view of divine grace went beyond that of his contemporaries, and his application of that view entailed a criticism of current communal beliefs and practices as a captivity. Lindbeck might respond to this objection that his own hermeneutic employs the christological and trinitarian rule of the early church as the lenses through which the Scriptures are read and as the canon that should be the basis of building communal consensus. To the extent that he would seek to put this into practice, he would be going beyond an anthropological thick description and would be making a specific norm the criterion to evaluate de facto communal practices and interpretations.

---

57. Francis Schüssler Fiorenza, "Pluralism: A Western Commodity or Justice for the Other," in *Ethical Monotheism, Past and Present: Essays in Honor of Wendel S. Dietrich* (ed. Theodore Vial and Mark Poster; New York: Oxford University Press, 2001), 278–306; idem, "The Challenge of Pluralism and Globalization to Ethical Reflection," *Concilium* (2001/4): 71–85.

In a similar vein, Lindbeck's theory of cultural-linguistic framework downplays differences among diverse Christian communities, even though these communities, both in the past and present, have had very different internal descriptions of their beliefs and have lived in different cultural and linguistic milieus. In response to this objection, it is argued that at least the well educated or spiritually disciplined will agree. Such a response, as Tanner notes, simply begs the question, especially if it assumes that the majority involved within a particular language game are not quite knowledgeable of its rules.[58]

Other challenges to theology as an interpretive thick description revolve around the implications of thick description and redescription as well as its polemic against the grounding or the apologetic function of theology. Jeffrey Stout claims that it exhibits "an irresponsible willingness to abandon public discourse and critical thought altogether."[59] Such a criticism may overlook the degree to which ad hoc public discourse or argument is possible. Nevertheless, it raises a significant question: What values do the warrants external to the Christian vision have for challenging elements of that vision? To the degree that this understanding of theology sees the world of the text absorbing the world outside the text, to that degree it overlooks that the world outside the scriptural text might not be able to be integrated within the world of the text. Such a resistance is often based not upon an appeal to some universal grounding or abstract reason, but upon concrete local knowledge and experiences. In fact, the resistance may be based upon nonfoundational pragmatic reasons, as pragmaticists argue.[60]

Reflective Equilibrium and Rhetorical Analysis

Elisabeth Schüssler Fiorenza's advocacy of feminist hermeneutics and critical rhetorical analysis sharply contrasts with the hermeneutical conceptions at the basis of the above conceptions of systematic theology. Her view of interpretation appeals to the critique of ideology within critical theory, and her evaluative rhetoric and feminist hermeneutic give a critical significance to criteria of praxis and to struggles for liberation. In refusing to abstract a text from its context, her rhetorical analysis attends to the diverse situations of the text: the historical argumentative situation, the implied or inscribed rhetorical situation, and the rhetorical situation of contemporary

---

58. Kathryn Tanner, *Theories of Culture: A New Agenda for Theology* (Guides to Theological Inquiry; Minneapolis: Fortress, 1997), 142.

59. Jeffrey Stout, *Ethics after Babel* (Boston: Beacon, 1988), 186.

60. Sheila Greeve Davaney, *Pragmatic Historicism* (Albany: State University of New York Press, 2000).

interpretations.[61] Her use of rhetorical analysis consequently entails diverse elements: a reader-response criticism that distinguishes between the actual writer/reader and the implied writer/reader; an analysis of how the rhetorical structuring of a text displays the text's argumentative strategies in relation to the author and the audience; and an analysis of the rhetorical question of a fitting response to the rhetorical situation. The interpretation of a text in terms of rhetoric means that interpreters cannot limit themselves either to a formalistic literary analysis of a text or to a historical critical analysis of the text's social location. Instead, understanding should develop a responsible ethical and evaluative theological criticism.

Not only do I agree with Elisabeth Schüssler Fiorenza's arguments on these points, but I have also been influenced by them.[62] In my view, systematic theology should be understood primarily as normative and reconstructive. Such a conception goes against any understanding of theology as primarily historical, hermeneutical, or descriptive. Theology should not be reduced to primarily a historical or hermeneutical task (as a reclamation of past theological figures and texts) nor should it be reduced to the task of redescription (as a thick description of the logic and rules implicit in a community's practices and beliefs). This claim does not deny the importance of the historical, descriptive, and interpretive undertaking, but it does affirm that the normative and reconstructive task is what makes systematic theology both theological and systematic. The execution of this theological normative and reconstructive task includes several elements that are mutually intertwined and interrelated: the reconstructive interpretation of a tradition, the examination of relevant background theories, the consideration of warrants from experience and practice, and the attentive engagement with diverse communities of discourse.[63]

The understanding of systematic theology as entailing a broad reflective equilibrium among diverse tasks does not so much play down the role of interpretation in all these tasks as it underscores the multiplicity of the tasks, the multiplicity of the sources, and the need for bringing these into relation with one another. Christian traditions with their beliefs and practices continuously intersect with other language games, background theories, and experiences of the world. They must deal with real and independent consequences that lead to differences from their own traditions just as they must deal with diverse communities of discourse. Interpretations and justifications of Christian beliefs and practices are interrelated not only internally,

61. Elisabeth Schüssler Fiorenza, *Rhetoric and Ethic: The Politics of Biblical Studies* (Minneapolis: Fortress, 1999), 109–11.

62. Francis Schüssler Fiorenza, "The Impact of Feminist Theology on My Thought," *Journal of Feminist Studies in Religion* 7 (1991): 95–105, responses on 106–26.

63. Concerning the method of broad reflective equilibrium and the relevant secondary literature, see Francis Schüssler Fiorenza, *Foundational Theology: Jesus and the Church* (New York: Crossroad, 1984); and idem, "Systematic Theology."

but also externally and in relation to many diverse warrants.[64] The reference to background theories, retroductive warrants, and communities of discourse does not appeal to these as elements that are independent of interpretation. There are no background theories, retroductive warrants, and communities of discourse that are not caught in the web of interpretation. This web of interpretation implies that they are interrelated with each other and can reciprocally challenge and critique one another.

All of this implies that the alternative that Frei or Lindbeck often poses of adapting the biblical world to the world outside the Scriptures (to which they object) or incorporating the outside world into the biblical world (which they advocate) is much too starkly and exclusively framed. It neglects other experiences and theories that have to be taken into account, and it overlooks that systematic theology involves challenges and warrants from diverse sources. Likewise, there is a difference between whether one considers diverse background theories of interpretation while interpreting a classic (thus focusing on methods of interpretation) or whether one considers the background theories about the human person, societal structure, origin of the human race, etc., and compares them with the background theories of classics or the Scriptures about these subject matters. In the latter case, one does not simply retrieve the disclosive power of the truth of the classic or the Scriptures, but one weighs the adequacy and significance of the diverse background theories, and one brings into consideration diverse warrants from experience and the insights of diverse communities of interpretation. Some of these warrants challenge and interrupt the claims of the classics.

This understanding of systematic theology as involving a broad reflective equilibrium adopts and modifies the category as it is used within political ethics in the discussions surrounding John Rawls's *Theory of Justice*.[65] Elisabeth Schüssler Fiorenza is critical of my appeal to broad reflective equilibrium as the method of systematic theology for two basic reasons. The first reason is that the category of broad reflective equilibrium is abstract and does not take sufficiently into account the subject or the agent of the broad reflective equilibrium. I seek to take this criticism into account by extending the category of broad reflective equilibrium to take into consideration the diverse communities of discourses. Reflection on the community of discourse would in this way take into account not only the content or subject matter, but also the agent or subject of theology.[66] From the perspective of Elisabeth Schüssler Fiorenza's work, this modification is inadequate because it fails to take sufficiently into account the standpoint of the theologian as an interpreter, constructor, and evaluator of the tradition. Not only is such

---

64. Justification and interpretation are often distinguished. The former deals with truth, the later with meaning. Nevertheless, to the degree that truth conditions affect meaning, they cannot be separated. Meaning and the truth conditions are interrelated.

65. John Rawls, *Theory of Justice* (Cambridge: Harvard University Press, 1971).

66. Francis Schüssler Fiorenza, "Systematic Theology."

a method formal and abstract, but even the inclusion of communities of discourse is abstract and fails to take power relations into account. The second reason for her critique is that such a method neglects to analyze critically the location and stance of the theologian who is reflecting upon the diverse elements and warrants with this method. What is significant for her rhetorical analysis is that one needs to take into account the preunderstanding and the stance of the exegete or the theologian and that one needs to take into account conditions of domination. The fallacy of scientism and objectivism not only within exegetical and historical studies, but also within theological studies, is that it fails to analyze critically the particular standpoint of the exegete, historian, or theologian.

It is in this context that Elisabeth Schüssler Fiorenza's rhetorical analysis is important for systematic theology. Though she does not discuss the nature of systematic theology as a theological subdiscipline, she does present a specific view of theology. "Theology is best understood," she writes, "not as a system, but as a rhetorical practice that does not conceive of language merely as signification and transmission, but rather as a form of action and power that affects actual people and situations."[67] She appeals to the image of "quilting" rather than "reporting" as a much more appropriate metaphor for her understanding of the historian's tasks.[68] Her understanding of theology goes beyond quilting, for theology as a form of action and power has a critical, evaluative, and emancipatory function. The conceptions of theology as the interpretation of Christian classics, interpretation of the plain sense of Scripture, and as thick description fail to take sufficiently into account not only the reconstructive and the constructive elements of theology, but also the evaluative and emancipatory rhetorical function of theology.

This evaluative aspect comes to the fore in Elisabeth Schüssler Fiorenza's elaboration of "a critical theo-ethical rhetoric." It comes through historically and systematically. Historically, she argues that the "validity and adequacy of this and of all historical reconstruction must be judged on whether it can make centrally present as historical agents and speaking subjects those whom the kyriocentric text marginalizes or excludes."[69] Systematically, she argues that the "central theological question today" is what kind of God (G*d) do the religious communities proclaim. Therefore, the task of theology in her view is to critically analyze and articulate a "rhetoric of God" or to critically reflect and evaluate how "the Scriptures, traditions, and believers speak about their G*d; and how their practices of *theo-legein* shape their self-understanding, worldviews, and social-political relations."[70] In her

---

67. Schüssler Fiorenza, *Rhetoric and Ethic*, 176.
68. Elisabeth Schüssler Fiorenza, "Quilting: Women's History: Phoebe of Cenchrea," in *Embodied Love: Sensuality and Relationship as Feminist Values* (ed. Paula M. Cooey et al.; San Francisco: Harper & Row, 1987), 35–50.
69. Schüssler Fiorenza, *Rhetoric and Ethic*, 142.
70. Ibid., 178.

view this task is multifaceted and includes not only a hermeneutics of systematically reflected experiences but also analysis, suspicion, evaluation, remembrance, imagination, and transformation.

The Normative Task of Theology

I would like to illustrate the "normative" task of theology by comparing systematic theology with ethics. Ethics is a normative discipline insofar as it does not merely describe the way we in fact conduct our lives or de facto interrelate with other people, communities, or societies. Instead ethics prescribes the way we *should* live our lives and interrelate with others. Likewise, ethical standards are normative in that they are not statistical descriptions of human behavior, but they present guides, recommendations, and obligations about human behavior that are good, right, and just. One cannot move directly from a description of how humans do in fact act to a normative claim about how humans should in fact live. Virtue and justice are ethical concepts that express normative values, obligations, and claims. To acknowledge the normative character of ethics raises complex questions: How does ethics derive its ethical standards for this normativity? Diverse moral systems compete with different claims and distinct grounds of normativity, for example, natural-law theories, intuitionism, utilitarianism, and various deontological approaches.[71] In addition, because following ethical standards is often difficult and in times may stand in opposition to natural inclinations and passions, the further question must be asked: How does ethics motivate individuals and societies to follow ethical standards?

The profiling of systematic theology as a normative discipline in relation to ethics as a normative discipline requires that the two be differentiated and that two misunderstandings be avoided. The argument is not that systematic theology is normative in the same sense that ethics is normative. Nor is the argument that the normativity of systematic theology is reduced to its ethical dimension — that dimension is only one of the many criteria. Instead, ethics illustrates the problem of the relation between facticity and normativity that I want to highlight for systematic theology, for this relation is much more clearly and sharply distinguished in ethics than in other disciplines such as linguistic usage, where the distinction is not as evident.

However, what may be true for linguistics is not true for ethics. In the twentieth century we witnessed the increased dichotomy between facticity and normativity. All too common in the last decades of the twentieth century were cases of genocide, practices of torture, uses of rape as an instrument of war, exploitation of children as soldiers, and the marketing

---

71. See C. D. Broad, *Five Types of Ethical Theory* (New York: Harcourt, 1930); and Christine M. Korsgaard, *The Sources of Normativity* (New York: Cambridge University Press, 1996).

of children and women as prostitutes. Yet at the very same time diverse cultures became increasingly critical of genocide, torture, rape, and sexual slavery. In these cases, one would not argue that the practice of genocide, the prevalence of torture, and the pervasiveness of sexual exploitation justify genocide, torture, and sexual exploitation. Normativity affects not only facticity but also possibility. The current debates in bioethics deal with normative questions about medical issues that deal with future possibilities for the human species through cloning and preembryonic genetic manipulation. What should be normative is not determined from what is factually possible, but from other considerations and criteria. The same should be true of normativity for systematic theology, though the criteria for normativity of action within philosophical ethics differ from the criteria for the normativity of belief within systematic theology.

Systematic theology raises normative questions about what we *should* believe and think about a wide range of religious and theological issues. Since these questions are normative in regard to the present and future of belief and thought, they cannot simply be answered by asking: How can we hermeneutically retrieve what Augustine, Aquinas, Calvin, Schleiermacher, Barth, or Rahner thought and apply it to our present situation? Though important, systematic theology goes beyond historical retrieval and application. It deals with questions whose normative answers require critique, reconstruction, and even construction. Such a process is indeed how Christian theologians have in fact proceeded in the past, and it shows how systematic theology should be done in the future. Two examples might help illustrate this point: the Christian understanding of creation and of marriage.

Creation: For the example of creation, I refer to Thomas Aquinas and the diverse and conflicting sources that influenced him. These included not only the Scriptures, but also Aristotle, Parmenides, Augustine, Boethius, Avicenna, Averroes, Pseudo-Dionysius, Peter Lombard, Albertus Magnus, and others. Although neo-Thomism traditionally stresses that Thomas interpreted creation with the help of Aristotelian causality, it is quite clear that Thomas was very much in dialogue with the Arabian receptions of Aristotle and Plotinus.[72] Moreover, it is quite clear that Aristotle would not have imagined a being beyond being or *esse* and would never have affirmed a transcendent efficient cause of being which is *ipsum esse per se subsistens* (whose very to be subsists through itself). It is quite clear that the idea of the being of the First Cause and the notion of its difference from its creatures stems from the *Plotiniana arabica*. These texts, foundational for Islamic philosophic, religious, and mystical thought, were the dialogue partners and sources that

---

72. See Pierre Hardot, "Dieu comme acte d'être dans le néoplatonisme: A propos des théories d' E. Gilson sur la métaphysique de l'Exode," in *Dieu et l'être* (Paris: Études augustiniènnes, 1978), 57–63.

influenced Thomas and in part were passed on to him through the *Book of Causes*, as is evident from his *Commentary on the Book of Causes*.[73] The Arabic tradition's understanding of the one as pure actuality and pure activity that transcended the finiteness of substance (as maintained by an earlier Greek tradition) was taken over by Thomas. Although he concurred with this Arabian Plotinian tradition that the First Cause is pure actuality and is properly alone creative, he integrated this view into his understanding of God as *ipsum esse* and *esse tantum*. He clearly combined both Aristotelian and Proclan notions of causality to shape a new understanding of causality and creation.[74]

In other words, the task of systematic theology was achieved not simply through the tradition of the interpretation of Christian classic, but took place in dialogue and conversation with other communities and traditions of discourse. This conversation and dialogue was not simply the application to the present of one's own tradition or of these philosophical traditions, but an attempt at a creative synthesis of diverse sources and background theories in order to reconstruct "constructively" the Christian faith. Thomas made normative arguments and reconstructed basic categories, all for the sake of a new understanding of creation. If one were to ask the systematic-theological question today, one might ask: How does one speak about God and God's creative activity in relation to the critique of metaphysics that stems not only from the metaphysical thinking within the Enlightenment and not only from Heidegger's criticism of onto-theological thought, but also in and through the encounter with Buddhism and other non-European religious conceptions of divine that are not as heavily indebted to Platonic and neo-Platonic sources as the Christian tradition has been? However, such questions by themselves do not suffice. Since the doctrine of creation is linked not only with convictions about the hierarchy of being and about the orders of creation and since these have societal and political implications, then the attention to kyriarchal structures of power that a critical rhetorical analysis employs in analyzing the action and practice of a belief is essential to systematic theology.

Marriage: Today, systematic-theological attempts to develop a theology of the sacrament of marriage within the Roman Catholic theological tradition might have to take a critical and reconstructive perspective both in

---

73. See Thomas Aquinas, *Commentary on the Book of Causes: Thomas Aquinas in Translation* (ed. and trans. Vincent A. Guagliardo, Charles R. Hess, and Richard C. Taylor; Washington, D.C.: Catholic University of America Press, 1996); and *Sancti Thomae de Aquino super Librum de Causis Expositio* (Textus philosophici friburgenses 4–5; Fribourg: Societé philosophique, 1954).

74. See Klaus Kremer, *Die neuplatonische Seinsphilosophie und ihre Wirkung auf Thomas von Aquin* (Leiden: Brill, 1971); and idem, "Die Creatio nach Thomas von Aquin und dem Liber de Causis," in *Ekklēsia* (ed. Klaus Kremer; Trier: Paulinus, 1962), 321–44.

regard to past tradition and current practices.[75] For instance, one does not simply attempt to retrieve interpretively the household codes in Ephesians and the Pastoral Letters. Instead, one has to examine them in the light of background theories about the status of male and female within the Greco-Roman Empire, in the light of apologetic rhetoric within the context of a patrimonial society, and with reference to the historical workings of these household codes throughout history. At the same time, one would have to take into account that in welcoming women and slave converts into the community, some early Christian voices were proclaiming in theory and in practice a vision of discipleship and membership in the Christian community that contrasts with the Greco-Roman values that came to the fore in the household codes.[76] In addition, the changes in the social roles within contemporary society also affect the interpretations of the household codes that subordinated women, slaves, and children to the male head of the house. Nevertheless, it has also to formulate its tradition in ways that critically address what in contemporary societies and practice should be criticized. In this example, systematic theology proceeds in a way that both takes into account the critical rhetorical analysis of the permeation of structures of power within the argumentative strategies of the tradition and attends to the diversity of background theories and warrants as a broad reflective equilibrium highlights.

These two examples seek to illustrate that some hermeneutical models of systematic theology, such as the model of the classic with its disclosure of an existential truth, the literary model with its emphasis on intratextuality, and the cultural linguistic model of thick description, do not capture what systematic theologians have done in the past or what they should do in the present. Such approaches fail to take into account the normative dimensions of systematic theology as it faces new challenges from different background theories, communities of discourse, practices, and reinterpretations of Christianity's diverse traditions. And such approaches fail to take into account that the normative dimension of systematic theology entails confronting the rhetoric and practice of power. The constructive element of systematic theology is intrinsically related to its ethical and practical task.

Theology and the Future of Religion

The normative tasks of theology embrace a range of religious and theological issues and include the attempt to deal with both the ongoing and new challenges that theology faces. The understanding of theology as both a broad reflective equilibrium and an ethical and rhetorical practice seeks to relate normative and reconstructive claims with practical normative issues.

---

75. Francis Schüssler Fiorenza, "Marriage," in *Systematic Theology: Roman Catholic Perspectives* (ed. Francis Schüssler Fiorenza and John P. Galvin; Minneapolis: Fortress, 1991), 2.305–46.

76. Schüssler Fiorenza, *In Memory of Her;* and idem, *But She Said.*

Whereas broad reflective equilibrium places emphasis upon the assertibil-
ity claims from background theories, from ongoing practices, and from
diverse communities of interpretation, a critical rhetorical analysis of liberation places much more emphasis upon the analysis of kyriarchal structures
of domination, and it articulates the normative in critique of such structures. Both approaches include the interpretive in all their tasks, but offer a
conception of theology that goes beyond the interpretation of a classic, the
intratextuality of plain sense, redescription, and thick description.

The normative task of Christian theology relates Christian theology to
the future. At the founding of the American Theological Society of America,
Eugene W. Lyman developed his vision of theology as concerned with the
future of religion. It has not only a historical concern with the transition
from the past to the present, but it has a future task: "It is concerned with
the point of transition from the present to the future. Its distinctive sphere
of operation is the birth and unfolding of religious life."[77] To the question,
what leads to this future development and to the transition from the past
to the future of religious life?, Lyman answers: the truth in religion.[78] He
attempts to substantiate this answer by showing the inadequacy of two alternative positions at the beginning of the twentieth century, namely, the
approach from the philosophy of religion and the scientific study of the history of religion, on the one hand, and the approach from Christianity in its
unicity and revelation, on the other hand. He argues for the interrelationship between both approaches but within the framework of a conception of
science and the scientific conception of history that had not yet been able to
learn from the advances of the twentieth-century hermeneutical theory.

This advance comes to the fore in the debate between Habermas and
Gadamer on the universality of hermeneutical tradition. Habermas points
out in relation to interpretation that there is not only the linguistic meaning, but there is also a subject matter (which we know something about) and
there are issues of norms and of power. All three additional elements (subject
matter, norms, and power) at the heart of the debate also come to the fore in
the task of systematic theology. The interpretation of the religious tradition
for the sake of the future of that religious tradition requires that an analysis of that tradition attend to social and political elements of the rhetorical
arguments within the past and the present. It also requires an attention to
warrants based on background theories and practice. If Gadamer's hermeneutical theory elevated practical judgment in the role of interpretation and
application, Elisabeth Schüssler Fiorenza's feminist hermeneutics and critical
rhetorical analysis underscore the centrality of the well-being of women.

---

77. Eugene W. Lyman. "What Is Theology? The Essential Nature of the Theologian's Task,"
American Journal of Theology 17.3 (1913): 329–44, quotation at 333–34.
78. Ibid., 336.

Theological reflection relates to a particular community in a way that philosophical ethics does not. The diverse paths of philosophical ethics, such as interpretation, discovery and construction, and discovery and interpretation,[79] are even more valid for systematic theology. They are not separate paths, but belong together with a critical and emancipatory perspective. Gadamer notes that the hermeneutical experience is not only an appropriation of the tradition, but it involves a change of oneself. Reaching an understanding in dialogue entails not merely a matter of asserting oneself or "successfully asserting one's own point of view, but being transformed into a communion in which we do not remain what we were."[80] If systematic theology aims for this goal by adjudicating diverse sources of warrants in dialogue with diverse communities of discourse, then in encountering Elisabeth Schüssler Fiorenza's feminist theology, systematic theology goes beyond "what we were" in its concern for the living future of religion. Elisabeth's Schüssler Fiorenza's feminist hermeneutic and critical rhetorical analysis with its concern for the well-being of women pushes systematic theology to go beyond interpretation for the sake of the future of religion and the future well-being of women.

---

79. Michael Walzer, *Thick and Thin: Moral Argument at Home and Abroad* (Notre Dame: University of Notre Dame Press, 1994). For an example of a constructive method in theology, see Gordon D. Kaufman, *An Essay on Theological Method* (Missoula, Mont.: Scholars Press, 1979); and idem, *In Face of Mystery: A Constructive Theology* (Cambridge: Harvard University Press, 1993).

80. Gadamer, *Truth and Method,* 360.

2

New Christendom
or Liberated World?

Theological Alternatives
for the Twenty-first Century

Harvey Cox

My friend and colleague (and neighbor down the hall here at Harvard Divinity School) Elisabeth Schüssler Fiorenza has not only clearly positioned herself within the movement of liberation theology. She has also fruitfully linked her feminist scholarship to that project in a creative way and has provided additional scholarly justification for the biblical basis of liberation theology. Even more, her voice has helped feminist liberation theologians all over the world to find their place in the larger theological and ecumenical conversation. Liberation theology is now an established and recognized stream within Christian (and other) theology. But that might not have happened. There were other, alternative movements in the wings as well, and they remain contenders. As we enter the twenty-first century, two conflicting visions of social theology are contending with each other in Catholic theology. One is liberation theology in all its many and varied expressions. The other is what I call here the "New Christendom" strategy. This essay focuses mainly on the sources and substance of the latter as the main alternative to liberation theology in our time.

The word *Christendom* combines the word *Christian* with the English suffix *dom* (or its equivalent in other languages), which means a place, province, or realm. Christendom is not the same as Christianity, or even institutional Christianity. Rather, it postulates a particular theory and practice of *how* Christianity should relate itself to a given culture. It is a normative vision of the appropriate relation of the church to the world and of the sacred to the secular. It suggests an earthly realm in which, in one way or another, Christian values hold sway, the faith is practiced, and the church benevolently guides the civil order. Restoration suggests simply that this correct relationship, Christendom, has been lost and must be reinstituted.

The emperor Constantine was probably the first architect of Christendom, but he was surely not the last. The vision, if not the reality, of a Christian realm inspired most of medieval Europe. It was never seriously challenged by the reformers, although Calvin trimmed its scope considerably when he restricted his own efforts to build such a realm mainly to Geneva. The idea fired the imagination of the Puritans who founded the Massachusetts Bay colony and of William Penn in his effort to construct a godly commonwealth through his "holy experiment" in Pennsylvania. It turns up again in the attempt of the American Social Gospel preachers to "Christianize the social order" and in T. S. Eliot's nostalgic vision of a Christian civilization.

The cornerstone of the Catholic Church's Restored Christendom strategy was the belief that, in the glorious thirteenth century and especially under the papacy of Innocent III, the divinely intended mutuality of the ecclesial and civil powers had been attained; that it had been undermined later by a series of attacks; but that the time had come to restore it. What this great medieval synthesis produced, according to its champions, was a civilization in which divine law was encoded into civil law, the natural and supernatural realms supported one another, and humans in their various stations — rulers, workers, bards, and warriors — all shared a single commitment to the one common good as taught by Mother Church. Christendom is the name for this unified Christian civilization which, though temporarily lost, could still be rebuilt. The fact that it never existed in actuality, not even under Innocent III, did not detract in the least from its power as a religious and political goal.

According to the Restored Christendom theory, the Reformation had struck a paralyzing blow to the blessings of a unified religious culture. By undermining the religious unity of Western civilization and by opening the door for further fragmentation, Luther's revolt undercut the possibility of a civil society united around a single spiritual core and under a single head. According to the view of history that underlies the Restored Christendom strategy, Christendom suffered another painful wound when the Enlightenment assailed the cherished doctrine of the faith and held the church's pious practices up to ridicule. The assault against Christian civilization reached a new peak of fury during the French Revolution and the subsequent rise of socialism and communism. These movements were propelling the world toward ever greater strife and discord and could end up only destroying the very fabric of human society. Only a restoration of a *Civiltà Cattolica* could rescue the world from such a disaster, and it was the vocation of the church to bend its every effort and expend its every resource to reestablish such a civilization. The beginnings of the Restored Christendom strategy go far back into modern history, but it came to classical expression when Leo XIII became pope in 1878 and initiated his reign by issuing an encyclical entitled *Inscrutabili Dei Consilio*. In it he eloquently set forth the ideal of

Christendom, chastised the fallen society of the present age which had seen fit to inflict its own laws on the church, and looked forward to "a time in which we will once again see that condition of things in which the designs of God's wisdom had long ago placed the Roman pontiffs." This would mean the reestablishment of the holy and venerable authority of the church, which in God's name rules humankind, upholding and defending all lawful authority. Here all the elements of a Restored Christendom theology are in place: there *was* a time when a right relation between the church and the secular realm existed; this fitting arrangement has been *lost;* it is the task of all Christians, led by the Roman pontiff, to *restore* it.

Leo XIII devoted his considerable energy and talent to this vision of a Restored Christendom. He issued numerous encyclicals devoted to current political and social issues. His famous *Rerum Novarum,* directed to the question of labor and capital, is read by some as an inspired attempt to reinstitute something like the medieval guilds in the modern age through a system of industrial councils. In order to dispel the many modern philosophical errors which had distorted people's thinking and action in all the other realms of life, Leo commended a return to Thomas Aquinas, the great thirteenth-century theologian, as the only true source of Catholic intellectual life. Leo's theological strategy was followed by all his papal successors up to Pius XII. The Restored Christendom theory reigned nearly undisputed for almost one thousand years. Only with John XXIII and the Second Vatican Council was it seriously challenged.

The Restored Christendom strategy is sometimes characterized as a "siege mentality," but this is a somewhat misleading metaphor. True, the symbolism of suffering and persecution, such as the image of the sword-pierced Sacred Heart of Jesus, once elicited great fervor among the masses of Catholics. But the strategy of restoration called for attack not retreat. It was a comprehensive campaign plan for a protracted battle against the forces of godlessness, secularism, and rationalism, seen as the mortal enemies of humankind. The reason the pope needed to be in unambiguous command had nothing to do with a siege. In the thick of march and countermarch, the bugle must not give an uncertain sound. Infallibility was needed in a church militant.

The metaphor of warfare had other advantages. It allowed for absorbing temporary setbacks, making tactical concessions, seeking compromise where necessary, finding allies where they could be found, and always keeping the long march in mind. In the nineteenth century the leaders of the Catholic Church felt themselves to be heading a new crusade, a *reconquista,* a global contestation in which every strategy available — whether diplomatic, cultural, political, or spiritual — should be marshaled to restore the lost provinces.

Who then was the enemy in this titanic contest of arms? Ultimately the Christendom advocates had no doubt that it was Satan himself, commanding his earthly legions. It is true that our own times are haunted by nightmares of a final holocaust, sometimes attuned to classical apocalyptic imagery. Still, it may be hard for us to imagine that the leaders of nineteenth- and early-twentieth-century Catholic Christianity had the same premonitions long before the mushroom cloud appeared. In his inaugural encyclical issued on 4 October 1903, Leo XIII's successor Pope Pius X declared that the age his hearers lived in might well be the "last days" foretold by the Apostle Paul in 2 Thess 2:3. The "Son of Perdition" or Antichrist, he warned, might well be in the world already. He discerned this Stygian evil in "the audacity and the wrath employed everywhere in persecuting religions, in combating the dogmas of the faith, in brazen efforts to uproot and destroy all relations between man and the Divinity." Humankind, the pontiff went on to say, "has with infinite temerity put [it]self in the place of God ... and made the universe a temple wherein [humanity it]self is to be adored."

This imagery may still appear overstated. But after two world wars, totalitarianism, the near destruction of European Jewry, and the threat of nuclear terror, it sounds somewhat more plausible than it did to the multitudes of optimists who criticized the pope at the time for his balefulness. In retrospect the pope sounds remarkably ingenuous. It is sobering to remember that only three years before Pius X fired this warning, liberal American Protestants had launched a journal whose title was meant to conjure not the great tribulation but the coming of the peaceable kingdom in the century then beginning. They named it *The Christian Century*. On balance the pope seems to have foreseen what was coming with considerably more perspicacity.

In view of his dark reading of the signs of his times, the pope announced that the guiding principle of his pontificate was to be *instaurare omnia in Christo* (to restore all things in Christ). Now the strategy had a name. The grand vision of a Restored Christendom of course required tactical consultation, training of the cadres, councils of war, and appropriate banners, songs, and martyrs. The remarkable feature of Catholic popular piety during the nineteenth century was not just how luxuriant it was, but that the hierarchy so brilliantly enlisted this fecundity in the overall struggle. Devotion to the Sacred Heart of Jesus, for example, and the celebrated appearances of the Virgin at Lourdes and Fátima all began as local devotional movements. But church leaders quickly and skillfully orchestrated them into the badges and ballads of the ongoing Armageddon. The cult of the Sacred Heart, which began with the fervently erratic visions of a young nun named Sister Mary Margaret and quickly spread to other convents, was transcribed into a Catholic alternative to the pathos of revolutionary sentiment. Priests placed a crown over the image of the Sacred Heart and encouraged Catholics to hold enthronement ceremonies in their homes. In Christendom, of course, only Christ is king, but monarchs seemed to recognize this better than prime ministers did; so the Restored Christendom strategy often took a monarchist turn. Still, republics were at least better than communes. The

metamorphosis of the popular devotion to the Sacred Heart into the counterrevolutionary symbol *par excellence* came with the construction of the
Église du Sacré Coeur in the Montmartre section of Paris as an expression
of penance for the Paris Commune of 1870.

Devotion to Mary was quickly enlisted as an antirevolutionary sentiment.
At Fátima, Portugal, where the Virgin had appeared to some peasant children, the church swiftly took charge of the resulting burst of piety and
announced that Our Lady had told the children they should pray without
ceasing for the conversion of Russia. A few years later, a Roman Catholic church was erected at Fátima in a style that carefully replicated the
onion-domed cupolas of Orthodox churches in Russia. For some visitors this
appeared to be a sort of architectural "sympathetic magic" and understandably gave rise to the question of just what kind of conversion the faithful
were asked to pray for. True, inside the faux orthodox edifice a wall painting
depicted a blue-clad Virgin standing above a fiery red Kremlin, but whether
the desired conversation was to be free from communism or from Orthodoxy or from both remained ambiguous. In any case what had started with
Ave Marias sung by innocent children who fervently believed they had seen
the Virgin had become a full-scale battle hymn.

Pius XII, who died in 1958, was the last pope to whom the Restored
Christendom strategy in its classical nineteenth-century form made any
sense. Eugenio Pacelli had grown up in the *realpolitik* of Vatican diplomacy
and had served as papal secretary of state. He devoted his pontificate to
shoring up the concordats that gave the church some elbow room within the
various national states, especially in such matters as education, and allowed
it to continue to be an actor on the international stage. He encouraged the
organization and growth of explicitly Catholic lay and professional organizations, Catholic political parties and trade unions, even Catholic bicycle
clubs and boy scout troops. He also took great pleasure in meeting with
delegations of physicians, journalists, and scientists and in writing detailed
encyclicals and elocutions about what it must mean to be a Catholic Christian in the modern world. For Pius XII, it meant to see one's post in the
civil society as an outpost in the great global effort not only to defend the
rights of the church but to restore to the world the serenity and unity of a
Christian civilization.

Even before Pius XII died, however, it had become evident to many
Catholic theologians that the Restored Christendom strategy was in need
of fundamental revision. All over Europe Catholic factory workers were
joining trade unions organized and led by socialists and sometimes even by
communists. Catholic artists, writers, poets, physicians, and scholars were
not content to remain within strictly Catholic clubs and associations. Within
the church itself a revival of biblical studies and investigations of the early
church fathers raised some questions about whether the very idea of Christendom was compatible with the Gospels. Theologians wondered whether

the blanket condemnation of the modern world might at least be made a bit more selective. All these issues had already reached a critical point when, shortly after succeeding Pius XII, Pope John XXIII issued his surprising call for an ecumenical council, which after hasty preparation assembled in Rome in 1962. It was clear to most of the bishops and theologians who gathered that their principal task was to find a new pastoral strategy to replace the *instaurare* theory.

Today, in retrospect, it is easier for us to understand why the old strategy was formulated than it was for many of its contemporary critics. Most liberation theologians also appreciate the fears and hopes that created it. Restored Christendom was, in short, an antimodernist strategy, and with the advantage of hindsight, many thoughtful people today can understand why it arose. Some even ask why the Catholic Church, which has been endlessly scolded for its stubborn opposition to "progress" and for its "siege mentality," might not better be commended for astutely foreseeing the disastrous consequences of many of the trends it was then opposing, especially rampant nationalism.

This is not to say that the church is always wise or even consistent in the enemies it singled out or in the tactics it devised to fight them. And its blanket condemnations of everything "modern" or "liberal" rightly seem excessive today. Still, at the start of the twentieth-first century, there are few people — again with the advantage of hindsight — who would deny that the nineteenth-century church had good reasons for its suspicion not just of nationalism, but also of individualism and the exaltation of science and technological progress into a quasi-religious status. Not one of these heroic emblems of the nineteenth century achieved its promise. Rather, each in its own way contributed to the explosive mixture that could destroy our civilization in an instant. Looking back on the nineteenth century today, it is easier to explain why the Catholic Church devised the seemingly negative strategy it did, with all its hyperbole and even obscurantism, than it is to explain why there were so few Kierkegaards and Dostoyevskys who warned about the disasters that were coming.

But according to the best Catholic ethical theory, good intentions are not enough. The bishops who gathered in Rome for the Second Vatican Council knew this, and many of them realized that the attempt to restore a lost Christendom, which had preoccupied the church for so many years, not only had not succeeded but had even inadvertently contributed to worsening the crisis it set out to address. Now the question was: What would the new pastoral strategy be?

Among the theologians who gladly accepted invitations to come to Rome and serve as *periti* (i.e., theological advisors to the bishops) was a brilliant young German scholar named Josef Ratzinger. Ratzinger was not then and is not now an advocate of a Restored Christendom. He knew as well as anyone gathered in the Holy City that Christendom, at least as it had been organized in the thirteenth century and as it existed in the minds of Leo XIII, Pius X, and Pius XII, could never be "restored." He and younger *periti* colleagues knew full well that to persist in trying to do so would only continue to create more undesired consequences, especially in view of what they saw as the worldwide threats of Marxism on the one side and consumer culture on the other.

By the time of the council, and especially in its aftermath, Ratzinger and a growing group of like-minded theologians, most of them French or German speaking, had begun to conceive of another grand strategy. The younger European bishops kept closely in touch with them and shared their ideas. What they hoped to do now was not to restore Christendom but to build a new religiously grounded civilization. Such a civilization would take into consideration the changes — not all of them bad — that had occurred in the world during the previous decades, including the more cordial relations between the Catholic Church and other religious traditions. But it would still be a church militant, vigilant about error, impatient with divisiveness, and fully cognizant of the strength of its mortal enemies.

The New Christendom strategy was not thought up quickly. Its sources go back far before the council to the creative ferment and dissatisfaction which erupted in the church during the 1930s and 1940s. It was created by some of the keenest minds and most cultivated spirits of the great European Catholic tradition. It represents a truly formidable and worthy alternative to the vision of the liberation theologians.

Meanwhile, however, while the seeds of the New Christendom strategy were sprouting, another set of historical events was in motion, which, though hardly foreseen by Pius XII or even John XXIII, became, during the years of the council and thereafter, the principal challenge to the New Christendom strategy. What happened was that during the same years the Catholic Church had bent its every effort to restore a Christian Europe, it had ceased to be a European church. The rapid growth areas of Christianity, both Catholic and Protestant, became Asia, Africa, and Latin America. This unforeseen change in venue, and not the forces the church set out to oppose in the nineteenth century, prepared the stage for the rise of liberation theology. This movement represents not the continuing power of the church's old foes, but the rise of a non-European theology that has its own vision of the mandate of the gospel, its own concept of the church's pastoral strategy, and its own register of who the enemies of Christ are and how they must be opposed. Ironically, both the New Christendom advocates and the liberation theologians recognized full well that the old-style Restored Christendom strategy was finished. What they disagreed on was what should come next.

The Second Vatican Council marked the end of the road for the advocates of a restoration of Christendom. The grand illusions of Leo XIII and Pius XII were gently set aside. No longer was the modern world viewed simply as the enemy. In the most widely cited of its documents, the famous "Schema 13" on "The Church in the Modern World," the bishops went so far as to proclaim that the "joys and hopes" of that world were also those of the church. But this was just the beginning. Now a debate began on what strategy the church should pursue in a world marked by cultural and religious pluralism, by new aspirations and hopes on the part of the poor, and by the terrible dangers posed by weapons of mass destruction. If the church did share these joys and hopes, then how should it share them?

The first clear answer to this question came, appropriately, from one of the French theologians that Pius XII had vociferously opposed, a Dominican named Marie-Dominique Chenu. Just as the council was closing in 1965, Chenu began publishing a series of books and articles on the mission of the church in the modern world. Chenu had been out of favor with Rome for three decades, but the Vatican Council became his vindication. He is basically a Thomist, but this had not prevented one of his books from being placed on the Index in 1938 because he had the bad judgment to suggest that Thomas Aquinas could be understood best if he were studied against his historical background. It probably did not help Chenu that he was reputed to be one of the closest advisors to the French "Worker-Priest" experiment of the postwar years. In 1950, Pope Pius XII's *Humani Generis,* his condemnation of the whole "French school" of theology, contained one passage that its readers knew was included especially for Chenu. Probably for this reason he was not invited to the council. But at the council itself, in part due to the influence of John XXIII, who had been papal nuncio in Paris when Pius XII's axe fell on the French theologians, the theology that Chenu and his fellow Frenchmen had continued to work on despite Rome's opposition was spectacularly resurrected. So in 1965 what Chenu had to say about "the Gospel in the current world" was deemed well worth listening to.

Chenu argued, as he had for years, not only that Christendom was gone, but that it was best for both the church and the world that it was. As a follower of Thomas Aquinas, he was not as upset over the alleged "disappearance of the sacral" as some others were. He believed that the natural and the supernatural realm, that the secular and the sacred, had discrete functions under God's providence and that it was important to keep them distinct. It was a mistake for the church to try to build a sacred world around itself because, as he argued, the more the world becomes the natural world that God intended it to be, the more the presence of God becomes just that — the presence of God and not some admixture of sacred and profane realms, a highly suspect alloy that Chenu identified with Christendom. Thus even though Christians had not actively sought desacralization or the disappearance of Christendom, still those developments had the positive effect of pushing Christians into the real world, out of what he called "the mental and institutional complex of Christianity." Chenu did not deny that

Christendom might once, long ago, have incarnated Christianity in a particular historical epoch. But he believed such an epoch was now gone and that Christendom was dead. It was time for a different strategy.

For Chenu the new strategy that the church needed was not to find some way to "Christianize the masses." What it needed, rather, was to respect the "autonomous processes" of the secular world. But this did not end the job. Resonating with some of the Protestant theology of the day, especially with that of Karl Barth and his followers, Chenu also voiced his confidence that, having accepted the God-given value of the world, the church itself would be freed from defending an expiring Christendom and would be in a stronger position to find ways to "maintain the primacy of God's Word over the whole." He stalwartly opposed any attempt by the church to "build for itself a Christian world alongside of the 'world.'" The church can rejoice that it no longer needs to be "the protector of a civilization" it had itself organized. The layperson can now venture into the secular world of work and politics with both feet. In making political choices laypeople can rely on the dictates of their own Christian consciences and need not lean on the advice of the hierarchy.

In Chenu's venturesome embracing of the secular world one can detect an understandable personal jubilation. He was obviously glad to get out from under the archaic system that had so intrusively monitored his own thinking for decades. One also suspects that his experience with the Worker-Priests taught him something about the freedom and responsibility of laypeople and both the risk and the promise of the declericalized world itself. However, in one of his writings Chenu used a phrase — though only in passing — that would lead to a great deal of puzzled discussion in the years that followed. Admitting that "the era of Constantine and of Western Christendom" was over, he nonetheless wrote that this condition "will lead to a new Christendom, it is a magnificent challenge: it underlies the whole of the Council." Chenu's phrase is hardly more than epigrammatic. How would this "new" Christendom differ from the old one that was dead? How would it be instituted? What strategy would it require? Chenu did not answer. Still, it cannot be denied that both the "preferential option for the poor" and the dream of a new Christendom are children of the council.

Chenu's fellow Frenchman Jean Daniélou did not agree with Chenu's strategy. Also brought under suspicion by *Humani Generis,* he too was passed over as a *peritus* at the council; so he shared the same sense of satisfaction when the theology that he had been writing found its way into the council documents. But Daniélou disagreed completely with Chenu's assessment of Christendom. As with most theologians, Daniélou's attitude about this can be gauged by his assessment of Constantine. In fact, that eccentric emperor's vision of the cross in the heavens inscribed with *In Hoc Signo Vinces* can almost serve as a kind of inkblot test of theologians. What they see or don't see in its smudgy silhouettes tells us a lot about their underlying presuppositions, especially about the idea of Christendom. Some Christians, beginning with the desert fathers, viewed the emperor's conversion as a skillful grandstand play and an unmitigated spiritual disaster: they fled to the wilderness to avoid such a traitorous compromise with Satan. Later, at the time of the Reformation, Protestant theologians interpreted it as a "fall of the church" corresponding to the fall of Adam. For Daniélou, it was — on balance — a positive development. He believed that the conversion of Constantine had "made the Gospel accessible to the poor," by which he meant that for Christianity to reach beyond minorities and elites it simply had to fuse itself with a culture. "The faith can really only take root in a country when it has penetrated its civilization," he argued, and "there can be no Christianity for the masses without a Christendom."

At first Chenu's and Daniélou's strategies seem to be diametrically opposed. But at another level there are important similarities. Daniélou recognized as well as Chenu that the dream of Christendom as it existed, or is thought to have existed, in the Middle Ages is no longer possible. But he still believed that the church must in some way suffuse the major institutions of a culture with Christianity; consequently he wanted to see certain "zones" of religion and sacrality preserved so that simple laypeople are not left without some social basis for their faith. Religion, Daniélou believed, had to be "in the calendar," with publicly recognized feast days and special occasions.

Chenu, on the other hand, was glad to see the old, clericalized Christendom go. But he was looking for a still undefined New Christendom. What separated the two was a different evaluation of the significance of the sacred in human life as such. Daniélou held that since secularization seemed to be spreading so rapidly, the church should place itself squarely on the side of the sacred wherever it appeared. He admitted that religion could be misused, but he feared that Christianity would make no sense in a world in which sacrality had drained away.

This defense of sacrality or transcendence has become, in the years since Daniélou wrote, a major theme in both Catholic and Protestant neoconservative religious thought. In this perspective, Christianity and the other traditions are all understood as species in the larger genus of religion, which is deemed essential to truly human life. The results of this subsuming are mixed. On the one hand, it results in a certain de-emphasis on the alleged uniqueness or superiority of Christianity, which is welcome after so many years of theological and ecclesial "triumphalism." On the other hand, it also produces a soft-pedaling of the critical and prophetic elements in Christianity and makes irreligion or atheism — rather than idolatry, fanaticism, or religiously sanctioned injustice — the main foe. The emphasis varies from writer to writer. Chenu, for example, saw the same picture that Daniélou saw from another angle. Recognizing how terribly sacral power was misused throughout history to keep people ignorant and servile, Chenu believed its decline was a hopeful sign. But he also wanted to maintain some fundamental sense of the mystery of life on which the gospel could build. From then on, the search for some specified quality of mystery or sacrality or — more commonly "transcendence" — became a hallmark of the quest for the New Christendom.

Today this quest for the sacral continues to motivate both the liberation theologians and their critics. But they approach it in different ways. Liberationists look for this spiritual energy where St. Francis did, among the poor. Their opponents hold that since traditional religion shores up custom and continuity amid the terrors of flux and uncertainty, Christianity should be its friend and ally wherever it is threatened. This represents what is often called the "priestly" view of religion. Liberation theologians, on the other hand, look at religion from a more "prophetic" perspective. They focus not just on the constructive role it plays but also on the perils that accompany its misuse and manipulation. They see religion *as such* as neither a positive nor a negative phenomenon but as a power fraught with possibilities for good or evil. Still, both agree that the sacred dimension is an indispensable ingredient in a truly human society.

The aim of advocates of the New Christendom is not to "restore all things" but to build something new. Although they may occasionally glance backward at one or another example of purportedly better times in the past, they do not pine for a golden era. They know the task they need to do will carry them into an uncharted future.

Still, as the New Christendom strategy — sometimes explicitly so-called but more often not — unfolds, it displays at least three features that reveal its underlying continuity with the old Restored Christendom approach. First, the New Christendom strategy relies heavily on a tightly ordered, hierarchically organized "prefectural" church. Whether one is restoring or building anew, it is clear that the question of who is in charge must not be left ambiguous. Accordingly, the New Christendom theologians are not particularly tolerant of dissent and, in the ongoing tension between a more papal and a more conciliar church, they tend to be strong papalists. Both Leonardo Boff and Hans Küng found themselves in hot water when they raised questions on this troubled front by advocating a less centralized church governance.

Second, New Christendom advocates, like their predecessors who strove "to restore all things in Christ," prefer to ally themselves with the existing and established secular authorities rather than to risk alliances with populist or opposition movements with uncertain prospects of success. As a rule they choose to advance their strategy by negotiating with those who hold power rather than with rebels, critics, and outsiders. One of the gifts of Pope John Paul II is his remarkable ability to encourage mass popular devotion and at the same time to negotiate one-on-one with heads of state. He knows that since he has no "divisions" the piety of millions of Catholics is his only power base. Still, he knows that when one is building for the future one must keep the long road and the powers-that-be in mind.

Finally, despite the sincere efforts of the New Christendom theologians to think globally and to take the newly expanded cultural diversity of the Catholic Church into consideration, a certain European quality still lingers in their mentality. Sometimes this results in a peculiar ambivalence. Thus in 1975, in his encyclical *Evangellii Nuntiandi,* Paul VI spoke of "the culture of a people" as the "fertile soil and starting point of theology and pastoral service." This sounds like a suggestion that Catholic theologians move away from a theology grown in Europe and then transplanted elsewhere and that instead they begin with the local culture, which he calls the "starting point." In his following sentence, however, the pope quickly added that the church had to "meet the challenge of her universality" but "without renouncing her first historical roots in a variety of peoples and cultures (Jewish, Greek, Latin, German) but, on the contrary, by thus enriching her common tradition" (§48). The vision here seems still to be that of a fundamentally European church whose "common tradition," which is Western, can now perhaps be "enriched." Somehow the vision of a truly universal church in which non-Western peoples share equally and where cultures begin to *constitute* the common tradition, not just enrich it, seems lacking.

As we enter the twenty-first century, the contest between theological advocates of a New Christendom and the champions of liberation theology still continues. It is clear, however, that the outcome will ultimately be decided not in Europe or America, but in the non-Western world where, ironically, a New Christendom that might be a liberationist one is coming to birth.

3

To Teach without a Net

Toward a Pedagogy of Imagination and Collaboration

John R. Lanci

> Won't you join me in this twirling, moving, spiraling dance of feminist biblical interpretation in the "imagined" and practiced radical democratic space of Divine Wisdom?
>
> — Elisabeth Schüssler Fiorenza, *Wisdom Ways*

"Why the glum face?" Chemise asks as I open the door for her. She's the first to arrive, and, as usual, she is weighed down with food, in this case a covered dish, a baguette, and a bouquet of wildflowers.

It's the essay, I tell her.

"It's not coming, I take it," she says as she slips past me into the living room and heads for the kitchen.

Oh, it is. But I'm not particularly happy with it.

"You're never happy with your writing," she says as she opens and shuts every cabinet in the kitchen. "Aluminum foil?"

Look down, I tell her.

"You love this stuff. You know you do," she says. "How'd you get into this business in the first place?"

I open my mouth to speak but she cuts me off.

"Wait! Make yourself useful while you're talking," she says. "Build a fire. It's freezing in here."

I head over to the woodstove, but before I begin, I ask her if I can read something to her — my latest introduction to the so-far-nonexistent text for this *Festschrift* — since it speaks to her question.

"Go for it," she grunts as she squats and shoves the casserole into the oven. "But then make the fire."

Okay, already. I begin:

A Memory

I am reading from a yellowed piece of paper covered with blurry purple letters; I think we called this ancient form of printing a "spirit-master":

> The Paraclete may be comprehended in terms of why he [*sic*] was created and (for pastoral purposes) by focusing on what it is that he [*sic*] does. From our work we have evolved a functional understanding of the Paraclete as (1) he [*sic*] who teaches the community of believers to recognize the presence of Jesus in their midst and (2) he [*sic*] who calls the community of believers to stand as the convictors of the world. Thus, the Paraclete is the Spirit of Truth which enlivens the community to recognize and become that which it should be.

I enrolled in my first Scripture course at the Catholic seminary on the campus of the University of Notre Dame in 1972. It was an M.Div. class on the Gospel of John taught by a professor recently arrived from West Germany. Her name was Elisabeth Fiorenza (as she was then known), and, according to the upperclassmen at our seminary, she was dangerous to your grade-point average and even your self-esteem, a *mulier fortis*, one of them called her. Don't be fooled by the smile, they warned.

We first-year guys were not fooled. We were petrified.

And never more so than when it was time for us to do our "group projects." This pedagogical tool was foreign to most of us. Topics were assigned, not chosen, and in that class on John, she handed me and my cohort a daunting one: we had to exegete the Paraclete passages in the Fourth Gospel. That in itself was bad enough for scriptural greenhorns, but it got worse. In addition to our research on the passages, we, like all the groups in all of her other seminary classes, had to present a "pastoral application" of the passage; in other words, we had to describe a situation in a parish, hospital, jail, or homeless shelter in which the Paraclete passages and our work on them would be relevant and helpful to our ministry.

Now we were petrified and clueless!

Doomed, we played it for laughs. Appearing in costume with scripts in hand, we presented a play burlesquing what Raymond Brown had to say in his then-recent Anchor Bible commentary about the origins of the Paraclete sayings. Furtive glances to the back of the room revealed our no-nonsense prof laughing out loud and shaking her head in disbelief at every pun. When the last living eyewitness was dispatched and the Final Redactor had completed his work, the players — our courage fortified by applause all around — regrouped at a table in the front of the room to present our pastoral implications.

I cannot now, thirty years later, recall what scam we attempted to perpetrate; we had absolutely no idea how the Paraclete sayings (as opposed to those of the more familiar Holy Spirit) might be relevant to pastoral life.

But I do remember that within minutes we were sweating cue balls as it was quietly but firmly pointed out to us that our textual exegesis (the play) had nothing to do with the pastoral ramifications we were proposing. Relenting a little in the face of evident terror, the object of that terror asked us more gently: why bother studying Scripture if it has no relevance to your future ministry?

Elisabeth and Francis Schüssler Fiorenza, alone among our Scripture and systematics professors, demanded that we make connections between the material covered in class and our work in the field.[1] It was this concern — that we never lose sight of the people we would be living and working with after ordination — that won a place for Elisabeth in our affections (we all called her Elisabeth even back then), despite our continued respect for her take-no-prisoners scholarly rigor. She became a dominant influence on her seminary students, a number of whom went on to become influential pastors, chaplains, professors, college presidents, and in one case (so far) a Catholic bishop.

I learned many years later of the admonition she had received on her arrival at Notre Dame: stick to critical exegesis, avoid theology, and "never allow your students to ask what is the religious or theological significance of biblical texts and interpretations for today."[2] I report for the historical record that, even as a newly minted *doktor,* she recognized really bad advice when she heard it and did just the opposite, embarking on exactly the road she was warned to avoid: the "slippery slope of relevance."

"She sounds like one tough woman to cross," Chemise says, arranging her flowers in a vase on the coffee table between us. Before I can respond the doorbell rings.

Imagining the Possibilities

What is regarded as "common sense" or plausible in a culture depends on the hegemonic ideological understandings of "how the world is...." Instead of asking if it is likely that wo/men shaped the Jesus traditions, one must ask if it is historically possible and thinkable that they did so. This shift requires scholars to prove that such a possibility did not exist at the time.

— Schüssler Fiorenza, *Jesus and the Politics of Interpretation*

1. While the liberational seeds of Elisabeth's later work were evident even then — note her students' gravitation toward a model of Christian community as "convictors of the world" — her pedagogy has evolved since the 1970s. So it is that she has moved beyond this exegesis/application "dichotomous hermeneutic model"; cf. Elisabeth Schüssler Fiorenza, *Wisdom Ways: Introducing Feminist Biblical Interpretation* (Maryknoll, N.Y.: Orbis, 2001), 2–3.
2. Elisabeth Schüssler Fiorenza, *Jesus and the Politics of Interpretation* (New York: Continuum, 2000), 56.

Wasn't it the literary experts who first labeled it "the end of modernity"? Maybe it was the philosophers. Now, scientific positivism and scholarly objectivity (justly) are on the ropes and even our once-venerable historical-critical methods for interpreting the Bible are found wanting and (perhaps a bit uncritically) dismissed. Some pastors, priests, and patriarchs decry a new "relativism," but other folk see a new opportunity to imagine. And imagination, to imagine the possibilities, is, I suggest, at the core of Elisabeth's work and must be at the center of our own.

In clerical circles, imagination has been cherished — think of traditional forms of prayer like the exercise of St. Ignatius or the *Lectio Divina* — cherished, that is, only if it is subject to strict supervision. But it's hard to control imagination, even with the help of a professional, sanctioned spiritual director.

In many parts of the academy as well, imagination still has a bad name. It leads to "soft scholarship" or worse: relevance, the danger flagged thirty years ago by Elisabeth's would-be mentor at Notre Dame.

And yet, as the evidence of our eyes and ears makes plain every day, without imagination, the people die. Without memory, that kindler of imagination, Jesus, becomes an idol in service of the status quo. Imagination is not the opposite of reality; fantasy is the opposite of reality. As my students' favorite theologian, Michael Himes, puts it, "Imagination is not about escaping from reality; it is precisely about making things real."[3] If, as Walter Brueggemann asserts, we live in a world in which "all claims of reality, including those of theologians, are fully under negotiation," we had better get those imaginative juices flowing in new pedagogical directions. Imagination? In Brueggemann's words, it is "the human capacity to picture, portray, receive, and practice the world in ways other than it appears to be at first glance when seen through a dominant, habitual, unexamined lens."[4]

You can see how well this dovetails with Elisabeth's call to investigate and articulate the possible rather than limiting one's imaginative enterprises to reconstructing — through "objective" research — the plausible.

Back to Chemise and company. A hermeneutical circle is about to convene.

The Conversation Heats Up

The doorbell rings again. Jeremy, Thad, and Marjorie have arrived. Let the conversation begin.

Actually, as I open the door I can tell that it already has. Jeremy and Thad are arguing as usual.

---

3. Michael J. Himes et al., *Doing the Truth in Love* (New York: Paulist Press, 1995), 137.

4. Walter Brueggemann, *Texts under Negotiation: The Bible and Postmodern Imagination* (Minneapolis: Fortress, 1993), 17, 13.

Friends! Come in and quiet down; you'll scare the cats.

"Spawn of Satan," Jeremy spits with genuine distaste at the thought of David and Jonathan, who, of course, adore him.

"It's freezing in here," Marj says, rubbing her hands to warm them up. "I'm building a fire." She moves to the woodstove.

"What can we do?" Thad asks.

"Dinner guests can sit down and look pretty," Chemise chimes in from the kitchen, and the two young men settle into the sofa.

"Is Yvonne coming?" Marj asks.

Not tonight. It's Paul's birthday and the kids are taking them out to dinner and a show in Boston. Neil Diamond, I think.

"Yuck," Thad says in evident disgust.

"Keep your juvenile comments to yourself," Marj says. She is in her middle forties now and old enough to be one of these students' parents. As are Chemise and I. The great divide.

Soft drinks all around and then our chef joins us and asks the guys what they were arguing about when they came in.

"What are we always arguing about?" Thad says. "Church."

"It's wonderful that people your age take these things seriously," Chemise says.

"How can you not?" Jeremy says to her. "Their church is imploding before the eyes of the world."

We are sitting in a town south of Boston, and as we speak, the Roman Catholic archdiocese, of which Thad, Marj, and I are ostensibly members, is entering a great dark night, the implications of which for the church as a whole are as yet unclear.

"It's not the Roman Catholic Church that's imploding," Marj says. "It's the clerical culture, the hierarchy."

"Precisely my point," Jeremy says. "In my church, we don't have this kind of clerical culture, as you call it."

Jeremy is a member of a nondenominational evangelical Christian church in nearby Brockton.

Thad turns to me. "I was citing the passage in Matthew where Christ designates Peter as the first pope," he says. "We just got out of Synoptics class and that was the text we discussed."

"And I was telling him," Jeremy is heating up, "that he is misrepresenting the passage. What's with the pope? That's not what the Scripture says."

"What does the Scripture say?" Marj asks as she sits on the floor by the woodstove.

Chemise reaches over to the bookshelf beside her and claims a copy of the New Revised Standard Version of the Bible.

"You have Bibles everywhere here," she says. "Where is that passage?"

"Matthew sixteen," Thad says. "Beginning with verse — "

"Got it," she says, and then reads:

Now when Jesus came into the district of Caesarea Philippi, he asked his disciples, "Who do people say that the Son of Man is?"

And they said, "Some say John the Baptist, but others Elijah, and still others Jeremiah or one of the prophets."

He said to them, "But who do you say that I am?"

Simon Peter answered, "You are the Messiah, the Son of the living God."

And Jesus answered him, "Blessed are you, Simon son of Jonah! For flesh and blood has not revealed this to you, but my Father in heaven. And I tell you, you are Peter, and on this rock I will build my church, and the gates of Hades will not prevail against it. I will give you the keys of the kingdom of heaven, and whatever you bind on earth will be bound in heaven, and whatever you loose on earth will be loosed in heaven."

Then he sternly ordered the disciples not to tell anyone that he was the Messiah.

Good. That's far enough.

A Methodological Interlude

It will soon become clear, I trust, why I have incorporated an imagined conversation into my text. But in case you find this or the conversational tone of the rest of this piece jarring or perplexing, permit me a few observations about method at this point.

This format of imagined conversation is hardly an original one, though it was developed independently and from scratch. But not by me. Several years ago I was engaged in a collaborative writing and research project with two undergraduates, Jenn Borden and Kevin Minoli. Our topic covered four centuries of women in early Christian tradition, and Jenn and Kevin found themselves confronted with a great deal of historical and methodological material that needed to be conveyed to college sophomores with little background in religious studies. After a few weeks of frustration and a couple of false starts, they hit upon an idea: to render the material comprehensible to nonspecialists, they would create a series of imaginary conversations in which we would clarify the denser aspects of biblical study.

Their strategy succeeded and in subsequent courses and writing projects, I and other undergraduate teaching assistants cultivated this technique of conversation in service of clarification. I find a certain elegance in this approach. For one thing, it renders on paper the very nature of biblical study, which is grounded in conversation within the community and between the community and the divine. For another, it places that study into a specific context. Thus, details are important: Jeremy, an evangelical with a fundamentalist bent, finds the satanic alive and well (is he just joking about those cats?) but turns out to have a heightened sensitivity for the oppressed; there is an age gap which can be significant to the group's deliberations; and there is a wider world in which the discussion takes place (in this case, a largely white, largely middle-class suburb of Boston).

But most important, a conversation so rendered can model the new pedagogy of collaborative work with undergraduates that has developed at many colleges and universities as well as at numerous adult church groups. I will "unpack" this a bit more later, but for now note that this pedagogy invites the "expert" to function as one who concentrates on facilitating the discussion and, while exerting little control over its content, helps the community place its insights within the wider tradition.

Back to Work!

By now the others have opened Bibles to Matthew, so I ask them: what do you see that's interesting in the text? What strikes you as odd?

"Well," Chemise says, "I'm wondering why Jesus is so insecure," and in response to Jeremy's quizzical frown, adds, "I mean, he's so concerned about how others see him."

"I was wondering why he asks the question in two different ways," Marj says. "First, he asks about the Son of Man and then about himself."

"Very good," Thad says, clearly impressed.

"What does this 'Son of Man' thing mean?" Marj asks. "Is it relevant to the passage?"

"Everything is relevant to the interpretation," Thad says, but Marj has had enough of Thad the Teacher.

"I know that," she says, cutting him off, and she turns to me.

Ah, yes, the Son of Man. Pretty deep topic. Do we want to go into it?

"Let's leave it for now," Jeremy says. "I want to get to Peter and the rock."

"Yeah," Thad says. "Besides, didn't we read that the title 'Son of Man' might just be another way of Jesus saying 'I'?"

Yes, or perhaps a traditional way of referring to himself as a human being, with perhaps a twist of end-of-the-world flavor. But what did you want to look at with regards to Peter here?

"This is what we were discussing," Thad says. "The class didn't come to any conclusion about Peter as the rock, the foundation of the church."

"That's because he wasn't," Jeremy says.

"No one claims that Peter was *not* central to the foundation of the church," Thad says. "Not even you evangelicals can deny how important he was."

"Or how important Matthew and the other writers make him out to be," Chemise says.

"But there's history behind those texts," Thad says. "Tradition can't be that consistent and still be wrong."

"Who says it's consistent?" Jeremy says with increasing heat, but before the lid blows, I steer the conversation back to the text.

Take a minute and martial your arguments, you two. Check your class notes if you have to.

While backpacks are opened and dueling notebooks consulted, Chemise observes, "I like Peter here. The others try to put Jesus into old categories and turn him into reincarnated dead people, but Peter comes up with a new insight."

"It's a revelation," Jeremy says. "That's why he's blessed by the Lord."

"And that is why he's given primacy," Thad says. "He is the rock, the foundation."

"Is he?" Chemise asks.

"What do you mean?"

"Well, even though I hail from California," she says, "I am not completely unchurched. And I have heard it said that the rock here is not Peter, but his insight, his identification of Jesus as Messiah."

"That's the point of contention," Thad says. "My church claims that the Spirit revealed this insight — that Jesus is the Messiah — first to Simon and that Jesus gave him the name 'Peter,' which means 'rock,' as a sign that he was to be the solid foundation of the Christian church."

This looks like a reasonable interpretation. Christian tradition very early on incorporated the notion that Peter was the rock, the base of the community, and that this charism, this designation, was passed on to Peter's successors as the bishop of Rome.

"And my church believes that the rock that Jesus talks about is not Peter but his profession of faith," Jeremy says. "What Thad calls his 'insight.' That is the foundation of the church, not the man."

This interpretation, too, rings true.

"Especially since elsewhere in the gospel, Matthew seems to go out of his way to put Peter in his place," Jeremy says with a glance at his notes. "In Matthew eighteen, verse eighteen, the whole community gets the authority to bind and loose; in chapter twenty-three, verses two through twelve, he warns against the concentration of power in the hands of a few, much less a single individual; and at the end of the gospel, the whole community is commissioned as a leadership group, not just Peter."[5]

"That is true, I grant you that," Thad says.

"Maybe there's some middle ground here," Chemise says.

How so?

---

5. Jeremy owes his listing of texts to Elaine M. Wainwright, *Shall We Look for Another?* (Maryknoll, N.Y.: Orbis, 1998), 99–100.

"Well, maybe Peter is the rock, but in his insight, he's meant to be a model for all followers of Jesus."

"I like that," Marj says. "All this stuff about Peter, putting him first and all. It seems to leave everyone else on the sidelines."

"Like who?" Thad asks.

"Well, Mary Magdalene for one," Marj says. "She was no slouch in the profession of faith department."

"And what's-her-name in the Gospel of John?" Chemise asks. "The sister of Lazarus who says the same thing that Peter does here, about Jesus being the Messiah."

"Martha," Jeremy says. "John eleven."

Interestingly, some of the early church fathers take Chemise's approach. They understood Peter as a model for believers. As one scholar puts it, following Origen of Alexandria, "Peter is the type of any person who has the ability to perceive the Word. The Word builds an indestructible church on such people."[6]

Chemise returns from the kitchen, where she has checked on dinner.

"We had better wind this down," she says.

So. What conclusions have we come to?

"Conclusions?" Jeremy says. "None. The experts don't agree."

"As usual for that crowd," Marj adds.

"Neither do the church fathers or the tradition," Thad says, glancing at his notes. "Tertullian and Cyprian would dissent from Origen's idea."

"We're back at square one," Marj says.

Perhaps. But we aren't done. We have only danced over the surface of some of the possible interpretations that other people have provided. I wonder if we might now look at the passage again, without the experts. If we do —

"Not now," Chemise warns and beckons us to supper. "And there will be no doing of theology at the table."

Perhaps after our meal we can take another look at this passage, without the notebooks and the "received wisdom."

Experts? What Experts? The Pedagogical Shift

If you have this volume in hand, you probably know that Elisabeth Schüssler Fiorenza found a place early on at the table of the foremost theologians of liberation and that the methodological starting points of liberation theology are these: that the work of theology begins with the experience and reflection of the people of G*d, rather than the privileged ruminations of the scholar or the pastor; and that "all theology knowingly or not is by definition always

---

6. Pheme Perkins, *Peter: Apostle for the Whole Church* (Columbia: University of South Carolina Press, 1994), 177; cf. Origen, *Commentary on Matthew* 12.10–11.

engaged for or against the oppressed."[7] Citing the groundbreaking work of the community at Solentiname, Elisabeth asserted almost twenty years ago that if " 'ordinary' members of the community can read, they are able to understand and interpret a text."[8]

This raises an obvious question for the educator: What is the role of the expert in this context? Rather than deny a place for the professionally trained, their participation must be reimagined. We scholars must become "critical transformative intellectuals," rather than the voice of authoritative interpretation and meaning.[9] In other words, rather than functioning as a gatekeeper or purveyor of information, the scholar becomes an assistant, a companion on the road, a resource to aid the community in its discernment.

In recent years I have had occasion to reflect upon the nature of excellent teaching at the level of the college or university. This is not the place to explore in detail the universe of scholarly literature and theory concerning how to teach well. However, one insight from this literature is pertinent: we are challenged to change our focus from the quest to be better teachers to a renewed concern for how students might more effectively learn. The difference here is between bringing knowledge to a student and guiding the student to knowledge.[10] The instructor invites each student to become a "partner in the tasks of analyzing, synthesizing, evaluating and monitoring the process of discovery."[11]

This shift in the expert's self-definition opens the door to a profound change in the learning situation: we and our students become members of a "community of learners."[12] The movement away from passive memorization and reproduction of facts is a journey toward deep learning, the kind of learning that is, in the words of Scottish education professor Noel Entwistle, "a way to establish personal meaning, by *transforming* the incoming information and ideas in relation to their existing knowledge and experience."[13]

This change to a teaching style in which vibrant discussion is the norm — and not merely an afterthought confined to the last few minutes of class —

---

7. Elisabeth Schüssler Fiorenza, *Bread Not Stone* (Boston: Beacon, 1984), 45.

8. Ibid., 134. Cf. Ernesto Cardenal, *The Gospel in Solentiname* (4 vols.; Maryknoll, N.Y.: Orbis, 1976–82).

9. Schüssler Fiorenza, *Jesus and the Politics of Interpretation*, 74–75.

10. C. Roland Christensen and Laura Ferguson, "Interview: A Community of Learners," *Harvard Gazette* (20 April 1995): 3.

11. Stephen C. Cooke, "Effective Use of Discussion Method Teaching," *Agricultural Education Magazine* 68 (1995): 6.

12. Christensen and Ferguson, "Interview," 3. Cf. J. T. Dillon, "Research on Questioning and Discussion," *Educational Leadership* 42 (1984): 50–56; and Richard G. Tiberius and Jane Tipping, "The Discussion Leader: Fostering Student Learning in Groups," in *Teaching Alone, Teaching Together* (ed. James L. Bess et al.; San Francisco: Jossey-Bass, 2000), 108–30.

13. Noel Entwistle, "Promoting Deep Learning through Teaching and Assessment," in *Assessment to Promote Deep Learning* (ed. Linda Suskie; Washington, D.C.: American Association for Higher Education, 2001), 10 (emphasis original).

is not as simple as gathering one's students in a circle and asking them what they think about today's readings. It involves retraining and a shift in one's way of thinking about what we do in the classroom and what roles we play there;[14] education theorists identify this as moving away from purveying information to passive receivers and moving toward offering students an opportunity for active learning, which leads to their transformation.[15]

And this is precisely where recent educational theory intersects with a century of rumination about how and why we do theology.[16] We see it everywhere in the literature. The pedagogy of passivity, an (unintended?) by-product of traditional modes of discourse that train the community to be a "competent" and "correct" reader of the Bible, is rejected in favor of interpretive strategies that invite the common reader (or hearer, since not all can read) into the center of the circle as a legitimate participant.[17]

Legitimate indeed! As Carlos Mesters declares, the people who come to Scripture study don't do so merely because they seek to interpret the Bible; they want to make sense of their lives with the Bible's assistance.[18] For these people, the Bible functions "as a channel, which it has observably been, between humankind and transcendence."[19] It reminds them of who they are; it uncovers them and displays for them their true identity.[20] Indeed they may even "suddenly discover the Bible reading them."[21]

And here we are, the experts in the middle of all this, lured away from our comfort zone, where we can control any discussion, and challenged to renegotiate all articulations of our alleged authority, "collaborating across

---

14. To be an effective discussion-based teacher, one is encouraged to explore the social context of teaching and learning and to study leadership theory, learning styles, the dynamics of teamwork, the stages of group development, and issues of diversity.

15. Jean MacGregor, "Collaborative Learning: Shared Inquiry as a Process of Reform," in *The Changing Face of College Teaching* (ed. Marilla D. Svinicki; New Directions for Teaching and Learning 42; San Francisco: Jossey-Bass, 1990), 19–30. See also the articles in other volumes in this series, especially in Kris Bosworth and Sharon J. Hamilton, eds., *Collaborative Learning* (New Directions for Teaching and Learning 59; San Francisco: Jossey-Bass, 1994); and Tracey E. Sutherland and Charles C. Bonwell, eds., *Using Active Learning in College Classes* (New Directions for Teaching and Learning 67; San Francisco: Jossey-Bass, 1996).

16. See, for instance, Sandra Schneiders's extended discussion of biblical interpretation for transformation rather than information: *The Revelatory Text* (2d ed.; Collegeville, Minn.: Glazier/Liturgical Press, 1999).

17. Fernando F. Segovia, "And They Began to Speak in Other Tongues," in *Reading from This Place*, vol. 1: *Social Location and Biblical Interpretation in the United States* (ed. Fernando F. Segovia and Mary Ann Tolbert; Minneapolis: Fortress, 1995), 1–32.

18. Carlos Mesters, "The Use of the Bible in Christian Communities of the Common People," in *The Bible and Liberation* (ed. Norman Gottwald; Maryknoll, N.Y.: Orbis, 1983), 128.

19. Wilfred C. Smith, "The Study of Religion and the Study of the Bible," in *Rethinking Scripture: Essays from a Comparative Perspective* (ed. Miriam Levering; Albany: State University of New York Press, 1989), 28.

20. Leander Keck, "The Presence of God through Scripture," *Lexington Biblical Quarterly* 10 (1975): 16–17; John P. Burgess, "Scripture as Sacramental Word," *Interpretation* 52 (1998): 381.

21. Chris Peck, "Back to the Future: Participatory Bible Study and Bible Theology," *Theology* 98 (1995): 355.

the power line."[22] Stepping away from the familiar, away from power and control, even away from the minimal comfort offered to us by adaptations of the Socratic method, we engage in a new high-wire act, what my colleague Mary Joan Winn Leith calls "teaching without a net."

Back to the Rock

David is stalking his prey.

"If that animal comes any closer to me," Jeremy says, "I'm gonna give it the opportunity to discover if there really is a kitty heaven."

"Oh, Jere," Marj says, as she sweeps up the red ball of fur. "Whoa," she says to the plump feline in her arms. "You are a little porker, aren't you?"

Let's get back to work. Back to Matthew sixteen. We've talked a bit about some of the interpretations provided by previous readers of the text. Now, let's look at it again. What do you see with your own eyes?

"What strikes me is the interpersonal interaction," Chemise says. "Between Jesus and Peter."

How so?

"Well, the way they name each other," she says. "Simon names Jesus Messiah and Jesus names Simon Peter."

That might be significant?

"Well, she says, "naming is a way of identifying someone.

"I agree," Marj says. "When I went into the convent, they wanted to give me a new name. I resisted."

"Why?" Chemise asks her.

"It was as though I would be giving them some power over me," Marj says. "Over who I was or how I saw myself."

"Ah, the power of naming," Chemise says. "Adam names all the animals and gets power over them."

"No one knows the name of G*d," Thad says. "YHWH, 'I am who am,' isn't exactly a name, is it?"

"And therefore," Jeremy says, "No one can have power over G*d."

"Women used to take their husbands' names," Chemise says.

"Right, and give their power to their men," Marj says. "Naming is about power."

"Are you saying that Peter gets power over Jesus here?" Jeremy asks.

Marj considers this for a moment. "No, not exactly," she says. "When the nuns wanted to rename me, it did seem a bit like a violation. But I didn't feel as though I was completely in their power. It was something else."

---

22. Karen T. Romer and William R. Whipple, "Collaboration across the Power Line," *College Teaching* 39 (1991): 66–70.

"Let me guess," Chemise says. "Power is present only in relationship, and I'll bet the violation you felt had something to do with that. With relationships."

"I guess," Marj says. "In a sense, by renaming me they were trying to put me into a different relationship with all the people who knew me before."

Thad has been listening but also looking at the text. "You could argue," he says, "that the rock here is relationship, the relationship between Peter and Jesus."

Say more.

"Could it be that the mutual naming that goes on here is a sign of a deepening intimacy between the two men?" he asks. "They've become more connected than they were before."

"That reminds me of Jesus and Mary Magdalene," Marj says. "At the tomb in the Gospel of John."

"Yeah," Thad breaks in. "He's just been raised from the dead. She doesn't know who he is."

"She thinks he's a gardener," Jeremy says.

"But when he calls her by her name, she recognizes him," Thad says. "And she names him back. What's the title she uses?"

" 'Rabboni,' " Jeremy says. "It means 'teacher.' "

Interesting parallel. But are we done? Let's pick up the passage where we left it before dinner. Chemise?

She opens to the text and reads:

Then he sternly ordered the disciples not to tell anyone that he was the Messiah.

From that time on, Jesus began to show his disciples that he must go to Jerusalem and undergo great suffering at the hands of the elders and chief priests and scribes, and be killed, and on the third day be raised.

And Peter took him aside and began to rebuke him, saying, "God forbid it, Lord! This must never happen to you."

But he turned and said to Peter, "Get behind me, Satan! You are a stumbling block to me; for you are setting your mind not on divine things but on human things."

We sit for a moment. Then Marj notes, "More naming."

"And a fight," Thad says. "Which means more intimacy, right?"

Marj looks perplexed but Jeremy understands. "No one fights as viciously as two brothers."

"Oh, I don't know about that," Chemise says. "Sisters can be pretty ferocious with each other, too."

"In either case," Thad says, "the better we know someone, the freer we are to let it all hang out, both the good and the bad, right?"

I like Thad's interpretation. The intimacy between these two, Jesus and Peter, is not sentimental and pseudo-pious; the road of their relationship is rocky and difficult. It involves not a moment here and there of holy revelation or prayer with Jesus, but real, robust give-and-take conversation.

Let's see if I can summarize what I think you're saying. Perhaps we can read this passage as the story of Peter's coming into mature relationship with Jesus, the Messiah. In this context, the rock is not Peter. It is also not some abstract theological concept like "faith."

"Right," Thad says. "The rock is the relationship between Peter and his friend, or the relationship between Peter and his Messiah."

This is a transformative reading. The reader is challenged not just to appropriate a piece of information about Peter or about the theological virtue of faith. No, we are invited to put ourselves in Peter's position, into a new relationship with Christ, not in a stance of admiration but of conversation, one of mutual intimacy, a relationship involving the whole person, not just the intellect. If we take this text in concert with the story of Mary Magdalene in the garden, we can discern a call to a profoundly intimate relationship — indeed, a love relationship — between the believer and Christ.

"I would take it a step further," Chemise says. "This story can remind people of the importance of any relationship, the significance of intimacy to each of us."

"And," Marj says, "the difficulty of maintaining right relationship with those we need and love."

Cornered: Interpretation for or Against

This all sounds nice, neat, and pretty tame. It is also pretty incomplete.

How so? our interlocutors might ask.

Well, even after we wrestle our egos to the mat and check control issues and messiah complexes at the church door, the work of liberation theology offers one tough final reminder to the traditionally trained pedagogue: in a liberational framework, there are no value-free deliberations.

Ah, but this is the postmodern world, and you are probably nodding in agreement with this key insight. Most of us — at least most of us reading this volume — long ago swept away notions of objectivity with respect to the work of interpretation. But if we are not vigilant, we can miss the obvious corollary to this widely acknowledged hermeneutical truth of ours and wind up in the same safe ivory tower as that inhabited by the proponents of positivistic objective scholarship (or maybe the next tower over!). Roberto Goizueta warns against the seductive peril of methodological rigor: "The reduction of theology to methodology absolves the theologian of ever having to commit him[self] or herself to a particular truth, or to any truth at all." And if we do articulate truth, it is liable to be an abstraction "not intrinsically linked to a particular appearance or form."[23] Even justice, as Gustavo Gutiérrez observes, can become an idol if allowed to drift into the realm of disembodied abstraction.[24]

Thus, the notion of the scholar/specialist as collaborator and resource for the community arrives with a challenge before which I, for one, still cringe: the expert becomes part of an advocacy stand for or against the oppressed. Not some category of generically oppressed people, but the specifically oppressed we find in our own context. In any biblical conversation, the professional must take sides.

I'll be honest with you: by temperament I am an irenicist, not a polemicist. Make love, not war, and all that. But as long as we are talking about an enterprise that is intrinsically based in the hard facts and living flesh of communities that aspire to some form of Christian discipleship, I don't see any way around this taking of sides.

We're cornered.

If we had time and space here, the after-dinner conversation might address this and move the discussion into a less individualistic interpretation of Matthew sixteen. It might begin something like this:

"I don't like it," Jeremy says, and our reflective flight of innovative thought comes back to earth with a thud.

"What's not to like?" Marj asks him.

"This idea that the rock is a love relationship between Peter and Jesus," he says. "It's too New Age for me."

"How so?" Marj asks him. Catholic though she is, she has an affinity for crystals.

"You're turning the story into something about me and my buddy Jesus," he says. "Jesus is not my buddy. He's my Savior."

"Actually, is he your Savior, Jeremy?" Thad asks him. "Or is he our Savior?"

"He's the Savior of the world!" Jeremy says with conviction.

"He's the Savior of the poor," Chemise murmurs under her breath.

Precisely, I would say to them. Now, let's take another look at the context for this encounter between Jesus and Simon Peter, especially what follows....

And what would follow might be a much edgier reading of this text in this group's context, a reading made possible by the first more intimate and comfortable discussion. The next step after that would be action. How could

---

23. Roberto S. Goizueta, "A Ressourcement from the Margins: U.S. Latino Popular Catholicism as Lived Religion," in *Theology and Lived Christianity* (ed. David M. Hammond; Mystic, Conn.: Twenty-Third Publications, 2000), 4, 7.

24. Gustavo Gutiérrez, *The Density of the Present: Selected Writings* (Maryknoll, N.Y.: Orbis, 1999), 141.

it not be? In this case, perhaps the action would involve joining other like-minded people to force the Roman Catholic archdiocese of Boston to make structural reforms and offer real support and healing to those whose lives have been ruined by the region's clerical culture.

"We have to take back our church," Marj might say, echoing the inhabitants of the pews in Boston, including some with whom I have used this dialogical method in recent months.[25]

The Dancing Has Just Begun

At the end of *Wisdom Ways* Elisabeth exclaims, "I hope that the 'dancing' has just begun."[26] But we have run out of time and I find the ending of this conversation — and this essay — to be unsatisfactory. Too many loose ends. Too many unanswered questions about method. But that is, in part, the point. The format developed by my students attempts to depict on paper this truth: the conversation does not end. The collaboration does not end. Nor does the messiness. Insights misfire. Clearly significant parts of texts never get addressed. ("Before we go, can't we talk about Peter getting the keys to heaven's realm in Matthew sixteen, verse nineteen?" Marj wonders. "Yeah," Thad says. "That's how we got into this discussion in the first place.") We wander off on tangents. One's sense of good order is regularly offended.

But that is the point: none of this ends until, as Walter Brueggemann puts it, the church becomes "a place where people come to receive new people, or old materials freshly voiced, that will...nourish, legitimate, and authorize a counterimagination of the world."[27]

I end this reflection with one last imagined scene. I remember the long, ivy-covered, stone building that housed the theology department at Notre Dame thirty years ago. In my mind's eye, I see what I admit to be a caricature of a dour man who scowls and warns his new colleague about the slippery road down into relevance. I imagine that her eyes flash but, uncharacteristically, she says nothing.

Later she passes through the dark foyer out of the building and into the late afternoon sunlight on the green of the south quad.

She is late for a meeting, but it's spring and there's a warm breeze here and she stops to enjoy the quiet scene. At this hour there are few people around to disrupt her solitude. She is thinking: avoid the slippery slope down.

She shrugs and flashes that smile we seminarians were warned about. She looks up, turns toward the giant marble depiction of Touchdown Jesus that flanks the south side of the library.

And she moves on.

---

25. For a fuller discussion of the method, see my *Texts, Rocks, and Talk: Reclaiming Biblical Christianity to Counterimagine the World* (Collegeville, Minn.: Glazier/Liturgical Press, 2002).

26. Schüssler Fiorenza, *Wisdom Ways*, 189.

27. Brueggemann, *Texts under Negotiation*, 20.

4

(Re)claiming *Oikoumenē?*

Empire, Ecumenism, and the Discipleship of Equals

Barbara R. Rossing

In her 1992 essay "A Discipleship of Equals: Ekklesial Democracy and Patriarchy in Biblical Perspective," Elisabeth Schüssler Fiorenza argues for a liberation-oriented use of the Greek term *basileia*.[1] She argues that the word has two meanings; while *basileia* "belongs to the royal-monarchical context of meaning that has as its sociopolitical referent the Roman empire," we can also retrieve another meaning, belonging to ancestral Israelite traditions in the prophetic milieu of the north, that asserts a "democratic countermeaning" to the royal meaning of the term. In Schüssler Fiorenza's view, Jesus' proclamation of the *basileia* of God appeals to this second, more democratic, meaning of the term. It is this meaning, she believes, that holds promise for ecclesial life today.

This essay will investigate the Greek word *oikoumenē* (world), asking whether a similarly liberating strand of the word *oikoumenē* in the biblical tradition can be retrieved for life in the *ekklēsia* as democratic assembly today.[2]

At first glance the answer would seem to be an obvious yes, affirming the promise of *oikoumenē*. For many feminist and liberationist Christians, involvement in the ecumenical movement has been one of the most progressive dimensions of ecclesial life. Third World women have found a haven in the ecumenical movement, most notably in the recent Ecumenical Decade of Churches in Solidarity with Women. The World Council of Churches, whose logo is a ship with the overarching slogan "Oikoumene," has been at the forefront of movements of liberation, promoting democratic visions.

---

1. Elisabeth Schüssler Fiorenza, "A Discipleship of Equals: Ekklesial Democracy and Patriarchy in Biblical Perspective," in *A Democratic Catholic Church: The Reconstruction of Catholicism* (ed. Eugene Bianchi; New York: Crossroad, 1992), 27.

2. *Oikoumenē* is the feminine passive participle of the verb *oikein* (to dwell or inhabit). Hence its meaning as "the whole inhabited world." The English word *ecumenical* derives from the adjective *oikoumenikos* (pertaining to the whole world).

Ecumenists trace their commitments back to the Greek notion of the *oikoumenē* or house that includes the whole inhabited world, which they have recently expanded to include all creation, not just the human world.[3]

In literature of the Roman era, however, the word *oikoumenē* carried an imperial meaning beyond its geographical meaning. More than "the earth as inhabited area" in a geographical sense, *oikoumenē* came also to mean "the world as administrative unit, the Roman Empire."[4] I will argue that throughout most of the New Testament *oikoumenē* carries this second or political connotation of the Roman Empire.

While in contemporary ecumenical discussions it can seem attractive to attempt to redefine *oikoumenē* in a positive sense, we need to recall that in earliest Christian literature *oikoumenē* was primarily a term of empire, rarely used in a liberating context. Indeed, the legacy of *oikoumenē* is so problematic that the question remains whether the term can be reclaimed apart from its kyriarchal and imperialist tendencies.[5] The challenge for ecumenism today must be to repudiate the imperial trajectory of *oikoumenē* and to seek alternative models that embrace ecclesial diversity and democracy.

Oikoumenē as the World Created by God: The Septuagint

In the Septuagint, *oikoumenē* is the translation for the Hebrew word *tēbēl* (world), often used in poetic parallelism with "earth" (Hebrew *'ereṣ*; Greek *gē*). God is the creator of the *oikoumenē*, the one who "has made the earth [*gē*] ... / who established the world [*oikoumenē*] ... / and has stretched out the heaven" (Jer 10:12; 51:15 [= 28:15 LXX]). The term *oikoumenē* is especially frequent in the Psalms: "The heavens are yours, the earth is yours, / and as for the world [*oikoumenē*] and its fullness, you founded them" (Ps 89:11 [= 88:12 LXX]). The apostle Paul's only usage of the word *oikoumenē* is a quotation from Ps 19:4 (= 18:5 LXX), where *oikoumenē* is parallel to *gē*: "Their line is gone out through all the earth [*gē*], / and their words to the end of the *oikoumenē*" (Rom 10:18).

Oikoumenē in the Septuagint encompasses the whole geographical world, both physical and human, that is accountable to God. God will "judge the

---

3. For a vision of *oikoumenē* as including all creation, see the essay by Konrad Raiser, "Ecumenism in Search of a New Vision," in *The Ecumenical Movement: An Anthology of Key Texts and Voices* (ed. Michael Kinnamon and Brian E. Cope; Geneva: World Council of Churches/Grand Rapids: Eerdmans, 1997), 76.

4. These are the first and second definitions of *oikoumenē* in Frederick William Danker, *A Greek-English Lexicon of the New Testament and Other Early Christian Literature* (3d ed.; Chicago: University of Chicago Press, 2000), 699.

5. The term *kyriarchal* was coined by Elisabeth Schüssler Fiorenza to describe the "social-political system of domination and subordination that is based on the power and rule of the lord/master/father"; *Sharing Her Word: Feminist Biblical Interpretation in Context* (Boston: Beacon, 1998), 190 n. 52.

world [*oikoumenē*] in righteousness" (Ps 9:8 [= 9:9 LXX]; 96:13 [= 95:13 LXX]; 98:9 [= 97:9 LXX]). God lays claim to the whole *oikoumenē*: "The world [*oikoumenē*] is mine" (50:12 [= 49:12 LXX]); "the earth [*gē*] is the Lord's and all that is in it; / the world [*oikoumenē*] and those who dwell in it" (24:1 [= 23:1 LXX]).

Oikoumenē as Empire

By the first century B.C.E., however, Rome also laid claim to the *oikoumenē*. In propaganda and iconography celebrating Rome's conquests of lands and peoples, *oikoumenē* was claimed not only to the ends of the world in a geographical sense but also in a political sense, as the ends of Roman imperial sway.[6]

In his landmark analysis of Rome's and Augustus's "ecumenical and ostentatious claims," Claude Nicolet argues that Rome's empire and its geographical knowledge developed hand in hand, as evidenced in the use of the Greek word *oikoumenē* and the Latin term *orbis terrarum*.[7] Already in the work of Greek historian Polybius (150 B.C.E.), Nicolet finds that geographical claims about the *oikoumenē* were "essentially political." Polybius possessed "extensive geographical knowledge (he is one of the geographers referred to and criticized by Strabo), and he devoted several important digressions and an entire book to geographical questions," yet Polybius frames his work with the political question of how "all the known parts of the inhabited world [*oikoumenē*] have come under the domination of Rome" (Polybius, *Histories* 3.1.4; see also 1.1.5; 1.2.7; 6.49.9).[8]

Romans were called "lords of the *oikoumenē*" (*kyrioi tēs oikoumenēs*; Plutarch, *Tiberius Gracchus* 9.6), a claim realized and further expanded through military conquests by Pompey, Julius Caesar, and Augustus. In 61 B.C.E. a huge trophy of the conquered *oikoumenē* was carried in triumphal procession in Rome to celebrate Pompey's three military victories over Libya, Europe, and Asia: "He [Pompey] celebrated the triumph in honor of all his wars at once, including in it many trophies beautifully decked out to represent each of his achievements, even the smallest; and after them all came one huge one, decked out in costly fashion and bearing an inscription stating that it was a trophy of the inhabited world [*oikoumenē*]" (Dio, *Roman History* 37.21.2).[9] Following the triumph, a permanent statue of Pompey

---

6. For the purposes of this essay I work with a definition of "geographical" as having to do with the *gē* (earth) and "political" as having to do with *polis* (city or empire). The distinction between the two terms is heuristic, since my point is to show that they are closely related.

7. Claude Nicolet, *Space, Geography, and Politics in the Early Roman Empire* (Ann Arbor: University of Michigan Press, 1991), 11.

8. Ibid., 30.

9. The translation of Dio's *Roman History* is by Earnest Cary in the Loeb Classical Library (Cambridge: Harvard University Press, 1954).

was erected in his theater, showing him holding a globe of the world in his left hand: "The globe, like his trophy, discreetly recalled that he had in principle 'conquered the world,' in the name of the Roman people."[10]

A bronze statue representing Julius Caesar's ecumenical domination was more overt, showing the emperor treading with his foot upon the *oikoumenē.* Dio's *Roman History* describes this statue as "mounted upon a likeness of the inhabited world [*oikoumenē*], with an inscription to the effect that he was a demigod," by decree of the Roman Senate. On the day of his triumph Julius Caesar "climbed up the stairs of the Capitol on his knees" until he reached the "image of the *oikoumenē* lying beneath his feet" (Dio, *Roman History* 43.14.16; 43.21.2). Coins from this period also depict the image of the emperor with the globe beneath his feet, an image of triumph.

Augustus made the most far-reaching ecumenical claims, as evidenced in his *Res Gestae,* his official list of global conquests prepared for posthumous publication on his mausoleum and on Greek and Latin inscriptions in cities throughout the empire. Beginning with a description of how "at the age of nineteen, on my own initiative and at my own expense, I raised an army," Augustus's *Res Gestae* sets his vision of *oikoumenē* within the context of his military conquests: "Wars, both civil and foreign, I undertook throughout the whole *oikoumenē,* on land and sea" (Augustus, *Res Gestae* 3).[11] Lists of conquered territory in Africa, Asia, and Europe substantiate Augustus's claim that he "extended the boundaries of all the provinces which were bordered by races not yet subject to our empire."

Art and architecture also proclaimed Roman sovereignty over the entire *oikoumenē.*[12] The Gemma Augustea, a carved cameo, personifies *Oikoumenē* as a feminine figure who places a crown on the head of Emperor Augustus.[13] Below, captive barbarians are depicted as bound and surrendering to Roman conquerors. The Great Cameo of France continues Augustus's ecumenical imagery into the reign of his adopted successor, Tiberius.[14] This three-tiered cameo portrays Augustus and Aeneas up in heaven, holding an orb or globe as a symbol of Rome's divinely sanctioned domination of the entire *oikoumenē* and giving their blessing to Tiberius who is below on earth. As in the Gemma Augustea, the lowest register of the Great Cameo of France portrays conquered barbarians. Together with coins showing the

10. Nicolet, *Space, Geography, and Politics,* 39.

11. The translation of Augustus's *Res Gestae* is by F. W. Shipley in the Loeb Classical Library (Cambridge: Harvard University Press, 1924).

12. See Paul Zanker, *The Power of Images in the Age of Augustus* (trans. Alan Shapiro; Ann Arbor: University of Michigan, 1988), on the "visual language" of Augustan imperial monuments.

13. The identification of the feminine figure as *Oikoumenē* in the Gemma Augustea in Vienna is debated. Fulvio Canciani categorizes as "probable" her identification as *Oikoumenē;* see "Oikoumene," *Lexicon iconographicum mythologiae classicae* (Zürich: Artemis, 1981), 17. Nicolet, Ando, and others accept the identification as certain.

14. See discussion in Clifford Ando, *Imperial Ideology and Provincial Loyalty in the Roman Empire* (Berkeley: University of California Press, 1990), 287–89.

emperor's foot on the globe and architectural assertions of ecumenical domination, such imagery symbolically lays claim to the *oikoumenē* in much more than a geographical sense.

Other ancient authors' usage of the term *oikoumenē* reflects such imperial perspectives. Aelius Aristides' *Roman Oration* lauds the harmony and unity that Rome brought to the whole *oikoumenē*, exemplifying the use of *oikoumenē* for imperial propaganda. Drawing on a medical analogy, Aristides argues that, prior to Roman rule, the "inhabited world [*oikoumenē*] was, as it were, ill" because of its many wars, factions, and rivalries (Aelius Aristides, *Orationes* 26.97).[15] In place of disunity, Rome brings universal good order. Local traditions and laws are superceded, as Rome organizes the entire *oikoumenē* into a "single household" under its rule. Aelius Aristides describes Rome's conquests of the landscape and its unifying of the *oikoumenē* in both geographical and political terms:

> What was said by Homer, "The earth was common to all," you have made a reality, by surveying the whole inhabited world [*oikoumenē*], by bridging the rivers in various ways, by cutting carriage roads through the mountains, by filling desert places with post stations, and by civilizing everything with your way of life and good order.... And now, indeed, there is no need to write a description of the world, nor to enumerate the laws of each people, but you have become universal geographers for all ... by opening up all the gates of the inhabited world [*oikoumenē*] ... and by organizing the whole inhabited world like a single household [*syntaxantes hōsper hena oikon hapasan tēn oikoumenēn*]. (*Orationes* 26.101–2)

The speech by King Agrippa II in book 2 of Josephus's *Jewish War* is a poignant example of the imperial context of the term *oikoumenē*. Agrippa underscores Rome's hegemony over the *oikoumenē*, as he seeks to persuade the Judeans of the futility of their revolt against Rome. Throughout the whole *oikoumenē* Roman power is undefeated, Agrippa tells his hearers (2.362). Peoples and nations who have submitted to Rome's rule include the Gauls, Greeks, Germans, and Britons (2.364). Finally Agrippa asks the Judeans: "What allies then do you expect for this war? Will you recruit them from the uninhabited [*aoikētou*] wilds? For in the habitable world [*oikoumenē*] *all are Romans*" (Josephus, *Jewish War* 2.388 [emphasis added]).[16]

---

15. The translation of Aelius Aristides' *Orationes* is by Charles A. Behr in *P. Aelius Aristides: The Complete Works* (2 vols.; Leiden: Brill, 1981). This oration dates to the mid-second century C.E.

16. The translation of Josephus's *Jewish War* is by H. St. J. Thackeray in the Loeb Classical Library (Cambridge: Harvard University Press, 1928).

Oikoumenē in the New Testament: Revelation

"In the *oikoumenē* all are Romans": this fact — mourned by Agrippa, celebrated by Aelius Aristides — describes the first-century context both geographically and politically, and it must be kept in mind as we investigate the meaning of *oikoumenē* in the New Testament. The word *oikoumenē* is used eight times in Luke-Acts and three times in Revelation, with fewer occurrences in Hebrews, Romans, and Matthew. The third edition of the *Greek-English Lexicon of the New Testament and Other Early Christian Literature* assigns the New Testament uses of *oikoumenē* to the geographical definition "the earth as inhabited area" or to the derived definition "inhabitants of the earth." We must ask, however, whether its second or more political definition of *oikoumenē* as "the world as administrative unit, the Roman Empire" is not also the predominant understanding of *oikoumenē* in the New Testament.

References to *oikoumenē* in the Book of Revelation exemplify the problem. Revelation uses the phrase *the whole oikoumenē* three times, always negatively. The question is whether these references are primarily geographical — that is, relating to the *gē* (earth) — in the tradition of the Septuagint and the first definition in the *Greek-English Lexicon of the New Testament,* or whether they are more political. Chilean liberation scholar Pablo Richard argues for the political reading of *oikoumenē* as Rome: "The inhabited world, or *oikoumenē*, is not all the earth, but the world that is organized and controlled by the Roman Empire. Everything else is the world of the barbarians."[17]

Revelation's first reference to *oikoumenē* is 3:10, in the letter to the Philadelphians. David Aune translates *oikoumenē* here as "earth," using the same word as he does for translating *gē* later in the same verse: "I will preserve you from the time of affliction which will come upon the whole earth [*oikoumenē*] to afflict the inhabitants of the earth [*gē*]."[18] The second reference to *oikoumenē* is 12:9, where *oikoumenē* is the world that has been deceived by Satan, Rome's surrogate: "The great dragon was thrown down... that deceiver of the whole *oikoumenē*, he was thrown down into the earth." Revelation's final reference to *oikoumenē* comes just before the anti-Roman chapter 17, in a description of the evil spirits that issue from the mouth of the dragon after the sixth bowl is poured out: "They are demonic spirits, performing signs, who go abroad to the kings of the whole world [*oikoumenē*], to assemble them for battle" (16:14).

---

17. Pablo Richard, *Apocalypse: A People's Commentary on the Book of Revelation* (Maryknoll, N.Y.: Orbis, 1995), 61, commenting on Rev 3:10.

18. David Aune, *Revelation 1–5* (Word Biblical Commentary 52; Dallas: Word, 1997), 228. Aune argues (239) that in Revelation the "whole *oikoumenē*" is synonymous with the "inhabitants of the earth," a phrase used also in 13:3. Charles Talbert likewise translates *oikoumenē* as "earth" in 3:10; *The Apocalypse* (Louisville: Westminster John Knox, 1994), 22.

Is Aune correct that *oikoumenē* is synonymous with "the inhabitants of earth" in Revelation? Does Revelation sustain the Septuagint's close parallelism between *oikoumenē* and *gē,* with *oikoumenē* having primarily a geographical meaning, or does the term take on a more anti-Roman political cast, as Richard suggests? Since Revelation contains only these three references to *oikoumenē* compared to its eighty-two references to *gē,* comparisons are difficult. Nonetheless, in my view, we can identify a crucial shift in the relationship between *oikoumenē* and *gē* from the Septuagint to the Book of Revelation, and indeed to the whole New Testament. While Aune is correct that there is a parallelism between *oikoumenē* and *gē* in Revelation when the terms are used negatively for judgment, what is missing from Revelation is any positive sense of *oikoumenē.*

Unlike the Septuagint, Revelation never asserts that the *oikoumenē* is God's creation. This is a crucial difference from *gē,* which does carry a positive sense in Revelation as God's creation and as an active agent of God's salvation.[19] Although the earth suffers judgment and tribulation, Revelation also always underscores that God created the earth (14:7) — a claim that is absent for *oikoumenē.* Earth plays a saving role in Rev 12, when earth rescues the woman from the dragon's river. God's saints will reign "on earth" (5:10), another positive reference. Revelation denounces Rome for destroying the earth, asserting that "the time has come ... to destroy the destroyers of the earth" (11:18). Most important, Revelation proclaims that the earth will be renewed in God's future world, as God's dwelling place, when God creates a "new earth" along with a new heaven (21:1). No such positive renewal is envisioned for the *oikoumenē.*

A political critique of Rome runs throughout the entire Book of Revelation, culminating in the indictment of Rome's imperial violence, idolatry, and unjust global commerce in Rev 13 and 17–18. Although the word *oikoumenē* does not occur in these overtly anti-Roman passages, it is linked to this critique. If Revelation refrains from referring to the *oikoumenē* as God's creation, it is because for Revelation *oikoumenē* represents the Roman Empire — an empire that must come to an end. In light of the book's overall anti-Roman polemic, the "hour of trial that is coming upon the whole *oikoumenē*" in 3:10 should be read not so much as a general eschatological tribulation that will come upon the earth, but more pointedly as the trial or judgment that God will bring upon *the entire Roman Empire* and on all those who benefit from Rome's injustice.[20]

---

19. For the argument that Earth (*gē*) plays a positive role in Revelation, see Barbara R. Rossing, " 'Alas for the Earth!' Lament and Resistance in Revelation 12," in *The Earth Bible,* vol. 5: *The Earth Story in the New Testament* (ed. Norman Habel and Shirley Wurth; Sheffield: Sheffield Academic Press, 2002), 183–95.

20. Such a political reading of Rev 3:10 mitigates against an escapist reading by which some use this verse as proof that they will be "raptured" up from earth before the tribulation. See, for example, Hal Lindsey, *The Rapture* (New York: Bantam, 1983), 119–24.

It is striking that Revelation never explicitly challenges Rome's claims over the *oikoumenē,* since Revelation vigorously contests Rome's claims to *basileia,* throne, *kyrios,* and many other political terms. Revelation asserts that "the kingdom of the world [*hē basileia tou kosmou*] has become the kingdom of our Lord and of his Christ" (11:15), a challenge to Rome's claims to kingship and lordship and a reclaiming of the term *basileia* for God. God — not the empire or emperor — is the true ruler who sits on the throne and is alone worthy to receive worship.[21] But Revelation does not attempt to reclaim the *oikoumenē* as belonging to God. *Oikoumenē* is portrayed rather as a realm supported by violence, a realm that has been deceived by Satan (12:9) and aligned with Rome and its kings for battle against God (16:14), a realm of future tribulation and judgment (3:10).

Oikoumenē in the Gospels and Acts

Paul's speech at the Areopagus in Acts 17 is a further example of the *oikoumenē* falling under God's judgment. The speech builds its argument on the basis of God's creation and people's desire for God, using the words *kosmos* (world) and *gē* (earth) to describe God's good creation. The author appears to go to great lengths, however, to avoid referencing the *oikoumenē* positively as God's creation: "God who made the world [*ton kosmon*] and everything in it, being Lord of heaven and earth, does not live in shrines... since he himself gives to all mortals life and breath and all things. From one ancestor, [God] made all nations to inhabit all the face of earth [*tēs gēs*]" (17:24–26). Not until the concluding warning about God's impending judgment of the world does Paul turn to the word *oikoumenē,* telling the Athenians that the time for repentance has come, because God "has fixed a day on which to judge the world [*tēn oikoumenēn*] in righteousness" (17:31, quoting Ps 9:8 [= 9:9 LXX]; 96:13 [= 95:13 LXX]; 98:9 [= 97:9 LXX]). In quoting here from the Septuagint, Acts selects only a single verse from the Psalms about God's judgment upon the *oikoumenē,* but does not quote any psalms that describe the *oikoumenē* as God's good creation.

Other references to the *oikoumenē* in Acts are clearly political, most notably the accusations against Paul and other Christians for disrupting civic order. A mob in Thessalonika attacks Jason's house and brings him before authorities on the grounds that "these people who have been turning the *oikoumenē* upside down have come here also.... They are acting contrary to the decrees of the emperor, saying that there is another king named Jesus" (17:6–7). In Caesarea the charge against Paul is that he is "an agitator among all the Jews throughout the *oikoumenē*" (24:5), while in Ephesus

---

21. For the argument that Revelation's throne room liturgies are parodies of Rome's imperial liturgies, see David Aune, "The Influence of Roman Imperial Court Ceremonial on the Apocalypse of John," *Papers of the Chicago Society of Biblical Research* 28 (1983): 5–26.

Paul is accused of disrupting the temple economy of the Ephesian Artemis "whom Asia and the *oikoumenē* worship" (19:27). The location of these charges in major cities of the Roman Empire is indicative of their political context.

The word *oikoumenē* is used infrequently in the Gospels, where it seems also to refer to the empire. Luke situates Jesus' birth alongside Augustus's imperial declaration in Luke 2:1: "In those days a decree went out from Caesar Augustus that the whole *oikoumenē* should be enrolled." Satan tempts Jesus by offering to give him the kingdoms of the *oikoumenē* (4:5). Both Matthew and Luke use the word *oikoumenē* in references to the end (*telos*) and to the tribulations that will come upon the nations: "And the gospel of the kingdom will be preached in the whole *oikoumenē*, as a testimony to all nations... and the end will come" (Matt 24:13–14); "there will be distress of nations... people fainting with fear and with foreboding of what is coming upon the *oikoumenē*" (Luke 21:25–26). These references to the *oikoumenē* in the context of the end should also be read in a more political sense — asserting the end of empire even more than the end of the geographical world or earth.

To summarize: in contrast to the Septuagint, the New Testament is strikingly silent regarding the *oikoumenē* as God's creation. Unlike the words *kosmos* or *gē*, there is no positive or ecological connotation to the term *oikoumenē*.[22] In the New Testament, as in other literature from the Roman period, the *oikoumenē* represents the world under Roman imperial hegemony, the entire world "organized as a single household" as Aelius Aristides describes. But whereas Aristides views that Roman household positively, most New Testament authors are critical of the Roman imperial *oikoumenē*. The New Testament refrains from any reclaiming of the *oikoumenē* for God.

Oikoumenē at Nicea and Today: Imperial Ecclesiology?

What are the implications of such a reading of *oikoumenē* for ecumenism and ecclesial life today? Does it matter that *oikoumenē* came to mean the Roman Empire or that the New Testament uses the term in this largely negative sense? Emperor Constantine convened the first ecumenical council of Christians in 325 C.E., summoning bishops from the whole *oikoumenē*. The church was now legitimized by the Roman Empire, creating an undeniable link between the church's use of the word *ecumenical* and Rome's claims over the *oikoumenē*. Jaroslav Pelikan observes the imperial context of Nicea and the double meaning of the term *ecumenical*: "That extension

---

22. An exception is Hebrews, which uses *oikoumenē* in reference to God's future world to come (Heb 2:5). First Clement 60.1 refers to the *oikoumenē* as God's creation.

of the 'apostolic council' to a position of universal authority created the concept of the 'ecumenical council,' with 'ecumenical' here taking the double meaning of 'for the general church as a whole' and 'imperial in scope and in authority' (*oikoumenē* meaning also, as noted earlier, at least 'the Roman Empire')."[23] The first ecumenical council at Nicea was itself a product of empire. Thus, when the modern ecumenical movement locates its work within this tradition, we need to ask whether and how it can appeal to *oikoumenē* without perpetuating an imperial view. As Pelikan notes, from its earliest ecclesial usage the term *ecumenical* had a dual meaning. The question is whether the two meanings can be sufficiently separated so that the church can avoid being "imperial in scope and in authority" while still working "for the general church as a whole." Or is an ecumenical understanding of the church and *oikoumenē* inevitably imperial, because it pursues globalized unity at the expense of local community?

Interestingly, some of the most vocal critiques of the use of the term *oikoumenē* within the ecumenical movement today are being raised by critics of economic globalization. The World Council of Churches' Harare assembly message includes an appendix on globalization contrasting the global market's "*oikoumenē* of domination" with "the *oikoumenē* of faith and solidarity that motivates and energizes the ecumenical movement."[24] Similarly, a recent Lutheran World Federation document on the global economy condemns globalization's hegemonic view of *oikoumenē* and proposes instead an alternative vision of *oikoumenē* that values plurality and cultural diversity:

> Globalization brings a competing vision of the *Oikoumenē,* the unity of humankind. But the unity of humankind being promoted by globalization is one of exploitation and domination, while the unity envisaged by the *Oikoumenē* is one characterized by solidarity and justice. Our vision of the *Oikoumenē* puts great value in plurality and cultural diversity for mutual enrichment and for affirmation of life experiences as expressed in different traditions.[25]

This is an attractive vision, but one must ask: Where, in the biblical or historical tradition, do we find the roots for such a vision of *oikoumenē* that "puts great value in plurality and cultural diversity"? Unlike the term

23. Jaroslav Pelikan, *The Excellent Empire: The Fall of Rome and the Triumph of the Church* (San Francisco: Harper & Row, 1987), 26.

24. "Policy Reference Committee II, Report 8.4, Appendix II: Globalization," in *Together on the Way: The Harare Report* (ed. D. Kessler; Geneva: World Council of Churches, 1998), 16.

25. "Engaging Economic Globalization as a Communion" (Geneva: Lutheran World Federation, 2001), 11. For a critique of economic and structural imbalance in the *oikoumenē* written already in 1984, see Jose Míguez Bonino, "Oikumene and Anti-Oikumene," repr. in *The Ecumenical Movement: An Anthology of Key Texts and Voices* (ed. Michael Kinnamon and Brian E. Cope; Geneva: World Council of Churches/Grand Rapids: Eerdmans, 1997), 227–30.

basileia, for which the New Testament provides a positive model in Jesus' proclamation of the *basileia* of God, there is no such positive precedent for *oikoumenē* in the New Testament. Not even the Septuagint uses the term *oikoumenē* in the sense of valuing diversity. Moreover, if one goes back to the Septuagint to reclaim a positive strand of the term *oikoumenē,* there is still the problem of the Christian kyriarchal use of the term through history. Christian ecumenical councils historically have embraced hierarchical and centralized models of unity in the *oikoumenē* more along the lines of Aelius Aristides' description of Roman rule — "organizing the whole *oikoumenē* like a single household" — rather than models of unity that respect plurality and cultural diversity.

Any attempt to reclaim or redefine the word *oikoumenē* for the agenda of ecumenism must begin by repudiating the imperial trajectory of the word, including the church's own imperial legacy. The emperor Constantine convened the first ecumenical council because he did not want to allow difference or dissent in the *oikoumenē.* Imperial Rome imposed its vision of a united *oikoumenē* by means of military conquest. Those who want to reclaim *oikoumenē* today must reject such kyriarchal models of unity and must also be attentive to critical issues that feminist and postcolonial liberation theologians are raising. The ecumenical history of the Roman Empire reminds us that those at the center will tend to construct a single unified household in which those at the margins are silenced for the sake of unity and universality. By contrast, we must seek decentralized models that stand with those at the "margins of the *oikoumenē*" (Rom 10:18), advocating what Brazilian theologian Vitor Westhelle calls a "strong case for a weak ecclesiology."[26]

When ecumenical documents cast the "problem" as disunity in order to urge more "visible unity," we need to approach such discourses with a hermeneutic of suspicion. Who decides which differences in the *oikoumenē* should be diagnosed as "sadly divided churches" rather than as legitimate and wonderful diversities of voices?[27] Are the criteria for disunity and unity to be defined by those at the center or by those at the margins? The first-century church at Corinth is often cited in ecumenical documents as a New Testament case study in disunity, for example — but this necessitates uncritically accepting the apostle Paul's diagnosis of the Corinthian *ekklēsia* as

---

26. Vitor Westhelle, unpublished manuscript (Carnahan Lectures, ISEDET, Buenos Aires, Argentina; October 2001). Translating *ta perata tēs oikoumenēs* in Rom 10:18 as the "margins of the *oikoumenē*" is Westhelle's suggestion.

27. "Sadly divided churches" is the description of William Lazareth and Nikos Nissiotis in their 1982 introduction to the World Council of Churches' Faith and Order Commission's statement on "Baptism, Eucharist, Ministry," repr. in *The Ecumenical Movement: An Anthology of Key Texts and Voices* (ed. Michael Kinnamon and Brian E. Cope; Geneva: World Council of Churches/Grand Rapids: Eerdmans, 1997), 177.

factionalized and divided.[28] Elisabeth Schüssler Fiorenza suggests another historical model for the situation in Corinth, arguing rather that "it is Paul, and not the Corinthians, who understand their debates as party or school divisions."[29] Instead of adopting Paul's rhetoric of unity/disunity that vilifies women and others in the Corinthian community, we might hypothesize that there was in Corinth a "broad theological movement of which Paul is a part." Then we can describe disputes in the *ekklēsia* in Corinth not as division or disunity but rather "in terms of *parrēsia* — the free speech of citizens."[30]

Schüssler Fiorenza proposes the model of the "discipleship of equals," a radically democratic vision of *ekklēsia* that has been foundational to her work for the past thirty years. Within this model she underscores that the word *equals* is intended to embrace diversity: "The modification of the word 'discipleship' with that of 'equals' must not be understood as advocating sameness under the guise of universality. Rather it seeks to underscore *equality in diversity* as the central ethos of discipleship."[31]

Applauding feminist critiques of discourses of unity and universality, ecumenist Konrad Raiser questions whether unity in the *oikoumenē* today can even be considered a desirable goal:

> "Unity"...still seems to have an unquestioned positive ring in the ecumenical movement....The notion of unity is part of a pattern of mind which has entered Christian thinking and practice through its inculturation in the classical Greco-Roman world....The orientation of thinking and practice towards achieving and maintaining unity almost inevitably leads to hierarchical systems of order which feminist analysis has described as one of the crucial features of "patriarchy...." In view of this questionable ancestry of the key notion of "unity," it is surprising that the question has been so seldom asked as to whether it is a suitable concept to express the ecumenical vision.[32]

Raiser recommends rather the goal of *koinōnia* (communion) that recognizes and values sharing and partnership in the *ekklēsia*.

If the image of the *oikoumenē* organized as a single household from the center is inevitably imperial, then from what other images can we draw to shape our ecclesial life? As Raiser notes, the image of *koinōnia* is widely

---

28. My own church's ecumenical statement, for example, cites 1 Cor 1:10–17 as an example of "disputes and divisions...in the earliest period of the church's existence." See *Ecumenism: The Vision of the Evangelical Lutheran Church in America* (1991): 2.

29. Elisabeth Schüssler Fiorenza, "Rhetorical Situation and Historical Reconstruction in 1 Corinthians," *New Testament Studies* 33 (1987): 395.

30. Elisabeth Schüssler Fiorenza, "Paul and the Politics of Interpretation," in *Paul and Politics: Ekklesia, Israel, Imperium, Interpretation* (ed. Richard A. Horsley; Harrisburg, Pa.: Trinity, 2000), 51, 54.

31. Schüssler Fiorenza, *Sharing Her Word*, 113.

32. Raiser, "Ecumenism in Search of a New Vision," 73.

embraced within the ecumenical movement today as a New Testament image that can address economic disparities in the *oikoumenē* as well as deepen communion across theological and ethnic diversities.[33] Marlene Perera, a Roman Catholic theologian from Sri Lanka, describes the *ekklēsia* in the Asian setting as multiplicity — women, men, children interacting together — rooted in local community:

> I see not one church but a multiplicity of churches that have been baptized by and taken root in the different faces of numerous human communities, manifesting the richness of the face of the immanent God walking with us on this pilgrimage. In this perspective it is the local church in all its richness and weakness which enters into deep communion with other churches, thus manifesting another profound visage of God. Communion is their unity in diversity.[34]

Drawing on the ecological paradigm of the diversity of life, Brazilian ecofeminist theologian Ivone Gebara proposes the ecclesial image of biodiversity.[35] In her view, the wonderful multiplicity of God's created world provides a model for embracing local diversity and pluralism in Christian community and ecclesial life as well. In our world, where rampant destruction of both the natural world and human community is accelerating, Gebara calls for renewed religious biodiversity as a way of "weaving qualitative ties among people through small communities":

> To speak of religious and cultural biodiversity is to attempt to give the human community a structure that will once again allow it to live out relationships that are more personal, closer to nature, and in deeper contact with the dreams and hopes of the great variety of human groups.... To bring biodiversity into theological reflection is to open ourselves up to pluralism in the expressions of Christian experience, and therefore to change our understanding of what "unity" is.... Biodiversity requires a new effort to form small faith communities.[36]

Like Gebara's image of biodiversity, I want to suggest an image for ecclesial diversity and community that is drawn from the realm of nature: the

---

33. But the discourse of *koinōnia* can at times be used to stifle debate in the name of unity, as in 1 Cor 1:9–10. For this critique see Barbara R. Rossing, "Models of Koinonia in the New Testament and Early Church," in *The Church as Communion* (ed. Heinrich Holze; Lutheran World Federation Documentation 41; Geneva: Lutheran World Federation, 1997), 65–80.

34. Marlene Perera, "New Models and New Praxis," in *Women's Visions* (ed. Ofelia Ortega; Geneva: World Council of Churches, 1995), 50–51; repr. in *The Ecumenical Movement: An Anthology of Key Texts and Voices* (ed. Michael Kinnamon and Brian E. Cope; Geneva: World Council of Churches/Grand Rapids: Eerdmans, 1997), 248–49.

35. Ivone Gebara, *Longing for Running Water: Ecofeminism and Liberation* (Minneapolis: Fortress, 1999).

36. Ibid., 207–8. See also David Rhoads, *The Challenge of Diversity* (Minneapolis: Fortress, 1996), on the analogy of biodiversity to ecclesial and theological diversity.

image of a braided stream. A braided stream is a river of many branches, crisscrossing, weaving together, and then dividing again — often found in glacial or mountain settings — making a pattern of ever-shifting water channels. From a distance a braided stream can look like beautiful strands of French-braided hair, with the sun sparkling off each strand. Unlike a tributary-stream model, where multiple branches feed into a single main channel, a braided stream divides as often as it joins together, flowing in a very wide channel.

If we apply the braided-stream image to ecclesial life, we can envision a model of unity that does not seek to funnel everyone into one monolithic channel, but instead cherishes the diverse ecclesial strands that crisscross and divide, braiding together across a wide spectrum. In a braided-stream model of *ekklēsia,* many diverse theological strands and perspectives will sparkle together as part of God's wide, pluriform, multivocal, flowing stream. Whatever our ecclesial images, whether *koinōnia* or biodiversity or the braided stream, it is models of diversity — rather than imperial models of *oikoumenē* — that must shape our ecumenical vision.

5

Faith and the
Public Intellectual

Ronald F. Thiemann

On Wednesday, 12 September 2001, Elisabeth Schüssler Fiorenza, Cornel West, and I entered a packed lecture hall at Harvard University to conduct the first class of our new course Christianity and Democracy. We had been anticipating this moment for more than a year, and the accomplishment of getting the three of us in the same room at the same time seemed remarkable. But none of us could have anticipated the impact that the events of the previous day would have upon this opening session. We took our seats on the raised platform at the front of the room and asked the hundred-plus students assembled there to engage in a moment of silence for the victims of the World Trade Center tragedy. Then each of us in turn offered reflections upon the meaning of that attack for the topic of our course. The coming months, we suggested, would be a time of testing for the basic principles of both Christianity and democracy. For the next hour we engaged in conversation with students who openly shared their fears and concerns about this new moment in American history. We did our best to respond to their questions and to offer some preliminary analyses of the situation. Our classroom had become a forum for the discussion of new and troubling issues, and we were inevitably cast into the role of public intellectuals seeking to apply the insights of our theological and philosophical scholarship to the events of the day.

That solemn beginning presaged one of the most remarkable intellectual experiences of my academic life — one that sadly will not be repeated due to Cornel West's untimely departure from Harvard University. Each Tuesday of the semester one of us would open the course with a lecture on the topic for the day, and then the other two would offer extemporaneous responses to the lecture. Our exchanges were candid, pointed, and spirited, as we explored the ramifications of our three quite different understandings of the relationship between Christianity and democracy. In a spirit of respectful collegiality and friendship, we engaged in rigorous dialogical conversation about the historical, normative, and contemporary dimensions of our topics.

It was without question the most stimulating set of exchanges I have ever had in a classroom, and I believe we modeled a kind of critical collegiality that students rarely glimpse in the specialized contemporary multiversity.

At Elisabeth's suggestion (actually, insistence) the first lecture from each of us provided an outline of our "intellectual framework." Thus from the beginning of the course we demonstrated the historical, social, cultural, and intellectual setting for our academic reflections. When my turn came to present this initial lecture I began with the juxtaposition of poems about America from Walt Whitman and Langston Hughes, two of America's greatest poets of the everyday. Despite their similar interests and political orientations, these two literary geniuses provide stark contrasts of the experience of being an American — a difference defined by America's "color line." When Elisabeth rose to make her critical comments she first thanked me for using poetry as one vehicle for the expression of my intellectual framework. "When I first prepared the manuscript of *In Memory of Her,*" she said, "I began each chapter with a poem from various feminist writers, but the publishers insisted that I delete that material for fear that scholars would not consider the book sufficiently serious if I employed poetry in this fashion."

Thus I am particularly happy that I can offer in this essay an analysis of the role of the public intellectual primarily through the discussion of the work of a woman poet, Anna Akhmatova. Elisabeth Schüssler Fiorenza is a pioneer in so many ways, not least in providing a model for what serious, theologically engaged, biblically informed, public intellectual work looks like. I am grateful for her intellectual leadership, her collegiality, and, most of all, her friendship.

In May 1944, Dietrich Bonhoeffer, writing from Tegel Prison in Berlin, wrote the following words in a letter commemorating the baptism of his namesake and godson, Dietrich Bethge:

> Today you will be baptized a Christian. All those great and ancient words of the Christian proclamation will be spoken over you, and the command of Jesus Christ to baptize will be carried out on you, without your knowing anything about it.... In [these] traditional words and acts we suspect that there may be something quite new and revolutionary, though we cannot as yet grasp or express it. That is our own fault. Our church, which has been fighting in these years only for its self-preservation, as though that were an end in itself, is incapable of taking the word of reconciliation and redemption to [hu]mankind and the world. Our earlier words are therefore bound to lose their force and cease, and our being Christian today will be limited to two things: prayer and righteous action.... All Christian thinking, speaking, and organizing must be born anew out of this prayer and action.... It is not for us to prophesy the day (though the day will come) when [we]

will once more be called so to utter the word of God that the world will be changed and renewed by it.... Till then the Christian cause will be a silent and hidden affair, but there will be those who pray and do right and wait for God's own time.[1]

Bonhoeffer was not able to witness that day for which he longed and to which he had dedicated his life because he was executed by the Nazis on 9 April 1945 at Flossenburg concentration camp for his role in the plot against Hitler's life. He joined the conspiratorial group that plotted Hitler's death out of his frustration with the Confessing Church, the small group of Protestant churches that resisted Hitler's attempt to Nazify German Christianity. Though the Confessing Church was notable for its courageous defense of the gospel against the heresy of the German Christian Movement, its members limited its struggle to a battle for control of the German Protestant church. Despite Bonhoeffer's strong urging, the Confessing Church never spoke out against the Nazi ideology itself or against the cruel anti-Semitism of Hitler's regime. So Bonhoeffer, a committed Christian pacifist, took the extraordinary step of joining a group buried deep within the German *Abwehr,* or military intelligence, that three times tried to assassinate Adolf Hitler. After two failed attempts early in 1944, the conspirators finally successfully detonated a bomb at Hitler's staff meeting on July 20 of that year. Unfortunately a partition on the large oak table at which the meeting was held partially shielded Hitler from the bomb's force. Although the room was badly damaged and Hitler's left arm seriously injured, he escaped with his life. Shortly after this failed attempt the members of the conspiracy were arrested, and all were executed before the end of the war.

Bonhoeffer's story became well known only in the decades following his death, primarily through the dedication of his biographer, Eberhard Bethge.[2] He has now become a model of courageous faith engaged in righteous action at a moment of grave international crisis. What makes Bonhoeffer's story so gripping is that he acted out of Christian convictions not just to save other Christians, but to bring to an end both the horrendous murder of European Jewry and the devastating world war that Hitler's hatred had spawned. Because Bonhoeffer was a true public intellectual motivated by spiritual and moral convictions, I have chosen him as one of four figures I will be treating in a book-length manuscript I am writing entitled "Prisoners of Conscience: Public Intellectuals at Time of Crisis." In addition to Bonhoeffer I am studying African American poet and playwright Langston Hughes, British novelist and essayist George Orwell, and Anna Akhmatova, one of the most important twentieth-century Russian poets. Each of these

---

1. Dietrich Bonhoeffer, *Letters and Papers from Prison* (New York: Macmillan, 1975), 300.
2. Eberhard Bethge, *Dietrich Bonhoeffer: A Biography* (Philadelphia: Fortress, 2000).

persons acted out of deep spiritual and moral belief, engaged in courageous and controversial acts of public protest, and addressed situations of profound human suffering. They did so because in some sense they "could do no other"; they were, as the title of my forthcoming book suggests, "prisoners of conscience," people so committed to doing justice in the world that when a situation of crisis emerged they were ready to act courageously and with a singularity of purpose we can only admire.

The four authors I am studying lived during the decades of international crisis, 1914–45, a period that saw the two world wars, the Communist triumph in Russia, the terror of the Hitler and Stalin regimes, and the Holocaust. When I first conceived of this project Americans were living in relative peace and prosperity and no single crisis of international proportion seemed to threaten us. After September 11, however, all that changed. As we now struggle to understand the threat posed by this faceless foe and we engage our own government's actions in fighting this elusive enemy, we look to find resources that can inspire us to a high moral and political vision for the nation. We are acutely aware that many of the spiritual and intellectual traditions that spawned the public intellectual witness of Akhmatova, Bonhoeffer, Hughes, and Orwell now lie in fragments. No single intellectual, moral, or political tradition seems capable of providing the resources needed for this difficult time. Many bemoan the disappearance of public intellectuals inspired by faith. Where, they ask, are the Sojourner Truths, Karl Barths, Dietrich Bonhoeffers, Reinhold Niebuhrs, Dorothy Days, and Martin Luther Kings of our own time? Is the great public intellectual an artifact of the bygone modern era, and must we, living in these postmodern days, carry on without the great spiritual, moral, and religious voices of earlier times? Will the religious public cause be today as in Bonhoeffer's time "a hidden and silent affair," or can genuine religious speech and activity emerge again from the crucible of "prayer and righteous action"? These are the questions I hope to address briefly in this essay.

The Public Intellectual
as Connected Critic

I want to set before you an understanding of the public intellectual as "connected critic." I used this notion, which I gratefully borrow from Michael Walzer,[3] in my book *Religion in Public Life: A Dilemma for Democracy* to capture the stance of critique I believe most appropriate for people of faith, disciples who are also citizens, within democratic societies.[4] I now want

---

3. Michael Walzer, *The Company of Critics: Social Criticism and Political Commitment in the Twentieth Century* (New York: Basic Books, 1988).
4. Ronald F. Thiemann, *Religion in Public Life: A Dilemma for Democracy* (Georgetown: Georgetown University Press/Century Foundation, 1996).

to expand upon this idea and propose it as a proper understanding of the person of faith as public intellectual.

Hear this word that the Lord has spoken against you, O people of Israel, against the whole family that I brought up out of the land of Egypt:

> You only have I known
>   of all the families of the earth;
> therefore I will punish you
>   for all your iniquities.
>   — Amos 3:1–2 (NRSV)

The judgment of God is upon the church as never before. If the church of today does not recapture the sacrificial spirit of the early church, it will lose its authentic ring, forfeit the loyalty of millions, and be dismissed as an irrelevant social club with no meaning. . . . I hope the church as a whole will meet the challenge of this decisive hour. But even if the church does not come to the aid of justice, I have no despair about the future. . . . We will reach the goal of freedom in Birmingham and all over the nation, because the goal of America is freedom. Abused and scorned as we may be, our destiny is tied up with the destiny of America. . . . We will win our freedom because the sacred heritage of our nation and the eternal will of God are embodied in our echoing demands.[5]

The prophet Amos and the prophet Martin capture the essential elements of connected criticism. Amos speaks to the people of Israel as a member of that "whole family . . . brought up out of the land of Egypt." He claims the authority of the God whose very "outstretched arm" had rescued the people from slavery and brought them into the land of promise. It is precisely as a member of the family of Israel, of the common religious and political community, that he speaks the judgment of God to his own people. So, too, Martin Luther King Jr. addresses the white clergy of Birmingham and through them the whole of the church and the whole of the nation as well. He speaks as a fellow Christian and citizen and announces the "judgment of God . . . upon the church." The authority for this word of judgment is the shared — though broken — covenant expressed in the prophets of Israel, the ministry of Jesus, and the founding documents of the nation. Though King condemns the pernicious segregation of racist America, he finds (or is it creates?) in the biblical and American traditions the sources of both

---

5. Martin Luther King Jr., "Letter from Birmingham City Jail," in *A Testament of Hope: Essential Writings of Martin Luther King Jr.* (ed. James Melvin Washington; San Francisco: Harper & Row, 1986), 300–301.

judgment and hope: "We will reach the goal of freedom in Birmingham and all over the nation, because the goal of America is freedom. . . . We will win our freedom because the sacred heritage of our nation and the eternal will of God are embodied in our echoing demands."[6]

Connected criticism of the public intellectual oscillates between the poles of critique and connection, solitude and solidarity, alienation and authority. Connected critics are those who are fully engaged in the very enterprise they criticize, yet alienated by the deceits and shortcomings of their own community. Because they care so deeply about the values inherent in their common enterprise, they vividly experience the evils of their society even as they call their community back to its better nature. Connected critics recognize that fallibility clings to the life of every political or social organization, and they seek to identify both the virtuous and the vicious dimensions of the common life in which they participate. Connected critics exemplify both the commitment characteristic of the loyal participant and the critique characteristic of the disillusioned dissenter. This dialectic between commitment and critique is the identifying feature that distinguishes acts of dissent that display genuine moral integrity from those that represent mere expediency or self-interest.

The connected critic is socially situated within the community to which her criticism is directed, yet still finds within the common life of the society principles of justice that serve as the basis for hope. Living in a state of "antagonistic connection," the public intellectual through an act of imaginative construction discerns the principles of justice that provide the basis for both critique and hope. Such an imaginative act is simultaneously a matter of discovery and creation. So Abraham Lincoln could *discern* within the founding documents of a nation "half slave and half free" the ideas of freedom and equality penned by the slaveholder Thomas Jefferson and so *create* a new understanding of citizenship within the republic. Likewise Martin Luther King Jr., sitting in his jail cell in Birmingham, Alabama, could *discern*, despite the segregated polity of the South, the freedom which is "the sacred heritage of our nation and the eternal will of God" and so *create* a new "birth of freedom" for African American citizens.

In the remainder of this essay I want to develop further this notion of the public intellectual as connected critic and apply it to those of us who live at a time when the voice of the genuine religious intellectual seems to have fallen silent. I am going to focus my analysis upon one of the figures I will be treating in my book-length manuscript, Anna Akhmatova. By looking in detail at this singular figure of the modern era, I hope that we might learn some lessons for our own time.

---

6. Ibid., 301.

Anna Akhmatova:
The Poet as Connected Critic

Anna Akhmatova, one of the greatest poets of twentieth-century Russia, was born in 1889 in a small town on the Black Sea near Odessa and died on 5 March 1966 in a nursing home near Moscow.[7] The date of her death was, ironically, the anniversary of the death of Stalin, a day she customarily celebrated as a personal holiday. Her life spanned the years of tumult in Russia, as she witnessed the demise of the tsarist regimes, the rise of Communist Party rule, the terror of the Stalinist purges, the two world wars, and the onset of the cold war between the nuclear superpowers. Recognized through her early poetry as a premier young literary artist, she, nonetheless, endured cycles of vilification and banishment as Communist Party leaders first condemned her poetry and then forbade her to publish for many years. Despite these harsh measures, she managed to write and share her poetry throughout her life and served as the voice and conscience of the nation during the horrors of the purges and the wars.

In her early years Akhmatova was a founding member of the Acmeists, a group of poets who opposed the mystical other-worldliness of the Symbolists, the dominant poetic force in early-twentieth-century Russia. Along with fellow Acmeists, Nikolay Gumilyov (her husband) and their friend Osip Mandelstam, Akhmatova focused her poetry on matters of the everyday, finding truth, beauty, and even the divine presence in aspects of the mundane and ordinary. In her memoir of her husband, Nadezhda Mandelstam described the basic orientation of the Acmeist movement:

> The poets and artists who rejected Symbolism d[id] not look down on ordinary, everyday life — on the contrary, it [wa]s a source of beauty for them.... By returning to earth ... [the Acmeists] considerably enlarged its horizon, and for [them] the world was no longer divided into ugly prose and sublime poetry. [They] did not seek to escape into some realm of pure spirit from the earthly confines of our here-and-

---

7. The English language literature on Akhmatova is extremely sparse. Among the best biographical treatments of her life written in English are Roberta Reeder, *Anna Akhmatova: Poet and Prophet* (New York: Picador, 1994); Amanda Haight, *Anna Akhmatova: A Poetic Pilgrimage* (New York: Oxford University Press, 1990); and Sam Driver, *Anna Akhmatova* (New York: Twayne, 1972). *The Akhmatova Journals,* written by her close friend Lydia Chukovskaya, have been translated into English (2 vols.; New York: Farrar, Straus & Giroux, 1994). The definitive edition of Akhmatova's poetry is Roberta Reeder, ed., *The Complete Poems of Anna Akhmatova* (trans. Judith Hemschemeyer; Boston: Zephyr, 1997). The task of translating Akhmatova, who employed a classic rhyming pattern in her poetry, is extremely difficult. While Hemschemeyer's translations are accurate and competent, I prefer the lyrical beauty of the translations of Haight and Stanley Kunitz. Special thanks to Inna Zolotarevskaya who advised me regarding translations and also provided one of her own original translations, which I employ in this essay.

now.... "The earth is not an encumbrance or an unfortunate accident but a God-given palace."[8]

Akhmatova's early work dealt primarily with the theme of love, as she poured her own experience into her poetry. Many of the poems collected in the volume entitled *Evening*, written during her husband's two-year-long absence in Africa, reflect her own sorrow and loneliness brought on by their separation and anticipate their final breakup and ultimate divorce:

> I wrung my hands under my dark veil
> "Why are you pale today, what makes you reckless?"
> — Because I have made my loved one drunk
> with an astringent sadness.
> I'll never forget. He went out, reeling,
> his mouth twisted, desolate.
> I ran downstairs, not touching the banisters,
> and followed him as far as the gate.
> Panting I cried: "I meant it all
> in jest. Don't leave me or I'll die."
> He smiled at me — oh, so calmly, terribly —
> and said, "Why don't you get out of the rain?"[9]

Or another brief poem that begins,

> How helplessly my breast grew cold
> yet my steps were light
> I put on to my left hand
> the glove from my right.[10]

The women in her poems are ordinary people steeped in the culture of Orthodox belief and practice, real persons through whom Akhmatova's own inner life, as well as the struggles of her countrywomen, are depicted. As her poetry matured, the themes of love, while still grounded in the personal and everyday, began to reflect larger aspects of Russian life and culture during the shattering and revolutionary years of the early twentieth century. Her second collection of poems, *Rosary*, published in 1913, continues the themes of the earlier collection, but the women depicted here, while still abandoned, now find new sources of strength and hope — in memory and in faith:

> To become a girl of the sea shore again,
> put shoes on my bare feet,
> wind my braid in a crown round my head
> sing with emotion in my voice.[11]

---

8. Nadezhda Mandelstam, *Hope against Hope* (New York: Random, 1999), 40.
9. Original translation by Inna Zolotarevskaya Hardison.
10. Haight, *Anna Akhmatova*, 21.
11. Ibid., 33.

Or again,

> There are many of us homeless
> Our strength lies in that
> for us the ignorant and blind
> God's house is bright.
>
> And for those who are bent down,
> altars burn,
> And up unto God's throne
> our voices rise.[12]

It would be a mistake to characterize even these early efforts as the depiction of helpless women who turn to religion as a mere palliative. Rather, the women depicted in *Rosary* are not unlike the African American women of the same era so powerfully portrayed in Evelyn Brooks Higginbotham's *Righteous Discontent,* who engaged in "everyday forms of resistance to oppression and demoralization,"[13] which draw upon and yet transform biblical and liturgical resources.

With outbreak of the war in 1914 Akhmatova's poetry captured the grief of a nation whose young were being slaughtered in increasing numbers on the battlefields of Europe. Drawing again upon her own emotional response, she provided the words for a nation in mourning as she employs the metaphor of a late spring frost to depict the tragedy of youth cut down in its prime:

> On the fresh turf the transparent shroud
> lies and thaws unnoticed.
> The cruel, cold spring is murdering
> the swollen buds.
> The face of this untimely death is so terrible
> I cannot look at God's world.
> I feel King David's grief, his regal bequest,
> passed down for a thousand years.[14]

As the Bolshevik revolution breaks into the already war-torn nation, uncertainty clings to both personal and public life. In the midst of the revolutionary and counterrevolutionary battles of the early years of Communist rule, Akhmatova's former husband and poetic colleague Nikolay Gumilyov is arrested and executed for alleged complicity in an anti-Bolshevik con-

---

12. Ibid., 34.
13. Evelyn Brooks Higginbotham, *Righteous Discontent: The Women's Movement in the Black Baptist Church, 1880–1920* (Cambridge: Harvard University Press, 1994), 2.
14. Haight, *Anna Akhmatova,* 48.

spiracy. A new sense of foreboding now characterizes her poetry, one that presages the more terrible events on the near horizon:

> Fear picks out objects in the dark
> and guides the moonbeam to an axe,
> Behind the wall is an ominous noise —
> What is it: rats, a ghost, a thief?
>
> Better to lie against the bare boards
> of a scaffold raised out on the green square
> and to the cries of joy and the groans
> pour out red blood to the end.
>
> I press the smooth cross to my heart:
> O God bring back peace to my soul.
> The sickly sweet smell of decay
> is given off by the cold sheet.[15]

The two volumes from which these poems are taken were published in 1921 and 1922 and were the final books of poetry that Akhmatova would be allowed to publish until the 1940s. As the Bolsheviks gained full political control of Russia they began systematic attacks on artists whose works did not support the new Communist ideology. Akhmatova and the Acmeists were accused of representing the reactionary values of tsarist and Orthodox Russia. G. Lelevich, a prominent Marxist critic, provided the political critique that would ultimately lead to the banning of her work for nearly twenty years. Relying on a classical gender stereotype he characterizes Akhmatova as

> not quite a harlot burning with passion, not quite a mendicant nun able to pray to God for forgiveness. . . . Akhmatova's poetry is a small and beautiful fragment of aristocratic culture. . . . The circle of emotions open to the poetess is exceptionally limited. She has responded to the social upheavals, basically the most important phenomenon of our time, in a feeble, and, at that, hostile manner. There is no broad sweep of vision or depth of understanding in Akhmatova's world.[16]

With that judgment Lelevich made clear that there was no place for Akhmatova in revolutionary Communist society. Despite her rejection by the Communist leadership, Akhmatova refused to join the many Russian artists who emigrated from the Soviet Union in the early 1920s. Her fate, she be-

---

15. Ibid., 58–59.
16. Ibid., 74.

lieved, belonged to that of her countrymen and countrywomen, and so she remained to face with them a most terrible time of suffering:

> I am not one of those who left the land
> to the mercy of its enemies.
> Their flattery leaves me cold,
> My songs are not for them to praise.
>
> But I pity the exile's lot.
> Like a felon, like a man half-dead,
> Dark is your path, wanderer;
> Wormwood infects your foreign bread.
>
> But, here, in the murk of conflagration
> where scarcely a friend is left to know,
> we, the survivors, do not flinch
> from anything, not from a single blow.
>
> Surely the reckoning will be made
> after the passing of this cloud.
> We are the people without tears,
> straighter than you ... more proud. ... [17]

Akhmatova continued to write poetry even though she had no chance of seeing her poems published. When asked later in life how she survived those years of official silencing, she responded: "I am poet, so I wrote poetry. What else could I do?" Still the pain of her silencing is obvious in a poem written in 1924:

> Oh had I known when, clothed in white,
> the Muse would visit my cramped abode,
> that my living hands would one day fall
> on to a lyre turned forever to stone.[18]

Despite the despair of those lines, Akhmatova continued to write; indeed, some of her most dramatic works were produced during the years of silence. She developed an affinity for biblical materials and turned her attention particularly to three biblical figures: Rachel, Lot's wife, and Michal, the daughter of Saul. In "Lot's Wife" she grants a powerful human presence to an otherwise obscure biblical figure. In Akhmatova's hands Lot's wife be-

---

17. Stanley Kunitz and Max Hayward, trans., *Poems of Akhmatova* (Boston: Little, Brown, 1967), 75.
18. Haight, *Anna Akhmatova*, 83.

comes not a symbol of disobedience or carelessness, but a poignant woman who gave up her life for a final glance toward home:

> And the righteous man followed God's messenger,
> huge and radiant, along the dark hill.
> while a restless voice of alarm spoke to his wife:
> "It's not yet too late, you still can look back.
>
> At the red towers of your native Sodom,
> at the square where you once sang, the spinning shed,
> at the empty windows of the tall house
> where your sons and daughters blessed your marriage bed."
>
> A single glance, a sudden dart of pain
> stitching her eyes before she made a sound. . . .
> Her body flaked into transparent salt,
> her swift legs rooted to the ground.
>
> Who will bewail this woman now?
> Does she not seem the least of the lost?
> Only my heart will never forget
> one who gave her life for a single glance.[19]

Like the unnamed woman at Bethany whose acts will be told "in memory of her," this woman known only by her husband's name is lifted up in Akhmatova's verse and becomes a symbol of all those who have mourned the loss of a home or homeland. Sentenced to exile within a land she no longer knows as home, Akhmatova finds in this biblical woman a figure for all those displaced by her country's increasingly tyrannical regime, and in so doing she transforms the biblical image itself, imbuing this woman with new meaning and significance.

For the next decade Akhmatova moved from place to place, accepting the kindness of friends who risked their own safety in offering her shelter. Plagued by recurring bouts of pneumonia and living in extreme poverty, she continued to keep in touch with others in her literary circle who lived under similar duress. In May 1934 her dear friend and colleague Osip Mandelstam was arrested for "crimes against the state" and sent to the work camps in Siberia, where he would soon die. In December of that same year, following the murder of a member of the Politburo, Stalin ordered the arrest of thousands of Russians who, because of their "terrorist acts," were denied any right of defense. Among those taken into custody was Akhmatova's son, Lev Gumilyov. Though he was released just a few days later, the terror con-

---

19. Ibid., 86.

tinued, and in early 1935 both her son and her husband, Aleksandr Punin, were arrested. Though terribly thin and weak, she would regularly go to the prison to join the long lines of people who hoped merely to catch a glimpse of the loved ones they were not allowed to visit. Later she would write about one particular encounter:

> In the terrible years of the Yezhov terror I spent seventeen months waiting in line outside the prison in Leningrad. One day someone in the crowd identified me. Standing behind me was a woman with lips blue from the cold, who had of course never heard me called by name before. Suddenly she awoke out of the benumbed condition in which we all found ourselves at that time and whispered in my ear (in those days we all spoke in whispers): "Can you put this into words?" And I said, "I can."[20]

Though the writing of the words was banned, the words themselves could not be silenced. She committed the words to memory and then taught them to her friends, who memorized them as well. Sometimes she would write the words on small scraps of paper and then burn them as soon as she knew they had been committed to memory. In this fashion one of the greatest poems she was ever to write, "Requiem," existed until finally in 1956 she was able to type it in full. Here the religious imagery of her imagination holds sway as she identifies herself and all of suffering Russia with the figure of Mary at the foot of the cross. But true to her instinct for the particular, she does not hide the concrete reality of her own Golgotha:

> Such grief might make the mountains stoop,
> reverse the waters where they flow.
> but cannot burst these ponderous bolts
> that block us from the prison cells
> crowded with mortal woe....
> For some the wind can freshly blow,
> for some the sunlight fades at ease,
> but we, made partners in our dread,
> hear but the grating of the keys,
> and heavy-booted soldiers' tread.
> As if for early mass, we rose
> and each day walked the wilderness,
> trudging through silent street and square,
> to congregate, less live than dead.
> The sun declined, the Neva blurred,
> and hope sang always from afar.
> Whose sentence is decreed?... That moan,

---

20. Kunitz and Hayward, *Poems of Akhmatova*, 99.

that sudden spurt of woman's tears,
shows one distinguished from the rest,
as if they'd knocked her to the ground
and wrenched the heart out of her breast,
then let her go, to reel, alone.
Where are they now, my nameless friends
from those two years I spent in hell?
What specters mock them now, amid
the fury of Siberian snows,
or in the blighted circle of the moon?
To them I cry, Hail and Farewell![21]

This extraordinary epic poem captures the unbearable pain of those women who waited, watched, and mourned for their loved ones during the eight long years of terror. By writing poetry in the midst of unspeakable horror Akhmatova gave words to the sighs and moans that would otherwise have gone unmarked. By keeping the memories alive through unwritten recitation of her powerful verse, the story was preserved in the hope that someday it might inspire her countrymen and countrywomen. In 1941, during the terrible siege of Leningrad, Akhmatova delivered a radio address to the women of Russia, urging them to resist the onslaught of the Fascist German troops. In response to this act Stalin lifted the publication ban in 1944. Akhmatova quickly set to work collecting and rewriting the poems she had composed during her twenty-year silencing. By 1946 a new collection of her poems was in production at a Moscow publisher when the dark clouds of censorship reappeared. Communist party boss Andrey Zhdanov, following the orders of Stalin, reinstated the ban and moreover expelled Akhmatova from the Soviet Writers Union, thus making it impossible for her to earn any money as a writer. Repeating the now classic slur, "Half nun, half harlot, or rather a harlot-nun whose sin is mixed with prayer," he condemned her work as incompatible with the postwar aims of the party and the state. The volumes in the Moscow publishing house were destroyed and Akhmatova entered one of the most difficult periods of her life. Most of her friends and colleagues were either exiled, imprisoned, or killed in the war. Her son, Lev, remained a prisoner in Siberia, and her own health continued to deteriorate:

This cruel age has deflected me,
like a river from its course.
Strayed from its familiar shores,
my changeling life has flowed
into a sister channel.
How many spectacles I've missed,
the curtain rising without me,

---

21. Ibid., 101.

and falling too. How many friends
I never had the chance to meet.
Here in the only city I can claim,
where I could sleepwalk and not lose my way,
how many foreign skylines I can dream,
not to be witnesses through my tears.
And how many verses have I failed to write![22]

It was not until 1956, when Nikita Khrushchev finally revealed the extent of the Stalin terror, that the ban on Akhmatova's poetry was finally lifted. For the final ten years of her life volume after volume of poetry flowed from the Russia presses, and the world could at last read two of the greatest poems of the twentieth century: "Requiem" and "Poem without a Hero." In 1964 she was allowed to travel to Italy to receive a literary prize from the Italian government, and in 1965 she received an honorary degree from Oxford University. With her words now available for publication and eagerly translated throughout the world, her unstinting commitment to the everyday cares and sorrows of the people of her country gave her worldwide notoriety. And so too the dark veil that had for so long been draped over her person and her poems began finally to lift as she gave expression to the hopes that were rekindled in the final years of her life in the poem "The Return":

The souls of all my dears have flown to the stars,
Thank God there's no one left for me to lose —
so I am free to cry. This air was made
for the echoing of songs.

A silver willow by the shore
trails to the bright September waters.
My shadow, risen from the past,
glides silently towards me.

Though the branches here are hung with many lyres,
a place has been reserved for mine, it seems,
And now this shower, struck by sunlight,
brings me good news, my cup of consolation.[23]

On Doing What We Do Best:
The Practice of Faith and Connected Critique

Anna Akhmatova, like Bonhoeffer, Hughes, and Orwell, exemplifies the essential qualities of the connected critic. Deeply grounded in the techniques

---

22. Ibid., 129.
23. Ibid., 127.

of her craft, in touch with her own emotional and intellectual life, and organically connected to the people, particularly the women, of her nation, she became the soul and conscience of Russia by simply doing what she did best, writing poetry. Her ability to see poetic drama in the ordinary everyday events of human life prepared her to chronicle the world-historical events of her time through the lives of women whose stories might otherwise never have been told. Her insight into the biblical narratives and her imaginative capacity to see herself and others as figures in a larger divine story enabled her to hold together the mundane and the cosmic without allowing one to overwhelm the other. Like many other great figures of faith, especially those in the Hebrew Bible, Akhmatova was a flawed and fallible person. She was by her own admission openly promiscuous in her sexual relationships. She seemed unable to find happiness in her relationships, going through three marriages and countless affairs without ever finding the love she so desperately sought. She was relentless in her sardonic criticism of those writers who failed to meet her high standards of literary excellence. She found motherhood extremely difficult. Having given up the care of her only son when he was eight months old, she had a distant and estranged relationship with him throughout her life, even after his return from the camps in the Gulag. To the ordinary eye she would not appear a candidate for spiritual heroism, but when the historic moment arose she became the chronicler of Russia's sorrow, because she shared the religious and cultural heritage of those for whom she spoke. Akhmatova's commitment to the Orthodox tradition and the legacy of Russian literary culture prepared her for the courageous acts of prayer and righteous action we glimpse in her poetry.

The connected critic needs to be deeply and self-critically grounded in the details, techniques, and substance of her craft. The connected critic must be organically connected to a living community of practice with whom and through whom the critic can speak publicly. The connected critic must have the intellectual capacity to interpret the events of the day through her craft and in relation to her community of practice, or she cannot have an authentic or authoritative voice. The connected critic must have sufficient lived experience with injustice, suffering, and alienation in order to express the pathos of those whose lives are threatened by such forces. And the connected critic must have the imaginative ability to discern and/or create principles of justice from the fragments of stories, traditions, and communities within which we all live.

And so we come to the questions posed at the outset of this essay. Is it possible for genuine public intellectuals motivated by spiritual concern to emerge in our fragmented, shallow, media-saturated culture? And if a new Akhmatova or Bonhoeffer were to emerge, would we even notice them in a world in which everything is played for the cameras and where "fifteen minutes of fame" is the most to which one can aspire? Will religious faith remain, as Bonhoeffer feared, a hidden and silent affair? As I continue my study of these four remarkable persons, I am struck by their uncanny ability to find elements of hope in situations desperate with suffering. A prison doctor who observed Bonhoeffer in prayer immediately prior to his execution wrote: "In the fifty years I have worked as a doctor, I have hardly ever seen a man die so entirely submissive to the will of God." And Akhmatova, who in her own life and in that of her nation experienced the most unspeakable horrors, still continued to write poetry as a life-affirming act in the midst of death. A condemned man calmly engaged in an act of prayer. A homeless and exiled woman engaged in the simple but courageous act of writing a poem. These are the signs of genuine faith and hope as manifested in the lives of true public intellectuals. These are persons who gazed deeply into the abyss of sorrow and death and emerged, nonetheless, as hopeful chroniclers of the human story.

I genuinely wonder whether those of us who practice our vocations in the university dare aspire to the role of public intellectual and connected critic. Michael Walzer suggests that university intellectuals are often forced to become "critics-in-the-small," because they have "given up any hope for social cooperation or political alliance." Cut off from any genuine communities of practice the aspiring intellectual becomes "not so much a professional critic as a critic in the little world of his profession, and the likely profession these days is academic; hence the critical wars [within the university] which have no echo outside the academy since the critics have no material ties to people or parties or movements outside. Academic criticism under these circumstances tends steadily toward hermeticism and gnostic obscurity; even the critic's students barely understand him."[24] If Walzer is correct, and I believe in large part that he is, then we may have to look to other institutions, particularly to local communities of faith, to find places where genuine public intellectual work might be fostered.

If there is to be a rebirth of the spiritually motivated public intellectual, then, as Bonhoeffer foretold, that renascence must, I believe, originate in prayer and righteous action. Only those public intellectuals who are genuine connected critics, people connected to real flesh-and-blood communities of commitment and engagement, can provide guidance for those of us who struggle to be faithful to our own spiritual commitments in a complex and challenging world. None of us can know when that moment of crisis might occur that will call forth the voice and leadership of a public intellectual who is a true connected critic. The role of public intellectual, like that of prophet, is not a self-appointed position; it is a vocation to which one must be called. For now we live "between the times." Indeed, philosophers tell us we live in a postmodern era, but that is a designation that indicates only what we are not, not who we are or what we shall become. So we too must

---

24. Walzer, *Company of Critics*, 228.

await the day of which Bonhoeffer spoke, a day "when [we] will once more be called so to utter the word of God that the world will be changed and renewed by it." For now our task is to nurture our communities of faith so that we might witness to hope in a world that is burdened by cynicism and despair. By engaging in prayer and righteous action, our communities of faith can provide the indispensable context within which true public intellectuals might be nurtured. Through acts of worship, education, and service we witness to our hope that the whole of God's creation "will be set free from its bondage to decay and will obtain the glorious liberty of the children of God" (Rom 8:21). Until that day may we be counted among "those who pray and do right and wait for God's own time."

Part 2

In Memory of Wo/men

6

Women Priestesses in the Apocryphal *Acts of Philip*

François Bovon

In honor of Elisabeth Schüssler Fiorenza and her significant contribution to the study of women's participation in the life of early Christian churches, I would like to draw attention to a new witness from late antiquity that argues for the existence of women in priestly ministry. The witness is part of the *Acts of Philip* attested in a neglected manuscript from Mount Athos, *Xenophontos* 32.[1]

Mentioned among the rejected books by the so-called *Decretum Gelasianum,* the *Acts of Philip* does not seem to have been very popular in antiquity, although it was not ignored in the Byzantine world.[2] Until recently, this noncanonical work was known for the most part only through *Vaticanus graecus* 824, discovered by Maximilien Bonnet at the end of the nineteenth century.[3] There is evidence in this manuscript of a tendency to censure the heretical nature of the original and to eradicate most of the elements concerning women's ministry. The end of the *Acts of Philip,* a section known as the *Martyrdom,* is better preserved; it is known in three recensions through several Greek manuscripts because the text was used regularly in the Byzantine Church on the feast of Saint Philip, which was celebrated on 14 November.[4] Konstantin von Tischendorf was the first to

---

1. See François Bovon, Bertrand Bouvier, and Frédéric Amsler, *Acta Philippi: Textus* (Corpus christianorum series apocryphorum 11; Turnhout: Brepols, 1999); Frédéric Amsler, *Acta Philippi: Commentarius* (Corpus christianorum series apocryphorum 12; Turnhout: Brepols, 1999).

2. See Wilhelm Schneemelcher, "General Introduction," in *New Testament Apocrypha* (ed. Wilhelm Schneemelcher; trans. R. McL. Wilson; Cambridge: Clarke/Louisville: Westminster/John Knox, 1991), 1.38–40.

3. Maximilien Bonnet, "Acta Philippi," in *Acta apostolorum apocrypha* (ed. Richard Adelbert Lipsius and Maximilien Bonnet; 2 vols. in 3; Leipzig: Mendelssohn, 1891–1903; repr. Darmstadt: Wissenschaftliche Buchgesellschaft, 1959), 2.1.vii–xv, 1–90.

4. Ibid., 41–90; Bovon, Bouvier, and Amsler, *Acta Philippi: Textus,* 342–431; Joseph Flamion, "Les trois recensions grecques du Martyre de l'apôtre Philippe," in *Mélanges d'histoire offerts à Charles Moeller* (Université de Louvain: Recueil de travaux publiés par les membres des conférences d'histoire et de philologie 40; Louvain/Paris: Bureau du Recueil, 1914), 1.215–25.

publish two forms of the *Martyrdom* in the middle of the nineteenth century.[5] With different degrees of intensity, all three recensions show traces of orthodox rewriting. The discovery of *Xenophontos* 32 gives us access to several acts that were at one time completely lost: the end of act 11 and complete versions of acts 12–15.[6] A comparison with *Vaticanus* 824 reveals that *Xenophontos* 32 has a second merit: it preserves a version of acts 1–9 in its more original, less-revised form.[7]

This essay focuses primarily on *Acts of Philip* 1, which takes place in Galilee, the point of departure for Philip's missionary journey. In the acts that follow, the evangelist travels alone to and through several countries, including Greece, Parthia, and Palestine. *Acts of Philip* 8 and following take place in Asia Minor, particularly in Phrygia. This second part narrates the story of a single, linear missionary journey that ends in Ophiorumos, which is identified with Hierapolis of Phrygia. On this particular journey Philip is accompanied by two companions, his sister Mariamne and his fellow apostle Bartholomew. According to the last part of the work, the *Martyrdom*, it is in Ophiorumos that Philip dies.[8] It is also in Hierapolis of Phrygia that, according to witnesses dated as early as the second century C.E., Philip's tomb was located. Veneration of Philip seems to have been particularly intense in this part of the ancient world. As a location for the writing of the *Acts of Philip*, then, Asia Minor seems probable, even certain.

Although scholars suggest that the work was written in the fourth or fifth century C.E.,[9] it is extremely difficult to assign a date to this work. Parts of the *Acts of Philip* may be earlier than the fourth century. Some prayers and stories, for example, go back to the third if not the second century C.E. Indeed the work is the result of a literary process that merged at least two cycles of stories, one related to Philip the evangelist of the canonical Acts (*Acts of Philip* 3–7) and the other related to the apostle Philip found in the Gospels and in the lists of Jesus' disciples (*Acts of Philip* 8/*Martyrdom*). In the final version of the work, these two figures constitute a single apostolic

---

5. Konstantin von Tischendorf, *Acta apostolorum apocrypha* (Leipzig: Avenarius & Mendelssohn, 1851), 75–104; see also idem, *Apocalypses apocryphae Mosis, Esdras, Pauli, Iohannis, item Mariae Dormitio, additis Evangeliorum et Actuum apocryphorum supplementis* (Leipzig: Mendelssohn, 1866; repr. Hildesheim: Olms, 1966), 141–56.

6. The work is preserved in the form of numbered acts. Unfortunately, the loss of several folios still deprives us of act 10 and the beginning of act 11; see François Bovon, "Les Actes de Philippe," in *Aufstieg und Niedergang der römischen Welt* (Berlin/New York: de Gruyter, 1988), 2.25.6.4472.

7. For *Acts of Philip* 8, we rely on a manuscript from Athens: *Atheniensis* 346. See the description of these manuscripts in Bovon, Bouvier, and Amsler, *Acta Philippi: Textus*, xiii-xxx.

8. While Amsler (*Acta Philippi: Commentarius*, 521–24) identifies Ophiorumos with Hierapolis, I suggest in "Les Actes de Philippe," 4521, that Ophiorumos may have been the city of the martyrdom and Hierapolis the city of the tomb, basing my judgment on the *Translation of Philip's Remains*. See M. R. James, "Supplement to the Acts of Philip," in *Apocrypha anecdota* (ed. M. R. James; Texts and Studies 2.3; Cambridge: Cambridge University Press, 1893; repr. Nendeln, Liechtenstein: Kravis, 1967), 158–63.

9. See Amsler, *Acta Philippi: Commentarius*, 437–39.

figure. Frédéric Amsler and Christopher Matthews demonstrate that *Acts of Philip* 2 is a later orthodox compilation,[10] and I am in agreement here. Amsler also suggests that *Acts of Philip* 1 was first an independent story.[11] In my opinion this may have been true in a preliterate stage, when the Act was an oral story, but it shares so much in common with the second half (*Acts of Philip* 8/*Martyrdom*) that I have decided to consider these sections together.

The first part of this essay considers act 1, which includes several interesting lists of Christian ministers who were members of the author's marginalized community. The second part treats the apostolic role of Mariamne and connects her role and example with the women ministers found in *Acts of Philip* 1.

The Christian "Priestesses" in *Acts of Philip* 1

Xenophontos 32, the most ancient version of *Acts of Philip* 1, presents the story of a young man who is the only son of a widow and who is miraculously resurrected by the apostle Philip at his mother's request. Differing from *Vaticanus* 824, this longer version includes a description of a tour of hell that the young man made during his short stay in the underworld, which he relates to the apostle at the instant of his resurrection (*Acts of Philip* 1.4–17).[12] Among the many punishments that confront his soul is the chastisement that people receive because they mistreated the leaders and the ascetics of another church. These leaders and ascetics are presented in three groups, divided according to gender. The result is three categories of two: priests and priestesses, deacons and deaconesses, eunuchs and virgins. This strange situation in the underworld most likely reflects a quarrel among competing Christian groups in this world. Those who are punished in hell are probably members of the majority church who while alive on earth abused their social standing and power to persecute members and ministers of the author's minority Christian community.

The writer's point of view is the one attested by the young hero and is recognized as legitimate by the apostle Philip as he listens to the narration of the tour of hell.[13] This point of view accords well with the perspective

---

10. See Christopher R. Matthews, *Philip: Apostle and Evangelist: Configurations of a Tradition* (Novum Testamentum Supplement 105; Leiden: Brill, 2002), 186–89; Amsler, *Acta Philippi: Commentarius*, 85–127.

11. Amsler, *Acta Philippi: Commentarius*, 25–83.

12. On the narrative of this tour of hell, see Richard N. Slater, "An Inquiry into the Relationship between Community and Text: The Apocryphal *Acts of Philip* 1 and the Encratites of Asia Minor," in *The Apocryphal Acts of the Apostles: Harvard Divinity School Studies* (ed. François Bovon, Ann Graham Brock, and Christopher R. Matthews; Religions of the World; Cambridge: Harvard University Center for the Study of World Religions, 1999), 281–306. See also Amsler, *Acta Philippi: Commentarius,* 50–70.

13. On the genre of the tour of hell, see Albrecht Dieterich, Νέκυια: *Beiträge zur Erklärung der neuentdeckten Petrusapokalyse* (Leipzig: Teubner, 1893); Martha Himmelfarb, *Tours of*

of a minority Christian community that can be called an ascetic community. For in the same act the apostle Philip sings the merits of ἁγνεία, a term difficult to translate but undeniably of an ascetic venue, meaning "purity, encratism, abstinence, continence." The type of asceticism to which the apostle, the mother, and her son adhere is more than an ethical obedience. In an explanatory sermon on the merits and virtues of ἁγνεία Philip says that through ἁγνεία God communicates with the Christian (αὐτῇ τῇ ἁγνείᾳ ὁ θεὸς ὁμιλεῖ; *Acts of Philip* 1.3).[14] Later in the work the reader discovers a similar saying: through ἁγνεία the believer can see God (ἡ ἁγνεία ὁρᾷ τὸν θεόν; *Acts of Philip* 4.1;[15] the influence of the Matthean beatitude ["blessed are the pure in heart, for they will see God"; Matt 5:8] is evident here, if only implicit). Asceticism is more than a moral attitude; it is a religious practice that draws the devotees closer to God, bringing them into intense communion with the deity.

The people who are punished, however, belong to an ecclesiastical organization that is less ascetic in nature. They correspond to the majority church, the mainstream of Christianity. They have probably used their political power to marginalize the ascetic community. Such a situation is not unfamiliar to fourth-century sources and is consistent with the struggle that the Great Church of the fourth century waged against ascetic minorities. Basil of Caesarea and Amphilochius of Iconium are typical examples, as we can see from Basil's letters and Amphilochius's fragment on the Apocrypha.[16] Such tension may have arisen only in the fourth century. We know very little about encratism in the third century C.E., but criticism that the majority church addresses against Montanism in the second century sounds very similar: appropriation of the Spirit, excessive ascetic practices, and women in leadership positions are among the usual accusations made against them. I would even suggest that the social and religious reality of such a group is not a late development of the Constantinian period, but represents on the contrary — not without alterations, of course — an archaic witness of an early Christian reality, like the anomalous block of stone that a receding glacier leaves behind in the middle of a meadow or on the beach beside a lake.

The depiction of punishments for those who mistreat ascetic leaders continues as the young hero exits through the door of hell. There he sees a man and a woman being attacked and eaten by the famous dog Cerberus. Taken

---

Hell: An Apocalyptic Form of Jewish and Christian Literature (Philadelphia: University of Pennsylvania Press, 1983).

14. In Bovon, Bouvier, and Amsler, *Acta Philippi: Textus*, 8–9, we translated: "C'est précisément en compagnie des purs que Dieu se complaît."

15. In ibid., 117, we translated: "La pureté voit Dieu."

16. See Basil the Great, *Epistulae* 188 and 199, in *Saint Basile, Lettres* (ed. and trans. Yves Courtonne; Paris: Les Belles Lettres, 1957–66), 2.120–31, 154–64; and Amphilochius of Iconium, *Contra Haereticos*, in *Amphilochii Iconiensis Opera* (ed. Cornelius Datema; Corpus christianorum series graeca 3; Louvain-Turnhout: Brepols, 1978), 181–214.

by pity, he tries to rescue the two people but the archangel Michael, his *angelus interpres,* urges him not to do so:

> Leave it as it is, because they also have pronounced blasphemy against priests [πρεσβυτέρους], priestesses [πρεσβύτιδας], eunuchs [εὐνούχους], deacons [διακόνους], deaconesses [διακονίσσας], virgins [παρθένους], accusing them wrongly of impudicity and adultery. Once they had done their misdeed, they met me, Michael, as well as Raphael and Uriel, and we gave them as food to this dog till the great day of judgment. (*Acts of Philip* 1.12)

At this point the young man is convinced of the couple's guilt and ceases his rescue attempt.

Several details in this episode are noteworthy. First, the man and the woman being punished are not identified as Christian ministers. Because of the phrase "they also," they are among those who participated, along with others previously mentioned, in these attacks and slanders. Second, the location of the couple in custody is surprising: they are close to the gate protected by Cerberus. Initially, the reader hesitates to consider them inside hell, but the next paragraph makes it probable that they are still inside the gate. This vagueness may suggest that the author considers them somewhat less guilty than the other sinners, who are strictly confined to the interior of hell. Third, there is a different order within the three groups of Christian leaders and ascetics who suffered vexation and persecution on earth. Because we have only one manuscript of the story, this anomaly is difficult to explain. However, the separation of the eunuchs from the virgins is probably accidental. This pair is mentioned in other passages in *Acts of Philip* 1, and at those times the sequence is coherent: the eunuchs and virgins form a group just as the deacons and deaconesses and the priests and the priestesses do.

It is well known that in antiquity many ascetic male Christians wanted to interpret literally Jesus' remark about the eunuchs and the kingdom.[17] Origen is not the only case in point here. The reaction of shock on the part of many bishops at the end of the second century C.E. and the first half of the third bears witness to the fact that not only a few Montanists but also many male Christians from the up-and-coming Great Church, particularly in Egypt (but not only in Egypt), wanted to eradicate the physical desire of the flesh and thus condemned sexuality and even marriage. That the females also felt a strong drift toward virginity is well attested. Even if we cannot be certain about the way in which the future *catholica* organized the young

---

17. See Ulrich Luz, *Das Evangelium nach Matthäus* (Evangelisch-katholischer Kommentar zum Neuen Testament 1; Zürich-Düsseldorf: Benziger/Neukirchen-Vluyn: Neukirchener Verlag, 1997), 3.88–89, 103–12.

and older virgins — both female and male — who wished to remain in celibacy, we do know that such ascetic Christians were highly venerated among the churches, particularly in minority Christian communities (sects or heresies in the traditional ecclesiastical historiography). It is not improbable that these young contempters of the flesh tried to participate in a kind of community life, creating an early form of monasticism. The risk they took was in refusing to separate the young women from the young men. The calumny of "impudicity and adultery," therefore, as attested in our text, was all too easy to level against them. The text does not imply that these two groups of ascetics were living apart from the local community; rather, they seem to have participated in the same common worship. Their precise ministerial status, however, remains uncertain.

We know from patristic and epigraphic evidence studied by A. Lambert, Georges Blond, Frédéric Amsler, and Richard N. Slater[18] that some ascetic and encratite communities of the fourth century c.e. did not distinguish secular life from monastic life. These witnesses also suggest that the organization of ministries within minority communities, including the Apostolics and Apotactics in fourth-century Asia Minor, was not so very different from the organization found in the Great Church. We are not surprised, therefore, to find in the minority church of the author the classical distinction between priests and deacons. There is, nevertheless, a major difference: in the Great Church of that time, the diaconate was still mixed, including deacons and deaconesses, but women were excluded from priesthood. The Council of Laodicea, Canon 11, is clear here: "About the fact that in the Church the so-called priestesses or female presidents should not be appointed" (περὶ τοῦ μὴ δεῖν τὰς λεγομένας πρεσβύτιδας ἤτοι προκαθημένας ἐν ἐκκλησίᾳ καθίστασθαι). In the minority communities, as attested by the *Acts of Philip*, πρεσβύτιδες rule beside πρεσβύτεροι. Priesthood was accessible to both sexes. Although Bertrand Bouvier and I published this new text in 1989[19] and Amsler presented the case in his Geneva dissertation published in 1999,[20] notice of this important witness has escaped the attention of recent studies on the role of women in ministry in antiquity.[21]

---

18. See A. Lambert, "Apotactites et apotaxamènes," in *Dictionnaire d'archéologie chrétienne et de liturgie* (ed. F. Cabrol; Paris: Letouzey et Ané, 1924), 1.2.2604–26; Georges Blond, "L'hérésie' encratite vers la fin du quatrième siècle," *Recherches de science religieuse* 32 (1944): 157–210; Amsler, *Acta Philippi: Commentarius,* 469–520; Slater, "Inquiry into the Relationship between Community and Text."

19. Bertrand Bouvier and François Bovon, "Actes de Philippe, I d'après un manuscrit inédit," in *Oecumenica et patristica: Festschrift Wilhelm Schneemelcher* (ed. Damaskinos Papandreou, Wolfgang A. Bienert, and Knut Schäferdiek; Chambésy-Geneva: Metropolie der Schweiz, 1989), 367–94, particularly 393–94.

20. See Amsler, *Acta Philippi: Commentarius,* 81–82.

21. The witness is absent from Karen Torjesen, *When Women Were Priests: Women's Leadership in the Early Church and the Scandal of Their Subordination in the Rise of Christianity* (San Francisco: Harper, 1993); and from Ute Eisen, *Amtsträgerinnen im frühen Christentum: Epigraphische und literarische Studien* (Forschungen zur kirchen- und Dogmengeschichte 61;

Several passages in *Acts of Philip* 1 mention ministers and ascetics in the minority community. In 1.6, for instance, the young man visits in hell a damned man who has been thrown into an infernal pit because he struck and slandered ἐπισκόπους ... καὶ πεσβυτέρους (bishops ... and priests). Then, in 1.7–8, he meets a young man, damned to lying on a bed of embers because he could not control his tongue when he was alive; he respected neither his parents nor the πεσβυτέρους (priests), and he insulted a παρθένον (virgin) by saying that she was not a virgin. Distressed by the extent of the punishment, the young traveler asks his guiding angel to lead him to τοὺς εὐνούχους καὶ τὰς παρθένους ... (the eunuchs and the virgins). He wishes to intercede with these elect on behalf of the damned so cruelly tortured. But once again the archangel Michael replies harshly, explaining that the young man will not obtain any softening of the punishment from the eunuchs and virgins (οὔτε εὐνούχους οὔτε παρθένους).

Later, in 1.10, the young man visits a bold, drunk man who is being punished by burning charcoal placed on his head. This damned man also tells him his story: the cause of his punishment, his sin, was that while drunk he could not resist criticizing bishops, priests, eunuchs, and virgins (κατὰ ἐπισκόπων καὶ πρεσβυτέρων καὶ εὐνούχων καὶ παρθένων). Again the young man would like to help, and he inquires as to the whereabouts of the virgins (αἱ παρθένοι). In response, he is told that unless he returns to the world of the living and is baptized he will not receive permission to see any eunuch or virgin (οὔτε εὐνοῦχον οὔτε παρθένον). Finally, near the end of his speech, the young man says (1.12, quoted above) that at the moment of leaving hell he saw a man and a woman being continually beaten by the guardian dog Cerberus at the gate of the underworld. Holding their liver in their hands, they implore the visitor for mercy. Having been moved slightly toward pity, the young man is once again rebuked by the archangel Michael, who tells him: "Leave it as it is, because they also have pronounced blasphemy against priests, priestesses, eunuchs, deacons, deaconesses, virgins, accusing them wrongly of impudicity and adultery."[22]

Until this point the young man in hell has visited only people who were not recognized as leaders of the majority church. Instead, they seem to be laypeople — we can imagine the population of Asia probably being largely Christianized by this time — who attacked the ascetic community because they considered it a sect or heresy. Just after he passes through the gate on his way back to earth, however, the young man sees an altar, and hypocrite ministers are celebrating at it (1.13). They seem not to be dead, and

---

Göttingen: Vandenhoeck & Ruprecht, 1996). Following my remarks, Eisen added mention of it in the English translation of her work; see Ute Eisen, *Women Officeholders in Early Christianity* (trans. Linda Maloney; Collegeville, Minn.: Liturgical Press, 2000), 136 n. 24a.

22. See the remarkable analysis of the tour of hell by Amsler, *Acta Philippi: Commentarius,* 24–83.

their negative actions are told in the present tense. The narrative is therefore skillful: it gives the impression of still being located in the underworld, but at the same time, it is present and reflects an actual situation in which priests and church leaders, divided among themselves, abuse their power. The next paragraph, representing the end of the young man's travel report, is more apocalyptic: it describes a beautiful throne and the trial of the guilty celebrants at the same altar mentioned in the previous paragraph. The judgment integrates the same criticisms made against the laypeople in the remainder of the tour of hell: the grievances against them are drunkenness, slander, hypocrisy, and wrath. The eschatological judge, visible only through a thunderbolt and a voice, quotes the Scriptures to condemn the wicked celebrants: they are called οἱ λειτουργοὶ τοῦ θυσιαστηρίου (the servants of the altar).

In this essay I have translated the term πρεσβῦτις as "priestess," but this is not the only possible translation. In Greek the term signifies first an aged woman, according to Liddell-Scott-Jones,[23] and a glance at Lampe's *Patristic Greek Lexicon*[24] indicates that in the Christian tradition the term was applied to senior widows and female presbyters. Lampe insists that for the masculine πρεσβύτερος "it is difficult to distinguish between this gen[eral] use of π[ρεσβύτερος], and its technical use to denote a member of a particular ministerial order."[25] In my opinion, what is true for the masculine must apply to the feminine.

To make the matter even more complex, we must be aware that Greek, in addition to the standard πρεσβῦτις, has two other feminine nouns with same root: πρεσβυτέρα and πρεσβυτερίς. The origin of the first is clear: it is an adjective in the comparative, used substantively. Its occurrence however is ambiguous: as does πρεσβῦτις, πρεσβυτέρα can mean an old woman or the head, or senior, of a women's community. The second noun, πρεσβυτερίς is probably a Christian neologism that was perhaps invented by Epiphanius; the word seems to be extremely rare. Epiphanius applies it to a female presbyter in a text written against the Collyridians, which condemns any woman whose status involves the exercise of priesthood or priestly functions: "Now it should be noted that church order required only deaconesses; it also included the name 'widows,' of whom the older were called 'eldresses,' but were never assigned the rank of 'presbytresses' or 'priestesses' " (χήρας τε ὠνόμασε καὶ τούτων τὰς ἔτι γραοτέρας πρεσβύτιδας, οὐδαμοῦ δὲ πρεσβυτερίδας ἢ ἱερίσσας προσέταξε; Epiphanius, *Panarion* 79.4).[26]

---

23. Henry George Liddell, Robert Scott, and Henry Stuart Jones, *A Greek-English Lexicon* (9th ed.; Oxford: Clarendon, 1961), 1462.

24. G. W. H. Lampe, *A Patristic Greek Lexicon* (Oxford: Clarendon, 1961), 1130.

25. Lampe also writes: "Accurate distinction between above sense [i.e., 'equivalent to ἐπίσκοπος, bishop'] and that of *priest* in threefold ministry is rendered difficult by long survival of inexact or untechnical terminology, by which πρεσβύτερος = *ruler in a church*."

26. On this passage see Eisen, *Amtsträgerinnen im frühen Christentum*, 115–19.

Epiphanius uses here πρεσβῦτις in the general meaning of an older woman and πρεσβυτερί in the technical meaning of a female presbyter. This distinction marks a divergence from the *Acts of Philip* and Canon 11 published by the Council of Laodicea.[27] With the Council of Laodicea, however, the bishop of Salamis reveals his hostility toward the ordination and sacerdotal functioning of women. The sect condemned by Epiphanius approves of this ministry for women, as does *Acts of Philip* 1. Epiphanius adds an interesting detail, stating that his adversaries were using Acts 21:9, among other biblical authoritative proof-texts, where mention is made of Philip's four prophesying daughters. Another apocryphal text, the *Martyrdom of Matthew*, mentions the appointment not only of a priest (πρεσβύτερος), but also of a priestess (πρεσβῦτις). If Matthew established the king as a priest and the son of the king as a deacon, "then he established the wife of the king as a priestess, and the wife of the king's son as a deaconess" (καὶ τὴν γυναῖκα τοῦ βασιλέως κατέστησεν πρεσβύτιδα, καὶ τὴν γυναῖκα τοῦ υἱοῦ αὐτοῦ κατέστησεν διακόνισσαν, *Martyrium Matthaei* 28).[28] The presence of women in these ministerial roles disturbs the community so little that the author concludes that there was a great joy in the church! To this list we can add epigraphic evidence that mentions a πρεσβῦτις by the name Epictos.[29] And as I discuss below, the *Acts of Philip* 8/*Martyrdom* valorizes another of Philip's female relatives, his sister Mariamne.

Ute Eisen is correct in saying that some early Christian churches accepted the ministry of women, not only at the level of virgins, widows, and deaconesses but also at the sacerdotal level of what I call "priestesses." She is probably not specific enough when she speaks repeatedly of the "church" or the "early church."[30] We should attempt to specify the period, region, and type of Christian community. One such community is the one found in the *Acts of Philip*, which was an ascetic movement in Asia Minor during the fourth, perhaps the third century C.E. The existence of this ministerial role for women in this community is confirmed in the second part of the book, *Acts of Philip* 8/*Martyrdom*.

---

27. See E. J. Jonkers, ed., *Acta et symbola conciliorum quae saeculo quarto habita sunt* (Textus Minores 19; Leiden: Brill, 1974), 88.

28. Maximilien Bonnet, "Martyrium Matthaei," in *Acta apostolorum apocrypha* (ed. Richard Adelbert Lipsius and Maximilien Bonnet; 2 vols. in 3; Leipzig: Mendelssohn, 1891–1903; repr. Darmstadt: Wissenschaftliche Buchgesellschaft, 1959), 2.1.259, lines 3–5. This is one recension of the text. The other recension, followed by the Latin translation, characterizes the two women as only deaconesses. This second recension and the Latin translation are printed below the first Greek version on the same page; ibid., lines 11–12, 28–29, 31.

29. The inscription from Thera, Greece, is presented by Eisen, *Amtsträgerinnen im frühen Christentum*, 123–25. In the same chapter, Eisen cites other inscriptions in which the evidence is less clear.

30. Ibid., e.g., 9, 23, 26; see the critical review of the English translation by Robin M. Jensen in *Journal of Early Christian Studies* 10 (2002): 135–38.

Mariamne as a Model of Faith and Leadership
in *Acts of Philip* 8/*Martyrdom*

Mariamne is introduced as Philip's sister in *Acts of Philip* 8.2.[31] She is said to have been active during Jesus' time, probably during the last supper: she prepared the bread and the salt, thus preparing the breaking of bread while Martha was busy with many other things. Mariamne is equated with Mary in the Lukan and Johannine episodes; she is Martha's sister (Luke 10:38–42).[32] Mariamne received another responsibility from the Savior: she is to carry the list of the countries to which the resurrected Jesus will send his disciples.[33] The Savior grants her a third responsibility as well: she is to accompany her brother in his apostolic ministry, and when he becomes weak and quick tempered, she is to be strong and calm. Mariamne is called upon right at the outset. When Philip hears the name of the city to which he is being sent, his courage melts at once. But Mary, who has — says the text — the body of a woman but — according to the ancient view — the spirit of a man, leads him on the right way and brings him back to the proper spiritual disposition. She does not console the weak apostle, but rather leads him to a mature understanding of his responsibilities.

Obeying a divine order, similar to logion 114 in the *Gospel of Thomas,* Mariamne must change her appearance: she has to cut the long summer outfit she wears and transform her appearance into that of a male.[34] She wears male clothing as she travels with her brother. But these two are not just traveling together as brother and sister. Following the two-by-two distribution commanded by Jesus in his missionary speech and respecting the grouping of the New Testament lists of the Twelve, Bartholomew is sent by the Lord also as the companion of Philip. The reader discovers, therefore, that the missionary expedition consists of a group of three people — Philip, his sister Mariamne, and his companion Bartholomew. As the text makes

---

31. See Amsler, *Acta Philippi: Commentarius,* 312–17.

32. It may be appropriate to mention here a strange apocryphal episode preserved in the so-called *Ecclesiastical Constitution of the Apostles* 26, where Christ refuses Mary and Martha the right to celebrate the Eucharist; see Adolf von Harnack, *Die Lehre der zwölf Apostel nebst Untersuchungen zur ältesten Geschichte der Kirchenverfassung und des Kirchenrechts; Anhang: Ein übersehenes Fragment der* Διδαχή *in alter lateinischer Übersetzung mitgeteilt von O. v. Gebhardt* (Leipzig: Hinrichs, 1884), 236; François Bovon, "Mary Magdalene's Paschal Privilege," in Bovon's *New Testament Traditions and Apocryphal Narratives* (trans. Jane Haapiseva-Hunter; Princeton Theological Monograph Series 36; Allison Park, Pa.: Pickwick, 1995), 234.

33. The Greek expression for this list is ἡ ἀναγραφὴ τῶν χωρῶν.

34. Instances of a woman's changing her clothing to that of a man in this work are not limited to Mariamne. In *Acts of Philip* 4.6 a girl named Charitini, who is healed by Philip, changes her garments and adopts a male dress. On the change of clothing, see Stephen J. Davis, "Crossed Texts, Crossed Sex: Intertextuality and Gender in Early Christian Legends of Holy Women Disguised as Men," *Journal of Early Christian Studies* 10 (2002): 1–36.

clear, these three together are called οἱ ἀπόστολοι (the apostles): Mariamne is an apostle as well as the other two; she also has been sent by the Savior.[35]

Mariamne's story does not differ from other early Christian traditions concerning Mary Magdalene. Actually, the name Mariamne is a Greek equivalent of Mary and not another name.[36] The connection between Mariamne and the postresurrection sending of the apostles in the *Acts of Philip* does not differ from what the New Testament presents with respect to the role of Mary Magdalene and the other women in their proclamation of the resurrection to the group of the Eleven. It is, in fact, identical with a very old tradition preserved by the Manichean Psalms, according to which Mary's courage brings the Eleven back together when they were ready to run away: she gives them back their courage.[37] This is exactly what Mariamne is doing when she cares for her cowardly brother, the apostle Philip.

Even a cursory reading of the sequence of episodes in the *Acts of Philip* reveals that at each step of the missionary journey Mariamne fulfills the duties and has the privileges of an apostle. If her preaching activity is limited even in *Xenophontos* 32, a manuscript not suspected of excessive orthodox editing, it is likely that in an earlier version of the text, which is now no longer recoverable, Mariamne must have been endowed with a full preaching load. What remains is still impressive. As soon as the apostolic group finds a location in Ophiorumos, she stays at the door of the house (actually an abandoned dispensary) and calls the passersby, inviting them to enter and hear Philip's apostolic message (*Acts of Philip/Martyrdom* 3 [recension Γ]). One of the passersby is Nicanora, the governor's wife. Syrian by birth, as were Mariamne and her brother — both being born at Bethsaida — Nicanora is happy to speak Aramaic or Hebrew with Mariamne. This female apostle begins to convince her of the Christian message. In the present form of the text this development provides an invitation to learn more from Philip, but in the original it was most likely Mariamne who provided the complete apostolic preaching, and this with no male mediation. A confirmation of my hypothesis is found in the later distribution of roles: Philip will baptize the male converts and Mariamne will baptize the women. The text is clear here. Mariamne does not just function as an adjunct for a sacrament performed by Philip her brother. She performs a sacrament as a minister.

---

35. This is noted with perspicacity by Ann Graham Brock, *Mary Magdalene, The First Apostle: The Struggle for Authority* (Harvard Theological Studies 51; Cambridge: Harvard University Press, 2003), 124n. 4, 126–27.

36. See my two articles: "Mary Magdalene's Paschal Privilege," 228; and "Mary Magdalene in the *Acts of Philip*," in *Which Mary?: The Marys of Early Christian Tradition* (ed. F. Stanley Jones; Symposium Series 19; Atlanta: Scholars Press, 2002), 75–89. Against the identification of Mariamne with Mary Magdalene, see Stephen J. Shoemaker, "Rethinking the 'Gnostic Mary': Mary of Nazareth and Mary of Magdala in Early Christian Tradition," *Journal of Early Christian Studies* 9 (2001): 555–95.

37. See Charles Robert Cecil Allberry, ed., *A Manichaean Psalm-Book*, part 2 (Manichaean Manuscripts in the Chester Beatty Collection 2; Stuttgart: Kohlhammer, 1938), 192; Bovon, "Mary Magdalene's Paschal Privilege," 154, 232.

Acts of Philip 8/*Martyrdom* also offers a description of other aspects of Mariamne's ministry.[38] She shares, for instance, in the healing ministry of Christ and his apostles (the *Acts of Philip* describes conversion as a process of healing, with numerous miraculous cures and successful exorcisms as medical symbols of salvation). What seems strange today, but did not seem strange to the evangelist Mark, is the use of saliva as a curative medication: like the saliva of the Markan Jesus, Mariamne's saliva that is dipped from her mouth by Philip's finger restores Stachys's sight (*Acts of Philip/Martyrdom* 14.7).[39]

Luke, the author of the canonical Acts of the Apostles, knew of feminine relatives around Philip the evangelist: his four daughters (Acts 21:9). Several other authors in the early centuries C.E. circulated traditions about these young women concerning their gift of prophecy, a resurrection story involving both them and Philip, and mention of their tombs in Hierapolis of Phrygia.[40] One finds such short allusions particularly among Christians who practiced prophecy. The number of daughters tends to vary, possibly indicating that Luke was not the only source of information about them. Some authors even claimed to know where one or the other had been buried. The Montanists relied on them as a warranty for their own religious experiences. According to Epiphanius, quoted above, the Collyridians found in Acts 21:9 justification for their practice of allowing female presbyters.

Orthodox writers could not censure the Lukan passage since this book had become canonical for them. They tried their best, however, to adapt its meaning to their own agenda. In a controversy not over prophecy but over asceticism, Clement of Alexandria rejoiced in the fact that Philip had daughters, even as Peter had a mother-in-law.[41] For Clement this meant that both apostles were married. A similar process of adaptation occurred for the ascetic community of the *Acts of Philip*. In a period when the Book of Acts was neither familiar nor canonized,[42] this community transformed the daughters into one sister.[43] By the same token, they identified this sister

---

38. See Bovon, "Mary Magdalene in the *Acts of Philip*."

39. I must add that this story shocked one reader into a drastic solution: to extract violently the rest of the story (the text breaks at the point when Philip dips his finger in his sister's mouth to anoint Stachys). We remember here also that the evangelists Matthew and Luke opposed two Markan narratives (Mark 7:31–37 and 8:22–26) that are similar to this one: they did not copy them, which is in effect also a form of censorship.

40. See Papias in Eusebius of Caesarea, *Ecclesiastical History* 3.39.9; see also Polycrates in 3.31.2–3 and 5.24.2, and the Montanist Proclus in 3.31.4.

41. Clement of Alexandria, in Eusebius of Caesarea, *Ecclesiastical History* 3.30.1. See Amsler, *Acta Philippi: Commentarius*, 7–9.

42. In the beginning of his first homily on the Book of Acts, John Chrysostom complains that in his time many people did not know the content of this biblical book; see John Chrysostom, *Homilies on Acts* 1.1 (Patrologia graeca 60.13); see my *De vocatione gentium: Histoire de l'interprétation d'Act. 10,1–11,18 dans les six premiers siècles* (Beiträge zur Geschichte der biblische Exegese 8; Tübingen: Mohr-Siebeck, 1967), 7–8.

43. Even the number four, with respect to four daughters (see Acts 21:9), is not consistent across the texts. Polycrates identifies their number as three; Papias and an anti-Montanist writer

with Mary Magdalene and with Mary the sister of Martha. The intention of such a manipulation is evident: in so doing, these Christians had at their disposal a first-rate female apostle, living proof of the validity of women's priestly ministry and the best advocate of strict asceticism. Philip is no longer married, and he can thus become for men the paragon of continence.

Conclusion

The connection between the πρεσβύτιδες in *Acts of Philip* 1 and the figure of Mariamne in *Acts of Philip* 8/*Martyrdom* is clear. If we accept that the community of the author of the *Acts of Philip* advocates for women's ministry in the church even at the level of priesthood, then the presence of a female apostle beside Philip, the evangelist and apostle of Phrygia (the apostle and the evangelist being one and the same person), becomes not only a possibility but a theological and ecclesiological necessity.

The community of the author lists among its members eunuchs and virgins, deacons and deaconesses, priests and priestesses. Such church order seems legitimate because in the beginning the apostles were sent out not only two by two, like Philip and Bartholomew, but also male and female side by side, like Philip and Mariamne. If the Great Church can claim that their threefold hierarchical system of bishops, priests, and deacons is biblical, then the ascetic community of Phrygia, like other marginal churches of that time, has the same right and the same authority to defend a church order that includes both men and women in priestly ministry.

Actually, the author of the *Acts of Philip* is less interested in canon law than in pastoral care and spiritual life. She or he needs an apostolic model for the present time. Models are not taken from legal documents, but from narratives. *A sa façon*, the work she or he writes or compiles, the *Acts of Philip*, fulfills this need. This literary composition gives legitimacy and courage to the marginalized, persecuted community.

The price paid is perhaps high: the distortion of apostolic memories. But who did not distort history in that time? And who is able to judge the distortion? Is the final victory granted to men, since Mariamne must wear male clothing? Perhaps so, but she is the strongest among those in her apostolic group. And her salvation is not due to her bearing children but to her practicing an ascetic life, ἀγνεία, a spiritual discipline that opens the eyes of faith to the vision of God.

---

do not specify their number at all (see Eusebius of Caesarea, *Ecclesiastical History* 3.31.2–3; 3.39.9; 5.17.3; 5.24.2).

7

The Identity of the Blessed Mary, Representative of Wisdom in *Pistis Sophia*

Ann Graham Brock

Attending seminary was a life-changing experience for me, in part because it was there that I first read Elisabeth Schüssler Fiorenza's book *In Memory of Her*.[1] The impact of this book on the community as a whole was such that the faculty of Trinity Lutheran Seminary chose hers as one of the books that all would read and discuss as a group that year. Through this book she transformed my understanding of early Christian history and especially the role of women in it.

It was therefore no small event when I later had the opportunity to take courses from Elisabeth or even work as a research assistant for her. The methods and approaches she taught, especially rhetorical analysis and the hermeneutics of suspicion and remembrance, provided me with some of the critical tools necessary to read ancient texts with an interpretive eye and with greater awareness of the suppression of women's roles. Schüssler Fiorenza's method of reading against the grain to look for vestiges of women's leadership that had been suppressed by layers of patriarchal memory has helped in my own research, especially as her example challenged me to explore further portrayals of women's early Christian leadership even in noncanonical texts and in languages such as Syriac and Coptic.

Elisabeth was particularly instrumental in the recovery and reconstruction of the leadership roles of some of the most pivotal early Christian female leaders, including Mary and Martha of Bethany, Mary of Magdala, Prisca, and Phoebe. One of the most prominent of those who transmitted wisdom in early Christianity was Mary Magdalene, a figure who in three of four gospels in the Christian canon received a special commissioning to tell others the good news (Matt 28:7, 10; Mark 16:7; John 20:17). As a result of Mary Magdalene's status as a resurrection witness, she became a role model for

---

1. Elisabeth Schüssler Fiorenza, *In Memory of Her: A Feminist Theological Reconstruction of Christian Origins* (New York: Crossroad, 1983).

many early Christians, some of whom called upon her example for the authority to preach or to teach. Since the first generations of early Christians, however, Mary Magdalene's role has suffered from misrepresentation and distortion through the conflation of her character with other female figures, including the penitent sinner, perhaps a prostitute, who anointed Jesus. Her role has also been diminished through the substitution of her character with less threatening or controversial characters named Mary, such as Mary the mother of Jesus.

Elisabeth's work helped to recover and reconstruct some of the pivotal role that Mary Magdalene initially played in early Christianity, one that earned for Mary the honorific title "apostle to the apostles."[2] The role that scholars such as Elisabeth reconstruct for Mary Magdalene, however, is being called into question by scholars such as Enzo Lucchesi and Stephen Shoemaker.[3] They challenge the interpretation that Mary Magdalene is the primary character in some of the most important early noncanonical texts, such as the *Gospel of Mary, Pistis Sophia,* and *Dialogue of the Savior,* and claim instead that this primary figure is Mary the mother of Jesus. In doing so they remove the threat of one of the most positive and empowering women and apostolic figures of early Christianity. They can do so because texts such as the *Gospel of Mary* and *Dialogue of the Savior* portray one of the primary characters as Mary, but do not provide much additional information concerning which Mary is being featured. Most scholars attribute this primary role to Mary Magdalene, despite the absence of a specific identification of her as "the Magdalene."[4] Without a hermeneutic of suspicion,

---

2. See, for example, Hippolytus's reference to Mary Magdalene in *De cantico* 24–26 (Corpus scriptorum christianorum orientalium 264.43–49). For more information on this title see Elisabeth Schüssler Fiorenza, "Mary Magdalene: Apostle to the Apostles," *Union Theological Seminary Journal* (April 1974): 22–24; and Rosemarie Nürnberg, "Apostolae Apostolorum: Die Frauen am Grab als erste Zeuginnen der Auferstehung in der Väterexegese," in *Stimuli: Exegese und ihre Hermeneutik in Antike und Christentum: Festschrift für Ernst Dassmann* (ed. Georg Schollgen and Clemens Scholten; Jahrbuch für Antike und Christentum: Ergänzungsband 23; Münster: Aschendorff, 1996), 228–42.

3. See Enzo Lucchesi, "Évangile selon Marie ou Évangile selon Marie-Madeleine?" *Analecta Bollandiana* 103 (1985): 366. Lucchesi suggests Mary the mother because of the tradition that Jesus appeared to his mother in the garden. The earliest that this tradition appears, however, is in Ephrem's commentary on the Diatessaron and may not be attributable to Tatian. See also Stephen Shoemaker, "Mary and the Discourse of Orthodoxy: Early Christian Identity and the Ancient Dormition Legends" (Ph.D. diss., Duke University, 1997); and its publication as *Ancient Traditions of the Virgin Mary's Dormition and Assumption* (Oxford Early Christian Studies; Oxford: Oxford University Press, 2002).

4. Schüssler Fiorenza, *In Memory of Her,* 51; Karen L. King, "The Gospel of Mary Magdalene," in *Searching the Scriptures,* vol. 2: *A Feminist Commentary* (ed. Elisabeth Schüssler Fiorenza; New York: Crossroad, 1994), 601–2; Anne Pasquier, *L'Évangile selon Marie* (Bibliothèque copte de Nag Hammadi, Section "Textes" 10; Quebec: University of Laval Press, 1983); Esther de Boer, *Mary Magdalene: Beyond the Myth* (Harrisburg, Pa.: Trinity, 1997), 81; and Antti Marjanen, *The Woman Jesus Loved: Mary Magdalene in the Nag Hammadi Library and Related Documents* (Nag Hammadi and Manichaean Studies 40; Leiden: Brill, 1996), 94–95. Marjanen, for example, points out that the only resurrection conversations involving Mary the mother and the Risen One are the *Questions of Bartholomew* and *Pistis*

however, it would previously not have been as much of a concern to me which Mary it was: the strong apostolic role of Mary Magdalene or the generally more acquiescent figure of Mary, mother of Jesus.[5]

This essay responds to this type of challenge to Mary Magdalene's role by reexamining these early texts, especially *Pistis Sophia,* since it is one of the more important texts in the argumentation for the unidentified Mary as the mother of Jesus. *Pistis Sophia* depicts female purveyors of wisdom in much higher proportion than the average canonical texts and in the process features a character named Mary, who functions as primary interlocutor with Jesus. This ancient piece of literature features revelation dialogue between Jesus and Mary, including queries, responses, and insights from both of them. The difficulty in specifically determining the identity of Mary lies in the way *Pistis Sophia* explicitly mentions both Mary Magdalene and Mary the mother of Jesus, but the vast majority of references to Mary do not explicitly distinguish which Mary is meant. This essay suggests that on the basis of numerous passages and implicit references one may nevertheless discern the identity of the primary Mary in *Pistis Sophia* as Mary Magdalene.

Mary in *Pistis Sophia* 1–3

The first essential step in examining *Pistis Sophia* is to nuance the discussion in terms of its composition. It should not be treated as a homogenous unity, as so frequently occurs. The text now called *Pistis Sophia* originally comprised at least two independent texts: *Pistis Sophia* 1–3, frequently dated to the second half of the third century, and *Pistis Sophia* 4, which Adolf von Harnack and others date to the first half of the third century.[6] No doubt this composite text consists of further layers of traditions and rewritings, but for the purposes of this discussion these two major divisions will suffice.

Sophia. The context of the *Questions of Bartholomew* is significantly different from the *Gospel of Mary,* and in *Pistis Sophia* "the mother of Jesus has an insignificant role compared to that of Mary Magdalene" (95 n. 2).

5. See her role, for example, in the *Questions of Bartholomew* in James Keith Elliott, ed., *The Apocryphal New Testament* (Oxford: Clarendon, 1993), 652–72.

6. Marjanen provides some good discussion (*The Woman Jesus Loved,* 171–72, esp. 172 n. 11) concerning the dating of these texts, stating that it is difficult to date the two texts with respect to each other based on the observations of Carl Schmidt. See previous work on this topic in Adolf von Harnack, *Untersuchungen über das gnostische Buch Pistis Sophia* (Texte und Untersuchungen 7; Leipzig: Hinrichs, 1891), 106–12; idem, "Ein jüngst entdeckter Auferstehungsbericht," *Theologische Studien: Festschrift B. Weiss* (Göttingen: [n.p.], 1897), 1. Other scholars agree with Harnack's dating of these two sections; see Carl Schmidt, *Pistis Sophia: Ein gnostisches Originalwerk des 3. Jahrhunderts aus dem Koptischen übersetzt* (Leipzig: Hinrichs, 1925), xl–lxxxi; idem, "Die Urschrift der Pistis Sophia," *Zeitschrift für die neutestamentliche Wissenschaft* 24 (1925): 218–40; Walter Till, *Die griechische christliche Schriftsteller der ersten [drei] Jahrhunderte* (Die griechische christliche Schriftsteller der ersten drei Jahrhunderte 45; 3d ed.; Berlin: Akademie-Verlag, 1959). For more information, see also Deirdre Good, "Pistis Sophia," in *Searching the Scriptures,* vol. 2: *A Feminist Commentary* (ed. Elisabeth Schüssler Fiorenza; New York: Crossroad, 1994), 678–707; and Michel Tardieu and Jean-Daniel Dubois, *Introduction à la littérature gnostique* (Paris: Cerf/CNRS, 1986), 1.80–81.

The following statistics concerning the variations of the forms of Mary's names confirm the necessity of treating these two texts of *Pistis Sophia* separately.[7] Whereas *Pistis Sophia* 4 apparently identifies only one figure named Mary and employs only one form of the name (ΜΑΡΙΑ), *Pistis Sophia* 1–3 features at least two Marys and employs multiple versions of the name: (1) ΜΑΡΙΑ (Maria) appears 175 times, (2) ΜΑΡΙΖΑΜ (Mariam) occurs 21 times, (3) and ΜΑΡΙΖΑΜΜΗ (Mariamme) appears 1 time (3.133). Although scholars try to determine Mary's identity according to the form of her name in the text, this form is not always reliable in determining which Mary is being discussed.[8] In fact, in Jesus' dialogue with what appears to be the same figure named Mary, two different forms of her name appear in the same scene (1.19 and 1.43; see also 3.108 and 3.128).

It is a challenging process to determine which Mary the text focuses upon and thus which figure, in conjunction with Jesus, holds the most prominent position. *Pistis Sophia* 1–3 uses the various forms of Mary's name at least 197 times, but only occasionally distinguishes them with an additional modifier such as ΜΑΡΙΑ ΤΜΑΓΔΑΛΗΝΗ (Mary Magdalene) or ΜΑΡΙΑ ΤΜΑΑΥ (Mary the mother). With only 12 such explicit references to Mary Magdalene and only 11 to Mary the mother,[9] the bulk of the references to Mary—a total of 174—do not provide either of these additional markers. However, their identities emerge more clearly than one might initially believe. This essay highlights some of the ways in which the text subtly provides additional identifiers. Although it is not unreasonable to call scholars into question for so often crediting Mary Magdalene with the bulk of the undesignated Marys in *Pistis Sophia*, the following analysis suggests some distinguishing factors that help to clarify which Mary is being discussed and confirm that the primary figure named Mary is, in all likelihood, Mary Magdalene.

Mary—Mother according to the Material Body

Mary the mother is first introduced in *Pistis Sophia* 1–3 as ⲘⲘΑΡΙΑ ΤΑΪ ΕϢΑΥΜΟΥΤΕ ΕΡΟⲤ ϪΕ ΤΑΜΑΑΥ ΚΑΤΑ ΠⲤⲰΜΑ ⲚⲐΥΛΗ (Mary, who is called my mother according to the material body; 1.8). Additional explicit references to her are the following: ΜΑΡΙΑ ΤΜΑΑΥ ⲚⲒⲤ (Maria, the mother of Jesus Christ; 1.59 twice, 61, 62), ΜΑΡΙΑ ΤΕΚΜΑΑΥ (Maria, your mother;

7. Some of these statistics also appear in a recent volume publishing the result of a scholarly discussion concerning the identity of the Marys in ancient texts at the 2000 national conference of the Society of Biblical Literature in Nashville. See *Which Mary? The Marys of Early Christian Tradition* (ed. F. Stanley Jones; Society of Biblical Literature Symposium Series 19; Atlanta: Society of Biblical Literature, 2002).

8. Stephen J. Shoemaker, "Rethinking the 'Gnostic Mary': Mary of Nazareth and Mary of Magdala in Early Christian Tradition," *Journal of Early Christian Studies* 9 (2001): 558.

9. I designate this Mary "the mother" instead of "the virgin" because the latter term reflects a later theological emphasis, and nowhere in *Pistis Sophia* is Mary the mother designated "the virgin." This epithet applies instead to "John the Virgin" (ⲒⲰϨΑΝΝΗⲤ ΠΠΑΡΘΕΝΟⲤ; 2.96) or the "Virgin of the Light" (ΤΠΑΡΘΕΝΟⲤ ⲘΠΟΥΟⲒⲚ; 1.59).

1.62 twice), and ⲙⲁⲣⲓⲁ ⲧⲉϥⲙⲁⲁⲩ (Maria, his mother; 1.59, 61, 62). Following these references to Mary as mother, the figure of Jesus responds to her several times with the words "excellent, well done, Mary" (1.59, 61, 62). A comparative analysis of this character's portrayal in the text as a whole, however, reveals that these words, albeit fine praise, do not really set this mother figure apart from the rest of the group in any special way. The phrase *excellent, well done* reflects instead the typical words with which Jesus responds throughout the volume, including, for example, in his reply to Martha (1.39), John (1.41), Thomas (2.70), Peter (2.65), James (2.68), and others.

All of the explicit references to Mary the mother are confined to the first book of *Pistis Sophia*. These few appearances of Mary the mother often bear the additional reference to her being part of the physical or material sphere, such as ⲙⲁⲣⲓⲁ ⲧⲁⲙⲁⲁⲩ ⲕⲁⲧⲁ ⲑⲩⲗⲏ ⲧⲉⲛⲧⲁⲓ̈ⲅⲟⲓ̈ⲗⲉ (Maria, my mother according to the matter to whom I was entrusted; 1.61), with this reference to "matter" echoing the vocabulary appearing in her introduction into the text as a "mother according to the material body" (1.8). Likewise, the text reiterates the concept of her being "entrusted" in the praise she receives from Jesus: "Truly, truly, I say that they will bless you from end to end of the earth for the pledge of the First Mystery was entrusted to you" (1.59). It is not from Jesus that this blessing comes, but from others who will bless her because of what was entrusted to her. Because the text tends to negate the physical realm, it frequently portrays Jesus encouraging renunciation, including "the whole world and all the matter in it" (2.95). This theme of renunciation appears throughout the text (see, for example, 1.33–35; 2.100; 3.104) and includes the command to "renounce the whole world... and all its relationships" (3.102, 106). Thus the status of Mary the mother, with its close connection to the material world, does not appear to be an especially high one. Her position is perhaps best encapsulated in Jesus' words to her: "From you has come forth the material body in which I exist, which I have cleaned and purified" (1.59). Such an attitude is not unusual in a text that tends to diminish the material world, including numerous exhortations to renounce "the world and all the matter in it." Once Jesus' origins are established here in the first of the four books of *Pistis Sophia*, no more explicit references to Mary the mother occur.

Mary Magdalene as "Superior to All My Disciples"

Pistis Sophia 1–3 registers the presence of a second character named Mary, clearly distinguishable from Mary the mother, in at least twelve passages that refer to her as "Mary the Magdalene" (2.83, 85, 87, 88, 90, 94, 96, 97, 98, 99; 3.127, 132). The explicit references to "the Magdalene" differ significantly from those to Mary mother of Jesus. For instance, just after ⲙⲁⲣⲓⲁ ⲧⲙⲁⲅⲇⲁⲗⲏⲛⲏ (Mary Magdalene) speaks, the text points out that "the Savior marveled greatly at the words she gave" (2.87). The author portrays

Mary Magdalene throughout this text as one who remains strong and intercedes on behalf of the others, "who have despaired completely" (2.94). In one example, she offers an interpretation for Salome, and the "power of light within Mary Magdalene welled up" (3.132). In response to one of Mary Magdalene's questions, Jesus promises, "I will fulfill you in all powers and all pleromas . . . so that you may be called the pleromas, fulfilled with all knowledge" (2.85). Such encomiums for this Mary continue to add up throughout the text as the Savior announces in another passage that "Maria Magdalene [ΜΑΡΙΑ ΤΜΑΓΔΑΛΗΝΗ] and John the Virgin [ΪѠ2ΑΝΝΗC ΠΠΑΡΘΕΝOC] will be superior to all my disciples" (2.96).

When one compares these explicit references of Mary Magdalene to Mary the mother, the ones that express especially high praise inevitably belong to Mary Magdalene. As these passages make clear, Jesus describes ΜΑΡΙΑ ΤΜΑΓΔΑΛΗΝΗ as superior, as filled with the power of light, and as providing explanations that evoke "marvel." The strength of these positive references suggests that Mary Magdalene is the primary interlocutor with Jesus in the text and thus is the Mary spoken of when her identity is unspecified. Although this evidence alone concerning the explicit references to Mary convinces many scholars that Mary Magdalene is the primary figure of the text, another interpretive tool exists that makes her identification even clearer. The text of *Pistis Sophia* 1–3 contains numerous descriptive phrases that in my opinion significantly diminish the ambiguity of Mary's identity. Although a thorough search of the text finds relatively few explicit identifiers of Mary as "the Magdalene" or "the mother," it does uncover an unusually high number of appositional phrases immediately following Mary's name, which seem to serve as supplementary identifiers. These identifiers include phrases such as "the other one," "the blessed one," and "the pure spiritual one."

"Mary—"the Other One," "the Blessed One," and "the Pure Spiritual One"

At one of the sites in which the Mary who is not the mother of Jesus first appears, the text refers to her as "the other Mary." Shoemaker argues that Mary the mother is the primary figure for this text in part because of the presence of this additional epithet: "Mary, the other one." He suggests that this phrase in all likelihood designates Mary Magdalene, thereby placing her in a secondary position in the text behind Mary the mother. I agree that "the other Mary" may well be Mary Magdalene, but I disagree with his conclusion that "implicit in this distinction is the notion that the name Maria, if otherwise unadorned, signifies the Virgin, while any 'other Maria' must be specified as such."[10]

I suggest an alternative explanation: this designation for Mary Magdalene is not a description to subordinate her to Mary the mother, but a literary

---

10. Shoemaker, "Mary and the Discourse of Orthodoxy," 185.

device to clarify and to make a transition back to the figure of Mary Magdalene after dialogue from Mary the mother. This phrase occurs twice in the text (1.59, 62), each time just after Mary the mother has spoken, but with no evidence of a diminished status for Mary Magdalene. In fact, at one point when the term ⲦⲔⲈⲘⲀⲣⲓ2ⲀⲘ (the other Mary) appears, the text includes another significant appositional phrase — it refers to her as "the other Mary, *the blessed one*":

ⲘⲀⲣⲓⲀ ⲦⲘⲀⲀⲨ ⲚⲓⲤ ⲠⲈⲬⲀⲤ....ⲦⲤ ⲠⲈⲬⲀ4 ⲬⲈ ⲚⲦⲞ 2ⲰⲰⲦⲈ ⲘⲀⲣⲓⲀ·
ⲦⲀⲓ ⲈⲚⲦⲀⲤⲬⲓ-ⲘⲞⲣФⲎ...ⲀⲨⲰ ⲀⲣⲈⲬ-ⲈⲓⲚⲈ...ⲚⲦⲞ ⲘⲚ ⲦⲔⲈⲘⲀⲣⲓ2ⲀⲘ
ⲦⲘⲀⲔⲀⲣⲓⲞⲤ:

Mary the mother of Jesus said,... Jesus answered, "You also, Mary, you have received form... and you have received likeness... you and the other Mary, the blessed one." (1.59)

These two descriptive phrases, "the other Mary" and "the blessed one," used in conjunction with each other provide a significant interpretive key for unlocking the identity of some of the otherwise unspecified references to Mary in the text that follows. The epithet ⲦⲘⲀⲔⲀⲣⲓⲀ (the blessed one) subsequently appears numerous times throughout the text and most likely serves as a supplementary identifier for a "Mary." Thus, by means of this particular passage (1.59), Mary "the blessed one" is clearly linked with the *other* one — that is, not the mother — who is most likely Mary Magdalene.[11]

The probability that the epithet "the blessed one" consistently refers to Mary Magdalene calls for careful examination of all the other references to "Mary, the blessed one." In *Pistis Sophia,* the first time the narrative mentions Mary without the designation "mother," Jesus addresses her with the following words: "Mariam, the *blessed one,* whom I will complete in all the mysteries of the height, speak openly, you are she whose heart is more directed to the kingdom of heaven than all your brothers and sisters" (1.17). Later, the text says that "Maria, the beautiful in her speech, came forward. The *blessed one* prostrated herself" (1.24). Shortly thereafter, Jesus affirms this Mary's words: "Excellent, Mariam, *the blessed one,* you pleroma or you all-blessed pleroma, who will be blessed among all generations" (1.34).

Shoemaker contends that the Mary in this last reference should be acknowledged as Mary the mother of Jesus because "blessed among all generations" is a description that "would surely prompt an ancient listener familiar with Luke's gospel to associate this Mary with the Virgin rather than

---

11. One has to acknowledge the possibility of a third Mary in *Pistis Sophia* 1–3. The presence of an unspecified Martha in the text, for example, at least raises the possibility of the presence of Mary of Bethany. However, based on the absence of any further designations or concrete indications of a third Mary, we will proceed with Mary Magdalene as the most logical choice for the "other Mary."

the Magdalene."[12] These references are not, however, "overlooked clues" that "interpreters failed to notice."[13] The problem with his suggestion lies in the fact that in the same sentence this Mary is also called the "pleroma or the all-blessed pleroma, who will be blessed among all generations." This designation as a "pleroma" or "all-blessed pleroma" is given explicitly to Mary Magdalene in a subsequent passage in which Jesus promises her: "I will fulfill you in all powers and all pleromas... so that you may be called the pleromas, fulfilled with all knowledge" (2.85). Another problem with the identification of this Mary as Mary the mother resides in the fact that the epithet ⲦⲘⲀⲔⲀⲢⲒⲀ (the blessed one) appears at least seventeen times in the text — in either the feminine or masculine form — but never in conjunction with explicit references to Mary the mother. Rather, in the case we have just seen, the reference to Mary as "the blessed one" explicitly refers to the Mary that is not the mother: Jesus spoke to his mother, saying, ⲚⲦⲞ ⲘⲚ ⲦⲔⲈⲘⲀⲢⲒϨⲀⲘ ⲦⲘⲀⲔⲀⲢⲒⲞⲤ (you and the other Mary, the blessed one; 1.59).

Further verification that "the blessed one" is a designation for the Mary that is not the mother occurs in a passage where the juxtaposition of speakers confirms the use of the term ⲦⲘⲀⲔⲀⲢⲒⲀ (the blessed one) as an identifier for the Mary that is not the mother: "Jesus says, 'Excellent, Mariam, the blessed one [ⲘⲀⲢⲒϨⲀⲘ ⲦⲘⲀⲔⲀⲢⲒⲀ], who will inherit the whole kingdom of the light.' After these things Mary the mother of Jesus Christ [ⲘⲀⲢⲒⲀ ⲦⲘⲀⲀⲨ ⲚⲒⲤ] *also* came forward and said, 'My Lord and my Savior, command me also that I answer this discourse' " (1.61). The text that follows this interchange presents more praise for the blessed Mary (who is not the mother), as it further singles her out, this time for a spiritual inheritance: ⲈⲨⲄⲈ ⲘⲀⲢⲒϨⲀⲘ ⲦⲈⲔⲖⲎⲢⲞⲚⲞⲘⲞⲤ ⲘⲠⲞⲨⲞⲈⲒⲚ (excellent, Mariam, you inheritor of the light; 1.62). The differentiation between the blessed Mary and Mary the mother of Jesus suggests that ensuing occurrences of the phrase "Mary, the blessed one" also refer to the Mary who is not the mother.[14] An additional passage supports this interpretation: the Savior heard the words of Maria (identified as Mary Magdalene in the preceding paragraph), and "he blessed her exceedingly" (3.132).

Perhaps one of the underlying messages of *Pistis Sophia* is that a disciple is called a "blessed one" for different reasons than being a mother. Against

12. Shoemaker, "Mary and the Discourse of Orthodoxy," 186. See Luke 1:42: "In a loud voice she exclaimed: 'Blessed are you among women' "; and 1:48: "From now on all generations will call me blessed."

13. Ibid., 186.

14. In addition to Mary Magdalene a few other disciples receive the description "the blessed one" (ⲦⲘⲀⲔⲀⲢⲒⲀ [fem.]/ⲠⲘⲀⲔⲀⲢⲒⲞⲤ [masc.]). Philip is the first male disciple to speak (1.22) and is given the special commission to record (1.43). He is subsequently identified as blessed (1.42; 2.82), as are Andrew (1.45), Thomas (2.70), Martha (2.80), and Peter (2.66), included in the plural ϨⲈⲚⲘⲀⲔⲀⲢⲒⲞⲤ (1.37). John, interestingly, is called ⲠⲘⲀⲔⲀⲢⲒⲞⲤ ⲀⲨⲰ ⲠⲘⲈⲢⲒⲦ (the blessed and beloved one; 2.90). James does not receive the epithet ⲘⲀⲔⲀⲢⲒⲞⲤ but is twice referenced as ⲠⲘⲈⲢⲒⲦ (the beloved; 2.68, 78). Lastly, none of the references specifically referring to Mary the mother designates her as ⲦⲘⲀⲔⲀⲢⲒⲀ, as the text does for Mary Magdalene.

Shoemaker, this reference in *Pistis Sophia* to Mary as "blessed among all generations" more likely represents the opposite evaluation of motherhood, which even the Gospel of Luke preserves: "When a woman from the crowd said to Jesus, 'Blessed is the womb that gave you birth and the breasts that nursed you.' Jesus replied, 'Blessed rather are those who hear the word of God and keep it' " (Luke 11:27–28).

The text not only points toward Mary Magdalene as "the other one" or "the blessed one," but also unquestionably designates this Mary with another epithet: ⲦⲈⲠⲚⲈⲨⲘⲀⲦⲒⲔⲎ ⲚⲌⲒⲀⲒⲔⲢⲒⲚⲈⲤ ⲘⲀⲢⲒⲀ (Maria, the pure spiritual one). This phrase occurs for the first time in the section in which ⲘⲀⲢⲒⲀ ⲦⲘⲀⲄⲆⲀⲖⲎⲚⲎ (Mary Magdalene) has just finished speaking and Jesus marvels at her answers (2.87). The text then explains the reason for his admiration: ⲈⲂⲞⲖ ⲬⲈ ⲚⲈⲀⲤⲢⲠⲚⲀ ⲦⲎⲢⲤ ⲚⲌⲒⲀⲒⲔⲢⲒⲚⲈⲤ (because she had become completely pure Spirit; 2.87). The Savior next praises her spiritual state: ⲈⲨⲄⲈ ⲦⲈⲠⲚⲈⲨⲘⲀⲦⲒⲔⲎ ⲚⲌⲒⲀⲒⲔⲢⲒⲚⲈⲤ ⲘⲀⲢⲒⲀ (excellent, Maria, the *pure spiritual one;* 2.87). In this case, the "pure spiritual" Mary is quite explicitly identified with numerous additional references that immediately follow and name her as Mary "the Magdalene" (see 2.88, 90, 94, 96, 97, 98, 99). Following this special designation as "a pure spiritual one" — specifically linked here to ⲘⲀⲢⲒⲀ ⲦⲘⲀⲄⲆⲀⲖⲎⲚⲎ — are additional references to "Mary, the spiritual one" that appear frequently thereafter, including the "all-blessed Mary — the spiritual one" (3.114), "Mary, the spiritual one of pure light" (3.116, 118), "Mary, the spiritual and pure one" (3.120), and simply "the spiritual one" (3.121, 122, 130). Once the text establishes these links between the "pure spiritual one" and Mary Magdalene, it seems logical that subsequent uses of the same phrase also refer to her. Indeed one would be hard pressed to attribute these references to Mary the mother since no explicit link between "a pure spiritual one" and Mary the mother ever appears in this text.

Thus these appositional phrases and additional epithets of Mary Magdalene significantly reduce the ambiguity of Mary's identity and add their weight to an already strong case for her prominence in the text of *Pistis Sophia* 1–3.

Mary in *Pistis Sophia* 4

Pistis Sophia 4 differs from *Pistis Sophia* 1–3 in that it seems to feature only one Mary, whose identity is more difficult to discern because there are no specific indicators or additional phrases to help specify this Mary. Interestingly, the most frequent form of the name Mary (ⲘⲀⲢⲒⲀ) in *Pistis Sophia* 1–3 (i.e., "Maria") never occurs in *Pistis Sophia* 4. Instead, every reference to the primary figure of *Pistis Sophia* 4 employs only the name ⲘⲀⲢⲒⳘⲀⳘ (Mariam), apparently referring to only one character. Although the name Mariam appears proportionately less frequently in *Pistis Sophia* 4 than in *Pistis Sophia* 1–3, it nevertheless still appears eight times (4.138,

139, 144, 145, 146, 148), a ratio of appearances significantly higher than
the names of all the other disciples in *Pistis Sophia* 4. Additionally, at least
one more reference to Mary must have existed, as the text states after a
large lacuna: "Mariam continued again and said" (4.144).[15] The use of her
name thus exceeds all other disciples (with four references to Thomas; two
to Andrew, Bartholomew, Philip, Peter, and John; and only one to James,
Simon the Canaanite, Philip, and Salome).

When scholars identify the Mary of *Pistis Sophia* 4 as Mary Magdalene, they do so primarily on the basis of literary parallels, especially to
the theme of Peter's challenging Mary. The author portrays tensions in *Pistis Sophia* 4 thus: ΠΕΧΑϤ ⲚϬΙ ΠΕΤΡΟC ΧΕ ΠΑΧΟΪC ΜΑΡΕ ΝΕ2ΙΟΜΕ 2Ⲱ ΕΡΟΟΥ
ΕΥϢΙΝΕ ΤΑⲢⲚ̄ϢΙΝΕ 2ⲰⲰⲚ· (Peter complains, "My Lord, let the *women* cease
to question, that we also may question"; 4.146). Jesus then turns to *Mary*
and the women and requests that they leave room for the CNHY Ⲛ̄2ΟΟΥΤ
(male brethren)[16] so that they may question also. Although it is possible
that Peter objects as a result of some theological differences with Mary and
the women, the instances in which references to gender occur in these controversy texts strongly support the argument that what is at stake in these
controversy scenes somehow involves gender and leadership roles.[17]

Analysis of the roles of the various disciples in *Pistis Sophia* 1–3 places
Peter in an adversarial role with respect to Mary, the blessed one, argued
here to be Mary Magdalene. In this text Peter first addresses Jesus with
these words:

ΑϤϤⲞ̄Ϥ ΕΒΟⲖ Ⲛ̄ϬΙ ΠΕΤΡΟC ΠΕΧΑϤ Ⲛ̄ΙⲤ̄ ΧΕ ΠΑΧΟΕΙC· ΤⲚ̄ΝΑϢ-ⲀΝΕΧΕ
ⲀⲚ Ⲛ̄ΤΕΪCⲀ2ΙΜΕ· ΕCΧΙ Ⲙ̄ΠΜΑ Ⲛ̄ΤΟΟΤⲚ̄· ΑΥⲰ Ⲙ̄ΠⲤ̄ΚΑ-ⲞΥΟΝ Ⲙ̄ΜΟΝ ΕϢΑΧΕ·
ⲀⲖⲖⲀ ΕCⲰ̄ⲀΧΕ Ⲛ̄2Α2 Ⲛ̄CⲞⲠ·

Peter said to Jesus, "My Lord we are not able to suffer this woman
who takes the opportunity from us and does not allow anyone of us
to speak, but she speaks many times." (1.36)

Peter's objection thus specifically refers to her being a woman.

Additional evidence of the gendered and confrontational nature of these
leadership controversies appears in the portrayal of Mary's objection to
Peter's role:

ΠΕΧΑC ΧΕ ΠΑΧΟΕΙC· ΠΑΝΟΥC ΟΥΝΟΕΡΟC ΠΕ Ⲛ̄ΟΥΟΕΙϢ ΝΙΜ ΕΤΡΑΕΙ·
ΕⲐΗ Ⲛ̄CⲞⲠ ΝΙΜ· ΤΑΤΑΥΕ-ⲠΒⲰⲖ Ⲛ̄Ⲛ̄ϢΑΧΕ ΕΝΤΑCΧΟΟΥ· ⲀⲖⲖⲀ ΕΪⲢ̄2ΟΤΕ
2ΗΤϤ Ⲙ̄ΠΕΤΡΟC ΧΕ ϢΑϤϤΑΠΙⲖΕΙ ΕΡΟΪ· ΑΥⲰ ϤΜΟCΤΕ Ⲙ̄ΠΕΝΓΕΝΟC·

---

15. A lacuna of eight pages or four leaves exists at this point in the text.

16. This reference is a good example of the author's understanding of the Coptic term CNHY
(often translated merely as "brothers") to be inclusive of both genders. Otherwise the author
would not have included the additional adjective Ⲛ̄2ΟΟΥΤ to point out that Jesus is speaking of
"male" brethren.

17. Schüssler Fiorenza, *In Memory of Her*, 305–6.

She says, "My Lord, my mind is understanding at all times that I should come forward at any time and give the interpretation of the words which she [Pistis Sophia] spoke, but I am afraid of Peter, for he threatens me and hates our kind/race." (2.72)

Scholars do not agree on the interpretation of the word ΓЄΝΟϹ, whether it refers to gender or some other type of rivalry.[18] Whatever the interpretation, it is clear that the issue is strongly contested since the passage employs the Coptic word ΜΟϹΤЄ, generally translated "hate."[19]

Another significant literary parallel, the *Gospel of Philip,* likewise portrays tension among the disciples because of the special status that Mary has within the group. This text is especially useful because it specifically identifies the Mary in the controversy scene as Mary Magdalene. The *Gospel of Philip* describes ΜΑΡΙΑ ΤΜΑΓΔΑΛΗΝΗ (Mary Magdalene) as the figure who holds a special status with respect to Jesus.[20] The text not only specifically identifies Mary Magdalene as the Mary who possesses a special status with Jesus, it also explains that this special status causes problems for some of the male disciples.[21] On a literary level, this conflict appears to be the result of some sort of jealousy on the part of the other disciples. It is difficult to determine what political or other factors could have motivated such a portrayal.

The *Gospel of Philip,* with its explicit identification of Mary Magdalene, lends strength to the identification of Mary in the controversy narratives of *Pistis Sophia* 4 as Mary Magdalene, and not Mary the mother of Jesus. This identification, based on parallel controversies, becomes more persuasive when one considers that no texts, at least to my knowledge, ever explicitly name Mary the mother of Jesus in conflict with Peter. In fact, numerous texts that feature Mary the mother portray just the opposite tendency. Texts such as the *Questions of Bartholomew* and certain Syriac works, for example, tend to portray Peter and Jesus' mother as particularly respectful to one another.

Mary the Mother in *Questions of Bartholomew*

The *Questions of Bartholomew* is one of the few ancient texts that explicitly features Mary the mother of Jesus as a primary figure in a resurrection

---

18. Marjanen, *The Woman Jesus Loved,* 180–3.

19. W. E. Crum, *A Coptic Dictionary* (Oxford: Clarendon, 1939), s.v. ΜΟϹΤЄ.

20. And the companion of the [...] Mary Magdalene [...loved] her more than [all] the disciples [and used to] kiss her [often] on her [...]. (*Gospel of Philip* §55 [111.32–37])

21. The rest of [the disciples...]. They said to him, "Why do you love her more than all of us?" The Savior answered and said to them, "Why do I not love you like her?" (*Gospel of Philip* §55 [111.36–112.5])

dialogue.[22] This text, composed in Greek, with an uncertain date between the second and sixth centuries, presents the dialogue of Mary the mother, Peter, Andrew, Bartholomew, and John and exemplifies how a text can feature a select grouping of disciples to fulfill specific roles.[23] Rhetorical analysis of this text reveals, for example, that the primary role that Mary the mother plays is as spokesperson for the authority of Peter over women. Examination of the dialogue attributed to this Mary is so rhetorically laden as to raise the possibility that the author is deliberately placing polemical or political narrative upon her lips. Among her first words in the narrative, for instance, is an acknowledgment of Peter's position in the group of the disciples: "She [Mary the mother] said to Peter, 'Peter, you chief, you great pillar, do you stand behind us? Did not our Lord say, "The head of the man is Christ [*Slav. Lat. 2* add: but the head of the woman is the man]"? Now, therefore, stand before me and pray' " (2.7). In another section Mary the mother declines the chance to speak to the Lord and asks Peter to go instead of her, addressing him with the words, "O stone hewn out of the rock, did not the Lord build his church upon you? Go first and ask him" (4.3). The author not only portrays this Mary as frequently deferring to Peter but doing so, in her own words, because he is a male "in the image of Adam" (4.5). Douglas Parrott, among others, intuits from the rhetoric of the text that the author may be using Mary the mother as a "counterpoint" or "foil" to Mary Magdalene.[24]

This examination of literary parallels includes the *Gospel of Bartholomew* because the attitude that Peter portrays in this text toward Mary, mother of Jesus, significantly differs from his interactions with the Mary of the controversy stories. For instance, Peter honors Mary the mother with the words: "You who are highly favoured, entreat the Lord to reveal to us the things that are in the heavens" (4.2). When she humbly declines, Peter tries again: "O tabernacle who are spread abroad, it behooves you to ask" (4.4). Mary's response accords women a secondary position, as she says to Peter: "You are the image of Adam; was not he first formed and then Eve?" (4.5). She goes on to describe the contrast between men and women: "Look upon the sun; according to the likeness of Adam it is bright, and upon the moon; because of the transgression of Eve it is full of clay" (4.5). Despite the way the author accords this Mary an authoritative role in this text, the result of the narrative, whether intentional or not, ultimately produces in Mary the mother a silenced purveyor of wisdom: "But Jesus appeared quickly [*Lat. 2:* and laid his hand upon her mouth] and said to Mary, 'Utter not this

---

22. For convenience, the English translation of *Questions of Bartholomew* is taken from Elliott, *Apocryphal New Testament*, 652–72. Another modern translation of this text, based on newer textual evidence, is available in Jean-Daniel Kaestli, "Questions de Barthélemy," in *Écrits apocryphes chrétiens* (Paris: Gallimard, 1997), 267–95.

23. Elliott, *Apocryphal New Testament*, 652.

24. Douglas M. Parrott, "Gnostic and Orthodox Disciples in the Second and Third Centuries," in *Nag Hammadi, Gnosticism, and Early Christianity* (ed. Charles W. Hedrick and Robert Hodgson Jr.; Peabody, Mass.: Hendrickson, 1986), 210, 211.

mystery, or this day my whole creation will come to an end. . . .' [*Lat. 2:* and the flame from her mouth ceased]. And the apostles were taken with fear lest the Lord should be angry with them" (2.22).

While this text silences the figure of Mary the mother, only three sentences later the narrative portrays Jesus as requesting his disciples to "ask me what you will that I should teach you, and I will show it to you" (3.3). Mary's role in this text is misleading because, although she has prominence as a primary actor, her role is a submissive one in which she acknowledges the authority of Peter and repeatedly defers to him. As Schüssler Fiorenza points out, however, the author may be employing Mary's words prescriptively rather than descriptively, since "ideological prescription and actual social reality do not always correspond."[25] This kind of supportive alliance between Peter and Mary, mother of Jesus, appears in other ancient texts, including Syriac and Coptic works, and diminishes the possibility that Mary the mother is the Mary figure in controversy with Peter.[26]

Conclusion

When I began working on the *Pistis Sophia* volumes, I initially believed a large proportion of the references to Mary left her identity somewhat ambiguous. I wondered why a text like *Pistis Sophia* 1–3, with at least two Marys, could not have offered more explicit identifiers and descriptions, as the *Gospel of Philip* does. After more intensive research, however, it became clear that in many subtle ways *Pistis Sophia* 1–3 does indeed provide such distinctions. It offers numerous additional distinguishing phrases, such as "the other one," "the blessed one," and "the pure spiritual one," that function as markers to help the reader identify this Mary. In each of these cases there are either explicit or implicit links to Mary Magdalene, making it quite difficult to argue instead for Mary the mother of Jesus as the primary figure in the text. If one takes into account not only the content of the explicit identifications of Mary Magdalene in the text but also the abundant implicit descriptions and epithets, one will find that the most persuasive and credible choice for the identity of the primary figure Mary in *Pistis Sophia* 1–3 is indeed Mary Magdalene. The arguments for identifying the Mary of *Pistis Sophia* 4 as Mary Magdalene are based primarily upon external criteria, especially literary parallels, and are therefore not quite as definitive as the arguments for Mary Magdalene in *Pistis Sophia* 1–3, which are based more upon internal criteria.

---

25. Schüssler Fiorenza, *In Memory of Her*, 310.

26. For more information on this dynamic, see Ann Graham Brock, *Mary Magdalene, the First Apostle: The Struggle for Authority* (Harvard Theological Studies 51; Cambridge: Harvard University Press, 2003). On the Syriac texts, see Robert Murray, *Symbols of Church and Kingdom: A Study in Early Syriac Tradition* (Cambridge: Cambridge University Press, 1975), 329–30.

Ancient texts such as *Pistis Sophia, Gospel of Philip,* and the *Gospel of Mary* preserve literary representations of prominent female figures who not only heard words of wisdom but were also instrumental in transmitting them. It is important to acknowledge that current debates concerning the identification of early Christian female leadership, especially the unspecified Marys, are more than merely scholarly exercises. They have implications for reconstructing women's role in early Christianity and female leadership within the early church. This is especially relevant with respect to Mary Magdalene, whose apostolic example has proven pivotal in the debate concerning women's ordination in many Christian congregations today.

8

High Priestesses of Asia and Emancipatory Interpretation

Steven J. Friesen

Elisabeth Schüssler Fiorenza articulates the task of feminist biblical interpretation in terms of a rhetorical-emancipatory model. This entails a change in the way we conceptualize ancient texts: "Rhetoric is aware that texts seek to persuade and to argue; they are address and debate, rather than objective statement and explanation."[1] It also involves a change in the way we envision the task of the interpreter: "Becoming a feminist interpreter means shifting your focus from biblical interpretation construed as an ever better explanation of the text to biblical interpretation as a tool for becoming conscious of structures of domination and for articulating visions of radical democracy that are inscribed in our own experience as well as in that of texts."[2]

In this essay I argue that Schüssler Fiorenza's conceptualization of text and interpreter has implications beyond the discipline of biblical hermeneutics and should be extended to the interpretation of archeological materials. I make the argument using the example of the high priestesses of Asia, who are known to us mostly from Roman imperial inscriptions. Debates have gone on for well over a century about the activities of these prominent women from malestream[3] society in the province of Asia. Does a feminist emancipatory interpretation shed light on this topic? Does it provide us with new ways to understand the persuasive character of archeological texts? Does it change our roles as interpreters of inscriptions, coins, and society? I argue that two concepts — "kyriocentrism" and "wo/men" — help us chart a more productive course in the interpretation of these materials. The first section of this essay describes some basic information about the high priestesses. After that I trace the kyriocentric history of interpretation and suggest future directions for an emancipatory engagement with the archeological materials.

---

1. Elisabeth Schüssler Fiorenza, *Wisdom Ways: Introducing Feminist Biblical Interpretation* (Maryknoll, N.Y.: Orbis, 2001), 3.
2. Ibid.
3. Malestream is a "term marking the fact that history, tradition, theology, church, culture, and society have been defined by men and have excluded wo/men"; ibid., 212.

Problems with Sources

The high priestesses of Asia came from the elite families of the province during the first three centuries of the Common Era. Their high priesthoods were part of the most prominent religious institutions of the time — the provincial imperial cults for the worship of the Roman emperors and their families. These particular provincial imperial cults were organized on a regional basis. The annual festivals included sacrifices to the Roman emperors and their families, athletic competitions, gladiatorial games, processions, and other standard features of religious celebrations.

A sizable body of data has accumulated about the elite women who served in these cults. We now have forty-four references to them from forty sources: thirty-nine inscriptions and one literary work.[4] The references mention approximately forty individual women. The exact number is uncertain because eight of the references are in generic statements about unnamed ancestors who served in these offices, and some of these could refer to more than one high priestess. Along with these eight anonymous references to ancestors are four more fragments of inscriptions that mention high priestesses of Asia with no names preserved. We are left, then, with references to twenty-eight women who can be identified by name or at least by the part of their name that is still extant.

Most of the evidence comes from texts inscribed on statue bases. The bases were rectangular stone pieces that originally supported images of various figures. Sometimes the statue portrayed the high priestess.[5] Other times it portrayed her husband,[6] her daughter,[7] her son,[8] her grandson,[9] her female benefactor,[10] or other famous figures. Along with statue bases, we also encounter references to high priestesses who contributed to building projects[11] or served as eponymous officials.[12] This information comes from the inscribed texts that were chiseled into stone and displayed in the plazas, streets, and buildings of the cities of Roman Asia.

---

4. The inscriptions and literary references can be found in the database available at web.missouri.edu/ religsf/officials.html. The database contains information on all the known references to high priestesses of Asia, high priests of Asia, and Asiarchs. I was able to build this database with support from the National Endowment for the Humanities Summer Stipend program and from the University of Missouri-Columbia Research Council.

5. For example, IGR 4.1571 was set up in Teos by the sons of Claudia Tryphaena and dedicated by the *boulē* and *dēmos* of the city in her honor.

6. CIG 2.2782 provides an example from Aphrodisias in which Flavia Appia's husband Marcus Ulpius Carminius Claudianus is honored by the *boulē, dēmos,* and *gērousia* of the city.

7. IGR 4.1571, from Teos.

8. TAM 5.2.944, from Thyatira.

9. IGR 4.1238, from Thyatira.

10. IvE 3.617 is an Ephesian inscription in which the high priestess Julia Atticilla honored her benefactor Desidiene Cincia, the wife of a Roman official.

11. Scaptia Firmilla, her husband, and her son paid for marble revetment in the Verulanus hall at Ephesus; IvE 2.430.

12. Vedia Marcia, from Ephesus; IvE 4.1017.

Twenty-eight women may seem to be an insignificant sample by the standards of modern demography, but for a historian of the Roman Empire it is a treasure trove of information. In spite of the amount of the data, however, quite a bit of confusion persists in discussions about the high priestesses of Asia. The debated topics include whether high priestesses actually participated in the provincial imperial cult rituals or merely held an honorary title; whether women could serve in cults for the male emperors or only in cults for female members of the imperial family; and whether high priestesses could serve in rituals without a male relative.

There are three main reasons for this confusion. One is that our evidence about the high priestesses is fragmentary; we know of only a small percentage of these women, and we have no surviving texts with overt descriptions of their responsibilities as high priestesses of Asia. But that is to be expected in historical investigation. We never have all the evidence.

The second reason for confusion is the debate about whether Asiarch was simply an alternative title for high priest of Asia, or whether Asiarch designated an office that was distinct from the office of high priest of Asia. I will return to this question below. At this point, I need to note only that some confusion in the secondary literature is due to arguments about the definition of the office of Asiarch because several high priestesses are known to have been married to Asiarchs. If Asiarch was another title for high priest of Asia, then all the sources about Asiarchs add to our information about the families of high priestesses. As long as the nature of the male office of Asiarch is debated, however, it clouds our interpretation of high priestesses of Asia.

The third source of confusion is one that is of particular interest in this context. Until the 1980s interpreters focused almost exclusively on the high priests and the male Asiarchs. In order to deal with the high priestesses of Asia, we must first contend with this malestream history of interpretation in which the lives of ancient women are normally considered important only if they provide information about the lives of ancient men. This history of interpretation is the main subject of the next section.

Kyriocentrisms, Ancient and Modern

It is no great revelation to observe that Roman imperial society was patriarchal. For the purposes of discussing elite women such as those who served as high priestesses in the imperial cults of Asia, however, patriarchy is a limiting concept. When domination is cast primarily as a question of gender, there is little room in our analysis for these elite women of antiquity. What shall we make of them?

Schüssler Fiorenza advocates kyriocentrism as an analytical tool for the analysis of society. The term describes a system of domination that is gendered but is not determined solely by gender. It defines normal society as a setting in which a variety of oppressive practices are exercised on the basis of several factors, including gender, wealth, class, race, etc. In the view of Schüssler Fiorenza, patriarchy places too much emphasis on oppression according to gender, which is a crucial determinant but not the only one. Kyriocentrism, on the other hand, helps us articulate a more complex analysis that recognizes that some women are involved in the perpetration of oppression and that some men are the victims of oppression. The fact that high priestesses of Asia were oppressors does not obviate the need for us to recognize that they were nevertheless subject to rules and practices that did not apply to their male counterparts.[13] The concept of kyriocentrism enables us to affirm these ambiguities as part and parcel of the "cultural-religious-ideological systems and intersecting discourses of race, gender, heterosexuality, class, and ethnicity that produce, legitimate, inculcate, and sustain kyriarchy."[14]

Kyriocentrism is useful not only for the description of ancient society, however. The concept also helps us see the gendered biases of modern interpretation of the ancient high priestesses. The interpretation of inscriptions and other archeological artifacts is often presented as though it were an objective, neutral enterprise that is concerned only with "the facts." A brief sketch of malestream interpretation during the last century and a half suggests otherwise. The "objective" description of the "evidence" actually drew attention away from ancient kyriocentrism while simultaneously promulgating modern forms of kyriocentrism.

The most prominent early interpreter of the high priesthoods of Asia was Theodor Mommsen. Mommsen published some notes on these offices as early as the 1850s, but his most accessible handling of the topic is now found in his *Die Provinzen, von Caesar bis Diocletian* (1885). Mommsen discussed the high priesthoods in his chapter on Asia Minor by proposing an odd hypothesis about the relationship between the titles high priest and Asiarch. He began with the assumption that the Asiarchs were the leaders of Asia's *koinon*.[15] While the high priests were responsible for the province's worship of the emperors, according to Mommsen the Asiarchs assumed responsibility for the associated festival and games. When Asia received a second provincial temple and another set of games, Mommsen assumed (without any evidence) that all the high priests of Asia were now called Asiarchs and that the civil responsibilities of the office receded. In this discussion, Mommsen devoted a part of one sentence to high priestesses, in which he assumed that high priestesses were all married to high priests. Mommsen's

---

13. Schüssler Fiorenza, *Wisdom Ways*, 117–24.
14. Ibid., 211.
15. This particular assumption is still popular, but the rest of his hypothesis is not. For a critique of the prevailing view, see Steven J. Friesen, "Asiarchs," *Zeitschrift für Papyrologie und Epigraphik* 126 (1999): 275–90.

point was that the male official no longer had governmental functions, so the wife could now participate fully in her husband's office.[16]

In 1872, I. Marquardt set out to update Mommsen's early work on provincial high priesthoods because the discovery and interpretation of Roman imperial inscriptions was accelerating rapidly in the second half of the nineteenth century and there were newly discovered texts to consider. Marquardt's study includes at least three major problems regarding the role of women in the provincial high priesthoods of Asia. First, he accepted Mommsen's assumption that women served only as a part of a married couple. Second, Marquardt followed the general trend of discussing high priestesses only if this concept clarified some issue about the activities of men. Third, Marquardt argued that high priestesses served only in provincial cults for wives of the emperors and suggested that this might have begun with the divinization of Augustus's wife Livia in 41 C.E.[17]

In 1885, Paul Monceaux revisited the question about the high priestess of Asia. His goal was the same as most interpreters — to understand the male officials — but he came to a somewhat different conclusion about the possibilities for women's involvement in public. Monceaux agreed with Mommsen that the provincial imperial cult included athletic competitions only once in a four-year cycle. When such a competition was involved, the high priest of Asia also functioned as the agonothete who sponsored the games, and he was given the title Asiarch.[18] For Monceaux, this explained why women were never called Asiarchs: they were not allowed to lead athletic competitions, so when their husband was an Asiarch, they were still called only high priestess of Asia.[19]

Five years later, E. Beurlier demolished Monceaux's argument about athletic competitions by showing that many inscriptions referred to women sponsoring games in various cults.[20] He also showed the flaw in Marquardt's argument that high priestesses led rituals only for divinized wives of emperors.[21] Beurlier asserted instead that women actually served in the provincial cults and that they did so in cults for emperors. He did not, however, question whether a woman could serve without her husband, nor did he show much interest in describing women's roles in these cults beyond what this

---

16. Theodor Mommsen, *The Provinces of the Roman Empire from Caesar to Diocletian* (trans. William P. Dickson; orig. 1887; repr. Chicago: Ares, 1974), 345–49.

17. I. Marquardt, "De provinciarum romanarum conciliis et sacerdotibus," *Ephemeris Epigraphica* 1 (1872): 200–14. This last argument was based on inscriptions from Hispania Citerior, and he assumed that the roles of women in public religion would be standard across the many provinces of the empire. In other words, evidence from the Iberian peninsula was used as evidence regarding high priestesses of Asia.

18. Specialists tend not to support this opinion any longer.

19. Paul Monceaux, *De communi Asiae provinciae (Koinon Asias)* (Paris: Thorin, 1885), 55–56.

20. E. Beurlier, *Essai sur le culte rendu aux empereurs romains* (Paris: Thorin, 1890), 127–28.

21. Ibid., 152–53.

might reveal about the men. His chapter on the high priesthoods is called "Les prêtres provinciaux" (The provincial priests), which leaves little conceptual space to consider the activities of women. The chapter is thirty-four pages long, and about a page and a half deals with high priestesses. So the amount of discussion regarding female officials is greater than the average, but the purpose of discussing the women at all was to develop an argument about the men (the high priests and the Asiarchs).

One year later, in 1891, something astonishing happened: Pierre Paris published a book about women in Asia Minor. The results, however, were not so astonishing. Paris dealt with a range of offices in the region. Regarding the high priestesses of Asia, he concluded that they would not have held governmental positions, but they did participate in the sacrificial rituals for the emperors and participated with their husbands in sponsoring competitions.[22]

So, as the nineteenth century drew to a close, a consensus about provincial high priestesses was taking shape: they normally served in the high priesthoods of Asia only with their husbands and had fewer duties than did their husbands. Within the space of twelve years, however, three important studies disagreed with the emerging consensus. At the end of his lengthy Pauly-Wissowa article "'Αρχιερεύς," C. Brandis asserted that high priestesses could fulfill any function of a high priest of Asia and that they did not always serve with their husbands.[23] Brandis did not argue for his point; he simply stated it as a postscript in the concluding sentence of his article. It was apparently enough, however, to convince Victor Chapot, who agreed — with similar brevity — that women could serve independently as high priestesses of Asia.[24] J. Toutain was also convinced, but distinguished himself by devoting several pages to the topic.[25] Citing extensive epigraphic evidence, he observed that it was a grave error to conclude that provincial high priestesses served only with their husbands.[26]

This history of interpretation in the late nineteenth and early twentieth centuries is hardly edifying (and it gets worse). I think it is instructive nevertheless. The review of important interpreters makes several points: modern "objective" scholars showed little interest in the roles played in public by ancient women; when high priestesses were discussed it was usually done for the purpose of proving something about high priests; and, many conclusions (both good and bad) were made on the basis of little or no evidence.

---

22. Pierre Paris, *Quatenus feminae res publicas in Asia Minore, Romanis imperantibus, attigerint* (Paris: Thorin, 1891), 112–13.

23. C. Brandis, "'Αρχιερεύς," in *Paulys Realencyclopädie der classischen Altertumswissenschaft* (ed. G. Wissowa; Stuggart: Metzler, 1896), 2.471–83.

24. Victor Chapot, *La province romaine proconsulaire d'Asie depuis ses origines jusqu'a la fin du haut-empire* (Paris: Bouillon, 1904), 470.

25. J. Toutain, *Les cultes païens dans l'empire romain* (Paris: Leroux, 1907), 141–69.

26. Ibid., 167.

These observations raise important issues about the ethics of archeological interpretation, for there is a cultivated aura of neutrality to this sort of discussion: specialists with classical training examine ancient stones and argue about correct answers. My review of the results, however, suggests that these scholarly discussions were far from neutral. One effect of the work of these scholars was to focus modern attention on elite men of the Roman imperial period and thereby to marginalize discussion of all the other inhabitants of the Roman Empire.

The mid-twentieth century interpretation of the high priestesses of Asia was not an improvement. David Magie's monumental two-volume work on Asia Minor is full of insight on many subjects and normally displays good sense and caution. On the topic of high priestesses (whom he calls "Chief Priestesses"), however, it is seriously deficient. The sum total of his analysis is this one sentence: "From the middle of the first century onward, the Chief Priest's wife enjoyed the privilege of being called Chief Priestess."[27] Many scholars take this to mean that Magie supported the "honorary high priestess" view; that is, the view that high priestesses had no actual duties but received the honorary title simply for being married to a high priest of Asia. The sentence might imply this, but the statement is brief and imprecise.

Jürgen Deininger was one of the most influential interpreters in the mid-twentieth century on the topic of the organization of Roman imperial provinces. On the subject of provincial high priestesses, however, his monograph is one of the worst contributions published to date. Fortunately, he devoted only a paragraph to the topic, but in this one paragraph he managed to introduce a new level of confusion into the discussion. Deininger noted that the epigraphic evidence is fragmentary and so we do not know whether all high priestesses were married to high priests. He then noted what he considered to be the most important observation on the topic: in no case can we prove that a provincial high priestess was not married to a provincial high priest.[28] This is an exceedingly strange criterion to impose on inscriptional evidence, because it is literally impossible to prove that a wealthy man (the only sort of male that appears in these inscriptions) was not a high priest. The epigraphic record is incomplete, and no inscription ever notes that someone did not hold an office. Moreover, Deininger asked the wrong question for his stated purposes. If one wants to examine what high priestesses did, one ought to ask about their activities. Instead, he asked whether it could be proved that they were not married, which is also impossible to prove in many cases.

---

27. David Magie, *Roman Rule in Asia Minor to the End of the Third Century after Christ* (Princeton: Princeton University Press, 1950), 1.449. Magie also includes a list of the twenty-one high priestesses known to him in the mid-twentieth century.

28. Jürgen Deininger, *Die Provinziallandtage der römischen Kaiserzeit von Augustus bis zum Ende des dritten Jahrhunderts n. Chr.* (Vestigia 6; Munich: Beck, 1965), 154.

In 1974 Margarete Rossner, the first woman to comment in print on the high priestesses of Asia, published an extensive and helpful catalogue of references to high priests of Asia, high priestesses of Asia, and Asiarchs that were known up to that time.[29] Like her male predecessors, Rossner was interested in the male officials and not the high priestesses, and so she entitled her article "Asiarchen und Archiereis Asias." Like most of her predecessors she also concluded that high priest of Asia and Asiarch were two titles for the same office. To the topic of high priestesses of Asia she devoted a mere paragraph. In that paragraph she took up Deininger's misbegotten argument and developed it: since no high priestess cannot be proved not to have been the wife of a high priest, we must conclude that only wives were high priestesses![30] The triple negative should have aroused suspicions among colleagues, but few questioned her conclusions. Thus, the first female to publish on the topic of provincial high priestesses prolonged the modern kyriocentric interpretation of an ancient kyriocentric institution.

Feminist Interpretation Makes a Dent in the Discourse

In the 1980s the arguments of feminists in several academic disciplines finally began to have an effect on descriptions of the high priestesses of Asia. Rosalinde Kearsley realized that a circular argument was at work in the secondary literature. The questionable logic runs like this: the fact that high priestesses were sometimes married to Asiarchs and sometimes to high priests of Asia proves that the two male titles refer to the same office; the "fact" that the two male titles are equivalent proves that the women served only with men; and the "fact" that the women served only with men proves that the two male titles refer to the same office. Laid out in stark terms like this, the argument looks ridiculous: a conclusion justifies the argument that originally led to the conclusion, and all of it is based on questionable observations and unverifiable assumptions about the roles of women in the Roman Empire. The argument is usually affirmed, nevertheless, because a disciplinary discourse validates this particular interpretation as a reasonable explanation of a body of admittedly difficult evidence.

How does one break into a circular argument like this? Kearsley first attacked the idea that high priestesses served only with their husbands.[31] She called attention to the special pleading in studies of the topic and pointed out several problems that are generally ignored or dismissed by specialists: high priestesses of Asia whose husbands are not attested as high priests

---

29. Margarete Rossner, "Asiarchen und Archiereis Asias," *Studii clasice* 16 (1974): 101–42.
30. Ibid., 102.
31. R. A. Kearsley, "Asiarchs, *Archiereis*, and the *Archiereiai* of Asia," *Greek, Roman, and Byzantine Studies* 27 (1986): 183–92.

of Asia; high priestesses who served more often than their husbands; and high priestesses who are honored in inscriptions without their husbands. In later articles Kearsley tried to break the circular logic of the general consensus by questioning the identification of the titles Asiarch and high priest of Asia.[32] Here she examined the careers of specific individuals and families, raised questions about discrepancies in titles, and pointed out the sheer absurdity of assuming that there were two titles — Asiarch and high priest of Asia — for the same office in Roman Asia. Kearsley's specific arguments and counterproposals were not well received,[33] but she raised several important problems of interpretation that had been conveniently neglected by earlier commentators, and she began to shift the focus of the discussion about high priestesses toward the high priestesses themselves.

My own entrance into this debate came in 1993 while I was working on a case study of the provincial imperial cult temple built in Ephesus during the reign of Domitian. In the course of the study I came upon this bewildering array of assumptions and circular arguments about Asiarchs, high priests, and high priestesses. In that context, I attempted to establish that high priestesses of Asia did indeed participate in provincial imperial cult rituals and called attention to an inscription in honor of Juliane, the first woman to serve in this function.[34] Her service, which was probably the first instance of a provincial high priestess anywhere in the empire, can be dated to the second quarter of the first century C.E. I did not overtly question whether high priestesses of Asia needed to be married to provincial high priests.

The next year an exceptionally well-documented study appeared. In 1994 Maria Campanile published a new catalogue of the known references to high priests of Asia, high priestesses of Asia, and Asiarchs. As a successor to Rossner's catalogue, Campanile's book is an extremely useful resource. The analysis of women's roles, however, was brief and cautious. Campanile tentatively sided with the traditional line of interpretation that high priestesses of Asia served together only with men. She responded to Kearsley's objection that some high priestesses served more often than their husbands

---

32. See R. A. Kearsley, "M. Ulpius Appuleius Eurykles of Aezani: Panhellene, Asiarch and Archiereus of Asia," *Antichthon* 21 (1987): 49–56; idem, "Some Asiarchs of Ephesos," in *New Documents Illustrating Early Christianity* (ed. G. H. R. Horsley; Sydney: Macquarie University, Ancient History Documentary Research Centre, 1987), 46–55; idem, "A Leading Family of Cibyra and Some Asiarchs of the First Century," *Anatolian Studies* 38 (1988): 43–51; and idem, "Asiarchs, Archiereis and Archiereiai of Asia: New Evidence from Amorium in Phrygia," *Epigraphica Anatolica* 16 (1990): 69–80.

33. For critiques of Kearsley's technical arguments, see Steven J. Friesen, *Twice Neokoros: Ephesus, Asia, and the Cult of the Flavian Imperial Family* (Études préliminaires aux religions orientales dans l'empire romain 116; Leiden: Brill, 1993), 84–85 n. 45, 88 n. 61, 102 n. 124, 111–12, 215–17; Michael Wörrle, "Neue Inschriftenfunde aus Aizanoi I," *Chiron* 22 (1992): 368–70; and Riet van Bremen, *The Limits of Participation: Women and Civic Life in the Greek East in the Hellenistic and Roman Periods* (Amsterdam: Gieben, 1996), 119–20.

34. Friesen, *Twice Neokoros*, 81–92.

by pleading special circumstances: perhaps these women inherited the titles from their mothers, or perhaps they served with husbands in a previous marriage.[35] While the second explanation might be possible, the first one is highly unlikely — and neither of them accounts for all the evidence.

The publication of Riet van Bremen's *Limits of Participation* in 1996 signaled a significant step forward in the discussions of the provincial high priesthoods of Asia and for the evaluation of women in public in the Greco-Roman world. The book does not simply evaluate a particular office or province. Instead, Bremen attempted to chart the broad evolution of the roles played by women in public offices in the eastern Mediterranean from the Hellenistic through the Roman imperial periods. Her arguments integrated epigraphic, numismatic, legal, and literary materials in a way that is both creative and judicious.

The gist of Bremen's argument is this. Everyone agrees that women became more prominent in the public record in the eastern Mediterranean during the Roman imperial period. The crucial question is how to account for this new prominence. Bremen rejected the idea that the public prominence of women was some form of liberation (contra Kearsley and others). Rather, Bremen accounted for the prominence of elite women in the public record by noting that these women of the imperial period were almost always portrayed as part of a married couple. This was apparently a new feature in discursive statements about gender in the Roman world. In the Hellenistic period, women had been honored as benefactors (in lesser numbers), but they did not appear as "the wife" in this period because the ideology of the married couple in service of the empire had not yet taken shape. In the Roman period, dynastic politics from the imperial center caused these local Hellenistic practices to develop in such a way that local aristocracies increasingly involved elite couples in public service, and women were increasingly portrayed as wives. According to Bremen, therefore, the prominence of women like the high priestesses of Asia was not due to emancipation from gendered restrictions; it was in fact a form of entrapment that restricted elite women to the role of the virtuous wife.[36]

Bremen's work took feminist interpretation of Roman imperial society to a new level by raising issues of imperial domination and by questioning the assumption that the appearance of women in the public record is equivalent to emancipation. A particularly important insight is her critique of modern, individualistic assumptions about power that are unconsciously imposed on the ancient world. Rather than settling for an evaluation of what individual women could "accomplish" in the Roman world, Bremen examined the overlapping and interlocking discursive systems of family, city, province,

---

35. Maria Domitilla Campanile, *I sacerdoti del koinon d'Asia (I sec. a.C.-III sec. d.C.): Contributo allo studio della romanizzazione delle élites provinciali nell'oriente greco* (Pisa: Giardini, 1994), 22–24.

36. For a summary of Bremen's thesis, see *Limits of Participation*, 115–20, 298–302.

and empire.[37] Thus, Bremen engaged in an examination of the structures of domination and explored gender issues in that context.

Provincial high priestesses played a crucial role in Bremen's argument because imperial cults seem to have been the first place where such joint office-holding of husband and wife occurred, making these cults the locus where the ideology of the married couple was first articulated. But is her conclusion about provincial high priestesses appearing primarily in couples correct? It is based on a testable axiom: "Since the great majority of *archiereiai* [high priestesses] we know of were the wives of the *archiereis* [high priests] with whom they held office, it is perfectly safe to say that this must have been the norm."[38] We can use the available evidence for Asia to see if this crucial point is valid.[39] Was it the case in Asia that the great majority of provincial high priestesses were married to high priests of Asia?

When we test this axiom, the larger thesis begins to unravel.[40] Two arguments are sufficient to dispel the idea that high priestesses normally served with their husbands. For the first argument, let us assume for the moment that Asiarch and high priest of Asia were equivalent titles. With this assumption in place, from the ancient evidence we can identify thirty-one couples where both spouses are known to us and where at least one spouse held the title Asiarch, high priest of Asia, or high priestess of Asia. Since we have evidence for both spouses in these cases, these thirty-one couples should fit the axiom. Of these thirty-one couples, however, only sixteen (or 52%) conform to the axiom. The fifteen couples who do not fit the theory include twelve couples where one spouse was listed with no provincial titles and three couples where husband and wife were listed with different numbers of terms of service. Therefore, in order for this theory to work 48% of the evidence has to be suppressed.[41]

We can push the issue further with a second argument that undermines the theory that the titles Asiarch and high priest of Asia were identical. If successful, this argument radically changes our perspective on the data about high priestesses of Asia. This second argument compares the office-holding pattern of wives of Asiarchs and the office-holding pattern of wives

---

37. Ibid., 45–46.

38. Ibid., 118–19.

39. The quotation from Bremen addresses a situation broader than the province of Asia, for other provinces had provincial high priestesses and high priests and offices similar to the Asiarchate. We can use Asia as a test case, however, because Asia is the only province for which we have a sizable amount of evidence and because conclusions about other provinces are usually based on comparisons with Asia.

40. For details regarding the statistics used in this paragraph, see Friesen, "Asiarchs," esp. 277–78.

41. Bremen appeals to an argument from silence here: the lost inscriptions would fill in the gaps in favor of her theory; *Limits of Participation,* 128–29. However, since half of the known examples do not fit the theory, it is equally probable that the lost inscriptions would invalidate the theory. Moreover, by selecting thirty-one couples for whom we have data, the appeal to lost data is irrelevant.

of high priests. If Asiarch and high priest of Asia are two titles for the same office, then the wives of these men should exhibit the same pattern of service as high priestesses of Asia, but this is not the case. From the hundreds of ancient sources we can identify sixteen wives of Asiarchs. Half (eight) of these Asiarch wives are not recorded with any provincial titles, and three more were high priestesses of Asia with a different number of terms of service than their husbands. This means that eleven of the sixteen known wives of Asiarchs (69%) do not fit the imperial-couple model proposed by Bremen. This is in striking contrast to the figures for wives of high priests of Asia. We can identify fourteen wives of high priests of Asia, eleven of whom fit the imperial couple model (i.e., only 21% of the examples are exceptions).[42] The office-holding patterns for wives of Asiarchs and for wives of high priests of Asia are so different that we have to conclude that the two male offices were not identical (i.e., Asiarch was not equivalent to high priest of Asia). Therefore, high priestesses who were married to Asiarchs did not serve only as part of a married couple. This means that only eleven of the forty known high priestesses of Asia can be shown to have served the same number of provincial high priesthoods as their husbands, and even these eleven examples are dubious evidence for couples serving together. Since eight wives of Asiarchs appear to have served without their husbands, the mere fact that eleven wives of high priests served *the same number of times* as their husbands does not mean that they served *with* their husbands in these offices.

What do these considerations allow us to say about the high priestesses of Asia? Let me suggest three conclusions. First, the idea that high priestesses of Asia served only with their husbands cannot be supported on the basis of evidence from the ancient world. We should not discard Bremen's argument about the ideology of the couple in the Roman world, for there is a good deal of evidence for some developments along these lines. But it is not safe to say that the normal pattern for wealthy Asian women was to serve as high priestesses in the provincial imperial cults with their husbands.

Second, the general direction pioneered by Bremen is profitable. Interpretation of the ancient world needs to take into account not only ancient individuals or simply empires, but also families and community institutions. Moreover, the overlap of these sectors of malestream society needs to be made explicit if we are to move beyond simple generalizations to nuanced appraisals of gender and domination. Such nuanced appraisals will need to follow Bremen's lead in focusing on families and wealth as significant indicators of power, but should be expanded using concepts like kyriocentrism as a heuristic method.

---

42. Two wives had no provincial titles, and one wife had a different number of terms of service than her husband.

Third, a convincing feminist interpretation of ancient materials needs as extensive a grounding as possible in the ancient evidence. This should not, however, be understood in positivistic terms. The inscriptions are not simply objective facts that, once gathered and counted, will give us the correct answer. The inscriptions are persuasive texts, previously embedded in ancient discourses of religion, politics, and domination but now resituated in modern discourses of gendered academic knowledge and political power. Any modern attempt to use the inscriptions constitutes a hermeneutic endeavor that has ethical consequences in the contemporary world of the interpreter.[43] It is to these ethical issues that I turn in the final section of the essay.

Wanted: An Emancipatory Rhetoric

A good deal of this essay is devoted to the history of interpretation. The reason for this strategy on my part is to suggest that the seemingly antiseptic sterility of epigraphic interpretation is actually fraught with ideological biases and ethical consequences. In much of the secondary literature and especially in the older writers, we find that the interpretation of provincial high priesthoods has had a deleterious effect on women. By focusing almost exclusively on the male officials, scholars reinscribed ancient kyriocentrism into their monographs. Readers were led to believe that the aristocratic men of old were the only topic worthy of consideration and that ancient women were primarily a resource for explaining the lives of men. Readers also were led to believe that only modern men had insights on such issues since they were (until recently) the only ones deemed worthy to publish on the topics.

We have seen that there was also an intermittent minority opinion in the secondary literature regarding high priestesses of Asia that sought to grant these ancient women more individual agency. This minority perspective appeared in underdeveloped form in the early twentieth century and reappeared in more vigorous forms late in the century. In my opinion this minority view was more helpful than that of the majority, because the minority view was more consonant with the extant evidence and because it was usually intent on promoting a more democratic vision of human communities. These writers, however, seldom made overt claims about the implications of their work for modern society because such "application" is defined as irrelevant to academic discourse. Nevertheless, the suggestion was often implicit in these writings that there should be more equality between men and

---

43. Schüssler Fiorenza expresses it this way (*Wisdom Ways,* 184): "All three phases of historiography — documentary research, explanation, and writing — must be rooted in a hermeneutics of suspicion, critical evaluation, and historical imagination. Historical understanding depends on analogy. It is narrative-laden and amounts to a remaking and retelling of reality; it is not reality itself nor a record of what actually happened. History and memory of the past always imbricate imagination and are imbricated by it."

women, even though the scholars did not advocate visions of radical democracy (with which this essay began). So we are left with one final question: is there a place for an emancipatory rhetoric in the study of ancient societies beyond the discipline of biblical studies?

A strategy of Schüssler Fiorenza might help us here. Her neologism *wo/men* might introduce a more profound level of insight into such discussions. She coined the term

> to indicate that the category "wo/man-wo/men" is a social construct. Wo/men are not a unitary social group but are fragmented by structures of race, class, ethnicity, religion, sexuality, colonialism, and age. This destabilization of the term "wo/men" underscores the differences between wo/men and within individual wo/men. This writing is inclusive of subaltern men who in kyriarchal systems are seen "as wo/men" and functions as a linguistic corrective to androcentric language use.[44]

By incorporating the term *wo/men* into discussions of Asia's provincial high priesthoods, we are constantly reminded of issues of wealth and class, issues that are mostly ignored in the secondary literature on high priestesses of Asia. Most of the secondary literature does not mention — let alone reflect on — the fact that the Asiarchs, the high priests of Asia, and the high priestesses of Asia all came from the wealthiest 1% of the inhabitants of the Roman Empire. By and large, the secondary literature discusses these officeholders as though they were in some way representative of the population, when in fact these ancient officials were crucial players in the structures of Roman domination.

A thorough discussion of the elite wo/men who served as high priestesses of Asia has not yet been undertaken. Such an emancipatory project could have a salutary effect in at least three ways. First, it would develop Bremen's insights into a more complex mode by raising even broader questions about the alleged liberation of wo/men in the Roman Empire. Bremen argued that the high priestesses were constrained into ideologies of marriage and family that were ultimately antithetical to the interests of those high priestesses. Schüssler Fiorenza's emancipatory rhetoric complicates the issues by portraying those same constrained wo/men as occupying the ambiguous position of oppressed oppressors, caught in the gendered machinations of aristocratic family politics while they also participated in the economic, political, and religious institutions that exploited the vast majority of the population. In this way, a discussion of Asia's high priestesses becomes a multidimensional discussion of the use and abuse of power.

A second salutary effect of an emancipatory rhetoric would be a shift in our focus from the wealthy fraction of the ancient population to the impoverished majority who could not endow monumental inscriptions for

---

44. Ibid., 216.

us to decipher. The standard scholarly practice in the academy has been too restricted to include them in our deliberations. We tend to read the inscription and perhaps even consider the statue atop the inscribed base without thinking about its ancient urban context. An emancipatory rhetoric challenges us to lower our gaze from the statue, to glance around the base, and to consider those whose labor and lives are implied by the monument but whose voices have been silenced by the dominion of wealth, class, and gender. An emancipatory rhetoric forces us to think about the masons who quarried the stone for a pittance, the day laborers who moved the finished product into place in order to keep their relatives from starvation, and the wo/men who struggled to sustain their families on such meager earnings. An emancipatory rhetoric requires that we supplement our studies of the aristocracy's artistic creations with an examination of the male and female wo/men passing by on the ancient boulevards, wo/men who were usually illiterate so they could not read the inscription and who were probably too tired to glance up at the statue overhead.

Third, an emancipatory rhetoric might help us use the study of archeological materials as a way to reflect on our own academic practices. After all, the wo/men of the Roman Empire lived in a world not unlike our own, where the underpaid work of the majority supported the lifestyles of the rich and famous. Will the academy continue to indulge in such kyriocentrism? Or will we find a way to address the concerns of the wo/men whose sacrifices are the prerequisite and foundation of effective domination?

Part 3

Rhetoric and Ethic: The Practice of Interpretation

9

The Landscape of Promise in the *Apocalypse of Paul*

Ellen Bradshaw Aitken

Depictions of landscape, real and imagined, pervaded the cultural and esthetic world of the Roman Empire. Landscape painting, favored in the
so-called Third Style of Roman wall painting, flourished in the Augustan
period and became part of the repertoire of generic types of wall painting
in the succeeding centuries.[1] Literary *ekphrasis* of landscape was itself an
art practiced by a wide range of Hellenistic and Roman authors to bring a
variety of natural scenes before their readers' eyes. Such depictions, whether
in the visual arts or the rhetorical arts, served not only decorative ends but
also political and ethical purposes inasmuch as they located the human and
human endeavor in relation to natural, idyllic, mythic, and sacral landscapes.

The third-century *Apocalypse of Paul* is notable among early Christian
apocalypses for its depiction of landscape, especially the landscape of the
land of promise in chapters 21–31, as part of the tour of heaven and hell
provided for the apostle Paul in this text.[2] Although the *Apocalypse of Paul*
most likely relies upon earlier apocalyptic literature such as the *Apocalypse*

---

1. I offer this essay with gratitude to Elisabeth Schüssler Fiorenza for many years of collegial
instruction, guidance, and friendship, as well as for her profound shaping of the landscape of
scholarship. Her insistence on the "visionary rhetoric" of the Apocalypse of John and on the
necessity of approaching it as a work of art (*Revelation: Vision of a Just World* [Proclamation
Commentaries; Minneapolis: Fortress, 1991], 32) inspires this offering in her honor. I also
thank the members of the 2001–2002 workshop on "Landscape and Memory," sponsored by
the Ford Foundation and organized in the Department of the Classics, Harvard University, for
their comments on a preliminary version of the ideas developed here.

2. For an English translation of the *Apocalypse of Paul*, see Hugo Duensing and Au-
relio de Santos Otero, "The Apocalypse of Paul," in *New Testament Apocrypha,* vol. 2:
Writings Relating to Apostles, Apocalypses, and Related Subjects (ed. Edgar Hennecke and
Wilhelm Schneemelcher; trans. R. M. Wilson; rev. ed.; Louisville: Westminster/John Knox,
1992), 712–48. The original Greek text survives in greatly abbreviated form; see Konstantin
von Tischendorf, *Apocalypses Apocryphae Mosis, Esdrae, Pauli, Iohannis item Mariae dormitio* (Leipzig: Mendelssohn, 1866), 34–69. The Latin recensions, together with versions in
Syriac, Coptic, Slavonic, Armenian, Ethiopic, Arabic, Spanish, Old English, and Old High
German, form the basis of our knowledge of the text. Of these, the Latin provides the most
complete form of the text; see Theodore Silverstein and Anthony Hilhorst, *Apocalypse of Paul:
A New Critical Edition of the Three Long Latin Versions* (Cahiers d'orientalisme 21; Geneva:

of Zephaniah and the *Apocalypse of Peter* for much of its scheme and many of its conventions,[3] it differs from earlier apocalypses in its attention to landscape alongside the cityscape of the heavenly city.[4] It is my purpose in this essay therefore to examine the depiction of landscape in the *Apocalypse of Paul* in the context of the literary and visual world of Roman landscapes. I argue that the depiction of landscape in this text forms part of the rhetorical strategy for inculcating the ethical stances advocated. It does so, I suggest, by its appeal to the imagination and by constructing a map for remembering scriptural traditions associated with a covenantal ethic. Informed by studies of Roman landscape, I ask in what ways and to what ends landscape features are present in this text. Landscape and memory are closely tied in Roman and Hellenistic rhetorical habits; thus I inquire into ways in which particular landscape features, as presented in the text, provoke memories and are in turn informed by those memories.[5] Finally, I ask how landscape functions rhetorically to ground the message of the text and to evoke a desire for virtue over vice.

To anticipate my conclusions, I propose that, corresponding to Roman conventions of "sacral-idyllic" and mythological landscapes, the *Apocalypse of Paul* creates a landscape rich in allusion to Scripture and ritual. In doing so, I emphasize the ways in which this text belongs to the Roman world and utilizes some of its strategies for instilling *pietas* and virtue. Much of the scholarship on the *Apocalypse of Paul* takes up questions of source criticism, apocalyptic genre, and reception history. Such work does not address how the text functions to communicate with an audience and to persuade an audience to certain attitudes and actions. The examination of the text in this essay goes in a different direction, that is, to investigate an aspect of the text's rhetoric and its persuasive strategy, an aspect that may indeed account for some of the text's popularity in later centuries.[6] This approach results in

---

Cramer, 1997), which supplements Silverstein's earlier edition, *Visio Sancti Pauli: The History of the Apocalypse in Latin, Together with Nine Texts* (Studies and Documents 4; London: Christophers, 1935). For a discussion of the manuscript traditions, see Pierluigi Piovanelli, "Les origines de l'*Apocalypse de Paul* reconsidérées," *Apocrypha* 4 (1993): 25–64; and Silverstein and Hilhorst, *Apocalypse of Paul*, 11–21. These questions are not, however, central to the present investigation. The dating of the text is also problematic, ranging from the early third to the mid-fourth century; for the purposes of my argument here it is not necessary to establish a more precise date.

3. Martha Himmelfarb, *Tours of Hell: An Apocalyptic Form in Jewish and Christian Literature* (Philadelphia: Fortress, 1985), 16–17, 140–51; see also idem, "The Experience of the Visionary and Genre in the *Ascension of Isaiah* 6–11 and the *Apocalypse of Paul*," *Semeia* 36 (1986): 97–111.

4. Himmelfarb, *Tours of Hell*, 147.

5. Simon Schama (*Landscape and Memory* [New York: Knopf, 1995], 14) writes that his exploration of the literary, artistic, and horticultural landscapes of modern Europe is "constructed as an excavation below our conventional sight level to recover the veins of myth and memory that lie beneath the surface."

6. Although Himmelfarb (*Tours of Hell*, 16) refers to the *Apocalypse of Paul* as "the longest lived and most influential of the tours of hell," it is important to note that its influence and popularity included the tours of heaven and paradise. See Piovanelli, "Les origines de l'*Apocalypse*

emphasizing what the text does, namely, how it motivates toward what it regards as the good and creates aversion to vice. It thus locates the rhetoric of the text in the ethical realm, rather than seeing it as concerned primarily with a theological problem. In other words, the deployment of landscape in the *Apocalypse of Paul* helps us to see that this is a text less about the future or present "fate of the dead"[7] and more about shaping the orientations and commitments of the Christian community in this life.

Recent studies of Roman landscape painting focus not only on matters of style but also on the rhetoric of place and space exercised in this art. Much as earlier styles of wall paintings played with perspective and architectural illusion, creating, for example, the impression of windows and stoas on a solid wall,[8] landscape painting is recognized as depicting, or rather constructing, the natural world with verisimilitude but in conformity with certain ideals. Nicholas Purcell, for example, points out how, in the depiction of bodies of water in Roman landscape painting and literary description, "Romans had refined the rhetoric of control over the landscape to express their power in the world."[9] He goes on to suggest that the depiction of damage from cataclysmic floods or in "subversive texts" such as the *Apocalypse of John* and the *Sibylline Oracles* attacks Roman power at just this point of control of the landscape.[10] Moreover, the Augustan ideal of the *locus amoenus*, that pleasant, cultivated place for the leisurely enjoyment of nature and the simple life, demonstrates how landscape at its best conforms to human interests.[11] The depiction of such a landscape in Augustan wall painting, as in Augustan poetry, thus serves as a vehicle for the values and ideals of the Augustan *saeculum aureum*. In addition, the placement of figures such as shepherds in such landscapes makes it clear that the *locus amoenus* is useful as well as pleasant for humans.[12] In other words, the construction of

---

de Paul," 25–26; on its influence on Dante, see Theodore Silverstein, "Did Dante Know the Vision of St. Paul?" *Harvard Studies and Notes in Philology and Literature* 19 (1937): 231–47.

7. That the *Apocalypse of Paul* is concerned with the "fate of the dead" is asserted by Richard Bauckham, "Visiting the Places of the Dead in the Extracanonical Apocalypses," *Proceedings of the Irish Biblical Association* 18 (1995): 89, who writes: "The pattern is that of a complete cosmic tour, but the sights to be seen concern exclusively the fate of the dead."

8. John R. Clarke, *The Houses of Roman Italy, 100 B.C.–A.D. 250: Ritual, Space, and Decoration* (Berkeley: University of California Press, 1991), 39–53.

9. Nicholas Purcell, "Rome and the Management of Water: Environment, Culture, and Power," in *Human Landscapes in Classical Antiquity* (ed. Graham Shipley and John Salmon; London/New York: Routledge, 1996), 206.

10. Ibid.

11. Mary Beagon, "Nature and Views of Her Landscapes in Pliny the Elder," in *Human Landscapes in Classical Antiquity* (ed. Graham Shipley and John Salmon; London/New York: Routledge, 1996), 286–89. On the importance of this in shaping villa design and the city *hortus* residence, see Nicholas Purcell, "Town in Country and Country in Town," in *Ancient Roman Villa Gardens* (ed. Elisabeth Blair MacDougall; Washington, D.C.: Dumbarton Oaks, 1987), 187–203.

12. Beagon, "Nature and Views of Her Landscapes," 291; see also Paul Zanker, *The Power of Images in the Age of Augustus* (trans. Alan Shapiro; Ann Arbor: University of Michigan Press, 1988), 286–87.

landscape becomes a means of displaying and popularizing an ideology of empire that makes possible a certain relationship between humans and the natural world.

Three general types of Augustan landscape painting can be distinguished.[13] Topographical settings of mythological scenes, such as the *Odyssey* landscapes found in a house on the Esquiline in Rome, portray narrative events amid vivid natural scenery. Architectural landscapes, a second type, have a broad panorama and foreground buildings, harbors, villas, and temples, most often in a loosely urban setting. Commonly cited examples of this type of landscape include the Yellow Frieze from the House of Livia in Rome and the slightly later paintings from the Villa alla Farnesina, also in Rome.

A third type, the sacral-idyllic landscape, focuses on a single scene, often set off on its own by framing techniques, rather than presenting a broad panorama. Typically included in this scene are both natural features, such as trees, rocks, and streams, and cultic monuments, such as temples, cult statues, and altars. Into these scenes may be set a few humans, some with small flocks or herds, and others depicted as pious worshipers bringing votive offerings. The shrine or sanctuary is often the visual focal point of the painting, and the style represents a combination of cultic ideals and the bucolic landscape of the *locus amoenus,* which thus becomes a sacred grove. Some of the best examples of this type come from the Villa at Boscotrecase, and there are also sacral-idyllic landscapes from the public room in Augustus's house on the Palatine in Rome.[14] Paul Zanker argues that, no less than in the mythological landscapes, *pietas* is the "principal message" of the sacral-idyllic landscapes that flourish in the Augustan period. It is, moreover, *pietas* tied to rustic simplicity and thus contrasted with the excesses of luxury, as is evident also in Vergil's *Georgics* and Horace's *Epodes.*[15]

Before we turn to the representation of landscape in literary texts, a few remarks are in order. First, although these types of landscape painting derive from the Augustan period and the best preserved examples date from the first century C.E., in the post-Augustan period, and into the second through fourth centuries, they become part of the "repertoire of fixed generic types" of wall paintings, friezes, and mosaics.[16] Thus, to correlate the conventions of these landscapes with a third-century text is not anachronistic.

---

13. I draw this threefold typology from Eleanor Winsor Leach, *The Rhetoric of Space: Literary and Artistic Representation of Landscape in Republican and Augustan Rome* (Princeton: Princeton University Press, 1988), 206–7. On the variations in style in Roman landscape painting, see also Roger Ling, "Studius and the Beginnings of Roman Landscape Painting," *Journal of Roman Studies* 67 (1977): 1–16.

14. Leach, *Rhetoric of Space,* 197–260, esp. 213–26.

15. Zanker, *Power of Images,* 285–87.

16. Leach, *Rhetoric of Space,* 209; Ling, "Studius and the Beginnings of Roman Landscape Painting," 16; Clarke, *Houses of Roman Italy,* 305–60 (on the late Antonine and Severan periods).

Second, the sacral-idyllic landscape, with its emphasis on *pietas* and the ideals of the Augustan golden age, has been identified as the "most prominent mode" of landscape painting in this period.[17] It is this type with which, as I shall argue, the landscape of promise in the *Apocalypse of Paul* shows the greatest similarity. Consequently, questions about the values and type of *pietas* that the *Apocalypse of Paul* displays and promotes will be important to consider.

A third consideration is that when we consider the "audience" of these landscapes, we should probably not think in terms of only the elite, even though the preeminent examples we have come, as a function of what kinds of buildings are best preserved, from imperial and senatorial houses. Wall painting from Herculaneum, Pompeii, and Ostia suggests that these conventions were imitated in households of many social strata. It is important to note, moreover, that it was the public rooms that often contained such landscapes, which would thus have been viewed by people from a range of socioeconomic groups and not least by slaves and freedpersons.

Fourth, Zanker indicates that what he characterizes as the "rapid transmission of the new style" in the household decorative arts depended upon the interrelation of political transformation under Augustus with the multiple uses of public images, such as coins, statues, altars, temples, and city plans. He thus locates the development of the genre of landscape painting within the cultural construction of an ideology of empire under Augustus.[18] The cultural materials available for the construction of empire remain available, moreover, for those who wish to be engaged in constructing and promoting the *imperium* of Christ.[19]

A literary landscape, however, is not the same phenomenon as a landscape depicted on a wall painting. Nevertheless, Roman authors such as Quintilian and Pliny recognized the two art forms as interrelated. It is on this basis that the rhetorical mode of *ekphrasis,* or the verbal depiction of a scene in such detail that it appears before the hearer's eyes, is compared to the visual arts.[20] Whereas verisimilitude was essential to a piece of art's ability

---

17. Leach, *Rhetoric of Space,* 197.

18. Zanker, *Power of Images,* 291.

19. One of many examples of this availability, but one which includes the conventions of an architectural landscape, is the apse mosaic in the Church of Santa Pudenziana in Rome. Completed in 390 C.E. and the earliest of its type in Rome, it depicts the apostles clothed as senators on either side of the enthroned Christ, with temples, baths, and other public buildings forming the architectural backdrop. See Richard Krautheimer, *Rome: Profile of a City, 312–1308* (Princeton: Princeton University Press, 2000), 40–41.

20. On *ekphrasis,* see, among other works, Don Fowler, "Narrate and Describe: The Problem of Ekphrasis," *Journal of Roman Studies* 81 (1991): 25–35; Ruth Helen Webb, "*Ekphrasis* Ancient and Modern: The Invention of a Genre," *Word and Image* 15 (1999): 7–18; and Andrew Sprague Becker, *The Shield of Achilles and the Poetics of Ekphrasis* (Lanham, Md.: Rowman & Littlefield, 1995). Following Becker (2), I use *ekphrasis* to refer to vivid description of any kind in literature and do not limit it to its more modern sense of a literary description of a work of visual art.

to communicate to the viewer, so *enargeia* was its counterpart in literary description, in *ekphrasis*. By *enargeia*, Quintilian (*Institutio oratoria* 8.3.62–66) means those techniques of vividness, distinctness, and clarity by which a literary description communicates to the reader or hearer. In order to be successfully persuasive, *enargeia* must act upon the audience by stimulating the audience's imagination, drawing upon the audience's ability to fill in missing details and to complete the narrative picture.[21]

In her work on the "rhetoric of space," Eleanor Winsor Leach proposes that texts that narrate or dramatize "acts of seeing and interpreting" can help in understanding the role of the spectator both of art and of literary *ekphrasis*.[22] In Jewish and early Christian apocalyptic literature, such narration of "acts of seeing and interpreting" are commonplace, in that there is frequent emphasis on what the "seer" sees in the vision or on the journey and *how* it is interpreted, as, for example, through dialogue with an interpreting angel. Following Leach, I suggest that such dramatizations foreground the rhetorical moment of *enargeia*, emphasizing for the audience the importance of their response and of their receiving the "vision" by means of what they bring to complete the scene. In particular, the mythopoetic language of apocalyptic calls upon the audience to exercise their imaginations and memories in responding to the literary *ekphrasis* of the vision.[23]

Literary description of landscape acts upon the audience in a distinctive fashion in that it typically creates space; that is, it constructs spatial relations and a scene in which action can take place.[24] Quintilian recognized "place" (*locus*) and *topographia* as particularly persuasive strategies (*Institutio oratoria* 4.2.36; 9.2.43–44), not least because the literary construction of space situates the readers or hearers and defines their perspective.[25] In addition, literary landscapes and topographies create for the audience mental maps in which meaning, memory, and imagination can be organized. Leach suggests that the conventions of cartography in the Roman world, whereby maps functioned as a means for organizing physical and practical knowledge, contributed to a literary landscape's capacity to persuade and to inculcate meaning.[26] The map of the landscape organizes knowledge for the audience, constructing a cohesive system of meaning and ethic.

---

21. This discussion is much indebted to Leach, *Rhetoric of Space*, 7–17, who writes (7): "*Enargeia* is directed by the speaker to the spectator. Although its artfulness derives from the speaker's verbal facility, its effects fall short of completion without the speaker's response. *Enargeia* differs from pictorial verisimilitude in the complexity of the receptive act it demands from the spectator. In responding to pictorial verisimilitude, he [*sic*] needs only to perform the two simple and interrelated mental functions of identifying the subject and acknowledging its likeness to life, but in responding to *enargeia* his [*sic*] cognitive faculties approximate the painter's act of giving form to the unseen."

22. Ibid., 18.

23. Schüssler Fiorenza, *Revelation*, 25–31.

24. Leach, *Rhetoric of Space*, 23.

25. Ibid.

26. Ibid., 89–90.

The construction of mental maps for journeying through space and ideas belonged to the orator's art in the Roman world. An orator organized a speech by means of a mental map in which each idea in turn was associated with a series of rooms in a house or a similar series of related spaces. This cartographic organization also provided the way whereby the orator "remembered" the speech. Here the journey through the oration proceeded through the association of place with concept.[27] Although discussions of this technique usually focus on its function for the orator, it is equally applicable in the case of literary landscapes and topographies to the audience's organization of what they hear. Leach draws an analogy between the orator's mental maps and the experience of the "viewer" of verbal and visual landscapes.[28] In other words, a literary landscape provides a map for the audience, allowing them to journey into the landscape and to create meaning in response to the description of particular places. By completing the scene in response to what is given in the description, the audience effectively places meaning, value, and invitation to action within the map of the landscape. In a text that evokes mythic and cultic traditions, such as the *Apocalypse of Paul,* the construction of a mental map not only allows a vision of the unseen world of the land of promise, but also furnishes a means of organizing the ethical demands of that world. Furthermore, when the drama of such a text involves not only landscape but also an otherworldly journey for the seer, this traveloguelike feature reinforces the cartographic rhetoric since, as the seer journeys, so too the audience proceeds through the landscape, responding to the depiction at each turn. As a persuasive strategy, such a map is successful to the extent that readers or hearers make it their own and adopt it as a guide for their own decisions and actions.

This consideration of landscape in the Roman world provides a framework for interpreting the *Apocalypse of Paul.* As I noted earlier, although the *Apocalypse of Paul* clearly participates in the world of earlier apocalypses, it is distinct in the emphasis placed upon describing features of the landscape, particularly in the depiction of the land of promise. Landscapes should also be distinguished from cityscapes; although other apocalyptic and prophetic texts portray the heavenly city or temple in great detail, they do not attend to the land surrounding the city. The city of Christ has prominence in the *Apocalypse of Paul* (22, 29–30), but it is situated within a larger landscape. We may ask, therefore, what contributions landscape makes to the rhetorical work of this text.

The *Apocalypse of Paul* presents itself as "the things revealed to the apostle Paul when he went up even to the third heaven and was caught

---

27. The classic work on this method is Frances A. Yates, *The Art of Memory* (London: Routledge & Kegan Paul, 1966; repr., London: Pimlico, 2000), 17–41; see also Jocelyn Penny Small, *Wax Tablets of the Mind: Cognitive Studies of Memory and Literacy in Classical Antiquity* (London/New York: Routledge, 1997).

28. Leach, *Rhetoric of Space,* 142.

up into Paradise and heard unspeakable words." In doing so, the text locates itself as an amplification of 2 Cor 12:2–4; we can thus understand
it as a narrative expansion of a peculiar enigma in an authoritative text.[29]
In this journey, much is revealed to Paul, the first-person narrator, as he is
taken on a tour of otherworldly places: heaven (*Apocalypse of Paul* 11),[30]
the "land of promise"[31] (21), and the place where the "souls of the godless
and sinners are" (31). Throughout the journey, Paul is accompanied by an
interpreting angel whose role is principally to identify various inhabitants
of heaven and hell and to name and interpret the places visited. Toward the
end of the journey (45), Paul is led back into paradise and introduced to
a series of "righteous ones," such as the Virgin Mary, Moses, Job, Elijah,
and Enoch. It would seem that this paradise is the same place as the land
of promise he visited earlier, since similar sets of rivers are named in both
instances and in both Paul meets Elijah and Enoch.[32]

Much of the text is devoted to descriptions of the inhabitants of these
places. Paul's journey to heaven and hell is similar to Odysseus's visit to
the Underworld in *Odyssey* 11 (the Nekyia) and Aeneas's in book 6 of
the *Aeneid*. The emphasis in the *Apocalypse of Paul* is clearly on persons,
their righteous or sinful deeds, their worship, or their capacity for repentance. This emphasis is framed at the start of the text by what amounts to a
prophetic call to Paul: "The word of the Lord came to me thus: Say to this
people: 'How long will you transgress and add sin to sin and tempt the Lord
who made you, saying that you are Abraham's children but doing the works
of the devil?'" (*Apocalypse of Paul* 3). This is followed by the protests of
the cosmic bodies (sun, moon, stars, and seas) over the sins of the people,
recalling the traditions of the covenant lawsuit in which the cosmic bodies
are the witnesses to the covenant.[33] The framing is completed toward the
end of the text (43), when Paul intercedes for the penitent sinners: "Lord

29. On narrative expansion as an interpretive response to peculiarities in the biblical text, see
James L. Kugel, *In Potiphar's House: The Interpretive Life of Biblical Texts* (2d ed.; Cambridge:
Harvard University Press, 1994), 247–51.

30. The "third heaven" is specified in the Syriac version (Duensing, "Apocalypse of Paul,"
744); in the Paris Latin manuscript it is simply "the place of saints," but when in chap. 21 Paul
is led down, it is from the "third heaven."

31. The Greek has ἡ γῆ τῶν πραέων (land of the meek), perhaps under the influence of the
succeeding quotation from Matt 5:5, but the more reliable long Latin versions read *terra* [or
locus] *repromissionis* (land of promise).

32. It must be admitted that there is a certain confusion over the divisions of heaven, oc-
casioned in part by differences among the versions, but also by the tension between the text's
interest in narrating what Paul sees and hears and what is said in 2 Cor 12:4, namely, that in
paradise he "heard things that are not to be told; that no human is permitted to speak." The
text resolves this tension at the beginning of *Apocalypse of Paul* 21 by isolating one part of
heaven about which nothing is reported. On this confusion, see A. Hilhorst, "A Visit to Paradise: *Apocalypse of Paul* 45 and its Background," in *Paradise Interpreted: Representations of
Biblical Paradise in Judaism and Christianity* (ed. Gerard P. Luttikhuizen; Leiden: Brill, 1999),
138–39.

33. See, for example, Deut 30:19; on the genre of the covenant lawsuit (*rîb*), see Frank M.
Cross, "The Council of Yahweh in Second Isaiah," *Journal of Near Eastern Studies* 12 (1953):

God, have mercy on what you have fashioned, have mercy on the children of humans, have mercy on your own image." This framework, with its emphasis on sin and repentance, marks the text as thoroughly interested in the ethical dimension of Christian life.

When we come to the depiction of the land of promise in *Apocalypse of Paul* 21–31, we find less interest in those who live there. Indeed, although Paul sees a few of the inhabitants (the patriarchs, the infants whom Herod slew, David), he is not introduced to them and does not converse with them, as he does in the second visit (46–51). Instead the description focuses on topographical features such as the river Okeanos surrounding the land, the rivers of milk, honey, wine, and oil, and Lake Acherusia, as well as on the vegetation, the trees, and the fruits they yield. The ethical dimension, however, is never far from sight, since what Paul sees is frequently interpreted in ethical terms: the fruits of the trees are for "the worthy," and the penitent are brought through Lake Acherusia (22). Moreover, the ethical, covenantal framework of the text as a whole implicitly also controls this section, even though landscape is in the foreground.

The land of promise is presented, in a certain sense, as a better version of earth, existing as a parallel, but yet unveiled, region. As the angel tells Paul: "When Christ whom you preach comes to reign, then by the fiat of God the first earth will be dissolved and this land of promise will then be shown and it will be like dew or a cloud; and then the Lord Jesus Christ, the eternal king, will be revealed and he will come with all his saints to dwell in it and he will reign over them for a thousand years and they will eat of the good things which I shall now show you" (*Apocalypse of Paul* 21). It is bounded by the river Okeanos, just as the earth was on Roman maps. The text provides a detailed depiction of the land, through the eyes of Paul, starting with a river flowing with milk and honey, along the edge of which are various kinds of fruit trees. In addition, in this land "brighter than silver" are tall palms trees full of fruit, luxuriant vines, each with "ten thousand branches, and each branch had on it ten thousand branches of grapes, and each bunch had ten thousand grapes" (22), and many other fruit-bearing trees. The scene evokes the river in the city of God in Rev 22:2, along which grow trees of life, and the similar river and trees in the heavenly temple in Ezek 47:12. But in the *Apocalypse of Paul* the riotous vegetation and abundant fruit become the primary focus, without a city or temple yet in sight. That the river flows with milk and honey links the landscape to the land of milk and honey, promised to the people of God throughout the exodus and wilderness journey in the Scriptures of Israel. Here the land of promise in the *Apocalypse of Paul* is defined in terms of the blessings of covenant faithfulness. This landscape thus invites the audience to fill it out with the associations of covenantal

---

274; and Herbert B. Huffmon, "The Covenant Lawsuit in the Prophets," *Journal of Biblical Literature* 78 (1959): 284–95.

blessing and abundance. We may also note in this first instance of *ekphrasis* how the vivid description prompts the visualization of the place.

Paul is then brought to a "river whose waters were very white, whiter than milk" (*Apocalypse of Paul* 22), which the angel names as Lake Acherusia, "where the city of Christ is." In Greek mythology, Lake Acherusia is the lake at the conflux of rivers at the entrance to the Underworld; here it is the means of access to the city of Christ, since in it the archangel Michael baptizes those who repent. Paul is put in a golden boat, however, and brought across the lake to the city, accompanied by three thousand hymn-singing angels (23). Again, the description invites visualization: the city on land across the brilliant white water, with the boat, Paul, and the angels. As the viewer moves with Paul closer to the city, it appears in greater detail with golden city walls, towers, and twelve gates. The four rivers that encircle the city, however, are prominently in view and subsequently identified more closely. Thus I maintain that the viewer's gaze is directed again toward the landscape and the situating of the city in the land. In this respect, the *Apocalypse of Paul* differs from the cityscape emphasis of Rev 21–22 or other apocalypses such as the *Apocalypse of Peter*. Even when Paul is within the gate, the emphasis is on the trees, which wondrously are bending over and straightening themselves; this action is interpreted as the trees' doing penance for those about to enter the city (*Apocalypse of Paul* 24). In terms of the conventions of Roman landscape painting, this is now a sacral-idyllic landscape; the depiction focuses on the sacred city, the shrine, but clearly is set in a broader natural landscape.

The four rivers that encircle the city bear the names of the four rivers flowing from Eden (Gen 2:10–14): Pishon (or Phison), Gihon, Tigris, and Euphrates (*Apocalypse of Paul* 23). These are further identified as, respectively, the rivers of honey, milk, wine, and oil. Paul is brought to each in turn, and each is commented upon in detail. The extended treatment of the rivers provides an important point of access to the rhetoric of the text. First, although the rivers are the biblical rivers of Eden, they also include two, the Tigris and Euphrates, that are regularly shown on Roman maps and are important in the Roman campaigns in the East. Second, the visual depiction of rivers, indeed groups of four rivers, formed part of the decorative program of Roman houses and baths into the late antique period. The Tigris and Euphrates were often included in these sets. For example, from a house in Seleucia, a mid- to late-second-century c.e. mosaic floor of a triclinium showed four portrait busts of rivers, of which only the Pyramos and the Tigris are preserved; it is thought that the Euphrates and the Kydnos completed the scene.[34] Named rivers were thus visualized and functioned to integrate landscape features into a decorative scheme.

---

34. Christine Kondoleon, *Antioch: The Lost Antique City* (Princeton: Princeton University Press, 2000), 152; the mosaic is from the House of Cilicia, room I.

In addition, in the depiction of rivers there is a cartographic dimension, whereby practical knowledge is organized in relation to a map of landscape features. The Nile Mosaic from the Temple of Fortuna at Praeneste provides an example of the depiction of a river used to show the whole region; it contains small scenes of topography, landmarks, people, occupations, and creatures typical of each area of Egypt and the Nile valley.[35] I suggest that the description of the four rivers in the *Apocalypse of Paul* provides a similar landscape map of paradise. As each river is taken in turn, the people particular to that region are identified, in most cases by means of mention of scriptural figures. Thus the river of honey is the region of the major and minor prophets who welcome those who follow the way of the prophets (*Apocalypse of Paul* 25); the river of milk is the region of the infants slain by Herod and then of "all who preserve their chastity and purity" (26). At the river of wine, to the north, are Abraham, Isaac, Jacob, Lot, Job, and other saints, and it is the place of "all those who have given hospitality to strangers" (27). Lastly, by the river of oil, to the east, are those who "rejoiced and sang psalms" and thus of "those who dedicated themselves to God with the whole heart and had no pride in themselves" (28).

In each case, the particular river serves as a locus for a rich web of illusions to Scripture, ethical orientation, and ritual practice. By indexing each river to a set of scriptural figures, the text invites the audience to complete the picture, as it were, with a set of narratives and scriptural characterizations. This is particularly true in the case of the infants slain by Herod and in the case of Abraham and Lot, where the stories of their hospitality are highlighted by the wider definition of who is greeted in that region. The rivers thus become a way of organizing scriptural experience. In addition, the ethical orientations advocated here by the *Apocalypse of Paul* — prophetic repentance, chastity and purity, hospitality to strangers, and whole-hearted dedication to God — are organized topographically. Here too the audience needs to complete the picture in terms both of the scriptural content to these ethical orientations and of further teaching and parenesis that they have experienced. The rivers also provide a way of organizing ritual experience, not only with the reference to those "who rejoiced and sang psalms," but by virtue of the liquids with which these rivers flow. Honey, milk, wine, and oil are all liquids used in early Christian ritual practice. As in the earlier river that flows with milk and honey, these liquids evoke the scriptural promises of the land of milk and honey, but also their use in some early Christian baptismal and eucharistic practice.[36] Wine is a frequent eucharistic liquid,

---

35. See Leach, *Rhetoric of Space,* 91–95. Leach dates the mosaic to the late Republican period, while recognizing a range of possibilities into the fourth century C.E.

36. See N. A. Dahl, "*La terre où coulent le lait et le miel,* selon Barnabé 6.8–19," in *Aux sources de la tradition chrétienne: Mélanges offerts à M. Maurice Goguel à l'occasion de son*

and oil was widely used for healing, exorcism, and chrismation of baptismal candidates and church leaders.[37]

The map of the rivers is, I propose, designed to provoke the audience to fill out the picture of each region with a set of ritual experiences, thus defining the landscape as a place of cultic activity. The conventions of Roman sacral-idyllic landscape merge with those of cartography and topographical décor to produce a way of linking and organizing multiple sources of authority (scriptural, ritual, ethical teaching). Moreover, because literary landscape draws the audience in, asking the audience to participate in the construction of the full picture at every turn, it produces a series of desires and a sequence of assents to the world portrayed. As a map for the memory, the landscape not only provokes appropriate recollections of scriptural, catechetical, and ritual experience, but also provides a guide for future action and for remembering on what basis certain choices have been made. Rhetorically it functions through the ritual markers to remind the audience of past decisions made for covenant faithfulness and to inculcate ethical patterns through the examples of the heroes of Scripture. The esthetic features of the literary landscape also, I suggest, aim at creating in the "viewer" desire and longing for the landscape portrayed. This provoking of desire is in stark contrast to the *ekphrasis* of the punishment of unrepentant sinners in the later portions of the *Apocalypse of Paul,* which function to incite aversion both to tortures and to the sinful actions. Landscape thus contains a rich array of strategies for persuading an audience to choose the good.

Roman landscape painting and literary *ekphrasis* of landscape, as we have seen above, provided vehicles for promoting the values associated with the Augustan golden age. Sacral-idyllic landscapes, with their prominent display of shrines, temples, and worshipers, accentuated the practices and orientations of *pietas*. In the *Apocalypse of Paul,* the landscape that surrounds the city of Christ similarly highlights the *pietas* of the Christian world as the ideal orientation of the earth. It does so in its portrayal of explicit acts of worship — the singing of psalms and the acts of penance — and its organization of the landscape through ritual markers. *Pietas,* moreover, includes ethical practices proper to the golden age, the mores of the ancestors in the case of the Augustan age, and the covenantal ethic that leads to the land of promise in the *Apocalypse of Paul.* In both cases, the ideal age was presented in order to motivate action in this world. In the age of Augustus and his successor the aim was to uphold the exercise of *imperium* in the Roman

---

soixante-dixième anniversaire (Bibliothèque théologique; Neuchâtel/Paris: Delachaux & Niestlé, 1950), 70; Andrew McGowan, *Ascetic Eucharists: Food and Drink in Early Christian Ritual Meals* (New York: Oxford University Press, 1999), 107–15.

37. John Halliburton, "Anointing in the Early Church," in *The Oil of Gladness: Anointing in the Christian Tradition* (ed. Martin Dudley and Geoffrey Rowell; London: SPCK, 1993), 77–91. There are a few indications that oil was also used in some eucharistic practices; see McGowan, *Ascetic Eucharists,* 115–17.

seek to discern the needs of the community that used the term. Martyn's explanation is not sufficient.

Other evasions or explanations also fail. Rudolf Bultmann, for example, ignores the gospel's anti-Judaism and emphasizes its philosophical and theological significance.[5] On the other hand, when historical-critical studies shed light on the roots of the problem, questions of theology and meaning still must be considered.[6] For example, clarifying that some, not all, Jews were hostile toward Jesus does not adequately address the gospel's opposition toward nonbelievers as a theological and ethical problem. Raymond Brown fails to address the deeper theological issue when he notes ethical problems in naming the Jews as children of the devil, while endorsing the universalized contrast of those who believe and those who do not: "There is a Prince of this world that is actively hostile to Jesus, so that the maxim *Christus contra mundum* (Christ against the world) is not without truth."[7] Attempts thus to neutralize the gospel's acid, therefore, shift attention to the "truth" of its message. This move leaves the ethical question unaddressed of whether such hostility to those who do not believe is ever justified. There is ethical danger, as well, in feminist linkages of the Johannine Word with Sophia without a deconstruction of the use of incarnational theology as an imperialist and anti-Jewish supercessionist tool.[8]

In this essay we explore a Samaritan bias in the Gospel of John and how this bias impacts the gospel's construction of its anti-Judaism. Though a Samaritan bias is noted by a variety of scholars, its implications for understanding the anti-Judaism of John have not been developed.[9] This Samaritan

---

of the Century," both in *What Is John? Readers and Readings of the Fourth Gospel* (ed. Fernando F. Segovia; Atlanta: Scholars Press, 1996), 1.111–38, 249–56. See also idem, *Befriending the Beloved Disciple: A Jewish Reading of the Gospel of John* (New York: Continuum, 2001).

5. See Rudolf Bultmann, *The Gospel of John: A Commentary* (trans. G. R. Beasley-Murray et al.; Philadelphia: Westminster, 1971), 69–83, 315–24, in which philosophy, theology, and myth are used to discuss the Jews, and historicity is set aside. See John Dominic Crossan, *Who Killed Jesus? Exposing the Roots of Anti-Semitism in the Gospel Story of the Death of Jesus* (San Francisco: Harper, 1995), 1–38, for a discussion of the problem of ignoring questions of historicity in connection with anti-Judaism in John.

6. Reinhartz, *Befriending the Beloved Disciple*, 75–76.

7. Raymond Brown, *The Community of the Beloved Disciple* (New York: Paulist Press, 1979), 66. Sandra Schneiders, *Written That You May Believe: Encountering Jesus in the Fourth Gospel* (New York: Crossroad, 1999), 34–35, 82, takes a similar position.

8. Elisabeth Schüssler Fiorenza notes: "One cannot overemphasize that this theological danger consisted not in the adoption of female language and G*ddess symbolism for G*d. Rather, it was that Jesus, who was a historical being, was now proclaimed in masculine mythological terms as a divine being and that the Galilean prophet and emissary of Sophia was now envisioned in kyriarchal terms as cosmic lord/master and sovereign comparable to Isis in universal power and world dominion"; *Jesus: Miriam's Child, Sophia's Prophet: Critical Issues in Feminist Christology* (New York: Continuum, 1995), 149.

9. Jarl E. Fossum, *The Name of God and the Angel of the Lord: Samaritan and Jewish Concepts of Intermediation and the Origins of Gnosticism* (Tübingen: Mohr, 1985), 152, notes the history of scholarship considering a connection between Samaritanism and John. Craig R. Koester, "The Spectrum of Johannine Readers," in *What Is John? Readers and Readings of the Fourth Gospel* (ed. Fernando F. Segovia; Atlanta: Scholars Press, 1996), 5–19, discusses the

bias transmits a preexisting enmity between two groups identified with Israel: the Samaritans and the Jews. Their enmity is rooted in centuries of oppression from a succession of empires and their own national aspirations. Considering this bias, we examine the impact of the gospel's interweaving of anti-Judaism with its theology.

The gospel provides explicit evidence for a Samaritan bias. All depictions of Samaria and Samaritans are unequivocally positive in John, whereas the depiction of Jews is overwhelmingly, though not exclusively, negative. The Samaritan woman in John 4 is placed in positive contrast to Nicodemus, a Pharisaic Jewish leader, in John 3. In John 8, Jesus is accused of being possessed by a demon and being a Samaritan; he denies having a demon but does not distance himself from the Samaritans. Other, more indirect evidence is elaborated below: its Christology, the relationship of Jesus to John the Baptist, Jesus' hostility to the Jerusalem temple, and the affirmation that Jesus fulfills the Samaritan expectation of the return of Moses.

The Meanings of Jew, Samaritan, and Christian

Scholarship about antiquity makes clear the difficulty of using the terms *Jew, Christian,* or *Samaritan* as simple religious designations in relation to the New Testament period. A number of groups in first-century Palestine traced their legendary ancestors back to Abraham; all could lay claim to being Israelites.

The term *Jews* is commonly understood to refer to various Israelite groups descended from returned exiles. Some grouped their loyalties around the Jerusalem temple, its priestly practices, and its alliances with Rome, and, many, though not all, resided in the Judean area. Others, while linked to the Davidic traditions of Jerusalem and their religious writings, rejected the cooptation of the Jerusalem temple and its leadership by the Romans. They were settled throughout much of Palestine.[10]

The term *Samaritan* in antiquity could refer to those who lived in the Samaria region, the leaders of and adherents to distinctively religious groups connected to the cultic centers of northern Israel and the Pentateuch, or to

---

readers — Samaritans among them — that John may have had in mind. Brown, *Community of the Beloved Disciple,* 36–40, suggests a series of historically successive communities that are spoken to simultaneously in the text, in which the first layer is a Jewish Christian community and the second is Samaritan. With some notable exceptions, such as Wayne Meeks, *The Prophet-King: Moses Traditions and the Johannine Christology* (Leiden: Brill, 1967), and Schneiders, *Written That You May Believe,* major twentieth-century works in Samaritan studies are not cited in the bibliographies or indexes of commentaries on the gospel.

10. A summary of scholarship on the meaning of *ioudaioi* is found in Naomi Janowitz, "Rethinking Jewish Identity in Late Antiquity," in *Ethnicity and Culture in Late Antiquity* (ed. Stephen Mitchell and Geoffrey Greatrex; London: Duckworth, 2000), 205–19. See also Shaye Cohen, *The Beginning of Jewishness: Boundaries, Varieties, Uncertainties* (Berkeley: University of California Press, 1999).

the general population of the region descended from the Assyrians, Canaanites, and others. During either the postexilic or Greek period, a group of residents of Samaria in the north near Shechem built a temple on Mount Gerizim. They also developed a canon of sacred texts comprised of the Pentateuch plus, with somewhat less canonical status, Joshua. Moses was their most important religious figure and only prophet; many awaited the return of Moses, as promised in Deut 18:18. Passover, with its relationship to Moses, became their central, perhaps most central, festival.[11] Samaritans ignored or were unaware of all documents having to do with Judean traditions: David, the Jerusalem temple, and the histories, prophets, and wisdom writings associated with the people of the exile.[12] The Samaritans' own history places them in Israel during the exile.[13] "The Samaritans regard themselves,... from an ethnic point of view, to this day as the direct continuation of the Ten Tribes of Israel."[14]

The term *Christian* rarely occurs in the New Testament and is absent in the Gospels. In the first and second centuries C.E., some Jewish and Samaritan communities identified themselves with Jesus. They were diverse and heterodox and used a variety of names.[15] The term *Christian* eventually comes into use to identify various Jewish, Samaritan, and Gentile followers of Jesus.

For the purposes of this essay, we use the terms *Jew, Samaritan,* and *Christian* advisedly, as a shorthand, while understanding the caution that

---

11. R. J. Coggins, *Samaritans and Jews: The Origins of Samaritanism Reconsidered* (Atlanta: John Knox, 1975), argues that the Samaritans were strict in Sabbath observance and were a conservative group that bore some resemblance to the Sadducees. Etienne Nodet's more convincing argument, *A Search for the Origins of Judaism: From Joshua to the Mishnah* (trans. Ed Crowley; Journal for the Study of the Old Testament Supplement 248; Sheffield: Sheffield Academic Press, 1997), 93–121, 380, 387–90, is that the weekly Sabbath was imported from Babylon and was not a long-standing Samaritan practice, for whom the lunar Sabbath was more traditional. The lunar system guaranteed that Passover would always fall on the Sabbath. Nodet also suggests that the Sadducees may have had Samaritan origins, adopting a weekly Sabbath after establishment in Jerusalem.

12. Nodet, *Origins of Judaism,* 154: "The narratives of the Hexateuch, which ignore the Judea of Bethlehem and Jerusalem, leave a major place for Shechem, from the time of the altar built by Abraham (Gen. 12.7) up to the great assembly of Joshua (Josh. 24), while treating in passing a solemn installation at Ebal and at Gerizim (Deut. 11.29–30; Josh. 8.30–33). In the genealogy of the patriarchs, Judah is a son of Israel, and consequently the northern kingdom has precedence. So the most official canonical tradition preserves very clear indications relative to the precedence of the North over the South."

13. Nodet, ibid., 93–153, discusses the probable origins of the Samaritans in relation to the formation of Judaism and the Pentateuch, which he believes was a deeply interactive process. He proposes that "the Samaritans of Gerizim were the most direct heirs of the ancient Israelites" (12). Nathan Shur, *History of the Samaritans* (New York: Peter Lang, 1989), and Coggins, *Samaritans and Jews,* provide comprehensive histories of the Samaritans.

14. Shur, *History of the Samaritans,* 32.

15. Walter Bauer, *Orthodoxy and Heresy in Earliest Christianity* (Philadelphia: Fortress, 1971), is one of the earliest accounts, among many, to discuss a wide variety of sects that can be identified as Christian.

religious, geographical, historical, and ethnic group identities are seen as contested and highly permeable by scholars of antiquity.[16]

Samaritan and Jewish Animosities

When the Babylonian exiles returned, they regarded the people in Samaria as foreigners, and interaction with them was forbidden. The Samaritans, in turn, would later regard Ezra's antiforeign bias negatively.[17] By sometime late in the Persian period or early in the Greek period, both the different geographical clusters, Samaritans and Jews, developed distinctive, but related, cultic identities.[18] The relationships of Samaritans with Jews were a mixture of tension and cooperation up to the Maccabean period.[19] Tensions between Samaritans and Jews escalated under Antiochus IV Epiphanes. A group of Samaritans at the temple in Shechem petitioned Antiochus in 166 B.C.E. in a letter separating themselves from the Jews:

> To King Antiochus Theos Epiphanes,... after droughts had desolated the country, our ancestors, obedient to a certain ancient religious scruple, adopted the custom of observing the day that the Jews call "sabbath." They had also erected on the mountain called Gerizim an unnamed temple, and they offered there appropriate sacrifices. These days, as you have treated the Jews as they deserved for their wickedness, the royal officers, thinking that as a result of our kinship with them we must do the same things, charge us with the same offences, whereas we are Sidonians by origin.... We therefore petition you, as our benefactor and saviour... not to harass us by bringing against us the same charges brought against the Jews, since to us they are aliens by race as well as customs.... In this way we will no longer be harassed, and being able from now on to attend in complete security to our work, we shall increase your revenues.[20]

---

16. Daniel Boyarin, *Dying for God: Martyrdom and the Making of Christianity and Judaism* (Stanford: Stanford University Press, 1999), chaps. 1–2, makes a compelling case for the permeability in the period of late antiquity of Israelite-based groups and the difficulty of using the binary terms *Christian* and *Jew*, as if there were two separate and easily distinguished groups. He suggests far more mutual adherence and permeability between those Israelites who followed the Nazarite, Jesus, and those who did not. The same caution applies to using Samaritan and Jew as binary terms.

17. Nodet, *Origins of Judaism*, 35.

18. Ibid., 122–53.

19. Ibid., chap. 6, has an extensive discussion of the events of the Maccabean period. Against this view, Shur, *History of the Samaritans*, 32–33, sees more intermingling between the groups: "The responsible Jewish halakhic authorities continued to regard the Samaritans from certain points of view still as Jews till late into the second century C.E.; some of the biblical psalms were in use among the Samaritans till the fourth century C.E. Thus the process of estrangement was a very slow one, spread over many centuries and completed only a millennium after it had started."

20. Nodet, *Origins of Judaism*, 142. Nodet regards Josephus's report of this petition as historically accurate. The use of the term *Sidonians* may have been used by the petitioners to

By this petition, the leadership at Shechem may have sought to protect themselves and their cultic practices by paying tribute to the Greek Empire.[21] When the Jews mounted an armed opposition to Greek rule during the Maccabean revolt, the Samaritan leadership maintained their alliances with the Greeks.

This Samaritan alliance was answered by Maccabean retaliation. Perhaps as early as 128 or as late as 110–107, the Hasmonean ruler in Jerusalem, John Hyrcanus, led an army into Samaria, destroyed the temple on Mount Gerizim (which was not rebuilt), conquered the cities of Samaria and Shechem, and destroyed them.

This Hasmonean hegemony was ended by Pompey in 63 B.C.E., but the intervening fifty-to-sixty-year period marks a time of hostility between the Samaritan leaders and their Jewish rulers. From 63 B.C.E. until the mid-40s, when Herod took it over, Samaria was annexed to the Roman province of Syria. The town of Samaria was rebuilt by Herod and called Sebaste, Greek for Augustus. Jews avoided Samaritan territories and contact with Samaritans and called them by the contemptuous epithet "Kuttim" (of Cuthean ethnicity), alluding to their heathen Mesopotamian ancestry described in 2 Kgs 17.[22] Despite these hostilities, the Samaritans appear to have been definitive for the formation of the Judaism of the first century B.C.E., and the two groups shared many religious practices in common, based in the Torah.[23]

Following the destruction of their temple on Mount Gerizim, the people of Samaria experienced profound religious crises. Many new sects offered responses to the loss of the temple and theologically reinterpreted its meaning.[24] These emergent groups reflected the influence of Hellenistic thought, developed during the time of Greek rule. By the Roman period, the relationship among various sects of Samaritans and Jews was deeply conflicted, with the Jerusalem temple as a major flash point:

> The temple in Jerusalem was called by [the Samaritans], instead of *"Beit Mikdash," "Beit Maktash"* — house of shame. They alleged that the Jews kept an image of a man hidden in the Holy of Holies, which they worshiped. . . . In the time of the first Roman procurator Coponius (6–9 [c.e.]) Samaritans infiltrated at night into the temple enclosure in Jerusalem and scattered there human bones in order to defile

---

create deliberate ambiguity surrounding their petition, since the term is used in the Mishnah to designate someone who is duplicitous, a term used against Samaritans by Jews.

21. Ibid., 146–47: "The Samaritans wanted to give an impression of submission, but . . . 'correctly understood, the petition of the year 166 in no way expressed a disavowal by the Samaritans of their paternal religion.'"

22. Ibid., 154–60; and Shur, *History of the Samaritans*, 43.

23. See Coggins, *Samaritans and Jews*, 157–61; and Nodet, *Origins of Judaism*, 380.

24. Fossum, *Name of God*, 45; Stanley Jerome Isser, *The Dositheans: A Samaritan Sect in Late Antiquity* (Leiden: Brill, 1978), 160.

and taint it and make it ritually unclean.... Further they endeavored to mislead the Jews in the areas beyond their district, by lighting beacons on the tops of hills on wrong dates, so as to confuse the Jewish calendar and make it impossible for them to keep the festivals at the correct dates.[25]

Later, Christian Samaritan sects claimed that the mission of Jesus was to destroy the God of the Jews.[26]

Samaritans and Jews maintained some cooperative interactions. Later rabbinic Judaism, with its interest in Torah, shared with Samaritans in late antiquity a link to Mosaic legacies. In 556 C.E. Jews and Samaritans joined together in one of their last uprisings against the Byzantine government.[27]

A Samaritan Gospel

Several New Testament documents indicate the existence of an early Christian Samaritan community that predates Paul's mission to the Gentiles, for example, Acts 8:5–13 and 9:31. John's Gospel suggests an early Christian Samaritan context and community in many ways, including its Christology, the activity of John the Baptist, the placement and theology of the Jerusalem temple demonstration, and the story of the Samaritan woman.[28]

The gospel's Christology emphasizes Jesus as the new Moses, a figure of singular importance to Samaritans, surpassing his importance in Judaism. While other New Testament texts, such as Matthew, link Jesus to Moses, they relate Jesus also to the Judean traditions of Davidic kingship. John ignores these traditions, except in 7:42–43, where the claim to Davidic lineage is described as dividing the community. John's exclusive focus on Moses and its fulsome and complex development of Mosaic themes are keys to the gospel's Samaritan character.

An example of the extensive Johannine use of Mosaic motifs is the association of water images with Jesus, which resonate with many of the stories of Moses and water. The River Jordan symbolizes passage into the Mosaic promise of new life in the land across the river found in Moses' farewell promise to the Israelites: if they take to heart the divine word, they will "live long in the land that [they] are crossing over the Jordan to possess" (Deut 32:47).

---

25. Shur, *History of the Samaritans,* 43–44.

26. Fossum, *Name of God,* 16, notes that Satornil, who came from the Samaritan school of Simon, "taught that 'Christ came for the destruction of the god of the Jews' (Iren. I.xxiv.2),... but... Satornil did not expressly equate the god of the Jews with the God of the Old Testament."

27. Shur, *History of the Samaritans,* 33.

28. This Samaritan thesis also has larger implications for the authorship, location, dating, and theology of the Gospel of John that need fuller investigation, which is beyond the scope of this essay.

The gospel presents John baptizing in "Aenon near Salim" (John 3:23), an area three miles east of the Samaritan holy site of Shechem, and in the wilderness east of Jordan (1:28; 3:26; 10:40), which was believed to be Moses' last earthly residence.[29] The Baptist proclaims Jesus as the one who is to come after him, suggesting a succession from John to Jesus that bound their respective followers into a coalition movement that used baptism in the River Jordan as a central rite of entry.[30]

Close on the heels of this opening baptism scene is the temple demonstration. John's Gospel places it at the beginning of Jesus' ministry in John 2, in contrast to the three Synoptic Gospels, which place the story just before Jesus' arrest, trial, and crucifixion.[31] In presenting Jesus' opposition to the Jerusalem temple so early, the gospel seems to signal to a Samaritan audience that Jesus shared their antagonism, as would many of his Galilean kin.

The Johannine temple account differs significantly from that of the Synoptic versions. It presents vivid details of Jesus' antagonism to the temple: with a whip he drives out the people selling animals for sacrifice and overturns the money-changers' tables. In addition, unlike the Synoptics, this account does not include an apocalyptic prediction of the future destruction of the Jerusalem temple.[32] This absence may indicate that the writer's theological concern is not the destruction of the Jerusalem temple in 70 C.E. Instead, the writer may be drawing on discourses in the aftermath of John Hyrcanus's destruction of the Samaritan temple.

Competing sects in Samaria imagined the renewal of their temple in differing ways.[33] Some expected a time of restoration in which the temple would

---

29. Fossum, *Name of God*, 114–17, discusses the connections of John the Baptist to the Samaritans.

30. The Baptist's movement is regarded by scholars as an alternative to the Jerusalem temple system, as was the Qumran community. Alternatives to the Jerusalem temple expressed an exodus-covenant model of salvation and Mosaic-covenant leadership. See Richard A. Horsley, *Jesus and the Spiral of Violence: Popular Jewish Resistance in Roman Palestine* (Minneapolis: Fortress, 1993), 288.

31. Crossan, *Who Killed Jesus?*; Horsley, *Jesus and the Spiral of Violence*; and E. P. Sanders, *Jesus and Judaism* (Philadelphia: Fortress, 1985), agree that the demonstration should not be called a "cleansing of the temple." Sanders (75) says, "He [Jesus] intended to indicate that the end was at hand and that the temple would be destroyed, so that the new and perfect temple might arise." Horsley (287, 300) disagrees with Sanders and concludes that "the Temple was functioning as an instrument of imperial legitimation and control of a subjected people.... Jesus' demonstration in the Temple was a prophetic act symbolizing God's imminent judgmental destruction, not just of the building, but of the Temple system." Crossan is closer to Horsley and places the accent on Jewish outrage against the oppressiveness of Rome and against the collusion with Rome by the priestly aristocracy.

32. See Matt 24:2, 15; Mark 13:1–8; Luke 19:44; 21:20–21. Neither John 2:19–20 nor 4:21 make reference to an apocalyptic prediction based in Daniel.

33. Fossum, *Name of God*, 45: "The crisis caused by the destruction of the Gerizim temple by John Hyrcanus was obviously a turning-point in the history of the Samaritans who then began to split up into several factions, giving divergent answers to the problem of how to re-establish religion."

be rebuilt.[34] Others said the new temple would be a spiritual indwelling of God's presence in the community or the arrival of the prophet like Moses.[35] Jesus' saying, "Destroy this temple, and in three days I will raise it up" (John 2:19), can be read as a sign to a Samaritan audience that their destroyed temple, the Mount Gerizim sanctuary, could be renewed in Jesus. The text says, "He was speaking of the temple of his body" (2:21).

Later passages in the gospel amplify the claim that Jesus is the Samaritan prophet who is to come. The first, and most crucial, instance of this claim is found in John 4:1–41, in the dialogue between Jesus and the Samaritan woman at Jacob's well. Jesus presents himself as the source of living water: "The water that I will give will become in them a spring of water gushing up to eternal life" (4:14).[36] The imagery suggests that Jesus is the return of Moses, who delivered living water for those wandering in the wilderness. Thus, Jesus fulfills the Song of Moses: "May my teaching drop like the rain, / my speech condense like the dew; / like gentle rain on grass, / like showers on new growth" (Deut 32:2).

The dialogue turns from water to conflicting claims between Jews and Samaritans about their holy mountains. The Samaritan woman initiates the topic, challenging Jesus to defend Jerusalem as "the place where people must worship" (John 4:20).

Jesus passes her test. He does not proclaim Jerusalem as the center, but promises a transformation in the places of worship: "The hour is coming when you will worship the Father neither on this mountain nor in Jerusalem.... True worshipers will worship the Father in spirit and truth. ... God is spirit, and those who worship him must worship in spirit and truth" (4:21–24). Jesus satisfies a Samaritan hope following the destruction of their temple.

This dialogue at Jacob's well evokes the memory of the ancestor who established Bethel, described in the Pentateuch as the first sanctuary. In an earlier passage Jesus says that people would "see heaven opened and the angels of God ascending and descending upon the Son of Man" (1:51). The imagery associates Jesus with Bethel, the place where Jacob saw the angels of God ascending and descending and built an altar, declaring: "This is none other than the house of God, and this is the gate of heaven" (Gen 28:17). Hearing Jesus proclaim the imminent hour of worship in spirit and in truth, the Samaritan woman refers to the coming Messiah who will "proclaim all

---

34. Isser, *Dositheans*, 141, 160.

35. John Bowman, *Samaritan Documents Relating to Their History, Religion, and Life* (Pittsburgh: Pickwick, 1977), 40–41.

36. Larry Paul Jones, *The Symbol of Water in the Gospel of John* (Sheffield: Sheffield Academic Press, 1997), suggests that living water is an allusion to Torah and that the dialogue at Jacob's well harkens back to the patriarchs who found wives at such wells, indicating the Jewish character of John's Gospel. These pentateuchal images are, however, more emphatically Samaritan, which may explain why a Samaritan woman and community are able to understand Jesus' message more readily than Nicodemus, who fails to understand fully.

things to us," a direct reference to Deut 18:18 (John 4:25). Jesus responds, "I am he, the one who is speaking to you" (4:26).[37]

The repeated use of the words *egō eimi* (I am) is a distinctive theological feature of the Gospel of John, occurring here in its first instance. Jesus announces to the Samaritan woman that he is the one awaited. Samaritan sects anticipating the return of Moses ascribed to his successor "the power of God's name, revealed to Moses at the burning bush."[38] To possess the power of the name "I am" was to manifest divine presence, creativity, and power — to be a dwelling place of God.[39] Jesus demonstrates this power by saying "I am."[40]

In this dialogue, Jesus is presented as the fulfillment of Samaritan hopes for the one who is to come. He brings eternal, life-giving water. He promises a renewal of worship that resonates back to the Hebrew patriarchs, challenging the hegemony of Jerusalem. The story concludes: "Many Samaritans from that city believed in him. . . . They asked him to stay with them; and he stayed there two days. And many more believed because of his word" (4:39–41).

It is noteworthy how little theological significance is attributed to the story of the Samaritan woman by most biblical scholars, evidence perhaps of subtle forms of sexism that dismiss stories of women as peripheral to the meaning of a text.[41] From our perspective, the Samaritan woman is one of the most important stories in the gospel.[42]

---

37. The well is usually interpreted through marriage symbolism as the place where many patriarchs found their wives. Schneiders, *Written That You May Believe*, 139–40, rejects a literal reading of the woman's five husbands which interprets the woman in sexual terms and ignores the legendary five Assyrian gods that Jews accused the Samaritans of worshiping. Her reading emphasizes the theological import of the story: "The exchange about the husband occurs . . . in the midst of [the theological discussion]. . . . The adultery/idolatry symbolism so prevalent in the prophetic literature for speaking of Israel's infidelity to Yahweh the Bridegroom would be a most apt vehicle for discussion of the anomalous religious situation of Samaria."

38. Fossum, *Name of God*, 294: "That Jesus was given the Divine Name when having ascended to heaven is in fact part of a primitive Christology predating Paul and appearing in the hymn in Phil. ii."

39. Samaritan liturgical practices included chanting the ten words of creation. The first word is "let there be light," and the tenth is the name of God given to Moses in the burning bush (Bowman, *Samaritan Documents*, 3). Fossum notes that "YHWH . . . inhabits the earthly temple, but not in person; he is present through the agency of his name" (*Name of God*, 84); "the Tetragrammaton, the 'Great Name,' is the original creative agent, by which the universe was filled and sustained" (87); and "Moses was the possessor of the Divine Name, and the eschatological prophet who was going to be like him would also be the owner of the Name" (126).

40. The "I am" statements in the gospel are central to Christian supercessionist claims that Jesus is the incarnation of God. A Samaritan reading offers a different theological purpose for these statements.

41. Schneiders, *Written That You May Believe*, 137: "As anyone familiar with the major commentaries on the Fourth Gospel knows, the treatment of the Samaritan woman in the history of interpretation is a textbook case of the trivialization, marginalization, and even sexual demonization of biblical women, which reflects and promotes the parallel treatment of real women in the church." Schneiders does an extensive analysis of this story and interprets its purpose in the gospel "to legitimate the presence of Samaritan Christians in the Johannine community and to affirm their equality with Jewish Christians" (139).

42. During field research in July 2002, we found many images of the Samaritan woman at the well depicted in the Roman catacombs, Ravenna mosaics and ivories, and Istanbul mosaics

This Samaritan element in John has long been recognized by scholars, but its implications have not been developed in any depth, nor has it significantly informed any major commentary published in the past fifty years.[43] Samaritan concerns, perspectives, and theological themes run throughout the Gospel of John. It is permeated with hexateuchal motifs but nearly devoid of themes outside the Hexateuch — a focus distinctive to Samaritans.

John's Jesus manifests the presence of God as Moses does. Mosaic themes of ascent to God and descent to the people mark Jesus' story, beginning with the descent in the prologue. Rather than cryptic parables, Jesus delivers long speeches, as Moses does, culminating in a parallel farewell discourse. Several of Jesus' miracles resemble those of Moses and have a similar enhanced dramatic quality. The "I am" speeches indicate that Jesus has the power granted to Moses at the burning bush. Jesus' mission, inherited from Moses, is to bring the divine word to the world with a new commandment. This coherence of identity between Jesus and Moses culminates in the farewell discourse when Jesus delivers a new commandment: "Love one another as I have loved you" (13:34; 15:12).

The Gospel of John's Anti-Judaism

The Gospel of John uses *hoi ioudaioi* (the Jews) in various ways. Sometimes the Jews are regarded favorably: salvation is said to come from the Jews (4:22), and many of Jesus' followers are Jews who "put their faith in him" (7:31; 8:30; 11:45; 12:11, 42). Sometimes the term designates neutral practices. The writer explains that Jews and Samaritans do not share vessels in common (4:9); and Jewish festivals are noted, such as Passover (2:13), as if the hearers were unfamiliar with them.

The negative picture of the Jews starts with Jesus' actions and condemnations (2:13–21; 3:11–21; 5:10–15). Beginning in 5:16, following these provocations, the Jews are described as persecuting and plotting to kill him. Throughout the rest of the gospel, Jesus confronts Jews as antagonists. His Jewish opponents include some members of the Sanhedrin (though not all), some temple guards (though not all), and some Pharisees (though not all). Caiaphas, the high priest of the Jerusalem temple, leads the plot to kill

---

and frescoes, from the first millennium of Christian art. She is also depicted in the earliest discovered house church in Dura Europos on the Euphrates in a frescoe painting, dated with certainty before the mid-third century C.E., when the Roman garrison outpost was destroyed. Yale University owns the frescoes.

43. For example, C. K. Barrett, *The Gospel according to St. John* (London: SPCK, 1978); Raymond Brown, *The Gospel according to John* (Anchor Bible 29–29A; New York: Doubleday, 1966–70), Bultmann, *Gospel of John;* C. H. Dodd, *The Interpretation of the Fourth Gospel* (Cambridge: Cambridge University Press, 1963); Robert Kysar, *The Fourth Evangelist and His Gospel* (Minneapolis: Augsburg, 1975); and Leon Morris, *The Gospel according to John* (Grand Rapids: Eerdmans, 1995).

Jesus (11:47–53). A crowd referred to as the Jews calls for Jesus' crucifixion (19:12, 14–15).[44]

The gospel's hostile portrait of Jews becomes grotesque in John 8 and beyond. In a dispute set in the temple court, Jesus accuses the scribes and Pharisees of plotting to kill him (8:40). He calls them the children of the devil, liars, and murderers, rather than authentic descendants of Abraham (8:39–47). The Jews protest and escalate their opposition (8:52–59; 9:16; 10:19–20, 31–33, 39). In John 11 Caiaphas declares that Jesus' death will prevent Romans from destroying their temple and their nation (11:47–53). Later, the Jewish crowd tells Pilate that no friend of Caesar would release Jesus (19:12), and the chief priests proclaim, "We have no king but the emperor" (19:15).

While the Gospel of John reports that Pilate, not the Jews, could lawfully put Jesus to death, the Roman procurator is portrayed as exercising this power reluctantly, responding to pressure from Jesus' opponents, the Jews (18:29–31). The text says that Pilate feared the Jews and agreed under protest to their demand that Jesus be crucified (19:1–7). It implies that Pilate anticipated a mass rebellion if he did not comply.

This relentlessly negative portrait of the Jews reiterates a long history of animosity between Samaritans and Jews. Major friction points of this animosity are illustrated in the gospel: controversy over the Sabbath (5:10–16; 7:22–23; 9:16), conflicting claims to true ancestry (5:45–47; 7:19, 42–43; 8:33–50, 58–59), competing temple systems (2:13–21; 4:20–24), different strategies for appeasing larger empires (11:47–53; 18:13–14; 19:15–16), and divergent messianic claims and national aspirations (4:13–26).

It is tempting to explain the gospel's anti-Judaism as a historical problem carried through the text from a prior period that is not essential to the gospel's message of truth. This might be possible were it not for the fact that the gospel itself inflates the historical animosity of Samaritans toward Jews into a cosmological principle of "the world's" hostility to receiving Christ. Jesus' Jewish opponents do not remain just Jews. They become the embodiment of the darkness that opposes the light.

The gospel text, from its opening prologue, sets up a cosmological drama between those who receive and believe the Word and those who do not (1:5, 10–12). The Word dwells in those who receive it (15:7; 17:6–8). They are born of God (1:12–13); they will know the truth and be free (8:32); they belong to Christ as friend (15:14) and are protected as his own (10:14–15); they are promised eternal life (3:36; 5:24–29; 6:51–58; 10:28; 11:25–26) and the gift of the Spirit's comfort and inspiration (7:39; 14:16–17, 25–26; 20:22). Those who believe have seen and heard (6:40, 45; 10:4; 14:7) and have come to the light (3:21; 8:12; 12:46).

---

44. Reinhartz, "Johannine Community," discusses various theories for John's complex use of the term *the Jews*.

The gospel characterizes those who do not believe as the opposite. They do not receive the Word (1:11; 3:12; 5:38–39) or love God (5:42); they are not of God (8:47) but are children of the devil, liars and murderers (8:44). They will not receive eternal life (3:36), but are condemned by God (3:18) as recipients of God's wrath (3:36) who will die in their sins (8:24). They will be pruned away and burned (15:2, 6). Their seeing and hearing is impaired (8:43–47; 9:39–49). They love darkness and their deeds are evil (3:19).

The cumulative effect of the gospel's portrait of the Jews is the transmutation of individual leaders who plot against Jesus into a theological caste that is cosmologically cast out. The gospel calls this caste evil: children of the devil, condemned, worthy of the wrath of God, denied life, darkness, the world that rejects God. In this transmutation, the gospel turns Jews into an image of transpersonal evil and establishes a Christian ethic of condemnation and murderous rage toward Jews and all others who do not believe.

Theological Reflection

Immersion in the corrosive hostility to Jews in John's Gospel does not lead beyond its rage to a purified theology. The gospel's theology imbeds its drama of light and darkness in a cosmological system that threatens wrath and violence to all who reject Jesus. In examining this theology below, we recognize that to demonize or condemn the text would be to endorse its own vituperative ethic.

As feminist theologians, we began a study of the Gospel of John because we found an early Christian voice that did not present Jesus' death as ordained by God to save the world.[45] Our feminist theological agenda is to expose how violence in Christianity is sanctioned by its theological construction of the atonement.[46] Our concern for victims of violence led us to consider the Johannine Jesus as a potential ally. His refusal to be a victim and his confrontation with those plotting to kill him provide an important counterpoint to images of Jesus whose silent submission to abuse is exemplary. At the point when he would appear most powerless, standing before Pilate, Jesus defiantly speaks from a center of power that violence cannot destroy. Testimony to such a center can be heartening for Christians who face violence or must recover from its effects.

---

45. The lack of atonement theology in John is noticed by a number of biblical scholars. See, for example, Gail O'Day, *Revelation in the Fourth Gospel: Narrative Mode and Theological Claim* (Philadelphia: Fortress, 1986).

46. Rita Nakashima Brock, *Journeys by Heart: A Christology of Erotic Power* (New York: Crossroad, 1988); Joanne Carlson Brown and Rebecca Ann Parker, "For God So Loved the World?" in *Christianity, Patriarchy, and Abuse: A Feminist Critique* (ed. Joanne Carlson Brown and Carole R. Bohn; New York: Pilgrim, 1989), 1–30; Rita Nakashima Brock and Rebecca Ann Parker, *Proverbs of Ashes: Violence, Redemptive Suffering, and the Search for What Saves Us* (Boston: Beacon, 2001).

John's Jesus, however, becomes a spokesperson for wrath against Jews and all who do not believe. The gospel suggests, in its theological scheme, that evil will be resolved by divine condemnation of all who oppose Jesus. The text thus reduces complex sources of human violence to issues of belief. At the same time, it minimizes violence as being of ultimate unimportance.

Reading John as a Christian Samaritan text places its anti-Judaism in a larger context of conflict and violence. But how the gospel relates to this larger context merits reflection. Samaritans and Jews created strategies for religious, political, economic, and national survival within divisive pressures of imperial domination. Their divergent strategies heightened the tensions between them and created a spiral of violence, as evidenced in sporadic violent exchanges in the first century C.E.[47]

The larger social and political context of imperial Rome was a constant destabilizing force in the area. Roman officials appropriated land for imperial use, dislocated populations, placed heavy taxes on its provinces, used spies and informants to monitor activity against their rule, frequently assassinated suspected traitors, and resorted to military action when other means failed to control populations.[48] Pilate, the Roman procurator of Judea based in Caesarea, regularly used crucifixion as a tool to intimidate the local population and quell uprisings against Roman rule. His use of mass murder eventually led to his recall to Rome.[49]

The gospel does not ignore the threat of imperial violence, but softens it in its picture of Pilate and subsumes that larger threat under the evil plotting of Caiaphas and his cohorts. In reducing the complexity of violence to one dimension of Samaritan experience, the gospel inflates those who have objections to Jesus into a cosmological principle of evil. In doing so, it uses its portrait of the Jews to mask imperial strategies, including violence, to control subject populations.

In confronting his Jewish opponents, the Johannine Jesus expresses a moral expectation that they recognize that what they do is wrong (8:42–47; 18:13–24). After his arrest, when he stands before Pilate, he makes no such demand of the Roman authorities (18:33–38; 19:10–11). The empire is neutralized. No critique of the justice or morality of the empire is made.

The text sidesteps any moral challenge to Roman domination and turns its focus of moral accountability solely on Jesus' Jewish opponents. In speaking to Pilate, Jesus asserts his own cosmological power, which makes the empire irrelevant. With this strategy, the gospel presents a duplicitous theology. On

---

47. Shur, *History of the Samaritans*, 44, suggests that the first century C.E. was the most violent in the entire history of Jewish-Samaritan relationships.

48. Arthur E. R. Boak and William G. Sinnigen, *A History of Rome to A.D. 565* (5th ed.; New York: Macmillan, 1965).

49. Josephus reports a massacre by Pilate of a group of Samaritans in 36 C.E. that led to the termination of his appointment; Shur, *History of the Samaritans*, 44; see also Crossan, *Who Killed Jesus?* 148–50.

the one hand, it condemns violence and threatens divine retribution for it. On the other hand, it attempts to minimize it as an insignificant power.

This gospel is true, not as a historical account of Roman behavior or as an ethical guide for Christians. Rather, it presents an honest accounting of how human communities often respond to violence and the trauma of its aftermath. In our study of the effects of violence, we learned that it impacts individuals and communities in complex ways. Sometimes people turn to lateral violence, neighbor on neighbor, while ignoring the larger system disrupting their relationships. Sometimes victims minimize violence, pretending that it has not really touched them. Sometimes a community feels helpless and turns to a more powerful other to vent its rage. Sometimes memories of violence are confused so that dissociated memory fragments combine with present reality and produce distorted experience and response. Sometimes experiences of injury are rationalized into universal principles or ideologies. Sometimes the trauma produces a hypervigilant paranoia, in which thinking becomes black and white, rigid, and obsessed with seeing the world through an all-encompassing orientation haunted by unhealed violence. The Gospel of John portrays all of these responses.

The history of Christian behavior toward Jews, heretics, and infidels reveals the incendiary ways that John's Gospel has contributed to violence. This history can neither be erased nor explained away. A redeemable Christianity cannot be extracted from it. While it may compensate for Christian complicity in the Shoah to remove the Jews from the list of those who should be converted, as the Catholic church has recently done,[50] shifting Jews from nonbelievers to believers leaves the problematic system unaddressed.

The problem for Christianity is not and never has been those who remain unpersuaded that Jesus is the Christ. The problem is the legacy and pervasiveness of violence. Theologies that inadequately understand violence and its sources reinscribe it and incite the use of violence as a solution to evil. This gospel can be a route to a greater understanding of ourselves, our limits, and our struggle to discern what will set us free from ongoing cycles of violence. For it to be so, we must read the gospel alongside the history of Christian anti-Semitism, which must never be laid aside, and alongside our own present human struggle to discern the sources of violence and to heal its effects. The gospel is neither our ally nor our enemy, but an uncomfortable witness to the peace we hope for and the violence we cannot deny.

---

50. Daniel J. Wakin, "Catholics, Jews, and the Work of Reconciliation," *New York Times* (15 September 2002): 4.3.

II

Nature, Law, and Custom in Augustine's *On the Good of Marriage*

Bernadette J. Brooten

The [classical Greek] theorists ... did not (so much) discover nature. ...
Rather they created, they invented, their own distinctive and divergent
ideas, often in direct and explicit confrontation with their rivals. The
concept was forged in controversy.
— G. E. R. Lloyd, *Methods and Problems in Greek Science*

Early Christian and other ancient Mediterranean conceptualizations are simultaneously strangely archaic to our own way of thinking and yet deeply
embedded in it. This is nowhere clearer than in the concept of nature.[1] The
methods and results of the contemporary natural sciences differ markedly
from those of ancient scientists, lawyers, philosophers, or theologians, and
modern scientific methods and results certainly persuade the general public
far more than does theology. Nevertheless, views about natural and unnatural sex deriving from ancient Mediterranean medicine, law, philosophy,
and theology continue to live on, in spite of modern acceptance of genetic
research and of scientific skepticism about religion. These ancient views of
nature were crucial in setting priorities for sexual ethics that continue to be
felt today.

Elisabeth Schüssler Fiorenza, through her writing, teaching, and public
speaking, challenges scholars to trace the impact of the Bible and of Christian
tradition on the lives of contemporary women and men. She especially urges
us to examine early Christian texts critically before making them the basis of

---

1. In addition to G. E. R. Lloyd, *Methods and Problems in Greek Science* (Cambridge:
Cambridge University Press, 1991), 431–32 (cited in the epigraph), others also recognize the
controversial character of the concept of nature. See Klaus Wengst on Rom 1:26–27: "Könnte
es nicht auch sein, daß etwas als 'natürlich' behauptet wird, was sich bei näherem Hinsehen
lediglich als eine bestimmte gesellschaftliche *Konvention* entpuppt?"; "Paulus und die Homo-
sexualität," *Zeitschrift für evangelische Ethik* 31 (1987): 75. See also John J. Winkler, who
titles his discussion of Artemidoros's categories of sexual intercourse "For 'Nature,' Read 'Culture' "; see *The Constraints of Desire: The Anthropology of Sex and Gender in Ancient Greece*
(New York: Routledge, 1990), 17. Both scholars implicitly refer to the Greek debate on the
boundaries between nature (*physis*) and law (*nomos*).

contemporary theology or ethics. In her own work, she extensively analyzes both ancient and contemporary frameworks that undergird societal values and norms. Schüssler Fiorenza was among the first feminist theologians to pay full attention to interlocking structures of oppression. She considers not only the domination of free women by free men, but also that of free women and men over enslaved women, men, and children, of citizens over noncitizens, and of the wealthy over the poor. She terms this interlocking system of domination "kyriarchy," a word that derives from the ancient Greek words *kyrios* (masculine) and *kyria* (feminine), which can mean "lord"/"lady," "slaveholder," "patron"/"patroness," and "legal guardian" (this last term applies only to men). In this essay, I will analyze how Augustine of Hippo, in his work *On the Good of Marriage,* draws upon an ancient system of classifying sexual acts based on whether they conform to nature, to law, and to custom. I hope to make clear that the sexual ethics of this highly influential early Christian treatise exemplify a kyriarchy made to seem universally self-evident through an appeal to what is natural. Augustine's comparisons of better and worse behaviors will disturb persons concerned with creating sexual ethics that are based on consent and mutuality and that thereby respect the full human dignity of all persons.

Ancient Mediterranean Classification of Sexual Acts

People in the ancient Mediterranean world, who thought of sexual relations as occurring between two unequal partners, classified sexual acts on the basis of whether they were in accordance with nature, law, and custom. By classifying certain acts as contrary to nature, they meant that all cultures and peoples would always reject them; when they classified other sexual acts as contrary to law or to custom, but in accordance with nature, they meant that some cultures might reject these acts, while other cultures might accept them. The categories of nature and law go back to philosophical discussions in ancient Greece.

Dream classifier Artemidoros, who apparently adopted the categories of nature, law, and custom from other thinkers, is a good representative of this ancient method of classifying sexual acts. Artemidoros came from Daldis in Asia Minor, today's Turkey, where, in the second century C.E., he composed a work in Greek entitled *The Classification of Dreams* (*Oneirokritika*), in which he classifies and interprets dreams on many subjects. Artemidoros (*Oneirokritika* 1.78–80) classifies sexual dreams according to three categories: "nature" (*physis*), "law" (the Greek word *nomos* could also be translated "convention"), and "custom" (*ethos*).[2] Artemidoros's schematization is as follows:

---

2. Roger A. Pack, ed., *Artemidori Daldiani Oneirocriticon Libri V* (Leipzig: Teubner, 1963), 86–99; for an English translation, see Robert J. White, *The Interpretation of Dreams:*

1. Natural (*kata physin*), legal (or conventional) (*kata nomon*), and customary (*kata ethos*) includes intercourse of a man with his wife or mistress, with a prostitute, with a woman whom the male dreamer does not know, with his male or female servant, and with a woman known to him and well acquainted with him. This category also includes the penetration of a female dreamer by a man known to her, intercourse between a richer man and a poorer man, intercourse between an older man and a younger man, and masturbation (i.e., for a man to stroke his own penis).

2. Illegal (or unconventional) (*para nomon*) consists primarily of incest: a man penetrating his son (distinguished as to age), being penetrated by his son, having intercourse with his daughter (distinguished as to age and marital status) or with his sister (which is not discussed, since it has the same meaning as intercourse with one's daughter), penetrating his brother, penetrating his friend, having intercourse with his mother (in a variety of positions, with a living or a dead mother, or with a mother from whom one is estranged), and having fellatio with his mother or with a variety of other people (as either the passive or the active partner in the act).

3. Unnatural (*para physin*) includes masturbation (i.e., for a man to "have sex with himself" — not differentiated from a man's stroking his own penis in category 1 above), kissing one's own penis, practicing fellatio with oneself, a woman playing the active or the passive role with another woman, sexual intercourse with a female or male deity, intercourse with a corpse (both active and passive — Artemidoros does not explain the mechanics of this latter category), and intercourse with an animal (both active and passive).

This system of classification, which I and others argue is older than Artemidoros and widely known in the Roman world, represents a coming together of several different principles of categorization, the most important of which is human social hierarchy. The single thing that the acts that Artemidoros classifies as natural, legal, and customary have most in common is that they represent a human social hierarchy: husband over wife; man over mistress, prostitute, or other woman; man over female or male slave; and older man over younger man and richer man over poorer man. Artemidoros also takes masturbation, seen here as hands stroking the penis, in a hierarchical fashion; thus, he sees the hands as like servants attending to the penis, which itself symbolizes the master's children.

Oneirocritica by Artemidorus (Park Ridge, N.J.: Noyes, 1975). For a fuller discussion, see Bernadette J. Brooten, *Love between Women: Early Christian Responses to Female Homoeroticism* (Chicago: University of Chicago Press, 1996), 175–86.

The illegal category includes acts against which some cultures might make laws and others might not. It consists mainly of incest, but also includes sexual relations between two male friends. Thus, Artemidoros classifies male homoerotic relations either as natural, legal, and customary if they represent a human social hierarchy, such as between a master and a slave, an older man and a younger man, or a richer man and a poorer man, or as illegal if they occurred between two partners of equal social stature, which people in this period included in the definition of friendship.

The unnatural category contains sexual relations that do not represent a human social hierarchy: between a human and a deity, between a human and an animal, between a live person and a corpse, and between two women. Notice that homosexuality and heterosexuality do not form a category in this ancient system of classification. Artemidoros defines male-male relations as natural, legal, and customary if they occur between two unequal partners or as illegal if they occur between two equal partners, but he sees all female-female relations as unnatural. This fits very well with the general difficulties that people in the Roman world had in trying to fit sexual relations between women into the normative cultural model that sex occurs between two unequal partners, one of whom penetrates the other.

Augustine's Classification of Sexual Acts

Augustine of Hippo in North Africa uses the nature/law schema documented in Artemidoros in order to adapt biblical sexual values to his own time and to classify certain types of sexual relations as better or worse than other types. Augustine's work, *On the Good of Marriage* (*De bono coniugali*; written in 401 C.E.), illustrates this process particularly well and will serve here as the basis for my analysis. *On the Good of Marriage* is directed against two views held by some of his contemporaries: (1) that marriage is as good as virginity and (2) that marriage is evil.[3] Augustine argues that marriage is indeed good, but that virginity is better. Augustine sets forth the three goods of marriage: offspring (*proles*), fidelity (*fides*), and the sacramental bond (*sacramentum*). With offspring, Augustine means that sexual activity within marriage becomes a moral good when it results in offspring (*De bono coniugali* 3.3). Fidelity means no intercourse that goes against the marriage compact. The bond is sacramental because it cannot be dissolved through divorce.[4]

---

3. Augustine directs himself here against Jovinian, who held that marriage is equal to virginity. Elsewhere, he argues against the Pelagian Julian of Eclanum, who held the same view. On the other hand, Augustine is at pains to distance himself from his own past as a member of the Manicheans, who held that marriage is evil because reproduction constitutes the imprisonment of souls in the material world.

4. For a detailed and subtle analysis of Augustine's teachings on married women, see Kari Elisabeth Børresen, *Subordination and Equivalence: The Nature and Rôle of Woman in Augustine and Thomas Aquinas* (trans. Charles H. Talbot; Washington, D.C.: University Press of

The Bible presents Augustine with the vexing dilemma of texts that apparently support or even require marriage; the narratives of the polygamous biblical patriarchs pose a particularly acute problem for him.[5] Augustine defends the biblical patriarchs for having more than one wife by setting forth his threefold criteria for legitimate sexual activity (*De bono coniugali* 25.33):

1. What is not done contrary to nature (*contra naturam*) is not a sin (*peccatum*), since they made use of their wives not for the sake of being wanton, but for procreation.

2. Nor against the customs (*contra morem*), because at the time those things were being done.

3. Nor contrary to the precept (*contra praeceptum*), because they were not prohibited by any law (*lex*).[6]

Augustine overlays the Christian concept of sin on the ancient schematization of sexual acts that are in accordance with or contrary to nature, law, and/or custom. He uses "custom" and "precept" rather straightforwardly, but with "nature" departs sharply from tradition. Nature is the most crucial of the three terms, since it alone counts as a universal category. According to Artemidoros's schema, the patriarchs' sexual relations with any number of women, whether or not married to them, would fully accord with nature, regardless of any wantonness and independent of any focus on procreation. Augustine's departure from legal doctrine is subtler. To support his position that procreation is the only legitimate purpose of sexual relations, Augustine states: "Among all peoples [*in omnibus gentibus*] marriage exists for the same purpose, namely to have children" (*De bono coniugali* 17.19).[7] He further elucidates by distinguishing between the universal norm and the specific norm applicable only to Christians: "The value of marriage, therefore, for all races and peoples, lies in the objective of procreation and the faithful observance of chastity. For the people of God, however, it lies also

---

America, 1981), 94–123. The English edition is a revision of the French original: *Subordination et equivalence: Nature et rôle de la femme d'après Augustin et Thomas d'Aquin* (Oslo: Universitetsforlaget/Paris: Maison Mame, 1968).

5. See Elizabeth A. Clark, *Reading Renunciation: Asceticism and Scripture in Early Christianity* (Princeton: Princeton University Press, 1999), 188. In this superb study, Clark analyzes how Augustine and other early Christian ascetic writers dealt with biblical texts that apparently contradicted their views.

6. Augustine notes that in his time, Roman law does not permit polygyny (*De bono coniugali* 7.7). Except as noted, translations of Augustine are taken from *Saint Augustine: Treatises on Marriage and Other Subjects* (trans. Charles T. Wilcox; Fathers of the Church 27; Washington, D.C.: Catholic University of America Press, 1969). Latin edition: Josef Zycha, ed., *Sancti Aureli Augustini* (Corpus scriptorum ecclesiasticorum latinorum 41.5.3; Vienna: Tempsky, 1940).

7. Translation from *The Works of Saint Augustine*, part 1, vol. 9: *Marriage and Virginity* (trans. Ray Kearney; Hyde Park, N.Y.: New City, 1999), 48.

in the sanctity of the sacrament" — which means that Christians are prohibited from divorcing and remarrying during the spouse's lifetime (32.24).[8] Roman, Jewish, Greek, and the other bodies of law probably known to Augustine defined procreation as central to marriage, but did not limit sex only to procreative acts and allowed for a number of extramarital sexual acts, particularly by men. By speaking of "all peoples," Augustine is alluding to the idea that marriage is laid down in natural law. One Roman jurist, who argues that nature taught natural law to all animals, not just to humans, defines marriage and the procreation and rearing of children as part of natural law.[9] Augustine differs from this view, however, because his focus is on marriage as existing for the procreation of children, not on nature's ordaining marriage as essential to society. In fact, he argues that "not marrying is better [than marriage, which is good] because to have no need of this task is better even for human society" (9.9).[10] Augustine also goes beyond the understanding of nature found in Roman natural-law theory, according to which humans, like animals, should join together in marriage to reproduce and raise their offspring; this leaves open extramarital relationships by Roman males (and presumably by animals), as well as nonprocreative sex within marriage. Thus, Augustine's universal claim that nature ordained that all humans should limit their sexual expression to procreative acts and that other sexual acts are "wanton" gains power from certain traditional understandings of nature, but actually differs considerably from them.

The criteria that Augustine sets forth in his justification of the biblical patriarchs' polygyny provide him with a means of classifying sexual acts and defining some as worse than others. We will see that procreation influences, but does not alone determine, how Augustine classifies sexual activity. Thus, Augustine imagines that without sexual activity, the relationship between husband and wife would have been "a kind of friendly and genuine union of the one ruling and the other obeying" (*De bono coniugali* 1.1). Augustine presents as universal the concept that a wife relates to her husband, as does a slave to a master or a human soul to God. This schema of ruler/ruled shapes Augustine's classification of various sexual couplings. Recall that Artemidoros classified sexual acts that represented a human social hierarchy as natural, legal, and customary and those that clearly did not as unnatural.

Beginning with the most immoral and proceeding to the least immoral, Augustine's scale is as follows:

---

8. Translation from ibid., 56.

9. Ulpian (second/third century C.E.) in *Corpus Iuris Civilis, Digesta* 1.1.1; see also *Corpus Iuris Civilis, Institutiones* 1.2.proem. Augustine employs precisely the same term for what Ulpian "call[s] marriage," namely the "joining of male and female" (*coniunctio maris et feminae*). The opening to *De bono coniugali,* with its focus on humans as social beings, is also quite reminiscent of Stoic natural-law theory (e.g., Cicero, *De officiis* 1.54).

10. Translation from Kearney, *Marriage and Virginity,* 41.

1. Unnatural sex, defined by Augustine as sex that cannot lead to pro-creation; he also refers to it as the unspeakable: "Those things about which, as the Apostle says: 'It is shameful even to speak'" (*De bono coniugali* 10.11–11.12; 8.8).[11]

2. Incest, specifically with one's mother (8.8).

3. Adultery (6.6; 8.8).

4. Fornication (presented as sex with a prostitute) (6.6; 8.8).

5. Marital intercourse "for the purpose of satisfying concupiscence," rather than for the purpose of having children. (Augustine argues that such intercourse, which is a venial sin, protects against the mortal sins of adultery and fornication, but he warns that, even so, it must not be so excessive that it takes time away from prayer (6.6; 10.11–11.12.)

Augustine's scale of sexual acts that are morally good is simpler:

1. Celibacy (the best).

2. Procreative sex within marriage and otherwise continence.[12]

While this scale seems to be based on nearness to God (best achieved through a celibate life of prayer, followed by chaste marriage with only pro-creative sex), a closer look reveals other criteria at work, as several examples can illustrate. Prostitutes are fully a part of Augustine's equation and some-times represent a morally better option than sex with one's wife. Female shame is the underlying criterion here (*De bono coniugali* 11.12):

1. The natural use (*usus naturalis;* i.e., coitus), when it goes beyond the marriage rights (i.e., beyond the need for procreation) is

   a. pardonable in a wife (*venialis . . . in uxore*)

   b. damnable in a prostitute (*damnabilis . . . meretrice*)

2. The use against nature (*contra naturam;* i.e., anal and perhaps oral sex) is

   a. abominable (*execrabiliter*) in a prostitute

   b. more abominable (*execrabilius*) in a wife (i.e., the wife is more shameful [*turpior*] if she permits this to take place with herself rather than with another woman)

---

11. Augustine interprets Paul in Rom 1:26–27 as prohibiting sex that does not allow for procreation, such as anal sex. (See also *De nuptiis et concupiscentia* 20.35.) He is unusual in the early church in taking Rom 1:26–27 this way; most others take the men being "consumed with passion for one another" to mean that Paul is referring to same-sex sexual relations. Elsewhere, Augustine does condemn homoerotic activity between women and between men (*Epistle* 211.13–14; *De opere monachorum* 32.40). The citation about the unspeakable is from Eph 5:12, which, within its context, could include same-sex sexual relations, as well as anal (or oral) sex between men and women and other acts deemed impure and idolatrous.

12. *De bono coniugali* 7.6: "Continence from all intercourse is certainly better than marital intercourse itself which takes place for the begetting of children." See also 8.8; 9.9; and 23.28.

Offspring, fidelity, and the sacramental bond — the three goods of marriage set forth by Augustine — do not explain this moral stratification. One might have thought that faithfulness to one's wife means that any sex with a prostitute is morally inferior to that with one's wife. Or one might have thought that all extramarital sex, none of which leads to the marital procreation that Augustine so espouses, would be equally morally turpitudinous. But another powerful ancient Mediterranean value — female shame — trumps procreation. In Augustine's view, this type of unnatural sex, which belongs to the realm of the impure, the impious, the perverted, the illicit, must call forth shame on the part of a virtuous matron. Although Augustine assumes and indeed ordains wifely subjection, and although he sees husbands as aggressors who demand sex of their wives beyond that necessary for procreation, here he presents the wife as having the final say on whether to allow herself to be penetrated anally. Augustine causes us to imagine a wife, confronted with the possibility of anal penetration, trying — in her shame — to ward it off by suggesting that her husband should better perform this abominable act with a prostitute. At this point, we are not far from Artemidoros's natural, legal, and customary category, which includes sex between a husband and his wife and between a man and a prostitute. While Augustine rejects anal sex as unnatural — in part because it is nonprocreative, a point that does not enter Artemidoros's radar screen — Augustine would accept Artemidoros's classification of prostitution as customary. And Augustine's teaching that such sex is more abominable with a wife than with a prostitute indirectly supports prostitution as an institution that serves to prevent the shaming of a Christian wife. Notice also that Augustine agrees with Artemidoros that coitus with a prostitute constitutes natural sex.

While Augustine disapproves of husbands who demand of their wives more vaginal intercourse than necessary for procreation, he expects their wives to indulge them. Some men, he states, are "incontinent to such a degree that they do not spare their wives even when pregnant" (*De bono coniugali* 6.6).[13] He assumes that the husband is an aggressor who may be overly demanding of his wife. Of such a husband, he states that "he sins much less than one who commits fornication even most rarely" (11.12). In other words, if what the husband demands is natural sex, his demands on his wife are sinful, since they go beyond what is necessary for procreation; but, unlike with unnatural sex, the wife presumably has no excuse to refer him to a prostitute. Augustine does not comment on how the subordinate wife should respond. Neither his treatise nor the laws and customs of his culture give her the genuine option of saying no should he become violent in his demands. Augustine's text contains no direct reference to the potential

---

13. Augustine continues: "In marriage, intercourse for the purpose of generation has no fault attached to it, but for the purpose of satisfying concupiscence, provided with a spouse, ... is a venial sin; adultery or fornication, however, is a mortal sin." Augustine shortly thereafter adds that both adultery and fornication are also crimes (*De bono coniugali* 7.6).

for such violence; whether violence accompanies sex within marriage is not relevant to his method of classifying sexual acts. If the sexual acts are natural and marital, then they are less sinful than sex outside marriage. Notice that, whereas in the case of unnatural sex, a prostitute can represent a less objectionable outlet; with natural sex, wedlock is meant to protect against fornication, which means that the wife is expected to endure excesses.

If the wife wishes to refrain from sex, however, she — like the husband, must do so only with the consent of the spouse. Paul is the basis for Augustine's teaching on this point; in 1 Cor 7:5, Paul directs married people to withhold conjugal rights only by mutual consent for a set time in order to have more time for prayer. Paul's principle for this directive is actually quite radical: "For the wife does not have authority over her own body, but the husband does; likewise the husband does not have authority over his own body, but the wife does" (7:4). The idea that wives have authority over their husbands' bodies is quite unusual in the Roman world. On the other hand, women's future economic security could depend on their offspring, so that a husband's refusal of sexual intercourse could tangibly endanger a wife's welfare. Paul may have been building upon ancient Jewish law, which recognized a wife's right to sexual intercourse for the sake of procreation and for her own sexual pleasure. For Augustine, sexual pleasure is at best peripheral and procreation inessential. But he retains the Pauline impulse to tread lightly in reducing sex within marriage, because marriage can help to keep sex within bounds. In both Paul's and Augustine's societies, however, free and freed women — the only women allowed to marry formally — did not have the same social, political, and legal power to exercise authority over their husbands' bodies that their husbands enjoyed over theirs. For this reason, marriage could cause wives to endure types of sexual behavior that protected their husbands from the sin of sex outside marriage, but did not protect them from their husbands.

Gender subordination as a value becomes even clearer when Augustine compares chaste concubines with lustful wives. Just as Augustine grants moral priority to an overly demanding husband over a fornicator, so too does he rank a concubine who has sex with a man only in order to conceive "and whatever she endures beyond the cause of procreation, she endures unwillingly" above matrons who "force their husbands to pay the debt of the flesh" (*De bono coniugali* 5.5). This further illustrates the role of gender subordination in Augustine. A man requiring excessive natural (i.e., vaginal) sex from his wife or concubine ranks morally higher than a man who fornicates (with an unmarried woman) or than a married woman who requires natural sex from her husband out of passion.

Augustine's discussion of polygyny and polyandry further illustrates the criterion of gender subordination. He states that the biblical patriarchs were allowed to have more than one wife for the sake of procreation, which was a higher priority in their time than in his, while emphasizing that polygyny is not legal in his time. Augustine does not, however, exclude the possibility of surrogacy, namely for a wife to consent to children being born by another woman from her husband's seed (*De bono coniugali* 15.17). In contrast, women are never allowed to have more than one husband, even for the purpose of procreation, as in the case of a fertile woman married to a sterile man: "For, by a hidden law of nature [*occulta lex naturae*] things that rule love singularity; things that are ruled, indeed, are subjected not only each one to an individual master, but also, if natural or social conditions [*ratio naturalis vel socialis*] allow, many of them are not unfittingly subjected to one master" (17.20). Thus, Augustine universalizes wifely subordination to one husband by postulating a hidden law of nature that guarantees to a ruler that he rule alone. Social customs build on this law of nature. In some societies, a slave owner customarily owns just one slave, while in others (such as the Roman Empire in which Augustine lived), owners possess many slaves. Similarly, in some societies, a man rules alone over one wife, while in others, he may rule over more than one. As Augustine sets it forth here, not only slavery per se, but also enslaving many human beings at one time can accord with both nature and custom (i.e., social conditions). Similarly, monogamy based on the rule of the husband over the wife accords with the law of nature, but so too does polygyny, which is "not against the nature of marriage [*natura nuptiarum*]" (17.20). Augustine makes a biological claim to substantiate this, which is actually a cultural claim: "Many women can conceive children by one man, but one woman cannot do so by many men" (17.20). Physically, of course, one woman can conceive by more than one man, but her doing so may create problems for some cultures. In addition to the comparison between a married (free) woman and a (male or female) enslaved person, Augustine compares married women to human beings in relationship with God: human souls can commit fornication with many false gods, but they do not thereby become fruitful. As the example of polyandry and polygyny shows, the subordination of free women to their husbands is a more fundamental principle than the good of procreation. Like the subordination of slaves to their owners, wifely subordination is grounded in immutable nature itself. Societies may create laws and customs, such as polygyny and surrogacy, that theoretically promote procreation, while other societies may create laws, such as monogamy, that limit it. Societies may also develop customs that relativize procreation, such as Christian celibacy or voluntary abstention within marriage. Augustine's acceptance of all of these schemes — polygyny, surrogacy, monogamy, celibacy, and voluntary abstention within marriage — demonstrates that procreation is not his priority. Instead, as sharply as Augustine differs from Artemidoros at one level, at another level, they agree. Free men's power to rule over free women and female and male slaves is grounded in nothing less than nature.

Where did sexual relations between slave-masters and their slave-women fall on Augustine's moral scale? Both Augustine and Artemidoros accept as a given the power of free men over enslaved women and men. In *On the Good of Marriage,* with its systematic comparisons of the morality of all manner of sexual acts, sexual relations between slave owners and their enslaved laborers are strikingly lacking. For Artemidoros, such relations are natural, legal, and customary. But Augustine may well have concurred with Artemidoros that sexual contact between a male owner and a slave-woman was, at the minimum, customary and, in the case of vaginal intercourse, also natural. We have seen that Augustine does not absolutely exclude surrogacy and, in the case of unnatural sexual acts, sees contact with a prostitute as less abominable than with one's wife. Both surrogate mothers and prostitutes could be enslaved women, which Augustine knew, even though he does not discuss it. But what of sex with one's own slave-woman? In two sermons, Augustine vehemently opposed sex between masters and their slave-women, stating that such masters would go to hell; his rhetoric implies that he was having difficulty dissuading them.[14] We cannot know why he does not address this question in *On the Good of Marriage.*[15]

Moral Problems Inherent in Augustine's Sexual Ethics

This closer look at several of Augustine's moral comparisons shows both how greatly he differs from the model set forth by Artemidoros and how closely he adheres to the ancient cultural categories of nature, law, and custom with respect to gender relations between free women and free men. Disturbing discrepancies between Augustine's assessments of female and male sexual behavior render his sexual ethics inadequate as a basis for contemporary sexual morality. Building on the dual values of female subordination and female shame, Augustine's system allows for the prostitution of women, for spousal rape, and for polygyny (where it is culturally acceptable and promotes procreation). None of these is contrary to nature or to law in Augustine's system.

Augustine's treatment of incest demonstrates the problems in maintaining ancient frameworks for thinking about sexual ethics. Augustine's classification resembles that of Artemidoros, for whom various incestuous acts form the bulk of his middle category, that is, those acts that are not legal or conventional, but are still nevertheless natural. While Augustine says too little for us to be sure, he also places incest in a middle category, namely as worse

---

14. *Sermons* 9 and 392, on which see Richard Klein, *Die Sklaverei in der Sicht der Bischöfe Ambrosius und Augustinus* (Forschungen zur Antike und Sklaverei 20; Stuttgart: Steiner, 1988), 178–79.

15. See *On Marriage and Concupiscence* (*De nuptiis et concupiscentia*), which contains many parallels to *De bono coniugali* and in which Augustine also does not address this subject. In *On Marriage,* as elsewhere in his writings, Augustine uses the docile slave as a metaphorical model, here, for self-control within the married state (*De nuptiis et concupiscentia* 13).

than adultery, but not as immoral as the things of which it is "shameful even to speak" (Eph 5:12; *De bono coniugali* 8.8).[16] This latter category parallels Artemidoros's unnatural category. Augustine, like others before him, may have seen incest as morally problematic, but nevertheless natural.[17]

We have seen Augustine's complex interaction with the cultural norms of his period, especially nature, law, and custom.[18] While Augustine may differ from Artemidoros as to which sexual acts he classifies as natural, legal, and customary, his assumptions about the relative value of nature, law, and custom coincide to a large extent with those of Artemidoros. The major difference, however, lies in Augustine's overall evaluation of sexual relations, including those that both saw as natural (and, therefore, legal and customary). Earlier Christian writers, such as Paul, Tertullian, and Clement of Alexandria, all assumed the sanctity of marriage, characterized by sexual intercourse between subordinate women and their husbands who instructed them. Augustine introduced the notion of original sin associated with sexual intercourse and passed on even to a child at the moment of conception. For Augustine, the problem is the sexual urge itself, which humans cannot control or subdue through their will. Thus, even a natural, procreative sexual act between a subordinate wife and her husband is characterized by sin.

The pattern found in Artemidoros and Augustine left a significant mark on history, as one example succinctly illustrates. Thomas Aquinas (thirteenth century) classifies sexual vices from worst to least bad; the sins that are contrary to nature are worse than those that are natural (*Summa theologiae* II-II Q. 154 art. 12). Thomas ranks the sexual sins against nature in this order: bestiality, sodomy (male with male or female with female), "lechery that does not observe the due mode of intercourse,"[19] and masturbation. Then he ranks the sexual sins that are not unnatural, but rather against "right reason on the basis of the principles of nature": incest, raping a virgin or raping a wife, seducing a virgin, seducing a wife into adultery, and "simple fornication" (*fornicatio simplex;* i.e., sex between two unmarried persons other than anal sex, incest, etc.). As in Artemidoros and Augustine, the principle distinction is between natural and unnatural. Bestiality and sodomy rank before all other sexual sins. Artemidoros, too, classified sex with animals as unnatural, as he did sex between women. (Likewise Paul,

---

16. Note that Augustine's immoral categories contain greater nuance and extend far beyond Artemidoros's classifications.

17. See, e.g., first-century Jewish philosopher Philo of Alexandria, who, in *On the Special Laws* 3, discusses incest, adultery, the rape of a widow, and the rape of a virgin, but does not define them as "unnatural," a term that he reserves for sex between a man and a menstruating woman, relations between a man and a boy, and relations between two species of animals (implying also between a human being and an animal). Philo strongly influenced early Christian writers.

18. See Brooten, *Love between Women*, 355.

19. Translation here and in what follows is from Thomas Gilby, *St. Thomas Aquinas, Summa Theologiae* (New York: McGraw-Hill, 1968), 249. Gilby includes the Latin text and an English translation.

who in Rom 1:26–27 reserves his strongest condemnation for same-sex sexual acts, which he defines as unnatural.) Thomas classifies incest as sinful, but natural, which recalls Artemidoros's classification of various forms of incest as illegal, but natural, and, before him, Paul's censure of the Christian living with his father's wife. Paul expresses strong disapproval, but stops short of defining such incest as unnatural (1 Cor 5:1–8).

This brief analysis demonstrates the longevity of an ancient pattern of classifying sexual acts along the axes of nature, law, and custom. Nature ostensibly denotes the universal and the immutable. The rhetoric of the natural succeeded so well that twenty-first-century persons find it persuasive. And yet the above examples show that these concepts of nature are deeply cultural, highly specific. Artemidoros classifies as natural, legal, and customary sexual intercourse between a man and his female or male enslaved laborers. Augustine refrains from calling a concubine an adulteress when her wealthier partner of higher social standing leaves her for a wife suited to his station — as long as she does not marry.[20] These cases can be viewed only as part of a slave-owning, highly stratified society. The understandings of femaleness and maleness are similarly culturally specific; female inferiority and wifely obedience are part of what is natural.

This pattern is clearly ancient, long-lived, and documented in such influential thinkers as the Apostle Paul, Augustine of Hippo, and Thomas Aquinas. But is this a tradition of which Christians can be proud? Should a way of thinking that is inextricably intertwined with inequality and hierarchy shape the future of Christian sexual ethics? Understanding how nature, law, and custom served to solidify social hierarchies — between women and men, between the poor and the wealthy, and between socially marginalized persons and the elite — better equips us to oppose these inequalities. For that is the real ethical challenge facing us today.[21]

---

20. Augustine defines the man as committing adultery against his concubine.

21. I encourage others to deepen and broaden what I set forth here. In order to develop a proper basis for contemporary Christian sexual ethics, we need a much fuller historical picture. Biblical scholars and church historians may investigate additional occurrences of this set of categories within and outside Christian literature, analyzing how these categories function in those texts. Other scholars may correlate this material with social, economic, and legal history. Cultural critics and ethicists can help us to disentangle ourselves from this web. It is essential that groups that have suffered from ethics based on these categories become part of the ecclesial process of learning how to make ethical decisions.

12

"Sell What You Have and Give to the Poor"

A Feminist Interpretation of Clement of Alexandria's
Who Is the Rich Person Who Is Saved?

Denise Kimber Buell

Elisabeth Schüssler Fiorenza persuasively insists that our present struggles and contexts inform our biblical interpretations and historical reconstructions. She locates her commitments most broadly in terms of present struggles to achieve "the *ekklēsia* of wo/men — understood as *the congress of full decision-making citizens.*" As she articulates it, "*Ekklēsia* is not just a Christian religious notion; rather it expresses a sociopolitical radical democratic vision," which "has never been fully realized in history since in Western traditions wo/men have not been accorded full citizenship and self-determination."[1] While not fully realized, neither has this vision been crushed.[2] It is revived and remade "in debates and emancipatory struggles to change relations of domination, exploitation, and marginalization."[3]

---

1. Elisabeth Schüssler Fiorenza, *Sharing Her Word: Feminist Biblical Interpretation in Context* (Boston: Beacon, 1998), 112. She elaborates further: "Thus the radical democratic belief that all are created equal, together with the notion of the *ekklēsia* as *the decision-making congress/assembly of full citizens,* stands in conflictive tension with the reality of classical and modern kyriarchy" (112). I follow Schüssler Fiorenza's use of the term *wo/men* to mean not only "all women but also... oppressed and marginalized men. 'Wo/men' must therefore be understood as an inclusive expression rather than as an exclusive universalized gender term"; Elisabeth Schüssler Fiorenza, *Jesus: Miriam's Child, Sophia's Prophet: Critical Issues in Feminist Christology* (New York: Continuum, 1994), 191.

2. As such, Schüssler Fiorenza is more radical than some contemporary postmodern thinkers who also give important attention to the porous and nonlinear relationship between past and present. For example, Slavoj Žižek provocatively suggests that "what the proper *historical* stance... 'relativizes' is not the past (always distorted by our present point of view) but, paradoxically, *the present itself* — our present can be conceived only as the outcome (not of what actually happened in the past, but also) of the crushed potentials for the future that were contained in the past"; Slavoj Žižek, *The Fragile Absolute — or, Why Is the Christian Legacy Worth Fighting For?* (London: Verso, 2000), 90.

3. Schüssler Fiorenza, *Sharing Her Word,* 112.

Struggles for socioeconomic justice are one facet of this emancipatory project. Given Schüssler Fiorenza's call to ground interpretations in the present, I begin from the need to contend with trends of increasing economic disparity in America,[4] a crisis that disproportionately disadvantages wo/men of color, wo/men in rural areas, wo/men in urban centers, single parents, children, and some lesbian wo/men. While Christian institutions have long been known for charity and poverty relief, these institutions have not led to a full realization of a radical democratic vision. In this essay I use Schüssler Fiorenza's emancipatory feminist rhetorical-critical interpretive framework to interpret the earliest surviving Christian text that offers an extended argument about the relation between wealth, poverty, and Christianness: Clement of Alexandria's homily on Mark 10:17–31, *Who Is the Rich Person Who Is Saved?* I show that we can reimagine struggles among Christians in the late second century over socioeconomic arrangements, especially over the significance of the injunction "sell what you have and give to the poor" (Mark 10:21).

Barbara Ehrenreich's best-selling book *Nickel and Dimed: On (Not) Getting By in America* offers an articulation of the contemporary socioeconomic crisis; she locates it in relation to the broader sociopolitical climate:

> The particular political moment favors what almost looks like a "conspiracy of silence" on the subject of poverty and the poor. The Democrats are not eager to find flaws in the period of "unprecedented prosperity" they take credit for; the Republicans have lost interest in the poor now that "welfare-as-we-know-it" has ended. Welfare reform itself is a factor weighing against any close investigation of the conditions of the poor. Both parties heavily endorsed it, and to acknowledge that low-wage work doesn't lift people out of poverty would be to admit that it may have been, in human terms, a catastrophic mistake.[5]

She reaches this conclusion by trying to survive briefly on the best "unskilled" low-wage jobs she could find. Her narrative style and tone, writing as an often astonished "participant-observer" of a world that is sharply different from her usual financially and physically comfortable social location, is crafted to move and challenge an implied audience of largely financially secure, educated readers:

> It is common, among the nonpoor, to think of poverty as a sustainable condition — austere, perhaps, but they get by somehow, don't

---

4. A recent article in the *New York Times* reports a continuation of the trend toward an increasing gap between the poorest and wealthiest residents of the United States; *New York Times,* 25 September 2002, A1, A18.

5. Barbara Ehrenreich, *Nickel and Dimed: On (Not) Getting By in America* (New York: Henry Holt, 2001), 217.

they? They are "always with us." What is harder for the nonpoor to see is poverty as acute distress: The lunch that consists of Doritos or hot dog rolls, leading to faintness before the end of the shift. The "home" that is also a car or a van. The illness or injury that must be "worked through," with gritted teeth, because there's no sick pay or health insurance and the loss of one day's pay will mean no groceries for the next. These experiences are not part of a sustainable lifestyle.... They are, by almost any standard of subsistence, emergency situations. And that is how we should see the poverty of so many millions of Americans — as a state of emergency.[6]

Ehrenreich's ethical wake-up call to the nonpoor to see that the labor and compromised lives of the working poor support the lives of the more privileged offers one articulation of a contemporary problem to be addressed. If the task implied by her study is a transformation of structures of socioeconomic oppression, how might a feminist historian of early Christianity contribute to it?

Schüssler Fiorenza argues that one crucial task of the feminist historian is to lift up and articulate the alternative visions, the struggles for justice in the past — especially of the communities who shaped what became Christianity. In formulating possible visions of how this crisis might be resolved to achieve justice for all wo/men, it is necessary both to examine the assumptions and structures that enable the current status quo and to articulate an alternative ethos.

Using Schüssler Fiorenza's dynamic framework, I take this urgency to address contemporary American ethical and material crisis as the starting point for analyzing and evaluating interpretations of Mark 10:17–31, a passage that directly addresses wealth in relation to salvation and discipleship. By examining one "moment" in its history of interpretation, I demonstrate that there are competing traditions within Christianity that help to understand how Christianity has been implicated in sustaining structurally unequal economic social arrangements but has also sustained alternative egalitarian visions. Clement's homily on this Markan text can be interpreted as containing competing Christian visions of just socioeconomic relations. Clement's world is not our world of global capitalism. Nonetheless, like Christians today, he uses the Gospel of Mark to formulate and authorize his teachings about wealth and poverty. The emancipatory materialist interpretations of Mark against which Clement argues might serve as alternatives against which contemporary interpretations of socioeconomic arrangements might be judged.

---

6. Ibid., 214.

The Struggle between Kyriarchy
and the Discipleship of Equals

In urging scholars to investigate both the rhetoric of interpretation in the present and in the past, Elisabeth Schüssler Fiorenza articulates an important ethical challenge: "An ethics of critical reading changes the task of interpretation from finding out 'what the text meant' to the question of what kinds of readings can do justice to the text in its historical context."[7] Because her approach presupposes multiple (though not infinite) readings of a text, the interpretive task cannot be to determine a singular meaning. Nevertheless, interpreters can limit and then evaluate the range of possible interpretations in part by persuasive reimaginings of the thought-worlds, sociopolitical arrangements, and imagined alternatives that flourished in the time that a given text was produced and used.

Crucially, Schüssler Fiorenza goes further. While reimagining the horizons of the "possible" for the producers and readers of biblical texts is vital for offering a persuasive reading of any text,[8] the modern interpreter's task does not end here. She also calls for an "ethics of accountability" that

> stands responsible not only for the choice of theoretical interpretive models but also for the ethical consequences of the biblical text and its subsequent interpretations. If scriptural texts have served — and still do — not only to support noble causes but also to legitimate war, to nurture anti-Judaism and misogyny, to justify the exploitation of slavery, and to promote colonial dehumanization, then biblical scholarship must also take the responsibility not only to interpret biblical texts in their historical contexts but also to evaluate the construct of their historical worlds and symbolic universes in terms of a religious scale of values. If the Bible has become a classic of western culture because of its normativity, then the responsibility of the biblical scholar cannot be restricted to giving "the readers of our time clear access to the original intentions" of the biblical writers. It must also include the elucidation of the ethical consequences and political functions of biblical texts and their interpretations in their historical as well as their contemporary sociopolitical contexts.[9]

These two tasks, attention to historical context(s) and to the contemporary one(s), are intimately intertwined since our very sense of the present is informed by both the dominant and suppressed possibilities of the past. There

---

7. Elisabeth Schüssler Fiorenza, *Rhetoric and Ethic: The Politics of Biblical Studies* (Minneapolis: Fortress, 1999), 27.
8. Elisabeth Schüssler Fiorenza, *Jesus and the Politics of Interpretation* (New York: Continuum, 2000), 51–53; see also 163–64.
9. Schüssler Fiorenza, *Rhetoric and Ethic,* 28.

is an intimacy between present, future, and past, but it is not a relation of causality or determinism.

In Schüssler Fiorenza's view there were no pure or singular beginnings to what became Christianity; rather, amid the range of perspectives was an emancipatory strand that she calls the discipleship of equals, as well as one characterized by a greater emphasis on hierarchical arrangements, which adapted existing hegemonic master-centered structures and values in shaping new communities (which she usually calls a kyriarchal impulse). Both strands, and their various combinations, have persisted in the Christian tradition — the relative success of one over another is a matter of ongoing ethical struggle rather than one of purity or originality. This is one of Schüssler Fiorenza's crucial insights: even when ethical struggles are *waged* in terms of claims of purity or originality, both emancipatory and kyriarchal strands are "authentic." Both are authentic, but not equally just.

Schüssler Fiorenza thus reconstructs and evaluates "the history of early Christian literatures and communities as the history of communicative persuasion, emancipatory struggles, and common visions."[10] These ancient struggles are not identical with those of wo/men in the present but imbricated in them. Making the link to scholarly practices, she adds: "Only a theoretical model that comprehends the ongoing conflicts and struggles between the vision and emancipatory practices of radical democracy, on the one hand, and those of kyriarchal social systems on the other...is able to make visible or conscious the submerged knowledges of the oppressed and to provide for a fragile historical continuity of emancipatory struggles."[11] It is not sufficient to identify the dominant perspectives and interpretations of texts; we must also read for unrealized, incipient alternatives. We must then evaluate these different possibilities for their ethical consequences. In Clement's *Who Is the Rich Person Who Is Saved?* we can reconstruct traces of an emancipatory legacy within Christianity.

Mark 10:17–31 and a Model of Struggle

And as he was setting out on his journey, a man ran up and knelt before him, and asked him, "Good Teacher, what must I do to inherit eternal life?" And Jesus said to him, "Why do you call me good? No one is good but God alone. You know the commandments: 'Do not kill, Do not commit adultery, Do not steal, Do not bear false witness, Do not defraud, Honor your father and mother.'" And he said to him, "Teacher, all these I have observed from my youth." And Jesus looking upon him loved him, and said to him, "You lack one thing; go, sell what you have, and give to the poor, and you will have treasure in

---

10. Ibid., 143.
11. Schüssler Fiorenza, *Sharing Her Word*, 113–14.

heaven; and come, follow me." At that saying his countenance fell, and he went away sorrowful; for he had great possessions.

And Jesus looked around and said to his disciples, "How hard it will be for those who have riches to enter the kingdom of God!" And the disciples were amazed at his words. But Jesus said to them again, "Children, how hard it is to enter the kingdom of God! It is easier for a camel to go through the eye of a needle than for a rich man to enter the kingdom of God." And they were exceedingly astonished, and said to him, "Then who can be saved?" Jesus looked at them and said, "With [humans] it is impossible, but not with God; for all things are possible with God." Peter began to say to him, "Lo, we have left everything and followed you." Jesus said, "Truly, I say to you, there is no one who has left house or brothers or sisters or mother or father or children or lands, for my sake and for the gospel, who will not receive a hundredfold now in this time, houses and brothers and sisters and mothers and children and lands, with persecutions, and in the age to come eternal life. But many that are first will be last, and the last first."

— Mark 10:17–31 (RSV)

Clement of Alexandria, a prolific late second-century Christian teacher, wrote a short treatise dedicated to an interpretation of Mark 10:17–31, *Who Is the Rich Person Who Is Saved?*[12] This text is the only extant Christian writing from the period before legalization (313 C.E.) to offer a sustained discussion of wealth in relation to salvation.[13] Although this text differs from Clement's other surviving writings in that it offers an extended reflection on one biblical text, it resembles them insofar as he writes as if his main readers are free and heads of households.[14] Although he makes clear in his multivolume work on more advanced Christian teachings, the *Stromateis*, that slaves and free wo/men of all backgrounds are capable of and should

---

12. For the critical Greek critical edition of this text, see Clemens Alexandrinus, *Stromata Buch VII und VIII, Excerpta ex Theodoto, Eclogae Propheticae, Quis Dives Salvetur, Fragmente* (ed. Otto Stählin; Die griechischen christlichen Schriftsteller der ersten drei Jahrhunderte; Leipzig: Hinrichs, 1909), 3.157–91. For an English translation, see Clement of Alexandria, *Exhortation to the Greeks; The Rich Man's Salvation; To the Newly Baptized* (trans. G. W. Butterworth; Loeb Classical Library; Cambridge: Harvard University Press, 1919 [repr. 1999]), 265–367. I follow Butterworth's translation quite closely, making some emendations. My interpretation of Clement's text develops some of the insights made in Denise Kimber Buell, "Ambiguous Legacy: A Feminist Commentary on Clement of Alexandria's Works," in *The Feminist Companion to Early Gnostic and Patristic Thought* (ed. Amy-Jill Levine; Sheffield: Sheffield Academic Press, forthcoming).

13. L. William Countryman, *The Rich Christian in the Church of the Early Empire: Contradictions and Accommodations* (New York: Mellen, 1980), 19, 47–48.

14. In the *Paidagogos*, for example, presented as a text for Christians in the "childhood" of their religious education, Clement offers detailed instructions for how women and men should live a proper Christian life. Many of his instructions presuppose that his listeners are wealthy, with access to luxury foods and goods, and slave-owning. See Buell, "Ambiguous Legacy." See also Countryman, *Rich Christian*, 48.

have access to the highest levels of Christian philosophizing (e.g., *Stromateis* 4.8.59.3; 4.8.68.2), his examples and exhortations are rhetorically shaped with a privileged male reader in mind.

In *Who Is the Rich Person Who Is Saved?* Clement crafts a position about material wealth, salvation, and Christian community that embodies the tensions that Schüssler Fiorenza suggests we imagine as a hallmark of early Christianity — namely, ongoing tensions between egalitarian vision/practices and kyriarchal social systems. If we read Clement's text as "taking sides in the emancipatory struggles of antiquity" and pay attention to the ways that Clement depicts conflicts among Christians, we can read his interpretation of Mark 10:17–31 as one strand in a broader struggle "between Hellenistic, Jewish, or early Christian 'egalitarian' movements and their dominant patriarchal Greco-Roman, Jewish, and emerging Christian sociopolitical contexts."[15] For his own part, Clement neither advocates a fully kyriarchal model nor a fully egalitarian one. His interpretation renders the entire Markan passage less effective in accomplishing radical egalitarian goals than the interpretation Schüssler Fiorenza offers of Mark 10:29–30. I shall suggest that Clement develops his arguments in a context of struggle in two ways: on the one hand, his own vision of Christianness contains both egalitarian and kyriarchal reasoning; on the other hand, he attempts to control rival visions of Christianity that foreground a more egalitarian, materialist reading of Mark 10:17–31.

Adopting Schüssler Fiorenza's analytical framework, I have two main aims for my examination of Clement's text. First, I show how his rhetorical strategies produce an interpretation of Mark 10:17–31 that supports a Christian ethos that preserves the value of economic disparity. While Clement challenges the kyriarchal logic of the Greco-Roman world insofar as he resituates the locus of authority,[16] his Christian vision also relies on kyriarchal structures to differentiate among Christians. His vision of Christianity contains within it a tension between egalitarian and kyriarchal impulses. Second, I show that by reading against the grain of Clement's rhetoric we can glimpse indications of a submerged alternative egalitarian ethos — one that interprets Mark to negotiate economic differences among Christians differently, with seemingly greater insistence on material redistribution of wealth.

Before turning to consider Clement's interpretation of Mark 10:17–31, it is useful to see how Schüssler Fiorenza reads Mark 10:29–30. She interprets this passage in light of emancipatory struggles, specifically a struggle to create a community of equal discipleship in contrast to community modeled

---

15. Schüssler Fiorenza, *Rhetoric and Ethic*, 145.

16. This shift moves the center of authority from those who wield power in the world according to status as well as wealth, to the "gnostic" Christian, the pinnacle of Christian development in Clement's understanding. Although few Christians attain this level, Clement views all humans as potentially capable of becoming gnostics.

upon the kyriarchal household.[17] She suggests that there is a "pre-Markan tradition which contrasts the patriarchal family with the community of equal discipleship. . . . Those who live the gracious goodness of God are Jesus' true family, which includes brothers, sisters, and mothers, but, significantly enough, no fathers,"[18] visible in the saying attributed to Jesus in 10:29–30: "Truly, I say to you, there is no one who has left house or brothers or sisters or mother or father or children or lands, for my sake and for the gospel, who will not receive a hundredfold now in this time, houses and brothers and sisters and mothers and children and lands, with persecutions,[19] and in the age to come eternal life." Schüssler Fiorenza sees this saying as advocating a communal vision of a "messianic community which brought together impoverished and marginal people, as well as 'houseowners' and 'farmers,' and bound them together in a new kinship and family based on radical discipleship."[20] In a more recent discussion of this vision, she emphasizes how its redefinition of kinship and family challenged kyriarchal definitions and institutions of these concepts, relating it to other gospel passages. She argues that this vision is

> antipatriarchal insofar as it required the breaking of household relationships. Those who followed the Jesuanic *basileia* vision were promised a new familial community in return. This new "family" of equal disciples was prohibited from calling anyone "father" (Mt 23:8–11) or according status on the grounds of motherhood (Lk 11:27–28). Insofar as this new familial community has no "fathers" it implicitly rejects patriarchal socioreligious power and status.[21]

In this excerpt, "fathers" serves as shorthand for those who occupy the master (*kyrios*) position over others, in keeping with ancient organization of households, which, unlike modern Western families, entailed not simply parents and children but also slaves and free persons who had ties through social, but not necessarily biological, reproduction.[22] This anti-kyriarchal vision of community refers to kyriarchal concepts but redefines them and their relationship to power. This redefinition bears especially on the concept of discipleship.

---

17. Elisabeth Schüssler Fiorenza, *In Memory of Her: A Feminist Theological Reconstruction of Christian Origins* (New York: Crossroad, 1983), 147–48.

18. Ibid., 147. This citation refers explicitly to Mark 3:31–35, a tradition that Schüssler Fiorenza also sees at work in 10:29–30.

19. Schüssler Fiorenza understands this phrase as a Markan addition; *In Memory of Her*, 147.

20. Ibid.

21. Schüssler Fiorenza, *Sharing Her Word*, 114–15. See also idem, *In Memory of Her*, 147–48.

22. On ancient household structures, see especially Elisabeth Schüssler Fiorenza, *But She Said: Feminist Practices of Biblical Interpretation* (Boston: Beacon, 1992), 114–20.

Schüssler Fiorenza locates the Markan unit within a longer discussion of discipleship and suggests that

> the child/slave who occupies the lowest place within patriarchal struc-
> tures becomes the primary paradigm for true discipleship. Such true
> discipleship is not measured on the father/master position but on that
> of the slave/child. This can be seen in the paradoxical Jesus saying:
> "Whoever does not receive the *basileia* of God like a child (slave) shall
> not enter it" (Mark 10:15). This saying is not an invitation to childlike
> innocence and naiveté but a challenge to relinquish all claims of power
> and domination over others.[23]

Mark 10:17–28 offers another frame of reference for thinking about discipleship in addition to child/adult or slave/master: namely, that of wealthy/
poor. In 10:17–28 it is neither the child nor the slave that exemplify
discipleship, but the giving up of possessions and distribution to the poor.

Schüssler Fiorenza does not discuss Mark 10:17–28, but some early
Christians read this passage as part of a unit with 10:29–31. I am interested
in how we might read it now and how it was read, especially in relation to
10:29–31.[24] Clement of Alexandria's reading of 10:17–31 shows that it is
possible to read this passage to preserve social arrangements characterized
by economic difference. But a feminist emancipatory rhetorical interpretation of Clement's text also shows that alternative interpretations of Mark
existed in Clement's day that represent the egalitarian strain that Schüssler
Fiorenza sees in 10:29–30.

"What *Koinōnia* Would Be Left among Humans if No One Had Anything?"

As the striking quotation in *Quis* 13.1 suggests, in *Who Is the Rich Person
Who Is Saved?* Clement encourages wealthy Christians to give to needy
fellow Christians but does not advocate a complete redistribution of wealth
or envision a community of common goods.[25] The structure of the text takes
its cue from the Markan passage, addressing primarily the questions of how
a rich person can have access to salvation and what the responsibilities of

---

23. Schüssler Fiorenza, *In Memory of Her,* 148.

24. Clement of Alexandria offers by far the most extensive interpretation of this Markan
passage in the surviving early Christian literature of the second and third centuries. For some
other examples, none of which treat the entire unit, see Justin, *Dialogue* 101.2; Tertullian,
On Monogamy 14.7; Pseudo-Clement, *Homily* 18.3.4. For additional examples, see *Biblia
Patristica: Index des citations et allusions bibliques dans la literature patristique* (Paris: CNRS,
1986), 1.305–7; 2.302.

25. Based on the Latin title *Quis dives salvetur, Quis* is the conventional short title
for Clement's *Who Is the Rich Person Who Is Saved?* Countryman also makes the point
about redistributing wealth, noting that "Clement did advocate voluntary equality among
Christians...but he never advocated communism of property"; *Rich Christian,* 60.

Christian teachers are in this process.[26] Clement states that many rich people, upon learning about Christianity, too often dismiss salvation as impossible for them. Building upon Mark 10:23–27, Clement characterizes the reaction of some rich people to Christian teaching:

> For some, after merely listening in an offhand way to the Lord's saying, that a camel shall more easily creep through a needle's eye than a rich person into the kingdom of heaven, despair of themselves, feeling that they are not destined to gain life. So, complying with the world in everything, and clinging to this present life as the only one left to them, they depart further from the heavenward way, taking no more trouble to ask who are the rich that the master and teacher is addressing nor how that which is impossible with humans becomes possible. (*Quis* 2.2)

Rhetorically, Clement sets the stage for exploring just these questions of Mark: Who are the rich anyway? How does the humanly impossible become possible? Through a combination of figurative interpretation and moral exhortation, he proceeds to (re)define the rich as those whose souls are bursting with passions and to describe the "impossible" transformation as the gradual eradication of these passions through a combination of individual effort, close supervision by a Christian leader, and the activity of God's will.

Although this reframing would seem to evade the question of material wealth entirely, earthly riches remain a focal point for Clement's arguments. The homily instead resituates wealth as an instrument that can be used in this process of training the soul and obeying the commandments. Material goods, he says, have no intrinsic moral value — what matters are the choices one makes in how to use them (*Quis* 14.1–4).[27] For Clement, the key to interpreting Jesus' teaching in Mark correctly is to distinguish between true and false wealth (as well as true and false poverty): he insists that material wealth is not at issue, but rather the wealth or poverty of the soul's passions that informs one's attitudes toward material wealth. Only those who cannot escape the clutches of passion for material goods should resort to surrendering their wealth (24.1). Clement's distinction between intentions (attitudes toward wealth) and the objects of use (goods, property, etc.) permits him

---

26. Countryman divides the structure of Clement's text into three main parts: introduction (1–3), argument that "Jesus did not exclude the rich from the Kingdom" (4–27), and instructions about "how the rich must act to further their salvation" (27–41) (*Rich Christian*, 49). I agree with Countryman's demarcation of a shift at §27. Here Clement states that he has finished demonstrating that the rich can be saved and shall now discuss "what hope it is that the Savior outlines for the rich." Since I read the rhetorical frame of the piece as indicating that Clement is addressing those who might teach rich people as much as he is addressing a hypothetical rich person, I interpret this portion of the text as having a dual function: to address an implied rich person and to "model" the kind of instruction that a Christian teacher ought to give a rich person.

27. This view of riches as *adiaphora* resonates with Stoic ethical teachings; see Countryman, *Rich Christian*, 52, 61–62.

to argue that one who is rich with worldly goods "must not fling away the riches that are of benefit to our neighbors as well as ourselves" (14.1). After all, he has just reasoned, "how could we feed the hungry and give drink to the thirsty, cover the naked and entertain the homeless, with regards to which he threatens fire and the outer darkness to those who have not done them, if each of us were already in want of these things?" (13.4).

Clement embeds the problem of wealthy people's perceptions of Christianity in a larger issue: namely, that of Christian views about wealth and wealthy people. He opens the text with a challenge to those who pander to the wealthy: "Those who offer speeches of praise as presents to the rich may rightly be classed, in my opinion, not only as flatterers and servile ... but also as impious and insidious.[28] They are impious because, while neglecting to praise and glorify the only perfect and good God ... they invest with [God's] prerogative men who are wallowing in a riotous and filthy life" (1.1–2). With this opening Clement positions himself in sharp contrast to this obsequious treatment of the rich, raising the question of what Clement's alternative stance will be. He states that the proper Christian response is to work with the rich to gain them salvation (1.4–5).

To explain what he means by working with the rich, Clement employs his preferred method of biblical interpretation, distinguishing between a literal/material and a spiritual level of the Markan text. After citing it in full, Clement introduces his interpretation by saying that, because "the Savior teaches his people nothing in a merely human way, but everything by a divine and mystical wisdom, we must not understand his words literally [sarkikos], but with due inquiry and intelligence we must search out and master their hidden meaning" (5.2). In Clement's view the hidden meaning of Jesus' command "if you will be perfect, sell all you have and distribute to the poor" is "strip the soul itself and the will of their lurking passions and utterly to root out and cast away all alien thoughts from the mind" (12.1).

Based on this figurative reading, Clement argues that there are two kinds of wealth and poverty: fleshly (or worldly) and spiritual. In his view, it is only spiritual wealth or poverty that bears on salvation. Spiritual poverty, which he correlates with the elimination of passions from the soul, is a state to be cultivated: " 'Selling all that we have' must therefore be understood in this way, as spoken with reference to the soul's passions" (14.6). The relative "wealth" of passions in one's soul determines the way one uses worldly wealth — the latter is a problem only if one is rich in passions: "The Lord admits the use of outward things, bidding us to put away, not the means of living, but the things that use these badly; and these are, as we have seen,

---

28. Because Clement does not specify who engages in such flattery, he leaves it to the reader to determine whether such people are other Christians or non-Christians. Nevertheless, he later advises Christians specifically against such behavior (*Quis* 3.1).

the infirmities and passions of the soul. Wealth of these brings death...but salvation when it is destroyed. Of this wealth one must render the soul pure, that is poor and bare" (15.6–16.1).

Clement offers yet another interpretation of the term *rich* in this text, one with a positive valence. While spiritual poverty is idealized as the goal for those removing passions from the soul, it paradoxically leads to riches, riches in "virtue" and "toward God." Spiritual poverty thereby enables the acquisition of "spiritual wealth." Clement offers another interpretation of Mark 10:17–23 to spell this out:

> To the one who is not poor in worldly goods and rich in passions, the one who is poor in spirit and rich toward God says, "Detach yourself from the alien possessions that dwell in your soul, that you may become pure in heart and may see God, which in other words means to enter the kingdom of heaven." And how are you to detach yourself from them? By selling them.... [And] in place of that which formerly dwelt in the soul you long to save, bring in another kind of wealth that makes you divine and provides eternal life.... In this way you make a good sale of...the many things that are superfluous and that shut heaven against you, while you receive in exchange the things that have the power to save. As for the first, let the fleshly poor who need them have them; but you, having received in their stead the spiritual wealth, will now have treasure in heaven. (*Quis* 19.3–6)

This passage suggests that those with material wealth can accomplish this process of spiritual impoverishment that leads to spiritual wealth in part through charitable distribution of material goods to the "fleshly poor" — a strategy often described as "redemptive almsgiving."

Clement describes this concept clearly later in the text. Echoing his earlier insistence on the proper attitude of indifference toward wealth, Clement specifies that material goods, and the differences between humans that they seem to create, are "by nature unrighteous *when one possesses them for personal advantage* — as entirely one's own — and does not bring them into the common stock for those in need" (31.6). He continues, shifting the emphasis from attitude of use to the soteriological consequences of using possessions wisely: "From this unrighteousness [of goods held for personal gain] it is possible to perform a deed that is righteous and salvific, namely, to give relief to one of those who have an eternal habitation [*skēnē*] with the father" (31.6). By giving their goods to needy Christians, rich Christians can thus advance themselves toward salvation.[29]

---

29. See also, "You give the perishing things of the world and receive in exchange for them an eternal abode in heaven" (*Quis* 32.1).

Clement's position makes sense within existing urban Greco-Roman practices of *leitourgia* — or public service[30] — and euergetism, whereby wealthy citizens accrued honor by acts of lavish spending partly through public works and festivals that could benefit others. He departs from the model of competitive euergetism, however, insofar as he redefines the goal as detachment from material concerns[31] and pursuit of salvation. Nonetheless, by preserving the notion that wealthy Christians have a role to play in using their wealth for good ends, Clement does not challenge the basic social structures that stratified people along an axis of have/have-not. To this extent, Clement's viewpoint sustains kyriarchal social arrangements.

After the legalization of Christianity, influential bishops such as Basil of Caesarea further developed the notion of redemptive almsgiving for wealthy Christians,[32] even though, as Susan Holman notes, Clement's "view against total divestment... did not become the prevailing view in the written texts that survive, and few later texts echo Clement's systematic caution against ascetic poverty."[33] That is, Holman shows that while many fourth-century Christians wrote in favor of ascetic poverty, individual and institutional practices more closely resembled those of redemptive almsgiving advocated by Clement: "The fact that liberal donations and Christian wealth in late antiquity did not necessarily mark one as a new convert suggests that the majority of Christians actually practiced a positive view of wealth more like Clement's."[34]

---

30. As Susan R. Holman notes, "In advocating that wealth is necessary to effectively serve one's neighbor and community, Clement echoes the ideals of the Graeco-Roman leitourgia, although he does not generally express his attitude toward the poor in civic terms"; *The Hungry Are Dying: Beggars and Bishops in Roman Cappadocia* (Oxford Studies in Historical Theology; Oxford: Oxford University Press, 2001), 53. Holman describes this civic context as follows: "Social assistance to the poor for the sake of justice did indeed exist as a cultural concept in the Greek, Hellenistic, and Roman worlds, although worthy recipients were perceived primarily in terms of civic identity rather than fiscal limitations. Consequently relief need not be expressed as 'charity' but rather in terms of maintaining civic order and the worthy members of its community, however community was defined" (11). This description fits well with Clement's emphasis on love of neighbor and his definition of Christian *koinōnia* not only as household of God, but citizenship in heaven. By redefining concepts of family, household, citizen, and citizenship, Christians could adapt traditional practices of civic obligation.

31. But even this reframing was consistent with the ethical principles of Stoicism; hence, as Countryman notes, Clement's ethical principles "were essentially identical with those of the *prevailing* philosophy of his day"; *Rich Christian*, 62 (emphasis original).

32. Holman, *Hungry Are Dying*, esp. 32–37, 54–55, 99–114.

33. Ibid., 52.

34. Ibid. Michele Renee Salzman interprets such donation practices as an instance of how "aristocratic" Roman values informed and influenced the emerging dominant forms of Christianity in the fourth and fifth centuries: "The church did not require radical changes in aristocratic behavior, and, in particular, evergetism. Instead, aristocrats could continue to exercise the privileges of their position and wealth while gaining spiritual rewards. Thus preexisting patterns of aristocratic gift-giving were encouraged, as was the possession of wealth itself, in ways that facilitated conversion without challenging the norms of aristocratic status culture"; Michele Renee Salzman, *The Making of a Christian Aristocracy: Social and Religious Change in the Western Roman Empire* (Cambridge: Harvard University Press, 2002), 205–9, quotation from 209.

Negotiating the Demands of Wealth and Family

Another facet of Clement's argument emerges especially in his interpretation of Mark 10:29–30 and a related passage about kin relations from Luke 14:26 ("whoever does not hate father, mother, and children, and even their own life [*psychē*], cannot be my disciple"). Clement defuses the apparent literal meaning of these passages about leaving one's family by saying that, unless it interferes with one's salvation, one should continue to honor one's father — as long as it is less than one honors Christ (*Quis* 22.5–7). Clement makes the passionate attachment to material goods that interferes with one's ability to gain salvation parallel to the worldly attachments to one's non-Christian kin that interferes with one's ability to follow one's "true" father (God); one need only reject those material goods or earthly kin who demand that you honor them over God (22–26).[35]

Clement's interpretation offers a vision of Christian community in possible tension with the demands of prevailing households. In addressing this tension, Clement supports an ethos that, at least incipiently, countervails customary ideas about kinship, household arrangements, and citizenship — even as his alternative ethos remains hierarchical rather than egalitarian. Clement's reading of Mark 10:29–30 differs significantly from the egalitarian perspective that Schüssler Fiorenza reconstructs. This is in part because he foregrounds the individual's need to eradicate passions, rather than to transform the prevailing social arrangements (including economic disparities), and partly because his understanding of the communal consequences of living as if all Christians were one's siblings in relation to a divine mother and father entails hierarchical stratification of the community into spiritually youthful and spiritually mature, rather than resulting in a "discipleship of equals" in which the child or slave (or the poor) serves as the paradigm of discipleship.

It is important to note how Clement characterizes the spiritually mature, however. He calls these "the more elect than the elect [*eklektōn eklektoteroi*]" (*Quis* 36.1), who "do not wish to be called holy," but are "the light of the world," the "salt of the earth," and the "seed" that is being collected by the Logos on God's behalf (36.1–2). The reader could easily infer that these most elect include the "army of God-fearing old men, of God-beloved orphans, of widows armed with gentleness, of men adorned with love" who are able to keep ships afloat, sickness at bay, fend off thieves, and exorcise demons (34.3); it is these Christians whom Clement says "seem to touch not your flesh but . . . soul, not to be talking with a sibling but with

---

35. Using a hypothetical law trial to clarify the matter, Clement notes that if one's father (he later adds "brother, child, wife, or anyone else") should appeal to family ties to encourage disobedience to "the law of Christ," one should let Christ's appeal win — an appeal arguing that God, via Christ, is one's true father and nurse (*Quis* 23.1–5). See Denise Kimber Buell, *Making Christians: Clement of Alexandria and the Rhetoric of Legitimacy* (Princeton: Princeton University Press, 1999), 100–104.

the eternal ruler who dwells in you" (35.2). Given that Clement associates this highest grade of Christians with some categories that would have been most socially vulnerable (although also well-known tropes from biblical traditions), it is possible to read his investment of authority in members of these groups as having subversive potential.

What Clement makes very explicit is that wealth does not entitle one to power, let alone invest one with it; rather, the appropriate authority figures are the "elect," the spiritual leaders of the church — these are the ones to be obeyed, by rich and poor alike. Although arguments about the use of wealth preserve economic differences within Christian communities, he insists that this does not mean that those with material wealth have authority over Christians who do not. Instead, he redefines the basis for social power and authority.

Clement recommends that wealthy Christians spend their excess funds on other Christians while constantly training themselves to cut away passions under the guidance of a "godly person" who can serve as their trainer (*aleiptēs*) and pilot (*kybernētēs*) (41.1). Part of what the wealthy Christian must learn is to "open your heart to all who are enrolled as God's disciples, not gazing scornfully on their bodies, not being led to indifference by their age. And if one appear needy or ill clad or ungainly or weak, do not take offense in your soul at this and turn away" (33.5). Clement turns this lesson in charitable distribution of funds simultaneously into a lesson about human nature: "This is a form thrown around us from without for the purpose of our entrance into the world, that we may be able to take our place in the universal school, but hidden within dwells the Father and his Son who died for us and rose with us" (33.6). Thus Clement argues both for a kind of spiritual equality of all Christians yet does not challenge the material distinctions per se as a hindrance to the realization of or participation in the heavenly city or kingdom.

Submerged Alternatives

Clement's argument sustains rather than assuages anxieties about his question: "What *koinōnia* would be left among humans if no one had anything?" (*Quis* 13.1). He offers a prescription for the use of wealth that envisions *koinōnia* as enabled by the wealth of some Christians. But does giving away one's material goods necessarily result in the impoverishment of all? If we turn to read against the grain of Clement's arguments, it becomes clear that Clement's opening remarks mask an important Christian alternative to both flattery of the rich and Clement's more conciliatory position: "It is the duty...of those whose minds are set on love of the truth and fellow-feeling, and *who do not behave with insolent rudeness toward the rich who have been called*...to banish from them their unfounded despair and to show...that the inheritance of the kingdom of heaven is not completely cut off from them" (3.1 [emphasis added]). While Clement more prominently contrasts his own position to those who would flatter the rich or "cling to them through personal love of gain" (3.1), his subsequent exegesis of Mark 10:17–31 suggests that he is also negotiating interpretations of this text that might have advocated renunciation of material wealth — an interpretive stance that might be caricatured by Clement as resulting in "insolent rudeness" to the wealthy.[36]

His preference for a "spiritual" interpretation of the first section of the passage (Mark 10:17–22) functions also to counter egalitarian readings.[37] Clement argues that when Jesus tells the inquiring man to sell all that he has, Jesus does not have material possessions in mind, but rather the passions of the soul. By contrasting his "spiritual" interpretation of Mark with a merely "fleshly" one, Clement structurally positions as inferior those who interpret 10:17–22 as a demand to surrender material riches and give them to the poor.

There are further indications that a materialist interpretation of Mark existed in Alexandria. Instead of just developing his spiritual interpretation, Clement entertains the idea of renouncing earthly wealth in order to dismiss it.[38] In reflecting on the command "sell what you have," Clement writes: "And what is this? *It is not what some rashly understand,* a command to fling away what one owns and part with one's wealth, but to exorcise from the soul one's ideas about wealth, its attachment to them" (*Quis* 11.2 [emphasis added]). He offers four main arguments against material divestment.

First, if it were necessary to renounce wealth to gain eternal life, then people who just happen to be destitute, "though 'ignorant' of God and 'God's righteousness' [Rom 10:3] [would] be most blessed and beloved of God and the only possessors of eternal life" (*Quis* 11.3). Conversely, he asks, "Why need wealth ever have arisen at all out of earth, if it is the provider and agent of death?" (26.5). These points are consistent with Clement's insistence throughout his writings that people are not naturally saved or

---

36. Countryman also raises the possibility that Clement is responding to an alternative Christian view here; *Rich Christian,* 51.

37. In her study of how early Christian writers authorized their programs of asceticism using biblical interpretation, Elizabeth Clark notes that Clement's interpretation of the renunciation of wealth offers a "classic example of how a 'spiritualized' reading might encourage a *weakening* of the ascetic rigor demanded by a more 'literal' exegesis"; Elizabeth A. Clark, *Reading Renunciation: Asceticism and Scripture in Early Christianity* (Princeton: Princeton University Press, 1999), 94 (emphasis original). She further notes that subsequent interpreters of this Markan passage, including Origen, Jerome, and the anonymous Pelagian author of *On Riches* all seek to control or counter spiritualizing interpretations that "*lessen* the demands of a rigorous asceticism" (95–99, quotation from 99). By situating interpretive tensions in the context of ascetic practices and ideals, Clark's study offers the important reminder that a reconstruction of egalitarian/kyriarchal struggles must be located in specific sociohistorical contexts. Ascetic ideals often countervailed hegemonic kyriarchal structures in antiquity, but were not necessarily egalitarian.

38. See also Buell, "Ambiguous Legacy."

perfected but must act on their natural *potential*. While silent about the possibilities for the involuntary poor to cultivate passionless souls (and thus gain heavenly riches), Clement seems here to devalue voluntary poverty.

Second, Clement notes that renunciation of wealth is not automatically linked with the search for eternal life. People like Anaxagoras, Democritus, and Crates all renounced their wealth "before the Savior's coming" for a range of allegedly less noble reasons: "To obtain leisure for study and for dead wisdom...for empty fame and vainglory" (11.4). It is noteworthy that Clement omits an important example that would have weakened his argument — the voluntary renunciation of wealth by Jewish women and men who joined the ascetic community of Therapeutrides and Therapeutai detailed by Philo of Alexandria.[39] Given Clement's extensive indebtedness to the writings and interpretive approach of Philo,[40] it is very likely that he was aware of this group. Those leaving Alexandria and other parts of Egypt to join the particular community that Philo describes are characterized as having holy, noble motivations — including their yearning for eternal life (*On the Contemplative Life* 13).

Clement's third argument against a materialist reading of Mark 10 is especially important because he contrasts his interpretation of Jesus' teaching with supposedly prior understandings (and practices) about wealth: "The people of former times [*proteroi*], in their contempt for outward things, parted with and sacrificed their possessions" (*Quis* 12.2). Because Clement defines Jesus' teaching about wealth to be directed toward removing passions, not worldly possessions, it is not surprising that he criticizes the practices of the *proteroi* as having led to an increase in the soul's passions: "For they become supercilious, boastful, conceited, and disdainful of the rest of humanity, as if they had accomplished something superhuman" (12.2). Even though Clement frames this argument with reference to interpretations and practices "before the Savior's coming," it is not at all clear that he is addressing only former practices. He has already stated that others "rashly" (or "ordinarily"; *procheirōs*) interpret Jesus' command to give all to the poor as a call to part with one's possessions. It seems possible that the practices of the *proteroi* may have been also those of some contemporary Christians.

---

39. See Philo of Alexandria, *On the Contemplative Life* (trans. F. H. Colson; Loeb Classical Library; Cambridge: Harvard University Press, 1941 [repr. 1995]), 9.112–69. Philo writes that "their longing for the deathless and blessed life" becomes so strong that "thinking their mortal life already ended they abandon their property to their sons or daughters or to other kinsfolk, thus voluntarily advancing the time of their inheritance, while those who have no kinsfolk give them to comrades and friends" (*On the Contemplative Life* 13). Philo goes on to compare the actions of the Therapeutai and Therapeutrides with the renunciations of Anaxagoras and Democritus, deeming the former superior for contributing to the needs of humans (not cattle, whom he claims were the sole beneficiaries of the latter) (§14).

40. See Annewies van den Hoek's comprehensive analysis of Clement's longest surviving work: *Clement of Alexandria's Use of Philo in the Stromateis: An Early Christian Reshaping of a Jewish Model* (Vigiliae christianae Supplement 3; Leiden: Brill, 1988).

Clement's negative depiction of these people as self-aggrandizing lacks force, as he leaves it undeveloped, but does bear some resemblance to the criticisms that he launches in the *Stromateis* against some contemporary Christians in Alexandria, whom he distances from "real" Christians (i.e., those in agreement with Clement) by calling them "Carpocratians," after Carpocrates (the Christian whose views these Christians allegedly follow). Clement paints in lurid terms the principles that these Christians advocate, condemning them for sexual immorality because they share common property: "Even reading Clement's descriptions with some skepticism, it appears that what Clement finds most offensive about the Carpocratians is that they apply the principle of equality in Christ (Gal. 3:28 and par.) to social relations."[41] Clement locates this egalitarian form of Christianity in his own backyard, as it were: "How can this fellow [Epiphanes, Carpocrates' son] still be listed in our church members' register when he openly does away with the Law and Gospels alike [through his biblical interpretations]?" (*Stromateis* 3.2.8.4).

Perhaps because he does not wish to fully acknowledge the presence of egalitarian forms of Christian thought and practice in his own surroundings, or because it would undermine the force of his arguments, Clement again fails to mention a possible counterexample from a source he respects. In Philo's description of the ascetic community of the Therapeutai and Therapeutrides, he links the renunciation of wealth to egalitarian goals (*On the Contemplative Life* 17) and emphasizes that members of the community reject many of the classifications of difference found in the rest of society, notably kin distinctions (§18), age (§67), and slave/free (§70). Clement would have been harder pressed to characterize this community as driven by pride and disdain. Furthermore, Clement nowhere in his entire corpus cites Acts 4:32, 34–35,[42] which could have been used to support a materialist, as well as egalitarian interpretation of Mark 10:17–31. Clement cites other portions of the Acts of the Apostles, but does not rebut the characterization of the community as holding possessions in common.

Finally, Clement also offers a fourth, quite different, diagnosis of the consequences of giving up material possessions. Clement now argues that renunciation of material possessions does not ensure that one will be free from material concerns: "It is possible for one, after having given up their property to be nonetheless continually preoccupied by the desire and longing for it.... For when one lacks the necessities of life, that one cannot fail

---

41. Buell, "Ambiguous Legacy"; in his critique, Clement focuses on the sexual and gendered implications of their views, but it is possible that their egalitarian vision was enacted more broadly. See also Countryman, *Rich Christian*, 60.

42. "Now the company of those who believed were of one heart and soul, and no one said that any of the things which [they] possessed was [their] own, but they had everything in common.... There was not a needy person among them, for as many as were possessors of lands or houses sold them, and brought the proceeds of what was sold and laid it at the apostles' feet; and distribution was made to each as any had need" (Acts 4:32, 34–35 RSV).

to be broken in spirit and to neglect the higher things, as they strive to procure these necessities by any means and from any source" (*Quis* 12.5); "one who has cast away worldly abundance can still be rich in passions" (15.2). Clement's interpretation is troubling because it locates the problem of wealth as one of individual attitudes rather than one of systemic structures of inequity that help to produce and reinforce such attitudes.

Conclusion

Clement develops arguments against voluntary renunciation of material wealth in response to those who rashly promote just such divestiture. The contours of this counterposition remain fuzzy and, indeed, need not be reduced to a single view, let alone tied to an identifiable social group like the so-called Carpocratians. Instead, it is more helpful to see that Clement's arguments contain within them the possibilities of alternative readings of Mark 10:17–31, which were likely sometimes organized into a set of social practices but may sometimes have remained unrealized.

My reading of Clement's text thus offers an instance of Schüssler Fiorenza's claim not only that Christianity was characterized by an ongoing struggle between kyriarchal and egalitarian visions, but also that we cannot know how fully the egalitarian ethos was realized in Clement's day. Even today, visions of egalitarian justice are challenging to put into practice.

In a world that is currently organized to support systemic economic disparities, though not in the same ways as Clement's, such struggles continue. America remains a context where "the horror of class stratification, racism, and prejudice is that some people begin to believe that the security of their families and communities depends on the oppression of others, that for some to have good lives there must be others whose lives are truncated and brutal. It is a belief that dominates this culture."[43] This belief dominates American culture, intertwined with other discourses and practices that reinforce systemic socioeconomic differences and other vectors of oppression. My reading of Clement's biblical interpretation must be evaluated (in the same way that I evaluated Clement) for its ability to address questions such as these:

> How has this text been used and how is it used today to defy or corroborate hegemonic political systems, laws, science, medicine, or public policy? How has biblical interpretation been used and how is the Bible still used either to challenge or to protect powerful interests and to engender sociocultural, political, and religious change? How is the Bible used to define public discourse and groups of people?

43. Dorothy Allison, "A Question of Class," in Allison's *Skin: Talking about Sex, Class, and Literature* (Ithaca: Firebrand, 1994), 35–36.

What is the vision of society that is articulated in and through biblical texts? Is, and how is, Scripture used to marginalize certain people, to legitimate racism and other languages of hate, or is it used to intervene in discourses of injustice? Such questions must become as central as exegetical-historical and literary-anthropological questions still are and have been.[44]

Reading Clement's text to expose the ways that biblical interpretations have material and ethical consequences does not itself provide a solution for contemporary problems of poverty and socioeconomic disparity. Nevertheless, by interpreting *Who Is the Rich Person Who Is Saved?* with a commitment to resolving these problems to accomplish justice for the most oppressed wo/men, it is possible to identify alternative perspectives to the dominant rhetoric of the text.

Schüssler Fiorenza's work allows us to see that the process of interpretation and the evaluation of our interpretations is part of ongoing struggles for justice. Her feminist emancipatory rhetorical framework insists that our interpretations of antiquity matter — for contemporary lives and discourses, as well as for how they allow us to imagine the future. We have seen that Clement is able to interpret Mark 10:17–31 as compatible with an inegalitarian socioeconomic system, even as he advocates charitable redirection of wealth through "redemptive almsgiving." So too, Christian communities have to choose whether to understand Christianity as consistent with global consumer capitalism and to examine whether even institutional practices designed to combat poverty function to sustain or transform structural inequities in social arrangements.[45] Schüssler Fiorenza's approach allows for the interpretation of an alternative egalitarian vision within Clement's text; this commitment to the ongoing possibilities of transformation presupposes that such alternatives can be imagined and realized today.

---

44. Schüssler Fiorenza, *Rhetoric and Ethic*, 33.

45. Although I specify Christian communities here, the challenge for critical self-examination and transformation is by no means limited to Christians, especially within the American context where so-called secular values are informed by biblical interpretations.

13

Bridging the Gap to "This Generation"

A Feminist-Critical Reading of the Rhetoric of Q 7:31–35

Melanie Johnson-DeBaufre

One of the remarkable things about Elisabeth Schüssler Fiorenza is her uncanny ability to see — simultaneously — both the forest and the trees. I have seen her at work in a seminar for doctoral students offering exegetical-textual insights that are refreshing and unexpected. She follows with a question: *why* are her proposals so unexpected? This presses her audience to consider the scholarly presuppositions that produce the "commonsense" interpretation of the text in question. When we are finished — if we have grasped it — we have witnessed the subtle, pervasive, and powerful interplay between interpretive frameworks and the results of interpretation, between our lenses and our readings. This persistent focus on both the forest and the trees is part of Schüssler Fiorenza's challenge to biblical scholars to recognize their own work as a rhetorical practice. This requires that scholars "study the pervasive and often only partly conscious set of value-laden dispositions, inclinations, attitudes, and habits of biblical studies as an academic discipline."[1] Practicing such critical reflexivity means that we "investigate not only the meaning of the Bible but also the meaning-making of biblical studies."[2] In honor of Elisabeth Schüssler Fiorenza's invaluable contribution to biblical studies, this essay offers a feminist-critical reading of Jesus' comparison between "this generation," the children in the marketplace, and Jesus and John in Q 7:31–35.[3] My interpretation attempts to demonstrate the

---

1. Elisabeth Schüssler Fiorenza, *Rhetoric and Ethic: The Politics of Biblical Studies* (Minneapolis: Fortress, 1999), 195.

2. Elisabeth Schüssler Fiorenza, *Jesus and the Politics of Interpretation* (London/New York: Continuum, 2000), ix.

3. Q (from the German *Quelle* for "source") is the hypothesized second source common to Matthew and Luke. Q verses are cited according to the common scholarly practice of using Luke's chapter and verse numbering.

exegetical and rhetorical possibilities created by a critically reflexive investigation that attends to both the intricacies of the text and the presuppositions and interests that shape that text's interpretation.

The Rhetoric and Ethics of Identity

Before turning to the particular trees of Q 7:31–35, it is important to glance at the forest of contemporary Q studies. It has become commonplace in the field of Christian Testament studies in the United States to say that earliest Christianity was diverse. We speak in pluralities — of communities and christologies and Judaisms of the first century c.e.[4] The reconstruction and interpretation of Q plays an important role in exploring the diversity of earliest Christianity. Some interpret Q as early evidence of " 'another kerygma' — one which had no special place for the death of Jesus and which, unlike Paul, did not view the vindication of Jesus through the apocalyptic metaphor of resurrection."[5] Some counter that "while Q may omit some things, it does not include anything really at odds with what Matthew or Luke held dear."[6] The lines in the debate over Q's "otherness" are drawn especially in terms of how scholars characterize Q's interpretation of Jesus. By locating Q's difference in relation to Q's presentation of Jesus, scholars replicate and amplify what I see as Q's own rhetorical move to center Jesus. This scholarly effort manifests itself in efforts to deploy Q to fix Jesus' identity — as a Cynic-like teacher or as an eschatological prophet — at the earliest layers of Q tradition. As I argue elsewhere, the issue at stake in the debates over Q is Christian identity in a diverse and pluralistic world. In the context of these debates, Jesus' identity is centered as the key to Christian identity.[7] The presupposition that runs through much historical-Jesus and Q scholarship is that, if we can say who Jesus was, we can know something about who (and how) Christians should be in this diverse world.

---

4. The discoveries of the Qumran and Nag Hammadi libraries have contributed a great deal to the development of diversity as a historical model for the reconstruction of ancient Judaism and Christianity.

5. Leif E. Vaage and John S. Kloppenborg [Verbin], "Early Christianity, Q, and Jesus: The Sayings Gospel and Method in the Study of Christian Origins," *Semeia* 55 (1991): 6. Vaage and Kloppenborg [Verbin] (5–6) attribute this "rediscovery of Q" as a "piece of theological reasoning in its own right" to the work of H. E. Tödt (*The Son of Man in the Synoptic Tradition* [German editions: 1959; 1963; trans. Dorothea Barton; Philadelphia: Westminster, 1965]) and Dieter Lührmann (*Die Redaktion der Logienquelle* [Neukirchen-Vluyn: Neukirchener Verlag, 1969]).

6. Dale C. Allison Jr., *The Jesus Tradition in Q* (Harrisburg, Pa.: Trinity, 1997), 45. Of course, this begs the question to some extent since Q — as far as we can reconstruct it — derives from the material that Matthew and Luke chose to preserve.

7. See Melanie Johnson-DeBaufre, "It's the End of the World as We Know It: Eschatology, Q, and the Construction of Christian Origins" (Th.D. diss., Harvard University, 2002).

I share the contemporary interest in reconstructing early Christianity as a diverse movement that included and negotiated a variety of practices, interpretations, and leaders. I argue, however, that this interest is undermined by the persistent focus on the identity of Jesus. This emphasis (both in Q and in modern scholarship) constructs early Christianity as a response to the work and vision of one great man. An interpretation of Q that centers the values and struggles of the movement around Jesus — rather than the identity of Jesus himself — can make important contributions to the reconstruction of early Christian diversity and to locating the values and visions that promote solidarity across lines of difference.[8]

In the context of a quest for Christian origins and the historical Jesus, early Christian gospels are not typically read in terms of the interests and values of the movement around Jesus so much as in terms of what they can tell us about the superlative value of Jesus himself. An approach that broadens the focus of inquiry from the identity of Jesus to the values of the communities around and after him is part of an explicitly feminist-critical framework. Such a framework attempts to give voice to the wo/men who "shape and have shaped culture and religion" even though their presence is often erased by kyriocentric texts.[9] Many feminist scholars argue that a process of reimagining is necessary to decenter the dominant rhetoric of texts as well as the prevailing reading practices that interpret their rhetoric as representing reality. As Schüssler Fiorenza argues, "A critical liberationist rhetoric maintains that one can break the hold of the androcentric text over the religious and historical imagination of its readers if one recognizes the agency of interpreters in reading texts as well as in reconstructing their socio-historical contexts."[10] I offer my interpretations of Q 7:31–35 in the context of a larger effort to imagine alternative possibilities for interpreting kyriocentric texts.

The reading of Q 7:31–35 presented here, therefore, presupposes certain things about language and texts that are part of a feminist rhetorical-historical approach to interpretation. This approach understands language "not as descriptive and reflective, as a window to reality," but as "polysemic" and "rhetorical-communicative."[11] It understands texts as rhetorical, that is, as determined "by rhetorical situations, arguments, persuasive goals, and visions."[12] Texts, therefore, are political discourses that attempt to persuade their audiences to accept their constructions of reality rather than records of things as they "really were." In the context of interpreting Q 7:31–35, this approach suggests that interpreters must imagine rhetorical

---

8. Schüssler Fiorenza proposes that this shift from Jesus to the movement around him is necessary for constructing an emancipatory historical-Jesus discourse; *Jesus and the Politics of Interpretation*, 21.

9. Schüssler Fiorenza, *Rhetoric and Ethic*, 138–39.

10. Ibid., 139.

11. Ibid., 196.

12. Ibid.

situations that make sense of the text as an act of persuasion rather than limit the text to meanings predetermined by an assumed polemical context of a conflict between the Q community and "this generation." My interpretation attempts to rethink how we tell the story of the Q community's relationship to their fellow Israelites. Using a feminist model of inquiry, I begin with the contemporary context of debates over religious pluralism and particularity and approach the text in light of the ethical imperative to articulate aspects of the tradition that envision solidarity across lines of difference around common visions and values. I suggest that the logic of the children-in-the-marketplace pericope does not have to depend upon or seek to negotiate the Q community's identity over and against Jewish outsiders.

Taking a feminist approach to interpretation means that I presuppose "that all texts, interpretations, and historical reconstructions are relative and perspectival. If what one sees depends on where one stands, social-ideological location and rhetorical context are as decisive as text for how one reconstructs historical realities or interprets biblical texts."[13] My examination of the scholarly discourse on Q 7:31–35, therefore, does not serve to identify and *eliminate* underlying interests and frameworks prior to interpreting Q, but rather to identify and *articulate* competing interests that have a bearing on one's interpretation of Q.

To What Shall We Compare "This Generation"?

In order to attend to both the forest and the trees, it is important to explore how interest in the identity of Jesus produces particular readings of Q 7:31–35. Schüssler Fiorenza challenges biblical scholars to engage in an ethics of interpretive practices that investigates "how interpretation is produced, authorized, communicated, or used."[14] It examines "problem formulation" and "patterns of interpretation." It asks "which boundaries and limits are constructed and maintained by a scholarly discourse," "which questions are not admitted," and "which arguments are silenced."[15] In what follows, therefore, I examine the common problems that Q scholars seek to address when interpreting Q 7:31–35. These problems and their typical solutions illustrate the central interest in the identity of Jesus in Q scholarship and the often pervasive expectation that the rhetoric of Q is primarily interested in Jesus' identity over and against "this generation."

The International Q Project reconstructs the Greek text of Q 7:31–35 as follows:[16]

---

13. Ibid., 138.
14. Ibid.
15. Ibid., 196–97.
16. James M. Robinson, Paul Hoffmann, and John S. Kloppenborg [Verbin], eds., *The Critical Edition of Q* (Hermeneia; Minneapolis: Fortress, 2000), 140–49 (my translation).

Q 7:31

τίνι ὁμοιώσω τὴ(ν) γενεὰ(ν) ταύτη(ν) [καὶ τίνι ἐ<στ>ὶν ὁμοί<α>];	To what am I to compare this generation and what is it like?

Q 7:32

ὁμοί(α) ἐ(στ)ὶν παιδίοις καθημένοις ἐν [[(ταῖς)]] ἀγορ[[(αῖς)]] ἃ προσφωνοῦ(ντα) [[(τοῖς ἑτέρ)]]οις λέγ(ουσιν)· ηὐλήσαμεν ὑμῖν καὶ οὐκ ὠρχήσασθε, ἐθρηνήσαμεν καὶ οὐκ ἐ[κλαύσατε].	It is like children seated in the marketplace/s, who, addressing the others, say: We fluted for you, but you would not dance; we sang a dirge,[17] but you would not cry.[18]

Q 7:33

ἦλθεν γὰρ Ἰωάννης μὴ ἐσθίων μήτε πίνων, καὶ λέγ[ετε]· δαιμόνιον ἔχει.	For John came, neither eating nor drinking, and you say: He has a demon!

Q 7:34

ἦλθεν ὁ υἱὸς τοῦ ἀνθρώπου ἐσθίων καὶ πίνων, καὶ λέγ[ετε]· ἰδοὺ ἄνθρωπος φάγος καὶ οἰνοπότης, τελωνῶν φίλος καὶ ἁμαρτωλῶν.	The son of humanity came eating and drinking, and you say: Look! A person [who is] a glutton and drunkard, a friend of tax collectors and sinners.

Q 7:35

καὶ ἐδικαιώθη ἡ σοφία ἀπὸ τῶν [τέκν]ων αὐτῆς.	But Wisdom is vindicated by [all][19] her children.

---

17. I translate θρηνέω as "sing a dirge" (first definition in Liddell-Scott-Jones) rather than using the International Q Project's "wail" (second definition in Liddell-Scott-Jones) in order to make the element of musical performance in the second phrase more apparent. See Henry George Liddell, Robert Scott, and Henry Stuart Jones, *A Greek-English Lexicon* (9th ed.; Oxford: Clarendon, 1961), 805.

18. The International Q Project selects Luke's ἐκλαύσατε (Liddell-Scott-Jones 955: "cry, wail, lament") rather than Matthew's ἐκόψασθε (Liddell-Scott-Jones 979: "beat one's breast or head through grief"; also "mourn" but usually with an accusative object). The Matthean version would make both verbs in the second half of each line into actions that involve moving the body. The evidence is strong either way. Whichever verb was in Q, the other verb choice may have been inspired by a line in the poem in Eccl 3 LXX about there being a time for everything: "A time to weep [κλαῦσαι] and a time to laugh / a time to mourn [κόψασθαι], and a time to dance [ὀρχήσασθαι]" (Eccl 3:4). This may indicate Q's having κόπτω (which parallels Ecclesiastes) or Matthew's changing Q to make it adhere more closely with Ecclesiastes. If Luke found the verb κόπτω unseemly, as Olof Linton argues ("The Parable of the Children's Game," *New Testament Studies* 22 [1975–76]: 162), then the verse in Ecclesiastes may have provided the alternative κλαίω.

19. Although the International Q Project prefers Luke's τέκνων to Matthew's ἔργων, it leaves aside Luke's πάντων as Lukan. In the context of the interpretation of Q 7:31–35 that I offer in this essay, Luke's πάντων reflects well the rhetorical interests of the Q passage.

Scholars often puzzle over the relationship between the three literary components of Q 7:31–35. The unit consists of (1) a simile that compares "this generation" with children sitting in the marketplace (7:31–32); (2) an application that gives a parallel comparison to the reception of John and Jesus (7:33–34); and (3) a concluding aphorism (7:35). As Arland Jacobson notes, "The problems with this pericope have less to do with reconstructing the Q text than with understanding the interrelationships of the various elements in the pericope."[20] Two problems commonly identified are the relationship between the simile and the application and the relationship between both of these and the concluding aphorism. As I will show, the predominant solutions to the problem of the interrelation of the three elements in Q 7:31–35 among Q scholars are shaped by the interpreters' expectation of a polemical gulf between Jesus/John and "this generation."

The first common problem is the fit between the simile in 7:31–32 and the application[21] to John and Jesus in 7:33–34.[22] John Kloppenborg Verbin admits that "although it seems apparent that the parable and its interpretation criticize 'this generation,' the *tertium comparationis* is far from clear."[23] As Ron Cameron summarizes:

> Are the uncooperative children those addressed by John and Jesus? Or do the children represent "this generation," calling unsuccessfully to John and Jesus? Does "this generation" represent *two* groups of children each calling to the other yet refusing to respond? Or are John and Jesus identified with one group which calls, and "this generation" with another which rejects their summons?[24]

In light of the application in verses 33–34, interpreters tend to rule out the possibility that "this generation" calls unsuccessfully to John and Jesus or that " 'this generation' represent *two* groups of children each calling to the

---

20. Arland D. Jacobson, *The First Gospel: An Introduction to Q* (Sonoma, Calif.: Polebridge, 1992), 120.

21. It may be more useful to describe Q 7:33–34 as an argument "from example" as Ron Cameron does in " 'What Have You Come Out To See?' Characterizations of John and Jesus in the Gospels," *Semeia* 49 (1990): 60. This would function to substantiate the truth of the simile by giving a concrete example from the realm of human behavior.

22. This perceived lack of fit has been a primary factor in the routine classification of the interpretation (Q 7:33–34) as secondary. See Paul Hoffmann, *Studien zur Theologie der Logienquelle* (Münster: Aschendorff, 1972), 227.

23. John S. Kloppenborg [Verbin], *The Formation of Q: Trajectories in Ancient Wisdom Collections* (Philadelphia: Fortress, 1987), 111.

24. Cameron, "What Have You Come Out to See?" 40 (emphasis original). This kind of list of possibilities also appears in Kloppenborg [Verbin], *Formation of Q*, 111; and Wendy J. Cotter, "The Parable of the Children in the Market-Place, Q (Lk) 7:31–35: An Examination of the Parable's Image and Significance," *Novum Testamentum* 29 (1987): 294. For a helpful elaboration of these interpretive options as they appear in scholarship before 1975, see Dieter Zeller, "Die Bildlogik des Gleichnisses Mt 11:16f./Lk 7:31f.," *Zeitschrift für die neutestamentliche Wissenschaft* 68 (1977): 252–57.

other yet refusing to respond."[25] For example, Kloppenborg Verbin argues that "the identification of John and Jesus with the children who do the calling, and 'this generation' with those who refuse to respond, seems the most *natural* interpretation, especially since v. 35 characterizes John and Jesus as children [τέκνα] of Sophia."[26] This reading aligns "this generation" with the addressees ("you") in both the parable and the application despite the direct comparison between the people of "this generation" and the children addressing other children in the marketplace in Q 7:31. Taking the simile — and its comparison between "this generation" and children who call to other children — at face value is not possible in this interpretation, given the expectation that John/Jesus and "this generation" are presented by the text as messengers and opponents respectively.

This solution also points to the second common interpretive problem for this unit: the relationship between the simile and application and the concluding aphorism. Where the previous problem aims at clarifying the identity and relationships of "this generation," the children, and Jesus and John, this problem asks, Who are the children of Sophia? Are they Jesus and John, as Kloppenborg Verbin suggests above? Or are they anyone who responds positively to Jesus and John? Or are they John, Jesus, and their followers? After an interpretation that links Jesus and John with the active children in 7:32 and "this generation" with the nonresponsive children, Christopher Tuckett is left with no choice but to posit that Jesus and John are the *implied* actors of 7:35. Once again, a wide range of possibilities are acknowledged but the interpretive framework leads to a narrow choice:

> It is hard to see how John and Jesus alone as "acknowledging Wisdom to be in the right" really fits the context. Much better is the idea of Wisdom's children as those responding to Wisdom's call (cf. Prov 8:32; Sir 4:11; 15:2) so that Wisdom's children provide the antithetical parallel to the people of this generation who have not responded. The saying in v. 35 thus provides a polemical thrust at the end of the pericope, *implying* that "this generation" do not comprise the true children of Wisdom by their rejection of the calls of Jesus and John. *Implicit* here is the idea that Jesus and John are messengers of Wisdom, and hence acceptance of their message is acceptance of Wisdom.[27]

For Tuckett, the saying's apparent focus on a wider group that justifies Wisdom cannot stand as the conclusion to the entire unit on John and Jesus (Q 7:18–35) because the purpose of the composition was already marked out as clarifying the relationship between John and Jesus. Therefore John

---

25. Cameron, "What Have You Come Out to See?" 40 (emphasis original).

26. Kloppenborg [Verbin], *Formation of Q*, 111 (emphasis added). Kloppenborg [Verbin]'s view is the dominant one. See further bibliography at 111 n. 39.

27. Christopher M. Tuckett, *Q and the History of Early Christianity* (Edinburgh: Clark, 1996), 178 (emphasis added).

and Jesus (and their perceived opponents in 7:31: "this generation") must be related to 7:35 *by implication*. When Tuckett concludes his discussion, the larger group — so apparent to him in the saying — has receded in favor of the *implied* foci: "The thrust of the small section in 7:31–35, and derivatively of the wider unit in 7:18–35, is thus that Jesus and John appear in parallel as messengers of Wisdom but shunned by this generation."[28]

The Rhetoric of "This Generation"

Since the work of Dieter Lührmann, scholars interested in the redactional history of Q have paid special attention to the expression "this generation." In his small but highly influential 1969 book, *Die Redaktion der Logienquelle*, Lührmann argues that the announcement of judgment against "this generation" is a "characteristic feature for determining the theology of Q."[29] For Lührmann, "this generation" stands for all of Israel and the conflict between Jesus, and "this generation" reflects the conflict between the Q community and Israel.[30] Citing the work of Max Meinertz,[31] Lührmann views "this generation" as a pejorative *terminus technicus*, which points to the people of Israel as chronically unrepentant and stubborn. According to Lührmann, "the announcement of judgment against this generation creates a decisive opposition between Jesus and the community on the one hand and Israel on the other: for Israel there remains only judgment."[32]

Kloppenborg Verbin builds on Lührmann's redactional insights in his *Formation of Q*. His own analysis concludes that the redactional structures of Q point to "the conflict between the Q group and their Jewish contemporaries over the preaching of the kingdom."[33] Interpreting "this generation" in a similar polemical vein, Jacobson links Q's use of "this generation" to its use of the deuteronomistic tradition to make sense of the rejection of Jesus

---

28. Ibid., 179.

29. Lührmann, *Redaktion der Logienquelle*, 93.

30. Ibid., 31.

31. Max Meinertz, " 'Dieses Geschlecht' im Neuen Testament," *Biblische Zeitschrift* 1 (1957): 283–89. Lührmann does not treat the term itself in any length. Evald Lövestam points out that Meinertz de-emphasizes the temporal aspects of "this generation" in favor of its negative moral characteristics because of his interest in Mark 13:30; see Evald Lövestam, "The ἡ γενεὰ αὔτη Eschatology in Mk 13:30 parr.," in *L'apocalypse johannique et l'apocalyptique dans le nouveau testament* (ed. Jan Lambrecht; Louvain: Leuven University Press, 1980), 403–13. Lövestam proposes that "this generation" derives from Jewish reflection on special "generations" in the history of Israel. The flood generation and the wilderness generation, for example, are characterized as demanding signs and ignoring the preaching of repentance and suffering the wrath of God as a result. Given the persistent emphasis in Q on the crucial significance of the present situation, Lövestam's proposals should be further explored for their value in interpreting "this generation" in Q.

32. Lührmann, *Redaktion der Logienquelle*, 93.

33. Kloppenborg [Verbin], *Formation of Q*, 167.

and the Q community by their fellow Israelites.[34] This theologizing reaches its climax in Q 11:49–51 where Wisdom declares that "this generation" will have to pay for its murder of the prophets. According to Jacobson, "the situation has reached crisis proportions; there seems to be not even a shred of hope for the conversion of Israel, for its reawakening. The polarization of 'this generation' and Wisdom's children seems to be understood in terms of God's judgment, in terms of the separation even now of those who respond from those blind ones who remain in darkness."[35]

The language about "this generation" in Q, therefore, is understood as polemical language that rhetorically reflects and constitutes boundaries between competing identity groups — particularly between the Q community and "Israel." Both Christopher Tuckett and Richard Horsley criticize Lührmann's understanding of "this generation" as all of Israel. They likewise identify "this generation" as a polemical expression, but argue that it has a more limited horizon in Q. For Tuckett, it points to "simply the non-responsive part of the Jewish people."[36] For Horsley, it refers to the scribes and Pharisees in particular and to the elite Jerusalem leaders in general who oppose Q's local program for the renewal of Israel.[37] Both Tuckett and Horsley attempt to deconstruct the dichotomy between the Q community and Judaism that is implied by Lührmann's interpretation of "this generation" in Q, but they retain a dichotomy between insiders (the Q community) and outsiders (those who reject the community or the message).

Much of the opacity created around the relationship between verses 31–32, 33–34, and 35 results from the interpretation of this pericope as part of Q's "announcement of judgment" against "this generation" for its rejection of Jesus' and John's messages. I suggest that by bracketing the interpretation of "this generation" as the monolithic recipient of Q's announcement of judgment via Jesus and John as messengers of Sophia, other possibilities come into view.

Fitting the Pieces of Q 7:31–34 Together

The traditional scholarly juxtaposition of John and Jesus over and against "this generation" presupposes that Q's Jesus is in contest or contrast with them. This results in interpretations that must find a way to reconcile the lack of contention in Q 7:18–35 with the expected jockeying for position

---

34. Jacobson (*First Gospel,* 72–76) draws here on the work of Odil Hannes Steck, *Israel und das gewaltsame Geschick der Propheten: Untersuchungen zur Überlieferung des deuteronomistischen Geschichtsbildes im Alten Testament, Spätjudentum und Urchristentum* (Wissenschaftliche Monographien zum Alten und Neuen Testament 23; Neukirchen-Vluyn: Neukirchener Verlag, 1967).

35. Jacobson, *First Gospel,* 183.

36. Tuckett, *Q and the History of Early Christianity,* 201.

37. Richard A. Horsley and Jonathan A. Draper, *Whoever Hears You Hears Me* (Harrisburg, Pa.: Trinity, 1999), 299.

between Jesus, John, and "this generation." This has the effect of render-ing certain interpretations unthinkable, for example, the possibility that Q presents John, Jesus, and "this generation" as all part of one group that should understand itself as enacting the vision of the *basileia* of God.

As I will show, the difficulty of the relationship between the simile and the application and even the concluding aphorism is overstated. There is complete structural similarity between the bipartite speech of the children in the marketplace and the sayings about John and Jesus. In addition, the introduction to the parable in 7:31 makes it very clear that "this generation" is likened to the children who address "the others." Thus the common in-terpretation that the children in the marketplace are Jesus and John calling to "this generation" is implausible. Although John and Jesus are the sub-jects of verses 33–34 (along with "you" plural), they are not the subjects of 7:31–32.[38] Analysis of the structure of each verse as well as an interest in resisting the dichotomy commonly constructed between Jesus and "this generation" and between Jesus and John will lead to alternative solutions to the perceived problems of the text.

If we begin with verses 33–34, one can see that the central verbal structures are strikingly parallel in their construction:

John	came	*not* eating and drinking	and you say	"he has a demon"
	ἦλθεν	μὴ ἐσθίων μήτε πίνων	καὶ λέγετε	
	ἦλθεν	ἐσθίων καὶ πίνων	καὶ λέγετε	
son of humanity	came	eating and drinking	and you say	"look, a glutton and a drunk"

The two verses speak about two people, each being negatively evaluated. They share two elements of similarity: (1) both have particular eating habits, and (2) both receive a negative response. The difference is the nature of the eating habits.[39] Thus the text constructs Jesus and John as two sides of the same coin. Whether they eat and drink, they are evaluated similarly by "you" (plural).

The children's speech in 7:32 attests a similar parallel structure:

we fluted for you	but you would not dance
ηὐλήσαμεν ὑμῖν	καὶ οὐκ ὠρχήσασθε
ἐθρηνήσαμεν	καὶ οὐκ ἐκλαύσατε
we sang a dirge	but you would not cry

---

38. Cotter, "Parable of the Children," 295.

39. Jesus also uses the expression *son of humanity* to refer to himself. There is some dispute over whether this alone elevates Jesus over John in Q 7:31–35. Given its recurrence throughout Q, this expression does function to mark Jesus' significance for the audience. As with the references to the "*basileia* of God," however, its meaning throughout Q is assumed rather than explicated.

As in 7:33–34, there are two similarities between the parts: (1) both speak of musical performance, and (2) both receive a negative response. As in 7:33–34, the first action is both similar and different: they both perform musically but one evokes celebration and one evokes mourning. Thus they are opposites — two sides of the same coin — in precisely the same way that Jesus and John eat or do not eat.

The recognition of this symmetry between the parts of verses 31–32 and verses 33–34 results in the simple conclusion that the two elements of the application correspond to the two elements of the simile. Their relationship is often described as a kind of ring structure (ABB′A′):

A	we fluted for you	but you would not dance
B	we sang a dirge	but you would not cry
B′	John came neither eating nor drinking	and you say, "he has a demon"
A′	the son of humanity came eating and drinking	and you say, "he is a glutton and a drunkard"

This structure creates a parallel between John's not eating and drinking and the children's singing a dirge and a parallel between Jesus' eating and drinking and the children's fluting.[40] Although the details are not always pressed, this is the most common interpretation of the relationship between the simile and the application.[41] This interpretation requires, however, that "this generation" represents the nonresponsive children and thus renders unintelligible the introduction to the simile, which directly links "this generation" to the children who flute and dirge.[42] The structure must twist the simile to fit the application. This reading also aligns "this generation" with the addressees ("you") in both the simile and the application. They will not dance or mourn and they call John and Jesus a demon and a glutton respectively. The association of "this generation" with "you" in both the simile and the application, however, introduces a disparity between the charge of passive recalcitrance leveled at "this generation" in verses 31–32 and the charge of active name calling in verses 34–35. The second offense (calling John and Jesus names) corresponds better with the charge that "this generation" is like children *addressing* other children in the marketplace. This reading,

---

40. Linking John with singing a dirge and Jesus with fluting has long been theologically attractive to Christian Testament interpreters who contrast John and Jesus as respectively dour and joyous. I argue that Q both constructs this dichotomy and seeks to undermine it.

41. See, for example, Burton L. Mack, *The Lost Gospel: The Book of Q and Christian Origins* (San Francisco: Harper, 1993), 157–58; Jacobson, *First Gospel*, 123; Majella Franzmann, "Of Food, Bodies, and the Boundless Reign of God in the Synoptic Gospels," *Pacifica* 5 (1992): 17–31. Although Séan Freyne ("Jesus the Wine-Drinker: A Friend of Women," in *Transformative Encounters* [ed. Ingrid Rosa Kitzberger; Leiden: Brill, 2000], 162–80) describes the structure as AB-A′B′ (172), his interpretation clearly depends on the AB-B′A′ structure.

42. So also Linton, "Parable of the Children's Game," 171–72; Cotter, "Parable of the Children," 295.

however, is commonly ruled out by the association of Jesus and John with the children who flute and dirge in 7:32.

This fog dissipates with two interpretive moves: (1) the structural relationship between the parts is ABA'B'(and not ABB'A'):[43]

A	we fluted for you	but you would not dance
B	we sang a dirge	but you would not cry
A'	John came neither eating nor drinking	and you say, "he has a demon"
B'	the son of humanity came eating and drinking	and you say, "he is a glutton and a drunk"

And (2) the antecedent of "you" in the simile is not the same as that of "you" in the sayings about John and Jesus. The children's first taunt claims that "we" ("this generation") fluted and "you" (other children) would not dance. The parallel application declares that, indeed, John would not dance (came fasting), but "you" ("this generation") say he has a demon. Similarly, "this generation" complains that they sang a dirge and the other children did not cry. The application concedes the point — Jesus did not mourn (he came feasting) and "you" ("this generation") say he is a glutton. Thus far, the result of this interpretation is that Jesus and John correspond to the "other" children in the parable.[44] The terms of the comparison lie in the criticisms — of the unresponsive children and of John and Jesus.[45] "This generation" is a judgmental generation. It judges John and Jesus because they do not play along.[46]

As Wendy Cotter shows, the sting of the parable lies in the image of the children itself. She notes the peculiar vocabulary associated with the children's behavior. Although the content of the taunts implies childlike games,

---

43. Allegorical interpretations attached to parables in the Synoptics follow a similar progressive structure (rather than a ring structure). See, for example, Mark 4:3–9, 14–20. Kloppenborg [Verbin] (*Formation of Q*, 110) describes Q 7:33–34 as an "attempt at allegorization of the parable," which nonetheless gets the procedure wrong insofar as "the interpretation, which refers to John first and then the Son of Man, does not accord with the order of the verbs in vv. 31–32 (αὐλέω . . . θρηνέω)." Kloppenborg [Verbin] confirms that the expected structure should be ABA'B', but sees a poor fit between the parable and allegory because he expects that John and Jesus should correspond to the active children in the parable.

44. This conclusion renders the choice between Matthew's τοῖς ἑτέροις (to the others) and Luke's ἀλλήλοις (to each other) in Q 7:32 insignificant for interpretation of the simile (*pace* Jacobson, *First Gospel*, 121). For discussion of this issue, see Johnson-DeBaufre, "It's the End of the World," 68 n. 35.

45. Zeller ("Bildlogik des Gleichnisses," 254) argues that this cannot be the case because early Christians would not associate John and Jesus with stubborn children.

46. This interpretation also retains the notion that Q 7:33–34 has some allegorical relationship to the parable. The allegory is commonly made between the fluting and Jesus' ministry and the wailing and John's ministry. My interpretation, however, links "not dancing" with John and "not mourning" with Jesus. There are clear parallels between the two-sided music and the two-sided approach to eating. Where interpreters have gone wrong is in the need to understand John and Jesus as the actors and subjects rather than as those who are acted upon.

the children are "seated" (καθημένοις) and formally "addressing" (προσ–
φωνοῦντα) "the others" in the marketplace. This vocabulary is consistently
used of adults who sit as judges in civic courts in the agora.[47] Thus, "no
matter how these 'children' adopt dignified behavior, it is plain from the
content of their objections, that they are, after all, only shallow children."[48]
In the application of the parable, therefore, the judgments made against
John and Jesus are equally childish in that they are now spoken by children
play-acting at being grown-up in the agora.

I argue that it makes the most sense to retain the sense of verses 31–32
that "this generation" is like children sitting in the marketplace addressing
other children (represented in the application by John and Jesus). It is common, however, to portray these two groups of children as active and passive
players: "this generation" flutes and wails, and "the others" just sit and are
judged for not playing along. There is, however, another possibility. What if
"this generation" is indeed two groups of children in the marketplace calling to each other? What if the groups of children each call and each reject
the other? If this were the case, then the structural relationship between the
simile and the application can be further nuanced. With this approach, the
two parts of the children's taunts (and the criticisms of John and Jesus) are
spoken antiphonally by opposing groups (represented in the chart by italic
and bold):

A		*we fluted*	and **you did not dance**
	B	**we sang a dirge**	*and you did not cry*
A′		**for John came not eating and drinking**	*and you say, "he has a demon"*
	B′	*the son of humanity came eating and drinking*	**and you say, "he is a glutton and a drunk"**

The accusations fly between two groups. One side (the italic group) calls
to the other (the bold group) and accuses them of not dancing when the
italic group fluted. Then the bold group retorts that they sang a dirge but
the italic group did not mourn. The application then applies this image of
the judgmental and uncooperative children to those who judge John and
those who judge Jesus on the basis of their eating practices. "Indeed," Jesus
says to the italic group, "John came not dancing and you ostracize him."
"Indeed," Jesus says to the bold group, "I (the son of humanity) came not
mourning and you criticize him (me)." In addition to the alternating structure (ABA′B′), there now is a chiastic relationship within each pair: in AB
the italic group both flutes and does not mourn, and the bold group both
refuses to dance and sings a dirge; in A′B′ the bold group (represented by
John) does not eat/drink and says that he who does is a glutton, and the
italic group eats/drinks and says that he who does not has a demon.

---

47. Cotter, "Parable of the Children," 295–302.
48. Ibid., 302.

Several textual and interpretive indicators make this interpretation possible:

1. If Matthew's τοῖς ἑτέροις was in Q 7:32, then Luke's ἀλλήλοις indicates at least that the author of Luke understood the simile as referring to two groups of children calling to each other. Indeed, Matthew's version also indicates two groups of children. Matthew's version simply does not say whether the second group of children is addressing the other group as well. It is thus also possible that Luke sought to fix and sharpen this already implied meaning.

2. Cotter shows well that the image of the parable plays on the juxtaposition of childish judgments and adults sitting in court in the agora. Cotter does not explain, however, why children would be doing that at all. Sitting around pretending to make serious judgments of other children who are not doing anything is hardly a game worth playing for very long. Interpreting the children as play-acting at court and judging each other with equal and opposite childishness lends even more vitality to the image.[49]

3. Scholars have long recognized that there seems to be some correspondence between the polar opposites of John's and Jesus' eating behaviors and that of the children who sing dirges and flute, respectively. But heretofore, Jesus/John could correspond to either the fluters/lamenters or the unresponsive mourners/dancers. As I have discussed, the former wreaks havoc with the relationship between the simile and its application. The latter is better but must leave aside the correspondence between the similar-but-opposite pairs: fluting/wailing and eating/not eating. Interpreting the children (and John and Jesus) as two groups, addressing and judging each other, accounts for both parallels. This creates the long-sought-after symmetry between the simile and application that has so far eluded interpreters.

The simile and the application make a case to the audience of Q that when they judge John or Jesus on the basis of their different eating practices, they are like children in the marketplace foolishly judging each other. It has long been recognized that there is no rivalry in 7:31–35 between John and Jesus.[50]

---

49. As Horsley (in Horsley and Draper, *Whoever Hears,* 123–27) argues, our ways of reading are formed by the print culture in which we live. Unlike oral-based cultures, we often read in silence rather than perform texts. Imagining the two criticisms as spoken by opposing groups is easier in the context of a dramatic reading of the text. At the literal level of the text, we have no indicator that "we" in each stanza might refer to different groups. If someone was performing this text, that reading might have emerged as a natural reading because it is inherently more dramatic.

50. Kloppenborg [Verbin], *Formation of Q,* 112; Jacobson, *First Gospel,* 122; Allison, *Jesus Tradition in Q,* 34; Tuckett, *Q and the History of Early Christianity,* 131; Ronald A. Piper, *Wisdom in the Q-Tradition* (Cambridge: Cambridge University Press, 1989), 126; Mack, *Lost Gospel,* 157; Leif E. Vaage, *Galilean Upstarts: Jesus' First Followers according to Q* (Valley

They are affirmed equally against their critics. What is unexpected, however, is the possibility that there is also no divide between "this generation" and John/Jesus, and thus no divide between "this generation" and the audience of Q.[51] The text argues for the equal legitimacy of John's practices and Jesus' practices within the larger group which they represent[52] and of which they are both a part. This interpretation places Jesus, John, and the audience in the same category as "this generation." Jesus asks, "What is this generation like?" To recast this question colloquially, Q's Jesus now asks, "What are the people of our time like? What's wrong with us?" The answer that Q's Jesus gives stings: we are like children sitting in the marketplace judging each other on the basis of our differences.

"Wisdom Is Vindicated by All Her Children"

The aphorism in Q 7:35 functions as concluding aphorisms do: it reverses "characterizations set up earlier in the unit."[53] Although "this generation" is characteristically factional and divisive along lines of difference, Wisdom is vindicated by all her children. Wisdom's children[54] are *all* children who vindicate her, that is, who prove her right or "acknowledge her to be right."[55] Without the divide between John/Jesus and "this generation," it is possible to read the aphorism in the way that we expect, that is, as affirming *both* John and Jesus and, therefore, all the "children" who flute or dirge as children who vindicate Wisdom. Their differences are insignificant given their common ground as children of Wisdom. Thus "this generation" can be like

Forge, Pa.: Trinity, 1994), 110 (for Q 7:33–34 only); idem, "More Than a Prophet, and Demon-Possessed: Q and the 'Historical John,'" in *Conflict and Invention: Literary, Rhetorical, and Social Studies on the Sayings Gospel Q* (ed. John S. Kloppenborg [Verbin]; Valley Forge, Pa.: Trinity, 1995), 183.

51. Several interpreters make a move similar to Kloppenborg [Verbin] in *Formation of Q,* 112, who sets aside the view that Q 7:31–35 deals with the opposition between John and Jesus in favor of an opposition between John/Jesus and "this generation": "Q 7:31–35 looks in retrospect at the careers of John and Jesus and at their lack of success with 'this generation....' Q 7:31–35 does not oppose John to Jesus, but both to 'this generation.'" See also, Lührmann, *Redaktion der Logienquelle,* 30; Jacobson, *First Gospel,* 122; Allison, *Jesus Tradition in Q,* 17, 53; Tuckett, *Q and the History of Early Christianity,* 135; Mack, *Lost Gospel,* 157; Vaage, *Galilean Upstarts,* 109.

52. Plural "you" in Q 7:32 does not contradict the reference to John and Jesus in the application since the criticisms of John and Jesus are presented as representative examples of the tendency of "this generation" toward factionalism.

53. Alan Kirk, *The Composition of the Sayings Source* (Novum Testamentum Supplement 91; Leiden: Brill, 1998), 375: "The appending of a concluding aphorism reversing characterizations set up earlier in the unit makes 7:31–35 parallel to 7:18–23 and 7:24–28." See also Cameron, "What Have You Come Out To See?" 61.

54. The shift from παιδίον to τέκνον may be because the aphorism in Q 7:35 was a well-known proverb (Lührmann, *Redaktion der Logienquelle,* 29). Given the deliberateness of the composition of Q 3:7–7:35, the link of the children of Abraham in Q 3:8 and the children of Sophia in Q 7:35 facilitates a larger compositional role for Q 7:35 as the conclusion not only to Q 7:18–35 but also to Q 3:7–7:35.

55. Piper, *Wisdom in the Q-Tradition,* 168.

children in a marketplace or like children of Sophia. Those like the former are judgmental of each other; those like the latter recognize that Wisdom is vindicated by all her children.[56]

The verb ἐδικαιώθη carries a forensic flavor[57] and, therefore, reverses the childish judgments made in the simile and application. The aphorism declares that John's and Jesus' eating practices, which are representative examples of the contentious differences among "this generation," both vindicate Wisdom. It attempts to move the audience to recognize this common ground. The saying thus rejects the infighting characterized by the negative judgments of John and Jesus. The defense of John and Jesus does not aim at establishing who John and Jesus were in contrast to each other (as Q 7:18 and many interpreters may lead us to think) or in contrast to "this generation," but rather at affirming their common ground as children of Sophia. The children of Sophia should not quarrel like children in the marketplaces, but rather vindicate her regardless of their differences.

But what, precisely, is the common ground between John and Jesus according to the text? They are both among the children of Sophia. But they are different insofar as John — and those like John — characteristically fasts (and metaphorically sings a dirge) and Jesus — and those like Jesus — characteristically feasts (and metaphorically pipes a dance). The text does not clearly state why both practices vindicate Sophia and are worthy of being recognized as such. In some ways, the aphorism simply declares by fiat that they both vindicate Sophia and calls the audience to act in accordance with that recognition.[58]

---

56. Patrick Hartin, " 'Yet Wisdom Is Justified by Her Children' (Q 7:35): A Rhetorical and Compositional Analysis of Divine Sophia in Q," in *Conflict and Invention: Literary, Rhetorical, and Social Studies on the Sayings Gospel Q* (ed. John S. Kloppenborg [Verbin]; Valley Forge, Pa.: Trinity, 1995), 155, notes: "It is important to stress this wider conception of the children of Sophia because there is the tendency to see the notion in a very individualistic way as relating to only John and Jesus." While I agree, Hartin does not explain how he includes both Jesus' and John's vindicating Sophia as her messengers and the community's vindicating Sophia by responding positively to John and Jesus in a saying with only two characters (Sophia and her children).

57. Lührmann, *Redaktion der Logienquelle,* 30–31; G. Schrenk, "Δικαιόω," in *Theological Dictionary of the New Testament* (ed. G. Kittel and G. Friedrich; trans. G. W. Bromiley; Grand Rapids: Eerdmans, 1964), 2.211–23; and Tuckett, *Q and the History of Early Christianity,* 178.

58. The juxtaposition of fasting versus feasting cannot be seen as inferring that John was somehow more religious or more Jewish than Jesus. As Linton points out ("Parable of the Children's Game," 175), both fasting and feasting are affirmed in Jewish tradition. The issue may be refusing to participate properly in one on account of overvaluing the other. The evaluation of people's eating practices was not peculiar to Judaism or any other ancient social identity. As Vaage shows, the Cynic philosophers were the target of dichotomized and equally criticized eating practices (*Galilean Upstarts,* 102; see also Cameron, "What Have You Come Out to See?" 42). But this shows that eating practices are significant across social identities, not that Jesus and John were or were not remembered as Cynics. Vaage ("More Than a Prophet," 191) overinterprets the helpful Cynic analogy and concludes that "at the level of Q's formative stratum, John was remembered as one more of those 'doggone' philosophers."

But perhaps there is more. "This generation" criticizes Jesus as a "glutton and a drunk"; he is a friend of tax collectors and sinners. According to the charge, Jesus' characteristic feasting leads to the slander that he is excessive in his consumption and a friend of disreputable people. Although the words φάγος καὶ οἰνοπότης are translated "glutton and drunkard,"[59] the English may emphasize the quantity of the eating and drinking over the quality of the crowd with which one eats and drinks.[60] Proverbs 23:20–21 (LXX) warns: "Do not be among winebibbers [οἰνοπότης], / or among gluttonous eaters of meat [ἐκτείνου συμβολαῖς κρεῶν τε ἀγορασμοῖς]; / for the drunkard and the glutton will come to poverty, / and drowsiness will clothe them with rags." It may follow from Jesus' being a "glutton and a drunk," therefore, that he keeps company with society's low-life types.[61] It may be significant, then, that the few words that do overlap in Luke 7:29 and Matt 21:31 are "John" and "tax collectors." Both state that it was these kinds of people who received John's baptism.[62] If John's fasting is related to his call to "bear fruit worthy of repentance" (Q 3:7–9), then John's eating habits may also lead to being surrounded by the wrong people. The aphorism in Q 7:35, therefore, would not only argue that John and Jesus vindicate Sophia (as all her children should), but that the socially undesirable people around them are children of Sophia as well.[63]

If the link between John's baptism and tax collectors (Luke 7:29‖Matt 21:31b) appeared in Q, then the accusation against Jesus may be a deliberate rhetorical effort to assert John's and Jesus' similarity.[64] The criticisms

---

59. These are *hapax legomena*. They may reflect the context of Deut 21:18–21, although the Greek is substantially different (LXX: συμβολοκοπῶν οἰνοφλυγεῖ). Howard Clark Kee, "Jesus: A Glutton and a Drunkard," *New Testament Studies* 42 (1996): 374–93, argues that not enough attention is paid to the Deuteronomic context of the rebellious son who is threatening to both his parents and the community (390).

60. Vaage ("More Than a Prophet," 189) sees a sharp contrast between the depiction of Jesus in Q 7:34 and the "messianic aura" of the previous portrait of Jesus' activities in Q 7:22: "Any scandal provoked by Jesus' person in 7:34 will not be due to eschatological surprise and wonder, but the direct result of his low-life associations." This view overlooks the fact that the "eschatological wonders" invoked in Q 7:22 *also* suggest association with society's "low-life," that is, the sick and the poor.

61. Vaage (*Galilean Upstarts*, 88) makes the common assumption that the criticism "glutton and drunk" means that "according to Q 7:34, [Jesus] apparently ate and drank well and often enough to be suspected of overindulgence." Vaage identifies the elements of Q 7:34b as two different criticisms of Jesus. This rules out the possibility that the extravagant criticism of Q 7:34b is generated not by excessive eating but by Jesus' keeping company with tax collectors and sinners.

62. Matthew's additional parable in 21:28–31a also confirms that the reputation of those who went out to John's baptism was a point of contention. Matthew's version also speaks of prostitutes who were baptized by John.

63. Piper (*Wisdom in the Q-Tradition*, 168–69) argues that Luke 7:29 was in Q and thus strengthens his interpretation of Q 7:35 as including anyone who accepts Jesus and John as children of Sophia.

64. There are several indications throughout Q 7:18–35 that Q creates parity between John and Jesus. If Luke 3:10–14 was in Q, this would be another case of the same phenomenon. Luke 3:10–14 is a speech attributed to John that summarizes Jesus' teachings in the inaugural

of John and Jesus in Q 7:33b and 7:34b are not parallel. While the slander against Jesus is a lampooning of his eating practices, the charge against John is more extreme[65] and the relationship to his fasting is unclear.[66] This may indicate that there is some interest here in refuting the marginalization of John (and those like him).[67] The two units in Q 7:18–28 also show an interest in affirming John by making him parallel to Jesus. James Robinson notes that "it is striking, and calling for some explanation, that the opening of Q would have been more suited to John's followers than to those of Jesus."[68] The persistent affirmation of John and Jesus as children of Sophia — along with the traditionally marginalized and anyone who will recognize the validity of what both John and Jesus are doing — stands in tension with Q's representation of Jesus as the central figure in the present and future of the people. John's status as a child of Sophia in Q fades in the light of Jesus' position in Q as the son of humanity who stands at the judgment. But the status of society's lowest members as children of Sophia is rendered completely invisible if we presuppose that Jesus' identity and his relationship to John and "this generation" is the only issue on Q's rhetorical horizon.

It is my view that the elements of the Q text come together when John/Jesus and "this generation" are understood as actors in the same group rather than foes. The entire unit critiques the addressees (and thus audience) as a faction-ridden group by comparing them all to mutually uncooperative children.[69] It also affirms them by concluding that they all have or are able to

---

sermon. A few scholars argue that this passage is non-Lukan and should be considered as in Q; see John Kloppenborg [Verbin], *Q Parallels* (Sonoma, Calif.: Polebridge, 1988), 10. In Luke 3:12, John speaks to the tax collectors who have come to be baptized.

65. Indeed this charge is made repeatedly against Jesus in the Gospel of John (7:20; 8:48–52; 10:20–21). In Mark 3:21, Jesus is accused of being "out of his mind" and then of being possessed by Beelzebul after he does not eat because of the gathering of the crowds.

66. Linton ("Parable of the Children's Game," 176) mentions that some people thought demons needed no food. Vaage (*Galilean Upstarts,* 88) discusses how Cynics were commonly called insane.

67. Hartin ("Yet Wisdom Is Justified," 154) argues that Q 7:33b and Q 7:34b primarily function to vindicate Jesus' practices: "Because the accusations against John are so unwarranted, the same conclusion is drawn with regard to Jesus. These statements demonstrate the unreasonable rejection of John and Jesus."

68. James M. Robinson, "The Sayings Gospel Q," in *The Four Gospels, 1992* (ed. Frans Van Segbroeck et al.; Bibliotheca ephemeridum theologicarum lovaniensium 100; Louvain: Leuven University Press, 1992), 1.362. Robinson is referring to John's speech in Q 3:7–9 and its lack of christological reflection. I would argue that the same can be said about the repeated rhetorical efforts in Q 7:18–35 to affirm John by making him parallel to — not less than — Jesus.

69. Freyne, Kee, and Franzmann all suggest that the slander against Jesus in Q 7:34b derives from Jewish religious leaders' "efforts to vilify the Jesus movement as being not just unobservant in regard to purity but as being un-Jewish in its basic affiliation" (Freyne, "Jesus the Wine-Drinker," 175). This interpretation views the central conflict being negotiated by this text as a conflict with religious authorities over religious identity. However, this interpretation must pass over the text's assertion that John is also defended from the slanderous evaluation of his eating practices. If the issue is proper religious rigor, why would the ascetic John be criticized as having a demon? Why would a text like Q seek to defend John's practices as equally vindicating Sophia? Kee suggests that "strict adherents to ritual, cultic and ethnic limits for participation

vindicate Sophia. Thus it argues for solidarity in the group across differences without calling for the obliteration of differences. The emphasis on *this* generation — that is all the people in the present of the text — points to a sense that *now* is the crucial time to recognize the common ground between John and Jesus (and thus those who are like them).

This interpretation of Q 7:31–35 makes sense of the passage as it stands in Q. While many of the pieces have been considered and argued, this comprehensive interpretation has not been proposed before now because our expectations about the meaning and goals of the text have removed this interpretation from the range of possible meanings.[70] Two major presuppositions ruled this interpretation out of court: (1) that there is a fundamental difference between John/Jesus and "this generation," and (2) that this pericope seeks to clarify the identities of John and Jesus. These expectations rest on an underlying interest in the identity of Q's Jesus vis-à-vis John and "this generation." This interest replicates Q's own concern to center Jesus in the rhetoric of Q. In the context of 7:31–35, Q's centering of Jesus appears only in his role as an authoritative speaker and in his self-designation as the son of humanity. Regardless of what this appellation meant to Q's audience, its recurrence throughout Q establishes it rhetorically as marking the significance of Jesus for those who remember him. This tension between the assumption of Jesus' central significance and an emphasis on the communal vision of the *basileia* of God echoes rhetorically throughout Q.[71]

Bridging the Gap to "This Generation"

The interpretation of Q 7:31–35 proposed in this essay supports the conclusion that the rhetoric of the unit does not announce irretrievable judgment on "this generation." Rather it diagnoses the problem with "this generation" and seeks to correct it. "This generation" is like children who refuse to play together because different groups compete to set the rules of the game. The concluding aphorism urges the solidarity of all the children of Sophia. Tuckett makes a similar observation about this passage: " 'This generation' is compared with grumbling children, but Wisdom is justified by her children: hence the message to the audience is not a statement about a judicial

---

in ... the people of God" would regard Jesus as rebellious and seditious like the son in Deut 21:18–21 ("Jesus: A Glutton," 391). But Kee attributes this same approach to defining the "people of God" to John (381) and thus does not explain why Q would equally defend John's practices in the context of this passage. Unfortunately, Franzmann's interpretation ("Of Food," 20–21) creates a sharp dichotomy between Jesus' inclusive Christian table fellowship and John's exclusive and boundary-setting Judaism. This does not take into account the common ground between John and Jesus created by the structure and content of Q 7:31–35.

70. Schüssler Fiorenza, *Rhetoric and Ethic*, 197.

71. See Johnson-DeBaufre, "It's the End of the World."

decision already made — rather, it is a call to the audience to stop behaving like the grumbling children of the parable."[72]

According to Tuckett, however, the audience can become Wisdom's children "by responding positively to Wisdom's envoys John and Jesus."[73] This view aligns Jesus and John with the children who pipe and dirge and focuses on the response to John and Jesus as the central problem being addressed by the unit. I argue, however, that the problem being addressed is not resistance to John and Jesus but rather the judgmental infighting of the people of "this generation," who play a divisive game when they judge each other on the basis of different eating practices. This interpretation assumes a common identity horizon between Jesus, John, and "this generation" and thus depends upon a rhetorical situation not of insider vs. outsider but rather of insider vs. insider. Most important, this interpretation suggests that the rhetoric of the text is not aimed at creating group boundary lines between insiders (as one might expect for insider vs. insider debate) but rather at persuading those groups to recognize their common cause.

This interpretation raises some important possibilities for the interpretation of "this generation" in Q 11:16, 29–32, and Q 11:49–51. Despite the increasingly negative tone of these units, I suggest that "this generation" in Q points to the self-reflection of the Q community as representative of the larger collective identity of "Israel," rather than a polemical critique of some Jewish "others" who have rejected the Q mission. Insofar as Q can be situated among Israelites facing the realities of Roman imperial rule, it should not be surprising to encounter rhetoric that seeks to resist the fragmentation and competition created among conquered people by colonizing power. A feminist rhetorical approach that centers the values and visions of the movement that shaped Jesus gives voice to that resistance and creates the possibility that for some interpreters — both ancient and modern — the rhetorical interests of Q are not primarily focused on asserting and negotiating Jesus' singular identity and value but rather on promoting solidarity across differences around the emancipatory vision of the *basileia* of God.

---

72. Tuckett, *Q and the History of Early Christianity*, 203.

73. Ibid. Horsley (in Horsley and Draper, *Whoever Hears*, 270) also interprets Q 7:31–35 as reflecting aggressive resistance to the movement.

14

The Rise of the Soul

Justice and Transcendence
in the *Gospel of Mary*

Karen L. King

In her groundbreaking book *In Memory of Her,* Elisabeth Schüssler Fiorenza not only put the feminist study of early Christian history on the intellectual map, she also laid out a research agenda for scholarship that continues to generate fruitful elaboration. One figure she treated was Mary Magdalene, "apostle to the apostles"[1] and "the most prominent of the Galilean disciples, because according to tradition she was the first one to receive a vision of the resurrected Lord."[2] Although patristic Christianity played down these roles, Schüssler Fiorenza demonstrated how others built on tradition "to claim the women apostles as apostolic authorities."[3] One of the works that these Christians produced was the *Gospel of Mary.*[4] In this essay, I want to build on Schüssler Fiorenza's work and consider how Mary's revelation of the ascent of the soul may provide resources for contemporary reflection about justice and transcendence.

In my brief commentary on the *Gospel of Mary* in Schüssler Fiorenza's *Searching the Scriptures,* I argued that the "*Gospel of Mary* unequivocally advocated women's leadership based on spiritual merit."[5] It teaches that sex/gender differences are irrelevant because they are inscribed on bodies that are destined to pass away along with the rest of the material world. As a result, spiritual maturity and proper understanding of the Savior's teaching are what matter for leadership, not a person's sex/gender. I suggested that the *Gospel of Mary* lets us hear a new voice in the early Christian debate over women's leadership, a voice that puts the canonical voice of 1 Timothy

---

1. Elisabeth Schüssler Fiorenza, *In Memory of Her: A Feminist Theological Reconstruction of Christian Origins* (New York: Crossroad, 1983), 332.
2. Ibid., 139.
3. Ibid., 305.
4. Schüssler Fiorenza discusses this work at some length, in particular its portrayal of strife between Mary and Peter; see *In Memory of Her,* 305–7.
5. Karen L. King, "The Gospel of Mary Magdalene," in *Searching the Scriptures,* vol. 2: *A Feminist Commentary* (ed. Elisabeth Schüssler Fiorenza; New York: Crossroad, 1994), 624.

and its attempt to silence women in a new perspective. First Timothy can no longer chime a monotone authority, but has to be heard as only one voice among others in the struggle to define women's roles in Christianity.

Yet at the same time, it seems to me that we could accept the *Gospel of Mary*'s argument only at a very high price: the denial that the body is the self. Such a position "appears to erase the possibility that women can exercise leadership *as women* and seems to ask people to denigrate their bodies. I argued that

> an ungendered, universal, transcendent view of ideal Humanity potentially removes us too far from lived human experience, differences in human conditions, and the realities of human diversity (not only gender, but class, race, age, sexual preference, and so on). This distance and forgetfulness are dangerous, since they can too easily wipe away consciousness both of privilege and oppression, and with them political action for justice and equity.[6]

In this essay I would like to reflect further on the meaning of transcending bodily differences in the *Gospel of Mary*. Does its teaching have nothing to offer contemporary women and men except another narrative of loss? I have begun to rethink my earlier position by asking: What if the *Gospel of Mary* "ties the erasure of difference to the simultaneous elimination of injustice and suffering"; that is, what if transcendence and justice are linked?[7] Might there be something for us in the *Gospel of Mary*—not a definitive solution, but a perspective we might engage critically and constructively? The *Gospel of Mary*'s teaching about the ascent of the soul is the best place to focus this reflection because it is there that we can best see what is at stake in rejecting the body as the self.

The Ascent of the Soul

The extant portion of the *Gospel of Mary* begins in the middle of a dialogue between the Savior and his disciples. When he finishes speaking, the Savior departs. All the disciples are distressed except Mary, who steps in and comforts them, turning their thoughts toward the words of the Savior. At this point, Peter asks Mary to tell the other disciples any words of the Savior that she remembers which they had not heard. She launches into an

---

6. Ibid.
7. Karen L. King, "Prophetic Power and Women's Authority: The Case of the Gospel of Mary Magdalene," in *Women Preachers and Prophets through Two Millennia of Christianity* (ed. Beverly Mayne Kienzle and Pamela J. Walker; Berkeley: University of California Press, 1998), 32.

extensive account of a revelation she received from the Savior, including an extended account of the soul's ascent to God.[8]

Unfortunately the first part of this passage is lost in a lacuna,[9] but the overall shape of the ascent is clear: the Savior's revelation recounts the soul's encounters with four Powers who seek to keep it bound to the world below. The missing beginning of the account must have included the soul's encounter with the first of the four Powers, probably named Darkness.[10] When the extant portion of the text resumes, the second Power, Desire, is addressing the soul, which replies and then ascends to the next level:

> And Desire said, "I did not see you go down, yet now I see you go up. So why do you lie since you belong to me?" The soul answered, "I saw *you*. You did not see *me* nor did you know me. You (mis)took the garment (I wore) for my (true) self. And you did not recognize me." After it had said these things it left rejoicing greatly. (*Gospel of Mary* 9.2–7)[11]

Desire attempts to keep the soul from ascending by claiming that it belongs to the world below and the Powers that rule it. Since Desire had not seen the soul descend, it charges that the soul's claim to belong to the world above is a lie. But the soul knows better and exposes the ignorance of the Power. It is true, the soul says, that you did not recognize me when I descended because you have mistaken the bodily garment of flesh I wore for my true spiritual self. But the soul did see the Power, proving that its capacity to discern the true nature of things is superior to that of Desire's clouded vision. That truth exposes Desire's impotence and lack of spiritual insight, and the soul gleefully ascends to the third Power:

> Again, it came to the third Power, which is called "Ignorance." [It] examined the soul closely, saying, "Where are you going? You are bound by wickedness. Indeed you are bound! Do not judge!" And the soul said, "Why do you judge me, since I have not passed judgment? I have been bound, but I have not bound (anything). They did not recognize me, but I have recognized that the universe is to be dissolved, both the things of earth and those of heaven." (*Gospel of Mary* 9.8–15)

---

8. See BG 15.1–17.9 (in Walter C. Till and Hans-Martin Schenke, *Die gnostischen Schriften des koptischen Papyrus Berolinensis 8502* [2d ed.; Texte und Untersuchungen 60; Berlin: Akademie Verlag, 1972]) and P.Ryl. 21.1–5 (in C. H. Roberts, "463: The Gospel of Mary," in *Catalogue of the Greek Papyri in the John Rylands Library* [Manchester: Manchester University Press, 1938], 3.18–23).

9. Four pages are missing, numbered 11–14 in the manuscript.

10. This speculation is based on the fact that darkness is the first of the seven powers of Wrath; see *Gospel of Mary* 9.18.

11. Translations of the *Gospel of Mary* are my own; the numbering of the passages follows my translation of "The Gospel of Mary," in *The Complete Gospels* (ed. Robert J. Miller; rev. ed.; Sonoma, Calif.: Polebridge, 1994), 357–66.

Again the Power attempts to stop the soul's ascent by challenging its nature. The Power judges the soul to be material and therefore bound by the wickedness of the passions, suffering, and death. The soul, Ignorance claims, has no right to judge anything. But the soul turns the tables: it is the Ignorance who is judging. It is the wicked domination of the Powers that binds the soul to the lower world — not the material nature — because the soul is spiritual. The soul is innocent precisely because it reflects the nature of the spirit: it does not judge others, nor does it attempt to dominate anything or anyone. It has knowledge of which Ignorance is ignorant; it knows that everything in the lower world is passing away, and so the Powers of that transitory world have no real power over the eternal soul.[12]

Earlier in the work, the Savior had clarified how the soul could be innocent when speaking to the disciples. Peter had asked him, "What is the sin of the world?" The Savior responded, "There is no such thing as sin" (*Gospel of Mary* 3.3); sin appears to exist only because of the domination of the flesh. Without the flesh — which is to be dissolved — there is no sin, judgment, or condemnation.[13] This insight frees the soul:

> When the soul had brought the third Power to naught, it went upward and saw the fourth Power. It had seven forms. The first is darkness; the second is desire; the third is ignorance; the fourth is zeal for death; the fifth is the realm of the flesh; the sixth is the foolish wisdom of the flesh; the seventh is the wisdom of the wrathful person. These are the seven Powers of Wrath.
>
> They interrogated the soul, "Where are you coming from, human-killer, and where are you going, space-conqueror?" The soul replied, saying, "What binds me has been slain, and what surrounds me has been destroyed, and my desire has been brought to an end, and ignorance has died. In a [wor]ld, I was set loose from a world [an]d in a type, from a type which is above, and (from) the chain of forgetfulness which exists in time. From this hour on, for the time of the due season of the aeon, I will receive rest i[n] silence." (*Gospel of Mary* 9.16–29)

The seven names of the Power of Wrath may correspond to the astrological spheres that control fate,[14] but above all they show the character of the Powers that attempt to dominate the soul.

---

12. The word *eternal* is not quite correct in this case, since the *Gospel of Mary* understands the final resting place of the soul to be beyond time and eternity.

13. As Anne Pasquier points out, three terms structure the dialogue of the third Power with the soul: ignorance, domination, and judgment. These three form the basis of the Power's illegitimate domination over entrapped souls; see *L'Évangile selon Marie* (Bibliothèque copte de Nag Hammadi, Section "Textes" 10; Quebec: University of Laval Press, 1983), 89–92.

14. See ibid., 80–83; Michel Tardieu, *Écrits gnostiques: Codex de Berlin* (Sources gnostiques et manichéennes; Paris: Cerf, 1984), 290–92. Concerning the origin of the Powers' names, see Pasquier, *L'Évangile selon Marie*, 80–86; Tardieu, *Écrits Gnostiques*, 234.

Like the other Powers, Wrath too seems disturbed at the soul's passage and questions both its origin and its right to pass by. Where Desire had charged the soul with lying and Ignorance had judged it to be wicked, Wrath charges it with violence, stating that it is a murderer and conqueror. The soul agrees — in part. It has cast off the material body and overcome the powers that bound it. This action is not portrayed as violence but as freedom: The soul says that it has been loosed from the world below and now traverses space toward its final resting place above. The soul dramatically contrasts the subjection to material bonds, desire, and ignorance which it has left behind, with the freedom of the timeless realm of silence and rest to which it ascends. At the end of the revelation, Mary, too, becomes silent, modeling in her behavior the perfect rest of the soul set free (compare *Dialogue of the Savior* logia 65–70).

We can interpret this account in (at least) two ways: as a topography of the perilous journey that every soul must take at death in its ascent to the divine, or as a guide to the stages of the soul's path to spiritual perfection in the here-and-now. The two are not mutually exclusive, and indeed the ability to ascend to the realm of the Good is dependent upon the soul's spiritual progress in this world.

Ascent as a Journey

Much could be said about the theme of the soul's ascent in antiquity,[15] but the most important point for our topic is that interpreting the ascent as a journey through space implies that the forces that seek to entrap the soul exist outside the true self. The *Gospel of Mary* teaches the reader the true character of these Powers. They claim to be able to discern the true nature of the soul and to judge it, but the dialogues between the soul and the Powers expose the fact that their attempts to dominate the soul are based on lies, ignorance, and false justice. Their condemnation of the soul for wickedness

---

15. The literature here is extensive. See, for example, Carsten Colpe, "Jenseitsreise (Reise durch das Jenseits)," "Jenseits (Jenseitsvorstellungen)," and "Jenseitsfahrt I (Himmelfahrt)," all in *Reallexikon für Antike und Christentum* (ed. Ernst Dassmann; Stuttgart: Hiersmann, 2000), 17.246–466, 490–543; Ioan Culianu, "Ascension," in *Death, Afterlife, and the Soul* (ed. Lawrence E. Sullivan; New York: Macmillan, 1987–89), 107–16; K. Kremer, ed., *Seele: Ihre Wirklichkeit, ihr Verhältnis zum Leib und zur menschlichen Person* (Leiden: Brill, 1984); April D. De Conick, *Seek to See Him: Ascent and Vision Mysticism in the Gospel of Thomas* (Vigiliae christianae Supplement 33; Leiden: Brill, 1996); Morton Smith, "Two Ascended to Heaven — Jesus and the Author of 4Q491," and Alan Segal, "The Risen Christ and the Angelic Mediator Figures," both in *Jesus and the Dead Sea Scrolls* (ed. James H. Charlesworth; New York: Doubleday, 1992), 290–332; Rodger Beck, *Planetary Gods and Planetary Orders in the Mysteries of Mithra* (Études préliminaires aux religions orientales dans l'empire romain 109; Leiden: Brill, 1988), 109; Naomie Janowitz, "Parallelism and Framing Devices in a Late Antique Ascent Text," in *Semiotic Mediation: Sociocultural and Psychological Perspectives* (ed. Elizabeth Mertz and Richard J. Parmentier; Orlando: Academic Press, 1985), 155–75; Rebecca Lesses, *Ritual Practices to Gain Power: Angels, Incantations, and Revelation in Early Jewish Mysticism* (Harvard Theological Studies 44; Harrisburg, Pa.: Trinity, 1998).

is rooted in spiritual blindness and lust for power. The soul opposes their lies with truth, their adultery with purity, their ignorance with knowledge, their judgment with refusal to judge, their blindness with true vision, their domination with freedom, their desire with peace, their mortal death with life beyond time and eternity. The soul's entire battle with the Powers focuses on overcoming their illegitimate domination.

So at one level, the *Gospel of Mary* invites the reader to discern the true character of power as it is exercised in the world. It insists that ignorance, deceit, false judgment, and the desire to dominate must be opposed by accepting the Savior's teaching and refusing to be complicit in violence and domination. People need to acquire the spiritual freedom, life, and peace that they already possess; the Savior admonishes his disciples to seek and find the Child of true Humanity (Son of Man) within. Knowing the truth about oneself and opposing the false powers that rule the world are foundational to achieving spiritual maturity and salvation.

Although it is quite possible that the revelation of the soul's ascent was originally a separate source only secondarily incorporated into the dialogue framework of the *Gospel of Mary,* it amplifies important themes raised in the Savior's teaching in the initial dialogue with his disciples. Salvation there, too, is conceived as overcoming the passions, suffering, and death associated with the physical body. The Savior's admonition not to lay down any law becomes more comprehensible as we see the judgment of the Powers working to condemn the soul in its struggle to escape their domination. Law, it seems, works on the side of those who wish to enslave the soul. The soul's refusal to be a judge is part and parcel of the refusal to be bound by unjust and ignorant laws. Those who judge, the Savior teaches, are ruled by laws that can then be used to condemn them. Such laws are really domination; such knowledge as they offer is really ignorance.

The entire dialogue between the soul and the Powers is characterized by a sharp contrast between the world above and the world below. The world above is the true kingdom of light, peace, knowledge, love, and life; the lower world is darkness, desire, arrogance, ignorance, jealousy, and the zeal for death. More is going on in this contrast than either a simple belief in the immortality of righteous souls or even the struggle against the arbitrary powers of fate. The dialogues instruct the reader about the true nature of reality by contrasting it with the deception that characterizes life in the world. By stressing the unjust nature of the Powers' illegitimate domination, the *Gospel of Mary* presents a biting critique of the way that power is exercised in the world.

Can we see any political motivation in this critique? The *Gospel of Mary* is clearly a *religious* work aimed at freeing the soul from the bonds of suffering and death; there is no outright call for political rebellion or explicit criticism of either local or imperial Roman domination. But does being a religious work necessarily *preclude* politics? Can it *also* contain a political message? In fact, I think if we overlook the political message, we are missing one of the *Gospel of Mary*'s most important elements, given that there was no separation of religion and politics in the Roman world, either in policy or in practice.

It has been a commonplace to exclude covert forms of resistance from consideration as real political activity. Indeed religious teaching that points the soul toward peace in the afterlife is often seen not only as *apolitical*, but as *antipolitical*, an escapist ideology that serves only to distract people from real political struggle by focusing on interior spiritual development and flight from the material world with all its troubling demands. New research among social scientists is changing this view dramatically. James C. Scott, for example, argues that the political resistance of subject peoples, such as those under Roman imperial rule, lies somewhere between quiescence and outright revolt. This political resistance, he argues, often takes the form of millennial imagery and symbolic reversals of folk religion; these "are the infrapolitical equivalents of public, radical, counterideologies: both *are aimed at negating the public symbolism of ideological domination.*"[16] It is just such opposition and reversal that characterize the soul's dialogues with the Powers. It recognizes that external forces exert power in part through ideological domination and in part through policies of violence. By offering an alternative view of reality, the *Gospel of Mary* sharply challenges their legitimacy.

That the *Gospel of Mary*'s critique is couched in the fantastic terms of the religious imagination should not lead us to ignore its potential political import. Its rejection of the body and the world, with its suffering and its ignorant, power-bloated rulers, draws its power precisely from envisioning a reversal of the pervasive understanding of law and justice in the Roman world. It is not aimed at escapist passivity, but at resistance of violent domination by cultivating a utopian vision of spiritual perfection and peace rooted in the divine good, beyond the constraints of time and matter and false morality. The main practical tool of resistance is preaching the gospel taught by the Savior, without fearing the violence the world will bring to bear against such a message.

In preaching the gospel, the disciples are cautioned by the Savior against setting any laws that may lead to domination in their own relations with each other. Elaine Pagels has suggested that the Savior's injunction to his disciples not to lay down any rule or law beyond what he determined for them was aimed directly against injunctions excluding women from ministry, such as 1 Cor 14:33–34, where Paul appeals to the law to silence women.[17] That Levi repeats the Savior's command in his defense of Mary against Peter provides support for this position. In response to Peter's accusation that

---

16. James C. Scott, *Domination and the Arts of Resistance: Hidden Transcripts* (New Haven: Yale University Press, 1990), 198–99 (emphasis added).

17. Elaine Pagels, conversation with author, November 2001.

Mary was lying, Levi points out to Peter that he is "contending against the woman like the Adversaries. For if the Savior made her worthy, who are you then for your part to reject her?" (*Gospel of Mary* 10.8–9). It would seem that Peter's accusation puts him in league with the Powers who attempt to bind the soul with their accusations and judgments. Levi's rejoinder to Peter implies that Peter is rejecting Mary because he does not consider her, a woman, to be worthy to teach the other disciples or preach the gospel. But in the end, the *Gospel of Mary* affirms that the Savior made her worthy. The controversy between Peter and Mary is aimed at instructing the disciples about how (and how not) to put the Savior's teaching into practice.

Ascent as a Spiritual Path

The ascent of the soul can also be read as a guide for following a spiritual path that leads from fear and instability of heart, such as the disciples evince after the Savior's departure, to unwavering faith and peace, modeled by Mary. In this scenario, the Powers represent the forces within the soul that it must overcome. Unfortunately we do not know what it took to overcome the first Power, since its encounter with the soul is lost in the lacuna. The second Power is overcome by the soul's knowledge of its own spiritual nature. By rejecting the body as the self, it can overcome the false power of desire. The Savior teaches the disciples that they sicken and die because they love what deceives them, that is, the bodily nature (*Gospel of Mary* 3.7–14). The true nature of humanity is not material, but formed according to the divine image within. If they seek and find the Child of true Humanity (Son of Man) within, they will come to know their own true spiritual nature (*Gospel of Mary* 4.3–7). This knowledge empowers the soul to defeat the power Desire. Rather than envision a moral system in which the mind rules over the passions and needs of the lower appetitive self, the *Gospel of Mary* rejects domination altogether — but at the cost of severing the self.

The third Power, Ignorance, is overcome by knowledge of the transitory nature of the world. The Savior teaches that matter will be dissolved back into its root (*Gospel of Mary* 2.2–4), understood in ancient cosmology either as primordial chaos or as nothingness. In either case, the current shape of the world is destined to pass away. The power of Ignorance falsely claims that this transitory nature binds the soul in wickedness and condemnation. In order for the soul to overcome this power, it must root itself in the Good by abandoning the moral economy of sin and judgment, which is tied to the world of the flesh. By turning to the Good, the soul establishes a foundation for the self's identity in what is enduring and true.

The final Power is the strongest, a combination of all those the soul had already faced, but now appearing united in the single countenance of Wrath. The seven names truly reveal the nature of rage: darkness, lust, ignorance, zeal for death, the realm of the flesh, foolish wisdom of the flesh, and wisdom of the wrathful person. Its tools are violence: killing and conquering. But what the soul has to realize is that violence is impotent. Whereas the power of Wrath claims that the soul belongs under its domination because the soul employs its own tools of violence — killing and conquering — the soul describes these acts as release from death, desire, and ignorance. The soul learns to reject violence and recognize that it is contrary to the spirit of the Good. The overt violence of wrath cannot harm the soul because the soul does not belong to the kingdom of the flesh, but to the realm of the Child of true Humanity.

The spiritual condition toward which the soul attains is characterized by light, stability of mind, knowledge, and life; the condition it must overcome is called darkness, desire, ignorance, and death. The true wisdom of the Savior opposes the foolish "wisdom" of the flesh, which thrives on false forces of wrathful judgment and violence. We see these contrasted in the *Gospel of Mary*'s portraits of Peter and Mary. Peter judges and condemns Mary out of his jealousy and his constant inclination to be hot tempered; his spiritual sight is clouded so that he is unable to see past the transitory distinctions of the flesh to the truth of Mary's teaching. Mary, on the other hand, shows stability of mind and teaches the words of the Savior, bringing comfort and knowledge to the other disciples. The contrast of these two characters illustrates the direction of the soul's inner ascent to spiritual perfection.

Reflections

The ascent of the soul is an act of transcendence. It is figured as the soul's escape from the suffering of the mortal body and the Powers that seek to bind it. Viewed as a purely external event, ascent could be pure escapism. But before the soul can ascend it must be prepared to face the powers of Darkness, Desire, Ignorance, and Wrath. This preparation involves recognizing one's own true spiritual nature, accepting the truth revealed in the teachings of the Savior, rejecting the false ideology of sin and judgment tied to domination by the flesh and the passions, and eschewing violence in any form. The capacity to overcome evil requires that one has perceived the Good-beyond-evil and molded oneself to its image and nature. One has to acquire peace within, find the Child of true Humanity within, and make no laws beyond those laid down by the Savior — lest the laws that are made come to dominate those who made them. Viewed as a purely internal event, ascent could be apolitical and individualistic. But by tying together these two meanings of the soul's ascent, the *Gospel of Mary* unites internal spiritual development with resistance to external forces of evil in the practice of preaching the gospel. The promulgation of an alternative ideology itself works as a force against the violent domination that leads the soul away from God.

The rejection of the reigning ideology of the body and the world is central to the *Gospel of Mary*'s critique of violent domination and its utopian vision of "the kingdom of God."[18] The vision is of an ungendered space where men and women proclaim the gospel, comforting and strengthening each in other in understanding of the Savior's teaching. In this vision, rejecting the body was an explicit rejection of the kyriarchal system, which appealed to the sexual distinctions of the flesh to argue that it was *natural* for women to be subordinated to men. The *Gospel of Mary* in contrast argues that sexual division is contrary to nature (3.10). One's true nature is spiritual and the material body is transitory, so the distinctions of the flesh are irrelevant for the spirit. The transcendence of the material world is offered as a perspective from which to rise above the current system and discern how leadership should be exercised among those who follow the teachings of the Savior. This discernment does not advocate escape from the world, but transformation of the world through the disciples' mission, which leads to the practice of the kingdom of the gospel of the Child of true Humanity. This practice is possible only for those disciples who have themselves overcome the rule of the unjust powers in their own lives, as is illustrated by the contrasting figures of Peter and Mary.

In having taken "the perspective of transcendence," the *Gospel of Mary* maintains that sexual differences are not valid determinants for teaching and preaching the gospel. It is true that the *Gospel of Mary* has not yet arrived at a point where it can celebrate differences or even critically reflect upon what differences might be necessary for the full life of a gospel community. But it might suggest to us that occasionally the transcendent perspective can be useful for our own critical thinking about the ascent of the soul to God — transcendence not as an objective view from nowhere, but as a mode of stepping back and assessing from a vantage point informed by enlarged critical perspectives. The work of Elisabeth Schüssler Fiorenza is devoted precisely to such critical and constructive vision. It is a great pleasure to dedicate this essay to her on the occasion of her sixty-fifth birthday.

---

18. I have generally resisted translating TMNTEPO as "kingdom" (using "realm" instead) precisely because the *Gospel of Mary* rejects the ideology of kingly domination. Here, however, I want to make it more clear that the *Gospel of Mary* is offering an interpretation of Jesus' teaching about the kingdom of God.

15

"Now I Know in Part"

Historiography and Epistemology
in Early Christian Debates about Prophecy

Laura S. Nasrallah

Elisabeth Schüssler Fiorenza's work consistently and radically challenges scholars to interrogate historiographies — our own production of history, as well as others' productions, ancient and modern — and to investigate the epistemological underpinnings of our work and of the ancient texts that we study. Schüssler Fiorenza frequently says that she wishes to provide "new lenses."[1] Her lenses offer clear sight, breathtaking views, and peripheral vision. She challenges scholars to put on these lenses and to interrogate rigorously the rhetoricity of ancient texts and also our own texts and ideas as ethical and rhetorical products. Not only her writings, but also her dedicated, persistent querying in classrooms and conversations draw the reader and student into the excitement and complexity of her ideas. I often find that this initial moment of discovery, face to face, when I thought I might have grasped her ideas fully, only leads to more such moments later as I return to Schüssler Fiorenza's ideas, and the depth and breadth of her vision unfolds.

Schüssler Fiorenza's concerns about historiography and epistemology undergird her model of struggle.[2] This model forms the basis for my analysis of three texts engaged in the debate over prophecy. Paul's 1 Corinthians and two early-third-century Christian sources, Tertullian and the Anti-Phrygian

---

1. For the metaphor of a "new optic," see Elisabeth Schüssler Fiorenza, *But She Said: Feminist Practices of Biblical Interpretation* (Boston: Beacon, 1992), 9; for other metaphors of vision, see 101, 214–16; regarding "hermeneutical binoculars," see Schüssler Fiorenza's *Jesus: Miriam's Child, Sophia's Prophet: Critical Issues in Feminist Christology* (New York: Continuum, 1994), 29.

2. Although the term *model of struggle* appears in several of Schüssler Fiorenza's works, including *Jesus and the Politics of Interpretation* (New York: Continuum, 2000), esp. 149–73, and *Rhetoric and Ethic: The Politics of Biblical Studies* (Minneapolis: Fortress, 1999), it is especially well explicated in "Re-Visioning Christian Origins: *In Memory of Her* Revisited," in *Christian Origins: Worship, Belief and Society* (ed. Kieran J. O'Mahony; London: Continuum International, forthcoming).

source in Epiphanius's *Panarion* 48.1.4–48.13.8, use a discourse of periodizing history.[3] They also demonstrate the way in which debates over prophecy are intricately tied to concerns about epistemology — who has access to what sort of knowledge, and when. Moreover, the early-third-century debate over prophecy employs a discourse of madness and rationality in order to draw boundaries around what can and should be known; Paul, too, uses this discourse, recast in terms of "folly" and "wisdom." Schüssler Fiorenza's historiographical model and her rhetorical-critical method, applied to these texts, allow us to recognize the multivocality and conflict present in the early Christian debate over prophecy.

The most frequent approach to the study of prophecy in early Christianity is the model of charismatic origins and subsequent decline into routinization or institutionalization. Although this Weberian paradigm has been challenged in recent historiography,[4] it remains dominant, explicitly and implicitly guiding the study of early Christian prophecy and of early Christianity in general, from Adolf von Harnack's *Mission and Expansion of Christianity* to David Aune's *Prophecy in Early Christianity.*[5] This model often reads ancient references to a decline in prophecy or charismata as transparent, rather than considering the rhetorical context of debate and polemic in which assertions about time and history are set forth.[6]

---

3. In using the concept of discourse, I am of course indebted to Michel Foucault's work, especially *Archaeology of Knowledge and the Discourse on Language* (trans. A. M. Sheridan Smith; New York: Pantheon, 1972). For an excellent explanation of the term, see Schüssler Fiorenza, *Jesus and the Politics of Interpretation,* 14–15.

4. Schüssler Fiorenza, "Re-Visioning Christian Origins"; idem, *Jesus and the Politics of Interpretation,* 29–51. See also Elizabeth Castelli and Hal Taussig, "Drawing Large and Startling Figures: Reimagining Christian Origins," in *Reimagining Christian Origins: A Colloquium Honoring Burton L. Mack* (ed. Elizabeth Castelli and Hal Taussig; Valley Forge, Pa.: Trinity, 1996), 2–20. For a challenge to other traditional historiographical approaches to the study of early Christianity, see Karen L. King, *What Is Gnosticism?* (Cambridge: Belknap, 2003).

5. Adolf von Harnack, *Mission and Expansion of Christianity in the First Three Centuries* (orig. 1908; trans. James Moffatt; repr. Gloucester, Mass.: Peter Smith, 1972), chap. 4. See also Cecil Robeck's discussion of Harnack: *Prophecy in Carthage: Perpetua, Tertullian, and Cyprian* (Cleveland: Pilgrim, 1992), 7; David Aune, *Prophecy in Early Christianity and the Ancient Mediterranean World* (Grand Rapids: Eerdmans, 1983), 189; David Hill, *New Testament Prophecy* (London: Marshall, Morgan & Scott, 1979), esp. chap. 8; James L. Ash Jr., "The Decline of Ecstatic Prophecy in the Early Church," *Journal of Theological Studies* 37 (1976): 227–37; James Dunn, *Jesus and the Spirit: A Study of the Religious and Charismatic Experience of Jesus and the First Christians as Reflected in the New Testament* (orig. 1975; repr. Grand Rapids: Eerdmans, 1997). In the 1950s, Hans von Campenhausen, in his *Ecclesiastical Authority and Spiritual Power in the Church of the First Three Centuries* (orig. 1953; repr. Stanford: Stanford University Press, 1969), attempted to intervene in the longstanding model of charismatic origins and subsequent routinization in early Christian history, but he contradicts himself at points (e.g., contrast arguments on p. 2 to those on p. 221).

6. The model of charismatic origins and subsequent decline comes to be written broadly onto the study of religion. Edward Tylor, writing at the turn of the twentieth century, presented an evolution of religion inextricably linked to ideas about human progress and to the colonialism and racism of his day. "Animism characterizes tribes very low in the scale of humanity," he states, which evolve in "unbroken continuity" into "high modern culture." These "tribes" existed in Africa and other colonized lands. See Edward B. Tylor, "Animism," in *Primitive Culture*

A different model is needed, one that displaces this binary of spirit versus institution, a binary that is diachronically mapped as charismatic spirit preceding and ossifying into organization and institution. Schüssler Fiorenza argues for a model of struggle in the study of the New Testament and early Christianity:

> To read early Christian history in terms of the reconstructive model of rapid decline from the heights of radical equality to the valleys of patriarchal institution is to overlook the continuing struggles that have been ongoing throughout Christian history between those who understand Christian identity as radically inclusive and egalitarian and those who advocate kyriarchal domination and submission.[7]

Schüssler Fiorenza's historiographical model of struggle illumines the study of early Christian prophecy by understanding ancient references to history not as pieces of evidence for a modern historigraphical project which argues for linear development toward a rational *telos,* but as instances of conflict and rupture, of negotiations of power and ideologies. Schüssler Fiorenza insists on the importance of writing history while at the same time interrogating that enterprise and admitting its provisionality: "A critical feminist history...challenges historical scholarship to recognize that it is a reconstructive and not positivist scientific practice which produces knowledges that sustain either domination or emancipation."[8] Here, *in nuce,* we find Schüssler Fiorenza's elegant weaving together of history and epistemology, her assertion that history is a discourse and that historiography, whether ancient or present-day, is rhetorically constructed and impinges upon and delimits knowledge. Schüssler Fiorenza's method of rhetorical criticism[9] therefore is also implicit in her model of struggle. Rhetorical-critical methodology insists that all texts attempt to persuade and convince audiences of their own worldviews, through classical forms of rhetoric and through the crafting of discourse and language more broadly.

(2d ed.; London: Murray, 1873); repr. in *Reading in Comparative Religion: An Anthropological Approach* (ed. William A. Lessa and Evon Z. Vogt; Evanston, Ill.: Row, Peterson, 1958), 13. Thus what seems to be a historiographical approach to religion becomes the grounds by which to classify other races, the colonized, or those who participate in spirit religion as primitive and even barely human. The model of charismatic origins and decline to institutionalization is especially fascinating and powerful insofar as it combines in itself two almost contradictory impulses. To put it crudely, a model that concludes with routinization and essentially the end of charisma is consoled by the recognition that a greater rationality and stability have emerged. At the same time the Enlightenment paradigm of increasing progress toward universal rationality is affirmed by this progress's origin in a spark of authentic religiosity, a pure moment of divine inbreaking.

   7. Schüssler Fiorenza, "Re-Visioning Christian Origins."
   8. Ibid.
   9. On rhetoric and rhetorical criticism, see especially Schüssler Fiorenza's *Rhetoric and Ethic.* While the book as a whole works out the theories of rhetorical criticism, a good example of this rhetorical practice is found in chap. 5.

Rhetorical-critical method and a model of struggle, applied to the mid-first-century 1 Corinthians and the early-third-century debates of Tertullian and the Anti-Phrygian, allow us to see the way in which ancient texts construct their own stance as continuous with prophetic traditions, apostolic succession, accurate and aware knowledge, the progress of truth, the development of orthodoxy. Such texts often point to the "heretic," the "other," or the person of an "unsound mind" as a moment of deviance from or rupture in the smooth attenuated lines of history in general and a Christian history in particular. Paul's 1 Corinthians dates to the 50s C.E.; Tertullian writes at the end of the second and beginning of the third century in Carthage; Epiphanius's Anti-Phrygian source in *Panarion* 48.1.4–48.13.8 dates to approximately the same time.[10] Tertullian and the Anti-Phrygian source do not speak directly to each other,[11] but their themes and interpretive concerns are similar and indicate participation in the same discourses of madness and rationality, as well as of history and time.[12] Although the third-century texts claim for themselves normativity and continuity with pure origins and correct practice of Christianity, a rhetorical-critical approach and a model of struggle reveal that these very claims are part of a larger discourse around history and spirit, as well as prophecy and ecstasy.

---

10. While this section of the *Panarion* is often called the "Anti-Montanist source," here I call it the "Anti-Phrygian source" in order to adhere closely to the vocabulary of the text and to avoid problematic scholarly constructions of Montanism. Moreover, the term *Anti-Phrygian* better signals the way in which this source utilizes the geographical marker of Phrygia — a province the source considers "barbarian" — to construct the "otherness" of this group's opinions. Regarding the extent of the source in the *Panarion,* see chapter 5 of Laura S. Nasrallah, *"An Ecstasy of Folly": Prophecy and Authority in Early Christianity* (Harvard Theological Studies 52; Cambridge: Harvard University Press, forthcoming). As I outline there in detail, several arguments point strongly both to Epiphanius's use of this source and to the source's late-second- or early-third-century date. See D. Richard Lipsius, *Zur Quellenkritik des Epiphanios* (Vienna: Braumüller, 1865), 221–31; Heinrich Voigt, *Eine verschollene Urkunde des antimontanistischen Kampfes* (Leipzig: Richter, 1891), 27–112; and Karl Holl, the editor of the first critical edition of Epiphanius's *Panarion*. See also Dennis Groh, "Utterance and Exegesis: Biblical Interpretation in the Montanist Movement," in *The Living Text: Essays in Honor of Ernest W. Saunders* (ed. Dennis Groh and Robert Jewett; New York: University Press of America, 1985), 73–95; Pierre de Labriolle, "Introduction," in *Les sources de l'histoire du montanisme: Textes grecs, latins, syriaques* (Freiburg: Gschwend/Paris: Leroux, 1913), xlviii–liv. The semantic field of *Panarion* 48.1.4–48.13.8 also supports the argument that Epiphanius uses a source. An investigation of some of the key terminology of *Panarion* 48.1.4–48.13.8 reveals that this particular vocabulary of reason and sound-mindedness is not widely replicated in other contemporary texts or elsewhere in the *Panarion*. See Nasrallah, *"Ecstasy of Folly,"* chapter 5.

11. Labriolle, too, does not see a direct relation between the texts; *Les sources,* liii.

12. While both are usually read together as part of the "Montanist controversy," this essay avoids the scholarly category of Montanism, which is not a self-appellation of Montanus, Maximilla, Priscilla, and those closely and loosely connected to their late-second-century prophetic renewal, some of whom seemed to call themselves the "New Prophecy." Instead, I investigate the discursive similarities between these two texts. On naming Montanism, see Christine Trevett, *Montanism: Gender, Authority and the New Prophecy* (Cambridge: Cambridge University Press, 1996), 2.

This essay shifts, then, between two theses. First, I argue that the discourse of rationality and madness in the ancient debate over prophecy and ecstasy is linked to claims about knowledge. What may appear to be arcane accusations of madness or skirmishes over prophetic episodes are struggles over who has access to what kinds of fields of knowledge. Especially after Foucault, we recognize that claims to knowledge are at the same time claims to power and authority. Growing up in Atlanta in the 1970s, I was told by teachers at my conservative elementary school, "If you're too open minded, your brain might fall out." This amusing image captures the way in which those adults sought to use their authority to constrain the kinds of knowledge to which young students might be attracted. Excessive interest in and seeking of knowledge might result in what was posited as its opposite: essentially, madness, the loss of one's mind.

The discourse of madness and rationality is found very clearly in Tertullian and the Anti-Phrygian source in Epiphanius's *Panarion*. Through them, I argue that in Greco-Roman antiquity the rhetoric of madness and rationality does not function to clarify the meaning of rationality, as we might expect, given the importance of Logos (reason) to the philosophies of the time. Instead, it functions, like the discourse of history, to delimit or extend realms of knowledge and to bolster the text's authority. To be more specific, the Anti-Phrygian attempts to constrain realms of knowledge, arguing that Montanus's and Maximilla's ecstasies and oracles are the products of unsound minds and thus by extension that the knowledge they reveal is spurious. At the same time, and in contrast, Tertullian seeks to justify and to extend realms of knowledge, even arguing that true Christian identity is constituted by spiritual gifts of prophecy or ecstasy, which he says are a form of *amentia* (madness). To put it another way, the discourse of madness and rationality within the debate over prophecy works not to define what madness and rationality are, but instead to delimit the realms of knowledge to which a community has access.

While Paul's use of a discourse of madness and rationality is more subtle than that of Tertullian or the Anti-Phrygian, he shares with them the rhetorical strategy of a discourse of time and history.[13] My second thesis is that these references to history cannot be read in a transparent way: they neither reveal something crystal clear about ancient understandings of history, deployed as they are in a polemical context, nor should they be adjusted to our own dominant concept of history. All three texts set forth arguments about history in order to make broader points about prophecy, charismatic gifts, and the limits of what most humans can know. Texts such as Tertullian's and the Anti-Phrygian's use a discourse of history as part of a larger debate about knowledge and Christian identity, although this discourse is

---

13. On Paul's use of "folly," "wisdom," and a discourse of rationality and madness, see Nasrallah, *"Ecstasy of Folly,"* chapter 2.

often misunderstood and used by later scholars as evidence of the decline of spiritual gifts. The Anti-Phrygian argued that prophecy and its realms of knowledge are a thing of the past, and Tertullian argued that prophetic gifts (and the knowledge they brought) were even more vivid in the glorious present time of the Paraclete. Paul in 1 Corinthians used a discourse of time or history in order to delimit the epistemes to which he thought that the Corinthians should have access, downplaying prophecy and knowledge, and insisting that some epistemes are a thing of the future — "but then, face to face" (1 Cor 13:12).

The Anti-Phrygian Source

Two aspects of the Anti-Phrygian's arguments are especially helpful in illuminating the discourse of madness and rationality and of time and history. First, the introductory argument challenges one of Maximilla's oracles, accusing her of an unsound mind and questioning her and her disciples' place within history. Second, the catalogue of "great men" makes a double-barreled argument about prophecy existing in the past, on the one hand, and the rationality of these past figures and irrationality of Montanus and Maximilla, on the other. Throughout, the Anti-Phrygian source shores up the authority of its argument and of its definition of Christian identity by demonstrating that the prophetic charismata are a thing of the past and by showing that Montanus's and Maximilla's oracles are the products of unsound and irrational minds — that is, they do not truly access new realms of knowledge in their prophetic ecstasy, but merely make such claims in wrongheaded and even crazed ways.

Panarion 48.1.4–48.3.2

The first text to which we will turn is *Panarion* 48.1.4–48.3.2,[14] which is best read as a struggle over prophetic gifts and where they fit into history. The source indicates that the sentence "it is necessary for us also to receive the gifts [*charismata*]" (δεῖ ἡμᾶς ... καὶ τὰ χαρίσματα δέχεσθαι) is a slogan of those who followed Montanus and Maximilla and immediately argues that it is "God's holy church" that has instead received the "real" gifts of grace. The Anti-Phrygian then continues the argument: "They cannot fulfill what they have contentiously promised," asking why "they no longer have prophets after Montanus, Priscilla, and Maximilla."

This question is indeed puzzling, given what we know of the continuing prophetic and ecstatic activities of the New Prophecy (which seems to be the group's self-appellation), unless it is read in the context of an

---

14. The Greek edition used is that of Jürgen Dummer: Epiphanius, *Panarion haer. 34–64* (Die griechischen christlichen Schriftsteller der ersten Jahrhunderte: Epiphanius 2; 2d rev. ed.; Berlin: Akademie-Verlag, 1980). Unless otherwise noted, all translations are my own.

oracle attributed to Maximilla, which the source discusses a little later: "After me, there will no longer be a prophet, but the end" or consummation (μετ᾽ ἐμὲ προφήτης οὐκέτι ἔσται, ἀλλὰ συντέλεια). The Anti-Phrygian (mis)reads the slogan "it is necessary for us also to receive the charismata" against Maximilla's oracle in order to argue that the New Prophecy is wrong and even unreasonable: how is it that this community must receive charismata in the present, when Maximilla herself declared that there is no more prophecy? Second, the source argues, "if those who prophesied prophesied up to a certain time, and [then] they prophesied no longer, then neither Maximilla or Priscilla prophesied after the prophecies which have been tested through the holy apostles in the holy church." The text seems to insist a priori that Maximilla and Priscilla could not have prophesied after a certain boundary (that of the "holy apostles")[15] and thus their prophecies are false.[16]

The argument concludes with a summary: either the Phrygians will prove that there are prophets after Maximilla or the disciples of Maximilla (οἱ περὶ Μαξίμιλλαν) will be found to be false prophets. The latter is given a fascinating explanation: if indeed prophets "no longer" speak after a certain time, then the disciples of Maximilla are false and audacious, having prophesied through demonic error "after the limit for the prophetic gifts" (μετὰ τὸν ὅρον τῶν προφητικῶν χαρισμάτων).[17] This reference to a "limit" or "end" must be understood in terms of Maximilla's oracle, which immediately follows in *Panarion* 48.2.4.[18] The Anti-Phrygian uses this oracle to demonstrate further that any disciple of Maximilla who claims to prophesy is immediately proved to be a false prophet, since Maximilla herself declared an end to prophecy. The Anti-Phrygian also uses this oracle to demonstrate the unreasonableness of Maximilla's prophecy. She is not like true prophets who speak "in full possession of their understanding, and their words have

---

15. The definition of "apostle" is not straightforward, but in the Anti-Phrygian source, it does not seem to apply to any present church leaders. See *Panarion* 48.1.6; 48.2.2.

16. Note that Eusebius's anonymous source is a close parallel: "And again after a little he goes on, 'For if the Montanist women succeeded to Quadratus and Ammia in Philadelphia in the prophetic gift, let them show who among them succeeded the followers of Montanus and the women, for the apostle grants that the prophetic gift shall be in all the church until the final coming, but this they could not show, seeing that this is already the fourteenth year from the death of Maximilla" (*Ecclesiastical History* 5.17; translation by Kirsopp Lake in the Loeb Classical Library; Cambridge: Harvard University Press, 1926 [repr. 1953], 1.484–85).

17. Ὅρος can denote a conceptual, spatial, or a temporal boundary; for example, it is used as the name of an eon among Valentinians, according to Irenaeus (see G. W. H. Lampe, *A Patristic Greek Lexicon* [Oxford: Clarendon, 1961], 974 §A.3); it can refer more generally to time (ibid., §A.2; cf. also Henry George Liddell, Robert Scott, and Henry Stuart Jones, *A Greek-English Lexicon* [9th ed.; Oxford: Clarendon, 1961], 1255 §I), a boundary or landmark (ibid., §I), or a limit or definition of the passions (Lampe, 975 §B).

18. It is likely that sourcebooks of Montanist prophecy existed and were used by heresiologists and adherents alike. See Frank Williams, trans., *The Panarion of Epiphanius of Salamis* (Nag Hammadi Studies 36; Leiden: Brill, 1994), 2.6 n. 1.

been accomplished and are still being fulfilled" (48.2.5),[19] since she wrongly predicted the "consummation."

I argue that the Anti-Phrygian source, with the phrase "after the limit of the prophetic charismata," also subtly launches another objection, a historiographical one. The source clearly argues that grace and gifts exist currently in the church. But it also believes that the *prophetic* charismata are indeed limited to the past. Nowhere else in this first argument (*Panarion* 48.1.5–48.3.2) is the adjective προφητικά attached to charismata. Although the Anti-Phrygian source argues strenuously that the "true" church received charismata, it never appeals to the correct behavior of prophets in its community or argues that its community engages in ongoing prophetic charismata.

The Anti-Phrygian begins its argument with terms that emphasize reality and truth over and against the Phrygians' error. It concludes this part of the argument with a description of the (true) church. The Lord sealed (ἐσφράγισε) it and filled it with gifts (<ἐν> αὐτῇ τὰ χαρίσματα). Two strategies surface here: discussion is restricted to the term *charismata* rather than prophetic charismata (or even *pneumatika,* spiritual gifts), and the discussion of prophecy is carefully sustained in the imperfect tense: "For when there was a need for prophets, the same saints were prophesying everything by a true spirit and a sound understanding and a conscious mind" (ὅτε γὰρ ἦν χρεία προφητῶν, ἐν ἀληθινῷ πνεύματι καὶ ἐρρωμένῃ διανοίᾳ καὶ παρακολουθοῦντι νῷ οἱ αὐτοὶ ἅγιοι τὰ πάντα ἐπροφήτευον). The Anti-Phrygian hints that true prophecy is a thing of the past. This is confirmed by the next argument, which is launched with the statement: "For by comparing what they have said and the prophecies which exist in truth and came to be in truth in the Old and New Testaments, let us examine what constitutes prophecy and what constitutes false prophecy" (48.3.3). And later, in *Panarion* 48.8.1, we find a reprise: "And although they will again wish to say that the first spiritual gifts are not like the last, whence are they able to prove this? For the holy prophets and the holy apostles prophesied in a manner similar to one another."[20] This further supports my assertion that the Anti-Phrygian wants to present prophetic gifts as a thing of the past: the source suggests that the first spiritual gifts are represented by the "holy prophets" and the last spiritual gifts are represented by the "holy apostles," thus shutting out the possibility of present prophetic gifts. In this introductory argument, therefore, the Anti-Phrygian uses both a discourse of history and a discourse of rationality and madness, comparing

---

19. Her oracle is wrong: 206 years (this is most likely Epiphanius's modification of the source's date) have passed, and the συντέλεια has not yet come.

20. Οὐχ ὅμοια τὰ πρῶτα χαρίσματα τοῖς ἐσχάτοις . . . ὁμοίως γὰρ ἀλλήλοις οἱ ἅγιοι προφῆται καὶ οἱ ἅγιοι ἀπόστολοι προεφήτευσαν. The interesting equivalence of apostle and prophet in this passage is reminiscent of *Didache* 12.

Maximilla to true and accurate prophets who speak "in full possession of their understanding."

The Catalogue of Prophets

The Anti-Phrygian source pursues this tack more persistently in a long catalogue of ancient prophets that it considers to be legitimate (over and against the new, irrational, false prophecy of Montanus and Maximilla and their followers). This catalogue serves as a counterpoint to a list of Montanus's and Maximilla's oracles, which the source later cites and refutes. A refrain resounds at the conclusion to the discussion of almost every great prophet. For example, *Panarion* 48.7.10 reads: "And you see how it is evident that everything was said in truth by the prophets, and by a sound mind and with sober reasoning, and not in madness." "Their" charismata, in contrast, are rhetorically constructed as τὰ ἀλλότρια, other than, or alien to, the true charismata. This accusation resonates with the source's constant statements that when the Phrygians prophesy, they lack sound understanding (ἐρρωμένη διάνοια) and awareness (παρακολουθοῦντες); they are "neither stable nor do they have an awareness of reason" (οὐδὲ εὐσταθοῦντες φανοῦνται οὔτε παρακολουθίαν λόγου ἔχοντες; 48.3.10–11). Their ecstasy is one of folly (ἐν ἐκστάσει γέγονεν ἀφροσύνης; 48.5.8).[21]

The Anti-Phrygian's catalogue refers to ten men and one group.[22] In this catalogue, the Anti-Phrygian avoids any present or recent prophets. Indeed, because of the discourse of history that the source employs and because of the authority associated with antiquity, the text constructs a catalogue that gains authority precisely because its prophets are historically located in some more God-infused distant time. For brevity's sake, I shall focus on only two figures. In the argument about Ezekiel and Peter, we see terminology that the Anti-Phrygian frequently uses in this text. Ezekiel is proven to have a mind that is sound and rational (ἐρρωμένην ἔχων τὴν διάνοιαν καὶ παρακολουθοῦσαν) because he resisted God's "threat" (ἀπειλή) regarding baking "bread on human dung."[23] Acts 10:14 is later cited because Peter similarly resists God's command to eat unclean animals: "He did not obey

---

21. The source reinforces by sheer repetition the importance of the true prophets' sound and sober thought, while never defining the criteria by which it selects the prophets in this catalogue. The catalogue reads almost like a word search for *ekstasis* in places. The list of Scriptures may have been first compiled by those who wished to use these references to ancient ecstasies to support their own practices.

22. The catalogue consists of Moses, Isaiah, Ezekiel, Daniel, Adam, Peter, David, Abraham, those who saw the angels as Christ ascended ("men of Galilee"), Agabus, and "Paul" (that is, quotations from 1 and 2 Timothy). A glance at this catalog is in itself surprising: some of the figures mentioned do not immediately come to mind as great prophets in Scripture. They may have represented important proof-texts in the ongoing discussion of ecstasy and prophecy. The Anti-Phrygian's catalogue also excludes any prophetesses.

23. The story of Ezekiel is full of such commands, which do sound like threats against his very life. See especially Ezek 3–4.

like a person of unsound mind, but told the Lord, 'Not so, Lord' " (*Panarion* 48.7.5; see also 48.8.3).[24]

These two examples of Ezekiel and Peter point to what bothers the Anti-Phrygian — the argument that God would compel humans. The Anti-Phrygian is concerned, as Origen will later be, that God did not impose upon the prophets' free will; and, indeed, the Anti-Phrygian asserts that no violence from God's hand befell the prophets, ancient and authoritative figures from the past. So also, God would not have compelled Maximilla, as she claimed, according to the Anti-Phrygian's record of (and bitter rejoinder to) one of her oracles:

> "The Lord has sent me to be a founder and revealer and interpreter of this labor and covenant and promise; I am compelled, willing and unwilling, to know the knowledge of God...." For see here she who so spoke, but was compelled and denounced herself unwillingly. Our Lord did not come unwillingly into the world. (*Panarion* 48.13.1, 3)[25]

Figures from the past — Ezekiel, Peter, and even "our Lord" — were not compelled, but Maximilla innovatively claims to have been under such compulsion, according to the Anti-Phrygian. Judged against such ancient figures, she is easily set aside as self-contradictory and self-denouncing.

In addition to an anxiety over the idea that the divine compels humans, the passages above reveal the Anti-Phrygian's two discursive strategies. First, ancient examples of rationality and clarity of mind are launched, but do little to advance a definition of rationality. Rather, the arguments are part of a rhetorical strategy that masks the source's deeper concern — the church's proper manifestations of charismata, its lack of compulsory or irrational behavior in prophecy, and thus its "true" or "real" Christian identity. Second, the Anti-Phrygian makes statements that reveal an underlying discourse

---

24. Regarding later interpretations of Acts 10 and the importance of 10:17 to texts associated with the "Montanist controversy," see François Bovon, *De vocatione gentium: Histoire de l'interprétation d'Act. 10,1–11,18 dans les six premiers siècles* (Tübingen: Mohr/Siebeck, 1967), esp. 92–165.

25. " Ἀπέστειλέ με κύριος τούτου τοῦ πόνου καὶ τῆς συνθήκης καὶ τῆς ἐπαγγελίας αἱρετιστὴν μηνυτὴν ἑρμηνευτήν, ἠναγκασμένον, θέλοντα καὶ μὴ θέλοντα, γνωθεῖν γνῶσιν θεοῦ." Although this oracle is spoken by Maximilla, the participles which describe her (ἠναγκασμένον [compelled] and θέλοντα καὶ μὴ θέλοντα [willing and unwilling]) are masculine. Holl believes this to be a "careless oversight" on the part of Epiphanius's source (*Panarion haer.*, 237). The Anti-Phrygian may indeed have carelessly elided the gender of the participles with the masculine of the preceding nouns (αἱρετιστὴν [founder], μηνυτὴν [revealer], and ἑρμηνευτήν [interpreter]). But masculine participles may be an intentional change from the feminine, making possible the source's later accusation (*Panarion* 48.13.7) that "she compelled the willing and the unwilling" (with the masculine singular as a generic). (See Williams's note [*Panarion of Epiphanius*, 2.19 n. 69], which explains the second reading of this phrase, in *Panarion* 48.13.7.) It is also possible, given the polemic immediately following, that Epiphanius's source knew that Maximilla's oracle was spoken in the voice of Christ — that is, that Christ through Maximilla proclaimed this oracle, necessitating masculine adjectives and pushing the Anti-Phrygian immediately to argue about "our Lord."

about a "limit" in history, a time when it was appropriate to know the "knowledge of God" through prophecy, as Maximilla's oracle states, and a present time when access to such knowledge has ceased.

The Anti-Phrygian's argument is rooted in a discourse of time and history that fits so well with our present-day understandings of chronological history that it is easy to universalize this idea of history, to employ again the model of charismatic origins and decline into institution, and to be unaware of the discursive nature of the Anti-Phrygian's presentation. A final example will demonstrate. Both Tertullian and the Anti-Phrygian argue strenuously from Gen 2:21, revealing that this verse and its setting are a subject of contentious debate in early-third-century Christianity:

> So the LORD God caused a deep sleep to fall upon the man, and he slept [the Septuagint reads: God cast an ecstasy upon Adam, and he slept; καὶ ἐπέβαλεν ὁ θεοἔκστασιν ἐπὶ τὸν Ἀδάμ, καὶ ὕπνωσεν];[26] then he took one of his ribs and closed up its place with flesh. And the rib that the LORD God had taken from the man he made into a woman and brought her to the man. Then the man said,
>
> > "This at last is bone of my bones
> > and flesh of my flesh;
> > this one shall be called Woman,
> > for out of Man this one was taken."
>
> Therefore a man leaves his father and his mother and clings to his wife, and they become one flesh. (Gen 2:21–24 NRSV)

Tertullian uses these verses to argue that Adam experienced a profound and prophetic ecstasy, a moment of sleep and ecstatic dreaming that become paradigmatic for all human experience of ecstasy thereafter. Discussing Adam's "prophecy" in Gen 2:21–24, Tertullian follows the interpretive strategy of texts such as Ephesians, which cites Gen 2:24, and then offers its own interpretation of the events of Adam's sleep and awakening: " 'For this reason a man will leave his father and mother and be joined to his wife, and the two will become one flesh.' This is a great mystery, and I am applying it to Christ and the church" (Eph 5:31–32 NRSV). Tertullian moves past an allegorical interpretation where husband and wife stand in for Christ and the church and argues that Adam in his ecstasy prophesied about Christ and the church. This prophecy is not due to Adam's naturally being a spiritual person, however, but to an *accidens* of the Holy Spirit. Such an *accidens* is possible for all humans (*De anima* 21; see also 11).[27]

---

26. The Septuagint text is quoted from *Septuaginta* (ed. Alfred Rahlfs; Stuttgart: Deutsche Bibelgesellschaft, 1979), 4.

27. For more on Tertullian's and the Anti-Phrygian's debate on Gen 2:21, see Nasrallah, *"Ecstasy of Folly,"* chapter 1.

The Anti-Phrygian, in contrast, insists that Adam experienced merely an "ecstasy of rest," not one of "wits" or mental capacities. The source grudgingly concedes that a prophecy occurred, but merely concludes that Adam "was aware" (ἐπέγνω) of the past (saying "bone of my bone" reveals that he knew what had happened as he slept) and of the present (that the woman was taken from his body) and that "he prophesied about the future, that 'for this a person will leave his father and his mother'" (*Panarion* 48.6.6). This knowledge and articulation of the past, present, and future gives the Anti-Phrygian further cause to emphasize: "These things are not from an ecstatic man, nor from one who does not follow (conceptually), but of one who has a sound understanding" (ταῦτα δὲ οὐκ ἐκστατικοῦ ἀνδρὸς οὐδὲ ἀπαρακολουθήτου, ἀλλὰ ἐρρωμένην ἔχοντος τὴν διάνοιαν; 48.6.6). Unlike Tertullian, who understands Gen 2:23 to refer prophetically to Christ and the church, the Anti-Phrygian's interpretation drains the text of its prophetic punch. Adam merely refers to the past, present, and future event of a man's leaving his family and joining his wife — the slow march of chronological, linear history.[28] While this view of history may seem natural to us — easy to skim over, and take at face value — we see here that it is launched in a polemical situation, in order to support the Anti-Phrygian's redefinition of ecstasy away from what it sees as the ecstatic follies of Montanus, Maximilla, and their disciples. The Anti-Phrygian's entire argument about ecstasy functioned in the same way: to recognize but downplay the term, to drain it of power, to insist that prophets and oracles have passed, to deny the possibility of present ecstasies or prophecies opening new realms of knowledge, and to accuse of mental instability those who presently make such claims.

Tertullian

Reading the Anti-Phrygian source in conjunction with Tertullian's writings, we find that the idea that the time of prophetic charismata had passed was not a matter of agreement, but a subject of debate in early Christianity. The Anti-Phrygian argued for a temporal limit to prophetic charismata. The great prophets existed in the past, while Maximilla's and Montanus's current-day attempts at prophecy consist of madness. Tertullian, in contrast, uses the term *amentia*, usually translated "madness," as a synonym for *ecstasis*, and argues that in the present, prophetic charismata are more vibrant than they ever could have been in the past, since the Paraclete has now come.[29] In fact, in *Against Marcion*, charismata, *amentia*, and ecstasy ("in ecstasi, id

---

28. This flat interpretation may also subtly support the Anti-Phrygian's promarriage stance in *Panarion* 48.8.6–48.9.10.

29. See also the introduction to the *Martyrdom of Perpetua and Felicitas,* which some think that Tertullian edited.

est in amentia"!) become a litmus test by which the legitimacy of Christian leadership and community is determined:

> Therefore let Marcion exhibit gifts of his god: some prophets, who have spoken, yet not from human sense, but from the spirit of God, who have both predicted future events and conveyed hidden things of the heart; let him produce some psalm, some vision, some speech, insofar as it is spiritual, in ecstasy — that is, in *amentia* — if, perhaps, he undertakes an interpretation of tongues. Let him show to me as well a woman who prophesies among them, from these his great holy women, I say. If I can proffer all these things easily, and assuredly these are in agreement with the rules and directions and instructions of the Creator, without doubt Christ and the spirit and the apostle belong to my God. (*Against Marcion* 5.8.12)[30]

Tertullian and the Anti-Phrygian source are thus engaged in the same discourse of madness and rationality, but use its terms in different ways. They do not seek to define rationality and madness, a sound mind and ecstasies of folly, but instead deploy this rhetoric to make larger arguments about epistemology and in order to construct and shore up their authority as true Christians.

While the Anti-Phrygian source made the Phrygians "other than" the true church by referring to their instability of mind and their lack of correspondence to a tradition of prophets, Tertullian attempts to construct and establish his community's identity (and that of his opponents) by drawing upon anthropological language — the person's status as fleshly (*animales*), as psychic or souled (*psychici*), or as spiritual (*spiritales*). Tertullian accuses his opponents of merely *claiming* to be *spiritales*, while not giving any real evidence of spiritual gifts at the present time.

This name-calling is part of a struggle to define Christianity authoritatively, but it is also part of Tertullian's attempt to settle definitely questions about the human soul and its epistemic capabilities. *De anima*, written late in Tertullian's life (ca. 210–13), both argues with and culls from every sort of philosophy in order to make Tertullian's point that the soul is unitary (not tripartite, as those following Plato would have it) and thus that it has a large range of epistemic possibilities. Since he does not privilege the mind as the highest part of the soul,[31] Tertullian, borrowing from Stoic philosophy, can argue for the epistemic value of sense perception. He does so vigorously in *De anima*, in an explicitly polemical context: "Don't the heretical seeds of

---

30. Except for *De anima*, translations of Tertullian's writings are made from the Latin text in Tertullian, *Opera* (Corpus christianorum series latina 1–2; Turnhout: Brepols, 1954).

31. See, e.g., *De anima* 12–15, where Tertullian argues not only about the unity of the soul, but also insists that the *hēgemonikon* is located in the heart, not the mind.

gnostics and Valentinians shine forth? For here they seize upon the distinction of corporeal senses from intellectual powers" (*De anima* 18.2–4).[32] He goes on to argue that sense perception is prior to intellectual perception: "For how can the intellect be given preference over sense perception, by which the intellect is instructed for the purpose of acquiring true knowledge?" (18.11).[33]

Tertullian's insistence on a broad range of valuable epistemes extends even further. For him, valuable knowledge can be gained through *amentia,* whether this occurs in dreams or in other contexts. For example, Tertullian uses information from a vision received by a "sister" in his community in order to support his idea that the soul is corporeal.[34] Thus Tertullian knows about the corporeality of the soul not only through the philosophical argumentation that pervades *De anima,* but also from evidence gleaned through continued charismata in his community:

> Currently, a sister among us receives gifts of revelation, which she experiences during the rites on the Lord's day....Indeed, truly, the materials for her visions are supplied according to the scripture which is read, or the psalms which are sung, or addresses which are offered, or the petitions which are made. It happened that we were discussing something about the soul — I don't know what[35] — when this sister came to be in the spirit. After the rites, when the people have left, we are accustomed to asking her what she saw (for we diligently set them in order,[36] and examine them). (*De anima* 9.4)

Although Tertullian carefully wishes to guarantee the epistemic worth of this vision (and so perhaps steers clear of the controversial term *amentia*), elsewhere he more easily introduces the idea that knowledge gained in *amentia* is valuable. Late in *De anima,* Tertullian explains that there are three kinds of dreams (*somnia*): those divinely sent, those from demons, and a third category. It is the latter that he has trouble explaining. He wishes to

---

32. Translations of *De anima* are made from the Latin text in Jan H. Waszink, *Quinti Septimi Florentis Tertulliani De anima* (Amsterdam: Meulenhoff, 1947).

33. Much of Tertullian's thinking is rooted in Stoic epistemology. See Émile Bréhier, *The Hellenistic and Roman Age* (trans. Wade Baskin; orig. 1931; repr. Chicago: University of Chicago Press, 1965), 38; Martha Nussbaum, "The Stoics on the Extirpation of the Passions," in Nussbaum's *The Therapy of Desire: Theory and Practice in Hellenistic Ethics* (Princeton: Princeton University Press, 1994), 359–401.

34. For this unusual and complex argument, see *De anima* 5–9.

35. That is, Tertullian himself was possibly reading from his writing or presenting a talk. See Waszink, *De anima,* 171.

36. Edwin A. Quain's translation reads: "All her visions are carefully written down" ("Tertullian *De anima,*" in *Tertullian: Apologetic Works; and Minucius Felix: Octavius* [Fathers of the Church 10; Washington, D.C.: Catholic University of America Press, 1962], 197), based in part perhaps on Waszink, *De anima,* 172. But this translation of *digeruntur* would then be based upon reading *De anima* 9 against mainly heresiological accounts of Montanists making written collections of their prophecies.

argue against what he characterizes as a typical Christian view, which asserts that dreams are "accidents of sleep and not insignificant disturbances of the soul" (45.1). He attempts to describe the third category of dreams:

> This power we call *ecstasis*, a departure of mental and sensory powers, which is an image of *amentia*. Thus, in the beginning, sleep was preceded by ecstasy, as we read: "And God sent an ecstasy upon Adam and he slept." Sleep brought rest to the body, but ecstasy came over the soul and prevented it from resting, and from that time this combination constitutes the natural and normal form of the dream. (*De anima* 45.3)[37]

Tertullian must explain, however, how it is possible that humans remember dreams, since he wants to argue that a dream (or an *amentia* or *ecstasis* — he uses the terms interchangeably) can be epistemically valuable:

> Therefore, in that (when) memory is present, the mind is sound; when a sound mind, with memory uninjured, is struck senseless [*stupeo*], a kind of *amentia* exists. For that reason, we do not call it "madness" but "dreaming"; therefore we are also wise and sensible, as at any other time. For although our faculty of knowledge is overshadowed, it is nevertheless not extinguished, except insofar as this very power [of knowing] also seems to be lacking at that time. For this likewise is ecstasy operating according to its own characteristics, so that it thus brings to us images of wisdom, even as it brings those of error. (*De anima* 45.6)

Tertullian's broad epistemology allows him both to participate in and to upend the discourse of madness and rationality in which the Anti-Phrygian engages. Tertullian surprises by using the term *amentia* easily, as a synonym of the transliterated Greek *ekstasis*. While *amentia* usually implies the departure of the mind, because Tertullian insists upon a unified soul *amentia* means something different: it is merely a marker of an ecstasy that opens

---

37. "Hanc vim ecstasin dicimus, excessum sensus et amentiae instar. Sic et in primordio somnus cum ecstasi dedicatus, et misit deus ecstasin in Adam et dormiit. Somnus enim corpori provenit in quietem, ecstasis animae accessit adversus quietem, et inde iam forma somnum ecstasi miscens et natura de forma" (*De anima* 45.3; Waszink, *De anima*, 62). This translation closely follows Quain, "Tertullian *De anima*," 280. Using Gen 2:21, Tertullian sets up three equivalent terms in the first sentence: *ecstasin, excessum sensus,* and *amentiae instar.* Quain translates *excessum sensus* as "a departure of sense." I think, however, that Tertullian is employing three different terms for the same thing: *ecstasis,* which is a transliteration of the Greek term; *excessum sensus* in order to explain further; and *amentia,* which is the Latin term he uses frequently as a synonym for Greek ἔκστασις. *Excessus* is defined as "a leaving of the mental powers, loss of self-possession = ἔκστασις." Moreover, after the Augustan period, *sensus* refers not only to perception, feeling, and sense, but also to "sense, understanding, mind, and reason"; it is a synonym of *mens* and *ratio*. *Instar* with the genitive can also be a term of equivalency: "like, in the form of, equal to" (Charlton Lewis and Charles Short, *A New Latin Dictionary, Founded on the Translation of Freund's Latin-German Lexicon* (New York: American Book Co., 1907), *s.v. excessus, sensus, instar*).

onto valuable realms of knowledge that are not solely intellectual, just as Tertullian already argued that the intellectual faculty is not the only or best faculty for knowledge gathering.[38] Tertullian makes this argument about the epistemic value of *amentia* in part through his sophisticated (and chaotic) arguments about the soul, but also because of his understanding of the periodization of time. For Tertullian and his intended interlocutors, the question of where they stood within history was vital.[39]

Tertullian has a very precise understanding of spiritual gifts and of history — that is, God's purpose and activity in the world from creation to the end of time — and this historiography helps to make sense of the accusations regarding the so-called *psychici*, who surely understood themselves at least to be on the road to the identity of *spiritales*, and their understanding of prophecy and spiritual gifts. In *On the Veiling of Virgins* 1.4, Tertullian argues that the law of faith is permanent, but that "new amendments" are possible because "it is evident that the grace of God operates and advances until the end" (*operante scilicet et proficiente usque in finem gratia dei*). Alluding to John 14, he states that "the Lord sent the Paraclete...since human mediocrity was not able to grasp all things at once." Through the Paraclete, discipline is regulated and "brought to perfection" (*ad perfectum perduceretur disciplina*). The role of the Paraclete[40] is "to direct discipline, to reveal scriptures, to reform the understanding, to make progress toward better things" (*On the Veiling of Virgins* 1.5). And then he sets forth the most interesting part of his argument, weaving Eccl 3:1 — "there is a time for everything" — with an appeal to all of creation, which "is advanced to fruit gradually." The created world progresses through many stages to become the ripe fruit: "So also righteousness...was at first in an originary state, when it revered God by nature; then it progressed in its infancy through the law and prophets, then it advanced in its youth by the gospel. Now through the Paraclete it is brought to maturity" (*On the Veiling of Virgins* 1.7). Tertullian's description conforms roughly to the historiographical paradigm, well established in antiquity, of the world's passing through stages of life just as a human does.[41]

In *On Fasting*, which is explicitly addressed to the so-called *psychici*, Tertullian exposes more of the problem.[42] He explains that the *psychici* are

---

38. Elsewhere, Tertullian is more ambiguous. Regarding his negative characterizations of the body in comparison with the soul, see *De anima* 53.

39. We see such an interest in a variety of texts in antiquity. Consider Polybius's *Histories*, Josephus's *Jewish Antiquities*, and Luke-Acts.

40. Tertullian is quoting John 16:12–13 here.

41. A. Momigliano, "The Origins of Universal History," in Momigliano's *On Pagans, Jews, and Christians* (Middletown, Conn.: Wesleyan University Press, 1987), 35–36.

42. In *On Monogamy*, Tertullian shifts his rhetoric, emphasizing that the Paraclete does not introduce novel practices, but defines more clearly what has already been set forth (*De monogamia* 3.10–12). It is clear that some claim that Tertullian and others ascribe "whatever is new and burdensome" to the Paraclete; the *psychici* even hint that such insights may come

not only in cahoots with heresy and pseudoprophecy, but they also argue that the Paraclete's prophets offer messages from the devil (*On Fasting* 11).[43] Moreover, it seems that the fixing of boundaries, temporal and otherwise, is disputed:

> But again you set boundaries for God, as concerning grace, so concerning discipline, as concerning charismata, so concerning rites, so that just as official observances have ceased, in the same way also God's benefits have ceased. And so you deny that duties are still imposed by God, because of this: "The law and the prophets were until John" [Luke 16:16]. (*On Fasting* 11.6)

Those whom Tertullian calls *psychici* must have used Luke 16:16 as an argument that charismata, including prophecy, had ceased at some point (probably after the time of Christ or the apostles, just as they claimed that certain "duties" ceased after John the Baptist).[44] Tertullian instead holds to a different tripartite division of history, which corresponds to infancy (the time of the law and the prophets), adolescence (the time of Christ), and maturity (the present period of the Paraclete). In his work we see that the periodization of time and arguments about Christian community's spiritual gifts are one discursive thrust in a larger struggle over authority and Christian identity in antiquity.

---

from a "rival spirit" (*ab aduersario spiritu*; 2.1–4; esp. 2.3). Moving focus off the hot topic of the Paraclete, Tertullian appeals to what they have in common: "Let us withdraw from mention of the Paraclete as having some authority for us. Let us unroll the common instruments of the original Scriptures" (4.1). Then, he says, all will see that the Paraclete is not an innovator but a restorer: monogamy (i.e., Tertullian argues against second marriages) is represented by figures from Noah to Peter (4–9). In this work on monogamy, Tertullian again sets history into three periods, as he did in *On the Veiling of Virgins*. He states that "hardness of heart reigned up until Christ, and weakness of the flesh had reigned up to the Paraclete. The new law removed divorce...; the new prophecy removed second marriage" (14.4). We can see that here, far from being a strange ethical rigorist, as most modern scholars characterize him (see, e.g., D. I. Rankin, "Was Tertullian a Jurist?" *Studia patristica* 31 [1997]: 335–42, esp. 338), Tertullian presents himself and his community as truly spiritual, as steering between those whom he characterizes as having no ethics at all (i.e., those who marry again and again) and Platonizing Christians ("heretics" in Tertullian's jargon) — those who twist ethics and anthropology so that they cannot see the goodness of the body and who deny all marriages. In the earliest age, there was "hardness of heart"; with the age of Christ came prohibitions on divorce; and in the age of the Paraclete second marriage is prohibited.

43. In *On Fasting* 12, Tertullian complains that his interlocutors will not accept the Paraclete in Montanus.

44. See also Ronald Heine, "Role of the Gospel of John in the Montanist Controversy," *Second Century* 6 (1987–88): 1–19. In his *Homilies on Luke*, Origen uses Luke 16:16 to insist that prophecy has come to an end; see Gunnar Af Hällström, *Charismatic Succession: A Study of Origen's Consept* [*sic*] *of Prophecy* (Helsinki: Toimittanut Anne-Marit Enroth, 1985), 32. For uses of Luke 16:16 in conjunction with Montanism/discussions of Cataphrygians, see Pseudo-Athanasius's *Sermon against All Heresies* and *Synopsis scripturae sacrae liber xvi: Canticum canticorum* (both found in Ronald Heine, *The Montanist Oracles and Testimonia* [Patristics Monograph Series 14; Macon, Ga.: Mercer University Press, 1989]).

Paul and I Corinthians

Tertullian and the Anti-Phrygian source are engaged in an early-third-century struggle over prophecy, ecstasy, and the limits of knowledge in Christian communities. To make their points, they engage in an ongoing discourse of madness and rationality, albeit in different ways. Paul, too, engages in this discourse, substituting the terms "folly" and "wisdom." First Corinthians also engages in the discourse of time and history in order to bolster its position that the epistemic benefits of certain spiritual gifts are not accessible in the present, but only in the future.

Like Tertullian and the Anti-Phrygian source, Paul is interested in de-limiting realms of knowledge. When the epistle is viewed as evidence of conflict between Paul and sectors of the Corinthians community, 1 Corinthians ceases to become a letter of Paul's correction of the Corinthians' incorrect, crazed, hubristic behavior.[45] Instead, it is a document that reveals intense conflict between the Corinthian community and Paul — a conflict that grew even more fierce, as the later materials in 2 Corinthians reveal. In 1 Corinthians, Paul's central response to this situation of struggle is to assert his authority by challenging the Corinthians' self-understanding as spiritual people (*pneumatikoi*), by upending their ranking of spiritual gifts and by insisting that love trumps knowledge.

In 1 Cor 1–4, Paul attempts to constrain the Corinthians' access to knowledge by challenging their self-understanding as *pneumatikoi*. He does so in part by insisting upon the incommensurability of human wisdom and divine wisdom and power.[46] God's wisdom is folly in human eyes, but "God's foolishness is wiser than human wisdom, and God's weakness is stronger than human strength" (1:25).[47] This sort of upside down logic fits well with the Corinthians' situation: "Consider your own call, brothers and sisters," Paul states:

> Not many of you were wise by human standards, not many were powerful, not many were of noble birth. But God chose what is foolish in the world to shame the wise; God chose what is weak in the world to shame the strong; God chose what is low and despised in the world, things that are not, to reduce to nothing things that are, so that no one might boast in the presence of God. (1 Cor 1:26–29)

Even if the status of the addressees, perhaps formerly set low, is now in the logic of God brought high, Paul still critiques them, stating that they are

---

45. See esp. Schüssler Fiorenza, "Rhetorical Situation and Historical Reconstruction in 1 Corinthians," in *Rhetoric and Ethic*, 105–28.

46. This discussion of wisdom reveals and emphasizes at every turn the gap between the human and divine. God's folly is wiser than humans, Paul states (1 Cor 1:25); what appears to be wise among this age and among the rulers of this age has nothing to do with God's secret and hidden wisdom, which was decreed before the ages (2:6–7).

47. All translations are from the New Revised Standard Version unless otherwise noted.

not mature, not privy to the "secret and hidden wisdom of God" (2:7). In fact, they are not πνευματικοί (people of spirit), not even ψυχικοί (people of soul), but are σαρκικοί (people of flesh) (2:13–3:3).

"Now we have received not the spirit of the world, but the Spirit that is from God, so that we may understand the gifts bestowed on us by God" (2:12), Paul states. It becomes clear from 1 Cor 12–14 — introduced with "now concerning spiritual gifts, brothers and sisters, I do not want you to be uninformed" (12:1)[48] — that Paul wants to assert that the Corinthians do not have a correct understanding of *pneumatika* and perhaps then do not really have the spirit of God. That is, the realms of knowledge that they believed themselves to have accessed were, in fact, false. It is also in these chapters that Paul drives a further wedge between the human and the divine. Paul does not want to state unequivocally that certain kinds of knowledge are inaccessible in the present, but he does argue later that complete epistemic transformation — perfection, or a resurrected life — is impossible in the here-and-now.[49]

The Corinthians clearly value the *pneumatika,* or spiritual gifts, manifest among them, in part for the knowledge and wisdom that emerge through those gifts. Paul, however, seeks to reorder and rank these gifts and thus to reconfigure the importance of knowledge. First Cor 12:14–26 argues for the significance of every member of the body, the "weaker" and those given more "honor," but this argument quickly flows into the larger argument about ranking gifts: "And God has appointed in the church first apostles, second prophets, third teachers; then deeds of power, then gifts of healing, forms of assistance, forms of leadership, various kinds of tongues" (12:28). Joop Smit points out that priority and rank are denoted by the use of ordinal numbers in 12:28 as various roles in the church are listed. He, among others, remarks that the ordering of *pneumatika* in 12:28 erodes the epistle's former emphasis on wisdom and knowledge — and concomitantly glossolalia and prophecy, charismata which the Corinthians held dear.[50]

---

48. The long debates over the gender of πνευματικῶν will not be rehearsed here. See Hans Conzelmann's convincing argument that it is neuter; *1 Corinthians: A Commentary on the First Epistle to the Corinthians* (trans. James W. Leitch; Hermeneia; Philadelphia: Fortress, 1975), 204. Paul's phrasing here is interesting: he purports to inform the Corinthians about something that is clearly already of great interest to them.

49. See Schüssler Fiorenza, "Rhetorical Situation and Historical Reconstruction," 122; see also Antoinette Clark Wire, *The Corinthian Women Prophets: A Reconstruction through Paul's Rhetoric* (Minneapolis: Fortress, 1990), 159–96, who argues that some members of the Corinthian community understood themselves already to be living in the resurrection, in a transformed life in the present. For a similar idea taken in a different direction, see Conzelmann, *1 Corinthians,* 14, who argues that the Corinthians espoused freedom, and thus ethical freedom and "moral and religious disorders" bound up with "religious enthusiasm."

50. Joop Smit, "Argument and Genre of 1 Corinthians 12–14," in *Rhetoric and the New Testament: Essays from the 1992 Heidelberg Conference* (ed. Stanley Porter and Thomas Olbricht; Journal for the Study of the New Testament Supplement 90; Sheffield: JSOT Press, 1993), 219. Throughout 1 Cor 12–14 we see Paul hierarchizing spiritual gifts; he delineates their importance as regards the "one body" to which he urges the Corinthians to strive. As

Immediately following this ranking, 1 Cor 13 offers an argument about spiritual gifts, knowledge, and time and history by setting forth three main and intertwined arguments: Paul puts the spiritual gifts most valued in the Corinthian community into a larger perspective and so downgrades some of them; he subordinates wisdom to love;[51] and he posits an as-yet-insurmountable gap between the human and the divine. He makes these arguments, which are fundamentally about epistemology, by means of a discourse of history, contrasting what is possible in the present with what will be seen at some future time, perhaps the eschaton.

Hans Conzelmann rightly points out that while 1 Cor 13 begins with values significant at Corinth, "these recognized values are then relativized":[52] "If I speak in the tongues of mortals and of angels, but do not have love, I am a noisy gong or a clanging cymbal. And if I have prophetic powers, and understand all mysteries and all knowledge, and if I have all faith, so as to remove mountains, but do not have love, I am nothing" (13:1–2). Paul comes back to glossolalia, prophecy, and knowledge as the main points of discussion.[53] He emphasizes that these three things which the Corinthians value most will all pass away, while "love never ends" (13:8).

Verses 4–8a may represent a pre-Pauline aretalogy of love, but I would assert that this material is used precisely to relativize the importance of wisdom in the Corinthian community and to critique the Corinthians for thinking that they already have access to certain epistemes. Aretalogies of wisdom (and less often of love) are found in Jewish as well as pagan sources;[54] a genre usually applied to wisdom is here applied instead to love. This praise of love may deliberately displace aretalogies of wisdom that are important to the community, working like 1 Cor 1–4 to control the Corinthian emphasis on wisdom. Thus glossolalia and prophecy, which the Corinthians likely understood as God's charismata, linked to knowledge and wisdom, are displaced, and with them, a knowledge of the divine is also displaced.

But not only does Paul offer an argument that holds up love in the face of wisdom and relativizes the importance of knowledge, tongues, and prophecy in the Corinthian community, he also presents an explicit argument

---

Conzelmann states (*1 Corinthians*, 233; see also 209), the argument here is "no longer a *critique* of πνευματικά . . . but their *classification*."

51. This opposition between love and knowledge is already found in 1 Cor 8:1.

52. Conzelmann, *1 Corinthians*, 221.

53. Conzelmann argues (ibid., 222) that in verse 2 "Paul follows the Corinthian order of merit in the spiritual gifts, which he will reverse in chap. 14." For a fascinating argument about the connection between 1 Cor 12:31b and 1 Cor 13, see Joop Smit, "Two Puzzles: 1 Corinthians 12.31 and 13.3: A Rhetorical Solution," *New Testament Studies* 39 (1993): 246–64, esp. 250–55, who concludes that 12:31b is an ironic and hyperbolic statement rooted in Paul's response to the Corinthians' competition for *pneumatika*.

54. Conzelmann, *1 Corinthians*, 218–19, esp. 219 n. 14; see 219–20 for an excursus listing parallels to 1 Cor 13; see also Margaret Mary Mitchell, *Paul and the Rhetoric of Reconciliation: An Exegetical Investigation of the Language and Composition of 1 Corinthians* (Louisville: Westminster/John Knox 1993), 57–58.

about epistemology. Paul severely limits the significance of spiritual gifts that bridge the human and divine. Verses 8b–13 solidly place the phenomena of tongues and prophecy and knowledge into the realm of the transitory. These things are not eternal, fixed: they will be abolished or rendered inoperative (καταργέω); they will cease. They are associated with the partial rather than the complete and perfect (v. 10); they are ranked developmentally with the child, and the "childish things" are similarly abolished. Verse 12 harshly exposes the inadequacy of human knowledge: βλέπομεν γὰρ ἄρτι δι' ἐσόπτρου ἐν αἰνίγματι, τότε δὲ πρόσωπον πρὸσ πρόσωπον· ἄρτι γινώσκω ἐκ μέρους, τότε δὲ ἐπιγνώσομαι καθὼς καὶ ἐπεγνώσθην (for now we see by means of a mirror, as by a riddle, but then face to face; now we know in part, but then we will know even as we are also known [my translation]). The riddling unclarity and distortion of mirrors in antiquity is a metaphor for the warping and inaccuracy of all present knowledge. Tongues and prophecy only barely mediate this higher knowledge; even tongues and prophecy, Paul is saying, are only partial glimpses of the divine. Divine knowledge (which understands humans fully) is different from the fragmentary nature of present human knowledge.

Schüssler Fiorenza's model of struggle helps us to see how 1 Corinthians, like Tertullian and the anti-Phrygian, is concerned about delimiting realms of knowledge in the debate over prophecy and spiritual gifts. One method for establishing a limit to what can be known is to draw upon an understanding of history. Paul thus engages in a discourse on history's periodization, as did our early-third-century sources. Paul nevertheless makes clear that certain realms of knowledge are not available in the present. They are off limits until some future date: "then, face to face."[55]

Conclusions

References to time, spiritual gifts, and prophecy in the Anti-Phrygian source, Tertullian's writings, and 1 Corinthians are best read as fragments of a discursive struggle over history, interconnected to issues of epistemology and authority. The Anti-Phrygian presents one view of history: prophetic charismata belong to the past, to the age of the prophets and apostles. Tertullian presents another grand narrative in support of his understanding of *amentia:* time has evolved through an age of infancy, with the law and the prophets, to an age of adolescence, with the coming of Christ, and now blooms into the age of the Paraclete, a time for greater spiritual gifts, especially ecstasy or prophecy. Paul, more than a century earlier, argued that certain realms of knowledge are inaccessible in the present, even through God's spiritual

---

55. Paul in 2 Corinthians, however, faces a more urgent rhetorical situation and retreats from the divide that he proposes in 1 Corinthians. Second Cor 12 indicates that he grudgingly will engage in discussions of the interpenetrability of the divine and human realms.

gifts; he shunted this knowledge into the divine realm and into the future, to a later time when one will see clearly and know perfectly.

In the early-third-century debate, the discourse of rationality and madness imbricates with or ties into the discourse of the periodization of history. The Anti-Phrygian rhetorically constructs its opponents as irrational while Tertullian uses the term *amentia* as a synonym to *ecstasis,* the prophetic ecstasy that for Tertullian is a key demonstration of a Christian community's status as spiritual people. Madness and rationality are not defined, but are deployed discursively to support a text's contention that its community is authentically Christian, while another community makes only spurious claims to charismata and true manifestations of Christian identity.

Although the Anti-Phrygian refers to a limit to prophetic gifts, and Tertullian challenges others to prove their true Christianity by means of *amentia* or ecstasy, and Paul refers to the cessation of prophecy and a future time of new realms of knowledge, these texts do not offer a key for tracing the evolution of early Christianity from charismatic origins to routinization and institutionalization (or evidence of heretical aberrations). Rather, they participate in a larger, centuries-long discourse that includes Christians, Jews, and Greco-Roman philosophy.[56] Using Schüssler Fiorenza's model of struggle and her method of rhetorical criticism, we have seen how all three texts use history discursively to draw boundaries around or to extend realms of knowledge and to shore up their own identity.[57] Schüssler Fiorenza's challenge to interrogate epistemology and historiography shatters the model of charismatic origins and subsequent institutionalization and gives us a vision of the complex and vivid negotiations of power in early Christianity.

---

56. See Plato's *Phaedrus* 244–49, with its four kinds of *maniai,* and Philo's *Who Is the Heir of Divine Things?* 258, which reworks this fourfold taxonomy and declares best a prophetic ecstasy in which the human mind is expelled and replaced by the divine mind. See Nasrallah, "Ecstasy of Folly," chap. 1.

57. An important discussion of the discourse of history, modern European hegemony over the definition of history as universal, unitary, linear, and chronological, and the ethics of history-writing is also found in postcolonial theorists; see Ashis Nandy, "History's Forgotten Doubles," *History and Theory* 34 (May 1995): 44–67; Dipesh Chakrabarty, *Provincializing Europe: Postcolonial Thought and Historical Difference* (Princeton: Princeton University Press, 2000). See also Schüssler Fiorenza's interactions with postcolonial theory, especially in *Rhetoric and Ethic,* 36–37.

Part 4

Rhetoric and Ethic:
The Politics of Meaning

16

Revelation 18

Notes on Effective History and
the State of Colombia

Allen Dwight Callahan

And I heard a voice saying unto me: Switch on the radio
And I did switch it on and heard: BABYLON IS FALLEN
BABYLON THE GREAT IS FALLEN....
And I heard another voice from heaven saying:
Go forth from her my people
Lest ye be contaminated...
By the Anthrax Bomb
. . . .
They will behold the great disaster on TV
For the Bomb is fallen on great Babylon.
—Ernesto Cardenal, "Apocalypse"

John's attempt to formulate the reality and meaning of eschatological
salvation in universal and symbolic symbols gains greater significance
again, at a time when those who share the author's experience of oppression and exploitation attempt to formulate their own theology of
liberation and to stake their life on it.
—Elisabeth Schüssler Fiorenza,
Invitation to the Book of Revelation

I.

Babylon the Great is fallen, and has become the habitation of devils,
and the hold of every foul spirit, and the cage of every unclean and
hateful bird. For all nations have drunk of the wine of the wrath of
her fornication, and the rulers of the earth have committed fornication
with her, and the merchants of the earth have grown rich from the
power of her luxury.   —Revelation 18:2–3 (author)

Presently the administration of George W. Bush is lobbying the United States Congress to approve the use of United States-trained soldiers against leftist guerrillas in Colombia.[1] Multinational firms are lobbying the White House and Capitol Hill assiduously to increase military aid to Colombia. "We could not survive in these remote areas without the protection of the Colombian military," says Lawrence Meriage, vice president for public affairs of Occidental Petroleum Corporation. Occidental Petroleum pays the Colombian government to keep an army base next to its refinery to protect it against guerrilla attacks. As a provision of the Emergency Supplemental budget bill, the House voted to allocate a $6 million advance on $98 million to finance a new Colombian army battalion to protect an oil pipeline used by Occidental.

Colombia is the eighth-largest supplier of crude oil to the United States and the third largest in Latin America after Mexico and Venezuela, shipping more than 330,000 barrels daily. After the terrorist attacks of 11 September 2001 and the subsequent instability in the Middle East, Ambassador Anne Patterson told the Bogota daily newspaper *El Tiempo*, "Colombia has great potential for exporting more oil to the United States, and now more than ever it is important for us to diversify our oil sources."

II.

Alas, alas that great city, which was clothed in fine linen, and purple, and scarlet, and decked with gold, and precious stones, and pearls!
— Revelation 18:16 (author)

Introduction: The Ethics of Interpretation

In her Society of Biblical Literature presidential address, Elisabeth Schüssler Fiorenza challenges biblical scholars to "learn how to examine both the rhetorical aims of biblical texts and the rhetorical interests emerging in the history of interpretation or in contemporary scholarship."[2] Here I reflect on the rhetorical aims and the rhetorical interests in the history of interpretation of one chapter in a biblical book that Schüssler Fiorenza's work illumines with such brilliance and erudition, the Book of Revelation. In what follows I offer a selective survey of the history of interpretation of chapter 18 of the Apocalypse, a brief account of the "rhetorical interests emerging in the history of interpretation or in contemporary scholarship" of recent Latin American biblical scholars. They, more than any other contemporary exegetes, insist that Rev 18 speaks as a Christian oracle for our time.

---

1. "U.S. Expects Wider War on Two Fronts in Colombia," *New York Times* (28 April 2002): 9.

2. Elisabeth Schüssler Fiorenza, "The Ethics of Biblical Interpretation: Decentering Biblical Scholarship," the presidential address delivered 5 December 1987 at the annual meeting of the Society of Biblical Literature and subsequently published in *Journal of Biblical Literature* 107 (1988): 3–17, quotation on 15.

Critique of Political Economy

Revelation 18, the climax of terrestrial judgment in John's visionary drama, is a critique in apocalyptic idiom of the political economy of imperial Rome. In the drama of Babylon's fall depicted in Rev 17:1–19:10 "the political and economic system is highlighted," comments Frederick J. Murphy, for the author of the Apocalypse "lived in the Roman Empire, a political and cultural system that many Christians saw as good, but that he saw as satanic."[3] Revelation 18 goes on to itemize the goods traded for the gratification of the powerful: luxuries — those commodities that all want, few have, and none need. "We may note that we have here (and especially in the subsequent verses 11–13)," comments Pierre Prigent, "the only allusion in the entire NT to the importance of the empire's commercial transactions."[4] François Bovon observes: "What strikes the reader is not the anticipated lamentation of the kings, the political actors, but the unexpected lament of the merchants, the economically powerful. Few New Testament texts reflect to the same degree an awareness of the link between political decline and economic collapse, and thereby a perception of the mutual implications of politics and economics."[5]

Schüssler Fiorenza highlighted the economic critique of the Apocalypse more than twenty years ago. "The author of Revelation is clearly on the side of the poor and oppressed," she comments, "insofar as he ... announces judgment and destruction for the rich and powerful of the earth." Her description of the political economy of Rome as the background for Rev 18 makes its relevance clear:

> The close economic ties between Rome and the provinces and the international commerce of the world-state fostered the growth of economic wealth not only in Rome but also in the provinces. ... Only the provincial elite and the Italian immigrants, especially the ship owners and merchants, were reaping the wealth of the empire's prosperity, while the heavy burden of taxation impoverished the great majority of the population. Thus a relatively small minority of the Asian cities benefited from the international commerce of the Roman empire, whereas

---

3. Frederick J. Murphy, *Fallen Is Babylon: The Revelation to John* (New Testament in Context; Harrisburg, Pa.: Trinity, 1998), 442.

4. "On notera que nous avons ici (et dans la suite du chapître notamment aux versets 11–13) la seule allusion de tout le NT à l'important mouvement commercial réalisé dans l'empire"; Pierre Prigent, *L'Apocalypse de Saint Jean* (Commentaire du Nouveau Testament 14; Geneva: Labor et Fides, 1988), 267–68.

5. François Bovon, "Possession or Enchantment: The Roman Institutions according to the Revelation of John," in Bovon's *New Testament Traditions and Apocryphal Narratives* (trans. Jane Haapiseva-Hunter; Princeton Theological Monograph Series 36; Allison Park, Pa.: Pickwick, 1995), 143.

the large masses of the city population lived in dire poverty or slavery (18:13).[6]

The theology of the Book of Revelation advocates "hope and encouragement for those who struggle for economic survival and freedom from persecution and murder."[7]

La Coyuntura

The transformations of global economy over the last fifteen years have persuaded exegetes in Latin America that the Apocalypse is urgently relevant to questions of political economy. Contemporary Latin American exegesis is informed by the commitment of liberation theology, as Karl Rahner once wrote to Cardinal Juan Landázuri Ricketts, archbishop of Lima: "The voice of the poor must be listened to by theology in the context of the Latin American church."[8] The commitment to hear the voice of the poor transcended the Marxist analysis that liberation theologians used as a tool in fashioning their theological critique of capitalism. With the demise of "real" socialism in the Eastern Bloc and the collapse of the Soviet Union itself in 1989, some European and North American theologians began writing the obituary of liberation theology. For Latin Americans, however, this proved presumptuous and premature. Indeed, false, as Enrique Dussell points out: "Liberation theology — as [the decade of 1990s would] show — is not in fact dependent on Marxism as a major source of inspiration."[9] The neoliberal capitalist regime has given rise to quotidian conditions even worse than the depredations of conquest,[10] a situation that Franz J. Hinkelammert calls "capitalism with no alternative."[11]

Systemic intensification of Latin American impoverishment and the violent reprisal against dissent accompanied neoliberal capitalist restructuring of the global economy in the post-Cold War era.[12] These were the attendant circumstances of all Latin American theological projects, including

---

6. Elisabeth Schüssler Fiorenza, *Invitation to the Book of Revelation: A Commentary on the Apocalypse* (New York: Doubleday, 1981), 172–73.

7. Ibid., 173.

8. In Alfred T. Hennelly, ed., *Liberation Theology: A Documentary History* (Maryknoll, N.Y.: Orbis, 1997), 351.

9. Enrique Dussell, "Recent Latin American Theology," in *The Church in Latin America: 1492–1992* (ed. Enrique Dussell; Maryknoll, N.Y.: Orbis, 1992), 399.

10. Pablo Richard, "El futuro de la iglesia de los pobres: Identidad y resistencia en sistema de globalización neo-liberal," *Pasos* 65 (1996): 9–10.

11. Franz J. Hinkelammert, "¿Capitalismo sin alternativas? Sobre la sociedad que sostiene que no hay alternativa para ella," *Pasos* 37 (1991): 11.

12. This restructuring, often mandated by the International Monetary Fund and the World Bank in their dealings with developing countries, was comprised of some combination of some or all of the following measures: cutting government spending and/or raising taxes to balance national budgets; privatization of government enterprises; so-called free trade through the elimination of tariffs, quotas, and subsidies; penetration of capital markets by foreign banks; and restructuring of foreign debt to further extend interest and principal payments.

biblical interpretation. Some theologians literally could not live under those circumstances. In November 1989 Salvadoran liberation theologian Ignacio Ellacuría was murdered. Ellacuría joined Archbishop Oscar Romero and tens of thousands of other Salvadoran martyrs. The actors who inadvertently proved most influential in exposing the economic and political underpinnings of Latin American poverty were not the Eastern Bloc and the Soviet Union, but the World Bank and the International Monetary Fund. The extraordinary foreign debt of Latin American countries resulting from the policies of these two institutions has been cause for ecclesiastical alarm since the late 1980s.[13]

The approach of Latin American exegetes typically begins with an assessment of the *coyuntura,* the "particular moment or period — which may cover weeks, months, or even years — and the way the forces in society line up and interact: the armed forces, the government, business groups, political parties, labor unions, organized peasants, students, the church, even the international context."[14] "We seek to interpret [Revelation] in a positive manner in its literal and historical meaning," writes Chilean biblical scholar and pastor Pablo Richard, "but we are likewise striving to interpret our present era in the light of Revelation."[15] Richard insists that the Apocalypse is "indispensable for building a theological, prophetic, and apocalyptic analysis of our present situation."[16]

Revelation 18 shows that the infernal assault on the peoples of the world is a systemic assault. "The effects of imperial Roman power," writes Néstor O. Míguez, "which produced a concentration of wealth among the privileged urban classes and oppressed the rest of the populace, are visualized in the pages of the New Testament as proclamations of total corruption that must be totally divested of its power."[17] Míguez is clear that the Apocalypse does not offer the kind of scientific analysis that is the Marxist's métier. Revelation 18 is not the first-century antecedent of *Das Kapital:* "Antiquity had no analytical science of economy," notes Míguez, and so "we cannot expect the New Testament texts to furnish us with a critique of today's oppressive mechanisms." Nevertheless the first-century Christians clearly

---

13. See Lynne Jones, ed., *The Debt Crisis: A Call to Action and Solidarity* (Debt Resource Material 1; Geneva: Commission on the Churches' Participation in Development/World Council of Churches, 1988); idem, *Taking a Stand: Highlights from the Ecumenical Hearing* (Debt Resource Material 2; Geneva: Commission on the Churches' Participation in Development/World Council of Churches, 1989). Latin American theologians were looking at the problem and already looking for solutions. See Franz J. Hinkelammert, *La deuda externa de America Latina: El autonomismo de la deuda externa* (San Jose, Costa Rica: DEI, 1988).

14. Phillip Berryman, *Liberation Theology* (Philadelphia: Temple University Press, 1987), 140.

15. Pablo Richard, *Apocalypse: A People's Commentary on the Book of Revelation* (Maryknoll, N.Y.: Orbis, 1995), 5.

16. Ibid., 173.

17. Néstor O. Míguez, "O Império e os pobres no tempo neotestamentário," *Revista de interpretação bíblica latino-americana* 5–6 (1990): 92.

understood "the real role of a system that turns into a 'deity.' "[18] The vision of Babylon's destruction is not a technical analysis of interlocking structures of oppression, but a recognition and indictment of those structures.

The indictment of economic structures that is the basic insight of Latin American interpretation of the Apocalypse is especially important because it presents a theological alternative to several influential modern traditions of interpretation that deny this critique of political economy. For different reasons respectively, Marxist, feminist, and premillennial dispensationalist readings of the Apocalypse tend to forestall the critique that Latin American exegetes read in Rev 18.

Engels Interpres

Friedrich Engels, the collaborator of Karl Marx, offers the classic Marxist interpretation of the Apocalypse. Though Engels considers Revelation to be the book of the New Testament that was most faithful to the sentiment of the first Christians, his reading of the Apocalypse disappoints expectations of economic analysis. Sustained class analysis is missing from his remarks on the Apocalypse in particular and his treatments of earliest Christianity in general.[19] Engels claims that "Christianity, like every great revolutionary movement, was made by the masses,"[20] but he does not argue that the early Christians undertook a revolution: "Despairing of material salvation," he explains, "the early Christians sought in its stead a spiritual salvation, a consolation in their consciousness to save them from utter despair."[21] Many were slaves, "deprived of . . . the possibility to free themselves, as the defeat of Spartacus had already proved."[22]

Engels's philosophy of history, with its strong residuum of Hegelian progressivism, did not countenance the revolutionary possibility of the early Jesus movements. Religion, in this instance early Christianity, became but a compensatory adjustment to the impossibility of revolution. The first Christians did not achieve revolutionary progress in ideology or in history. In Engels's view the consciousness of the early Jesus movements was limited to recognition of grievances without redress and, most important, without revolution. History was not yet ready for these miserable proletarians to successfully rebel. Late antiquity did not possess the material conditions suitable for revolution. Engels's historical criticism informs his interpretation of Revelation as truly reflective of its historical moment and the power relations that distinguished it. Yet his historical sensibility, a sensibility we

---

18. Ibid., 91.

19. David McLellan, *Marxism and Religion* (London: Macmillan, 1987), 43.

20. Friedrich Engels, "The Book of Revelation," in Karl Marx and Friedrich Engels, *On Religion* (New York: Schocken, 1964), 206.

21. Engels, "On the History of Early Christianity," in *On Religion*, 330.

22. Engels, "Ludwig Feuerbach and the End of Classical German Philosophy," in *On Religion*, 199.

now call Marxist, renders the Apocalypse as irrelevant to the present as it was reflective of the past.

The Clothed Woman

Feminist hermeneutics makes it clear that we must read the female image of Babylon in Rev 18 with careful attention to the threat of biblical misogyny. Some contemporary feminists argue that the figural violence that God visits upon Babylon is therefore violence visited in figure against a woman's body and, as a corollary, theological license for violence visited against women.[23] In the Israelite prophetic metaphor of the adulterous woman, her promiscuity represents the nation's sin. Sexual violence against her public exposure and rape represent divine retribution:[24] "These texts direct the reader's eye to images of sexually insatiable women, who fornicate with multiple lovers and are then stripped naked and sexually violated in public."[25] These metaphors perceive "women's sexuality as deviant and threatening to the status and well-being of men"[26] and "stress that [women's] sexuality is and ought to be an object of male possession and control."[27] Following T. Drorah Setel's characterization of Hosea's imagery as pornographic,[28] several feminist biblical scholars apply the term *pornoprophetic* to this misogynous imagery in the Hebrew Bible.[29] It is precisely this pornoprophetic imagery, however, that is missing from the female personification of Babylon. Babylon is the sign of international domination in the symbolic lexicon of the classical prophets; the female figure thus represents heathen empire, not apostate Israel.

---

23. Tina Pippin, *Death and Desire: The Rhetoric of Gender in the Apocalypse of John* (Louisville: Westminster/John Knox, 1992), 105.

24. See Hos 1–3; Jer 2:23–3:20; Ezek 16; 23 for the more egregious instances.

25. Alice A. Keefe, "Stepping In/Stepping Out: A Conversation between Ideological and Social Scientific Feminist Approaches to the Bible," *Journal for the Study of the New Testament* 73 (March 1999): 20.

26. Renita Weems, *Battered Love: Marriage, Sex, and Violence in the Hebrew Prophets* (Minneapolis: Fortress, 1995), 41.

27. Fokkelien van Dijk-Hemmes, "The Metaphorization of Woman in Prophetic Speech: An Analysis of Ezekiel 23," in *A Feminist Companion to the Latter Prophets* (ed. Athalya Brenner; Sheffield: Sheffield Academic Press, 1995), 253.

28. T. Drorah Setel, "Prophets and Pornography: Female Sexual Imagery in Hosea," in *Feminist Interpretation of the Bible* (ed. Letty Russell; Philadelphia: Westminster, 1985), 86–95.

29. See van Dijk-Hemmes, "Metaphorization of Woman in Prophetic Speech"; Athalya Brenner, "On Prophetic Propaganda and the Politics of 'Love': The Case of Jeremiah," in *A Feminist Companion to the Latter Prophets* (ed. Athalya Brenner; Sheffield: Sheffield Academic Press, 1995), 256–74; idem, "Pornoprophetics Revisited: Some Additional Reflections," *Journal for the Study of the Old Testament* 70 (1996): 63–86; idem, *The Intercourse of Knowledge: On Gendering Desire and "Sexuality" in the Hebrew Bible* (Leiden: Brill, 1997); Cheryl Exum, "The Ethics of Biblical Violence against Women," in *The Bible in Ethics: The Second Sheffield Colloquium* (ed. John W. Rogerson et al.; Sheffield: JSOT Press, 1995), 248–71; idem, "Prophetic Pornography," in *Plotted, Shot, and Painted: Cultural Representations of Biblical Women* (Sheffield: Sheffield Academic Press, 1996), 101–28. For a critical review of the literature, see Keefe, "Stepping In/Stepping Out," 20–22.

Nor does the text linger on the details of the woman's destruction: "After the courtesan is eliminated by her admirers…the curtain can fall. And this is what happens in chapter 18, which tells nothing more concerning the woman victim, but states her death and allows lamentation by three groups amongst her partisans."[30] The fornicating woman of Rev 18 is a prostitute: her sexual relationships are neither rebellion nor adventure. Sex is neither compulsive nor gratuitous. It is business — the business of political economy.

The whore's attire signifies the prosperity of the Asian cities under Flavian rule.[31] Thus the text highlights the woman's attire, not her nakedness. Her adornments, not her body, are the focus of the imagery. The luxuriantly illustrated commentary by Spaniard Beatus of Liebana is emblematic of how pictorial images translated the female image of Babylon in the effective history of the Apocalypse. Beatus published his *Commentarius in Apocalypsin* at the end of the eighth century. The copious illustrations of the *Commentarius* made it a celebrated work of medieval culture. It is known from thirty-two medieval manuscripts dating from the ninth to the thirteenth century. As Beatus announces in the preface to the work, it is a compendium of centuries of commentary tradition that he has dutifully compiled, innocent of any explicit attempt to emend, update, or reconcile the opinions of the authors he has excerpted. Consequently they do not reflect the *Sitz im Leben* of the editor, who labored under the conservatism of his era. More reflective of contemporary temper are the illustrations, which signal the increasing hostility toward the Muslim presence on the Iberian Peninsula that marked Spanish Christendom in the tenth century.

Madrid Biblioteca Nacional manuscript Vitrina 14–1 of the *Commentarius* is from the earlier branch of the manuscript tradition dating from the ninth century. In it the whore of Babylon is dressed in traditional royal garb and is seated on a throne that straddles diverging streams. The iconography renders the details of Rev 17:1–3. But in New York Pierpont Morgan Library manuscript Morgan 644, a tenth-century revision, the woman bears an ornamented crown and sits on a divan of stacked cushions. The streams are absent. The illustration depicts the whore as a royal Andalusian lady.[32] Even as the Spaniards came to hate the Moors, they came to admire them. Córdoba in Andalusia was not merely the capital of a caliphate and the center of three Islamic dynasties: it boasted the acme of medieval European art, architecture, and learning. Spain had been conquered by the Muslim sword, but thereafter by the architectural grandeur of the great mosque of Mezquita, the finest gold craftsmanship in all of Europe, and a university

---

30. Bovon, "Possession or Enchantment," 142–43.

31. See David Magie, *Roman Rule in Asia Minor* (Princeton: Princeton University Press, 1950), 583–86.

32. See John Williams, "The Purpose and Imagery in the Apocalypse Commentary of Beatus of Liebana," in *The Apocalypse in the Middle Ages* (ed. Richard Emmerson and Bernard McGinn; Ithaca: Cornell University Press, 1992), 217–33, esp. 219, 231.

library of over 400,000 volumes — precious gems that bedecked Muslim hegemony in southern Spain.

The adornments of Moorish dominion cover the body of the woman in these illustrations of Beatus's commentary on the Apocalypse. The illustrators tacitly understood that the adornments and the allure of their luxury, and not the woman *in se*, are the point of the biblical imagery. As I argue elsewhere,[33] Rev 18 does not share the erotic imagery of the prophetic traditions that it emulates and radically modifies. The reader's attention is turned to the whore's clothing, not her lack thereof. The vocabulary of her destruction, as Barbara R. Rossing shows,[34] is comprised of the military terminology of urban siege: it is not pornographic at all but martial. Babylon is not stripped naked as the lascivious women of Ezekiel's oracles. She is denuded and barren, a city stormed by a celestial assault. Babylon, celebrated and desired as a woman, is destroyed as an imperial metropolis.

Escapist Literature

According to premillennialist dispensationalism, developed in the nineteenth century by British biblical scholar John Nelson Darby (1800–82) and widely influential in popular Anglophone interpretations of the Apocalypse,[35] the church is snatched up out of history, "raptured," before the judgment of Babylon is consummated. This great eschatological escape, informed by 1 Thess 4:17, removes Christians from the challenge and danger of the Babylonian regime. The rule of this oppressive order, called the tribulation period, becomes irrelevant to the true believers, now safely ensconced in heaven.

But Rev 18:4 presents a problem for a rigorous premillennialism because of its direct address to "my people," an audience that, according to premillennialist eschatology, has been transported to heaven in the rapture. Darby admits as much: "Chapter xviii, announces the judgment. The one difficulty here is verse 4, coming where it is." Darby makes exegetical virtue of necessity in finessing a solution: "But, as every difficulty in Scripture, leads into further light."[36] Because the warning comes from heaven and is not

---

33. Allen Dwight Callahan, "Apocalypse and Political Economy: Some Notes on Revelation 18," *Horizons in Biblical Theology* 21.1 (June 1999): 55–57.

34. Barbara R. Rossing, "A Choice between Two Cities: A Wisdom Topos in the Apocalypse" (Ph.D. diss., Harvard University, 1998), 122–34; published subsequently as *A Choice between Two Cities: Whore, Bride, and Empire in the Apocalypse* (Harrisburg, Pa.: Trinity, 1999), esp. 87–97, where she treats feminist critiques of the imagery.

35. John Nelson Darby, *Synopsis of the Books of the Bible* (London: Gregg, 1857), 5.516–602. Darby's influence on fundamentalism has been pervasive. See Ernest R. Sandeen, *The Roots of Fundamentalism* (Chicago: University of Chicago Press, 1970; repr. Grand Rapids: Baker, 1978), xix, 173; Larry V. Crutchfield, *The Origins of Dispensationalism: The Darby Factor* (Lanham, Md.: University Press of America, 1992). Darby's complicated dispensationalist hermeneutics and premillennialist eschatology, explicated in thirty-four volumes, were popularized just before the turn of the century by William Kelly Mackintosh and through the copious annotations of the Scofield Bible.

36. Darby, *Synopsis of the Books of the Bible*, 5.583.

sounded by an angel of judgment on earth, it "supposes spiritual apprehension of heaven's mind. This is the case when it is simply a voice from heaven. This call, then, was a spiritual call, not a manifest judgment."[37] The heavenly cry is merely an eleventh-hour echo from above — "heaven's mind" — before the catastrophic demise of the condemned empire.

Premillennialist dispensationalism thereby commends an eschatological quietism that views the evils of seductive empire from a sheltered, celestial vantage. Darby's reading renders the judgments of the Apocalypse superfluous to the present age. Thus the intellectual heritage of premillennialist dispensationalism is the most reactionary influence in the *Wirkungsgeschichte* of the Book of Revelation. And this heritage is most prevalent in much of modern Anglophone interpretation, especially in the United States.

Revelation 18: Justice and Judgment

Latin American exegetes, however, insist on the urgent relevance of the Apocalypse and particularly of Rev 18. Brazilian Paulo Augusto de Souza Nogueira argues that Rev 18 is a prophetic denunciation of global violence in response to the outcry of those who are suffering and oppressed: the issue for the Seer and ultimately for God is justice that is concrete, economic, and political.[38] For Günter Wolff, another Brazilian, "the entire chapter accentuates the economic question as being the key to the whole empire. The attack is against the economic system, the viability of which requires the political order. Both [the system and the order] are of the devil."[39]

In 1989, the same year that the fall of the Berlin Wall sounded the death knell of Marxist socialism in Eastern Europe and the ascendancy of neoliberal capitalism, Argentine scholar Ricardo Foulkes argued that the intercourse in which those trafficking with Babylon amass enormous fortunes is "an idolatrous cult of Mammon, a cult that can only merit the name 'fornication.'" The murderous dominance of transnational wealth and the elites who trade in it constitutes both John's world system and our own. Foulkes correlates the "emphasis on the economic dimension prevalent throughout chapter 18" and the contemporary dominance of global capital: "It is as though this chapter describes our contemporary situation."[40]

---

37. Ibid., 5.583–84.

38. Paulo Augusto de Souza Nogueira, "A realização da justiça de Deus na história — algumas considerações sobre a tradição da inversão escatológica no Apocalipse 18," *Revista de interpretação bíblica latino-americana* 11 (1992): 98–104 (Spanish edition = 113–21).

39. "Todo o capítulo acentua a questão econômica como sendo a chave de todo o império. O ataque é contra o sistema econômico que para se viabilizar necessita do poder político e os dois são do diabo"; Günter Wolff, "A utopia do fim e não o fim da utopia!" *Estudos bíblicos* 49 (1996): 86–87.

40. "El regodeo con ella que embelesaba a los magnates y a los presidentes de la tierra tenía raíz financiera, pero los enredaba necesariamente en un culto idolátrico a Mamón, culto que sólo merece el nombre de 'fornicación.' Parece como si este capítulo describiera en detalle

One year after the publication of Foulkes's commentary, Dagoberto Ramírez Fernández, Chilean Methodist minister and former dean of the Evangelical Theological Seminary in Santiago, interpreted Rev 18 as the divine condemnation of multinational corporations. He argues that the multinationals are agents of a neoliberal capitalist "economic model [that] has left the countries of the Third World with the weight of tremendous foreign debt that has become impossible to repay."[41] Ramírez Fernández undertakes an analysis of Rev 18 "because...the characteristics of the reigning political power [of the Roman Empire] and the expression of the economic project that sustained it are reflected in this chapter."[42] "The economic aspect dominates that text," he observes, and "the political aspect is also present and closely linked.... One cannot be understood without the other."[43]

In this understanding of the text, Rev 18 is not merely an allegory of contemporary neoliberal rapacity in Latin America. It is a critique of the first-century Roman imperial economy. This is, according to Ramírez Fernández, one element of "the theological message" of the chapter. The other element, however, is "the conditions under which the Christian community develops a message that constitutes a prophetic witness that transcends history."[44] The identification of Roman imperial economy with contemporary global capitalism is not allegorical, not a one-to-one correspondence of ancient, apocalyptic signifiers and neoliberalist restructuring as the exclusive signified of those signifiers. The identification is analogical: the injustice, poverty, and mass death of the Roman regime corresponds to the injustice, poverty, and mass death of our global economy. Interpretation renders the "prophetic witness" of Rev 18 not by decoding its signs but by extending them: "The text as literature comes from a historical situation. Once transformed into a written text, however, it gains independence from the original historical situation and can be extended, in this case, to the contemporary situation that we want to illuminate."[45] The sign of the beast, for all its contemporary relevance, remains open. The prophetic witness is transcendent: as all witnesses that are truly prophetic, it bears a testimony for its time, for our time, and for all time.

---

nuestra situación actual"; Ricardo Foulkes, *El Apocalipsis de San Juan: Una lectura desde américa latina* (Buenos Aires: Nueva Creación/Grand Rapids: Eerdmans, 1989), 189.

41. Dagoberto Ramírez Fernández, "The Judgment of God on Multinationals: Revelation 18," in *Subversive Scriptures: Revolutionary Readings of the Christian Bible in Latin America* (ed. and trans. Leif E. Vaage; Valley Forge, Pa.: Trinity, 1997), 75. Originally published as "O juizo de Deus contra as transnacionais—Apocalipse 18," *Revista de interpretação bíblica latino-americana* 5–6 (1990): 49–67.

42. Ibid., 78.
43. Ibid., 97.
44. Ibid., 78.
45. Ibid., 96.

Papal Denuncio

Latin American interpreters insist that the image of Babylon remain semi-
otically open to identify contemporary powers of oppression. José Comblin
argues that Babylon is a sign for any power "that arises against God, inspired
by Satan," and "is not incarnated only in Rome": "Some may find today that
Babylon the Great is those groups of global financiers who rule the capitals
and direct the market of global financial speculation. Therein is the great
power of oppression that keeps humanity in a state of misery and abjection,
leaving the benefits for a small elite of collaborators in the world system."[46]
This semiotic openness in Latin American interpretations of the beast of the
Apocalypse is distinctive in the effective history of the Book of Revelation.
Other traditions of interpretation demand a one-to-one correspondence of
the beast and the woman with a putative evil power. Though the Greek
Orthodox Church omitted the Apocalypse from its canon for a millennium,
the book received unprecedented attention after the fall of Constantinople.
After 1453, Greek exegetes began to read the Apocalypse as a book of oracles being realized in their own time: twenty Greek commentaries on the
Book of Revelation were written in the period of Turkish rule.[47] For these
Greek exegetes, Revelation described their own time, for they were living in
the last days. From the vantage of Turkish oppression, Greek interpreters
believed that they enjoyed the ultimate hermeneutic privilege of reading a
book about the eschaton as they lived through the eschaton: they could even
understand things in the text that their predecessors either misunderstood
or failed to notice.[48]

The following excerpt from the work of Anastasius of Gordion, *Treatise on Muhammad and against the Romans* (*Syngramma peri Moameth
kai kata Lateinon*, 1717–18), is typical of Byzantine "historical method,"
which identified contemporary persons and events with figures in the
Apocalypse:

---

46. "Roma representa naquela época a presença do pecado no mundo, dum pecado global,
estrutural, social. No decorrer da história esse poder que se levanta contra Deus, inspirado
por Satanás, não se encarna somente em Roma. Hoje em dia alguns achariam que a Grande
Babilônia são os grupos financeiros mundiais que dominam os capitais e dirigem o mercado da
especulação financeira mundial. Ali está a grande força de opressão que mantém a humanidade
num estado de miséria e de prostração deixando os benefícios a uma pequena elite de colab-
oradores do sistema mundial"; José Comblin, "O Apocalipse de João e o fim do mundo,"
Estudos bíblicos 59 (1998): 49.

47. On this resurgence of interest in the Apocalypse in a tradition that, until its ordeal
with foreign oppression, had no use for it, see Stergiou Argyriou, "The Use of the Historical
Method as the Preeminent Method of Interpretation of the Apocalypse of John in the Time of
Turkish Rule" (in Greek), in *The Apocalypse of John: Philological, Historical, Hermeneutical,
and Theological Problems* (ed. I. Karabidopoulos et al.; Leukosia, Cyprus: Archepiscopate of
Cyprus, 1991), 65–77; also idem, *Les exégèses grecques de l'Apocalypse à l'époque turque
(1453–1821)* (Thessalonike: Hetaireia Makedonikon Spoudon, 1982).

48. Argyriou, "Use of the Historical Method," 66.

Behold... it is coming to pass today just like the other things of the Antichrist, because over in the east you can hear nothing but "Allah, Allah, Prophet Muhammad." And nowhere is there the Word of God.... Go also to the west, and you will not hear anything there except, "O Pope, O Pope," and, "Have faith in the Pope!" And nowhere is there Christ or the Word of God.[49]

A great cloud of witnesses would join Byzantine interpreters in the *Wirkungs-geschichte* of Rev 18 who saw the Roman papacy ruling Babylon. Among the earliest readings of the Babylon imagery of the Apocalypse as an indictment of the Roman papacy in Western Europe is the allusion to the Apocalypse in Dante's *Divine Comedy*. The venal popes in lines 106–8 of canto 19 of the *Inferno* are "shepherds the Evangelist accused / When she that sits upon the waters / committing fornication with kings was seen by him."[50] Dante was a Catholic royalist who thought that the pope had no business in affairs of state. He offered his critique in the spirit of Saint Francis, that is, in the spirit of Catholic reform. Dante identified the popes as "the kings of the earth" in light of his denial of papal authority in temporal affairs—a sentiment that caused his work to be listed in the *Index* in 1554, where it remained for over three centuries until it was removed by Pope Leo XIII.

Later antipapal polemic in the effective history of Rev 18 flourished with the Protestant Reformation and its legacy, where it waxed obsessive and vicious. Martin Luther's first preface to the Apocalypse, written in 1521, is disparaging and dismissive.[51] But in his second preface, written after his excommunication, the sack of Rome by Charles V, and the diets of Augsburg and Worms, the reformer had radically changed his opinion of the book. A text of weird ciphers now teemed with the apocalyptically veiled enemies of ecclesiastical history and personal experience: the Revelation was for Luther, as for the Greek exegetes under Turkish rule, an encryption of the life story of the church. For Luther, the two beasts of Rev 13 were the Holy Roman Empire and the Roman Catholic papacy; the second and third woes of 11:14 were, respectively, "in the East, Mohammed and the Saracens" and "in the

---

49. Ibid., 69: "Ἰδού... ἐνεργεῖται τήν σήμερον καθὼς καί τά ἄλλα τά τοῦ Ἀντίχριστου. Διότι, πέρασε εἰς τά μέρη τῆ Ἀνατολῆς καί δέν θέλεις ἀκούσει ἄλλο παρα· Ἀλλαχ, Ἀλλαχ, Μεχμέτ ρασούλ. Καί οὐδαμοῦ Λόγος Θεοῦ.... Ἄμε καί εἰς τά μέρη τῆς Δύσεως, καί οὐδέν θέλεις ἀκούσει καί ἐκεῖ ἄλλο εἰμή· Πάπα, Πάπα καί πιστεύεις εἰς τόν Πάπαν. Καί οὐδαμοῦ Χριστός ἤ Λόγος Θεοῦ." In the history of interpretation of the beasts in the Book of Revelation, bestiality proves to be in the eye of the beholder. Italian abbot Joachim of Fiore understood Babylon to symbolize not Rome but Constantinople and the Greek Orthodox Church (*Expositio in Apocalypsim*, fols. 192rb–193rb). Turnabout is fair play. In a *coyuntura* not so long ago and not as far away, however, Latin American theologian León Muñoz identified the beast of Rev 13 as neoliberal capitalism. See his "El neoliberalismo—resopla el monstruo de las siete cabezas," *Centro de estudos bíblicos informativo* 17 (1993): 17–20; and idem, "El nombre de la bestia es capitalismo liberal," *Itacate* (November 1993): 16p.

50. Dante accepts the traditional identification of John of Patmos with the author of the Fourth Gospel.

51. *Works of Martin Luther* (Grand Rapids: Baker, 1982), 6.489.

west, papacy and empire."[52] Revelation 18 depicted for the Reformer the destruction of the papal court, whose "courtesans...rob endowments and steal the incomes."[53] Luther's economic critique begins and ends with the accusation of papal malfeasance.

Once commentators begin pointing the finger at the pope they have little interest in other features of the text. We see an outstanding instance of this myopic mode of interpretation in British activist Granville Sharp (1735–1813). Sharp was among the cadre of British abolitionists whose agitation against slavery contributed to the British Empire's ostensible exit from the transatlantic slave trade in the second quarter of the nineteenth century. Sharp was a lay Bible scholar with an obsessive interest in the apocalyptic oracles of biblical prophecy. His extended tract, *An Inquiry, Whether the Description of Babylon, Contained in the 18th Chapter of the Revelations, Agrees Perfectly with Rome as a City?*,[54] answers the question posed in its title emphatically in the affirmative. Sharp's seventy-page anti-Catholic screed is exclusively concerned to identify the "scarlet-colored beast" of Revelation as the Roman Catholic Church.

Sharp's hermeneutical key to Rev 18 is anti-Catholicism. Though 18:13 mentions slavery explicitly, a reference not lost on some abolitionists in the United States crafting biblical arguments against slavery,[55] Sharp, the career abolitionist and comrade of William Wilberforce, glosses the sale of souls as the traffic of Catholic indulgences. He interprets the "prophets and saints" in 18:24 as those who have fallen by the Catholic sword: for Sharp the verse is an indictment, among other offenses, of the thirteenth-century crusade in southern France against the Albigensians and the mass executions of Huguenots. Oblivious to the rapacity and violence of British oppression in Ireland, Sharp paints the Irish Rebellions of 1641–43 as treacherous attacks on innocent Protestants. Sharp's enthusiasm for the interpretation of apocalyptic signs and his hatred of the Roman Catholic Church, common sentiments among Britons in the eighteenth and nineteenth centuries, rendered him deaf to what the text of Rev 18 could be saying about slavery and colonialism of his own time.

The antipapal polemic fails to engage the economic and ethical elements that are so prominent in the text. As Schüssler Fiorenza argues, the ethical-political interest of Revelation "prohibits Christians from projecting 'evil' only on others, while holding themselves exempt from it. Revelation speaks not only of judgment against the dehumanizing antidivine powers but also

---

52. Ibid., 6.484.
53. Ibid. (slightly modified).
54. Granville Sharp, *An Inquiry, Whether the Description of Babylon, Contained in the 18th Chapter of the Revelations, Agrees Perfectly with Rome as a City?* (London: Calvert, 1805).
55. For some citations of Rev 18:13 in American abolitionist exegesis, see Callahan, "Apocalypse and Political Economy," 60 n. 45.

warns Christians not to succumb to their concrete pressures."[56] Unlike the Byzantines, Luther, and Sharp, Latin American interpreters indict their own elites as complicit in the violence and injustice of the world system. The prostitution of Rev 18 is not a victimless crime: the "johns" also share the guilt and the fate of the whore.

Wolff makes explicit the analogy of the political economy condemned in Rev 18:5–8 and Latin American "national security states":

> God is going to judge the entire system based on its actions against life. Though it has received power from the devil, there is no deliverance from the judgment of God. Nothing and no one delivers from the judgment of God. The oppressive system always goes along as if it cannot be called to account by justice and does everything with impunity. We see this in the actions of Latin American dictatorships, where there is almost no condemnation of torture, murder, and especially for the entry of international capital (something that continues still today) that gave rise (and still gives rise) to poverty and death among the people.[57]

"In every age," writes Ramírez Fernández "the community of the faithful is called to separate itself from any political-economic system that does not have the well-being of all humanity as its ultimate goal."[58] Revelation 18 suggests that the "prophetic role of the church in our time" is "to denounce the hidden intentions of any system that seeks total hegemony through the imposition of an economic system that assumes idolatrous characteristics."[59]

Contemporary Latin American interpretations of Rev 18 offer an ecumenical indictment of the principalities and powers of oppression in this and every era. These interpretations are ecumenical in their embrace of the victims of oppression as well as in their indictment of the principalities and powers. The violence of global capital is no respecter of persons. The list of martyrs mentioned in Rev 18:24 stretches from the Roman imperial period to today to include those great and small who have paid with their lives for their testimony against injustice. "In relation to these 'martyrs,'" insists Foulkes, "it is important to observe that John's protest is not limited to the slaughter of the followers of Jesus; he laments the loss of other lives cut down for their dedication to high ideals.... John mourns not only the assassination of Monsignor Romero in El Salvador but that of Benigno

---

56. Schüssler Fiorenza, *Invitation to the Book of Revelation,* 30–31.

57. "Deus vai julgar todo o sistema baseado em ações contra a vida. Mesmo tendo recebido o poder do diabo, não está a salvo do julgamento de Deus. Nada e ninguém estão a slavo do juízo de Deus. O sistema opressor sempre age como se não pudesse ser alcançado pelo justiça e faz tudo para ficar impune. Vejam-se as ações das ditaduras latino-americanas onde quase não houve julgamento pelas torturas e assassinatos e principalmente pela entrega da economia ao capital internacional (algo que continua ainda hoje) que gerou (e ainda gera) pobreza e morte entre o povo"; Wolff, "A utopia do fim e não o fim da utopia!" 86.

58. Ramírez Fernández, "Judgment of God on Multinationals," 99.

59. Ibid., 99–100.

Aquino in the Philippines."[60] On this reading, the text of Rev 18 is a complex apocalyptic oracle against the interlocking directorates of corporations and governments, the worship of wealth, the complicity of local elites, and the murderous exploitation of the wretched of the earth from late antiquity to the present.

III.

And in you was found the blood of prophets and of saints, and of all who have been slaughtered on earth.

— Revelation 18:24

On 12 March 2002 paramilitary gunmen killed two leaders of the union representing Colombian employees of the United States-based coal-mining firm Drummond Ltd. in northern Colombia. The killers, presumed members of United Self-Defense Forces of Colombia, pulled local union president Valmore Locarno Rodríguez and vice president Víctor Hugo Orcasita off an unmarked company-chartered bus and shot them. On 8 April 2002 Diafanol Sierra Vargas, director of the Sindicato Nacional de Trabajadores de la Industria de Alimentos (the Food-Workers Union) and member of the Organización Femenina Popular, or Popular Women's Organization, was assassinated by paramilitaries. He was dragged into the street from his home and shot dead in front of his family.[61] That same day right-wing paramilitaries pulled Alfredo Zapata Herrera off a bus and killed him. The military and the police knew that Zapata, a leader in the local construction workers' union, had been targeted for assassination, but did nothing to protect him. He was the forty-fifth union organizer killed in Colombia in 2002. Six more have been killed since.

Amnesty International is now concerned for the safety of the president of the Organización Femenina Popular, Yolanda Becerra. The paramilitary group Autodefensas Unidas de Colombia (AUC), or the United Self-Defense Forces of Colombia, is reportedly planning to kill her. Members of the Union Sindical Obrera (USO), the petroleum worker's union, have been informed by credible sources of a plot to kill Becerra. She has been threatened in the past and may have been targeted because her organization continues to denounce human rights violations committed by Colombian paramilitary groups.[62]

Three of every four union organizers killed around the world are killed in Colombia. According to figures by the country's leading labor organization, the Unified Labor Confederation (CUT), right-wing paramilitary

60. Foulkes, *El Apocalipsis de San Juan*, 193.
61. *www.rabble.ca/news_full_story.shtml?x=1118a&url=*.
62. Ibid.

groups have killed over 1,500 labor leaders in Colombia since 1995. In 2001 at least 129 trade unionists were murdered.[63] Four thousand civilians have been murdered for political reasons — up from 1,187 in 2000. The vast majority were assassinated for speaking out for political and economic justice or massacred to scare their neighbors into abandoning land coveted by oil companies, cattle ranchers, or cocaine traffickers. Increasing oil production in Colombia to meet the demands of the United States will inevitably require forcing more farmers and indigenous people off their land. Escalating the war achieves this end — as do crop fumigations, massacres, and assassinations financed directly and indirectly by the United States government.[64]

Latin American interpreters read Rev 18 as a text that traces the ties that bind dollars to death in Colombia and other countries in Latin America. In its text is written in blood the testimony of all who have been slaughtered by the present victory of global capital. That blood cries out against markets, governments, and corporations as they conspire to coerce and seduce the peoples of the world.

---

63. *United Steel Workers of America* (16 March 2001).
64. *www.commondreams.org/views02/0531-07.htm.*

17

The Gnosis Issue in Contemporary European Scholarship

A Problem of Psychopathology, Politics, or Human Rights?

Dieter Georgi

Elisabeth Schüssler Fiorenza has always sought to reopen closed chapters of history and to assist people to speak who have been silenced. In honor of her, this paper attempts to readdress an issue allegedly settled and to give voice to persons and issues whose memory has been defaced if not altogether wiped out.[1] Their movement was hushed and caricatured because it protested too much. Many women had been active in that movement. I speak of gnostics and the movement of gnosis.

Presently, Berlin is an oasis in a desert of European gnosis research. In earlier days, Germany was a center in that field. Critical editions of gnostic texts and interpretations of both known texts and documents newly discovered by German researchers dominated the field. They presented constructive views of the religious, philosophical, theological, and social reality of Gnosticism and the people behind them as represented by these texts. Today, the situation is almost entirely the opposite. With a few admirable exceptions in Berlin and the work of some individuals elsewhere who devote their time and energy to this now outlandish field (especially Professor Kurt Rudolph in Marburg), Germany's gnosis research has become an underdeveloped country.

As a result, the Nag Hammadi documents today find little attention in the land of Bousset and Bultmann. The principal challenge that these texts present to the views of the heresiomachs of old concerning the gnostics is not sufficiently recognized. Instead, the ideologically biased perceptions of Irenaeus and his followers about the form and content of gnostic writings

---

1. A version of this essay was read at the International Meeting of the Society of Biblical Literature, 19–22 July 2002, at Humboldt University in Berlin, Germany.

still form much of the theological mindset about the "heresies" of old. Famous German publications on gnosis of years past have received mausoleum status and are thus neutralized. Neither in contemporary German theology nor in the German public at large is there any serious recognition of the fact that Gnosticism was once a major world religion with links to Judaism, Christianity, Hellenistic-Roman paganism, and Eastern religions.

There seems to be some force behind this contemporary marginalization and active neglect among German theologians inside and outside the university. Its proficiency shows in the swift negative reaction that the term *gnostic* evokes today. The negative reaction to that term works as if it were an invocation of threat and fear. Almost a millennium after the final end of active Gnosticism, the invocation *gnostic* still evokes the same feelings the likes of Irenaeus and Hippolytus had and that they attempted to create among their readers as well. Something like an active dememorization of the gnostics exists in established university and church quarters.[2] This dememorization is advertised as an act of sanitation of the scholarly and the ecclesial mind, for the future protection of reason and faith.

Contemporary gnosis research, especially in Europe, is still dominated by the agreements of the Messina conference of 1966.[3] This conference is frequently quoted as evidence for the present German disbelief in an early origin of Gnosticism and the rejection of its relevance for the evolution of Judaism and Christianity during the first three centuries C.E. The 1966 Messina conference essentially confirmed five major claims of Irenaeus and his heresiomachic colleagues and successors:

1. Gnosticism was basically a dualistic ideology, in fact, a ditheistic *Weltanschauung*.

2. Gnosticism was based on revelation.

3. An objectified mythical narration was essential for this gnostic *Weltanschauung*.

4. Gnostic ideology was mainly a perverted secondary development within the church.

5. Gnosticism was organized in different systems.[4]

The Nag Hammadi find, however, presented the world with original gnostic documents by any definition of "Gnosticism." Several documents had

---

2. There seems to still exist a lasting trauma that causes aggressive feelings as protective means.

3. Ugo Bianchi, ed., *Le origini dello gnosticismo, Colloquio di Messina, 13–18 Aprile 1966: Testi e Discussioni* (2d ed.; Studies in the History of Religions, Supplement to Numen 12; Leiden: Brill, 1970).

4. A thorough reading of the essays collected in Bianchi's *Le origini dello gnosticismo* shows, however, that the *communis opinio* present at this conference was not as unified and consistent as the later references to the "Messina resolution" usually pretended.

no traces of Christian thought, some were more Jewish, and a few even had pagan character. Others obviously were Christianized but only superficially. And some were clearly Christian-gnostic documents as well. In many ways, the disparity of the Nag Hammadi tracts is immense — even among those that the majority of scholars consider gnostic. Distilling an objective definition or common ideology from these documents, Christian or not, is impossible. There is neither a clear shared myth nor a clear systematic structure, much less a common system. In fact, the mythical narrations, wherever and whatever they are in these documents, are anything but consistent. Indeed, much of it appears to be rather confused. This is, however, not because of a general craziness, as the church fathers wanted the gnostics to appear to their readers. This confusion is intentional — intending to deobjectify anything that might come across as objective information. Even those texts that show resemblances to the alleged systems of the heresiomachs never present such systems in full, even less in any systematic form. In addition, the resemblances are accompanied by differences, sometimes rather strong ones. Were the Nag Hammadi texts our only evidence, no one could imagine gnostic systems, let alone reconstruct them.[5]

The Messina conference of 1966 had devastating consequences for gnosis scholarship, especially on the biblical side. It has become fashionable, allegedly more scholarly, to discredit the exegetical and historical assessment that the old guard gave to the presence of gnosis and gnostics in the New Testament. Younger scholars do not even dare to mention the terms *gnosis* or *gnostics* positively in their publications on New Testament or intertestamental exegesis for fear of not getting a job. Even in patristic scholarship the gnosis issue is marginalized.

I find this slowdown on the patristic front particularly astonishing. Take for instance, the amazing eradication of Günther Bornkamm's introduction to the *Acts of Thomas* from the fifth edition of Hennecke-Schneemelcher's *New Testament Apocrypha*.[6] Bornkamm had written his introduction for the third edition of this work, and it was also included in the fourth edition. As an assistant of Bornkamm at Heidelberg University, I became involved in the final stages of his work on the text and introduction of the *Acts of Thomas* for the then-new edition of Hennecke-Schneemelcher. My main task was the arrangement of the final text, which I based on the preliminary work of my predecessor, Gerhard Iber, and some additions that Ulrich Wilckens provided. This task was not eased by the request of the publisher and editor

5. It is very surprising that even in the collection of essays edited by Kurt Rudolph under the title *Gnosis und Gnostizismus* (Wege der Forschung 262; Darmstadt: Wissenschaftliche Buchgesellschaft, 1975), gnosis is still looked at under the aspect of a "mythical *Weltanschauung*." This is even the case in the contribution of Hans Jonas to that collection: "Typologische und historische Abgrenzung des Phänomens der Gnosis," 626–45.

6. Wilhelm Schneemelcher, ed., *Neutestamentliche Apokryphen*, vol. 2: *Apostolisches, Apokalyptisches und Verwandtes* (5th ed.; Tübingen: Mohr/Siebeck, 1989). The 3d and 4th editions were published by the same publisher in 1959 and 1968.

to retain the earlier edition's text of the *Acts of Thomas* as much as possible. Practically speaking, this increased the labor and the headaches. Bornkamm came in only at the end of these laborious efforts of mine with spot-checks of some questionable passages and issues I had singled out. In addition, he and I collaborated on a new translation of the *Hymn of the Pearl*. Here the text of the earlier edition had too many shortcomings.[7] Our text of the *Hymn of the Pearl* and of the *Acts of Thomas* is almost entirely reprinted in the fifth edition. The introduction, however, is gone. There is no argument given for the removal of Bornkamm's introduction. Was it the gnostic attribution of the *Acts of Thomas* by Bornkamm that caused the elimination, that made it too dated for the editor?

As in his dissertation, Bornkamm based his interpretation of the *Acts of Thomas* in his introduction on its peculiar literary character. Hans J. W. Drijvers in his new introduction agrees with this, however without reference to Bornkamm:

> Die unterschiedlichen Erzählungen, deren Reihenfolge sicherlich nicht willkürlich ist, können deshalb auf eine symbolisch-typologische Weise gelesen und gedeutet werden, für die jedes Detail einen Sinn inner-halb des Ganzen hat.... Zu dieser kunstvoll durchdachten literarischen Struktur und Ordnung gehört auch die mehrfache Verwendung bes-timmter Wörter und Termini in verschiedenen Kontexten, die jedoch aufeinander verweisen und dem Ganzen einen ganz bestimmten Sinn verleihen, weil sie sich gegenseitig erhellen.[8]

In this reference, Drijvers does not name the real author of this stylistic observation. He points, though, to the dissertation of my student Michael LaFargue.[9] In his dissertation on the *Acts of Thomas*, LaFargue himself builds on Bornkamm's work and cites his indebtedness to my former teacher. In what follows, however, Drijvers does not pursue this important, indeed decisive, literary observation at all but falls back on the rather dated toolbox of anti-gnostic ideologizing. What he presents as the theology of Thomas is

---

7. Here the most stunning confounding of reality has occurred. Hans Drijvers reprinted Bornkamm's and my translation of this hymn with no change. He adds, however, a footnote (*Neutestamentliche Apokryphen*, 2.343 n. 155) to Bornkamm's edition, regarding his and my translation. For this footnote, Drijvers copies (without credit) parts of Bornkamm's lengthy footnote from the third edition on the particular problems of the text of the *Hymn of the Pearl* (303 n. 1). Drijvers edits that footnote not only by cutting out essential elements but by adding three more recent works and by the following initial remark: "Die hier gebotene Übersetzung ist im großen und ganzen mit der von G. Hoffmann, 'Zwei Hymnen der Thomasakten,' in: ZNW 4, 1903, S.273ff. gelieferten identisch." Why this drastic change of Bornkamm's note through this addition, which contradicts what Bornkamm says about the use of Hoffmann? Bornkamm and I used the reconstructed text given by Hoffmann and consulted his translation as we did others too. Does Drijvers want to accuse Bornkamm indirectly of plagiarizing? Drijvers's hiding and modifying of texts and facts is truly astounding.

8. Schneemelcher, *Neutestamentliche Apokryphen*, 2.292.

9. Michael LaFargue, *Language and Gnosis* (Harvard Dissertations in Religion 18; Philadelphia: Fortress, 1985).

a kind of systematizing of relatively simplistic theologumena. Yet the literary makeup of these acts works aggressively against such confusion of theology with organized information. Drijvers does not notice this since he neglects the forms and style of this complex work despite the initial reference quoted above. Drijvers instead offers material arguments against the gnostic character of the *Acts of Thomas* that are not convincing at all. He calls up Tatian and Bardesanes as comparable to the *Acts of Thomas,* as if they were definitely non-gnostic, and this, despite a number of scholars — even conservative ones — who allege them to be gnostic. Drijvers also invokes as the *Sitz im Leben* of the *Acts of Thomas* the magic blanket term of conservative anti-gnostics of the 1950s to the 1980s: "encratism." In addition, he brings in "Middle Platonism," the hodgepodge of the history of Hellenistic philosophy.

Within all of this mix, the *Acts of Thomas* loses its profile. Its peculiar style, initially referred to by Drijvers, is deprived of its guiding force, a force that taken seriously would demonstrate powerfully the intentional transcending of all objectifying language in the *Acts of Thomas,* not only that of romance and myth but also that of theological and philosophical conceptuality and of alleged dogmatic objectification. Such a deobjectifying tendency, characteristic for the *Acts of Thomas,* is also significant for all gnostic literature. The deobjectifying tendency of gnostic texts is a major instrument of their overturning of the sense of reality. It is a tool of gnostic hermeneutics of interpretation of traditions and of its hermeneutics of existence. The literary nature of the *Acts of Thomas* should have given strong signals that storytelling and mythicizing mingled — myth not of the old type but of a new, consciously artificial type. With this mingling, both reality and illusion were turned topsy-turvy.[10] The driving force in these gnostic ventures was not "gnosis" as informative knowledge but as existential knowledge. "Existential" here is not understood in a Heideggerian sense, that is, merely as individualistic, but also with a strong cosmic dimension, therefore more precisely translated and defined as "consciousness" in the most comprehensive and complex sense of the term.[11]

---

10. See Dieter Georgi, "Das Wesen der Weisheit nach der 'Weisheit Salomos,'" and "Ergänzende Beobachtungen zum Thema 'Gnosis und Politik,'" both in *Gnosis und Politik* (ed. Jacob Taubes; Religionstheorie und politische Theologie 2; Munich: Fink & Schöningh, 1984), 66–81, 90–91.

11. Drijvers would have done better had he heeded my advice that I gave at the end of Bornkamm's introduction to the *Acts of Thomas* in the third edition (308). I speak there (in criticism of Klijn's commentary on the *Acts of Thomas*) of the fact that what we now call Orthodoxy in Syria had been clearly a very late phenomenon presupposing strong gnostic movements: "Diesen Prozeß zeigen gerade die ATh aufs deutlichste in ihrer unbefangenen Aufnahme gnostischer Mythen und Gedankengutes in Liedern, liturgischen Stücken und Erzählungen, der Verkleidung von Mythen und Legenden, aber auch ihrer Überarbeitung im Sinne einer Orthodoxie, in der die später als häretisch geltenden Stellen geändert oder ausgemerzt wurden (Textgeschichte). Diesen Vorgang vermag nur eine Analyse aufzuzeigen, die anders als es bei Klijn geschieht, weiter gespannte religionsgeschichtliche, literarische und formgeschichtliche

The replacement of Bornkamm's introduction to the *Acts of Thomas* in the 1989 fifth edition of Hennecke-Schneemelcher amounts literally to what we call in German *totschweigen* (to silence unto death). A famous scholar who had just died was buried once more. A *damnatio memoriae* of sorts was committed against him. Such an impression of tendentiousness in this case could have been avoided only if all introductions to the third and fourth edition of Hennecke-Schneemelcher and their authors had been replaced in the fifth edition. However this was not the case.

Another interesting example of the mildew-producing effect of the Messina conference on German scholarship with respect to the study of Gnosticism is the fact that even the exegesis of a scholar who is not totally anti-gnostic is affected. In his commentary on 1 Corinthians, Wolfgang Schrage quotes the Messina conference as he discusses the possible gnostic background of the congregation in Corinth and of the letter.[12] Moved by that conference Schrage opts for a Gnosticism *in statu nascendi,* or better for "gnosticizing pneumatics," whatever that means. He then separates the discussion of wisdom from the discussion of Gnosticism. This makes him helpless vis-à-vis the combination in 1 Cor 2 of the motifs of wisdom with those of cross, mystery, revelation and hiding, governing powers, deception by the divinity, tradition, "depths of divinity," spiritual insight and power. The dialectics of Paul's interpretive procedure are not grasped by Schrage because he evades the gnostic perspective, where all these factors would best find their connections and come to a point. The very fact that Paul's style in 1 Cor 1–2 comes especially close to the forms of the gnostic approach to texts, traditions, and reality is not sufficiently recognized by Schrage. The high degree of dialectic, paradox, irony, and outright satire in these passages is not adequately appreciated, even less the closeness of this linguistic format to the style of gnostic texts. This corresponds to the fact that stylistic and form-critical questions and observations rarely inform hermeneutical perceptions in contemporary presentations of the gnosis issue in Germany.

Untersuchungen vereint und mit der Textgeschichte verbindet." Drijvers's least cogent argument in his anti-gnostic treatment of the *Acts of Thomas* is the claim that the *Hymn of the Pearl* is based on the Synoptic parables of the prodigal son and of the pearl (Luke 15:11–32; Matt 13:45–46). This unfounded argument has been proven wrong many times. The significance of these two parables is not so much their being about a pearl or about a lost son. Rather, their main point is the way those phenomena are talked about. The author of the hymn is skilled in vocabulary, syntax, and poetic style. The author traces, establishes, and maintains narrative strands and their proper presentation not just as narrative but as a narrative that includes critically reflective elements in a refined fashion. The author works with tensions and suspense in a masterful fashion. Would not this author have observed that neither in content nor in form does this hymn have anything to do with the parables mentioned by Drijvers? Why should he have known the New Testament at all? Is the burden of proof principle here not turned on its head?

12. Wolfgang Schrage, *Der erste Brief an die Korinther* (Evangelisch-katholischer Kommentar zum Neuen Testament 7.1; Zürich/Brunswick: Benziger/Neukirchen-Vluyn: Neukirchener Verlag, 1991), 52.

This proves that here as much as elsewhere in German exegetical scholarship, given the character of gnostic texts and their use, the real gnosis is very much off.

The influence of the Messina conference of 1966 continues also in Schrage's dealing with the gnosis issue as such, namely, in his deliberation on whether there could be "gnosticizing" or "pre- or proto-gnostic" elements in 1 Corinthians at all. He concurs with those who doubt an early date of Gnosticism. However, such chronological deliberations with respect to the dating of gnosis strike me as very curious. The same doubts are completely forgotten as soon as the same persons deal with the New Testament, with the church in the first century, and with Judaism during the first century B.C.E. and first century C.E. These scholars, so skeptical of an early dating of gnosis, easily speak of Christians and Christianity in the first century, although most New Testament texts do not know these terms. If the gnosis skeptics would raise the same questions or apply the same criteria of doubt with respect to Christians and Christianity in the first century, their very existence would have to be denied. Even in the case of Jewish texts and groups of the first century B.C.E. and first century C.E., their identity with Jews and Judaism of the second and third centuries C.E. could not be easily claimed.

However, the more conservative the scholars are who pronounce on Gnosticism the less they raise such questions. Still, it is without doubt that the theology of Paul cannot be reconstructed from the writings of the second century, least of all from the so-called Catholic authors. To a slightly lesser degree this is also true with the Synoptic Gospels, yet certainly with respect to the Gospel of John. The differences between the Mishnah tractates and Jewish texts that can be dated with confidence before 100 C.E. are staggering too. Still, in those cases continuity is taken to be a matter of course, and none of those scholars who are so doubtful about early gnostics would speak of pre-Christian or proto-Christian texts in the first century C.E. or pre-Jewish or proto-Jewish texts between 200 B.C.E. and 100 C.E. Indeed there is still a sizable number of conservative scholars, not only in Judaism, who take the mishnaic and the postmishnaic texts as a measuring stick for judging the Jewishness of texts of the intertestamental period and of the first century C.E.[13]

The denial of gnostic influences on the New Testament in contemporary exegesis is marked by claims of the existence of curious antitheses and of alternatives to gnostic options. In the prevailing anti-gnostic argumentation, extremely generalized alternatives to gnosis are invoked, such as

---

13. In passing, I could mention as an illustration of such rather ideological inconsistency in dating the very pertinent issue of the temporal relationship between the Septuagint and Masorah as textual complexes and the ease with which particularly conservative scholars breeze beyond the difficulties of the difference in age and time, making a text-complex that in its present text form is medieval, namely the Masorah, more relevant than a text-complex dating much before the third century C.E., namely the Septuagint.

the Old Testament, Jewish wisdom, Qumran, Hellenistic Judaism, Jewish mission, pagan Christianity, Christian-diaspora Pharisaism, Elkasaites, Encratites, and magic — all of them much too imprecise and thus betraying an essential descriptive helplessness. In these anti-gnostic arguments, it is also common to appeal to an antithesis between allegory and typology. In reality, this is a way to deny the existence of allegorical elements in the Bible and in much of patristic literature.[14] The same is true with the antithesis between mythical and symbolic. Ancient people would not have understood this alleged contrast. For them, gnostic or not-gnostic, symbol and myth would be intimately interrelated.[15] The distinction made by Drijvers and others is clearly a modern apologetic one. Even the antithesis between dualistic and monistic is not as significant and heuristically relevant as is often claimed, because no gnostic text speaks definitely of dualistic division as an eternal division. Instead, in the primeval past only one divine reality is presupposed, and wherever an end is spoken of at all it is also the one and only reality of the (good) deity.

Another important argument has been brought into the discussion during the last thirty years, most prominently by Hans Jonas. Jonas places Gnosticism into the anti-Jewish box and draws lines from the first gnostics to Heidegger and other crypto-fascist thinkers of modern days. For him and for those conservative scholars who adopted this kind of argument with pleasure, any argument that spoke of a proximity between early Gnosticism and Judaism was implicated as anti-Semitism, even more those that dared to speak of a Jewish origin of Gnosticism.[16] The view of Judaism behind such argumentation is contrary to fact. Not unity but an almost countless variety is the characteristic mark of Judaism of the intertestamental and

---

14. This understanding of typology is a very imprecise, indeed unwarranted, conversion of the Philonic understanding of typology that has little if anything in common with what apologetic Protestant theology more than a millennium later, especially since the nineteenth century, understood as typology. Christian apologists use the term *typology* not only in order to avoid the term *allegory* but also and even more in order to escape the terms *mythical* or *mythological,* which a proper theologian must not find in Christian literature. Of course, it appears by the buckets in the Old and New Testaments. As a former student of Rudolf Bultmann, this strikes me as especially curious if not ridiculous. Many scholars who take this antimythical stance are also very strongly anti-Bultmann. However, in reality they demythologize the New Testament and Christian theology thereafter even more radically than Bultmann ever did. Their denying of mythical elements in the Bible and in Christian literature leads to outright denial and elimination of essential theological data, such as preexistence as a christological given in Pauline and pre-Pauline texts.

15. The symbolic and the spiritually materialistic are similarly interrelated in the understanding of baptism by John the Baptist or by Paul or as we see it in the presentation of the Lord's Supper in its various versions in the New Testament.

16. There is no doubt that gnostic ideas are picked up and furthered by people who subscribe to anti-Judaism and world-hatred and promise themselves and their ideas as saving agents. In his book *Die Gnostiker: Der Traum von der Selbsterlösung des Menschen* (Frankfurt: Eichborn, 1992), Micha Brumlik gives in the latter part of this very readable study a fascinating and also horrifying picture of this *Unheilsgeschichte* of Gnosticism in the modern era. In con-

New Testament periods. Monotheism was a philosophical principle found neither in the Bible nor in intertestamental literature, only in philosophical texts like those of Philo. There are definitely polytheistic elements in Israelite religion, in preexilic times as well as in postexilic ones. And there is more than once the issue of God against God, not only between Israel's God and another God but also within the Israelite deity itself.[17] Prophetic and Wisdom literature of the Bible is full of radical criticism of Israel, Israelites, and their institutions. There are rebellious texts in Israelite and Jewish literature, rebellious against the established religion and their power figures.[18] The sapiential and psalmic literature also have strong anticultic and even antinomistic elements.[19]

The prominence of the power issue in these texts raises another question, namely, why liberation theologians have not yet taken the gnosis phenomenon more seriously. No one in the ancient world discussed the problems of power as frequently and as critically as the gnostics. These texts critique power in all of its forms and in its intimate relationship with reality, in particular the intimate relationship between power claims, power mongering, and assertions about reality. That liberation theologians do not yet deal much with this potent object of interest appears to be caused by fear that

---

trast to ancient gnosis, these new forms and borrowings lack much if not all of the style and hermeneutics of the original gnosis and their true followers into the high Middle Ages. In contrast, they possess more than enough of that which the ancient gnostics thoroughly and consistently attacked: dogmatism, more or less authoritarian, and the accompanying worship of power. There is even more than a chance that this authoritarian perversion of Gnosticism took hold of the Roman Catholic Church through one of its most important teachers, Augustine, a converted Manichean. Was he fully and truly changed? Brumlik's discussion of Carl Schmitt (70–86) evokes the question whether the Christian authoritarian state, perhaps since its Byzantine formation, had not been and still is a thoroughly gnostic creation, yet in its solipsistic dogmatic structure and the accompanying actions bereft of all critical means of gnosis proper. Was this not a kind of dualism too — namely one between a reality defined by force and for the sake of power and a reality of powerless nature declared unreal by the power figures and power brokers, real, however, for the powerless? Is not Andersen's tale "The Emperor's New Clothes" a good caricature on that enforced claim of the reality of power, unmasking it as mere farce holding its illusionary fetters only as long as people believe the manipulators? Is all of this reigning confusion of realities of actual power not a belated revenge of those persecuted and killed and yet turning their opponents' reality of force into a persiflage and into a curse?

17. This appears most prominently in Job, not only in 19:26 but throughout the work.

18. See Prov 1–9, Job, psalms such as Ps 22, and Ecclesiastes. See Dieter Georgi, "Interpretation of Scriptures in Wisdom of Solomon," in *Jüdische Schriften in ihrem antik-jüdischen und urchristlichen Kontext* (ed. Hermann Lichtenberger and Gerbern S. Oegema; Studien zu den jüdischen Schriften aus hellenistisch-römischer Zeit; Gütersloh: Gütersloher Verlagshaus, 2002), 304–32.

19. I certainly do not want to argue that these texts were pre-gnostic or gnostic. What I want to point out strongly is that Israelite and Jewish literature was anything but conformist. Not only preexilic but also postexilic literature has left innumerable traces of turbulence, tumult, conflict, and rebellion. Within such atmosphere the gnostic rebellion of the second century B.C.E. could take its beginning, alongside as well as against apocalyptic wisdom, another rebellious movement within Judaism, although with links to the pagan world as well.

dealing positively with the gnosis issue still draws a stigma of impropriety, one that has persisted for almost two thousand years.[20]

The gnosis phobia that I have described thus far is amazing. At the latest, by the time of Constantine, the winning branch of the church could count on the power of the state to support its merciless pursuit, discreditation, and elimination of the gnostics. Any revival, real or imagined, was repressed in unrelenting fashion. It is amazing that the denunciations of the gnostics found in the heresiomachic literature are still repeated today, and not by church representatives alone. Even the argument made by the heresiomachs that the gnostics cowardly avoided martyrdom is still read today in scholarly literature — and this despite the evidence of physical liquidation of gnostics before and after Constantine. The collaboration between the later winning branch of the church and state authorities in their efforts of persecution is also obvious. The denunciatory nature of the heresiomachic literature has thus far been neglected.[21] The Roman police must have enjoyed reading the writings of the heresiomachs, and people like Tertullian had sufficient legal knowledge and political experience to know that their giving of "evidence," arguments, and allegations would provide ideal material for the persecuting Roman authorities in their attempts to wipe out religious groups that could threaten the state.

It is high time to go beyond psychoanalyzing either the gnostics or modern scholars. Irenaeus and his successors put their political interests quite openly on the table. The modern historian has to take this into account and take issue with it, revealing his or her own political perspective too. The range of options as well as questions and suggestions concerning gnosis and gnostics should be opened widely, also in full knowledge that the naming of things is always a matter secondary to the precision of presenting the differentiated nature of the textual and historical phenomenon at hand. Whether a certain text or document is Jewish, Christian, or gnostic is of secondary importance. Primacy should be given to the exact presentation of what a document says and also what it does not say, how it is said and how not. Characterizing the relationship of the texts analyzed to larger phenomena is also necessary, but it is always secondary. Whatever is Jewish, Christian, or gnostic is a consequence stemming from the given texts and other historical data, not

---

20. Rose Horman Arthur demonstrates in her book *The Wisdom Goddess: Feminine Motifs in Eight Nag Hammadi Documents* (Lanham, Md.: University Press of America, 1984) that among feminist scholars in the United States a change for the better was in the making on the other side of the Atlantic Ocean — fighting against the spores of the anti-gnostic mildew that had crossed the Atlantic Ocean too. This is further proven by the comments on certain Nag Hammadi documents by Anne McGuire, Ingvild Saelid Gillius, Karen L. King, Pheme Perkins, and Deirdre Good in *Searching the Scriptures,* vol. 2: *A Feminist Commentary* (ed. Elisabeth Schüssler Fiorenza; New York: Crossroad, 1994).

21. See Dieter Georgi, "Das Problem des Martyriums bei Basilides: Vermeiden oder Verbergen," in *Secrecy and Concealment: Studies in the History of Mediterranean and Near Eastern Religions* (ed. Hans Kippenberg and Guy Stroumsa; Leiden: Brill, 1995), 247–64.

the other way round. It is, for instance, wrong to argue that Paul must have meant or must not or could not have meant certain things because he was a Christian. He never said that he was a Christian — and what does "Christian" mean anyway? All of this, in my opinion, is a matter of promoting courageous as well as imaginative scholarship, unfettered by any dogma of the past. It is even more an issue of human rights. First of all are those who were unfairly and unjustly treated during their lifetime and whose memory was tainted if not entirely wiped out. This has been and still is the noblest business of historical criticism maintained by the author of *In Memory of Her.* Speaking up for those who had been and are victims of an unjust history and its power systems has been and is the mission of Elisabeth Schüssler Fiorenza. This essay argues that the gnostics of the past belong to those who were and are not allowed to defend themselves and are looking for defenders today who are ready to speak not only for the victims of today but also for those who are dead already and have their memory distorted or even stricken. Our future and that of our children depends on such courageous and imaginative interference with the distortion and liquidation of memory. Such disfiguring and purging of memory was and is an essential element in the continuous process of corrupting the present and the past for the purpose of manipulating the future for the benefit of those who hold the reins of power now. Historians are called upon to resist and resurrect.

18

Feminist Scholarship and Postcolonial Criticism

Subverting Imperial Discourse and Reclaiming Submerged Histories

Richard A. Horsley

Elisabeth Schüssler Fiorenza, outstanding biblical interpreter and theologian, has become the most prominent New Testament scholar in recent times insisting on the political engagement and public accountability of biblical interpretation. She inspired, informed, and mentored a whole new generation of feminist biblical scholarship. Throughout her articulation of a feminist hermeneutic of liberation, moreover, she points out persistently that power relations of gender are closely interrelated with other political-economic power relations and that gender is generally constructed to sustain the multiple interrelated structures of domination that sustain the prevailing sexual, racial, political-economic, and cultural-religious distribution of power. Among biblical scholars, she is the most conversant with broader feminist scholarship and closely related areas of investigation. In writing an essay in honor of Elisabeth I aim to follow her lead in reading more widely than I have previously, particularly among third-world feminist critics and what has come to be called postcolonial criticism, in order to explore these interrelated power relations in New Testament literature and its historical context.

Deconstructing Dominant Discourse to Recover Submerged Peoples' Struggles

Feminist scholars generally, like Schüssler Fiorenza and others in the New Testament field, have been instrumental in widening the recognition that academic scholarship, like culture more generally, is not a closed sphere of life, separate from and innocent of politics and power. Scholarship is not merely the production of knowledge about particular subjects, but is itself a discursive political practice. Insofar as previously dominant scholarship in various fields obscured or completely hid women under generic androcentric concepts, feminist scholarship mounted disruptive interventions into the general hegemonic discourse of academe. Feminist scholarship in various fields challenged, resisted, and partially replaced the dominant imperial forms of knowledge/power. Insofar as feminist scholarship is generated within Western academe, which it challenges, resists, and subverts, it is also implicated in the continuing domination of other peoples by Western forms of knowledge. Yet having mounted an effective challenge to dominant forms of knowledge/power in one important respect, feminist scholarship and theory, such as that of Schüssler Fiorenza in New Testament studies, can serve as a model for expansion of the challenge to those dominant forms of knowledge/power in other respects.

In the last few decades non-Western feminists, finally getting a hearing in the West, are making unavoidably clear how scholars embedded in Western-generated academic fields still engage in cultural colonization by distorting, appropriating, or even submerging and eliding non-Western wo/men's lives and history.[1] These critiques by non-Western feminists parallel and overlap other non-Western scholars' "postcolonial" criticism of Western cultural production for its construction of the world according to its imperial interests. While sometimes striking for its failure to attend to issues of gender and class, postcolonial criticism attempts to challenge dominant discourses and master narratives in order to recover previously submerged histories. In this regard it is important to listen to the voices of non-Western feminist scholars and postcolonial critics in other fields. And Schüssler Fiorenza shows the way toward fuller inclusion of precisely these concerns in pressing the agenda of feminist interpretation more comprehensively in the field of biblical studies.

In a significant critical review of Western (feminist) treatments of Third World women up to about twenty years ago, Chandra Mohanty argues that "the [analytic] assumption of women as an already constituted, coherent group with identical interests and desires, regardless of class, ethnic, or racial location" served to perpetuate rather than challenge Western imperial cultural domination.[2] Over against ahistorical classifications such as "Arab women" or "African women," she calls for attention to the material reality of particular local groups of women and the consideration of interrelated factors in power relations. Correspondingly, Mohanty objects to abstract

---

1. E.g., Chandra Talpade Mohanty, "Under Western Eyes: Feminist Scholarship and Colonial Discourses," in *Third World Women and the Politics of Feminism* (ed. Chandra Mohanty et al.; Bloomington: Indiana University Press, 1991), 51–80; cited from the version repr. in *Contemporary Post-colonial Theory: A Reader* (ed. Podmini Mongia; London/New York: Arnold, 1996), 172–97; and Valerie Amos and Pratibha Parmar, "Challenging Imperial Feminism," *Feminist Review* 17 (1984): 3–19.

2. Mohanty, "Under Western Eyes," 175, 183.

generalizations such as "*the* Arab familial system" or "*the* Islamic code" without further attention to particular social situations, relations, and locations.[3] The implication is that a separate singular patriarchal kinship system or legal code is what constitutes another separate and given entity, women, as oppressed: "Arabs and Muslims, it appears, don't change at all. Their patriarchal family is carried over from the times of the prophet Mohammed. They exist, as it were, outside history."[4] Western Orientalism thus, for example, obscures the lives of particular groups of Iranian Shi'ite women, the situation they were forced into precisely by the CIA's overthrow of the elected reformist government of Mosaddeq in 1953 and the United States' sponsorship of the Shah's forced capitalist "development" and Westernization programs in the 1960s and 1970s and the remarkable role that both Western-educated middle-class women and their lower-class sisters in Tehran and elsewhere played in the revolution of 1979.[5] Western academic discourse robs particular groups of wo/men of their historical political agency. Similarly, Marnia Lazreg suggests that it is virtually an academic ritual for scholars to appeal "to religion as *the* cause of gender inequality just as it is made the cause of underdevelopment in much of modernization theory."[6]

Mohanty insists instead that women are not so much subject to some kinship system or code as they are produced through particular political, economic, and social relations. Wo/men are also implicated in forming and participating in those relations, such that their activities acquire meaning through concrete social interactions.[7] It simply perpetuates the Orientalism that submerges and denies wo/men's history, for example, to "treat Islam as an ideology separate from and outside social relations and practices, rather than a discourse which includes rules for economic, social, and power relations within society."[8] Instead of perpetuating a discourse in which wo/men are defined as objects outside social relations, we could rather examine how wo/men are constituted through and act in social relations.[9] Mohanty calls for a "mode of local, political analysis which generates theoretical

---

3. Ibid., 177.

4. Ibid., 181.

5. Brief summary with references in Richard A. Horsley, "Religion and Other Products of Empire," *Journal of the American Academy of Religion* 71 (2003), 13–44.

6. Marnia Lazreg, "Feminism and Difference: The Perils of Writing as a Woman on Women in Algeria," *Feminist Issues* 14 (1988): 87.

7. Mohanty, "Under Western Eyes," 179.

8. Mina Modares, "Women and Shi'ism in Iran," *m/f* 5–6 (1981): 61–82. For a sophisticated analysis of how Western imperial forms of knowledge and culture and both misogynist and feminist politics are implicated in Muslim women's struggles in and against the power relations in which they have been situated, see Meyda Yegenoglu, *Colonial Fantasies: Towards a Feminist Reading of Orientalism* (Cambridge: Cambridge University Press, 1998); and idem, "Sartorial Fabrications," in *Postcolonialism, Feminism, and Religious Discourse* (ed. Laura Donaldson and Kwok Pui-lan; London: Routledge, 2002), 44–61.

9. Mohanty, "Under Western Eyes," 190.

categories from within the situation and context being analyzed" and results in "careful, historically specific generalizations responsive to complex realities."[10] Reflecting on another Western intellectual product, the postcolonialism that opposed social theory that employed general categories such as gender, race, and class, some of the more critical Western feminist theorists also insist upon "theory that would be explicitly historical, attuned to the cultural specificity of different societies and periods and to that of different groups, ... comparativist rather than universalizing, ... treating gender as one relevant strand among others [such as class and race]."[11] With more concrete reference, other Western feminist theorists argue that, insofar as the world capitalist system, particularly in colonial situations, transformed the household in accordance with its needs to extract labor, feminist theory and political strategy must critically consider how so-called traditional patriarchal relationships may be effected by that system, as mediated by state policy.[12]

Like other Western-developed academic fields, New Testament studies has been "colonialist." The field is full of essentialist constructs, universalist generalizations, and abstract dichotomies that obscure or simply submerge ancient women in virtually any circumstances, and particular groups and movements in particular locations. The field even has its equivalent of Orientalism in the fundamental essentialist modern construct of Judaism, Western Christianity's other, often dichotomized with the equally essentialist Hellenism. Simply to add women back into the New Testament and "mix and stir" still leaves intact a field that obscures and submerges wo/men's lives and struggles. It also leaves intact an essentialist Judaism as the field's other. Schüssler Fiorenza was one of the first to caution against the demonization of Judaism and to insist on deconstruction of such essentialisms in a more critical investigation of overlapping factors in systems of domination. It was precisely to comprehend how ancient Mediterranean patriarchy was embedded in the wider Greco-Roman political-economic power relations, of course, that Schüssler Fiorenza coined the concept of kyriarchy.

---

10. Ibid., 184, 188.

11. Nancy Fraser and Linda J. Nicholson, "Social Criticism without Philosophy: An Encounter between Feminism and Postmodernism," in *Feminism/Postmodernism* (ed. Linda J. Nicholson; London: Routledge, 1990), 19–37, quotation at 34. Micaela de Leonardo, "Introduction: Gender, Culture, and Political Economy: Feminist Anthropology in Historical Perspective," in *Gender at the Crossroads of Knowledge: Feminist Anthropology in the Postmodern Era* (ed. Micaela de Leonardo; Berkeley: University of California Press, 1991), 17–27, 30–31, provides a similar criticism of poststructuralism/postmodernism as problematic for more comprehensive feminist analysis, along with a parallel agenda for feminist investigations and interpretation.

12. Joan Smith, "The Creation of the World We Know: The World-Economy and the Recreation of Gendered Identities," in *Identity Politics and Women: Cultural Reassertions and Feminism in International Perspective* (ed. Valentine M. Moghadam; Boulder, Colo.: Westview, 1994), 27–41; and June Nash, "Cultural Parameters of Sexism and Racism in the International Division of Labor," in *Racism, Sexism, and the World-System* (ed. Joan Smith et al.; New York: Greenwood, 1988), 11–36.

It should be possible to follow the lead of Schüssler Fiorenza in further deconstructing the dominant discourse and grand narrative of established New Testament studies in order to recover submerged histories/struggles of groups of wo/men involved in various "Jesus movements." Like postcolonial reclamation of people's histories, over against the grand narrative of our field (Christianity superceding Judaism), we can investigate the life situation and resisting struggles of wo/men involved in local (Roman Palestinian) political, economic, and social power relations. Admittedly our sources are limited in the extreme. Nevertheless, as postcolonial theorist Gayatri Spivak suggests, we can adapt the Gramscian maxim — "pessimism of the intellect, optimism of the will" — by combining a philosophical skepticism about recovering any subaltern agency with a political commitment to representing as conscientiously as possible the situation and perspective of multiply oppressed people.[13]

The Village-Based Social Renewal Movement Addressed/Articulated in Mark's Gospel

Once we cease reading the Gospel of Mark through the dominant discourse of established New Testament studies it reads like a story of Galilean and other peoples' struggle for renewal of their community life under the recently established Roman imperial order in Palestine.[14] It is impossible to separate the gender, class, and ethnic aspects of power relations present in the narrative, suggesting that those aspects not be separated in what must be multidisciplinary analysis. The risk, of course, is that specifically feminist analysis and interpretation may be blunted or even resubordinated. The hope, however, is to discern both ways in which multiple forms of oppressive power relations work in the kyriarchy of Roman Palestine and ways in which wo/men formed a sustained movement of resistance in assertion of their own agenda of societal renewal.

Only in the grand narrative of Western Christian theology is Mark the story of the origin of a universal spiritual and largely Gentile religion of Christianity from the overly political religion of Judaism obsessed with its parochial law. Most of the story focuses on Jesus' mission among villagers of Galilee as well as villagers beyond Galilee in the territories of Tyre, Caesarea Philippi, and the Decapolis. In contrast to upper, particularly priestly, classes, for whom ethnic and purity boundary definitions would have held considerable importance, cultural differences would have far less importance

---

13. Gayatri Spivak, "Can the Subaltern Speak?" in *Marxism and the Interpretation of Culture* (ed. C. Nelson and L. Grossberg; Basingstoke: Macmillan, 1988), 308; Ania Loomba, *Colonialism/Postcolonialism* (London: Routledge, 1998), 234.

14. The following is based on the more extensive analysis in Richard A. Horsley, *Hearing the Whole Story: The Politics of Plot in Mark's Gospel* (Louisville: Westminster/John Knox, 2001).

for Galilean and nearby peasantries than the political-economic subordination and exploitation to which they were all subjected under the Roman imperial order. Indeed, cultural difference, like the political-economic division, was mainly between the village communities and the newly built cities housing the palatial residences and the tax-gathering administrations of the Roman-educated client rulers such as Antipas and Herod Philip. The episode telling of how the prophet of covenant renewal, John the Baptizer, was executed mocks the dehumanizing practices (the kyriarchal lasciviousness as well as the cavalier violence) of the royal court. In the middle of the story, Jesus and his followers exhibit a rather free movement back and forth between villages apparently rooted in Israelite tradition and those who are not already "children" (of Israel). In the only episode in which someone bests Jesus in debate, the Greek-speaking Syrophoenician woman insists, against Jesus' own parochialism, that other peoples also receive the blessings of healing now available in Jesus' mission (Mark 7:24–30).

Much of Jesus' teaching and healing/exorcism takes place in synagogues, which were local assemblies of the villages in Galilee, not the houses of worship of "Judaism," which had not yet developed in Palestine as a religion.[15] The father of the twelve-year-old woman close to death (whose name "Jairus" is not mentioned in early manuscripts) is not a "ruler" of the Jews, but the chairperson or head of such a local assembly. There is no sharp division between a "Jewish" and a "Gentile" side of the Sea of Galilee. As Judean historian Josephus states (*Antiquities* 13.318–19), Galilee and Galileans had been taken over by the Hasmonean high priestly regime in Jerusalem/Judea in 104 B.C.E., little more than a generation before the Romans took control of the whole area of Palestine and Syria.[16] Judeans, unmentioned in the story except for the Roman crucifixion of Jesus as "king of the Judeans," apparently live in Judea, in which Jerusalem is situated, down from which the scribes and Pharisees come to challenge Jesus. Mark's story thus does not portray Jesus or Jesus' movement as opposing or breaking away from Judaism. The dominant division in the story is rather between rulers, the Romans and their Herodian and high priestly clients in Jerusalem and Sepphoris or Tiberias, on the one hand, and villagers in Galilee and surrounding territories, on the other, as compounded by the regional difference between Galilee and Jerusalem.

The conflict between Jesus and the scribes and Pharisees in Mark's Gospel is not over "the Jewish law" so much as over which or whose version of

---

15. For a preliminary argument that the *synagogai* of late second-temple Palestine were local assemblies, contrary to the standard traditional belief that they were religious buildings of "Judaism," see Richard A. Horsley, *Galilee: History, Politics, People* (Valley Forge, Pa.: Trinity, 1995), chap. 10.

16. For a provisional attempt to reconstruct the history of Galilee in Hasmonean times, see Horsley, *Galilee,* chap. 2.

Israelite tradition Jesus and the Galileans observe.[17] In episodes throughout the story, Jesus speaks as representative of the popular Israelite tradition and covenantal commandment of God over against the Pharisees, who accuse Jesus and his followers of not obeying the official tradition, which includes "the traditions of the elders" as well as Deuteronomic law, both apparently based in Jerusalem. Thus, for example, Jesus insists on observance of the covenantal commandment of God to "honor your father and mother," keeping local economic resources in local families as economic support for the elderly, against the scribes' and Pharisees' demand that local economic resources be "devoted" to God (*korban*) in support of the temple in Jerusalem (Mark 7:1–13). And Jesus insists on the inviolability of marriage as the central bond of the family that constituted the fundamental social-economic unit of the people, thus also guaranteeing women's economic rights, against the Pharisees' liberalization of divorce based on Deut 24:1–4, which facilitated consolidation of landholdings for the Herodian and other elite, but undermined the economic security of women and children (10:2–9).[18]

At key points in Mark's story women play representative and instrumental roles. Particularly in the juxtaposition of women in positive roles over against the twelve disciples as paradigms of misunderstanding and lack of faith, women appear to be the models of what the movement is about.[19] In their interwoven stories, the woman who has been hemorrhaging for *twelve* years and the *twelve*-year-old woman (whose father is head of a village assembly) are not simply individuals, but figures representative of Israel, which is being bled under the Roman imperial order and indeed is virtually dead. Through the hemorrhaging woman's own trusting initiative, she is healed, while the young woman who is dying just as she reaches child-bearing age is restored to life, presumably including reproductive power.

The episodes of the story presumably are interrelated, therefore to be heard together. Closely related to the situation of particular women and of the people generally, as represented by these two women, therefore, is the collective trauma suggested in the one Mary's provenance, Magdala. As Josephus reports, in 52 B.C.E. Galileans in the area of Magdala/Tarichaeae, like those in the area of Nazareth two generations later in 4 B.C.E., had experienced severe military violence and mass enslavement at the hands of

---

17. The points in this paragraph are argued more fully in Horsley, *Hearing the Whole Story*, chaps. 7 and 9.

18. This observation should not be misunderstood as a reversion to the Christian anti-Judaism about which Schüssler Fiorenza and other feminist scholars caution. To modern liberal individualists, Mark's Jesus may appear as a "conservative," while the Pharisees are the "liberals." My principal concern is to take into account the effects of the political-economic-religious kyriarchy of ancient Roman Palestine.

19. Fuller presentation is given in Horsley, *Hearing the Whole Story*, chap. 9, which in turn is heavily dependent on Elisabeth Schüssler Fiorenza, *In Memory of Her: A Feminist Theological Reconstruction of Christian Origins* (New York: Crossroad, 1983), 316–23.

Roman armies (*Jewish War* 1.180; 2.68; *Antiquities* 14.119–20; 17.288–89). And under the efficient tax collection of Antipas's newly built capitals directly in Galilee during the lifetime of Mary Magdalene and other figures in Mark's story, the heightened economic pressures on subsistence households would surely have had disintegrative effects on families (noted above in connection with the Jerusalem scribes' demand for *korban*). Interestingly enough, later in the story, Jesus condemns the scribes for "devouring widows' households," followed by an illustrative episode of how a widow gives away her whole subsistence living in responding to the scribes' encouragement to give to the temple. Not surprisingly, therefore, as discerned some time ago by Schüssler Fiorenza, in the episode for which his own mother and brothers serve as foils, Jesus calls for the whole village to form a "familial" community, in which the patriarch is conspicuously missing among mother, brothers, and sisters, to pick up the supportive functions that would ordinarily have been filled by the family.[20] Along with reempowering the people through healings and exorcisms, Jesus' "kingdom of God" program focuses on renewal of Mosaic covenant community, featuring the covenantal marriage bond centering the fundamental social economic unit of the family, "becoming like a child" in humble cooperation as community member, observance of nonexploitative covenantal economic relations, and commitment to egalitarian political relations, including leadership (Mark 10:1–45). Although not explicit in the episode that calls for leadership as service, it seems clear that the implicit paradigm of leadership is the service role of women in the patriarchal family, now being held up against the male disciples who represent the imperial model of exploitative power and privilege. Ironically, of course, in "malestream" interpretation ecclesial as well as secular kyriarchs have turned Mark's model of leadership, originally held up against would-be kyriarchs, against women as a scriptural warrant for subordination and servile roles.

As the political counterpart of the social revolution of renewing village-based society in covenantal community, Jesus both (literally) demonstrates and pronounces prophetic condemnation of the temple and the high priestly regime, the face of indirect rule that the Roman imperial forces present to the Palestinian Israelite people(s) (Judeans and Galileans). A women then steps into the prophetic role of anointing Jesus, and some of the many women who had been with Jesus throughout the campaign of renewal in Galilee witness not only the crucifixion but the empty tomb as well — after Peter and the Twelve had betrayed, denied, and abandoned Jesus and, perhaps by the time Mark was being performed, had set themselves up as head honchos of a wider movement, based now in Jerusalem (as in Acts 1–15).

It would be anachronistic to claim Mark's Jesus as a hero of a utopian egalitarian social order. Mark's story rather represents a people's movement

---

20. Schüssler Fiorenza, *In Memory of Her*, 140–51, esp. 147.

in Galilee and beyond in which gender relations are inseparable in operation from political-economic power relations and in which wo/men engage in struggle against oppressive structures and practices in the conditions in which they find themselves. In such circumstances of the disintegration of traditional patriarchal social forms such as the family and village, women commonly take leading roles, in contrast to what may happen among aristocratic or bourgeois classes.[21] In village communities, where families live in tiny two-room facilities opening off common courtyards, there is far less separation between public and private space and roles than in the ancient urban aristocracy (e.g., of first-century Jerusalem), where wealthy families build private mansions, or in modern middle-class civil society. Even what minimal separation there is, however, breaks down in colonial or imperial situations, as the family becomes both the location and the symbol of public anti-imperial activity.[22] Since the basic social forms in which the people were constituted in ancient Galilee and surrounding areas were the family and the village community, the form that renewal of the people and resistance to oppression by the Romans and their client rulers took was revival and strengthening of families and village communities. That required mutual social-economic cooperation and support, the emergence of local leadership, including those women in Galilee, and occasionally some aggressive innovation, as in the case of the Syrophoenician woman.

The Diversity and Deployment of Syncretism

When we move to the Jesus movements' mission beyond Palestine in cities such as Antioch, Philippi, Corinth, and Ephesus, the interrelations between gender, class, and ethnicity become more complex, while the sources for particular groups become more fragmentary. It is again necessary to challenge and deconstruct the dominant discourse, particularly the essentialist construct of Hellenism or Hellenistic syncretism into which the remarkable cultural diversity and local histories of the eastern Roman Empire have been submerged and homogenized. And again it is impossible to separate and extricate power relations of gender from those of class and ethnicity. In this regard recent discussion of postcolonial identity in terms of hybridity, and especially critical qualifications of the concept,[23] may be useful for

---

21. In Israelite biblical tradition, the Song of Deborah (Judg 5) provides a dramatic illustration. See also Tamis Hoover Renteria, "The Elijah/Elisha Stories: A Socio-cultural Analysis of Prophets and People in Ninth-Century B.C.E. Israel," in *Elijah and Elisha in Socio-Literary Perspective* (ed. Robert B. Coote; Atlanta: Scholars Press, 1992), 75–126.

22. Loomba, *Colonialism/Postcolonialism*, 217.

23. E.g., Homi K. Bhabha, "Remembering Fanon: Self, Psyche, and the Colonial Condition," in *Colonial Discourse and Postcolonial Theory* (ed. P. Williams and L. Chrisman; New York: Columbia University Press, 1994), 112–23; Loomba, *Colonialism/Postcolonialism*, 173–83; Benita Parry, "Signs of Our Times: Discussion of Homi Bhabha's *The Location of Culture*," *Third Text* 28–29 (1994): 5–24.

New Testament studies, both in cutting through the essentializing construct of Hellenistic syncretism and in opening historical inquiry to the varying circumstances of the peoples who participated in the expanding Jesus movements in various cities.

Prominent postcolonial theorists celebrate the hybridity of culture and identity, partly as acceptance of the impossibility of reverting to the precolonial past. The celebration of hybridity, however, has come in for a good deal of criticism from those concerned with historical continuity and political resistance. The concept fails to distinguish the different ways in which colonial power affected peoples in different contexts according to various factors such as class, gender, and race: "forced assimilation, internalized self-rejection, political cooptation, social conformism, cultural mimicry, and creative transcendence."[24] Without critical attention to neoimperial power relations, affirmation of hybridity runs the risk of "sanctifying the fait accompli of colonial violence."[25] Hybridity appears as a postmodernist "carnivalesque collapse and play of identities," possible mainly for "the migrant intellectual" who "thus dispenses with a sense of place, of belonging, of some stable commitment to one's class or gender or nation.[26] The idea "that one is free to invent oneself . . . as one goes along, is usually an illusion induced by availability of surpluses, of money capital or cultural capital or both."[27]

This last point calls attention to the way in which cultural contents are today torn from their original social and historical contexts and transformed into commodities, from which multicultural consumers can piece together their hybrid identities — or acquire one after another with each passing fad or fancy. It does not take much political-economic analysis to realize that the force behind all the hyperavailable cultural diversity is global capital, which has recently begun to cannibalize culture to satisfy its insatiable appetite for profits. One of the principal motive forces of the recent rise of multiculturalism is the need of transnational corporations to deal with their own multicultural work force. But those multinational corporations also now thrive on multiculturalism, both in the contents of what it markets and in the marketing of those contents: "Hybridity and in-betweenness . . . facilitate

---

24. Ella Shohat, "Notes on the 'Post-colonial,'" *Social Text* 31–32 (1993): 109–10; Loomba, *Colonialism/Postcolonialism*, 15.

25. Shohat, "Notes on the 'Post-colonial,'" 109.

26. Aijaz Ahmad, "The Politics of Literary Postcoloniality," *Race and Class* 36 (1995): 13–14. Homi Bhabha, the principal postcolonial advocate of "hybridity," asserts: "I want to take my stand on the shifting margins of cultural displacement — that confounds any profound or 'authentic' sense of a 'national' culture or 'organic' intellectual"; *The Location of Culture* (London/New York: Routledge, 1994), 21. A significantly different conception was operative in the convening of an international conference in biblical studies; see the papers published in *Reading from This Place: Social Location and Biblical Interpretation* (ed. Fernando F. Segovia and Mary Ann Tolbert; 2 vols.; Minneapolis: Fortress, 1995).

27. Ahmad, "Politics of Literary Postcoloniality," 18.

the transnational operations of global corporations.... By itself, multiculturalism and an affirmation of hybridity do not point to a way out of existing structures of power, only to modifications within it."[28]

Questions of multiculturalism and hybridity therefore must be asked critically in relation to imperial power relations: Who, with what power, is mobilizing what cultural contents or identities or representations with what vision or goal or for what purpose or effect? Some people threatened with virtual annihilation may feel compelled, for their very survival, to assert a nearly lost cultural heritage in relatively essentialist form. To revive and reformulate precolonial languages and cultures may be some peoples' only way of not simply yielding to the effects of colonial violence.[29] Maintaining or recovering historical vision may be crucial in this regard. Multihistoricalism could be substituted for multiculturalism. That would enable already hybridized people (most of us) to draw upon different historical trajectories out of different pasts, providing outside viewpoints from which to evaluate contemporary power relations and the ideologies that authorize them. Indeed, it might even be possible to recover histories that have been suppressed by European colonialism and the neoimperialism of global capital as a way of envisioning a future in terms of alternative historical trajectories.[30]

In broadly analogical terms, these criticisms of postcolonial celebration of hybridity can be applied to Hellenistic syncretism in New Testament studies. Like hybridity, *syncretism* is conceived as having been largely a cultural phenomenon. Acknowledged perhaps, but usually left unexamined, is the often violent application of imperial power that pried cultural contents loose from the indigenous peoples who originally produced them — and whose collective life they provided with coherence and meaning — and/or removed people themselves from their ancestral lands and communities. The unabashed Orientalism that dominated the "history of religions" as well as the New Testament field is evident in one of the basic required textbooks in graduate training.[31] The "East," in its "political apathy and cultural stagnation" prior to its takeover by Alexander the Great, had sunk into a state of "passivity, docility, and readiness for assimilation." Yet Eastern cultural contents could be salvaged, for "Greece had invented the *logos*... [and] made it available to the East, whose self-expression could now benefit from it." Salvageable cultural contents could now be "disengaged from their native soil, abstracted into the transmissible form of teachings." Thus "the first cosmopolitan civilization known to history... was made possible by catastrophes overtaking the original units of regional culture."

---

28. Arif Dirlik, *The Postcolonial Aura: Third World Criticism in the Age of Global Capitalism* (Boulder, Colo.: Westview, 1997), 9, 17.

29. Shohat, "Notes on the 'Post-colonial,'" 109–10.

30. Dirlik, *Postcolonial Aura*, 18–19.

31. Has Jonas, *The Gnostic Religion* (Boston: Beacon, 1958). The following excerpts are from 11, 13–14, 15–17, 21–22.

A more critical approach would lead us to inquire after the dislocations of people and culture by Hellenistic and Roman imperial power, which led to Hellenistic syncretism. Then questions of the creative use of syncretism (and ancient multiculturalism) must be asked critically in relation to Roman imperial power relations: Who, with what power, is mobilizing what cultural contents or identities or representations with what vision or goal or for what purpose or effect? The wealthy and powerful elite of the Greek cities, with the cooperation of the early emperors, developed the emperor cult (with statues, temples, shrines, games, etc.) on the basis of the traditional civil religion of their *poleis* into one of the dominant ways that imperial power was constituted.[32] Recent investigation into the official establishment of the cult of the Magna Mater in a central civil location in Rome invites further critical analysis of the political uses of religious syncretism.[33] The Roman elite's eager devotion to the exotic Egyptian goddess Isis and initiation into her mysteries (portrayed in Apuleius, *The Golden Ass* 11) appear to be a cooptation and "commodification" of subjugated indigenous people's culture/religion for the spiritual enjoyment of the imperial elite (reminiscent of New Age phenomenon among contemporary Western elites).[34] On the other hand, syncretism could be used by subjected peoples in resistance to the dominant Roman imperial order. This would appear to be what the mission of some of the movements focused on Jesus did in various ways. We can focus on a few "Hellenistic Jewish" leaders in the mission of the Jesus movement that we have at least minimal information for: such as Prisca of Rome, Saul of Tarsus, and Apollos of Alexandria, marshalling available information to help illuminate their circumstances and creative actions.

Diaspora Jews Leading an Anti-imperial Movement Based in History of Israel

Roman political violence and Hellenistic-Roman cultural pressure affected peoples in different situations in different ways. Roman enslavement of tens of thousands of Syrians, Galileans, and Judeans in vengeful conquests and reconquests left them in a situation of "natal alienation."[35] The tiny minority who survived the brutality of slavery to become emancipated were left deracinated and socially and economically dependent on their former masters. It is likely that some Diaspora Jews who joined communities of Jesus believers were enslaved Judeans and Galileans or their descendants.

---

32. Simon R. F. Price, *Rituals and Power: The Roman Imperial Cult in Asia Minor* (Cambridge: Cambridge University Press, 1984).

33. Lynn E. Roller, *In Search of God the Mother: The Cult of Anatolian Cybele* (Berkeley: University of California Press, 1999), chap. 10.

34. Explored in Horsley, "Religion and Other Products of Empire."

35. Orlando Patterson, *Slavery and Social Death: A Comparative Study* (Cambridge: Harvard University Press, 1982).

Perhaps at the opposite end of the spectrum of imperial power relations from such forced assimilation was the defensive posture of cultural mimicry evident in the treatises of Philo of Alexandria. He and other Jewish social and intellectual elite in Alexandria came to understand the true message of the Jewish Scriptures in Greek in terms of a mystical devotion to heavenly Sophia/Logos, which afforded the enlightened soul immortality and a spiritually aristocratic status as truly noble, wealthy, and powerful. Luke's and Paul's characterization (in Acts 18 and 1 Cor 1–4) of Apollos, who was also from Alexandria, as eloquent and well versed in Scripture suggests that he came from just such a social-cultural context.

The impact of imperial power relations must have been quite different, depending on the local circumstances. The Hellenistic hybridity of Saul of Tarsus, the Levite Barnabas from Cyprus, and Stephen and other "Hellenist" Jews from various Diaspora communities such as Cyrenaica, must have been very different from that of Philo of Alexandria. How else can we explain how readily some of those Hellenists, who had presumably settled in Jerusalem after coming on pilgrimage to the holy city, enthusiastically joined an Israelite peasant renewal movement focused on an executed Galilean prophet and led by a few Galilean country bumpkins like Peter, James, and John?

Similarly, far from imagining a homogenous Hellenistic culture consistent from place to place, we must also reckon that Hellenistic hybridity was different in the various "cities" of the Pauline mission. Corinth, destroyed by Roman armies in 146 B.C.E., had become the site of a colony of freed slaves and other "surplus populace" from Rome in 44 B.C.E. and because of its central commercial location would have been a humming cosmopolitan center of uprooted peoples and cultures. One can easily imagine the cultural pluralism and anxious individual quest for status and identity in such a cultural crossroads. On the other hand, the Roman impact on Macedonia, including two successive military colonies imposed on Philippi, would have left the "indigenous" population of the smaller provincial towns of Thessalonica and Philippi perhaps unusually receptive to a movement with anti-imperial overtones. One should hardly think in terms of a tranquil and homogenous social order and culture in either Thessalonica or Philippi.[36] We can now similarly investigate local hybridized cultural histories that have previously been submerged in essentialist concepts in order to ascertain the particular situations into which the Jesus movement and Pauline mission spread.

Another factor that surely affected the purpose and effect of cultural syncretisms in the Roman imperial order was how they may have been related to social formations. The Romans apparently allowed the Diaspora Jewish communities in many cities a measure of self-governance in their *synagogai*

---

36. See further Abraham Smith, " 'Unmasking the Powers': Toward a Postcolonial Analysis of 1 Thessalonians," in *Paul and the Roman Imperial Order* (ed. Richard Horsley; Harrisburg: Trinity Press International, forthcoming).

(assemblies). Such ethnic communities would have acted as important medi-
ators of the impact of cultural hybridity and social power relations. Jewish
ethnic communities would have provided some shielding and protection of
ethnic culture and social relations for wo/men, in contrast to the situation
of either Jewish female or male slaves, to whom the Roman imperial order
allowed their masters sexual access, or even compared with the rootless urban poor who belonged to no such supportive community. Diaspora Jewish
synagogues may well have provided enslaved Judeans and Jewish freedpersons a supporting community that mitigated the worst effects of their natal
alienation and deracination as slaves. Again, we cannot but help wonder
about Prisca's background in this connection.

Many of those communities appear to have spoken Greek and to have
cultivated their cultural tradition in Greek, using the Septuagint. We should
not imagine, however, that all Greek-speaking Diaspora Jews cultivated the
same philosophically informed allegorical interpretation as did the Alexan-
drian Jewish elite such as Philo. Some "Hellenistic" Jews apparently still
thought in terms closer to the historical orientation evident in Psalm of Solomon 2 or even in "apocalyptic" terms, as in some of the *Sibylline Oracles*.
It is entirely possible, as in modern imperial relations, that some subordinate peoples were using the imperial master's cultural "toolbox" (language,
rhetorical forms, etc.) to subvert the empire and imperial power relations.
And/or their cultural hybridity might be a veneer of language, idioms, and
rhetorical forms that only superficially decorate an orientation deeply rooted
in an imperially subordinated cultural tradition.

Just as strong opponents of Western and/or global imperialism today
reject hybridity as a cultural response/strategy, so opponents of Roman imperialism rejected Hellenistic syncretism and other forms of Romanization.
The Jesus movement(s) strongly reasserted Israelite traditions in a bid to
renew Palestinian peoples over against Roman imperial and Roman client
rulers. Even Diaspora Jews who in various ways and degrees had become
acculturated to Roman-Hellenistic society, such as the "Hellenists" Stephen
and Barnabas who joined the Jesus movement early on, opted to identify
with and reassert what might to others have seemed an irretrievable past.[37]
Indeed, even before they joined the Jesus movement, Hellenists such as Saul
had been involved in a movement of Jewish cultural revival poised sharply
over against Hellenism.

This must be what Paul is referring to when he writes about "my earlier life in *ioudaismos*," in which he was "advanced... beyond many among
my people of the same age, ... zealous for the traditions of my ancestors"
(Gal 1:13–14). *Ioudaismos*, which has long been misunderstood in modern

---

37. This observation holds even if we view Stephen as a representative figure in whose mouth
Luke placed a "speech in character," on the Greek and Hellenistic historiographical pattern of
what a given figure would likely have said in a certain situation.

religious terms as "Judaism," would appear to have been a program of renewal of what its proponents understood as the traditional Jewish/Israelite
way of life in direct opposition to *hellēnismos,* the cultural program that
had long been forced upon the Jews, first by Seleucid and then by Roman
imperial power. It is perhaps somewhat ironic for standard New Testament
studies' understanding of Paul and his mission as the "Hellenization" of the
Jesus movement to realize that leaders such as Paul, Barnabas, and Stephen
were almost certainly acculturated Diaspora Jews who had begun to identify with more traditional Palestinian Israelite culture in direct opposition
to the Roman imperial order. They were evidently rejecting their previous
Hellenistic hybridity.

We can ask about Paul and other leaders of early Jesus movements the
question that their critics pose to advocates of postcolonial hybridity:[38] Who
is mobilizing what in the articulation of the past and deploying what identities in the name of what vision and goals? Paul and apparently other
Diaspora Jews such as Prisca and Stephen who led the movement focused
on Jesus Christ as Lord, however acculturated they were in the hybridity
of Hellenistic culture, mobilized Israelite tradition for a movement whose
identity was rooted in Israelite history and sharply opposed to the Roman
imperial order and its syncretistic Hellenistic culture. They spearheaded a
recovery of Israelite history that was in the process of being suppressed in the
multicultural melting pot of Hellenistic hybridity, the culture of the Roman
imperial order in the eastern Mediterranean. Moreover, their efforts helped
to open a way to thinking about the future in terms of an alternative historical trajectory to the pax Romana that was oppressive for subject peoples,
slaves, and the vast urban underclasses even as it provided "peace and security" for the pro-Roman urban elites. Perhaps it could be said that Paul
and others were exploring a new possibility of cultural identity, understood
as a project that constituted a key aspect of the struggle for liberation that
it informed.[39]

The shift in identity that Saul made to Paul (via his *apokalypsis* of Jesus
Christ/commissioning by God; Gal 1:12–16) was a move from a defensive
program to shore up a subject culture being threatened with submergence
to an offensive use of cultural hybridity and plurality (i.e., multiculturalism)
in organizing an alternative society where identity was no longer primarily ethnic/religious/separate cultural tradition, but ancillary to the project
of establishing an alternative social order. For Stephen and Peter as well as
for Paul, the project was based in a history different from and alternative to
Rome's, that of the now subjected people of Israel. But Paul then understood
that history as having opened onto a new phase of fulfillment on an international basis, among other subject peoples, in which no particular culture

---

38. Shohat, "Notes on the 'Post-colonial,'" 109.
39. Dirlik, *Postcolonial Aura,* 15.

(boundary definition) was definitive, in which participation was not con-
ditional on adherence to a particular cultural boundary definition. Other
Diaspora Jews such as Prisca evidently agreed with and shared in the leadership of this program, whereas Barnabas and others did not make the same
move.[40] The movement's group identity, no longer primarily cultural, was a
political-economic-social-cultural project-in-progress symbolized by the formula pronounced in the baptismal ritual of incorporation: "No longer Jew
or Greek, no longer slave or free, no longer male and female."

In the letters that Paul wrote to communities he (along with Prisca and
others) helped to catalyze, we have at least fragmentary indications of how
he attempted to shape the project-in-progress on these three interrelated issues. Again, with feminist and postcolonial critics, it is important to get out
from under the standard Western imperial discourse and master narrative
of the established field that touts Paul as the very paradigm of enlightened
liberal universalist Christian theologian, on the one hand, and of a sober
social conservative, on the other. The former construction is based heavily
on a standard (mis)reading of Paul's argument about eating meat offered to
idols in 1 Cor 8–10. The latter is based mainly on deutero-Pauline letters,
which in turn influence a standard (mis)reading of one mistranslated statement about slavery in 1 Cor 7:21 and the standard reading of the letter to
Philemon.

Western Christian interpreters, of course, are eager to claim Paul for
their own enlightened point of view. They thus find in these paragraphs
an enlightened Paul who, having himself seen through the parochialism of
the Jewish legalistic scruples about idols and meat offered to them, urges
other enlightened believers to refrain from eating in consideration of their
weaker fellow believers' scruples, in a generous gesture toward less enlightened points of view. Paul's argument in 1 Cor 8–10, however, especially
when read in the context of his overall argument in the letter, clearly goes
the other direction.[41] He comes to his main point in the paragraph constituted by 10:14–22 (and not in 10:23–30). He adamantly insists on the
traditional Jewish/Israelite strictures against idols as representative of other
gods and lords — and imposes them on non-Israelite Corinthians who have
joined the assembly in Corinth — against the tolerant hybridity of enlightenment Hellenistic philosophy and Hellenistic Jewish enlightenment theology.
Those other gods are not only real but dangerous. The jealous God of Israel demands the believer's exclusive loyalty. And this is a social-political
matter, not simply an issue of theological belief. The Corinthians owe exclusive loyalty to Christ as their Lord: "You cannot drink the cup of the Lord

---

40. Although in very different historical circumstances, Paul's and others' projects bear a
striking similarity to the formation of Islam, which built on Arabic tradition/culture, but aimed
to transcend and unite previously conflicting tribes/peoples.

41. Sketched more fully in Richard A. Horsley, *1 Corinthians* (Abingdon New Testament
Commentaries; Nashville: Abingdon, 1998), 115–51.

and the cup of demons. You cannot partake of the table of the Lord and the table of demons" (10:21). Paul flat-out rejects the principle of enlightenment Hellenistic multicultural hybridity that "all things are lawful/permissible for me!" Paul was adamant in his letter to the Galatians that Galatians and other non-Israelite peoples not be required to join Israel (by the males undergoing circumcision) in order to receive the blessings promised to all peoples through Abraham's seed, that is, adopting as children of God, along with Israelites. But he is equally adamant in 1 Corinthians that the God of Israel demands exclusive loyalty, to the point that believers cannot possibly participate in ritual expressions of other social-political solidarities. Other peoples can share in the blessings to Abraham, but cultural hybridity must yield when it poses a threat to political solidarity.

Given the importance of slavery in the political economy of the Roman Empire as its central mode of production and in the modern Western world as a subsidiary mode of production, it was important that Western academic discourse not seriously undermine its cultural acceptance. Even after it distinguished critically between the genuine letters of Paul and the deutero-Pauline letters that adjusted back into the dominant imperial order, the basically conservative field of New Testament studies simply perpetuated the misreading of 1 Cor 7:21 ("even if you can gain your freedom, make use of your present condition now more than ever").[42] It also continued to read Paul's letter to Philemon as concerned with the blatant cultural stereotype of a "thieving runaway slave." The latter may not even be about a slave, much less about a fugitive slave, hence not relevant to the issue.[43] And the only possible reading of 1 Cor 7:21 is as an exception to the general principle enunciated in 7:17, 20, 24: "But if you have the opportunity to gain your freedom, by all means make use of it (take the opportunity).... You were bought with a price; do not become slaves of human masters!"[44] The issue of slave and free overlapped considerably with that of male and female. Particularly in urban areas such as Corinth and Ephesus, the majority of household slaves would likely have been women, whereas large gangs of male slaves were deployed in mining and latifundial agriculture. As on the issue of other gods, which involved issues of political loyalty, again on the issue of slavery, Paul appears to oppose, not support, the dominant imperial order. It is not clear whether Paul condemned slavery itself, on which the metropolitan Roman economy was based, which would be analogous to condemning capitalism, on which the modern imperial economy is based. In

---

42. For an reexamination of standard Pauline interpretation on this and other issues of Paul's "social conservatism," see Neil Elliott, *Liberating Paul: The Justice of God and the Politics of the Apostle* (Maryknoll, N.Y.: Orbis, 1994), 32–52.

43. See the important revisionist treatment of Paul's letter to Philemon by Allen Dwight Callahan, *Embassy of Onesimus: The Letter of Paul to Philemon* (New Testament in Context; Valley Forge, Pa.: Trinity, 1997).

44. See further Horsley, *1 Corinthians*, 100–103, 113; and idem, "Paul and Slavery: A Critical Alternative to Recent Readings," *Semeia* 83–84 (1998): 153–200.

encouraging slaves to become free if possible, however, Paul was drawing on Israelite covenantal tradition, which opposed chattel slavery and included provisions for the release or redemption of debt-slaves, in opposition to the Roman imperial order, in which subject peoples who resisted imperial domination, such as Judeans and Galileans, were enslaved.

On the issue of male and female Paul appears to have been less insistent on the ideals of the project-in-progress than on the issue of slaves and free. Indeed, in his deep-seated Israelite concern about permissive Greek cultural sexual practices, he appears to persuade women to sacrifice their newly gained gender equality with men in order to ward off the danger of potentially uncontrollable male sexual desires, as leading feminist scholars demonstrate.[45] Paul is clearly familiar with the rhetoric of equality, as in the balanced phrases of 1 Cor 7:1–16 and especially the statement of 7:4, which is remarkable for any place and time. It is all the more striking, therefore, that he uses that rhetoric in attempting to manipulate married women, who apparently wished to be free of their traditional conjugal obligations, to provide an outlet for their husbands' unrestrainable sexual desire, the specter of which he has evoked in the previous two arguments of the letter (1 Cor 5; 6:12–20). In the second half of his argument about sex and marriage, Paul abandons all pretense of egalitarian rhetoric, addressing men only (7:25–38).

In the longer run, of course, the project-in-progress was adjusted to the power relations of the Roman imperial order, as later generations of Christian leaders explicitly advocated the dominant social-economic form of the patriarchal slaveholding family. Correspondingly, those identified as "Greeks," whose predecessors had joined a movement based in the history and tradition of Israel and surely identified initially as a "Jewish" movement, came to dominate the *ekklēsia* that acted more and more like what we think of as a religion.

Texts and History

In her 1987 presidential address to the Society of Biblical Literature, Elisabeth Schüssler Fiorenza states that "an *ethics of historical reading* changes the task of interpretation from finding out 'what the text meant' to the question of what kind of readings can do justice to the text in its historical contexts."[46] The critical perspectives and scholarship of feminist scholars and postcolonial critics are making it clear that readings rooted in established Western academic fields that developed in close connection

---

45. Antoinette C. Wire, *The Corinthian Women Prophets: A Reconstruction through Paul's Rhetoric* (Minneapolis: Fortress, 1990).

46. Elisabeth Schüssler Fiorenza, "The Ethics of Biblical Interpretation: Decentering Biblical Scholarship," *Journal of Biblical Literature* 107 (1988): 14 (emphasis original).

with Western imperialism and Orientalism cannot comprehend the multiple interrelated facets of power relations involved in ancient texts or modern imperial situations. These perspectives consistently and systematically submerge other people's histories and knowledges. As Schüssler Fiorenza herself, other feminist scholars, and postcolonial critics argue, that is not simply because those fields are patriarchal, but more comprehensively because they are kyriarchal. The conception and construction of gender relations are integrally related to the conception and construction of other power relations such as those of class and ethnicity. The problem for New Testament interpreters in particular is not just that New Testament texts and their Roman imperial contexts are kyriarchal, but that the academic field in which we have been trained is kyriarchal, Western imperial as well as patriarchal. As long as we continue to perpetuate essentialist foundational constructs such as "Christianity" and "Judaism" and project peculiar modern Western assumptions of religion as separate from political-economic life, for example, we will continue the epistemic violation that compounds the Roman imperial violence imposed on ancient wo/men of various subject peoples and their struggles of political resistance and social renewal.

Perhaps it is implicit in doing justice to texts, but Schüssler Fiorenza and other feminist and postcolonial scholars seem to be engaged in a recovery of submerged histories as well as textual interpretation. This seems all the more important in our current situation, as global capital expands its domination of cultural expression in general and cannibalizes subject peoples' culture while simply making their history "disappear." This subversive agenda of feminist and postcolonial scholarship has multiple dimensions.

Implicit in both feminist scholarship and postcolonial criticism is the subversive enterprise of driving a wedge between texts and the textual communities that claim authority over and authorization by those texts, predominantly academic fields produced during and by Western imperialism. In some cases this enterprise also involves liberating the texts from textual communities. This involves a historicizing at least of the textual communities/academic fields and often also of the texts as well. The reading of New Testament texts presented above attempts to do this. The use of the Gospel of Mark discussed above insists that it was an ancient "Third World" story and neither addressed to the ancient Roman imperial metropolis nor intended for appropriation by the modern Western imperial academic field that claimed it was addressed to Rome. The use of Paul's letters discussed above insists that they do not address *homo religiosus* as constructed by universalist Western Christian theologians who take Paul as authoritative and normative, but formative communities in an ancient anti-imperial movement among subject peoples. In both cases these texts are being used not as literature to be directly appropriated by modern Western readers, but as sources for and/or reflections of ancient histories of peoples that must be reclaimed and reconstructed because they have been submerged.

Feminist scholarship also demonstrates how, once free of essentialist modern Western scholarly constructs, texts can be read in order to reconstruct the history of struggles within movements, as leaders and other participants attempt to embody an alternative to the dominant power relations. In this way leaders who were elevated to positions of authority in later canonization processes and other moves by an established imperial religion to consolidate its own authority can be put back in their place in the originary struggles. Mark's story appears to be criticizing the position of, while more or less still recognizing the historical role of, Peter and the Twelve, who had set themselves up as the authorities of a wider movement headquartered in Jerusalem. Mark presents women in the narrative in juxtaposition with the commissioned but fearful, misunderstanding, and faithless Twelve as paradigms of the renewal movement and models of its assumption of mutual responsibility and solidarity.

Especially in his more polemical letters Paul, simply assuming authority over assemblies that he claims to have founded, is attempting to counter and even suppress other views and voices with which he disagrees. In opposition to Western imperial theologians who claim Paul as the authoritative correction of alternative, "heretical" views, feminist scholars demonstrate how, with sophisticated rhetorical criticism, Paul's letters can be used as sources for the voices that Paul was trying to "correct" or submerge.[47] Paul's letters were attempts at persuasion, one side of ongoing conversations, even contentious arguments. Just as Paul was one leader among many, sometimes in sync, sometimes in conflict with one another or with the assemblies they catalyzed, so his arguments give voice to one position among many. And because he is often trying to persuade by speaking directly to other positions and even articulates his arguments in others' language, we can often discern those other voices through Paul's arguments. Equipped with rhetorical criticism, therefore, we can use Paul's letters as windows into the struggles of people with various positions and concerns, struggling with each other as they work out their project-in-progress.[48] In New Testament studies feminist scholarship thus shows the way to discern in our texts how, at more than one level, the histories of women and (other) imperial subjects are "histories of resistance and opposition and not just histories of oppression.[49]

It is important generally to affirm the centrality of history, given its neglect by much contemporary cultural criticism, after the "linguistic turn" in

---

47. Elisabeth Schüssler Fiorenza, "Rhetorical Situation and Historical Reconstruction in 1 Corinthians," *New Testament Studies* 33 (1987): 386–403; Wire, *Corinthian Women Prophets*.

48. See further Elisabeth Schüssler Fiorenza, "Paul and the Politics of Interpretation," in *Paul and Politics; Ekklesia, Israel, Imperium, Interpretation* (ed. Richard A. Horsley; Harrisburg, Pa.: Trinity, 2000), 57.

49. Loomba, *Colonialism/Postcolonialism*, 50.

Western academic scholarship. The increasing consolidation of global capital's cultural as well as political hegemony on a global scale is "producing among the professional intelligentsia a characteristic loss of historical depth and perspective."[50] To reclaim submerged people's histories, suppressed by the dominant order, may be particularly important to enable us once again "to conceive of the past not merely as a route to the present, but as a source of alternative historical trajectories that had to be suppressed so that the present could become a possibility."[51] The struggles of movements that attempted to counter multiple interrelated oppressive power relations, including replication of such power relations within the movements, may then be highly informative and valuable to today's alliances of groups attempting to counter multiple interrelated power relations of a new imperial order. Recovering those submerged histories will contribute toward new efforts to reimagine and pursue what Schüssler Fiorenza calls unfulfilled historical possibilities.

---

50. Aijaz Ahmad, *In Theory: Classes, Nations, Literatures* (London/New York: Verso, 1992), 16.
51. Dirlik, *Postcolonial Aura*, 3.

19

Rethinking Authorship
in the Letters of Paul

Elisabeth Schüssler Fiorenza's Model
of Pauline Theology

Cynthia Briggs Kittredge

Elisabeth Schüssler Fiorenza proposes decentering Pauline theology from an unblinking focus on Paul to a broader reconstruction of early Christian communities. Her challenge has not been accepted by most Pauline theologians.[1] In making her proposal Schüssler Fiorenza is taking on a powerful tradition of interpretation and arguing for a major shift in the enterprise of biblical theology and study of Paul's theology. Her interpretive approach to the letters marks a change in the way Paul is viewed both as the "author" of the letters and as the authoritative voice in early Christian communities. One of the ways that those who try to advance this project attempt to re-focus attention beyond Paul is to attribute the origin of early traditions, particularly hymns, creeds, and baptismal prayers, to other Christians. Using form criticism, source criticism, and rhetorical criticism, these feminist interpreters claim that some statements within the letters represent theological expressions of communities, rather than original statements of Paul.[2] In so doing, they begin to question the model of Paul as the single author and the one authority who speaks from the letters. This essay places the work of Elisabeth Schüssler Fiorenza, Antoinette Clark Wire, and myself in dialogue with the well-published work of the Pauline Theology Group of the Society of Biblical Literature.[3] The difference between the manner in which inter-

---

1. Recent books devoted to Pauline theology maintain a Paul-centered approach to describing Paul's theology. See, for example, Lauri Thurén, *Derhetorizing Paul: A Dynamic Perspective on Paul and the Law* (Harrisburg, Pa.: Trinity, 2000); Michael Gorman, *Cruciformity: Paul's Narrative Spirituality of the Cross* (Grand Rapids: Eerdmans, 2001).

2. Antoinette Clark Wire, *The Corinthian Women Prophets: A Reconstruction through Paul's Rhetoric* (Minneapolis: Fortress, 1990); Cynthia Briggs Kittredge, *Community and Authority: The Rhetoric of Obedience in the Pauline Tradition* (Harrisburg, Pa.: Trinity, 1998).

3. The essays are published in four volumes entitled *Pauline Theology,* vol. 1: *Thessalonians, Philippians, Galatians, Philemon* (ed. Jouette M. Bassler; Minneapolis: Fortress, 1991); vol. 2: *1 and 2 Corinthians* (ed. David M. Hay; Minneapolis: Fortress, 1993); vol. 3: *Romans* (ed. David M. Hay and E. Elizabeth Johnson; Minneapolis: Fortress, 1995); and vol. 4: *Looking Back, Pressing On* (ed. E. Elizabeth Johnson and David M. Hay; Atlanta: Scholars Press, 1997).

preters name and evaluate early traditions is closely bound up with their picture of Paul as an author and theologian. I suggest that a change of focus away from Paul as the central author is difficult and yet is vitally necessary and ethically responsible, given our present interpretive context.

In her essay "Pauline Theology and the Politics of Meaning," Schüssler Fiorenza proposes that biblical theology be reconceived not as a neutral objective enterprise in which interpreters "describe" the theology of Christian Testament authors, but as a rhetorical practice in which scholars engage in a "critical hermeneutical process that is able to investigate the rhetoric of a text or tradition in terms of the ethics of liberation."[4] She argues that claims to describe Paul's theology operate with the politics of "othering," the politics of "identity," and the politics of "identification." Critics employ the politics of othering when they construct Paul's letters in terms of orthodoxy and heresy or in terms of Paul versus his opponents. The politics of identity seeks to interpret Paul's theology as consistent and coherent. Interpreters engage in the politics of identification when they become spokesmen and advocates for Paul's theology and thus take on for themselves Paul's authoritative voice.[5] The result of such interpretive moves is the presentation of an heroic figure. Rather than constructing an individual figure, distinct from his context, who demands emulation or adulation, Schüssler Fiorenza sees Paul as a prophetic voice who can be challenged by other inspired speakers in order to be a catalyst for change. In contrast to perpetuating the heroic model, Schüssler Fiorenza proposes a model that decenters Paul and reconstructs the early Christian communities that the letters represent.

The Pauline Theology Group — The Single-Author Model

An influential discussion of Pauline theology occurred within the Pauline Theology Group of the Society of Biblical Literature. In seminars that met between 1986 and 1995, the members of this group gave sustained attention to the task of describing Paul's theology. They planned to build up a description of the theology of Paul by focusing on each letter of Paul apart from the others, beginning with the earliest and proceeding to the latest. The collected papers published over the course of the years of its meetings give a sense of the conversation and a fascinating picture of the promises and

---

4. Elisabeth Schüssler Fiorenza, *Rhetoric and Ethic: The Politics of Biblical Studies* (Minneapolis: Fortress, 1999), 176.

5. Schüssler Fiorenza's critique of interpreters of Paul identifying with Paul is akin to her analysis of historical-Jesus scholars who "inhabit" the symbolic construct of the historical Jesus in a way in which women cannot. In addition, her description of the way in which historical-Jesus scholars tend to separate Jesus from the movement of which he is a part is parallel to her criticism that Pauline scholars separate Paul from what precedes him and what follows; Elisabeth Schüssler Fiorenza, *Jesus and the Politics of Interpretation* (New York: Continuum, 2000), 11–12.

frustrations of the project as it was defined. Although the Pauline Theology Group did not explicitly engage Schüssler Fiorenza's proposal to reconceive Pauline theology, their methodological discussions reveal a tension between the goal of the group to understand Paul's theology as a dynamic process and its methodological focus on Paul as a single author.

The group agreed to understand the task of identifying Pauline theology to be a primarily descriptive task rather than a rhetorical enterprise.[6] However, very early in the work of the group, the question of what model to use in order to describe Paul's theology emerged as a central methodological question.[7] Throughout their discussions the members of the group used different working definitions of theology. These definitions included "Paul's thought world," "the communication of Paul's thoughts in his letters to the various churches," "Paul's appropriation and application of scripture and Christian traditions to the specific situation," and many others.[8] Despite their different working definitions, most of the scholars agreed that Paul's theology was not so much a system as a process of "theologizing."[9] Their efforts revolved around delineating the distinctive roles played by "convictions," "assumptions," and "contingent situations" within that process.

In his summary and review of the discussion, James D. G. Dunn proposes that the process whereby contemporary communities of faith interpret Scripture might provide a model for conceiving of the way Paul does theology: "Our best insights into the complexity of Paul's theology as activity may well come from reflection on our own activity in theologizing."[10] Within a community, in relation to a community's traditions, theology is dialogic. It is the manner in which theologians debate and discuss their convictions: "In addition we need to recall that most theologizing is undertaken within a community (and/or communities) and in relation to a community's traditions, life, needs and opportunities. This means that theology is unavoidably dialogic in character."[11] Dunn's suggestion that our own communal enterprise of interpretation might be an analogue for Paul's theologizing raises the issue of the relationship between the contemporary interpretive context and our reconstruction of Paul's theology. For Dunn, that means that we should imagine Paul as being in dialogue with his traditions and the communities in the same way that contemporary communities of faith are in dialogue with their traditions. In a response to Dunn, Stephen J. Kraftchick raises the significant objection that our contemporary context is so unlike Paul's first-century context that our contemporary experience cannot be a model for

---

6. Schüssler Fiorenza, *Rhetoric and Ethic,* 178.

7. Essays focusing on methodology are found in *Pauline Theology,* vols. 1, 2, and 4.

8. Some of the working definitions are summarized by James D. G. Dunn, "In Quest of Paul's Theology: Retrospect and Prospect," in *Pauline Theology,* 4.95–96.

9. See especially ibid., 98, 99, 101.

10. Ibid., 101.

11. Ibid., 102.

Paul's.[12] The exchange between Dunn and Kraftchick on this point raises the issue of how our present theological and ecclesial contexts shape our view of Paul in the past. Kraftchick points out that the community theologizing that Dunn imagines in the present is really a process in which the question of God is a critical problem and that in the contemporary context the authority of Paul is not assumed or required.[13] Although they take opposite positions on the question of how closely our interpretive context resembles Paul's, both Dunn and Kraftchick are attending to the interplay between present context for interpretation and the way we picture the past. Dunn appears to be arguing for a picture of theological discussion in the present that is critically self-reflective, interactive, lively, and dialogic — that is, a fundamentally social activity.[14]

Other scholars of Paul emphasize the communal aspects of contemporary biblical interpretation. For example, in the conclusion to his essay on biblical theology in "Fragments of an Untidy Conversation," Luke Johnson makes a plea that theology be reconceived as an "ecclesial process of discernment" in the reading of Scripture.[15] Stephen E. Fowl and Gregory L. Jones argue persuasively that the context for reading Scripture is the "Christian communities striving to live faithfully before God."[16] In the communal models of Dunn, Johnson, and Fowl and Jones, the picture is of communities of interpretation being in dialogue and discussion with the diverse texts and authors of Scripture. However, the model of Paul constructed by the Pauline theologians favors the individual and univocal over the communal and dialogical.

One factor that works against the effectiveness of Dunn's proposal to use our own process of theologizing as an analogy for Paul's is the identification of the locus of theology in the mind of Paul. The descriptive task of the theologians is highly focused on the mind of Paul and lacks the communal dimension emphasized by Dunn. For example, Jouette M. Bassler's description of the process emphasizes Paul's sensibility:

> The *raw material of Paul's theology* (the kerygmatic story, scripture, traditions, etc.) passed through *the lens of Paul's experience* (his common Christian experience as well as his unique experience as one "set apart by God for the gospel") and generated a *coherent (and characteristic) set of convictions.* These convictions were refracted through

---

12. Stephen J. Kraftchick, "An Asymptotic Response to Dunn's Retrospective Proposals," in *Pauline Theology,* 4.138–39.

13. Ibid., 133.

14. Dunn, "In Quest of Paul's Theology," 102.

15. Luke Timothy Johnson, "Fragments of an Untidy Conversation: Theology and the Literary Diversity of the New Testament," in *Biblical Theology: Problems and Perspectives: Essays in Honor of J. Christiaan Beker* (ed. Steven J. Kraftchick, Charles D. Myers Jr., and Ben C. Ollenburger; Nashville: Abingdon, 1995), 287. See also Luke Timothy Johnson, *Scripture and Discernment: Decision Making in the Church* (Nashville: Abingdon, 1983), 57–58.

16. Stephen E. Fowl and L. Gregory Jones, *Reading in Communion: Scripture and Ethics in Christian Life* (Grand Rapids: Eerdmans, 1991), 21.

a prism, Paul's *perception of the situations that obtained in various* communities, where they were resolved into specific *words on target for those communities.*[17]

D. M. Hay reconstructs Paul's interior state of mind: "Theology emerges as Paul listens to the doubts of others and those in his own mind, reflects on essential convictions, and ponders which warrants preserve 'the fear of the Lord' and are likely to persuade."[18]

Imagining the locus of Paul's theology to be in his own mind means that efforts to reconstruct the process are focused individually rather than socially. Despite frequent statements about Paul's indebtedness to shared convictions, the role of other Christians in the theological process is not emphasized. Paul W. Meyer emphasizes the "creative singularity of Paul." Quoting Leander Keck, he states this position in an extreme form: "Paul had no Christian teacher. He was nobody's pupil, but was an *autodidact,* that is, a self-taught thinker who, while indebted to traditions, *never appealed to an authoritative teacher.* Nor did Paul's thinking develop in a collegial context as Johannine theology did, assuming that this tradition was formed in a school."[19] In this model, the origin and energy of the theological process is Paul himself. Despite their desire to imagine a contemporary social and communal context for biblical interpretation, the persistent attention of the commentators is on the mind of Paul, and the locus of "theology" is in the person of Paul. By restricting the theological process to the individual, the dialogical aspects of theologizing, such as response to other voices, discussion, and dispute, are bounded and contained.

Modifying the View of Paul as Author— Early Christological Traditions in Paul

In order to explore the difference between traditional and feminist approaches to Paul as author, we will look at how scholars interpret the early church traditions "quoted" by the author, Paul. Important to all theologians who are trying to reconstruct Paul's process of theologizing are the Christian formulas, prayers, and creeds that are incorporated into Paul's letters. These elements stand out from their context in the letters because of their distinctive vocabulary, literary form, or theological perspective. Because these units appear to be able to stand on their own, critics posit that they circulated independently or were used in different liturgical contexts by early

---

17. Jouette M. Bassler, "Paul's Theology: Whence and Whither?" in *Pauline Theology,* 2.11 (emphasis original).

18. D. M. Hay, "The Shaping of Theology in 2 Corinthians: Convictions, Doubts, and Warrants," in *Pauline Theology,* 2.155.

19. Paul W. Meyer, "Pauline Theology: A Proposal for a Pause in Its Pursuit," *Pauline Theology* 4:159 (emphasis by Meyer). Leander E. Keck, "Paul as Thinker," *Interpretation* 47 (1993): 28.

Christians other than Paul. Scholars label these elements "pre-Pauline traditions," "early Christian creeds," "christological hymns," and "baptismal formulas." Some of these texts, like Phil 2:6–11, have been highly valued in the history of interpretation because of their contribution to the theological tradition and because of New Testament scholarship's fascination with the earliest form of the tradition.[20] As with study of sayings traditions in the Gospels, analysis of the manner in which the author of the letter calls on and cites these traditions can give insight into both Paul's technique of theologizing and the beliefs and practices of other Christian communities. In his argument for reconstructing the theological process as a dialogue, Dunn refers to the importance of "allusion" to common convictions shared by Paul and his audience. The allusions contribute to the bonding power of community discourse.[21] The way that interpreters of Paul name, describe, and evaluate these early traditions is an important key to showing how they are constructing Paul's relationship and role in early Christian communities. Their aims and priorities shape the way they describe this process, how they attribute authorship, and how they judge the relationship between Paul and the traditional element.

James D. G. Dunn's *Theology of Paul the Apostle* provides an example of how one Pauline theologian treats early christological traditions in the letters. Dunn asserts strongly that Paul's teaching assumes the common Jesus tradition shared with the recipients of his letters. Dunn uses the image of Paul entering a conversation already well underway.[22] The regular occurrence of the preexisting formulas "suggests a commonality of faith and of expression of that faith. Which in turn suggests that summary formulations like this were indeed in fairly widespread use in the earliest Christian churches."[23] Dunn emphasizes that Paul's central christological claims were in direct continuity with the gospel that was preached before his conversion.[24] The summary of the gospel in 1 Cor 15:3–4 shows that Christ's resurrection was the "bedrock on which the common faith of Christians was built."[25] At the same time, Dunn privileges Paul's use of the tradition over any earlier interpretation of it. For example, in commenting on Phil 2:6–11, Dunn de-emphasizes the passage's earlier existence: "For most of this century Phil. 2.6–11 has been designated a pre-Pauline hymn. The description is fitting, but does not greatly affect us, since Paul presumably

---

20. Ralph P. Martin, *Carmen Christi: Philippians ii.5–11 in Recent Interpretation and in the Setting of Early Christian Worship* (Society for New Testament Studies Monograph Series 4; Cambridge: Cambridge University Press, 1967).

21. Dunn, "In Quest of Paul's Theology," 103.

22. Dunn, *The Theology of Paul the Apostle* (Grand Rapids: Eerdmans, 1998), 189.

23. Ibid., 176.

24. Ibid.

25. Ibid., 236.

made use of it as an appropriate expression of his own theology."[26] Similarly, Dunn argues against those who claim that the assertion of Gal 3:28 expresses Paul's views on women in ministry.[27] He claims that "it would be unwise to draw out an applied theology from the principle without regard for the way in which Paul himself actually theologized in practice."[28] Thus, in the description of Paul's theology, Paul's use of earlier traditions and his practice take precedence over the tradition itself.

Despite Dunn's insistence on the close connection between Paul's convictions and the belief of other Christians, Dunn constructs Paul as the original and singular source of the key terms of Christian theology: "gospel," "grace," and "love."[29] Dunn's treatment of Paul's use of early Christian traditions shares common features with discussions among many scholars of Paul. In order not to separate Paul from the Jesus tradition that precedes him, scholars emphasize the link between Paul and both the early stratum of the gospel tradition and the christological hymns and creeds.[30] But in keeping with their focus on the theologizing process within Paul, they subordinate earlier use of the tradition to Paul's employment of it.[31] The assumption of Paul's centrality pushes the expressions of others to the margins.

The marked difference in the way that Schüssler Fiorenza and other feminist scholars of Paul analyze and evaluate these early Christian traditions reveals differences between their aims and assumptions and those of Dunn and the other members of the Pauline Theology Group. Both the christological hymns and the baptismal formula in Gal 3:28 are especially valuable to Schüssler Fiorenza's project to reconstruct the environment of debate and discussion within early Christian communities because they preserve early liturgical material that can be used to reconstruct the developing history of these communities.[32] Wire develops the baptismal formula as an expression

---

26. Ibid., 281 n. 64.

27. Dunn (ibid., 592 n. 138) cites Schüssler Fiorenza and Wire.

28. Ibid., 592.

29. Ibid., 733.

30. Fitzmyer asserts that "fragments of the primitive kerygma" in Paul's letters show that Paul joined a movement and was dependent on the "apostolic tradition of the early church"; Joseph A. Fitzmyer, *Paul and His Theology: A Brief Sketch* (Englewood Cliffs, N.J.: Prentice-Hall, 1989), 32.

31. Some suggest that the Christ hymn was composed by Paul. See Larry W. Hurtado, "Jesus as Lordly Example in Philippians 2:5–11," in *From Jesus to Paul: Studies in Honour of Francis Wright Beare* (ed. Peter Richardson and John C. Hurd; Waterloo, Ont.: Wilfrid Laurier University Press, 1984), 113–26. See also Gordon D. Fee, *Paul's Letter to the Philippians* (New International Commentary on the New Testament; Grand Rapids: Eerdmans, 1995), 193–94.

32. See Elisabeth Schüssler Fiorenza, "Wisdom Mythology and the Christological Hymns of the New Testament," in *Aspects of Wisdom in Judaism and Early Christianity* (ed. Robert L. Wilken; Notre Dame: University of Notre Dame Press, 1975), 17–41; idem, *Jesus: Miriam's Child, Sophia's Prophet: Critical Issues in Feminist Christology* (New York: Continuum, 1994), 139–54; idem, *Rhetoric and Ethic*, 149–73 (a chapter entitled "Ideology, Power, and Interpretation, Galatians 3:28").

of the self-understanding of the women prophets in Corinth.[33] In my work on Philippians, I claim that the Christ hymn in Philippians expressed the self-understanding of a community before it is used by Paul.[34] These interpreters value these traditions not only in order to maintain that Paul is in continuity with the earlier Jesus traditions, but because they give insight into what the theological perspective of these earlier Jesus traditions might be. Taking their character as "pre-Pauline" seriously, these critics are much more likely to attribute their origin and use to other Christians besides Paul. For example, for Schüssler Fiorenza, the christological hymns speak to a theological movement that spoke of Jesus' life and death in terms of Wisdom-Isis theology and expressed the hope for liberation and participation in a heavenly divine world.[35] Wire stresses that the women prophets' theology was part of the faith in Christ that developed in the Hellenistic cities before Paul.[36] In my reconstruction of the historical situation, I attribute the origin of the hymn to women and men in community who had a vital history of leadership with Euodia, Syntyche, Epaphroditus, and Clement.[37] Thus, in contrast to those who de-emphasize the earlier life of the traditions in favor of Paul's employment of them in the letters, Schüssler Fiorenza, Wire, and I attribute these traditions to other Christians. We propose alternative "authorship" for these traditions, that is, the collective Christian community in worship, which includes individuals whose names the letters of Paul do not reveal.

Feminist scholars stress the existence and participation of other leaders in the communities before Paul and during Paul's ministry and identify them as "authors" of the christological hymns or baptismal formulas. As a result, these critics have another way of explaining contradictions between perspectives in Paul's letters. When scholars using a Paul-centered approach attribute to Paul all Christian language, contradictions among statements must be explained as a result of a change in Paul's mind or as a response to a changed situation in the community or audience. Disparate statements of Paul on one topic may be summarized in a general way that minimizes the differences among them.[38] For those who consider that some of Paul's statements, especially the allusions and quotation of early baptismal prayers, hymns, or creeds, may have not only originated with others but also continue to be proclaimed at the time of the writing of the letters, the tensions in Paul's statements can be read as evidence of diverse theological perspectives.

---

33. Wire, *Corinthian Women Prophets*, 184–88.
34. Kittredge, *Community and Authority*, 77–83.
35. Schüssler Fiorenza, *Jesus: Miriam's Child*, 148.
36. Wire, *Corinthian Women Prophets*, 185.
37. Kittredge, *Community and Authority*, 86.
38. For example, see the discussion of the way theologians treat the topic of "obedience" in Paul's letters in ibid., 13–29.

Once diversity within the functioning Christian communities is accepted as an imaginative possibility, then one is able to reconstruct these positions as Christian visions of community with which Paul is in dialogue, rhetorically trying to encourage, modify, or circumscribe. Schüssler Fiorenza develops this possibility with the baptismal formula in Gal 3:28 and later Pauline restriction of it.[39] Wire demonstrates how Paul's arguments in 1 Corinthians are responses to a baptismal understanding held by women prophets in Corinth. I argue that the tradition quoted in the Christ hymn in Philippians has an allusive meaning beyond the rhetorical use to which Paul puts it in Phil 2:12. I argue that the hymn is evidence of perspectives on leadership in the community that are not in harmony with Paul.[40]

Schüssler Fiorenza, Wire, and I operate with a model of theologizing in which communities of worship and praxis are in the process of working out how the gospel will be embodied, rather than a model in which one man's mind must be shown either to be consistent or to have reasonable factors that "changed" it. This model allows us to imagine conflict between aspects of Paul's vision and elements of other Christian visions. Both perspectives on Paul seek to explain the same evidence — the early traditions quoted by Paul that originated with others, and the diverse statements in Paul's letters about the role of women, the status of marriage, the preexistence of Jesus, his exaltation, the meaning of his death on the cross, and other aspects of the gospel. One argument brought to bear against the reconstructive position of feminist scholars is that it is illegitimate to speculate about the meaning of hypothesized earlier forms in the text.[41] Another is that it is unreasonable to use a statement like Gal 3:28 as a statement of Paul's principle when his practice clearly violates it.[42] Other objections claim that it is improbable that early Christians could ever imagine the relativization of patriarchal marriage or of human existence as freedom rather than slavery. Presuppositions about reasonableness or probability prevent interpreters from envisioning Christian women and men as vigorous and challenging co-workers with Paul.

The difference between these interpretations of the same evidence results from one's convictions about Paul's centrality and authority. Because some see Paul as the originator of the gospel language, traditional Pauline theologians do not picture other leaders as very important. Congregations are generally construed as passively receiving Paul's instructions or heretically opposing them. However, some see Paul alluding to the language of the wider Christian community whose missionaries and leaders generated this

---

39. Schüssler Fiorenza, *Rhetoric and Ethic,* 149–73.
40. Kittredge, *Community and Authority,* 40.
41. This criticism is typical of those interpreters who stress a canonical perspective in which only the latest form of the text is to be considered.
42. Dunn, *Theology of the Apostle Paul,* 592 n. 138.

language in their worship and praxis. Reading the ample evidence in the letters that Paul's authority with the churches was contested, these interpreters construe the congregations as active and engaged in formulating what is coming to be tradition in the *ekklēsia*. In their imagined reconstructions, the first position assumes Paul's authority and centrality, and the second does not.

It is possible to see each of these options as mutually exclusive but essentially unrelated choices about how to approach Paul's letters. The first strategy has in its favor the whole history of Western theological tradition since the Reformation in which Paul has been a source of doctrine and a heroic person who could be admired and imitated and whose "mind" could be plumbed and analyzed by other minds. The historical credentials of this traditional model make this approach appear more effective than the alternative that sees the broader community movement as the focus of attention. Before I present the benefits of a model where Paul's authority is decentered, I want to explore the reasons for the persistence of the Paul-centered model of Pauline theology, which is closely related to the idea of Paul as author.

Tradition of Paul as Original Author and Single Authority

The proposal to decenter Paul faces enormous resistance among biblical scholars because, although Jesus is the central subject of the New Testament, Paul is its primary author. Paul as the authoritative figure for a community and Paul as author have been closely connected both in ancient times and in the present.[43] While the Gospels are interpretations of Jesus mediated by the evangelists, their association with apostolic authors was made at a later time in the canonization process. Paul as the author and "character" in the letters is associated by definition with the writings from their inception. Because the letters of Paul have an author, interpreters of Paul are able to focus on explaining, discussing, and speculating about authorial intention in a way that interpreters of the Gospels are not. The effort to explain psychologically why Jesus did what he did or said what he is recorded to have said in the Gospels is greatly modified by awareness of the narrated and literary character of the Gospels. In Paul's letters, historical projections about the author play a role in the interpretations of the letters themselves more than in the Gospels.[44] That Paul is the only accepted and identifiable author in the New Testament may explain why even the recognition of his letters as

---

43. David G. Meade, *Pseudonymity and Canon: An Investigation into the Relationship of Authorship and Authority in Jewish and Early Christian Tradition* (Grand Rapids: Eerdmans, 1987).

44. Robert Morgan ("New Testament Theology," in *Biblical Theology: Problems and Perspectives: Essays in Honor of J. Christiaan Beker* [ed. Steven J. Kraftchick, Charles D. Myers Jr., Ben C. Ollenburger; Nashville: Abingdon, 1995], 117) criticizes the primacy of history over

"conversations in context" does not appreciably modify focus on Paul as the center of interest.[45] Scholarly focus on Paul as author is exemplified by the attention given to the disputes over Pauline authorship of Ephesians and Colossians and of the Pastoral Epistles. The desire to preserve Paul as an authoritative author motivates both those who want to claim Ephesians and Colossians as written by Paul and those who want to sharply distinguish the "genuine" Paul from "early catholicism." Theories about interpolations in the letters are undergirded by the belief that if Paul is not the author of 1 Cor 14:34–35, then that statement cannot be authoritative.[46]

The high value placed on Paul and his letters by the Protestant theological tradition is another feature of Paul's letters that works against any attempt to view the letters without Paul at the center. Theologians have read the history of Christian theology as the reaction of key thinkers to the influence of Paul.[47] Because of the dominant understanding of Paul as the hero of the Reformation, with recovery of Paul's insight of justification by faith as its crux, modern interpreters of Paul continue to identify with Paul as the authoritative figure, whose theology they are describing and advocating, even if they do not see justification by faith as the interpretive key.[48] In designating Paul's opponents, interpreters often reconstruct Paul's historical situation in analogy with their own.[49] Troels Engberg-Pederson convincingly outlines the conflation of description and advocacy in the scholarship on Paul since the rise of historical criticism.[50] To describe the theology of Paul that closely mirrors the one advocated by the commentator is to gain an irresistibly

---

theology: "The temptation to substitute history for theology, historical reconstruction for theological reflection on the NT texts is strongest in relation to Paul, because in these Epistles, far more than in the Gospels, historical projections about the author are both possible and essential to plausible interpretations of the documents themselves."

45. The metaphor of "conversation" is frequently used to describe Paul's letters. See, for example, Calvin J. Roetzel, *The Letters of Paul: Conversations in Context* (Louisville: Westminster/John Knox, 1991).

46. Non-Pauline authorship of Ephesians, Colossians, the Pastorals, and interpolations in the "genuine" Pauline letters is a key basis for Neil Elliott's argument for a liberative reading of Paul in *Liberating Paul: The Justice of God and the Politics of the Apostle* (Maryknoll, N.Y.: Orbis, 1994), 26–31.

47. John D. Godsey, "The Interpretation of Romans in the History of the Christian Faith," *Interpretation* 34 (1980): 3–16.

48. See the classic expression of this critique of the interpretation of Paul in Krister Stendahl, "Paul and the Introspective Conscience of the West," *Harvard Theological Review* 56 (1963): 199–215; repr. in idem, *Paul among Jews and Gentiles, and Other Essays* (Philadelphia: Fortress, 1976), 78–96. See also Richard A. Horsley, "Krister Stendahl's Challenge to Pauline Studies," in *Paul and Politics: Ekklesia, Israel, Imperium, Interpretation* (ed. Richard A. Horsley; Harrisburg, Pa.: Trinity, 2000), 1–16. See also Stanley K. Stowers's criticism of traditional interpretation of Romans in *A Rereading of Romans: Justice, Jews, and Gentiles* (New Haven: Yale University Press, 1994), 13–15.

49. Robert Jewett, "Major Impulses in the Theological Interpretation of Romans since Barth," *Interpretation* 34 (1980): 17–31.

50. Troels Engberg-Pederson, *Paul and the Stoics* (Louisville: Westminster/John Knox, 2000), 19.

powerful ally.[51] Both those who claim that Paul's social conservatism means that women should not be church leaders and those who claim that Paul is advocate for equality of women in the church are operating with the model of Paul as the ultimately authoritative voice.

Attempts to relativize the importance of Paul either in the present or in historical reconstruction threaten the longstanding tradition of Paul as primary authority for theology. For exegetes and theologians in the Protestant tradition, Paul is the center of the canon — if not the canon itself. Hendrikus Boers states Paul's importance in the canon most emphatically: "What is significant about Paul is that in him the full range of the tension of the canon comes to expression. He may be regarded as *the* canon, not *a* canon in the canon."[52]

In addition to the influential history of Paul's being revered as the hero of the Reformation's revolt against legalism, another force works against decentering Paul. Since the Reformation, there has been a strong emphasis on the contributions of the individual creative genius. Developed in the Romantic period and exemplified by Schleiermacher, this view of the creative individual emphasized novelty and innovation. John Thiel describes the "romantic paradigm":

> The romantic conception of theological authorship was born in this ascription of authorial ability, and thus authority, to the individual theologian. At least in the founding assumptions of the romantic paradigm, the theologian possesses a sort of ecclesial genius — a talent exercised in the sensitive discernment, the felicitous expression, and the careful guidance of ecclesial truth in history. Since this development was primarily accessible in and through experience, the importance accorded to individual creativity in theological reflection was remarkably enhanced. The theologian's task was no longer seen as the mimetic *representation* of an objective revelation but as the imaginative *construction* of the historical experience of salvation. This shift in conceptions about the very nature of the theological enterprise was one that highlighted the theologian's creativity and gave rise to the romantic paradigm of theological responsibility.[53]

Even among interpreters of Paul's theology who would not identify themselves with the "romantic" or "liberal" tradition, the conception of Paul's

---

51. For an analysis of the relationship between the authority of the commentator and the authority of Paul in the treatment of mimesis, see Elizabeth Castelli, *Imitating Paul: A Discourse of Power* (Louisville: Westminster/John Knox, 1991), 23–31.

52. Hendrikus Boers, "Paul and the Canon of the New Testament," in *Biblical Theology: Problems and Perspectives: Essays in Honor of J. Christiaan Beker* (ed. Steven J. Kraftchick, Charles D. Myers Jr., and Ben C. Ollenburger; Nashville: Abingdon, 1995), 208.

53. John E. Thiel, *Imagination and Authority: Theological Authorship in the Modern Tradition* (Minneapolis: Fortress, 1991), 21.

theologizing in which inherited convictions are refracted through Paul's experience as apostle and interact in the mind of Paul is thoroughly shaped by this romantic paradigm. Although inherited traditions and pre-Pauline traditions are given a role as the raw material for Paul's production, these communal expressions play a subsidiary role in the active originating author. The impulse for commentators to identify with this figure, to describe him in their image, and to "borrow" his authority has been thus far too strong to overcome.

Recovering Community Authorship

The contemporary interpretive situation shapes how we view the past, and our present questions determine who or what receives our attention in the ancient world. For example, it was possible for historical criticism to "discover" diversity in the New Testament in the context of increasing recognition of the diversity of Christian denominations and of religious pluralism in general. The scholarly attention to the origins of the separation between orthodox Christianity and rabbinic Judaism in the first century grew out of the questions raised by the Holocaust about the historic relationship of Christian theology to anti-Semitism. As the exchange between Kraftchick and Dunn indicates, scholars continue to debate whether Pauline theology can be done with only Christian concerns in mind. Interpreters of Paul who are in some measure responsible to communities of faith are more explicit about how theological questions in the present shape the way they explore the past than those who claim to be neutral historians or classicists. Therefore, I would justify the interpretive choice to decenter Paul on the basis of what kind of interpretive community we want to envision. Because we imagine a contemporary community of interpretation in which diverse positions are negotiated in light of shared commitments and beliefs, then our reconstruction of the early Christian communities must be one in which Paul and other Christian leaders share responsibility for expressions of theological conviction and faith.

Despite the pressure of a long history and tradition of the Paul-focused approach to Pauline theology, the choice of a model that decenters Paul, reconstructs Christian positions in addition to those of Paul, and imagines those expressions in tension and debate is a necessary shift to make in light of the character of our contemporary interpretive context. Dunn suggests that we use our own model of theologizing as an analogy in order to reconstruct Paul's. Kraftchick objects that significant differences in basic presuppositions make it difficult to treat Paul's theologizing as resembling our own. However, both positions indicate a close relationship between our models of community interpretation and our reconstructions of early Christian communities. In order to encourage interpretive communities of dialogue and deliberation such as those that Dunn, Johnson, and Fowl and Jones urge, it is necessary to use a model for the study of ancient communities that acknowledges the role of the community in the production of creedal and doxological statements and that recognizes the ongoing role of the present community as interpreter of Scripture. This model must be able to recognize diversity and even disagreement among and within early Christian communities and to understand sympathetically how such diverse positions could be contained within the legitimate variety of Christian expressions. Employing this model, interpreters would reconstruct arguments on behalf of these ancient positions, rather than simply claiming ongoing authority for them by attributing them to Paul as a single authoritative author. A model that envisions early Christian communities as true conversations within the *ekklēsia* can function more helpfully in creating dialogical interpretive communities in the complex contemporary hermeneutical context.[54] A model in which Paul is a participant but not the center can function to envision a democratization of contemporary interpretive communities.

When Schüssler Fiorenza, Wire, and I make the choice to attribute the origin of portions of Paul's letters to other Christians, we claim that Paul is neither the single author or the central authority in the early Christian movement. Rather, the community experience of the gospel, which for many Christians was unrelated to Paul, is an equally important source for Christian language as well as a resource for theological reflection. This approach recognizes the role of community in producing and employing religious language. Allowing liturgical formulas, hymns, and doxologies to keep some status, independent of their use in Paul's letters, is one way of upholding the role of the community in the production of Scripture and the creation of the canon. In their focus on individual authors, particularly Paul, scholars overlook the role of community and tradition in shaping Scripture.[55] The move of various commentators to insist that the only legitimate object of study is Paul's use of early Christian traditions causes the loss of the communal dimension of these traditions.

Recognizing these traditions as at one time independent of Paul recovers them as possible resources for alternative early Christian visions. Our critique of the underlying romantic notion of authorship focused in one individual attempts to recover the shared expression of the community and to recognize that some of those visions were not passed on unaltered by Paul. Rather than effacing the author completely as some deconstructive positions would,[56] our approach allows authorship and authority to be envisioned

---

54. For example, those who argue for leadership of women in the church by claiming that Paul supports it base their stance on an appeal to Paul's authority rather than claiming the validity of other authoritative criteria such as their contemporary experience, ethical norms, other statements in the New Testament, or other criteria.

55. See, for example, Meade's critique of individualistic views of inspiration of canonical Scripture in *Pseudonymity and Canon*, 209.

56. See, for example, the critique of the author in Mark C. Taylor, *Erring: A Postmodern Altheology* (Chicago: University of Chicago Press, 1984), 74–93. For discussion of Taylor's

in a more democratic manner. This move is related to the impulse of other feminists to expand the canon beyond the books of the Bible based on the criterion of "usefulness" rather than particular authorship. Rather than going outside the canonical books to find useful traditions, by fracturing the unified view of Paul, we find theological resources within the canonical letters of Paul.

Modifying the view of Paul as the single author implies a corresponding shift in the picture of Paul as the central theological authority, either in his specific statements or in his process of theologizing. While Dunn takes Paul's authority as a given in the interpretive community, Kraftchick responds that it would be possible to describe Paul's theology without granting it authority.[57] Wire argues that viewing Paul's letters as arguments requires a shift in the view of the Bible's authority from one in which authority is determined independently from the text to one in which the authority operates through the meeting between persuasive arguments and the convictions of readers.[58] The Paul-focused model reads back into the letters a view of Paul's central authority that is anachronistic in the first century and that is becoming obsolete within our increasingly pluralistic and postmodern Christian communities. The alternative places the locus of theologizing in the interaction of Christians in the *ekklēsia* instead of in the mind of the individual. This decentering of Paul creates a change of position for the Pauline theologian. Rather than being a spokesperson for Paul's authoritative position, the interpreter brings her own questions and priorities into discussion with the singers of the Christ hymn, the ascetic followers of Paul, and the other voices in the canon. Responsibility for visions of community is taken by the community rather than placed onto one authoritative individual. Such a decentering of the commentator is more likely to create an interpretive community that acknowledges "disagreements within Christian communities about how best to understand and perform scripture."[59]

Recent work in Pauline theology increasingly emphasizes Paul's process of theologizing and the importance of recognizing and creating communities of theological interpretation of Scripture. This work also maintains a highly individualized focus on the mind of Paul. This focus on Paul at the center is exemplified by an approach to the christological traditions that privileges Paul's use of the tradition over any earlier form of it. The choice of feminist interpreters to attribute the christological traditions to the community is one element in a strategy to broaden the focus of Pauline theology from one centered around Paul as the authoritative author to another that

---

position see Thiel, *Imagination and Authority,* 143–50. See also A. K. M. Adam, "Author," in *Handbook of Postmodern Biblical Interpretation* (ed. A. K. M. Adam; St. Louis: Chalice, 2000), 8–13.

57. Kraftchick, "Asymptotic Response to Dunn's Retrospective Proposals," 129.
58. Wire, *Corinthian Women Prophets,* 10.
59. Fowl and Jones, *Reading in Communion,* 84–86.

reconstructs Christian communities in their tension and diversity. This reorientation acknowledges shifts in understanding of authorship and authority in our contemporary context. Sharing with theologians of Paul who use a traditional model the understanding of Paul's theology as a process, feminist scholars reconceive this process to include "authors" and speakers besides Paul in order to contribute to the creation of lively communities of scriptural interpretation.

20

Ethical Issues in Reconstructing Intrareligious Violence in Antiquity

The Gospel of Matthew as a Test Case

Shelly Matthews

One of the crucial aspects of Elisabeth Schüssler Fiorenza's scholarship is her call for biblical scholars to incorporate into their critical work "the elucidation of the ethical consequences and political functions of biblical texts and their interpretations in their historical as well as in their contemporary sociopolitical contexts."[1] This call is both a gift and a challenge: a gift in the sense that it offers to the discipline an opportunity for relevancy; a challenge in that it requires its practitioners to step outside the dominant discursive modes of biblical scholarship. This essay attempts to answer this call by focusing on ethical and political issues raised by depictions of early followers of Jesus as subject to violent persecution at the hands of Jews in the Gospel of Matthew. It builds on several argumentative strands articulated throughout Schüssler Fiorenza's work. First, it embraces her critique of academic discourses that pose as objective and value-neutral quests for historical facts and her constructive understanding of historiography as rhetorical practice.[2] Second, it does not understand the historical-Jesus movement as a movement *over and against* Judaism, but as one of several renewal movements *within* Judaism.[3] Third, it adopts her understanding of systems of domination as kyriarchal rather than patriarchal. This neologism, derived from the Greek terms *kyrios* (master) and *archē* (rule), signals that "domination is not simply a matter of patriarchal, gender-based dualism but of more comprehensive, interlocking, hierarchically ordered structures of domination, evident in a variety of oppressions, such as racism, poverty,

---

1. Elisabeth Schüssler Fiorenza, *Rhetoric and Ethic: The Politics of Biblical Studies* (Minneapolis: Fortress, 1999), 28.

2. See, for example, Schüssler Fiorenza's works on Revelation, such as *Revelation: Vision of a Just World* (Minneapolis: Augsburg Fortress, 1991).

3. See, for example, Elisabeth Schüssler Fiorenza, *Jesus and the Politics of Interpretation* (New York/London: Continuum, 2000).

heterosexism, and colonialism."[4] This notion of hierarchical, interlocking oppressions, useful for destabilizing binaries of all sorts, is one means of challenging the binary Jew/Christian in reconstructions of violence in the community for whom the Gospel of Matthew is written.

The Problem

Christian narratives of self-identity often include depictions of Jews instigating violence against them. Someone wishing to chart the history of such narratives would begin with accusations of Christ-killing in New Testament literature and also include references to the church fathers and the early Christian martyr texts in which Jews hold pride of place as initiators of persecutory activity. Such a history would take note of the numerous accusations, like this one from Justin Martyr directed at his Jewish dialogue partner Trypho: "For in truth your hand was lifted high to do evil, for even when you had killed the Christ you did not repent, but you also hate and murder us" (*Dialogue with Trypho* 133.6). It would expose the unreflective incorporation of such ancient accusations into nineteenth- and twentieth-century histories of early Christianity, noting, for example, this assessment in Adolf von Harnack's monumental study *Mission and Expansion of Christianity:* "As a rule, whenever bloody persecutions are afoot in later days, the Jews are either in the background or the foreground.... By a sort of instinct they felt that Gentile Christianity was their particular foe."[5] A historian attuned to the workings of Roman imperial power would note the tragic scapegoating of Jews for Christian political gain in the empire, perhaps citing Luke as an early example of a Christian apologist who depicts the Jews as agents of violence while simultaneously exculpating Roman officials.[6]

Histories of this sort, of course, have been and continue to be written. The tragedy of the Holocaust provoked scholars to rethink nearly every aspect of early Jewish and Christian historical reconstruction, including the

---

4. Schüssler Fiorenza, *Rhetoric and Ethic,* ix.

5. Adolf von Harnack, *The Mission and Expansion of Christianity in the First Three Centuries* (orig. 1908; trans. James Moffatt; repr. New York: Harper, 1961), 58. See discussion in Judith Lieu, "Accusations of Jewish Persecution in Early Christian Sources, with Particular Reference to Justin Martyr and the *Martyrdom of Polycarp,*" in *Tolerance and Intolerance in Early Judaism and Christianity* (ed. Graham N. Stanton and Guy G. Stroumsa; Cambridge: Cambridge University Press, 1998), 279–95.

6. Note, for example, how the arrest of Paul by the Roman tribune in Acts is depicted as a "rescue," a means of preventing him from being killed by Jews (Acts 22:30–23:30; cf. 21:30–35). On depiction of Roman involvement in Acts, see Klaus Wengst, *Pax Romana and the Peace of Jesus Christ* (Philadelphia: Fortress, 1987), 89–105. Justin Martyr also casts Romans as peacemakers, preventing Jews from acting upon their murderous inclinations. He says to the Jew Trypho: "For you do not have authority to act murderously against us, *on account of those who now hold power,* but as often as you were able, that you did" (*Dialogue with Trypho* 16.4 [emphasis added]).

(re)inscription of the Jew as Violent Other in ancient and modern historiography.[7] Much New Testament scholarship on Jews as agents of violence,
including some of the most methodologically sophisticated, focused on the
"Christ-killing" charge — the historical details of the crucifixion of Jesus and
the theological and ethical implications of speaking about this execution, in
Judea, under Pontius Pilate. The works of Elisabeth Schüssler Fiorenza, John
Dominic Crossan, and James Carroll are notable for their attention to theological and ethical issues pertaining to narratives of this death.[8] Given the
currency of the Christ-killing charge as justification for Christian violence
against Jews in history, such focus is necessary and laudatory. The sophis-
tication of this scholarly output on the death of Jesus, however, is not yet
matched by work on a closely related issue: the numerous New Testament
depictions of Jews as agents of violence subsequent to the crucifixion.[9] The
problem I begin to explore in this essay is how to responsibly interpret New
Testament texts suggesting such violence.

The idea that (some) Jews either have or will persecute those who follow Jesus pervades nearly every layer of the New Testament tradition.[10]

---

7. Elisabeth Schüssler Fiorenza was among the vanguard of biblical scholars facing the issue
of anti-Semitism squarely and self-reflectively. Among her many contributions to this discussion,
see, for example, *Jesus: Miriam's Child, Sophia's Prophet: Critical Issues in Feminist Christology* (New York: Continuum, 1994), esp. 67–111; *Jesus and the Politics of Interpretation,*
115–44.

8. Schüssler Fiorenza, *Jesus: Miriam's Child,* 67–111; John Dominic Crossan, *Who Killed
Jesus? Exposing the Roots of Anti-Semitism in the Gospel Story of the Death of Jesus* (San
Francisco: Harper, 1995); James Carroll, *Constantine's Sword: The Church and the Jews*
(Boston/New York: Houghton Mifflin, 2001).

9. A stark example of the difference between treatments of New Testament narratives relating to the death of Jesus and those relating to subsequent violence directed against Jesus'
followers is found in Carroll's popular history, *Constantine's Sword.* Carroll subjects the gospel charges of Jewish responsibility for the death of Jesus to serious exegetical and theological
reflection for several chapters. Then, in an unexamined move and without further comment,
he places the murders of Stephen and James by the Jews alongside the execution of Jesus under
Pontius Pilate as part of the litany of "facts" of early Christian history (70; cf. also 108, 130,
132, 135). For other important treatments of the question of Jews as agents of violence in post-
New Testament martyrdom literature, see E. Leigh Gibson, "Jewish Antagonism or Christian
Polemic: The Case of the *Martyrdom of Pionius,*" *Journal of Early Christian Studies* 9 (2001):
339–58; Daniel Boyarin, *Dying for God: Martyrdom and the Making of Christianity and Judaism* (Figurae: Reading Medieval Culture; Stanford: Stanford University Press, 1999), esp.
127–30; Lieu, "Accusations of Jewish Persecution."

10. The usage of the terms *Christian, Jew,* and *Jewish* when speaking of New Testament
texts and other first-century phenomena is problematic and currently the focus of much discussion; see Boyarin, *Dying for God;* idem, "On the Prehistory of the *Ioudaioi;* or, Was St. John
a Christian?" in *Pauline Conversations in Context: Essays in Honor of Calvin J. Roetzel* (ed.
Janice Capel Anderson, Philip Sellew, and Claudia Setzer; Sheffield: Sheffield Academic Press,
forthcoming); John W. Marshall, *Parables of War: Reading John's Jewish Apocalypse* (Studies
in Christianity and Judaism 10; Waterloo, Ont.: Wilfrid Laurier University Press, 2001). While
I make no claim to have discerned a problem-free solution for how to speak of religious phenomena of this time period traditionally considered under the categories of Jew, Christian, or
some hyphenated version thereof, I will adopt the following procedure here: I will use the terms
Jew and *Jewish,* in general, to speak of phenomena of this period that are associated with the
social group of persons whose religious, cultural, and political practices are bound up with the

Paul states that in his "earlier life in Judaism [*en tō ioudaismō*]" he was "violently persecuting the church of God . . . trying to destroy it" (Gal 1:13), refers to a lashing at the hands of the *ioudaioi* in the hardship catalogue in 2 Cor 11:24, and makes general references to being persecuted in his letters, notably in the Corinthian and Galatian correspondence.[11] In the eschatological discourse of Mark 13, Jesus warns, "They will hand you over to councils; and you will be beaten in synagogues" (13:9). The Markan discourse on future persecution is taken over by Matthew in the mission discourse in Matt 10:16–23, which also speaks of beatings in the synagogues. Frequently the inscription of (some) Jews as persecutory makes them also murderous. The Q tradition indicts Israel for its perpetual murdering of the prophets (e.g., Q 11:49–51; 13:34–35); Matthew further embellishes this tradition by including the prediction that Pharisees will continue to kill, as well as "crucify . . . and flog in [the] synagogues" (Matt 23:34). The infamous, possibly interpolated statement of 1 Thess 2:15 also picks up the topos of Israel's murdering the prophets, noting that *ioudaioi* killed "both the Lord Jesus and the prophets, and drove us out; they displease God and oppose everyone by hindering us from speaking to the Gentiles." The Gospel of John contains several references to *ioudaioi* throwing stones and the infamous expulsion-from-the-synagogue passages, the last of which concludes with the ominous prophecy that "an hour is coming when those who kill you will think that by doing so they are offering worship to God" (John

---

God of the temple of Jerusalem and this God's laws (cf. Shaye J. D. Cohen, *The Beginnings of Jewishness: Boundaries, Varieties, Uncertainties* [Berkeley: University of California Press, 1999], 14). In recognition that Christianity is not a distinct, clearly definable religious category in the first century, I will not use this free-standing term when speaking of first-century texts. When referencing New Testament texts in which separations of Christians from Jews has not occurred, I will speak of those whose lives are marked by a particular reverence for and commitment to Jesus as Messiah as "followers of Jesus" or "disciples of Jesus." (I am aware that Marshall [*Parables of War*] argues that this is problematic in the case of the Apocalypse, which document I do not treat here.) When it is clear that those with such reverence are Jewish and not Gentile, I may speak of them as Christian-Jews or Jewish followers of Jesus. Because in many biblical texts in which Jews are designated as agents of violence, the referent is muddled (does the author mean only Jewish leaders? all Israel? Pharisees? Jews of "this generation"?), I will signal the ambiguous nature of this referent by qualifying the term *Jews* in this way: "(some) Jews." Likewise, I will often use "(some) Jews" when referring to discussions in secondary literature. When I reference a New Testament text in which the specific term *ioudaios* or *ioudaioi* is used, I will generally leave it untranslated in my text, in order to signal that the author using this term does not mean to designate all persons belonging to the social group whose religious, cultural, and political practices are bound up with the God of the temple of Jerusalem and this God's laws, but a subset thereof. The exception to this rule will be in my references to the Book of Acts, in which case I will use the specific terms *Jew* and *Judaism, Christian* and *Christianity.* While these terms were still not fixed impermeable categories at the time of the writing of Acts, I understand the author of this text to be writing in the second century and to be ideologically committed to marking a break between two distinct and separate religious/social/political communities, whom he designates as Jews and Christians.

11. Here and throughout this essay, English translations of the Bible are from the New Revised Standard Version.

16:2). In Acts the portrait of venomous, murderous Jews pulses through the narrative like a drumbeat. Before his Damascus experience, Paul is depicted as "breathing threats and murder" against the disciples of the Lord (Acts 9:1), imprisoning them and voting to sentence them to death (26:9–11). According to Acts, the Sanhedrin wishes to kill the apostles (Acts 5); Jews — in riotous lawlessness — kill Stephen (Acts 7); Jews foment violence at virtually every stop along Paul's journeys; and Jews plot to kill Paul from Acts 20 onward.[12]

In distinction to recent scholarly treatments of the role of Jews in the death of Jesus cited above, exegetical treatments of these passages depicting Jewish persecution of Jesus followers are frequently plagued by two problematic and overlapping hermeneutical assumptions: (1) These New Testament texts are read positivistically as unmediated evidence that early Jesus followers were violently persecuted; and (2) the persecuted are categorized as Christians and the persecutors as Jews, as if it were possible to reconstruct distinct separate religious groups bearing these fixed identities in the first century. As a representative indication of the pervasiveness of these two assumptions, even among leading New Testament scholars, consider the following example taken from a reader in early Christianity edited by Bart Ehrman.[13] To introduce a chapter entitled "The Attack on Christianity: Persecution and Martyrdom in the Early Church," Ehrman first notes the difficulties many first-century Jews would have with messianic claims about Jesus. He continues: "Understandably, then, the earliest persecution of Christians was by Jews. This is clear from the oldest historical account of the incipient Christian movement, the Book of Acts, and from the writings of Paul, who indicates that as a Jewish Pharisee he had persecuted Christians (Gal 1:13) and that later, as a Christian, he himself was punished by Jewish authorities (2 Cor 11:24)."[14]

---

12. The pervasiveness of the idea in the New Testament that the followers of Jesus are suffering from persecution is relevant to the thesis elaborated by Judith Perkins in *The Suffering Self: Pain and Narrative Representation in the Early Christian Era* (London/New York: Routledge, 1995) on the subjectivity of early Christians. Perkins argues that Christianity formed its political and social unity and achieved its institutional power around the image of the suffering self. In her view, the representation of the self as a body that suffers and is in need of care signals a new subjectivity being produced through the cultural discourses of the late first and early second centuries. This representation of self as sufferer challenges another traditional Greco-Roman image of the self as soul/mind controlling the body. Unfortunately, Perkins limits her discussion to Christian literature of the second century and beyond. For further discussion of this phenomenon (and further invitation to work out its implication for the reading of New Testament texts), see Brent D. Shaw, "Body/Power/Identity: The Passion of the Martyrs," *Journal of Early Christian Studies* 4 (1996): 269–312.

13. Bart D. Ehrman, ed., *After the New Testament: A Reader in Early Christianity* (New York/Oxford: Oxford University Press, 1999). For a pernicious and elaborate formulation of the violent Jew/violated Christian binary, see Robert G. Hamerton-Kelly, *Sacred Violence: Paul's Hermeneutic of the Cross* (Minneapolis: Fortress, 1992).

14. Ehrman, *After the New Testament*, 25.

The most egregious instance of positivism here is the demarcation of the Book of Acts as the "clear," "oldest" (and therefore most reliable), "historical" account of incipient Christianity. Through this move, Ehrman invites the reader to accept Act's narratives of murderous Jews as a fact of history, offering not the slightest indication of the heavy-handed ideological, often overtly anti-Jewish, tendencies of this author.[15] Moreover, the citation of Gal 1:13 and 2 Cor 11:24 without further comment also allows these verses to stand unproblematically in a continuum of violent actions against Jesus followers culminating in the deadly persecutions this chapter in Ehrman's sourcebook narrates.

In this (not uncommon) way of formulating the problem of Jewish responses to followers of Jesus, "Jew" and "Christian" are marked as stable, impermeable categories, belonging to the same taxonomic level of classification, one violent, the other violated. That is, these terms are assumed to signify two distinct religions into which aggressors and victims can be neatly slotted. When Paul was a Jew, he persecuted Christians; after he became a Christian, Jews persecuted him. This move occludes the fact that Christianity neither exists in Paul's time nor for several decades after his death and that many proto-Christianities evolving in the first and second centuries are best understood as sects within Judaism.[16] The ethical flaw of such formulations lies in the inscription of Jew as originary persecutor (murderer) and Christian as originary (sacrificial) victim.[17]

The analysis of these passages depicting Jews as agents of violence against members of the Jesus movement and systematic ethical reflection upon their

---

15. Compelling arguments for the novel as the most appropriate genre for Acts are made by Richard Pervo, *Profit with Delight: The Literary Genre of the Acts of the Apostles* (Philadelphia: Fortress, 1987). But even those (except for the most conservative) who argue that Acts falls more properly under some variation of the historical genre would not consider the portrait of Jews in Acts as a mirror representation. On the ideological function of the depiction of Jews in Acts, see especially Lawrence M. Wills, "The Depiction of the Jews in Acts," *Journal of Biblical Literature* 110 (1991): 631–54. Compare also Jack T. Sanders, *The Jews in Luke-Acts* (Philadelphia: Fortress, 1987).

16. On the problem of connotations of "Christian" when speaking of first-century religious phenomena and the taxonomic status of this term in much secondary literature, see especially Marshall, *Parables of War*, esp. 25–67. Ehrman himself knows, on some level, that "Christianity" is not a proper designation for first-century phenomena, as he indicates in his elaboration on first- and second-century "proto-Christianities" in his textbook *The New Testament: A Historical Introduction to the Early Christian Writings* (2d ed.; New York/Oxford: Oxford University Press, 2000), 2–7. Nevertheless, he reverts to the problematic Jew/Christian binary in his reader. This move would be less lamentable if his reader were not targeted, as it is, at a large undergraduate student audience that will readily digest and reinscribe this Jewish/Christian binary.

17. I use the term *originary* intending to invoke Michel Foucault's critique of the historiographic quest for pure origins/essences. See Foucault's "Nietzsche, Genealogy, History," in *Language, Counter-Memory, Practice: Selected Essays and Interviews* (ed. D. F. Bouchard; Ithaca: Cornell University Press, 1997), 139–64. I further suggest that in Christian discourse, narratives of Christians being murdered by Jews have *sacrificial* overtones in the sense that they are generally inscribed as the practice of *imitatio Christi*, whose death is most often assigned a sacrificial function.

interpretations, while a desideratum in New Testament scholarship, cannot be fully undertaken here. In the remainder of this essay I focus specifically on persecutory passages in the Gospel of Matthew and their interpretations by New Testament scholars. After identifying these passages, I note literary and theological issues that inform their construction. I then suggest alternatives to the historical positivism and the employment of a Jewish/Christian binary that feature so prominently in contemporary scholarship on violence in Matthew.

Persecution in Matthew

The idea that Jesus followers are persecuted is pervasive in Matthew. Blessings are pronounced in the Sermon on the Mount on those who are persecuted for righteousness' sake (5:10–12); the long string of woes directed against the Pharisees in Matt 23 culminates in predictions that they will "kill and crucify,...flog in...synagogues and pursue from town to town" (23:34); the parable of the banquet in 22:2–10, widely read as an allegorical rendering of the Matthean community's own situation, implies that "servants of the king" (i.e., Matthean missionaries) will be killed by those to whom they are sent (22:6). Especially notable for the way it serves to "normalize" the phenomenon of persecution is Matthew's adaptation of the Q mission discourse in Matt 10. By inserting the eschatological persecution predictions of Mark 13:9–13 — which for Mark are part of the "birth pangs" marking the end of the age — into the charge to the disciples as they go from town to town, Matthew makes all missionaries potential targets of persecution. That is, while for Mark persecution is the *extraordinary* sign that the end is near, for Matthew persecution is the *ordinary* expectation, the routine, for anyone sent out into mission by Christ.[18]

While Gentile persecutors are occasionally in view in this gospel,[19] key passages in Matthew identify the agents of violence as belonging to the house of Israel.[20] This is explicit in the woes to the "scribes and Pharisees" in Matt

---

18. Cf. Matt 10:7–16 with the similar discourse to the disciples in Luke 10:2–12. Note that Matthew extends the discourse by adding warnings of persecution (10:17–23), adapted from Mark 13:9–13. The routinization of the perception "we will be everywhere persecuted" in Matt 10 demonstrates Perkins's thesis in *Suffering Self*.

19. See, for example, Matt 24:4–14 on the destruction of the temple and the end of the age. Presumably the "governors and kings" before whom the disciples will be dragged (10:18) are also Gentile persecutors. For conflicting views on this point, compare Douglas Hare, *The Theme of Jewish Persecution of Christians in the Gospel according to St. Matthew* (Cambridge: Cambridge University Press, 1967), 101–9, with Ulrich Luz, *Matthew 8–20* (trans. James E. Crouch; Hermeneia; Minneapolis: Fortress, 2001), 88–89. For reconstruction of Gentile persecution of the Matthean community, see David C. Sim, *The Gospel of Matthew and Christian Judaism* (Edinburgh: Clark, 1988).

20. For a different characterization of the agents of persecution in Matthew that privileges class conflict as a primary factor in Matthean inscriptions of violence, see Warren Carter,

23, for it is specifically these who are predicted to kill, crucify, flog, and pursue (23:34). That Matthew draws the net larger here in order to include more than these religious leaders is suggested by his indictment, following immediately after the woes, of "this generation" (23:36) and of all "Jerusalem" (23:37). The further utilization of the topos of Israel persecuting its own prophets in 5:11–12 and 22:1–10 places Israel in the role of persecuting Jewish followers of Jesus in these two passages. The explicit instruction for the Twelve in Matthew's mission discourse to "go nowhere among the Gentiles...but...rather to the lost sheep of the house of Israel" (10:5–6), makes clear that those who will "arrest and flog" (10:17) and "persecute from town to town" (10:23) are of that same house.

The *pervasiveness* of the accusation that Israel persecutes, kills, or intends to kill Jesus followers in Matthew is matched by the *evasiveness* of the details — the charges, the motives, the causes, the specific agents of the persecution. The lack of explanatory detail is succinctly acknowledged by Douglas Hare in his classic book on persecution in Matthew. He notes that Matthew avoids sociological causes for persecution: "Only the theological cause, the obduracy of Israel is of interest to the author. Nor is the mystery of Israel's sin probed, whether in terms of dualistic categories or in terms of predestinarianism. Israel's sin is a fact of history which requires no explanation. It is the sufficient cause of the persecution. For Matthew no other explanation is necessary."[21]

Literary Convention

While sociological details are absent, the "fact" of Israel's sin in Matthew does conform to a literary topos. According to this literary convention, suggested first in Deuteronomic literature and elaborated more fully in early Judaism, Israel has always persecuted its prophets. As Odil Steck demonstrates, in its fullest expressions the prophet-persecution topos contains the following elements: (a) Israel, from the beginning, has been a disobedient people; (b) Yahweh repeatedly sends prophets to rebuke disobedience and call for repentance; (c) Israel repeatedly resists these prophets, often through persecution and murder; (d) thus inciting the wrath of Yahweh.[22]

"Constructions of Violence and Identity in Matthew's Gospel" (paper presented at the annual meeting of the Society of Biblical Literature, Toronto, Ontario, 25 November 2002).

21. Hare, *Theme of Jewish Persecution*, 145.

22. Odil Hannes Steck, *Israel und das gewaltsame Geschick der Propheten: Untersuchungen zur Überlieferung des deuteronomistischen Geschichtsbildes im Alten Testament, Spätjudentum und Urchristentum* (Wissenschaftliche Monographien zum Alten und Neuen Testament 23; Neukirchen-Vluyn: Neukirchener Verlag, 1967), esp. 60–80. For earlier treatments, see Hans-Joachim Schoeps, *Die jüdischen Prophetenmorde* (Symbolae biblicae upsalienses 2; Uppsala: Wretmans, 1943); and H. A. Fischel, "Martyr and Prophet," *Jewish Quarterly Review* 37 (1947): 265–80, 363–86. For this motif in the Hebrew Bible, see especially Neh 9:16–31 and 2 Chr 36:11–21 and the discussion in Steck, *Israel und das gewaltsame Geschick der Propheten,*

This topos is present in Q material that Matthew incorporates into his narrative. For example, the blessing upon the persecuted in 5:12 is further elaborated: "In the same way they persecuted the prophets who were before you" (cf. Luke 6:23). Jerusalem is castigated as the city that kills the prophets (Matt 23:37; cf. Luke 13:34). The scribes and Pharisees are linked to the murderers of all the righteous from all times: "Therefore I send you prophets, sages, and scribes, some of whom you will kill and crucify . . . so that upon you may come all the righteous blood shed on earth, from the blood of righteous Abel to the blood of Zechariah son of Barachiah, whom you murdered between the sanctuary and the altar" (Matt 23:34–35; cf. Luke 11:50–51).[23]

Matthean redaction also conforms to the prophet-persecution topos in the instance of the parable of the wedding banquet in 22:2–10.[24] Matthew's version of this parable differs from the Lukan version by adding that after the king's invitation to the marriage feast is declined some of the invitees "seized his slaves, mistreated them, and killed them" (22:6). Compare the similarity between this parable and Josephus's reworking in *Antiquities* 9.263–65 of an invitation sent by King Hezekiah: Josephus notes that Hezekiah, after purifying the temple, sent messengers throughout the southern kingdom, and also to the northern kingdom of Israel, exhorting them to come to Jerusalem and join with him in the celebration of the festival of unleavened bread. In these details, Josephus follows the story as it is told in 2 Chr 30. However, Josephus also adds the following details, not found in the Chronicler's version: "When [the king's] envoys came and brought them this message . . . the Israelites were not only not persuaded, but even laughed at

---

60–80. This is a theme common to the Hellenistic Jewish work *Lives of the Prophets*, where six of the twenty-three named prophets are said to have died by unnatural means, and the *Martyrdom of Isaiah*, which narrates that Isaiah was sawn in two (cf. Heb 11:37b). For discussion of rabbinic elaborations on this theme, see Fischel, "Martyr and Prophet." Steck includes discussion of rabbinic as well as Muslim and later Christian elaborations; *Israel und das gewaltsame Geschick der Propheten*, 86–109.

23. The violent death of the Zechariah, first mentioned in Chronicles, is frequently elaborated in Second Temple and rabbinic employments of the prophet-persecution topos. Compare 2 Chr 24:17–22; Josephus, *Antiquities* 9.168–69; *Lives of the Prophets* 23; Luke 11:51; Targum to Lamentations 2:20; and Babylonian Talmud, tractate *Giṭṭin* 57b. See Sheldon H. Blank, "The Death of Zechariah in Rabbinic Literature," *Hebrew Union College Annual* 13 (1938): 327–45; Schoeps, *Jüdischen Prophetenmorde*, 17–21.

24. Matt 22:2–10: "The kingdom of heaven may be compared to a king who gave a wedding banquet for his son. He sent his slaves to call those who had been invited to the wedding banquet, but they would not come. Again he sent other slaves, saying, 'Tell those who have been invited: Look, I have prepared my dinner, my oxen and my fat calves have been slaughtered, and everything is ready; come to the wedding banquet.' But they made light of it and went away, one to his farm, another to his business, while the rest seized his slaves, mistreated them, and killed them. The king was enraged. He sent his troops, destroyed those murderers, and burned their city. Then he said to his slaves, 'The wedding is ready, but those invited were not worthy. Go therefore into the main streets, and invite everyone you find to the wedding banquet.' Those slaves went out into the streets and gathered all whom they found, both good and bad; so the wedding hall was filled with guests."

his envoys as fools; and, when their prophets exhorted them in like manner and foretold what they would suffer if they did not alter their course to one of piety toward God, they poured scorn upon [the envoys] and finally seized them and killed them" (*Antiquities* 9.265).[25] In their depiction of the persecution and murder of the prophets who are sent with "the king's" message, Matthew and Josephus adhere to the same formula.

Theological Necessity

The sufferings that Matthew predicts to come upon his community conform to the sufferings of Christ he also narrates. Note the similarity between the address to disciples in Matt 10:17–18:

> Beware of them, for they will hand you over [*paradidōmai*] to councils [*synedria*] and flog [*mastigoō*] you in their synagogues; and you will be dragged before governors [*hēgemonoi*] and kings because of me, as a testimony to them and the Gentiles.

and the prediction/narration of Jesus' passion:

> See, we are going up to Jerusalem, and the Son of Man will be handed over [*paradidōmai*] to the chief priests and scribes, and they will condemn him to death; then they will hand him over to the Gentiles to be mocked and flogged [*mastigoō*] and crucified. (20:18–19a)

> Now the chief priests and the whole council [*synedrion*] were looking for false testimony against Jesus. (26:59)

> They bound him, led him away, and handed him over [*paradidōmai*] to Pilate the governor [*hēgemōn*]. (27:2)

For Matthew, as for many authors of the New Testament, the suffering of followers of Jesus is a positive phenomenon in the sense that it is necessary for the shaping of their self-understanding and for community formation. To be a disciple of Jesus is to take up the practice of *imitatio Christi*. Matthew 10 is particularly steeped with this sentiment, with its predictions of impending persecution highlighted above (10:16–23); its warning that the community will be hated by all (10:22); and its exhortations for disciples to be like their teachers (10:24–25), to bear the cross, and to lose their lives (10:38–39). The welding of suffering to Christ belief is often cast in positive terms by commentators as well. This is how Ulrich Luz summarizes his commentary on the persecution of the disciples in 10:16–23:

> The central point of the whole text is Matthew's conviction that proclaiming the kingdom, including following Jesus, *of necessity* involves

---

25. The translation of Josephus is by Ralph Marcus in the Loeb Classical Library (Cambridge: Harvard University Press, 1937), 6.141.

suffering. For this reason the church's experiences in the mission to Israel that are expressed with the aid of Mark 13:9–13 are given a fundamental significance. Luther correctly translates the spirit of v. 22 (*esesthe misoumenoi hypo pantōn*), "And you *must* be hated by everybody." On this point there is a deep convergence between Matthew and Paul. The "apostolate" is "essentially — not merely fortuitously — ... active suffering and ... suffering activity."[26] In vv. 24–25 Matthew will indicate the christological basis of this conviction; in vv. 26–39 he will develop it.[27]

While the critiques of how Paul's/Matthew's/Luther's privileging of suffering has been used to justify Christian complacency in the face of oppression are multiple and crucial, I will not elaborate them here.[28] What I wish to point out at present is (1) how such a statement — "the apostolate is essentially, not merely fortuitously, active suffering and suffering activity" — muddles distinctions between theological affirmation and historical reconstruction in Luz's (and like-minded) commentary; and (2) how "persecuting Jews" function as the unspoken complement to "persecuted Jesus followers" in such formulations. First, if Matthew needs to communicate, for theological purposes, that the suffering of disciples is essential and inevitable, then he *must* depict these followers in his narrative as suffering or about to suffer. Likewise, if modern interpreters of Matthew affirm his theological claim, then they *must* reconstruct the historical situation of the Matthean community as one involving persecution. Such predeterminism undermines the task of historical reconstruction, because it disallows raising the question of the historical possibility of such persecution. Second, if Jesus followers *must* suffer, then it is necessary for outside agents to inflict suffering upon them. Because in Matthew these agents are most often (some) Jews, the unspoken corollary to understanding suffering as essential in this text is to understand (some) Jews as predestined to persecute.

Of course, one may respond to this argument by suggesting that in Matthew's case, history preceded theology. That is, an actual historical situation of persecution by (some) Jews prompted Matthew to make the best of a bad situation by finding some theological good in that suffering, the affirmation that it is Christlike. Nevertheless, the language of *essence* and *inevitability* found in Matthew, replicated and affirmed in Christian scholarship,

---

26. Here Luz (*Matthew 8–20*, 94) is citing Jürgen Moltmann, *The Church in the Power of the Spirit* (New York: Harper & Row, 1977), 361.

27. Luz, *Matthew 8–20*, 94 (emphasis original). Compare the tenor of Luz's entire discussion (95–122) of Matt 10:24–42.

28. See Anthony B. Pinn, *Why Lord? Suffering and Evil in Black Theology* (New York: Continuum, 1999); Schüssler Fiorenza, *Jesus: Miriam's Child*, 98–107; Joanne Carlson Brown and Carole R. Bohn, eds., *Christianity, Patriarchy, and Abuse: A Feminist Critique* (New York: Pilgrim, 1989); Rita Nakashima Brock, *Journeys by Heart: A Christology of Erotic Power* (New York: Crossroad, 1988).

elides the two-step process of historical experience followed by theological reflection, substituting a form of predestinarianism in its place.

Grounded in the Text

In spite of the fact that Matthew's narrative of routine persecution conforms to the literary convention of the persecuted prophet and serves a heavily weighted theological need,[29] most biblical scholars assume that at root there lies an originary historical phenomenon, beyond the crucifixion of Jesus, of violent persecution and — some would say — even death at the hands of (some) Jews. To put it another way, while the narrative of persecutory Jews in Matthew cannot pass the criterion of dissimilarity on either end (the prophet-persecution topos precedes, and the *imitatio Christi* theology develops quickly after Jesus' death), most scholars do not doubt its historicity.[30]

Perhaps they are right. Intra-Jewish violence in Hellenistic and Roman times is suggested in several documents. Literary, epigraphic and archeological remains attest to the pervasiveness of violence in the provinces of imperial Rome. If one were building on a theoretical model that could account for violence in the Matthean community within the framework of this larger historical complex of violence or on an analogy to the working of violence in a comparable sociological setting, the argument that Matthew's text reflects a historical situation of persecution by (some) Jews might indeed be

---

29. And — if one finds Perkin's thesis compelling — a psychological need as well.

30. Distinctions are made among Matthean scholars about the nature and scope of Jewish persecution. Robert H. Gundry has the most "global" view of Jews as persecutors of Christians. In the second edition of his commentary on Matthew, he foregrounds the pervasiveness of Jewish persecution in the Matthean community by changing his subtitle from "A Commentary on His Literary and Theological Art" to "A Commentary on His Handbook for a Mixed Church under Persecution" and by noting in the introduction to the new edition: "Persecution does not have its source in Roman government, but among Jewish leaders in Jerusalem"; *Matthew: A Commentary on His Handbook for a Mixed Church under Persecution* (2d ed.; Grand Rapids: Eerdmans, 1994), 5. Daniel Harrington is cautious regarding the extent of persecution, but still assumes its historical reality. He notes of Jewish persecution of the Matthean community: "What persecution there was seems . . . to have been local and sporadic — but nonetheless real for those who suffered"; and further: "Jewish persecution of early Christians should not be exaggerated. By no means does it equal Christianity's record in persecuting Jews over the centuries. Moreover, the 'persecution' alluded to in Matt. 10:17 pitted Jew against Jew; it took place within Judaism and was not the action of one religion against another"; *The Gospel of Matthew* (Sacra pagina 1; Collegeville, Minn.: Liturgical Press, 1991), 147, 148. Sim argues similarly to Harrington, reconstructing Jewish persecution of Matthew's "Christian Jews" as "unofficial and sporadic" and stressing the conflict as *intrareligious; Gospel of Matthew and Christian Judaism,* 151–63. Both Hare (*Theme of Jewish Persecution*) and Luz (*Matthew 8– 20*) argue that after 70 c.e. the church is no longer persecuted by Jews but that Matthew looks back to pre-70 persecution of Christ believers by Jews when shaping his gospel. Graham N. Stanton disputes this, arguing for post-70 Jewish persecution as well; *Gospel for a New People: Studies in Matthew* (Edinburgh: Clark, 1992), 159–60.

a compelling one.[31] One potential ethical good to come from such a reconstruction would lie in recalling to First World biblical scholars, who generally
work in isolation from sites of violence in our own regimes of domination,
the violence to which marginalized peoples in kyriarchal systems are subject,
then as now.

However, the positing of a Matthean community that was persecuted by
(some) Jews is seldom based on a theoretical model rendering such violence
possible. Rather, the more common procedure is to rely solely on biblical citation as "evidence" of such violence. This positivistic framework leads to an
interpretive process akin to fundamentalist proof-texting. Many arguments
that (some) Jews persecuted members of the Matthean community can be
reduced to the reasoning, "they must have done it, because the biblical text
says so."

Most acknowledge that not all Matthean passages on persecution and
martyrdom of early Christ followers can be read as transparently referen-
tial,[32] and therefore a particular passage or phrase — or sometimes only one
word — will be excised as hyperbolic. However, the remaining text, free of
excision, is cited as historical evidence that (some) Jewish persecution of
Matthean community members took place. Interpretations of Matt 23:34
illustrate this procedure. This verse, which ends Matthew's long series of
"woes" addressed to the Pharisees, reads: "Therefore I send you prophets,
sages, and scribes, some of whom you will kill and crucify, and some you
will flog in your synagogues and pursue from town to town." Because commentators generally agree that Pharisees did not have power to crucify, this
verse is plucked from the list, and either assigned to a later interpolator[33]
or attributed to another motive, such as "the evangelist's fears for the future."[34] But rather than asking whether the whole string of persecutory acts
might also be hyperbolic, the verbs *kill, flog,* and *pursue* are left to stand as
indicators of actual harassment and murder.

Jack Sanders follows a similar procedure, excising many verses and re-
taining others as historically reliable, without offering rationale for these
judgments. Here, for example, is his assessment of 22:3–6, a text describing the fate of the king's servants in the parable of the wedding
banquet:[35] "In Matt 22:3–6 we likely have a reference to the killing of,

---

31. Carter takes steps in this direction by making analogies between the Matthean community and millennialist sectarian groups who are subject to persecution from establishment
forces. See his "Constructions of Violence and Identity in Matthew's Gospel."

32. Gundry, *Matthew,* is an exception here; see above.

33. Hare, *Theme of Jewish Persecution,* 83–93.

34. Sim, *Gospel of Matthew and Christian Judaism,* 160. Cf. Luz who suggests that the verb
to crucify is added so that suffering of disciples conforms to that of Christ; *Das Evangelium
nach Matthäus* (Evangelisch-katholischer Kommentar zum Neuen Testament 1; Neukirchen-
Vluyn: Neukirchener Verlag, 1997), 3.371–72 n. 27.

35. For discussion of the literary topos of the persecuted prophet after which this parable is
patterned, see the discussion on pp. 341–43 above.

first, Israelite prophets and, second, Christian missionaries, since these are the probable identities of the groups of servants sent in the parable to the invited guests. Thus, while John's allusion to the killing of Christians is…subject to doubt, *Matthew's seems to be more precise.* Matthew therefore attests…persecution…along with ostracism (as in John), *with possible occasional killing added.*"[36]

Circular arguments are frequently employed to make the case for Jewish persecution of the Matthean community: texts outside Matthew are assumed to be transparent and then cited to prove the transparency of Matthew's own texts on violence.[37] Graham Stanton makes his argument that Jewish persecution of Christians extended into the post-70 era by citing John 16:2: "They will put you out of the synagogues. Indeed, an hour is coming when those who kill you will think that by doing so they are offering worship to God." He also cites "evidence" from 1 Clement, where *zēlos* among Jewish opponents of Christianity leads "literally" to death.[38] Luz, in a footnote to his commentary on Matt 10, directs the reader interested in the question of "the persecution of the Matthean community by Judaism" to consult Douglas Hare's work on persecution in Matthew, along with "Gal. 4:29, 6:12, I Thess 2:15–16, etc."[39] The "etc." here is apparently meant to suggest the boundless number of passages that could be cited.

To be clear, I repeat that I do not mean to suggest that the only possible reconstruction of Matthean community is one that is "violence free." I argue here, rather, that reconstructions of Matthean history need to be made on the basis of theoretical models, rather than proof-texts. To be persuasive, reconstructions positing violence against Matthean community members should assess how the literary, theological, and psychological needs pressing on the author, such as I outlined here, contribute to the depictions of a suffering community. Such reconstructions would also need to engage the recent work of New Testament scholars who theorize that not all texts depicting violent persecution have their rhetorical exigency in historical persecutory acts.[40] Furthermore, in order to be ethically responsible, such arguments

---

36. Jack T. Sanders, "The First Decades of Jewish-Christian Relations," *Aufstieg und Niedergang der römischen Welt* (Berlin/New York: de Gruyter, 1988), 2.26.3.1050 (emphasis added). See similar argument in his *Schismatics, Sectarians, and Dissidents* (London: SCM, 1993).

37. Circular arguments plague reconstructions of Jews as violent persecutors. On their employment in the case of the martyrdom of Pionius, see Gibson, "Jewish Antagonism or Christian Polemic."

38. Stanton, *Gospel for a New People,* 159–60.

39. Luz, *Matthew 8–20,* 90 n. 47.

40. Jan Willem van Henten, "Martyrs as Heroes of the Christian People: Some Remarks on the Continuity between Jewish and Christian Martyrology, with Pagan Analogies," in *Martyrium in Multidisciplinary Perspective: Memorial Louis Reekmans* (ed. M. Lamberigts and P. van Deun; Bibliotheca ephemeridum theologicarum lovaniensium 117; Louvain: Leuven University Press, 1995), 303–22; Leonard A. Thompson, *The Book of Revelation: Apocalypse and Empire* (Oxford: Oxford University Press, 1990).

would need to avoid the dualistic inscription: Jewish/persecutor and Christian/persecuted. Rather than inscribing incidents of persecution as unique and "essential" to Christian origins, such reconstruction would need to place them on a continuum of hostile acts directed toward sectarian groups preceding, concurrent with, and subsequent to the writing of the Gospel of Matthew.[41] I conclude this essay with attention to this task.

Destabilizing Binaries

In an effort to resist the dichotomous inscription, Jew/persecutor and Christian/persecuted, some recent scholars are careful to signal that when they speak of Jewish violence directed against the Matthean community they are speaking of *intra-Jewish* violence.[42] Furthermore, in an effort to reconstruct a Matthean community situation in which points of tension are not merely between Christian Jews and non-Christian Jews, careful attention is being paid to the ways in which Roman imperial power comes into play in this community.[43]

I suggest that another fruitful way to complicate the narrative of intra-Jewish persecution in the Gospel of Matthew is to begin with a story outside the New Testament: Josephus's narration of the death of James. The story is embedded in an evaluation of the high priesthood of Ananus II:

> Ananus thought that he had a favourable opportunity because Festus [Roman governor] was dead and Albinus [succeeding Roman governor] was still on the way. And so he convened the judges of the Sanhedrin and brought before them a man named James, the brother of Jesus who was called the Christ, and certain others. He accused them of having transgressed the law and delivered them up to be stoned. Those of the inhabitants of the city who were considered the most fair-minded and who were strict in observance of the law were offended at this. They therefore secretly sent to King Agrippa urging him, for Ananus had not even been correct in his first step, to order him to desist from any further such actions. Certain of them even went to meet Albinus, who was on his way from Alexandria, and informed

---

41. My argument that reconstructions of persecution in the Matthean community should not posit such violence as "originary/essential" but on a continuum with other incidents of persecution within Greco-Roman and early Jewish cultures is analogous to Schüssler Fiorenza's argument that egalitarian impulses in the Jesus movement should not be seen as "originating" with Jesus, but rather in line with several ancient social movements and emancipatory struggles against kyriarchal relations of exploitation. See her "Revisioning Christian Origins: *In Memory of Her* Revisited," in *Christian Origins: Worship, Belief and Society* (ed. Kieran J. O'Mahony; London: Continuum International, forthcoming).

42. Harrington, *Gospel of Matthew,* 147–48; Sim, *Gospel of Matthew and Christian Judaism,* 151–63.

43. Warren Carter, *Matthew and Empire: Initial Explorations* (Harrisburg, Pa.: Trinity, 2001).

him that Ananus had no authority to convene the Sanhedrin without his consent. Convinced by these words, Albinus angrily wrote to Ananus threatening to take vengeance upon him. King Agrippa, because of Ananus' action, deposed him from the high priesthood which he had held for three months and replaced him with Jesus the son of Damnaeus. (*Antiquities* 20.200–203)[44]

This remarkable vignette is the only extant first-century text speaking of intra-Jewish violence involving followers of Jesus that is not written by a Jesus follower. I do not mean to suggest that Josephus offers to us the "true" story of early relations between Christian and non-Christian Jews; he is as ideologically driven as any historiographer. Unlike authors of early Christian literature, however, Josephus has no interest in crafting the subjectivity of Jesus followers or in defending their cause. For these reasons, his text offers us a different, useful angle from which to begin a reconstruction of the possible dynamics of violence directed at Jesus followers in the first century.

The high priest Ananus notes that the interim between the death of one Roman governor and the arrival of another gives him opportunity to convene the judges of the council (or Sanhedrin), to charge James and others with transgressing the law, and to have them stoned. This passage is generally studied for what it might reveal about the power of the Sanhedrin to execute and therefore for what bearing it might have for understanding the trial of Jesus. But for understanding the relationship between non-Christian Jews and Christian Jews subsequent to Jesus' death, it is the next sentence that is most intriguing. Josephus notes that those inhabitants of the city who were considered the most fair-minded and who were strict in the observance of the law were "offended at this" — or better, "burdened with grief over this" (*bareōs ēnegkan epi toutō*).[45] These fair-minded and strict interpreters of the law seek to have Ananus deposed for his flagrant lawlessness.

If this were the only extant historical document regarding relations between Christian Jews and non-Christian Jews in the first century, we would conclude that Christian Jews, such as James, had important and sympathetic non-Christian Jewish friends. The strict observers of the law are "burdened with grief" at Ananus's reckless use of power and the resulting death of the brother of Jesus and certain others. They use their influence to convince Rome to depose a priest who has put at least one follower of Jesus to death.[46] Grief prompts political action, resulting in a measure of justice.

---

44. The translation of Josephus is by Louis H. Feldman in the Loeb Classical Library (Cambridge: Harvard University Press, 1965), 10.107, 109.

45. I am indebted to Steve Mason for this translation. For his discussion of this passage, see *Josephus and the New Testament* (Peabody, Mass.: Hendrickson, 1992), 175–81.

46. It is not clear whether the "certain others" (*tinai heteroi*) executed were also followers of Jesus. Mason suggests that *heteroi* might suggest others "of a different kind" (*Josephus and the New Testament*, 177). If so, this passage in itself underscores my argument that reconstructions of violence against Jesus followers should not inscribe such violence as "unique" to this group.

This text does not inscribe the binary (Jewish) persecutors/(Christian) persecuted, nor even the triangle Jew-Christian-Roman. Rather, it depicts (1) a Jewish high priest hostile to (2) the brother James, who is executed, and (3) certain others (perhaps non-Christian Jews), also executed; (4) a prominent non-Christian Jewish group sympathetic to and politically motivated on behalf of the executed; (5) the Jewish client king; and (6) the Roman overlord.

At the very least, the multiple subjects in this text should prevent interpreters from citing it as an instance of Jews responsible for the death of Christians.[47] Furthermore, since James is generally regarded as holding a position similar to Matthew on law observance, one could argue by analogy that similar alliances hold — or, perhaps better — once held, in this community as well. Matthean scholars who wish to reconstruct hostility, even murderous violence, directed at followers of Christ by "strict observers of the law" must also account for a text suggesting that, in at least one instance, these two groups were united in common grief.

---

47. Though this is a common practice. See, for example, Luz, *Evangelium nach Matthäus,* 3.371.

21

African American Churches and Galatians 3:28

A Brief Assessment of the Appropriation of an Egalitarian Paradigm

Demetrius Williams

There is no longer Jew or Greek, there is no longer slave or free, there is no longer male and female; for all of you are one in Christ Jesus.
—Galatians 3:28 (NRSV)

Elisabeth Schüssler Fiorenza in her classic work *In Memory of Her,*[1] which offers a creative feminist theological reconstruction of Christian origins, examines Gal 3:28 as a central vision for the early Christian missionary movement. It appears that these missionaries believed, on the basis of the baptismal saying of 3:26–28, that they had transcended (at least within the Christian assemblies) the three traditional categories of human division and oppression. They formulated this slogan according to the language of their day: "There is no longer Jew or Greek [race/ethnicity], there is no longer slave or free [class], there is no longer male and female [gender], but all are one [equal] in Christ." This vision of Christian freedom and unity in Christ offered enormous implications for social relations within the Christian communities. On the basis of this baptismal formulation, Schüssler Fiorenza argues that

> Gal 3:28 not only advocates the abolition of religious-cultural divisions and of the domination and exploitation wrought by institutional

---

1. Elisabeth Schüssler Fiorenza, *In Memory of Her: A Feminist Theological Reconstruction of Christian Origins* (New York: Crossroad, 1983). It was this work that inspired and sparked my interest in exploring the use and function of Gal 3:28 in the African American religious context. If the vision of Gal 3:28 offered, for some early Christians, potentially radical challenges to the Greco-Roman social order (wherein slavery and social stratification were the order of the day), I could not imagine that African Americans would not have also seized this paradigm in their own challenges to the social order of American slavery and racism. To my delight, they certainly did!

slavery but also of domination based on sexual divisions. It repeats with different categories and words that within the Christian community no structures of dominance can be tolerated. Gal 3:28 is therefore best understood as a communal Christian self-definition rather than a statement about the baptized individual. It proclaims that in the Christian community all distinctions of religion, race, class, nationality, and gender are insignificant. All the baptized are equal, they are one in Christ.[2]

Paul apparently inherited and accepted from this pre-Pauline mission the egalitarian baptismal statement on Christian unity and equality and attempted to incorporate its tenets into his pastoral and missionary activity, at least in some instances.[3] Some interpreters suggest that Gal 3:28 had far-reaching sociopolitical implications for Paul and for those "in Christ."[4] For Richard Horsley the implications of Paul's preaching and mission among Gentile communities actually entailed the establishment of counterimperial communities, which indicates that "the principle forms of social domination that prevailed in Roman imperial society were supposedly transcended in the new alternative society. Presumably this formula expressed at least the ideal social relations in the new movement, the *ekklēsia,* for Paul and his own mission."[5]

Just how far-reaching the social implications of this vision are, especially for Paul, however, is a matter of great debate. While Paul utilized the statement in Gal 3:28 in its entirety, he is far from unequivocal on the social implications of it when the Corinthians themselves apparently sought clarity on this matter (e.g., Paul excludes the pair "no longer male and female" in 1 Cor 12:13).[6] Despite the language of unity and equality expressed in Gal 3:28, Paul was willing to stand firm on only the "no longer Jew or Greek" reality.[7] The reason is clear: on this question hangs the very success of his mission to the Gentiles. He was not willing to compromise this aspect of his mission at any cost, and this was the only category for which he formulated a plan of action (justification by faith alone). Thus Paul's ambiguity on the social reality for all the elements of the statement seems apparent. Nevertheless, the vision of human unity and equality expressed in Gal 3:28

---

2. Ibid., 213.

3. Ibid., 220.

4. Hans Dieter Betz, *Galatians: A Commentary on Paul's Letter to the Churches in Galatia* (Hermeneia; Philadelphia: Fortress, 1979), 190; Richard Horsley, "Paul and Slavery: A Critical Alternative to Recent Readings," *Semeia* 83–84 (1998): 153–200.

5. Horsley, "Paul and Slavery," 177.

6. Elisabeth Schüssler Fiorenza, "Rhetorical Situation and Historical Reconstruction in 1 Corinthians," *New Testament Studies* 33 (1987): 37.

7. While Horsley ("Paul and Slavery," 177) disagrees with this position, he concedes that "by scholarly consensus, Paul was adamant that there be 'no longer Jew or Greek' in the assemblies he helped organize among the people of Asia Minor and Greece."

offered great appeal for future generations confronted with the realities of human divisions, oppression, servitude, and social fragmentation.

African Americans faced with the realities of racism and class oppression centuries later found a biblical statement such as Gal 3:28 quite appealing. Although African Americans, like the ancient Corinthians, have had to deal with Paul's ambiguity on the social implications of this saying, they did not cast him aside as useless.[8] The egalitarian vision of Gal 3:28 certainly did not escape the attention of African Americans as they combed the Scriptures to find biblical support in their quest for freedom and equality. To be sure, the vision of human unity and equality that Gal 3:28 espoused had enormous impact upon enslaved blacks. Although this apparent fact is stated and acknowledged by several contemporary African American scholars, theologians, and interpreters of the Bible,[9] no adequate elaboration of the political-religious uses of Gal 3:28 in African American discourses of unity and equality has been explored.[10] What I hope to offer here is a brief examination of some of the uses of Gal 3:28 in African American rhetoric concerning the unity of humanity, freedom, and equality.

The African American Religious Tradition and Galatians 3:28

Vincent Wimbush, one of the leading voices in African American biblical hermeneutics, in an insightful overview of the use of the Bible in the African American experience, notes that during the late eighteenth and early nineteenth centuries — during the period of the American Revolution — African Americans sought to institutionalize an ethical and moral principle that

---

8. Allen Dwight Callahan, " 'Brother Saul': An Ambivalent Witness to Freedom," *Semeia* 83–84 (1998): 235–50.

9. See, for example, Latta R. Thomas, *Biblical Faith and the Black American* (Valley Forge, Pa.: Judson, 1976); Amos Jones Jr., *Paul's Message of Freedom: What Does It Mean to the Black Church?* (Valley Forge, Pa.: Judson, 1984); Cain H. Felder, *Troubling Biblical Waters: Race, Class, and Family* (Maryknoll, N.Y.: Orbis, 1989); Vincent L. Wimbush, "The Bible and African Americans: An Outline of an Interpretive History," in *Stony the Road We Trod: African American Biblical Interpretation* (ed. Cain H. Felder; Minneapolis: Fortress, 1991), 81–97.

10. Vincent Wimbush, who has been one of the trailblazers in the emerging field of African American biblical hermeneutics, certainly mentions the significance of Gal 3:28 for African Americans in two important works (cf. "Bible and African Americans," 90; and "Reading Texts through Worlds, Worlds through Texts," *Semeia* 62 [1993]: 129–39, 62). He also expounds briefly upon the African American historical context and the hermeneutical framework in which the passage's import emerged. But he does not provide an analysis of the function of Gal 3:28 within African American religious-political rhetoric from actual sermons, speeches, or narratives. He does, however, provide samples of speeches and statements employing seminal quotes and allusions from Acts ("Reading Texts through Worlds," 132–36), which were used in conjunction with Gal 3:28 to support the overall principle of human unity and equality. These observations, to be sure, do not diminish Wimbush's contributions in this area at all, but allow room for the lacuna to be filled, if even in a cursory fashion.

stressed the ideal of Christian unity.[11] Interestingly, despite the classic paradigms of liberation in the Old Testament (in particular, the exodus-promised
land saga), they found a small selection of passages from the New Testament
that embodied their aim. Wimbush elaborates further in another study:

> The historical intent in the dramatic narratives of the Old Testament
> notwithstanding, there was a certain cluster of passages from the New
> Testament, especially Galatians 3:26–28 and Acts 2; 10:34–36, that
> provided the evocative rhetorical and visionary prophetic critique and
> the hermeneutical foundation for this dominant "mainstream" African
> American "reading" of the Bible and American culture. These passages
> were important on account of their emphasis upon the hope for the
> realization of the universality of salvation. They were often quoted
> and paraphrased in efforts to relate them to the racial situation in the
> U.S. by generations of African Americans — from the famous to the
> unknown.[12]

To be sure, Gal 3:28 and the passages from Acts[13] were used time and
again to level protest against injustices in American religion and society and
to offer an alternative vision to the present state of affairs.[14] These select
passages were also important because they confirmed within African Americans the idea of "the equality of all people before God." This idea was
seized not only by literate blacks in the North, but also by illiterate (and
the small minority of literate) slaves in the South. The majority of enslaved
blacks, lacking literary skills, were nevertheless exposed initially to the idea
of the equality of all people before God from evangelical Christianity in the
form of prayers, sermons, and exhortations at camp and revival meetings.
Through these means, evangelical Christianity impressed upon both master
and slave that they were sinners equally in need of salvation. So impressive
was the idea of "the equality of all people before God" that it became for
African Americans the basic source of authority, and they have been unre-
servedly committed to this biblical anthropology.[15] According to Peter Paris,
who explores this idea in some detail, this notion represents "that tradition

---

11. Wimbush, "Bible and African Americans," 90.

12. Wimbush, "Reading Texts through Worlds," 132.

13. The Holy Spirit's descent at Pentecost and the prophecy of Joel, "your sons and daughters
shall prophesy" (Acts 2:17); "God is no respecter of persons" (10:34–36); God "hath made of
one blood all nations of men for to dwell on all the face of the earth" (17:26) (all quotations
from the King James Version).

14. Wimbush, "Bible and African Americans," 90.

15. Peter Paris, *The Social Teachings of the Black Churches* (Philadelphia: Fortress, 1985),
11. Paris states further: "Their raison d'être is inextricably tied to the function of opposing the
beliefs and practices of racism by proclaiming the biblical view of humanity as they have appropriated it, that is, the equality of all persons under God. Thus their moral aim is theologically
grounded. The doctrine of human equality under God is, for them, the final authority for all
matters pertaining to faith, thought, and practice. In short, its function in the black experience
is categorical, that is, it is unconditional, absolute, and universally applicable" (14).

governed by the principle of non-racism, which [is called] the black Christian tradition. The fundamental principle of the black Christian tradition is depicted most adequately in the biblical doctrine of the parenthood of God and the kinship of all peoples — which is a version of the traditional sexist expression 'the fatherhood of God and the brotherhood of men.' "[16]

The black Christian tradition's most useful function was not only to give African Americans a fundamental principle with which to critique American oppression and society, but more important a means of justifying and motivating the endeavors for survival and the social transformation of society. The discovery of this principle revealed to African Americans the contradictions implicit in the religion of white Americans, whose practice of racism and oppression over their fellow human beings contradicted this biblical understanding of humanity. Thus the black Christian tradition utilized all available means to effect religious and moral reform in the society at large. In effect, it posited the most stinging moral and religious dilemma to the soul of white America and its practice of Christianity, and it was born in opposition to that problem. For this reason the black Christian principle has been employed by oppressed African Americans in their efforts to press America to live up to its rhetoric of "freedom, liberty, and justice for all." Paris states that the principle of "the equality of all people before God" was so important that "apart from [this] tradition it is doubtful that blacks would have been able to survive the dehumanizing force of chattel slavery and its legacy of racial oppression."[17]

In accordance with their endeavors for survival, African Americans seized this understanding of God and humanity as a revolutionary hermeneutic for understanding Scripture, starting with the slaves and continuing into subsequent generations.[18] Moreover, based upon this understanding of God, enslaved African Americans were able to practice a nascent "hermeneutics of suspicion" long before this idea was articulated as a modern hermeneutical method.[19] They were suspicious of white interpretation of the Bible and

---

16. Ibid., 10.

17. Ibid., 10–13.

18. Gayraud S. Wilmore, *Black Religion and Black Radicalism* (2d ed.; New York: Orbis, 1983), 37.

19. Cf. Elisabeth Schüssler Fiorenza, *Bread Not Stone* (Boston: Beacon, 1985), 15–18. Schüssler Fiorenza herself was influenced by and engages with the history of African American hermeneutics. This is expressed clearly in her edited volume, *Searching the Scriptures*, vol. 1: *A Feminist Critical Introduction* (New York: Crossroad/Herder & Herder, 1997), which is dedicated to the memory of Anna Julia Cooper, a nineteenth-century black feminist/womanist of great learning and of committed advocacy for women's rights and equality. In this volume Schüssler Fiorenza informs her readers: "Singling out *The Woman's Bible* as *the* milestone in the history of women's biblical interpretation not only risks overlooking the contributions of women of color to biblical hermeneutics. It also continues white feminist gender discourse inscribed in *The Woman's Bible* that does not recognize the constitutive kyriarchal *differences* among and within women. In so doing, it is not only in danger of perpetuating a feminist historical discourse that celebrates the work of those nineteenth-century feminists with 'fair skin' and forgets or represses feminist achievements of women from the 'Dark Continent' but

white practice of Christianity, both of which were used to support slavery and racism. They felt so strongly about this notion that they set out to form religious organizations where they could actualize this idea of equality and freedom, even if it could be realized only within the confines of independent black churches. In this way, the principle of the equality of all people before God became institutionalized within the emergent independent black churches.[20] Galatians 3:28; Acts 2; 10:34–36; and 17:26 provide important biblical authority and rhetorical foci through which this principle could find expression in their political and religious rhetoric for freedom and equality.

In the following overview I will explore Gal 3:28 (and some select passages from Acts) under four rubrics: issues related to the unity of humanity, issues related to race, issues related to class, and issues related to gender/sex. It will be apparent that Gal 3:28, in some cases, can be used in the same breath with one of the kindred passages from Acts. The reason is clear: all of the passages support the central theme of human equality and unity under God. Nevertheless, the use of Gal 3:28 in African American political-religious discourses, while governed by this general theme, is not by any means monolithic.

Galatians 3:28 and Issues Relating to the Unity of Humanity

The equalitarian vision of Gal 3:28 provided a powerful means for African Americans to argue for a universalism that included them unequivocally within the human family regardless of their race, class, or social status. God is, they argued, the common "father" and creator of all humanity and shows no partiality among creation. An ex-slave, G. W. Offley, expresses this reality by claiming "that he learned from his mother and father the potentially revolutionary doctrine 'that God is no respecter of persons, but gave his son to die for all, bond or free, black or white, rich or poor,' and that 'God protects those whom he chooses to sanctify for some task.' "[21] Offley, or the tradition he received, elaborates upon the categories that are relevant to the contemporary situation. The unique aspect of this saying is that it combines two important passages that were important elements of the building block for the notion of human equality for African Americans — Gal 3:28 and Acts 10:34 ("God is no respecter of persons"). First, God's impartiality is addressed. Second, the gospel relates that Jesus' death was "for all," and this again underscores God's impartiality. Finally, Offley expresses the categories that are relevant to American social situation: "bond or free, black

---

also in danger of perpetuating the cultural myth of 'true womanhood. . . .' As long as feminist interpretation focuses on the universalizing of gender discourse, its vision remains one-sided and partial" (12).

20. Wilmore, *Black Religion*, 78; Paris, *Social Teachings*, 10.

21. Albert J. Raboteau, *Slave Religion* (New York: Oxford University Press, 1978), 305.

or white, rich or poor." Interestingly enough, the statement "neither male and female" is missing! Nevertheless, it would seem that in the same way as in the deutero-Pauline tradition (cf. Col 3:11), this saying was so versatile that it could be modified to fit various contextualized visions of unity and equality.[22]

Offley's use of this saying combines a trope of Gal 3:28 with Acts 10:34. However, the Rev. Reverdy C. Ransom, an eloquent and influential bishop of the African Methodist Episcopal Church (AME) from 1924 to 1952, in a sermon titled "Golden Candlesticks Shall Illuminate Darkest Africa,"[23] emphasizes the unity and equality of humanity through the declaration of Acts 17:26 that all humanity stems from "one blood." Important for him is the connection of the principle of the equality of all people before God with American democratic principles, which are not based upon race, creed, or any other factor. For Ransom the idea of the equality of all people before God has concrete political implications — equal opportunity for all regardless of race, creed, color, or nationality:

American democracy is founded upon the Bible; its chief cornerstone rests upon the fact that God is the common father of all mankind. All men are brothers; if brothers, then all men are equal. This is the very foundation upon which American democracy stands. Upon this conception we have established our American democracy. We do not seek by force of arms to dominate the world, but to give equal opportunity and freedom to each and all. To achieve without limit legal handicaps, to the extent ... of their capacity and ability. Our democracy is not based upon race, creed, color, wealth, or nationality, but upon cooperation in the spirit of brotherhood.[24]

After stating his case for the biblical foundation of American democracy based upon the notion of the equality of all under God, Ransom alludes to Acts 17:26 (God "hath made of one blood all nations of men for to dwell on all the face of the earth") in order to impress upon his hearers the social and political implications of this familiar passage: "Since all the families of the earth are now one through their daily contacts upon the land, sea, and the air, they are in a position now to receive and accept the 'One Blood Doctrine,' as a final link in a chain that not only reveals the sovereignty of God, but also unites all the peoples of the earth by affirmation of the 'One

---

22. Although in the deutero-Pauline tradition of Col 3:11 the freedom of women and slaves is curtailed by the household codes (3:18–4:1). But the author of Colossians does expand upon the ethnic categories and in this way emphasizes particularly the "neither Jew or Greek" pair. Perhaps this author recognized Paul's own unequivocal commitment to this category in particular.

23. Reverdy C. Ransom, "Golden Candlesticks Shall Illuminate Darkest Africa," in *Making the Gospel Plain: The Writings of Bishop Reverdy C. Ransom* (ed. Anthony B. Pinn; Harrisburg, Pa.: Trinity, 1999), 170–76.

24. Ibid., 173–74.

Blood Doctrine,' which means the brotherhood, freedom, and equality of all mankind."[25] The "one blood doctrine," as Ransom termed it, was another important means of underscoring the central theme of the unity of humanity as well as the equality of all people before God.

In Howard Thurman we find a further development of the theme of human unity and equality. He takes the theme to its logical conclusion: not only are all physical characteristics insignificant — all racial, ethnic, cultural, religious, and sex distinctions are eradicated before God. Only the human spirit is important. He says: "It is my belief that in the Presence of God there is neither male nor female, white nor black, Gentile nor Jew, Protestant nor Catholic, Hindu, Buddhist, nor Moslem, but a human spirit stripped to the literal substance of itself before God."[26] Thurman, to his credit, does not delete the aspect of Gal 3:28 that is related to sex/gender, but places it first in his elaboration. Thurman was the consummate mystic and philosopher and perceived all seeming physical, religious, or cultural differences as facile. His trope of Gal 3:28 advanced both some traditional and personal themes for him. What is important to him is the human "spirit." His spiritualizing of the saying fits well with his philosophy and ministerial aspirations. Beneath the guise of corporeal differences lies the true essence of the unity of humanity — the human spirit.

Galatians 3:28 and Issues Relating to Race

African Americans did not only find it necessary to argue for their inclusion into the human family as free and equal members and hence to be treated with civility and fairness, they were also forced to address racism and a constellation of arguments for their inferiority. In this cause too, the egalitarian themes of Gal 3:28 could find expression in their discourses.

Along these lines, J. W. C. Pennington, a black abolitionist and preacher, delivered a speech at Exeter Hall, London, England, before the British Foreign Anti-Slavery Society on 21 June 1843, in which he evoked Col 3:11 (already an early modification and elaboration of Gal 3:28 by a deutero-Pauline author). A variety of participants attended the gathering, since the London World's Anti-Slavery convention had closed one day before. Included were "political leaders, a few colonial administrators from the West Indies, and a sprinkling of European anti-slavery activists. The gathering was notable for the 'large party of ladies' present... [and] several 'gentlemen of color' attended."[27]

Before an audience so composed Pennington delivered his ad hoc speech in which he protested in particular England's sanction of emigration from

---

25. Ibid., 176.
26. Howard Thurman, *The Creative Encounter* (New York: Harper & Row, 1954), 152.
27. C. Peter Ripley, ed., *The Black Abolitionist Papers*, vol. 1: *The British Isles, 1830–1865* (Chapel Hill: University of North Carolina Press, 1985), 129.

Africa to the West Indies, but in general slavery as a whole.[28] After touching upon the injustice of England's policy, he concludes:

> Though I have a country that has never done me justice, yet I must return to it, and I shall not recriminate. It has pleased God to make me black and you white, but let us remember, that whatever be our complexion, we are all by nature laboring under the degradation of sin, and without the grace of God are black at heart. (Hear, hear.) I know of no difference between the depraved heart of a Briton, an American, or an African. There is no difference between its colour, its disposition, and its self-will. There is only one mode of emancipation from the slavery of sin, from blackness of heart, and that is by the blood of the Son of God. (Hear, hear.) Whatever be our complexion, whatever our kindred and people, we need to be emancipated from sin, and to be cleansed from our pollution by the all-prevailing grace of God. I bless his name, that in Christ there is neither Jew nor Greek, Barbarian nor Scythian, bond nor free, but all are one.[29]

Pennington in his conclusion, according to Abraham Smith, "relegates all persons — whether black or white — to a common bondage of sin and exploits Gal 3:27 [*sic*] to support his claim of the common humanity of all persons despite the societal labels of bond persons and free persons."[30] He also universalizes the concept of blackness. While Pennington and his kindred people were created black in complexion, all of humankind labor under the "blackness of heart" on account of sin. Although it is unfortunate that Pennington adopts the pejorative connotation of blackness, as is common in Western culture, he at least universalizes this notion to all people. It might also have been rhetorically advantageous for him to trope this theme in order to address racial attitudes concerning blackness that were prevalent in

---

28. Pennington was not scheduled to offer a speech, but after being well received and greeted by a hearty applause from the audience, he offered a resolution that took the form of a speech: "Pennington's remarks typified the tendency of black abolitionists to turn public discussions on any issue into a forum for considering slavery"; Ripley, *Black Abolitionist Papers*, 1.129.

29. "Speech by J. W. C. Pennington, Delivered at Exeter Hall, London, England, 21 June, 1843," in *Black Abolitionist Papers*, 1.129–33, quotation at 132.

30. Abraham Smith, "Putting 'Paul' Back Together Again: William Wells Brown's *Clotel* and Black Abolitionists Approaches to Paul," *Semeia* 83–84 (1998): 251–62, quotation on 255. While Smith states that Pennington exploits Gal 3:27 (surely Smith means 3:28), Pennington is most likely alluding to Col 3:11. Pennington's quotation of Col 3:11 works better than the archetypal paradigm of Gal 3:28, it would appear, because in the context of Col 3:11 the deutero-Pauline author encourages his readers to put to death the practice of various sins and selfish behaviors (3:5–8) that are a part of the "old humanity" and to become participants in the "renewal" through Christ: "Seeing that you have stripped off the old self with its practices and have clothed yourselves with the new self, which is being renewed in knowledge according to the image of its creator. In that renewal there is no longer Greek and Jew, circumcised and uncircumcised, barbarian, Scythian, slave and free; but Christ is all and in all!" (Col 3:9–11 NRSV). The context of this passage, referring to human sinfulness and the need for renewal, fits Pennington's rhetorical purposes in his speech quite well.

his day. In this way, through the lens of Col 3:11 and its reformulation of Gal 3:28, he can claim a common humanity of all people and at the same time covertly attack racist attitudes about black humanity.

Florence Spearing Randolph, born in Charleston, South Carolina, on 9 August 1866, was a renowned AME Zion minister, missionary, suffragist, lecturer, organizer, and temperance worker. She would emerge as one of a handful of women affiliated with a mainline black denomination to hold a regular pastorate of a church. In her sermon "If I Were White," she speaks out directly against racist attitudes.[31] In this sermon she posits that, if she were white and believed in God, Jesus, and the Bible, she would prove her "true race superiority" by her willingness to live out the principles of the equality of all people under God as delineated in the Bible. This means taking up the cause of the oppressed and marginalized. She grounds her attack against racism upon the "one blood" saying of Acts 17:26:

> If I were white and believed in God, in His Son Jesus Christ, and the Holy Bible, I would speak in no uncertain words against Race Prejudice, Hate, Oppression, and Injustice. I would prove my race superiority by my attitude towards minority races; towards oppressed people. I would remember that of one blood God made all nations of men to dwell upon the face of the earth.[32]

In the final analysis, Randolph infers that race really means nothing in the sight of God. All humanity shares a common ancestry. Randolph also offers a challenge to those white Americans who want to claim a racial superiority: if such a thing exists, it would be based upon how one treated those who are oppressed and on the fringes of society, because all are equal before God through a common origin by the plan of God.

In a similar manner, Mary McLeod Bethune, indefatigable educator and founder of Bethune-Cookman College, touches upon this well-established theme of the equality of all people before God in her argument against racism and its accompanying evil — black inferiority. In recounting her early childhood realization of self-worth, she relates the account of her teacher who read to her of God's love from John 3:16. In recounting her moment of enlightenment, she tropes Acts 9 and Paul's Damascus Road experience.[33] In this same narrative, she also tropes Gal 3:28 when in her moment of self-discovery, she realizes that "[her] sense of inferiority, [and her] fear of handicaps, dropped away."[34] It was the word *whosoever* through which she

---

31. Florence Spearing Randolph, "If I Were White," in *Daughters of Thunder: Black Women Preachers and Their Sermons, 1850–1979* (ed. Bettye Collier-Thomas; San Francisco: Jossey-Bass, 1998), 129.

32. Ibid.

33. Callahan, "Brother Saul," 244.

34. Gerda Lerner, *Black Women in White America: A Documentary History* (New York: Vintage, 1973), 136.

saw herself joined to a common humanity through God's love that ignited her determination and passion: " 'Whosoever,' it said. No Jew nor Gentile, no Catholic nor Protestant, no black nor white; just 'whosoever.' It meant that I, a humble Negro girl, had just as much chance as anybody in the sight and love of God. These words stored up a battery of faith and confidence and determination in my heart."[35]

Like those before her, Bethune sought to validate her aspirations for self-realization and equal opportunity through the essential principle of human equality under God, using Gal 3:28 as the focal point. Although she does not include the "neither male and female" reference so important for black women's arguments for preaching and pulpit ministry, it can be inferred through her reference to herself, "a humble Negro girl," who had not even reached womanhood, "had just as much chance as anybody" in God's sight. Thus, like Pennington and Randolph, Bethune also combats racist notions using the vision of human unity and equality as espoused in Gal 3:28.

Galatians 3:28 and Issues Relating to Class

Marxist and socialist thought began to influence the African American consciousness and surfaced in their political-religious discourse in the early decades of the twentieth century.[36] A small cadre of African Americans believed that the idea of a classless society was one solution to American racism and classism. Even socialist idealism could be bolstered by reference to Gal 3:28. I turn again to Ransom. In his speech "The Paraclete of God the Only Hope for Brotherhood and Peace,"[37] he argues that since all humanity is the creation of God, they should be free not only to marry whom they please, but also to have access to the freedoms outlined in the Declaration of Independence. The problem was that America has not lived up to the principle of the equality of all people under God as outlined in its charter document and the biblical account of creation (which declares that all humanity is created in the image of God). Therefore, "the progress of African Americans in the United States is necessary in order to bring about the truth of the declaration and its connection to Scripture."[38]

On the point of a common human origin in creation and its connection with the Declaration of Independence, Ransom says:

> From the marriage of one man to one woman stem families, tribes, nations, states, and empires. But these do not invalidate the fact that

---

35. Ibid., 39.
36. Cf. Cornel West, *Prophesy Deliverance: An Afro-American Revolutionary Christianity* (Philadelphia: Westminster, 1982), 39–41.
37. Ransom, "Paraclete of God," in *Making the Gospel Plain* (ed. Pinn), 166–70.
38. Ibid., 166.

"all men are created equal," equal in the sense of having a common origin and fatherhood by the creative act of God. There is but one race, the human race. It follows then, there can be no such thing as "mixed marriages." More than that, they are endowed with certain unalienable rights, among which are "life, liberty and the pursuit of happiness." Thomas Jefferson was inspired in his choice of words when he said, "created equal." This was an act of the Creator God. Now this does not mean equal in the sense of equally wise, equally endowed or equally powerful and resourceful.[39]

Interestingly, Ransom has to clarify what he means by "created equal." He clarifies this point above in the negative, by explaining what he feels equality is not — not equally wise, endowed, powerful, or resourceful. What he means positively by "created equal" is the freedom to pursue life, liberty, and happiness without the restrictions of laws and customs that unduly thwart these "God-given" pursuits. Ransom alludes to Gal 3:28 to underscore this idea in terms of a classless society:

Our chief weapon is that we have here in America a "classless" society. There is neither Jew, Gentile, white, black, consumer, producer, farmer, laborer, or capitalist but because he is a man and possesses the personal God-given integrity of each free man in the American "classless" society.

For added emphasis I declare that God created all men free to develop, achieve, and pursue any line of human activity [they] may desire. No human law is valid that seeks to divide or to segregate mankind into "classes," "minority groups," "labor," "industry," "white," or 'black."[40]

Ransom recasts Gal 3:28 to reflect the themes of socialism: "neither... consumer, producer, farmer, labor, or capitalist." And also to reflect that of a race-conscious society: "[neither] 'white' [n]or 'black.'" These points emphasize that "Ransom's reading of the world was class- and race-specific."[41] To be sure, while he seeks to emphasize the issue of classism, class and race have always been unified partners in the American socioreligious and political contexts. This reality has been equally true for racism and sexism, as we shall see, when African American women in particular employ Gal 3:28 in their arguments for equality and open access for all people regardless of sex within the church and larger society.

---

39. Ibid., 167.
40. Ibid.
41. Wimbush, "Reading Texts through Worlds," 137.

Galatians 3:28 and Issues Relating to Gender/Sex

African American male church leaders often recognize the importance of black women's active support in the churches and denominational bodies, as well as black women's efforts toward racial self-help and self-reliance. Nevertheless, many traditionally have not recognized their leadership potential or their confessed callings to pulpit and pastoral ministry: "Thus tainted by the values of the larger American society, the black church sought to provide men with full manhood rights, while offering women a separate and unequal status."[42] African American men and women from slavery to freedom, however, rejected scriptural texts that in any way supported human bondage and race prejudice. While in their quest for human freedom and equality many African American men (in particular, but not exclusively as we have seen) are apt to quote from Galatians — "there is neither Jew nor Greek, slave nor free" — African American women call attention to the implications of Gal 3:28 in its more complete form: "There is neither Jew nor Greek, slave nor free, male nor female, but all are one in Christ Jesus."[43] That is, African American women seek to use Gal 3:28 not only to address issues of race and class, but also issues of gender/sex. African American women agree fully that the principle of the equality of all people before God should entail the eradication of racism and classism. Why should this principle not extend to sexism? They certainly think it did and in accordance with the interpretive tradition use Gal 3:28 and the salient passages from Acts to support their convictions.

Julia A. J. Foote, a member of the AME Zion church and lay preacher of the nineteenth century with Holiness influences, uses the baptismal confession in her nineteenth-century biography. In her use the category "male and female" was *the* essential element of the saying. In arguing for her calling and right to preach the gospel in Holiness circles she says:

> We are sometimes told that if a woman pretends to a Divine call, and thereon grounds the right to plead the cause of a crucified Redeemer in public, she will be believed when she shows credentials from heaven; that is, when she works a miracle. If it be necessary to prove one's right to preach the Gospel, I ask of my brethren to show me their credentials, or I can not believe in the propriety of their ministry. But the Bible puts an end to this strife when it says: "There is neither male nor female in Christ Jesus."[44]

---

42. Evelyn Brooks Higginbotham, *Righteous Discontent: The Women's Movement in the Black Baptist Church, 1880–1920* (Cambridge: Harvard University Press, 1993), 3.

43. Ibid., 122.

44. William L. Andrews, *Sisters of the Spirit: Three Black Women's Autobiographies of the Nineteenth Century* (Bloomington: Indiana University Press, 1986), 208–9.

For Foote "neither male nor female" entailed an end to the debate over women preachers. She apparently recognized that if the black Christian tradition agreed that concrete implications should be expected from the first two elements of Gal 3:28, the same equally applied to the third element without further qualification (as she states emphatically: "The Bible puts an end to this strife").

Virginia Broughton, a black Baptist churchwoman of the late nineteenth century, employs Gal 3:28 to support women's roles inside and outside the church. In her defense of women's work in the church, she describes the biblical judge Deborah as a woman with a task that was independent of the will or control of her husband. God alone uses whom God pleases without distinction, so long as they have a willing heart. Along these lines Broughton asserts:

> Her work was distinct from her husband who, it seems, took no part whatever in the work of God while Deborah was inspired by the Eternal expressly to do His will and to testify to her countrymen that He recognizes in His followers neither male nor female, heeding neither the "weakness" of one, nor the strength of the other, but strictly calling those who are perfect at heart and willing to do his bidding.[45]

Surprisingly, Broughton does not condone women preachers. According to Evelyn Brooks Higginbotham, "Despite the broad number of roles that Broughton believed the Bible authorized and her rather unusual autonomy within her own household, she explicitly warned women against the danger of aspiring to roles that had no female precedents in the Bible. She denied that women should have access to the clergy or perform the clergy's role of establishing new churches, baptizing converts, and administering the Eucharist."[46]

Thus for Foote the "neither male and female" element of the baptismal saying settles the problem related to women in the preaching ministry. For Broughton, on the other hand, the saying can open the doors of opportunity for women to use their gifts in various ways in the church as long as it does not counter the traditional understanding of the biblical injunctions to women's roles. In their separate ways, they recognize the implications that could be drawn from Gal 3:28 to empower women for ministry. While "no longer male nor female" means for Broughton widening the doors of opportunity for women to serve in the church within traditional parameters, for Foote, in particular, it represents a new pattern of relationships that rested on equality between men and women in terms of the roles for preaching, ministry, and service within the church.

---

45. Higginbotham, *Righteous Discontent*, 135.
46. Ibid., 133.

The same reality is expressed by Florence Spearing Randolph (discussed above). Like Foote before her, she was a member of the AME Zion Church, the first black denomination to grant women suffrage (1876) and full clergy rights (1894). Randolph was among a small group of women in the late nineteenth century who functioned as evangelists, received license to preach, and were ordained as deacons and elders in the AME Zion church. In the same way as her sisters before her, in her pursuit of a preaching career she defied gender conventions and went against the wishes of her husband, family, and friends. She excelled above her peers by receiving appointments to pastor a number of churches. Ultimately, her crowning achievement was serving as pastor of Wallace Chapel AME Zion Church in Summit, New Jersey (1925–46). Beginning her ministry in the late 1880s, she was profoundly influenced by the holiness teachings and example of Foote.[47]

In her sermon "Antipathy to Women Preachers," Randolph begins by referring to the women in Jesus' ministry who remained faithful throughout his career and were witnesses to his crucifixion and resurrection. Because of their unwavering faith these women were granted the privilege of being the first preachers of the resurrection: "You have been faithful, you persevered for the truth and hence you are honored by God and are first commissioned." She goes on to say:

> But notwithstanding the fact that the first gospel message was delivered to the women, there always has been and still is great antipathy to women preachers. But God, with whom there is neither Jew nor Greek, bond nor free, male nor female, in His wonderful plan of salvation has called and chosen men and women according to His divine will as laborers together with Him for the salvation of the world.[48]

Randolph quotes all three pairs of the saying to stress not only the call of women to ministry, but also to emphasize the mutual work of ministry that men and women are to share together in God's plan of salvation. Used in its fullest form by African American women, Gal 3:28 reflects their concerns to push its meaning to include not only issues of sex/gender discrimination, but also the mutual work and collaboration of men and women in the plan of salvation without distinctions based on sex.

Our last example, Quinceila Whitlow, another woman preacher/evangelist of note during her day, was born in Mercer, Tennessee. Before entering the ministry, she spent several years in the nursing profession after graduating from the Chicago School of Nursing. Although little else is known about her life or her career as an evangelist, in 1940 the editor of the CME *Christian*

---

47. Collier-Thomas, ed., *Daughters of Thunder,* 126.
48. Ibid.

Index described her as "an Evangelist of high standing," whose "lectures are splendid and far-reaching. Those who hear her can never forget."[49]

It is fortunate, however, that at least one of her sermons in which she cites Gal 3:28 is left to posterity. In this sermon, "The Woman in the Ministry of Jesus Christ," Whitlow affirms women's right to preach the gospel and in the process applauds women's changing status in the church. Her sermon also "reflects the rhetoric of campaigns to recruit women into the workplace during World War II, declaring that there is a 'growing spirit of equality' in the country as 'new fields of labor' open to women." Therefore, just as in the world of labor, the church needs to recognize the talents and gifts of women and develop a more open policy of leadership toward them. As will be evidenced in the following quotation, she echoes the arguments of many black female preachers before her. In her argument she confirms "that gender is irrelevant when it comes to doing God's work; conversion and sanctification, not gender, truly qualify someone for the ministry." Whitlow asserts:

> We need in our churches today eager and alert women, talented and accomplished women, skilled and artistic women, but far more than that we need Christian women, who with trusting faith and undaunted hope, will behold the Saviour despised and rejected of men, a man of sorrow and acquainted with grief.... No one has done so much for womanhood as Jesus. When His words proclaimed that in Him there is, "neither male nor female["] but He is the Saviour of all that blessed truth that became the Christian constitution for womanhood.
>
> The position which woman occupies today under the elevating influence of Christianity and the growing spirit of equality is a matter of rejoicing among the best and most thoughtful minds in all classes. The new fields of labor that are opening to her, the widening spheres of influence which she is entering and filling with highest credit to herself and with greatest benefit to mankind. This cannot but awaken gratitude and hope in the heart of womanhood.
>
> Can you not see why womanhood has found a powerful appeal in the Gospel of Jesus Christ[?] May God save the woman of the Gospel from the brazen rejection of the narrow minded critic.... Let the woman stand fast in her calling. We cannot sit idly by while modern denial continues to rain blasphemous blows upon our Saviour. We must plead His cause and stand up for His truth. We must be prepared to stand alone to uphold the glorious truth of the Gospel.... I am praying to God that the ministers of our churches will help to stamp out this false doctrine that is being practiced in our churches today.[50]

---

49. Ibid., 211–14.
50. Ibid., 213.

In Whitlow's sermon, she attributes the baptismal saying directly to Jesus, because for her and several other African American women Jesus is the ultimate source of liberation for women. For Whitlow, the gospel of Jesus Christ contained the essence of what came to fruition in Paul's (and the early Christian missionary movement's) declaration of human unity and equality. This connection is what makes it possible for her to proclaim that "womanhood has found a powerful appeal in the Gospel of Jesus Christ." While Whitlow's use of the term *womanhood* is understandable in view of the time in which she writes, it is important to recognize that contemporary womanists and feminists no longer resort to such a term like "womanhood" because of its essentialist connotations. They recognize instead that all women are different because of the combination of variables — race, class, geography, and sexual status — that inform them.[51] At any rate, Whitlow sought to encourage those who were opposed to women preachers to help stem the tide of "antipathy" and end the "false doctrine" that women cannot practice ministry in the church. Again, like the women before her, Gal 3:28 served as the crux of her argument.

These few examples serve to highlight the importance of Gal 3:28 (especially, the pair "male and female") in black women's interpretive traditions of the Bible. They used it to call the church to live out the full implications of Gal 3:28.

Galatians 3:28 and the African American Religious Tradition: A Brief Assessment

What this brief analysis of Gal 3:28 in the African American religious tradition reveals is that free blacks, slaves, and subsequent generations used the fundamental principle of "the equality of all people before God" or the "gospel of equality" as a hermeneutical key both to understand Scripture and their social situation. They also used it as a rhetorical strategy in their discourses against racism, classism, and sexism. As far as the African American tradition and churches are concerned, race and class oppression are evil and against the will of God. In terms of the baptismal saying of Gal 3:28, then, the most important aspects for African Americans historically have been "no longer Jew or Greek, no longer slave or free" — that is, issues related to *race* and *class*. This has been evident in African Americans' religious and political rhetoric throughout their history in America. For it was out of the crucible of racial injustice and class oppression that independent black congregations arose to institutionalize a nonracist and nonclassist appropriation of the Christian faith as they had come to know it. In spite of the insight of individuals like Foote, Thurman, Randolph, and Whitlow that Gal 3:28 and other biblical teachings on equality applied to women as well

---

51. This notion is central to Schüssler Fiorenza's work; cf. *Searching the Scriptures*, 1.11–12.

as men, black churches *as a whole* did not exploit this insight in order to self-critically analyze their own sexist notions and practices. This is where the African American religious tradition and churches failed in their actualization of Gal 3:28, for, like Paul, they too have had their own agenda, which excluded the particular issues related to gender/sex. The problem was, according to Paris, that for blacks in general the race issue was considered the most overriding obstacle to black freedom:

> Though the doctrine of human equality under God implies that none —
> including blacks — are justified in their attempts to subordinate the
> humanity of others, its application to blacks is often obscured by the
> prevalence of white racism in all walks of life. Thus, although blacks
> are guilty of oppressing other blacks..., the churches generally give
> their attention to the fact that all blacks are oppressed by the greater
> force of white racism, which is considered the greater evil and possibly
> the source of all sin.[52]

Bettye Collier-Thomas suggests that, given the high percentage of black women in African American churches, they themselves might effectively be able to eliminate sexism and gender discrimination in the church. The African American religious tradition provides evidence that black Christian women consistently raised their voices in print, in the pulpit, and in the pew against these forms of discrimination. However, it seems that for the most part many black women agreed with the tradition that racism posed the greater threat than sexism. For this reason, many chose to devote their energies almost exclusively to eradicating racism. Nevertheless, African American women continue to be divided over which is of greater importance — racism or sexism.[53]

For the most part, this assessment is true. Black women have historically not opted to vigorously challenge the black churches to consider their laxity on sexism because the evil of racism had precedent over sexism. But if the black churches are going to be faithful to their interpretive tradition of the equality of all people before God as a challenge to racism and classism, it cannot continue to ignore this same principle vis-à-vis sexism. Black churches must be willing not only to admit the inequity of sex discrimination against women, but also act to challenge the sexist attitudes of the churches and society. It is a contradiction for the black religious tradition

---

52. Paris, *Social Teachings*, 16; cf. also Elsie Johnson McDougald, "The Double Task: The Struggle of Negro Women for Sex and Race Emancipation," *Survey Graphic* 6 (March 1925): 691 (quoted in Lerner, *Black Women in White America*, 171): "The feminist efforts are directed chiefly toward the realization of the equality of the races, the sex struggle assuming a subordinate place.... The wind of the race's destiny stirs more briskly because of her striving."

53. Collier-Thomas, ed., *Daughters of Thunder*, 279; cf. also Cheryl Townsend Gilkes, "Some Mother's Son and Some Father's Daughter's: Gender and Biblical Language in Afro-Christian Worship Tradition," in *Shaping New Visions: Gender and Values in American Culture* (ed. Clarissa Atkinson et al.; Ann Arbor: UMI, 1987), 77.

and churches to protest racism and classism in the white churches and society and then fail to critique sexism in black churches and society. It must be taken into consideration that sexism has a reality and significance peculiar to itself for black women because it is a "form of oppression suffered by black women at the hand of black men."[54]

If the "equality of all people before God" is to be carried out in terms of sexism just as it has for racism and classism, what then is the role of black churches in this struggle? Since the black churches have a long history of struggle against racism and classism, it should be in the vanguard of the struggle against sexism — for it too is oppression on the same level as racism. If this is done, black churches can fulfill the complete vision of Gal 3:28: a vision that has influenced their own development, contributed to their understanding of "the equality of all people before God," and inspired their religious-political rhetoric of "freedom and justice for all, regardless of race, creed, or color."

The call for such action to end sexism in black churches is nothing new in the African American religious tradition, although the challenge was issued only after slavery's end. In 1899 the Rev. J. Francis Robinson issued such a clarion call to the churches on behalf of women. I will let him have the last word:

> The slaves have been emancipated; now let us emancipate women! The unconditional and universal and immediate emancipation of womanhood is the demand of the age in which we live; it is the demand of the spirit of our institutions; it is the demand of the teachings of Christianity; it is her right, and, in the name of God, let us start a wave of influence in this country that shall be felt in every State, every county, every community, every home and every heart.[55]

---

54. Pauli Murray, "Black Theology and Feminist Theology: A Comparative View," in *Black Theology: A Documentary History, 1966–1979* (ed. Gayraud Wilmore and James Cone; New York: Orbis, 1979), 422.

55. Quoted in Higginbotham, *Righteous Discontent*, 148.

Bibliography of the Writings of Elisabeth Schüssler Fiorenza

Books

Der vergessene Partner: Grundlagen, Tatsachen und Möglichkeiten der Beruflichen Mitarbeit der Frau in der Heilssorge der Kirche. Düsseldorf: Patmos, 1964.

Priester für Gott: Studien Zum Herrschafts- und Priestermotiv in der Apokalypse. Neuetestamentliche Abhandlungen n.s. 7. Münster: Aschendorff, 1972.

The Apocalypse. Chicago: Franciscan Herald Press, 1976.
[Translation: Spanish]

Hebrews, James, 1 and 2 Peter, Jude, Revelation. With Reginald H. Fuller et al. Proclamation Commentaries. Philadelphia: Fortress, 1977.

Invitation to the Book of Revelation: A Commentary on the Apocalypse, with Complete Text from the Jerusalem Bible. New York: Doubleday, 1981.

Lent. With Urban T. Holmes. Proclamation II: Aids for Interpreting the Lessons of the Church Year, Series B. Philadelphia: Fortress, 1981.

In Memory of Her: A Feminist Theological Reconstruction of Christian Origins. New York: Crossroad, 1983. Tenth Anniversary Edition, 1994. 2d edition. London: SCM Press, 1995.
[Translations: French, German, Dutch, Spanish, Korean, Italian, Portuguese, Swedish, Japanese, Indonesian]

The Book of Revelation: Justice and Judgment. Philadelphia: Fortress, 1985. 2d edition with a new epilogue, 1998.

Bread Not Stone: The Challenge of Feminist Biblical Interpretation. Boston: Beacon, 1985. Tenth Anniversary Edition, 1995.
[Translations: German, Dutch, Japanese]

Revelation: Vision of a Just World. Proclamation Commentaries. Minneapolis: Augsburg Fortress, 1991.
[Translations: German, Italian, Spanish]

But She Said: Feminist Practices of Biblical Interpretation. Boston: Beacon, 1992.
[Translation: Spanish]

Discipleship of Equals: A Critical Feminist Ekklēsia-Logy of Liberation. New York: Crossroad, 1993.
[Translation: Portuguese]

Jesus: Miriam's Child, Sophia's Prophet: Critical Issues in Feminist Christology. New York: Continuum, 1994.
[Translations: German, Italian, Dutch, Spanish]

Sharing Her Word: Feminist Biblical Interpretation in Context. Boston: Beacon, 1998.

Rhetoric and Ethic: The Politics of Biblical Studies. Minneapolis: Fortress, 1999.
Jesus and the Politics of Interpretation. New York: Continuum, 2000.
Wisdom Ways: Introducing Feminist Biblical Interpretation. Maryknoll, N.Y.: Orbis, 2001.

Books and Journals Edited

Aspects of Religious Propaganda in Judaism and Early Christianity. Notre Dame: University of Notre Dame Press, 1976.
The Holocaust as Interruption. Edited with David Tracy. Concilium 175. Edinburgh: T. & T. Clark, 1984.
Journal of Feminist Studies in Religion. Co-founded and co-edited with Judith Plaskow, 1985–1995. Co-edited with Emilie M. Townes, 1995–2000. Co-edited with Kwok Pui-lan, 2001–present.
Women, Invisible in Theology and Church. Edited with Mary Collins. Concilium 182. Edinburgh: T. & T. Clark, 1985.
Women, Work, and Poverty. Edited with Anne Carr. Concilium 194. Edinburgh: T. & T. Clark, 1987.
Interpretation for Liberation. Edited with Katie G. Cannon. Semeia 47. Atlanta: Scholars Press, 1989.
Motherhood: Experience, Institution, Theology. Edited with Anne Carr. Concilium 206. Edinburgh: T. & T. Clark, 1989.
The Special Nature of Women? Edited with Anne Carr. Concilium 1991/6. Philadelphia: Trinity Press International, 1991.
Searching the Scriptures: A Feminist Introduction and Commentary. 2 vols. New York: Crossroad, 1993–94.
[Translation: Japanese]
Violence against Women. Edited with M. Shawn Copeland. Concilium 1994/1. Maryknoll, N.Y.: Orbis, 1994.
Feminist Theology in Different Contexts. Edited with M. Shawn Copeland. Concilium 1996/1. Maryknoll, N.Y.: Orbis, 1996.
The Power of Naming: A Concilium Reader in Feminist Liberation Theology. Maryknoll, N.Y.: Orbis, 1996.
Women's Sacred Scriptures. Edited with Kwok Pui-lan. Concilium 1998/3. Maryknoll, N.Y.: Orbis, 1998.
The Non-ordination of Women and the Politics of Power. Edited with Hermann Häring. Concilium 1999/3. Maryknoll, N.Y.: Orbis, 1999.
In the Power of Wisdom: Feminist Spiritualities of Struggle. Edited with M. Pilar Aquino. Concilium 2000/5. Maryknoll, N.Y.: Orbis, 2000.

Articles

"Beispiele zur exegetischen Methode." Pages 359–81 in *Wort und Botschaft: Eine theologische und kritische Einführung in die Probleme des Alten Testaments.* Edited by Josef Schreiner. Würzburg: Echter, 1967.
"The Eschatology and Composition of the Apocalypse." Translated by Mary Buckley and Elisabeth Meier. *Catholic Biblical Quarterly* 30, no. 4 (1968): 537–69.

"Der Anführer und Vollender unseres Glaubens: Zum theologischen Verständnis des Hebräerbriefes." Pages 262–81 in *Gestalt und Anspruch des Neuen Testaments.* Edited by Josef Schreiner and Gerhard Dautzenburg. Würzburg: Echter, 1969.

"Gericht und Heil: Zum theologischen Verständnis der Apokalypse." Pages 330–47 in *Gestalt und Anspruch des Neuen Testaments.* Edited by Josef Schreiner and Gerhard Dautzenburg. Würzburg: Echter, 1969.

"Saints Alive Yesterday and Today." *Brooklyn Tablet* (7 December 1972).

"Die tausendjährige Herrschaft der Auferstandenen (Apk 20,4–6)." *Bibel und Leben* 13 (1972): 107–24.

"Apocalyptic and Gnosis in the Book of Revelation and Paul." *Journal of Biblical Literature* 92, no. 4 (1973): 565–81.

"Images of Jesus." Pages 65–69 in *Teaching Religion to Undergraduates: Some Approaches and Ideas from Teacher to Teacher.* Edited by Luke Timothy Johnson. New Haven: SHRE, 1973.

"Mary Magdalene, Apostle to the Apostles." *Union Theological Seminary Journal* (April 1974): 22–24.

"Redemption as Liberation: Apoc 1:5f. and 5:9f." *Catholic Biblical Quarterly* 36, no. 2 (1974): 220–32.

"Religion und Politik in der Offenbarung des Johannes." Pages 261–72 in *Biblische Randbemerkungen: Schülerfestschrift für Rudolf Schnackenburg zum 60. Geburtstag.* Edited by Helmut Merklein and Joachim Lange. Würzburg: Echter, 1974.

"Feminist Theology as a Critical Theology of Liberation." *Theological Studies* 36, no. 4 (1975): 605–26.
   Repr. pages 29–50 in *Woman: New Dimensions.* Edited by Walter Burghardt. New York: Paulist Press, 1977.
   Repr. *Mission Trends* 4 (1979): 188–216.
   Repr. pages 46–66 in *Churches in Struggle: Liberation Theologies and Social Change in North America.* Edited by William K. Tabb. New York: Monthly Review Press, 1986.

"Symposium: Toward a Theology of Feminism." *Horizons* 2 (1975): 117–18.

"Wisdom Mythology and the Christological Hymns of the New Testament." Pages 17–41 in *Aspects of Wisdom in Judaism and Early Christianity.* Edited by Robert L. Wilken. Notre Dame: University of Notre Dame Press, 1975.

"Women Studies and the Teaching of Religion." *Occasional Papers on Catholic Higher Education* 1 (1975): 26–30.

"Cultic Language in Qumran and in the New Testament." *Catholic Biblical Quarterly* 38, no. 2 (1976): 159–77.

"Eschatology of the NT." Pages 271–77 in *The Interpreter's Dictionary of the Bible: Supplementary Volume.* Edited by Keith Crim. Nashville: Abingdon, 1976.

"First Fruits, NT." Page 337 in *The Interpreter's Dictionary of the Bible: Supplementary Volume.* Edited by Keith Crim. Nashville: Abingdon, 1976.

"Interpreting Patriarchal Traditions of the Bible." Pages 39–61 in *The Liberating Word: A Guide to Nonsexist Interpretation of the Bible.* Edited by Letty Russell. Philadelphia: Westminster, 1976.

"Miracles, Mission, and Apologetics: An Introduction." Pages 1–25 in *Aspects of Religious Propaganda in Judaism and Early Christianity.* Edited by Elisabeth Schüssler Fiorenza. Notre Dame: University of Notre Dame Press, 1976.

"Revelation, Book of." Pages 744–46 in *The Interpreter's Dictionary of the Bible: Supplementary Volume*. Edited by Keith Crim. Nashville: Abingdon, 1976.

"Die Rolle der Frau in der urchristlichen Bewegung." *Konzilium* 7 (1976): 3–9.

"Women Apostles: The Testament of Scripture." Pages 94–102 in *Women and Catholic Priesthood: An Expanded Vision: Proceedings of the Detroit Ordination Conference*. Edited by Anne Marie Gardiner. New York: Paulist Press, 1976.

"Women in the New Testament." *New Catholic World* (November–December 1976): 256–60.

> Repr. Pages 6–13 in *Scripture and the Church*. Edited by Robert J. Heyer. New York: Paulist Press, 1976.

> Repr. as "Women in the Early Christian Movement," pages 84–92 in *Womanspirit Rising: A Feminist Reader in Religion*. Edited by Carol Christ and Judith Plaskow. San Francisco: Harper & Row, 1979.

"The Apostleship of Women in Early Christianity." Pages 135–40 in *Women Priests: A Catholic Commentary on the Vatican Declaration*. Edited by Leonard Swidler and Arlene Swidler. New York: Paulist Press, 1977.

"Composition and Structure of the Revelation of John." *Catholic Biblical Quarterly* 39, no. 3 (1977): 344–66.

"Judging and Judgment in the New Testament Communities." Pages 1–8 in *Judgment in the Church*. Edited by William Bassett and Peter Huizing. Concilium 107. New York: Seabury Press, 1977.

> [Translation: German]

"The Quest for the Johannine School: The Fourth Gospel and the Apocalypse." *New Testament Studies* 23 (1977): 402–27.

"The Twelve." Pages 114–22 in *Women Priests: A Catholic Commentary on the Vatican Declaration on the Ordination of Women*. Edited by Leonard Swidler and Arlene Swidler. New York: Paulist Press, 1977.

"Understanding God's Revealed Word." *Catholic Charismatic* (1977): 4–10.

"Feminist Spirituality, Christian Identity, and Catholic Vision." *National Institute for Campus Ministries Journal* 1 (1978): 29–34.

> Repr. pages 136–48 in *Womanspirit Rising: A Feminist Reader in Religion*. Edited by Carol Christ and Judith Plaskow. New York: Harper & Row, 1979.

"Für eine befreite und befreiende Theologie: Theologinnen und feministische Theologie in den USA." *Konzilium* 8 (1978): 287–94.

> [Translation: English]

"Women in the Pre-Pauline and Pauline Churches." *Union Seminary Quarterly Review* 33 (spring–summer 1978): 153–66.

> [Translation: German]

"For the Sake of Our Salvation: Biblical Interpretation as Theological Task." Pages 21–39 in *Sin, Salvation and the Spirit: Commemorating the Fiftieth Year of the Liturgical Press*. Edited by Daniel Durken. Collegeville, Minn.: Liturgical Press, 1979.

> Repr. pages 40–61 in *Pastoral Hermeneutics and Ministry*. Edited by D. F. Beisswenger and D. C. McCarthy. N.p.: Association for Theological Field Education, 1983.

"Marriage and Discipleship." *The Bible Today* (April 1979): 2027–34.
[Translation: German]

"Study of Women in Early Christianity: Some Methodological Considerations." Pages
30–58 in *Critical History and Biblical Faith in New Testament Perspectives.*
Edited by T. J. Ryan. Villanova, Pa.: CTS Annual Publication, 1979.

"Word, Spirit, and Power: Women in Early Christian Communities." Pages 29–70
in *Women of Spirit: Female Leadership in the Jewish and Christian Traditions.*
Edited by Rosemary Radford Ruether and Eleanor McLaughlin. New York:
Simon & Schuster, 1979.

" 'You Are Not to Be Called Father': Early Christian History in a Feminist Perspective." *Cross Currents* 29, no. 3 (1979): 301–23.
Repr. pages 394–417 in *The Bible and Liberation: Political and Social Hermeneutics.* Edited by Norman Gottwald. Maryknoll, N.Y.: Orbis, 1983 and pages
462–84 in the rev. ed. Edited by Norman Gottwald and Richard A. Horsley,
1993.

"Apokalypsis and Propheteia: The Book of Revelation in the Context of Early Christian Prophecy." Pages 105–28 in *L'Apocalypse johannique et l'Apocalyptique
dans le Nouveau Testament.* Edited by Jan Lambrecht. Bibliotheca ephemeridum
theologicarum lovaniensium 53. Gembloux, Belgium: Duculot, 1980.

"Der Beitrag der Frau zur urchristlichen Bewegung: Kritische Überlegungen zur
Rekonstruktion urchristlicher Geschichte." Pages 60–90 in *Traditionen der
Befreiung: Sozialgeschichtliche Bibelauslegungen.* Vol. 2: *Frauen in der Bibel.*
Edited by Willy Schottroff and Wolfgang Stegemann. Munich: Kaiser, 1980.

"The Biblical Roots for the Discipleship of Equals." *Duke Divinity School Review*
45 (Spring 1980): 87–97.
Repr. *Journal of Pastoral Counseling* 14 (spring-summer 1979): 7–15.

"To Comfort or to Challenge: Theological Reflections on the Pre-Conference Pro-
cess." Pages 43–60 in *New Woman, New Church, New Priestly Ministry:
Proceedings of the Second Conference on the Ordination of Roman Catholic
Women (Nov. 10–12, 1978, Baltimore, Maryland).* Edited by Maureen Dwyer.
Rochester, NY: Women's Ordination Conference, 1980.

" 'A History of the Victims': Response to Charles Davis." *Commonweal* (1 February
1980): 52–53.

"Rassurer ou Deifier? Reflexions theologiques feministes." Pages 43–78 in *"Et vox
filles prophetiseront" (Acts 2,17): Deux theologiennes americaines parlent de
l'eglise de demain.* Edited by Marie Denis. Recherche et Vie 20. Brussels: n.p.,
1980.

"The Vision of Galatians 3:28." *National Catholic Reporter* 16, no. 17 (22 February
1980): 12.

"Sexism and Conversion." *Network* 9 (1981): 15–22.

"Toward a Feminist Biblical Hermeneutics: Biblical Interpretation and Liberation
Theology." Pages 91–112 in *The Challenge of Liberation Theology: A First
World Response.* Edited by Brian Mahan and L. Dale Richesin. Maryknoll,
N.Y.: Orbis, 1981.
Repr. pages 354–82 in *Readings in Moral Theology 4: The Use of Scripture
in Moral Theology.* Edited by Charles E. Curran and Richard A. McCormick.
New York: Paulist Press, 1984.

"We Are Still Invisible: Theological Analysis of the Study of Women and Ministry." Pages 29–43 in *Women and Ministry: Present Experience and Future Hopes*. Edited by D. Gottmoeller and R. Hofbauer. Washington, D.C.: Leadership Conference of Women Religious, 1981.

"Discipleship and Patriarchy: Early Christian Ethos and Christian Ethics in a Feminist Theological Perspective." Pages 131–72 in *The Annual of the Society of Christian Ethics: Selected Papers*. Edited by Larry Rasmussen. Waterloo, Ont.: Council of the Study of Religion, 1982.

Repr. pages 143–60 in *Women's Consciousness, Women's Conscience: A Reader in Feminist Ethics*. Edited by Barbara Hilkert Andolsen, Christine E. Gudorf, and Mary D. Pellauer. Minneapolis: Winston, 1985.

"The Ecclesia of Women: Towards a Feminist Catholic Sisterhood." *Probe* (NAWR Newsletter) 11, no. 3 (1982): 1–3.

"Feminist Theology and New Testament Interpretation." *Journal for the Study of the Old Testament* 22 (fall 1982): 32–46.

"Gather Together in My Name: Toward a Christian Feminist Spirituality." Pages 11 and 25 in *Women Moving Church*. Edited by D. Neu and M. Riley. Washington, D.C.: Center of Concern, 1982.

Repr. *Benedictines* 38.1 (1983): 46–51.

"Luke 2:41–52: An Exposition." *Interpretation* 36 (October 1982): 399–403.

"Tablesharing and the Celebration of the Eucharist." Pages 3–12 in *Can We Always Celebrate the Eucharist?* Edited by Mary Collins and David Power. Concilium 152. Edinburgh: T. & T. Clark, 1982.

"Emanzipation aus der Bibel: Gegen patriarchalisches Christentum." *Evangelische Kommentare* 16 (1983): 195–98.

"From Study to Proclamation: Response to W. J. Burghardt, S.J." Pages 43–55 in *A New Look at Preaching*. Edited by J. Burke. Good News Studies 7. Wilmington, Del.: Michael Glazier, 1983.

Repr. as "The Silenced Majority Needs to Come to Word." Pages 51–60 in *Preaching Better*. Edited by Frank J. McNulty. New York: Paulist Press, 1985. Repr. pages 68–77 in *Preaching: The Art and the Craft*. Edited by Walter J. Burghardt. New York: Paulist Press, 1987.

"The Phenomenon of Early Christian Apocalyptic: Some Reflections on Method." Pages 295–316 in *Apocalypticism in the Mediterranean World and the Near East: Proceedings of the International Colloquium on Apocalypticism, Uppsala, August 12–17, 1979*. Edited by David Hellholm. Tübingen: Mohr, 1983, 2d edition, 1989.

"To Set the Record Straight: Biblical Women's Studies." *Horizons* 10 (spring 1983): 111–21.

Repr. pages 21–31 in *Mainstreaming: Feminist Research for Teaching Religious Studies*. Edited by Arlene Swidler and Walter E. Conn. Lanham, Md.: University Press of America, 1985.

"Claiming the Center: A Critical Feminist Theology of Liberation." Pages 293–309 in *Women's Spirit Bonding*. Edited by Janet Kalven and Mary Buckley. New York: Pilgrim, 1984.

"Contemporary Biblical Scholarship: Its Roots, Present Understandings, and Future Directions." Pages 1–36 in *Modern Biblical Scholarship: Its Impact on Theology and Proclamation*. Edited by Francis Eigo. Villanova, Pa.: Villanova University Press, 1984.

"Continuing the Conversation." Response to a special section entitled "*In Memory of Her:* A Symposium on an Important Book." Edited by Susan Setta. *Anima* 10, no. 2 (1984): 109–12.

"For the Sake of the Truth Dwelling among Us: Emerging Issues in Feminist Biblical Interpretation." Pages 33–54 in *Christian Feminism: Visions of a New Humanity*. Edited by Judith Weidman. New York: Harper & Row, 1984.

"For Women in Men's Worlds: A Critical Feminist Theology of Liberation." Pages 32–39 in *Different Theologies, Common Responsibility: Babel or Pentecost?* Edited by Claude Geffré, Gustavo Gutiérrez, and Virgil Elizondo. Concilium 171. Edinburgh: T. & T. Clark, 1984.

Repr. pages 181–88 in *Yearning to Breathe Free: Liberation Theologies in the United States*. Edited by Mar Peter-Raoul, Linda Forcey, and Robert F. Hunter, Jr. Maryknoll, N.Y.: Orbis, 1990.

"Patriarchal Structures and the Discipleship of Equals." *Probe* (NAWR Newsletter) 12, no. 2 (1984): 4–6.

"Phoebe." *Bibel Heute* 79 (1984): 162–64.

"The Quilting of Women's Early Christian History." Pages 22–29 in *Lessons from Women's Lives*. Maxwell Summer Lecture Series. Syracuse: Syracuse University Press, 1984.

"Breaking the Silence — Becoming Visible." Pages 3–16 in *Women, Invisible in Theology and Church*. Edited by Elisabeth Schüssler Fiorenza and Mary Collins. Concilium 182. Edinburgh: T. & T. Clark, 1985.

"Claiming Our Authority and Power." Pages 45–53 in *The Teaching Authority of Believers*. Edited by J. B. Metz and Edward Schillebeeckx. Concilium 180. Edinburgh: T. & T. Clark, 1985.

"The Discipleship of Equals." *Commonweal* (9 August 1985): 432–37.

"The Followers of the Lamb: Visionary Rhetoric and Social-Political Situation." Pages 144–65 in *Discipleship in the New Testament*. Edited by Fernando Segovia. Philadelphia: Fortress, 1985.

Repr. in Early Christian Apocalypticism: Genre and Social Setting. *Semeia* 36, no. 1 (1986): 123–46.

"Remembering the Past in Creating the Future: Historical-Critical Scholarship and Feminist Biblical Interpretation." Pages 43–63 in *Feminist Perspectives on Biblical Scholarship*. Edited by Adela Yarbro Collins. Chico, Calif.: Scholars Press, 1985.

"[Contribution to] Roundtable Discussion: On Feminist Methodology." *Journal of Feminist Studies in Religion* 1, no. 2 (1985): 73–76.

"Die theologische Sprachlosigkeit überwinden." Pages 58–64 in *Nennt uns nicht Brüder!* Edited by Norbert Sommer. Stuttgart: Kreuz Verlag, 1985.

"The Will to Choose or to Reject: Continuing Our Critical Work." Pages 125–36 in *Feminist Interpretation of the Bible*. Edited by Letty Russell. Philadelphia: Westminster John Knox, 1985.

"A Feminist Critical Interpretation for Liberation: Martha and Mary: Luke 10:38–42." *Religion and Intellectual Life* 3, no. 2 (1986): 21–36.

"Missionaries, Apostles, Coworkers: Romans 16 and the Reconstruction of Women's Early Christian History." *Word and World* 6, no. 4 (fall 1986): 420–33.
    Repr. pages 57–71 in *Feminist Theology: A Reader*. Edited by Ann Loades. London: SPCK, 1990.
"So Far, So Bad." *Commonweal* (31 January 1986): 144–46.
"The Sophia-God of Jesus and the Discipleship of Women." Pages 261–73 in *Women's Spirituality: Resources for Christian Development*. Edited by Joann Wolksi Conn. New York: Paulist Press, 1986.
"Die Anfänge von Kirche, Amt und Priestertum in feministisch-theologischer Sicht." Pages 62–95 in *Priesterkirche*. Edited by Paul Hoffmann. Düsseldorf: Patmos, 1987.
"Elisabeth Schüssler Fiorenza." Interview with Annie Lally Milhaven. Pages 42–63 in *The Inside Stories: Thirteen Valiant Women Challenging the Church*. Edited by Annie Lally Milhaven. Mystic, Conn.: Twenty-Third Publications, 1987.
"The Quilting of Women's History: Phoebe of Cenchreae." Pages 35–49 in *Embodied Love: Sensuality and Relationship as Feminist Values*. Edited by Paula M. Cooey, Sharon A. Farmer, and Mary Ellen Ross. San Francisco: Harper & Row, 1987.
    Repr. *International Christian Digest* 3 (1989): 14–16.
"Rhetorical Situation and Historical Reconstruction in 1 Corinthians." *New Testament Studies* 33, no. 3 (1987): 386–403.
"Theological Criteria and Historical Reconstruction: Martha and Mary: Luke 10: 38–42." Pages 1–12 in *Protocol of the Colloquy of the Center for Hermeneutical Studies in Hellenistic and Modern Culture 53: 10 April 1986*. Edited by H. Waetjen. Berkeley: Center for Hermeneutical Studies in Hellenistic and Modern Culture, 1987.
"The Ethics of Biblical Interpretation: Decentering Biblical Scholarship." *Journal of Biblical Literature* 107, no. 1 (1988): 3–17.
    Repr. pages 107–23 in *Reading the Bible in the Global Village: Helsinki*. Edited by Heikki Räisänen et al. Atlanta: Society of Biblical Literature, 2000.
"Eine feministisch-kritische Befreiungshermeneutik." Pages 13–44 in *Feministische Theologie: Perspektiven zur Orientierung*. Edited by M. Kassel. Stuttgart: Kreuz, 1988.
"1 Corinthians." Pages 1168–89 in *Harper's Bible Commentary*. Edited by James L. Mays. San Francisco: Harper & Row, 1988; rev. ed. 2000.
"Liberation, Unity, and Equality in Community: A New Testament Case Study." Pages 58–74 in *Beyond Unity-in-Tension: Unity, Renewal, and the Community of Women and Men*. Edited by Thomas F. Best. Geneva: WCC Publications, 1988.
"A Response to 'The Social Functions of Women's Asceticism in the Roman East' by Antoinette Clark Wire." Pages 324–28 in *Images of the Feminine in Gnosticism*. Edited by Karen L. King. Philadelphia: Fortress, 1988.
"'Waiting at Table': A Critical Feminist Theological Reflection on Diakonia." Pages 84–94 in *Diakonia*. Edited by Norbert Greinacher and Norbert Mette. Concilium 198. Edinburgh: T. & T. Clark, 1988.
"Women as Paradigms of True Discipleship." Pages 111–29 in *The Gospels*. Edited and with an introduction by Harold Bloom. New York: Chelsea House, 1988.

"Biblical Interpretation and Critical Commitment." *Studia theologica* 43, no. 1 (1989): 5–18.

"Commitment and Critical Inquiry." *Harvard Theological Review* 82, no. 1 (1989): 1–11.

Repr. in *Harvard Divinity Bulletin* 18 (winter 1989): 8–10.

Repr. pages 267–77 in *Readings in Modern Theology: Britain and America.* Edited by Robin Gill. Nashville: Abingdon, 1995.

"Les Douze dans la communauté des disciples egaux: contradiction ou malentendu?" *Foi et vie: Cahier biblique* 88 (1989): 13–24.

"In Search of Women's Heritage." Pages 29–38 in *Weaving the Visions: New Patterns in Feminist Spirituality.* Edited by Judith Plaskow and Carol P. Christ. San Francisco: Harper & Row, 1989.

"The Politics of Otherness: Biblical Interpretation as a Critical Praxis for Liberation." Pages 311–25 in *The Future of Liberation Theology: Essays in Honor of Gustavo Gutiérrez.* Edited by Marc Ellis and Otto Maduro. Maryknoll, N.Y.: Orbis, 1989.

"Revelation." Vol. 2, pages 367–81 in *The Books of the Bible.* Edited by Bernhard W. Anderson. New York: Scribner, 1989.

"Revelation." Pages 407–27 in *The New Testament and Its Modern Interpreters.* Edited by Eldon J. Epp and George W. MacRae. Philadelphia: Fortress/Atlanta: Scholars Press, 1989.

"Text and Reality — Reality as Text: The Problem of a Feminist Historical and Social Reconstruction Based on Texts." *Studia theologica* 43, no. 1 (1989): 19–34.

"Theological Education: Biblical Studies." Pages 1–19 in *The Education of the Practical Theologian: Responses to Joseph Hough and John Cobb's Christian Identity and Theological Education.* Edited by Don S. Browning, Don Polk, and Ian S. Evison. Atlanta: Scholars Press, 1989.

"Biblical Interpretation in the Context of Church and Ministry: A Perspective on Theology for Christian Ministry." *Word and World* 10 (fall 1990): 317–23.

"Changing the Paradigms." *Christian Century* 107 (5–12 September 1990): 796–800.

Repr. pages 75–87 in *How My Mind Has Changed.* Edited by James M. Wall and David Heim. Grand Rapids: Eerdmans, 1991.

"Daughters of Vision and Struggle." Pages 15–21 in *Toward a Feminist Theology.* Edited by Elaine Lindsay. Hellensburgh, N.S.W.: Conference Proceedings, 1990.

"Frauenkirche — eine Exodusgemeinschaft?" *Romero Haus Protokolle* 31 (November 1990).

"Justified by All Her Children: Struggle, Memory, and Vision." Pages 19–38 in *On the Threshold of the Third Millennium.* Edited by the Foundation. Concilium 1990/1. London: SCM Press, 1990.

"Zu ihrem Gedächtnis . . . Frühchristliche Frauengeschichte als Geschichte der Nachfolgegemeinschaft von Gleichgesinnten." Excerpt of *In Memory of Her.* Pages 172–81 in *Gott in dieser Zeit: Eine Herausforderung der Theologie.* Topos Taschenbücher Band 200. Mainz, Germany: Matthias-Grünewald, 1990.

"Auf den Spuren der Weisheit: Weisheitstheologisches Urgestein." Pages 24–40 in *Auf den Spuren der Weisheit: Sophia, Wegweiserin für ein neues Gottesbild.* Edited by Verena Wodtke. Freiburg: Herder, 1991.

"The Rhetoricality of Apocalypse and the Politics of Interpretation: Epilogue." Pages 205–36 in *Revelation: Vision of a Just World*, by Elisabeth Schüssler Fiorenza. 2d edition. Minneapolis: Fortress, 1991.

"Zur Methodenproblematik einer feministischen Christologie des Neuen Testaments." Pages 129–47 in *Vom Verlangen nach Heilwerden: Christologie in feministisch-theologischer Sicht*. Edited by Doris Strahm and Regula Strobel. Fribourg/Lucerne: Exodus, 1991.

"A Discipleship of Equals: Ekklesial Democracy and Patriarchy in Biblical Perspective." Pages 17–33 in *A Democratic Catholic Church: The Reconstruction of Roman Catholicism*. Edited by Eugene C. Bianchi and Rosemary Radford Ruether. New York: Crossroad, 1992.

"Feminist Hermeneutics." Vol. 2, pages 783–91 in *Anchor Bible Dictionary*. Edited by David N. Freedman et al. New York: Doubleday, 1992.

"The Twelve and the Discipleship of Equals." Pages 109–21 in *Changing Women, Changing Church*. Edited by L. M. Uhr. Newtown, Australia: Millennium Books, 1992.

"Foreword." Pages 7–9 in *Let the Oppressed Go Free: Feminist Perspectives on the New Testament*, by Luise Schottroff. Translated by Annemarie Kidder. Louisville: Westminster John Knox, 1993.

"Die Frauen gehören in's Zentrum." Pages 13–22 in *Streitfall: Feministische Theologie*. Edited by Britta Hübener and Hartmut Meesmann. Düsseldorf: Patmos, 1993.

"Leggere la Bibbia nel 'villaggio globale': riflessioni teologiche femministe." *Protestantismo* 48, no. 2 (1993): 80–93.

"Neutestamentlich-frühchristliche Argumente zum Thema Frau und Amt: Eine kritische-feministische Reflexion." *Theologische Quartalschrift* 173, no. 3 (1993): 173–85.

   Repr. as "Mujer y Ministerio en el cristianismo primitivo." Translated and edited by María José de Torres. *Selecciones de Teología* 33, no. 132 (1994): 327–37.

   Repr. pages 32–44 in *Frauenordination: Stand der Diskussion in der katholischen Kirche*. Edited by Walter Gross. Munich: Wewel, 1996.

"The Practice of Biblical Interpretation: Luke 10:38–42." Pages 172–97 in *The Bible and Liberation: Political and Social Hermeneutics*. Rev. ed. Edited by Norman K. Gottwald and Richard A. Horsley. Maryknoll, N.Y.: Orbis, 1993.

"Transforming the Legacy of the Woman's Bible." Vol. 1, pages 1–24 in *Searching the Scriptures*. Edited by Elisabeth Schüssler Fiorenza. New York: Crossroad, 1993.

"Der 'Athenakomplex' in der theologischen Frauenforschung." Pages 103–11 in *Für Gerechtigkeit streiten: Theologie im Alltag einer bedrohten Welt*. Edited by Dorothee Sölle. Gütersloh: Kaiser, 1994.

"The Bible, the Global Context, and the Discipleship of Equals." Pages 79–98 in *Reconstructing Christian Theology*. Edited by Rebecca Chopp and Mark L. Taylor. Minneapolis: Fortress, 1994.

"Love Endures Everything: Toward a Critical Hermeneutic of Proclamation." The 1993 Jacob L. Morgan Lecture. *Taproot: The Journal of the Lutheran Theological Southern Seminary* 10 (1994): 16–34.

"Remember the Struggle: Introduction to the Tenth Anniversary Edition." Pages xiii–xlii in *In Memory of Her,* by Elisabeth Schüssler Fiorenza. New York: Crossroad, 1994.

"The Rhetoricity of Historical Knowledge: Pauline Discourse and Its Contextualizations." Pages 443–69 in *Religious Propaganda and Missionary Competition in the New Testament World: Essays Honoring Dieter Georgi.* Edited by Lukas Bormann, Kelly Del Tredici, and Angela Standhartinger. Novum Testamentum Supplement 74. Leiden: Brill, 1994.

"Spiritual Movements of Transformation? A Critical Feminist Reflection." Pages 221–26 in *Defecting in Place: Women Claiming Responsibility for Their Own Spiritual Lives.* Edited by Miriam T. Winter, Adair Lummis, and Allison Stokes. New York: Crossroad, 1994.

"Transgressing Canonical Boundaries." Vol. 2, pages 1–14 in *Searching the Scriptures.* Edited by Elisabeth Schüssler Fiorenza. New York: Crossroad, 1994.

"A Critical Theory and Practice of Feminist Interpretation for Liberation Revisited." Pages 151–79 (afterword) in *Bread Not Stone,* by Elisabeth Schüssler Fiorenza. Tenth Anniversary Edition. Boston: Beacon, 1995.

"Feminist/Women Priests — An Oxymoron?" *New Women, New Church* 18, no. 3 (1995): 10–13.

"Feminist Studies in Religion and a Radical Democratic Ethos." *Religion and Theology* 2, no. 2 (1995): 122–44.

"Jesus — Messenger of Divine Wisdom." *Studia theologica* 49, no. 2 (1995): 231–52.

"Maria und die Frauenbefreiungsbewegung: Eine kritische-feministisch-theologische Sichtung." Pages 91–119 in *Was willst du von mir, Frau?: Maria in heutiger Sicht.* Theologische Berichte 21. Edited by Josef Pfammater and Eduard Christen. Fribourg, Switzerland: Paulusverlag, 1995.

"Patriarchale Herrschaft spaltet/Feministische Verschiedenheit macht stark: Ethik und Politik der Befreiung." Pages 5–29 in *Women Churches: Networking and Reflection in the European Context.* Edited by Angela Berlis et al. Yearbook of the European Society of Women in Theological Research. Mainz, Germany: Matthias-Grünewald, 1995.

"Ties That Bind: Domestic Violence against Women." *Voices from the Third World* 18, no. 1 (1995): 122–67.
    Repr. pages 39–55 in *Women Resisting Violence: Spirituality for Life.* Edited by Mary John Mananzan et al. Maryknoll, N.Y.: Orbis, 1996.

"Wartime as Formative." *Christian Century* 112 (16–23 August 1995): 778–79.

"Das zwiespältige Erbe der Woman's Bible." *Bibel und Kirche* 50, no. 4 (1995): 211–19.

"Challenging the Rhetorical Half-Turn: Feminist and Rhetorical Biblical Criticism." Pages 28–53 in *Rhetoric, Scripture, and Theology: Essays from the 1994 Pretoria Conference,* part 1: *Rhetorical Method and Interpretation.* Edited by Stanley E. Porter and Thomas H. Olbricht. Sheffield: Sheffield University Press, 1996.

"Discipleship and Patriarchy: Early Christian Ethos and Christian Ethics in a Feminist Theological Perspective." Pages 33–63 in *Feminist Ethics and the Catholic Moral Tradition.* Edited by Charles E. Curran, Margaret A. Farley, and Richard A. McCormick. Readings in Moral Theology 9. New York: Paulist Press, 1996.

"The Ekklesia of Women: Revisioning the Past in Creating a Democratic Future." Pages 239–55 in *The Call to Serve: Biblical and Theological Perspectives on Ministry in Honour of Bishop Penny Jamieson*. Edited by Douglas A. Campbell. Sheffield, England: Sheffield Academic Press, 1996.

"Gerechtigkeit leidenschaftlich lieben." *Neue Wege* 90 (1996): 43–46.

"G*d at Work in Our Midst: From a Politics of Identity to a Politics of Struggle." *Feminist Theology* 13 (summer 1996): 47–72.

"Rivendichiamo il potere della visione: *l'ekklēsía* delle don/ne." Translated by Maria Assunta Sozzi Manci. Pages 299–312 in *Cammino e visione: Universitalità e regionalità della teologia nel 20 secolo: Scritti in onore di Rosino Gibellini*. Biblioteca di teologia contemporanea 88. Edited by Dietmar Mieth, Edward Schillebeeckx, and Hadewych Snijdewind. Brescia, Italy: Queriniana, 1996.

"Ruma ao Discipulado de Iguais: A Ekklesia de Mulheres." *Estudos-teologicos* 36, no. 3 (1996): 281–96.

"Struggle Is a Name for Hope: A Critical Feminist Interpretation for Liberation." Extracts from a paper prepared for Colloquia on Feminist Hermeneutics, Australia, August 1995. *Women Church* 18 (1996): 22–27.

"Die werfe den ersten Stein: Zum strukturellen christologischen Antijudaismus." *Schlangenbrut* 14, no. 53 (1996): 23–26.

1995 Selwyn Lectures. Edited by Janet Crawford. Auckland, New Zealand: The College of St. John the Evangelist, 1997.

"Born of a Woman." *Journal of Women's Ministries* 12, no. 3 (1996–97): 4–5.

"Bread/Rice of Wisdom: Biblical Interpretation for Liberation." *Ewha Journal of Feminist Theology* 2 (1997): 101–25.

"Communicating across Boundaries." Pages 12–14 in *Interreligious Dialogue at Harvard Divinity School: Experiment and Experience*. Edited by Robin L. Zucker. Cambridge: Harvard Divinity School, Office of Student Life, 1997.

"Discipleship of Equals: Reality and Vision." Pages 1–11 in *In Search of a Round Table: Gender, Theology and Church Leadership*. Edited by Musimbi R. A. Kanyoro. Geneva: WCC Publications, 1997.

"Elisabeth Schüssler Fiorenza: Feminist Perspectives on Jesus, Discipleship and Church." Interview by Robert A. Becker. *Cathedral Age* 73, no. 2 (1997): 10–13.

"Jesus and the Politics of Interpretation." *Harvard Theological Review* 90, no. 4 (1997): 343–58.

"The Praxis of Coequal Discipleship." Pages 224–41 in *Paul and Empire: Religion and Power in Roman Imperial Society*. Edited by Richard A. Horsley. Harrisburg, Pa.: Trinity Press International, 1997.

"Reading the Bible as Equals." Pages 57–70 in *In Search of a Round Table: Gender, Theology and Church Leadership*. Edited by Musimbi R. A. Kanyoro. Geneva: WCC Publications, 1997.

"Speaking about G*d." *The Living Pulpit* 6, no. 1 (1997): 20–21.

"Struggle Is a Name for Hope: A Critical Feminist Interpretation for Liberation." *Pacifica* 10 (June 1997): 224–48.

"Celebrating the Struggles/Realizing the Visions." *Journal of Women and Religion* 16 (1998): 16–27.

"Elisabeth Schüssler Fiorenza: An Interview." With Alice Bach. *Biblicon* 3 (May 1998): 27–44.

"The Emperor Has No Clothes." *New Women, New Church* 21, no. 3 (1998): 7–8.

"Gender." Pages 290–94 in *The Encyclopedia of Politics and Religion*. Edited by Robert Wuthnow. Washington, D.C.: Congressional Quarterly Books, 1998.

"Die Macht des Wortes beanspruchen: sich als Subjekt von Theologie begreifen." Interview with Annebelle Pithan and Ilana Nord. Pages 121–28 in *Wie wir wurden, was wir sind: Gespräche mit feministischen Theologinnen der ersten Generation*. Edited by Gerburgis Feld, Dagmar Henze, and Claudia Janssen. Gütersloher Taschenbücher 548. Gütersloh: Gütersloher Verlagshaus, 1998.

"Theologin der Befreiung." Interview. *Publik-Forum* 13 (1998): 24–26.

"Vollbürgerinnen in Theologie und Kirche." Pages 157–65 in *There Were Also Women Looking on from Afar*. Edited by Nyambura J. Njoroge and Irja Askola. Geneva: World Alliance of Reformed Churches, 1998.

"Wer sagt ihr, dass ich bin? Anfrage an Christologie zum Thema: Globalisierung — Solidarität oder Barbarei?" *Das Argument: Zeitschrift für Philosophie und Sozialwissenschaften* 228 (1998): 839–50.

"Ecclesia Semper Reformanda: Theology as Ideology Critique." Pages 70–76 in *Unanswered Questions*. Edited by Christoph Theobald and Dietmar Mieth. Concilium 1999/1. Maryknoll, N.Y.: Orbis, 1999.

"The Emperor Has No Clothes: Democratic Ekklesial Self-Understanding and Kyriocentric Roman Authority." Pages 58–65 in *The Non-ordination of Women and the Politics of Power*. Edited by Elisabeth Schüssler Fiorenza and Hermann Häring. Concilium 1999/3. Maryknoll, N.Y.: Orbis, 1999.

"A feminista teológia" (in Hungarian). Translated by Dévény István. *Egyházfórum* 14, nos. 2–3 (1999): 41–51.

"Gleichheit und Differenz: Gal 3,28 im Brennpunkt feministischer Hermeneutik." *Berliner theologische Zeitschrift* 16, no. 2 (1999): 212–31.

"Liberation: A Critical Feminist Perspective." *Theology Digest* 46 (Winter 1999): 327–36.

"To Follow the Vision: The Jesus Movement as *Basileia* Movement." Pages 123–43 in *Liberating Eschatology: Essays in Honor of Letty M. Russell*. Edited by M. A. Farley and S. Jones. Louisville: Westminster John Knox, 1999.

"Die Worte der Prophetie: Die Apokalypse des Johannes theologisch lesen." *Jahrbuch für biblische Theologie* 14 (1999): 71–94.

"Christlicher Antijudaismus aus feministischer Perspektive." Pages 56–70 in *Das christlich-jüdische Gespräch: Standortbestimmungen*. Edited by Christina Kurth and Peter Schmid. Stuttgart: Kohlhammer, 2000.

"Defending the Center, Trivializing the Margins." Pages 29–48 in *Reading the Bible in the Global Village: Helsinki*. Edited by Heikki Räisänen et al. Atlanta: Society of Biblical Literature, 2000.

"Paul and the Politics of Interpretation." Pages 40–57 in *Paul and Politics: Ekklesia, Israel, Imperium, Interpretation: Essays in Honor of Krister Stendahl*. Edited by Richard A. Horsley. Harrisburg, Pa.: Trinity, 2000.

"Resident Alien: Dazugehören und doch fremd bleiben." Pages 69–83 in *Zwischen-Räume: Deutsche feministische Theologinnen im Ausland*. Theologische

Frauenforschung in Europa 1. Edited by Katharina von Kellenbach and Susanne Scholz. Munster: Lit, 2000.

"Speaking Out: Toward the Millennium of Wo/men." *Journal of Feminist Studies in Religion* 16, no. 1 (2000): 91–94.

"Yeast of Wisdom or Stone of Truth: Scripture as a Site of Struggle." Pages 67–89 in *Caminos inexhauribles de la Palabra (Las relecturas creativas en la Biblia y de la Biblia)*. Edited by Guillermo Hansen. Buenos Aires: Grupo Editorial Lumen, 2000.

"Preface." Pages 1–5 in *A New Thing on Earth*, by Gabriele Dietrich. Bombay: ISPCK, 2001.

"The Rhetorics and Politics of Jesus Research: A Critical Feminist Perspective." Pages 259–82 in *Jesus, Mark, and Q: The Teaching of Jesus and Its Earliest Records*. Edited by Michael Labahn and Andreas Schmidt. Journal for the Study of the New Testament Supplement Series 214. Sheffield: Sheffield Academic Press, 2001.

"The Struggle for the Catholicity of Theology." *Bulletin ET: Zeitschrift für Theologie in Europa* 12 (2001): 207–28.

"Unterscheidung der Geister: Schriftauslegung als Ideologiekritik, theologische Rhetorik und Interpretationsethik." Pages 149–64 in *Interdisziplinäre Ethik: Grundlagen, Methoden, Bereiche: Festgabe für Dietmar Mieth*. Edited by Adrian Holderegger and Jean-Pierre Wils. Freiburg: Herder, 2001.

"The Words of Prophecy: Reading the Apocalypse Theologically." Pages 1–19 in *Studies in the Book of Revelation*. Edited by Steve Moyise. London: T. & T. Clark, 2001.

"The Ethos of Interpretation: Biblical Studies in a Postmodern and Postcolonial Context." Pages 211–28 in *Theological Literacy for the Twenty-first Century*. Edited by Rodney Petersen with Nancy Rourke. Grand Rapids: Eerdmans, 2002.

"Foreword." Pages 13–15 in *The Lost Coin: Parables of Women, Work, and Wisdom*. Edited by Mary Ann Beavis. Sheffield: Sheffield Academic Press, 2002.

"Lettera aperta a Miriam IV, la successore di Pietro e di Maria di Magdala." Pages 115–40 in *L'agenda del nuovo papa: Dai cinque continenti ipotesi sul dopo Wojtyla*. Edited by Luigi De Paoli and Luigi Sandri. Rome: Editori Riuniti, 2002.

"Method in Wo/men's Studies in Religion: A Critical Feminist Hermeneutics." Pages 207–41 in *Methodology in Religious Studies: The Interface with Women's Studies*. Edited by Arvind Sharma. Albany: State University of New York Press, 2002.

"Public Discourse, Religion, and Wo/men's Struggles for Justice." *DePaul Law Review* 51 (Summer 2002): 1077–1101.

"*The Journal of Feminist Studies in Religion*: A Q & A with Elisabeth Schüssler Fiorenza." E-interview in *Religious Studies News/SBL Edition* 3.3 (March 2002): *www.sbl-site.org/Newsletter/03_2002/index.html*.

"Religion, Gender and Society: Shaping the Discipline of Religious/Theological Studies." Pages 85–99 in *The Relevance of Theology: Nathan Söderblom and the Development of an Academic Discipline*. Edited by Carl Reinhold Bråckenhielm and Gunhild Winqvist Hollman. Uppsala, Sweden: Uppsala Universitet, 2002.

"Thinking and Working across Borders: The Feminist Liberation Theologians, Activists, and Scholars in Religion Network." *Journal of Feminist Studies in Religion* 18, no. 1 (2002): 71–74.

"Der wirkliche Jesus? Feministische Anfragen an die sozialwissenschaftliche Jesusforschung." Pages 23–32 in *Jesus in neuen Kontexten.* Edited by Wolfgang Stegemann, Bruce J. Malina, and Gerd Theissen. Stuttgart: Kohlhammer, 2002.

"Neutestamentliche Wissenschaft als kritisch-emanzipatorische Wissenschaft." Pages 347–60 in *Neutestamentliche Wissenschaft.* Edited by Eve-Marie Becker. Tübingen: Francke Verlag, 2003.

"Rethinking the Educational Practices of Biblical Doctoral Studies." *Teaching Theology and Religion* 6 (April 2003): 65–75.

"Re-Visioning Christian Origins: *In Memory of Her* Revisited." Pages 225–50 in *Christian Beginnings: Worship, Belief and Society.* Edited by Kieran O'Mahony. London: Continuum International, 2003.

"G*d the Many Named: Without Place and Proper Name." In *Gott.* Edited by Hermann Häring. Münster: Lit. Verlag, forthcoming.

Grenzen uberschreiten. Der theoretische Anspruch feministischer Theologie. Ausgewählte Aufsätze. Münster: Lit Verlag, forthcoming.

Radio and Television Interviews (Selected)

Panel: "Aspects of Women in Religious History." WAMU/FM, Washington, D.C., 1981.

Interview: "Distinguished Theologians and Their Work." Swiss Television Series, 1990.

Interview: "Perspectives — Faith in Our Times." Sylvan Productions, 27 April 1990.

Interview: "Feminist Theology and Interpretation." BBC, 1992.

Discussion: "Freedom and Entrapment: Women Thinking Theology." Australian Broadcasting Corporation, 1995.

Interview: "Brot und Bibel." Swiss Television, 1998.

Interview: KRO and KTRO. Belgium Television, 1998.

Hessischer Rundfunk, Führende Theologinnen des 20. Jahrhunderts, June 2000.

Radio and Television Interviews in Graz, August 2001.

Contributors

Ellen Bradshaw Aitken, Harvard Divinity School

François Bovon, Harvard Divinity School

Ann Graham Brock, Iliff School of Theology

Rita Nakashima Brock, Starr King School for the Ministry

Bernadette J. Brooten, Brandeis University

Denise Kimber Buell, Williams College

Allen Dwight Callahan, Macalester College

Harvey Cox, Harvard Divinity School

Francis Schüssler Fiorenza, Harvard Divinity School

Steven J. Friesen, University of Missouri, Columbia

Dieter Georgi, Johann Wolfgang Goethe-University in Frankfurt

Richard A. Horsley, University of Massachusetts, Boston

Melanie Johnson-DeBaufre, Luther College

Karen L. King, Harvard Divinity School

Cynthia Briggs Kittredge, Episcopal Theological Seminary of the Southwest

John R. Lanci, Stonehill College

Shelly Matthews, Furman University

Laura S. Nasrallah, Occidental College

Rebecca Ann Parker, Starr King School for the Ministry

Barbara R. Rossing, Lutheran School of Theology at Chicago

Ronald F. Thiemann, Harvard Divinity School

Demetrius Williams, Tulane University